OECD ECONOMIC OUTLOOK

57

JUNE 1995

ORGANISATION FOR ECONOMIC CO-OPERATION AND DEVELOPMENT

The Organisation for Economic Co-operation and Development (OECD)

was set up under a Convention signed in Paris on 14 December 1960, which provides that the OECD shall promote policies designed:

- *to achieve the highest sustainable economic growth and employment and a rising standard of living in Member countries while maintaining financial stability, and thus to contribute to the development of the world economy;*
- *to contribute to sound economic expansion in Member as well as non-member countries in the process of economic development; and*
- *to contribute to the expansion of world trade on a multilateral, non-discriminatory basis in accordance with international obligations.*

The original Member countries of the OECD are: Austria, Belgium, Canada, Denmark, France, Germany, Greece, Iceland, Ireland, Italy, Luxembourg, the Netherlands, Norway, Portugal, Spain, Sweden, Switzerland, Turkey, the United Kingdom and the United States. The following countries became Members subsequently through accession at the dates indicated hereafter: Japan (28 April 1964), Finland (28 January 1969), Australia (7 June 1971), New Zealand (29 May 1973) and Mexico (18th May 1994). The Commission of the European Communities takes part in the work of the OECD (Article 13 of the OECD Convention).

FOREWORD

The *OECD Economic Outlook* provides a periodic assessment of economic trends, prospects and policies in OECD countries. It appears twice a year, in June and December.

Each issue contains an overall analysis of the latest economic trends and short-term projections. This survey is the joint work of members of the Economics Department. The journal also occasionally contains special studies by members of the Department or other divisions of the Organisation designed to assist the interpretation of economic trends. Reference statistics are included. The French version of the *OECD Economic Outlook* is entitled *Perspectives économiques de l'OCDE.*

The *OECD Economic Outlook* is published on the responsibility of the Secretary-General of the OECD. The assessments given of countries' prospects do not necessarily correspond to those of the national authorities concerned.

TABLE OF CONTENTS

LIST OF NUMBERED TABLES AND FIGURES

OECD ECONOMIC OUTLOOK AND POLICIES

General Assessment of the Economic Situation

Investment in the Current Upswing in a Longer-Term Context

Effects of Ageing Populations on Government Budgets

DEVELOPMENTS IN SELECTED NON-OECD COUNTRIES

Central and Eastern European Countries and the Russian Federation

Table

China and the Dynamic Asian Economies

Figure

South and Central America

Table

ANNEX

Reference Statistics and Annual Projections

Annex Table

Demand and Output

Wages, Costs and Inflation

Labour Force, Employment and Unemployment

Business Sector

Saving

LIST OF OTHER TABLES AND FIGURES

CHALLENGES AND POLICY PRIORITIES

DEVELOPMENTS IN INDIVIDUAL OECD COUNTRIES

ANNEX

CONVENTIONAL SIGNS

$	US dollar	.	Decimal point
c	US cent	I, II	Calendar half-years
£	Pound sterling	Q1, Q4	Calendar quarters
mbd	Million barrels per day	Billion	Thousand million
..	Data not available	Trillion	Thousand billion
0	Nil or negligible	s.a.a.r.	Seasonally adjusted at annual rates
–	Irrelevant	n.s.a.	Not seasonally adjusted

Summary of projections[a]

Seasonally adjusted at annual rates

	1994	1995	1996	1994 I	1994 II	1995 I	1995 II	1996 I	1996 II
				Percentage changes from previous period					
Real total domestic demand									
United States	4.7	3.3	1.8	5.1	4.4	3.2	2.3	1.6	1.6
Japan	1.0	2.4	3.1	1.0	1.5	2.1	4.0	2.9	2.9
Germany	2.6	2.5	3.3	3.3	1.9	2.5	3.2	3.3	3.5
OECD Europe	1.9	2.8	3.2	2.4	2.3	2.9	3.1	3.2	3.2
Total OECD	3.0	2.5	2.6	3.5	3.0	2.3	2.6	2.6	2.7
Real GDP									
United States	4.1	3.2	2.3	4.3	4.3	3.0	2.6	2.3	2.2
Japan	0.6	1.3	2.3	1.0	1.0	0.8	2.7	2.2	2.3
Germany	2.9	2.9	2.7	3.8	2.0	3.3	3.0	2.6	2.6
OECD Europe	2.4	3.0	3.0	2.9	2.7	3.2	3.1	3.0	2.9
Total OECD	2.9	2.7	2.7	3.2	3.2	2.5	2.7	2.7	2.7
				Per cent					
Inflation[b]									
United States	2.1	2.0	2.7	2.4	2.1	2.0	2.2	2.8	2.9
Japan	0.1	–0.3	0.2	0.4	–1.6	0.3	–0.1	0.3	0.4
Germany	2.2	2.1	2.3	2.3	1.7	2.3	2.3	2.3	2.4
OECD Europe (excluding Turkey)	2.6	2.8	2.9	2.5	2.5	2.9	3.0	2.9	2.9
Total OECD (excl. Mexico and Turkey)	1.9	2.0	2.4	2.0	1.6	2.1	2.2	2.4	2.5
Total OECD	3.9	4.1	3.7	4.3	3.9	4.4	3.9	3.8	3.6
				Per cent of labour force					
Unemployment									
United States	6.1	5.6	5.7	6.4	5.8	5.6	5.7	5.7	5.8
Japan	2.9	3.1	3.1	2.9	2.9	3.1	3.1	3.1	3.1
Germany	9.6	9.2	8.7	9.7	9.5	9.3	9.0	8.8	8.7
OECD Europe	11.3	11.0	10.6	11.3	11.2	11.1	10.9	10.7	10.5
Total OECD	8.1	7.8	7.6	8.2	7.9	7.9	7.8	7.7	7.6
				Per cent of GDP					
Current balances									
United States	–2.3	–2.7	–2.5	–2.1	–2.5	–2.6	–2.8	–2.6	–2.5
Japan	2.8	2.5	2.2	3.0	2.6	2.5	2.4	2.2	2.1
Germany	–1.1	–0.7	–1.2	–0.6	–1.7	–0.9	–0.5	–1.0	–1.4
OECD Europe	0.7	0.9	0.8	0.8	0.6	0.8	0.9	0.8	0.8
Total OECD	–0.2	–0.1	–0.1	0.0	–0.3	–0.1	0.0	–0.1	–0.1
				Per cent					
Short-term interest rates[c]									
United States	4.3	5.9	6.4	3.6	4.9	5.7	6.2	6.4	6.4
Japan	2.3	1.7	1.6	2.2	2.3	2.0	1.4	1.5	1.6
Germany	5.4	4.8	5.2	5.6	5.2	4.9	4.7	5.0	5.4
Major 4 European countries[d]	6.3	6.9	6.9	6.3	6.3	7.1	6.7	6.8	7.0
				Percentages changes from previous period					
World trade[e]	9.8	8.9	7.8	10.0	11.5	8.2	7.9	7.7	7.7

a) Assumptions underlying the projections include:
- no change in actual and announced policies;
- unchanged exchange rates from 2 May 1995; in particular $1 = Y 83.73, DM 1.38;
- dollar price (OECD fob imports) for internationally traded oil of $16.5 per barrel for 1995 I, and rise in line with manufactured export prices thereafter;
- the cut-off date for other information used in the compilation of the projections was 10 May 1995.

b) GDP deflator, percentage changes from previous period.
c) United States: 3-month Treasury bills; Japan: 3-6 month CD; Germany, France, Italy, United Kingdom: 3-month interbank rates.
d) Unweighted average of Germany, France, Italy and the United Kingdom.
e) Growth rate of the arithmetic average of world import volumes and world export volumes.

Challenges and policy priorities

The current economic situation

The economic situation in most Member countries (see table on facing page) has improved substantially after several difficult years in the early 1990s. Expansions of output are well established virtually everywhere, Japan being a striking exception. World trade is growing robustly. Unemployment in the area is falling. Inflation has dropped to rates not seen since the 1960s. Beyond these favourable conjunctural developments, much has been done to lay the foundation for sustained improvement in economic performance over the longer term. Competition in product markets is being strengthened internationally by agreements to reduce barriers to trade, notably the implementation of the European Single Market, NAFTA and the Uruguay Round, including the establishment of the World Trade Organisation, while regulatory reform and technological innovation continue to increase competition and efficiency, in particular in financial markets. A number of countries have also made some progress in enhancing the flexibility of their labour markets. Outside the OECD area, growth is robust in many Asian economies, many of the economies in transition have returned to growth and, despite the effects of the crisis in Mexico on countries in Central and South America, longer-term prospects in that area remain bright.

Medium-term challenges

Notwithstanding these achievements, many issues will have to be confronted in the coming years to ensure that high economic growth with sustained increases in employment and productivity is achieved within the OECD area and outside, and that rising living standards and increased prosperity are shared, both across countries and among individuals within countries.

Sustained increases in employment and permanent reductions in unemployment are essential, since they would contribute both to the growth of output by reducing the waste of human resources which is now occurring, and to the reduction of the social distress which high and prolonged unemployment causes. Rapid progress in implementing the recommendations in the Jobs Study is a matter of urgency in all countries. (For a review of progress and priorities, see *The OECD Jobs Study: Implementing the Strategy*, distributed with this *OECD Economic Outlook*.)

More rapid increases in productivity growth will require: open competitive markets, which put producers under continuous pressures to improve efficiency and to innovate; high levels of research and development and of new investment which embodies new technologies and ensures that they are adequately diffused; and a more highly skilled labour force. The adverse effects on particular groups or individuals of the rapid changes sometimes associated with competitive markets and technological advances can be addressed by enhancing OECD societies' capacity to adapt constructively, rather than attempting to slow the pace of change. In the final analysis, the productivity improvements which competitive processes and technological advance generate are the main source of rising living standards. They will also provide the means for increased support for the displaced and the excluded, and in particular for programmes to help re-integrate them.

Further productivity growth and an efficient allocation of the world's real resources will also depend on the free movement of financial resources. The challenge here is to maximise the benefits of globalised and liberalised financial markets while ensuring that any associated costs are minimised. In recent years, these markets have at times experienced large and unexpected pressures, often leading to abrupt movements in exchange rates and long-term interest rates. In many cases, pressures have reflected a justified loss of market confidence in macroeconomic policies and prospects. However, once a loss of confidence has occurred, the timing and magnitude of the market reactions cannot be fully attributed to changes in underlying economic conditions. The large short-term swings which sometimes result can destabilise domestic economic conditions and aggravate financial fragility. As well, prolonged misalignments of currencies can lead to large movements in trade balances and give rise to tensions in international trade and payments systems, which may contribute to protectionist pressures.

Strengthening the open multilateral rules-based trading system, and bringing international investment into a similar framework, will boost growth by raising productivity through better allocation of resources across sectors and countries, and thus contribute to continued increases in living standards. Notwithstanding the successful conclusion of the Uruguay Round, protectionist pressures still exist. At the time of writing, trade relations between the United States and Japan are undergoing a period of particularly intense tension. Other trade-related issues involving competition policies, direct investment, environment and labour standards are under discussion in a number of fora, including the OECD. It is important that solutions be found – including to the issue of lowering the level of immediate specific trade tensions between the United States and Japan. Such solutions must be consistent with an open multilateral and rules-based approach that is conducive to more open competitive markets and more efficient international resource allocation.

Macroeconomic policy requirements

Achieving and maintaining a stable macroeconomic environment will provide a supportive backdrop for sustained growth. The gains made in lowering inflation must be preserved. A difficult but vital task will be to reduce high public deficits and debt-to-GDP ratios, particularly in view of the expected increase in fiscal burdens associated with ageing populations.

Success over the longer term first implies dealing with any short-term problems in a way that is compatible with longer-term objectives. The OECD Secretariat currently projects reasonably robust growth to the end of 1996, but this outcome cannot be taken for granted. There are risks associated with: the possible negative effects of foreign-exchange turbulence in recent months; further adverse financial market reaction to the poor state of public finances in many countries (i.e. higher interest rates than assumed); and, possibly, more restrained consumer spending than projected. These risks must be contained.

In the present macroeconomic situation, the requirements of non-inflationary growth point to the need for monetary policy to moderate demand where margins of spare capacity have virtually disappeared or substantially narrowed, while it should support a recovery of activity where such margins remain large and there is little risk of inflation. The recent decline of the external value of the US dollar against other major currencies has raised additional policy issues. In the United States, the sharp fall of the dollar, if maintained, could add somewhat to price pressures which already show some signs of rising. In Japan, the current strength of the yen could compromise a recovery that has already been delayed. In Europe, the dollar's weakness against the Deutschemark has been reflected in pressures on other currencies, both within and outside the ERM. Some countries, particularly those with weak budget positions or poor inflation records in the past, have needed to raise interest rates to defend the currency at a time when unemployment is still high and economic recovery is incomplete.

Closely co-ordinating interest rate policy in the largest three OECD economies with the primary objective of exchange rate stability could generate significant domestic costs. Given the divergence of cyclical positions, the underlying external pressure could be translated into higher interest rates than would be implied by purely domestic considerations. In large economies, for which the relative size of the foreign sector is fairly small, it would not be advisable to adopt the exchange rate as a target of monetary policy. However, even in these economies, the exchange rate should be used as one important indicator when designing monetary policy, together with a number of domestic economic and financial variables. In the current situation, such a broad set of indicators relevant to the assessment of appropriate stance of monetary policy suggests that:

- In the United States, the monetary authorities will have to watch developments carefully, remaining vigilant to potential inflation pressures and being ready to raise short-term interest rates further in the event that signs of resumption of strong growth are detected in incoming data or that a weak exchange rate appears to pose an inflation risk.
- In other countries where large currency depreciations have occurred and whose economies are more exposed to external influences than the United States (such as Italy, the United Kingdom, Mexico, Spain and Sweden), even greater care would be needed in the conduct of monetary policy to prevent the currency depreciation from triggering a price/wage spiral.
- In Germany, if the underlying forces of expansion maintain their strength over the coming twelve months in the face of the Deutschemark appreciation, an increase in interest rates is likely to be required. In France, on the other hand, short-term market rates should be reduced closer to the German levels as soon as exchange market tensions subside.
- In Japan, the existing margin of unused capacity, the projected strength of domestic demand, and on-going balance sheet adjustments of banks point to the need for flexible use of existing, though limited, room for further cuts in short-term rates, unless a significant reversal of the yen exchange rate overshooting takes place quickly through market forces.

Over the longer term, it is necessary to strengthen further the credibility of commitments to non-inflationary monetary policy in order to lower interest rate premia for inflation and inflation uncertainty, as well as provide a favourable backdrop for decisions about current resource allocation and new investment. This would improve productivity performance and help reduce the extent of financial market volatility. There are a number of measures which would contribute positively in this regard, all of which are desirable in their own right. Considerable progress has been made in many countries in terms of emphasis on inflation control when formulating monetary policy objectives, the ambitiousness of these objectives and transparency in communicating them to the public. A number of countries – the United Kingdom, Canada, Finland, New Zealand and Sweden – have established explicit inflation targets and several others, including Germany, France, Italy, Australia, Greece, Portugal, Spain and Switzerland, have announced medium-term inflation objectives. Others have established effectively fixed exchange rates *vis-à-vis* low inflation countries. Greater autonomy for central banks in their operations is also enhancing institutional pressure for maintaining price stability in a number of countries – for example in some EU countries and New Zealand. Further progress in these areas would help central banks to build successful track records and contribute to the development of public support on which these commitments ultimately depend.

Fiscal consolidation continues to have a key role to play. Chronic budget deficits and rising debt-to-GDP ratios in many countries suggest widespread unsustainability of present fiscal policies. Measures to address this problem are being taken in most countries, and these efforts need to be maintained, or, in some cases, intensified. In several countries, for example Italy, Canada, Spain and Sweden, concern about the size of deficits has at times contributed to premia on interest rates and downward pressure on currencies. In the United States, chronic budget deficits together with relatively low private saving have resulted in a continuous deterioration in the net foreign position. Reducing deficits can be expected to raise national saving, which would help ease upward pressures on interest rates, to finance increased investment and to promote sustainable growth in the medium term. It will also allow greater room for manoeuvre and help underpin the credibility of official commitments to price stability. In view of medium-term pressures from pension commitments and health care programmes, which will rise as populations age, it is all the more critical to address fiscal imbalances as soon as possible.

Since the scope for increasing taxation in many countries is limited by political resistance and the increased economic distortions that higher taxes imply, the main burden of adjustment will have to fall on expenditure. Some more specific policy recommendations, which differ from country to country, are presented in the General Assessment chapter of this publication. More generally, recent experience in a number of countries indicates that the adjustments which deficit reduction will require are easiest for the economy to absorb if action is taken during an upswing in activity, even though pressure to act may then be less. Governments should, therefore, seize the opportunity which the current situation offers, in order to avoid much more difficult conditions when the expansion slows. Action to reduce spending may be most effective where budgetary processes combine credible and binding limits on expenditure with efforts to improve the efficiency of public activities. Beyond this, it is necessary to achieve reductions in social exclusion and marginalisation, and an equitable distribution of income, both among those currently alive and between current and future generations. Such achievements will be important factors in obtaining and maintaining broad political support for the actions required in all areas, in particular action to bring about significant improvements in budget positions.

Key structural reform issues

Reforms to reduce structural rigidities in both labour and product markets would make wage and price formation more responsive to market conditions and speed the adjustment to changing price signals, enhancing the ability of economies to adjust to changes such as shifts in demand patterns or technological advances. At the moment, rigidities in labour and product markets have the effect of channelling pressures that arise in these markets into more flexible sectors of the economy, in particular financial markets. More flexible labour and product markets will also contribute to the job creation which is necessary to reduce long-term unemployment. Improved job creation performance will assist in creating the climate necessary to address problems of marginalisation and exclusion. In these ways, the favourable impact of structural reforms on productivity and the social costs of adapting to change would increase the credibility of stable monetary and fiscal policies.

Financial markets in OECD countries are now all essentially liberalised. The potential benefits of liberalised financial markets are substantial, and include: allowing savers greater protection against inflation; facilitating portfolio diversification both within countries and internationally; providing access to financing often lacking in the past; enlarging the scope for the end users of capital to make productive investment in activities that are judged to yield the highest return over the longer term; increasing the operating efficiency of financial institutions and reducing intermediation margins; and encouraging innovative methods of risk management. To maximise these benefits it is essential that market participants be subject to the disciplines which markets impose as well as having access to the rewards they offer to ensure that they prudently balance risk-taking and the search for high returns. In particular, care must be taken to avoid a situation (often described as ''moral hazard'') in which participants' investment or financing decisions or government policies are distorted by the perception that they are effectively guaranteed against risk or are underwritten by domestic taxpayers or the international community.

The volatility which financial markets have displayed has led to suggestions that the process of deregulation should be reversed or that measures, such as transaction taxes, should be introduced to ''slow'' financial markets. In view of the adverse economic effects caused by the distortions associated with much of past regulation, reversing the trend towards liberalisation is not a solution, and in any case is unlikely to be feasible. To be effective, transaction taxes and regulations would have to be applied virtually worldwide, which would require a degree of international co-ordination that is probably not achievable. A large pool of funds to stabilise excessive currency movements has also been suggested, but it would create moral hazard problems on the part of both private sector market participants and governments, undermining healthy market discipline on their behaviour and policies.

OECD governments cannot, however, be complacent about financial market behaviour. The full benefits of liberalised markets will be realised only if the necessary information is available for market participants to make decisions wisely and for the relevant authorities to assess institution-specific and systemic risks. This points to the need to enhance transparency in both private and public sectors: by devising more accurate and informative accounting methods – notably for derivatives and other new financial instruments; through earlier and more comprehensive disclosure of financial situations by both private market participants and national governments; and by improving the quality of relevant economic and financial data. There is also scope for improving prudential supervision of financial institutions and markets, as well as for ensuring adequate consumer protection and continued vigorous competition in the financial system.

The current expansion in the OECD area has the potential to mature into a phase of durable growth of employment and incomes in a stable, non-inflationary environment. Ensuring this desirable outcome, however, will require policy initiatives across the full range of actions outlined above. Exploiting to the full the mutually-reinforcing effects of good macroeconomic policies and good structural policies is crucial to achieving the objective of rising and equitably distributed global living standards.

1 June 1995

OECD ECONOMIC OUTLOOK AND POLICIES

GENERAL ASSESSMENT OF THE ECONOMIC SITUATION

Economic prospects for most of the OECD area remain good, although the steady improvements in the outlook which have occurred during the past year or so appear to be running their course. Output is projected to expand at 2¾ per cent in 1995 and 1996. Employment should rise in virtually all countries, a development not seen since the late 1970s, and unemployment rates should fall. Nevertheless, unemployment will remain high, especially in Europe. Inflation is projected to remain low nearly everywhere. Ensuring the sustainability of the expansion will require continued efforts towards establishing a sound macroeconomic environment. In particular, budget deficits and debt-to-GDP ratios need to be reduced. The credibility of monetary authorities' commitments to price stability over the medium term also needs to be strengthened. Such macroeconomic policy endeavours, together with greater transparency in financial markets, will contribute to confidence in financial markets and reduce the likelihood of abrupt disturbances and turbulence such as those that have occurred on a number of occasions in recent years. Finally, further progress in structural reform is essential. Priority needs to be given to improving the functioning of labour markets and to extending the reach of competition in product markets. It is particularly important that the open, multilateral, rules-based trading system not be compromised.

RECENT DEVELOPMENTS AND PROSPECTS FOR 1995-96

Economic activity and financial market developments since late 1994

Six months ago, when *OECD Economic Outlook 56* was published, the OECD area appeared to be expanding steadily at close to 3 per cent per annum and was projected to continue to do so during 1995 and 1996. It is now clear that activity in North America and Europe, particularly in the second half of 1994, was more robust than was apparent at the time. Consequently, despite some delay in the Japanese recovery, activity in the area as a whole turned out somewhat stronger during 1994 than projected (Table 1). However, during the past six months, a number of developments have occurred whose overall impact on short-term growth prospects in the area appears to be negative. The most important of these have been the Mexican crisis which has unfolded since last December and the deflationary impact of exchange-rate appreciation in Japan and, to a lesser extent, in Germany and some smaller countries whose currencies have moved closely with the Deutschemark. As a result, growth in the area is now projected to be somewhat lower in 1995 and 1996 than expected earlier, at around 2¾ per cent.

Most of the negative economic forces that have emerged in recent months either have been reflected in turbulence in foreign exchange markets or appear to be consequences of it. The Mexican crisis, which began with the collapse of the peso at the end of last year, occurred against the background of a rising current account deficit and increasing political instability in

Table 1. **Growth projections compared**

Per cent

Date of projection	1994		1995		1996	
	December 1994[a]	June 1995	December 1994[a]	June 1995	December 1994[a]	June 1995
North America	3.9	4.1	3.2	2.8	2.3	2.5
of which:						
United States	3.9	4.1	3.1	3.2	2.0	2.3
Mexico	2.9	3.5	4.0	–2.9	4.3	3.0
Japan	1.0	0.6	2.5	1.3	3.4	2.3
OECD Europe	2.3	2.4	3.0	3.0	3.2	3.0
of which:						
Germany	2.8	2.9	2.8	2.9	3.5	2.7
Total OECD	2.8	2.9	3.0	2.7	2.9	2.7

a) OECD Economic Outlook 56, December 1994, Paris.

Mexico. The situation there has necessitated restrictive fiscal and monetary policies which are projected to bring about a recession. Market concern about the United States' external position, partly associated with the adverse consequences of the Mexican crisis, and partly due to changes in market expectations about relative monetary conditions in the three largest economies, triggered a sharp decline in the US dollar against the Japanese yen and the Deutschemark in recent months. In Canada and a number of European countries, political uncertainties and doubts about fiscal prospects eroded financial market confidence, and exchange-rate turbulence spread to markets in these countries.

By early May 1995, when exchange-rate assumptions underlying the projections presented here were fixed, the Japanese yen and the Deutschemark had appreciated against the US dollar by 15 and 8½ per cent, respectively, since last November (Table 2), while many European currencies had depreciated by varying amounts against the Deutschemark. In effective terms, the appreciation of the yen and the Deutschemark amounted to 13 and 5¼ per cent, respectively. Other European currencies have also registered pronounced movements since late 1994, including the Italian lira, the pound sterling, the Spanish peseta, and the Swedish krona, which all depreciated in effective terms. At the same time, the Swiss franc and currencies of most countries participating in the European Exchange Rate Mechanism (ERM) have appreciated broadly in line with the Deutschemark. Despite the dollar's large depreciation against the yen and most ERM currencies, its stability against the Canadian dollar and its rise of more than 40 per cent against the Mexican peso, the currencies of two of the United States' largest trading partners, meant that it fell by much less on an effective basis.

These pronounced variations in exchange rates have translated into large changes in relative competitive positions across OECD countries, which in turn are expected to have an important influence on net export performance and activity in the major regions over the next two years (Table 3). In the United States, while the contribution from net exports to growth is projected to turn positive in the course of 1995, this is likely to occur later and to a smaller extent than expected previously due to the immediate impact of the crisis in Mexico. In Europe, lower export growth in countries whose currencies have appreciated is not projected to be fully offset by stronger exports in depreciating countries, as some of them are facing capacity constraints in exporting sectors. In Japan, reflecting the effects of the yen appreciation,

Table 3. **Contributions to real GDP growth**[a]

Per cent of real GDP in the previous year

	1994	1995	1996
United States			
Total domestic demand	4.7	3.3	1.8
of which:			
Business investment	1.6	1.9	0.9
Net exports	–0.7	–0.2	0.5
GDP	4.1	3.2	2.3
Japan			
Total domestic demand	1.0	2.4	3.1
of which:			
Business investment	–1.7	0.2	0.5
Net exports	–0.4	–1.1	–0.8
GDP	0.6	1.3	2.3
OECD Europe			
Total domestic demand	1.9	2.8	3.2
of which:			
Business investment	0.2	0.8	0.8
Net exports	0.8	0.4	–0.0
GDP	2.4	3.0	3.0
Total OECD			
Total domestic demand	3.0	2.5	2.6
of which:			
Business investment	0.6	1.1	0.8
Net exports	–0.2	0.1	0.1
GDP	2.9	2.7	2.7

a) May not sum up due to rounding.

Table 2. **Developments in nominal and effective exchange rates in selected OECD countries**

Percentage change between 2 November 1994 and 2 May 1995[a]

	Vis-à-vis US dollar[b]	In effective terms[c]
A. Depreciating countries		
United States	–	–0.8
Italy	–7.8	–12.5
United Kingdom	–1.3	–5.5
Australia	–1.9	–6.7
Mexico	–41.4	–42.3
Spain	1.4	–2.1
Sweden	–0.8	–5.3
B. Appreciating countries		
Japan	15.1	13.0
Germany	8.5	5.3
Austria	8.6	3.0
Belgium	8.1	3.9
Denmark	8.0	3.7
Netherlands	8.5	4.2
New Zealand	9.4	6.4
Switzerland	9.9	5.5

a) 2 November 1994 and 2 May 1995 are the dates for fixing exchange-rate assumptions underlying projections reported in *OECD Economic Outlook 56* published in December 1994, and in this issue of the *OECD Economic Outlook*, respectively.
b) Percentage change in one unit of each currency per US dollar.
c) Percentage change in indices of nominal effective exchange rates, 1991 = 100.

net exports are projected to continue to act as a drag on output growth throughout the projection period. Since many non-OECD countries in Asia are among the principal beneficiaries of yen appreciation, in terms of competitiveness, only a part of the positive counterpart to the negative impact of exchange rate turbulence on Japan will be felt within the OECD area.

Monetary policies have also had a restraining influence on demand in many countries. Where the expansion has been under way the longest and tightening began during 1994 to avoid capacity-related price pressures before they emerge, domestic demand appears to have started to slow (United States, United Kingdom, Canada, Australia, and New Zealand), in some cases more rapidly than expected earlier. In a number of other countries which have experienced downward pressures of varying severity on their currencies, particularly *vis-à-vis* the Deutschemark (France, Italy, Belgium, Denmark, Spain and Sweden), policy-controlled interest rates were increased in early 1995. While there has been some reversal of these increases in some of these countries, short-term interest rates in most appear unlikely to be as low, on average, during 1995 as assumed six months ago by the OECD Secretariat. On the other hand, in Japan and Germany policy controlled interest rates and money market rates have eased significantly.

On the positive side, long-term interest rates have generally declined since their peaks in the autumn of 1994 (Figure 1). By mid-May 1995, 10-year bond yields had fallen by around 1 to 1½ percentage points in the major countries, with the exception of Italy, and in several smaller ones. The decline in long-term rates has been more pronounced in the United States and Japan than in Germany, and the differential between US and German rates has now been reversed.[1] However, in Italy and some other smaller European countries, where budget deficits remain large and currencies have been under pressure, the decline in bond yields has been less marked or, as in Spain, has not occurred at all, and the differential *vis-à-vis* Germany has increased to around 4 to 5 percentage points.

POLICY AND TECHNICAL ASSUMPTIONS UNDERLYING THE PROJECTIONS

Fiscal policy assumptions are based on announced measures and stated policy intentions, where they are embodied in well-defined programmes.

Policy-controlled interest rates are assumed to be set in line with the stated policy priorities of the national authorities with respect to inflation (and in some cases to support recoveries). In the United States and the United Kingdom this is assumed to entail some further increases; in Germany and most other continental European countries they are assumed to start rising toward the end of 1995, with differentials *vis-à-vis* Germany in most cases declining; and in Japan they are assumed to remain low.

The most important technical assumptions and external factors which affect the projections are the following:

- The projections assume unchanged exchange rates from those prevailing on 2 May 1995. The fixed exchange rate assumption is modified for Greece and Turkey to allow for continuous exchange rate depreciation, reflecting the OECD Secretariat's interpretation of "official" exchange rate policies.
- The average dollar price (OECD fob imports) of internationally traded oil is estimated to be $16.5 in the first half of 1995 and is assumed to rise in line with OECD manufactured export prices thereafter.

While the overall outlook is somewhat weaker than it appeared six months ago, the central projections based on a set of technical assumptions (described in the Box, and which include stability of nominal exchange rates) remain favourable, with a major exception of Japan. In the United States, growth has already slowed from its 1994 pace of more than 4 per cent to 3 per cent in the first half of 1995 and is projected to fall to 2¼ per cent in 1996. The projected slowdown in growth is consistent with the objective of putting the economy on a more sustainable path after three years of rapid expansion at rates exceeding potential growth. The near-term strength of business fixed investment and improving net exports are projected to cushion cautious spending behaviour on the part of households and weak inventory investment. In Europe, output growth may rise somewhat from 2½ per cent in 1994 to around 3 per cent in both 1995 and 1996, as business investment increasingly takes over from exports as the main engine of growth. In Japan, on the other hand, growth will remain low in 1995 at around 1¼ per cent. Provided that the yen stabilises and that household confidence is sustained, however, strengthening domestic demand – led by private consumption and continued buoyancy of government spending – should provide increasing support for activity and growth in 1996 could rise to 2¼ per cent.

Figure 1. **Short- and long-term interest rates**

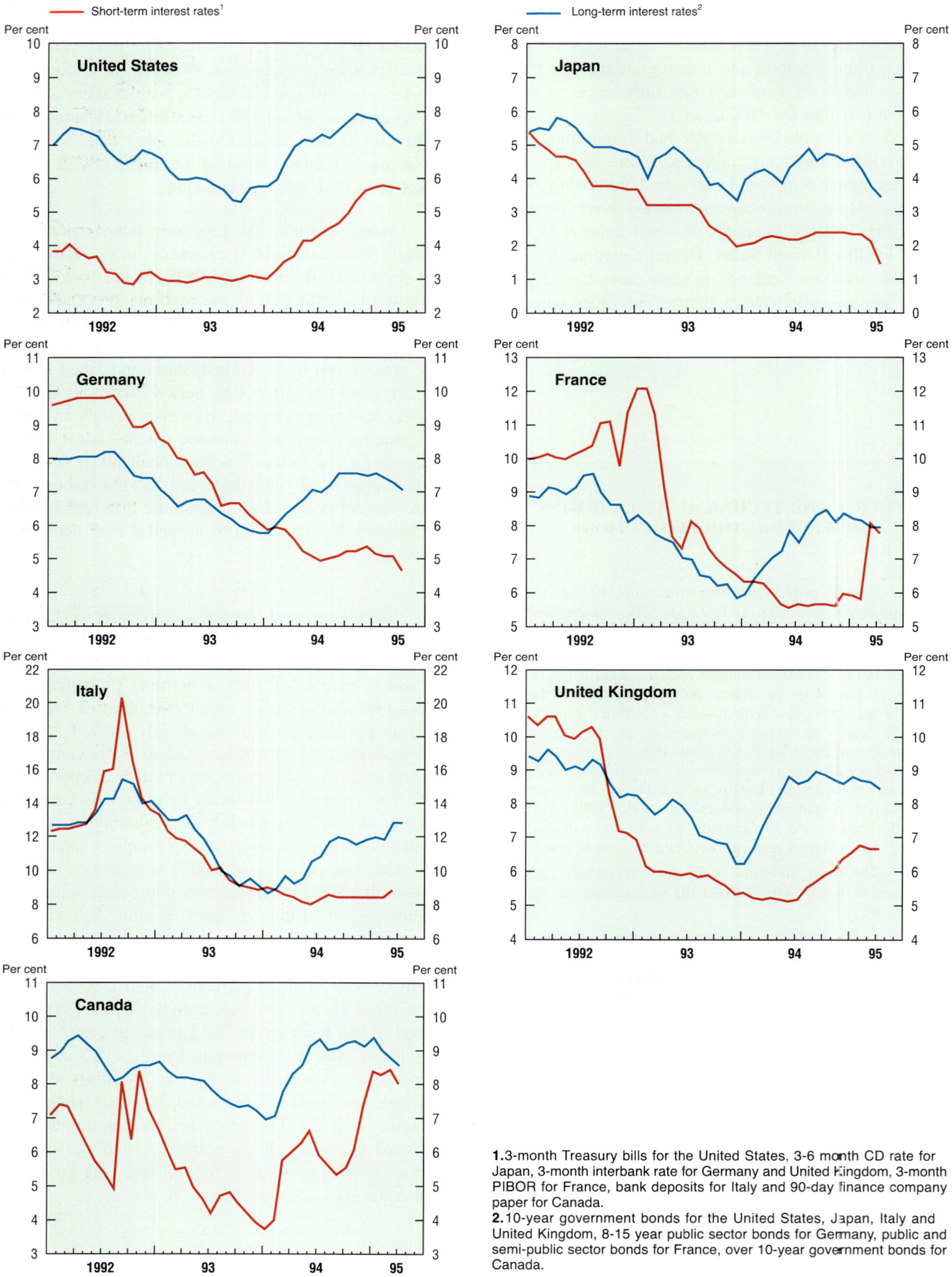

1. 3-month Treasury bills for the United States, 3-6 month CD rate for Japan, 3-month interbank rate for Germany and United Kingdom, 3-month PIBOR for France, bank deposits for Italy and 90-day finance company paper for Canada.

2. 10-year government bonds for the United States, Japan, Italy and United Kingdom, 8-15 year public sector bonds for Germany, public and semi-public sector bonds for France, over 10-year government bonds for Canada.

Figure 2. **Recoveries in employment**

Index, troughs[1] = 100

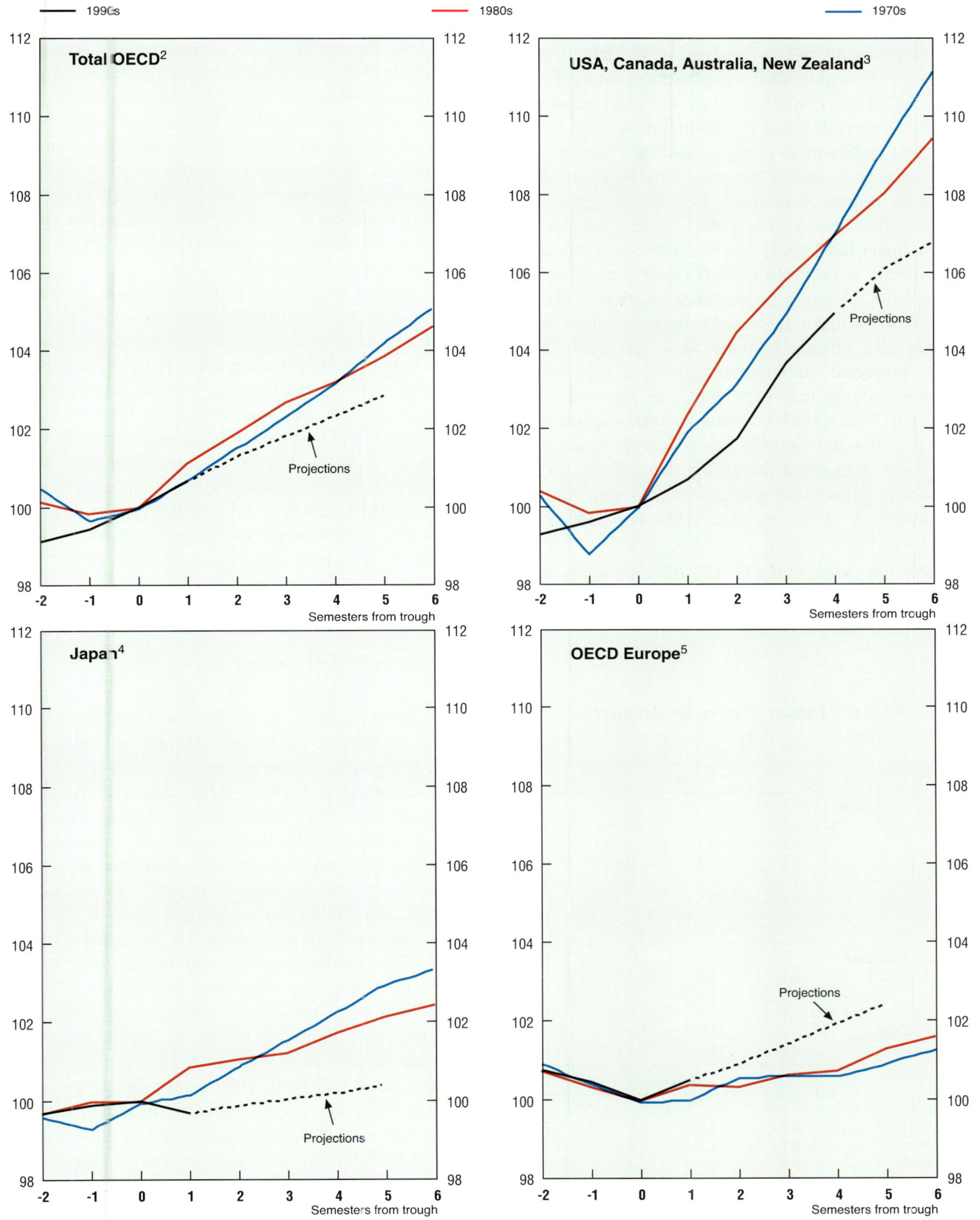

1. Troughs of economic activity are identified as the point in time when the largest negative value of the output gap is observed.
2. Recoveries beginning in 75-II, 83-I and 94-I. Excluding Mexico and Turkey.
3. Recoveries beginning in 75-II, 83-I and 92-II.
4. Recoveries beginning in 75-II and 84-I. For the current economic cycle, the trough is not projected to be reached before the end of the projection period. However, for comparison purposes, employment developments in Japan between 93-I and 96-II are shown.
5. Recoveries beginning in 75-II, 83-I and 94-I. Excluding Turkey.

Labour market and inflation developments

Against the backdrop of rising economic activity, area-wide unemployment, which peaked in early 1994, should continue to fall. As a share of the labour force, unemployment is projected to decrease to about 7½ per cent by the end of 1996 (Table 4), a level last recorded in 1991. It is noteworthy that for the first time since the late 1970s total employment is expected to increase in every OECD country in both 1995 and 1996. However, large differences in rates of unemployment across regions will persist. In the United States, the cyclical reduction in unemployment has largely run its course, and the unemployment rate is expected to start rising during 1995 as activity slows. In Japan, employment creation is likely to be too weak to make any significant dent in the unemployment rate, already high by Japanese standards. In Europe, projected employment growth is on average somewhat stronger than experienced in previous cycles (Figure 2). Widespread declines in unemployment are expected, although there will be cyclical increases in the labour force throughout the region. Nevertheless, European unemployment will probably remain above 20 million persons in 1996, or about 10½ per cent of the labour force.

The low point in the OECD inflation cycle seems to have been reached in 1994, when private consumption deflators in the area (on average, excluding Mexico and Turkey) are estimated to have risen at a rate of just over 2 per cent (Table 5). However, no significant generalised acceleration is projected in the near term: area-wide inflation on this basis is expected to remain around 2½ per cent until the end of the projection period, although with a slight upward drift. (Inflation is projected to be slightly lower as measured by the GDP deflator, but the general profile over time is similar.) Indicators of wage inflation, such as changes in private compensation per employee and unit labour costs, are also projected to creep upwards during this year and next as labour markets tighten in several countries. Commodity price increases are projected to be similar to those of overall prices, having peaked in the early months of 1995.

Within this broad picture, inflation performance will be affected by recent currency movements. Appreciation will limit price rises in Germany and those European countries which maintain a fairly tight exchange-rate link to the Deutschemark, while in Japan the overall price level may fall slightly during 1995 and remain stable in 1996. On the other hand, where currencies have depreciated, as in Italy, the United Kingdom, Mexico, Spain, Sweden and Turkey, rises in import prices may directly affect consumer price inflation. The risk will be especially serious where export booms have led to high levels of industrial capacity utilisation (Italy, United Kingdom, Portugal, Spain and Sweden).

Table 4. **Labour market developments**

	1993	1994	1995	1996
	Per cent			
Employment growth				
United States[a]	1.5	3.1	1.9	1.1
Japan	0.2	0.1	0.1	0.3
Germany	–1.8	–0.9	0.0	0.5
OECD Europe	–1.7	–0.8	0.9	1.1
Total OECD	–0.1	0.9	1.2	1.1
	Per cent of labour force			
Unemployment rate				
United States[a]	6.8	6.1	5.6	5.7
Japan	2.5	2.9	3.1	3.1
Germany	8.9	9.6	9.2	8.7
OECD Europe	10.7	11.3	11.0	10.6
Total OECD	8.0	8.1	7.8	7.6
	Millions			
Unemployment				
United States[a]	8.7	8.0	7.5	7.7
Japan	1.7	1.9	2.1	2.1
Germany	3.4	3.7	3.5	3.4
OECD Europe	20.3	21.4	21.1	20.4
Total OECD	33.9	34.3	33.6	33.1

a) Break in series as of January 1994.

Foreign trade and balance of payments

World trade was buoyant in 1994, increasing at nearly 10 per cent in real terms (Table 6). It is projected to keep rising by around 9 per cent in 1995 and to lose pace only slightly in 1996, mainly due to slowing domestic demand in the United States. Strong world trade growth reflects rising trade flows both between OECD countries and with countries outside the area, whose imports may rise by around 10 per cent annually, on average, over the projection period.

International imbalances are expected to remain large. The United States' current-account deficit is projected to increase by more than $35 billion in 1995 to more than $190 billion (2¾ per cent of GDP) and to decline only slightly in 1996. In Japan, the current-account surplus is projected to fall from its peak of 3.2 per cent of GDP in 1992 to around 2¼ per cent of GDP in 1996. The surplus will also decline in yen terms, but it will remain broadly unchanged in dollar terms, at around $125 billion in 1996, reflecting the sharp depreciation of the US dollar against the yen. The main counterparts to the continued deterioration in the United States' current-account position are found in a significant

Table 5. **Inflation indicators in selected OECD countries**

Per cent

	Change in private consumption deflator from previous period			Change in private compensation per employee from previous period			Change in unit labour cost in the business sector from previous period			Output gaps[a]		
	1994	1995	1996	1994	1995	1996	1994	1995	1996	1994	1995	1996
United States	2.1	2.8	3.4	3.4	2.9	3.7	1.8	2.1	2.4	1.2	1.8	1.4
Japan	0.3	–0.6	0.0	1.2	2.5	2.5	0.6	1.2	0.3	–1.4	–2.9	–3.1
Germany	2.7	2.3	2.1	3.7	3.9	4.7	–1.0[b]	0.7[b]	2.5[b]	–1.1	–0.9	–1.0
France	1.8	1.6	1.7	1.2	2.6	3.3	–1.5	0.4	1.1	–3.6	–2.8	–1.9
Italy	4.7	5.4	4.7	4.4	4.8	5.1	0.1	1.7	2.9	–4.0	–3.0	–2.1
United Kingdom	2.5	2.9	3.1	2.6	3.6	4.4	–0.1	1.7	2.6	–3.1	–2.1	–1.6
Canada	0.7	2.0	2.0	2.0	2.5	3.0	–0.6	1.0	2.0	–3.2	–1.9	–1.1
Australia	1.4	2.6	3.7	2.0	3.8	4.5	–0.3	2.9	3.6	–0.4	0.4	0.7
Belgium	2.4	1.9	2.0	2.5	2.7	2.8	–0.3	0.3	1.0	–2.5	–1.9	–1.7
Finland	1.6	2.1	2.6	2.6	5.2	5.5	–2.0	3.6	3.8	–5.7	–3.7	–2.5
Netherlands	2.2	1.7	1.8	1.7	2.0	2.0	–1.3	–0.2	0.2	–1.5	–0.9	–0.9
New Zealand	0.5	2.9	2.0	1.7	3.5	3.1	2.5	3.1	1.9	..	..	..
Norway	1.4	2.8	2.6	3.1	3.3	3.8	0.6	2.1	2.7	–1.5	–0.9	–0.7
Spain	5.1	4.7	4.1	3.5	3.9	4.6	0.3	1.9	3.0	–3.0	–2.6	–2.3
Sweden	3.0	3.3	2.8	5.4	5.3	3.9	1.8	5.0	3.1	–3.5	–2.7	–2.3
OECD Europe (excl. Turkey)	3.1	3.1	2.9	3.3	3.8	4.3	–0.2	1.4	2.3	–2.7[c]	–2.0[c]	–1.6[c]
Total OECD (excl. Mexico and Turkey)	2.2	2.4	2.6	2.9	3.2	3.7	0.8	2.4	2.6	–1.0[d]	–0.7[d]	–0.6[d]
Total OECD	4.1	4.6	4.0	4.5	5.1	5.1	2.4	3.6	3.3	–1.0[d]	–0.7[d]	–0.6[d]

a) Difference between actual and potential output. No estimates of potential output are available for New Zealand. For further details, see Giorno C. *et al.*, "Potential output, output gaps and structural budget balances", *OECD Economic Studies*, No. 24, Paris, 1995.
b) Western Germany only.
c) OECD Europe less Iceland and Turkey.
d) Total OECD less Iceland, Mexico, New Zealand and Turkey.

Table 6. **Trade and payments summary**

	1993	1994	1995	1996
	Percentage changes from previous period			
A. Merchandise trade volumes				
World trade[a]	3.6	9.8	8.9	7.8
intra-OECD trade[b]	0.3	10.1	8.3	6.9
OECD exports to non-OECD	8.7	9.6	10.4	9.1
OECD imports from non-OECD	7.4	9.4	8.9	8.0
Exports				
OECD total	2.6	9.6	8.9	7.4
United States	4.6	11.0	10.2	11.5
Japan	–1.9	1.6	2.7	4.9
OECD Europe	1.9	10.1	8.9	6.4
Non-OECD total	7.4	9.7	8.9	8.5
Imports				
OECD total	1.6	10.3	8.4	7.2
United States	11.7	15.2	10.2	5.7
Japan	3.8	13.7	13.2	10.3
OECD Europe	–2.8	7.6	7.7	7.3
Non-OECD total	8.6	9.5	10.4	9.5
B. Terms of trade				
United States	0.7	0.2	–2.8	–1.6
Japan	8.9	7.5	2.9	–0.5
OECD Europe	0.5	–1.0	–0.7	–0.1
OECD terms of trade with rest of the world[c]	2.2	1.6	–0.8	–0.3
	$ billion			
C. Current balances				
United States	–104	–156	–193	–188
Japan	132	129	135	127
OECD Europe	22	52	79	78

a) Growth rate of the arithmetic average of world import volumes and world export volumes.
b) Simple arithmetic average of intra-OECD export and import volumes implied by total OECD trade volumes and estimated trade flows between OECD and the non-OECD areas. Historical figures are based on the 1991 structure of trade by value, deflated by total OECD export prices.
c) Prices of OECD exports to the non-OECD as a ratio of prices of OECD imports from the non-OECD.

increase in the European surplus, which is projected to rise by some $25 billion in 1995, and in sharp reductions in the current-account deficits of Canada and, especially, Mexico.

RISKS TO THE OUTLOOK AND TENSIONS IN THE CURRENT SITUATION

Notwithstanding the generally favourable projections for most countries, a number of features of the current situation imply risks in the short term to non-inflationary growth and in the longer term to macroeconomic stability, productivity and employment performance and the open multilateral rules-based trading system. Failure to manage these risks successfully will threaten the ability of OECD countries to achieve their ultimate goals of raising the living standards of their citizens and reducing marginalisation and exclusion.

In countries which had both gone into recession and emerged from it earliest, the margin of spare capacity has been declining rapidly and monetary policies have generally been tightened to prevent a resurgence of inflation. In a number of countries there is some evidence that monetary tightening is already having its intended effect. However, in the United States, where economic slack appears to have been virtually eliminated, the central projections embody a resumption of demand growth in the latter half of 1995 which may increase inflation pressure unless it is contained by a further monetary tightening. If such action is not taken in the face of stronger demand, a more pronounced cyclical swing (a boom and bust) similar to those observed in the past may become more likely. Elsewhere, the somewhat weaker prospects for Japan, Germany and some smaller European countries with close currency linkages with Germany could adversely affect countries such as France and Italy. Given that area-wide growth appears to have passed its peak, these considerations suggest that the risks attached to the prospect of stable non-inflationary growth which progressively absorbs cyclical unemployment throughout the area may now be more evenly balanced than six months ago.

Should recent exchange rate movements be reversed quickly, the balance of risks would be more positive. In countries where currencies have depreciated, inflation pressures would be less likely to emerge and would allow somewhat more relaxed monetary policy stances. In Japan, Germany and some smaller European countries, which have experienced significant exchange rate appreciation in recent months, the favourable impact of correction of misaligned currency relationships might not be confined to the beneficial effects on trade flows. It could also lead to higher levels of business and consumer confidence, with positive implications for private spending.

There have been a number of episodes of financial market turbulence in recent years – of which the recent disturbance involving the decline in the dollar against the yen and the Deutschemark and pressures on intra-European exchange rates is only one. This turbulence has generally indicated a lack of confidence in either economic policies or prospects or both. It has frequently reflected market reactions to inappropriate macroeconomic policies, structural imbalances, possible conflicts between structural policy objectives and other goals, or inconsistencies in policies across countries. Such market reactions have often acted as a useful discipline on policies. However, on a number of occasions they have also operated in a disruptive manner which has had – or has threatened to have – widespread ramifications which could put the financial deregulation process itself into question, or increase political pressures that could lead governments to resort to counter-productive measures to "slow" the markets in some way.

Public finances are in poor shape in most OECD countries. This poses risks of a short- and a long-term nature. The unsustainability of current budget positions and the rapid increases in government debt which they imply have already contributed to negative reactions from financial markets in several countries, notably Italy, Spain, Sweden and Turkey. These reactions, which have been reflected in high long-term interest rates and persistent exchange rate weakness against currencies of major trading partners, could affect confidence more widely and require restrictive policies which could put the expansion at risk in the near term. However, avoiding such a risk by delaying necessary policy adjustment might worsen longer-term economic performance. In other countries, the risks are of a longer-term nature, as commitments to spending on public pensions and health care as populations age will put fiscal positions under increasing stress.

While employment is projected to rise in every OECD country during the coming two years, unemployment will remain far too high in many of them. At the same time, there is growing concern about the social consequences of rising inequality, even in countries where employment prospects are generally favourable. These developments – persistent high unemployment and rising inequality – are likely to put pressure on social safety nets which are designed to minimise marginalisation and to provide some protection against poverty. In this context, debate has taken place about foreign trade, particularly with non-OECD countries, as a cause of both high unemployment and rising income inequality in OECD countries.

These risks and tensions pose challenges which will require responses covering a broad range of policy areas. The section below considers three areas where both short-run and medium-term policy action in OECD countries could contribute to better functioning of the open economies: fiscal policies, monetary policies and policies towards financial markets. A final section considers the influence of international trade on labour markets. Policy action in labour and product markets in individual countries are examined in the recently published monograph *The OECD Jobs Study: Implementing the Strategy*.

MAKING OPEN ECONOMIES FUNCTION MORE EFFICIENTLY AND SMOOTHLY

Fiscal policy priorities

Budget prospects on current fiscal policy settings

The improvement in budget positions which began in 1994 in many countries is projected to continue, but the pace of consolidation is likely to remain modest over the next two years. For the OECD area as a whole, the general government deficit is projected to continue falling by nearly ½ per cent of GDP per year. Yet at around 3½ and 3 per cent of GDP in 1995 and 1996, respectively, it will remain high (Table 7). Consolidation efforts are generally projected to be insufficient to

Table 7. **Actual and structural general government financial balances**

	Actual financial balances, as a percentage of nominal GDP				
	1989	1993	1994	1995	1996
United States[a]	–1.5	–3.4	–2.0	–1.8	–2.0
Japan	2.5	–1.4	–3.5	–4.1	–4.2
Germany[b]	0.1	–3.3	–2.5	–2.3	–2.2
France	–1.2	–6.1	–6.0	–5.0	–4.1
Italy	–9.9	–9.6	–9.0	–7.8	–6.9
United Kingdom	0.9	–7.9	–6.5	–4.2	–2.6
Canada	–2.9	–7.1	–5.3	–3.7	–2.4
Total of smaller countries[c]	–2.1	–6.4	–5.6	–4.9	–3.9
Total of European countries[d]	–2.5	–6.5	–5.7	–4.8	–4.0
Total OECD[c]	–1.2	–4.5	–3.9	–3.4	–3.1
General government financial balances excluding social security					
United States[a, e, f]	–2.5	–4.2	–2.9	–2.8	–3.0
Japan[e]	–0.8	–4.9	–7.0	–7.6	–7.7
	Structural financial balances,[g] as a percentage of nominal potential GDP				
	1989	1993	1994	1995	1996
United States[a]	–2.3	–3.2	–2.4	–2.5	–2.6
Japan	2.0	–1.6	–2.9	–2.8	–2.8
Germany[b]	0.0	–2.7	–1.9	–1.8	–1.7
France	–1.9	–3.8	–3.9	–3.4	–3.0
Italy	–10.6	–7.9	–7.4	–6.7	–6.1
United Kingdom	–2.0	–5.6	–4.8	–3.0	–1.7
Canada	–4.7	–4.1	–3.4	–2.7	–1.7
Total of smaller countries[c]	–3.3	–4.9	–4.4	–4.1	–3.4
Total of European countries[d]	–3.5	–4.9	–4.3	–3.8	–3.2
Total OECD[c]	–2.1	–3.6	–3.3	–3.1	–2.8

a) Excludes deposit insurance outlays.
b) Includes balances of the German Railways Fund from 1994 on, and of the Inherited Debt Fund from 1995 on.
c) Excluding Iceland, Luxembourg, Mexico, New Zealand, Switzerland and Turkey.
d) Excluding Iceland, Luxembourg, Switzerland and Turkey.
e) OECD Secretariat estimates, derived from fiscal year data converted to a calendar year basis. The coverage of the social security systems is not the same in the United States and Japan.
f) Includes the surplus of state and local government pension schemes.
g) For a description of the methodology used to calculate structural balances, see Giorno, C. *et al.*, "Potential output, output gaps and structural budget balances", *OECD Economic Studies*, No. 24, Paris, 1995.

stabilise or reduce debt levels and the OECD area's gross debt-to-GDP ratio is likely to rise further from around 70 per cent in 1994 to 74 per cent in 1996.

In the United States, unless discussions taking place in Congress result in a medium-term deficit reduction agreement that has a significant immediate effect, the general government deficit in 1995 and 1996 appears set to remain broadly unchanged from its 1994 level of around 2 per cent of GDP. In Japan it is projected to increase during 1995 to just over 4 per cent of GDP, as a result of earlier packages aimed at stimulating the economy and the recent programme to deal mainly with the Kobe earthquake. In most other countries, considerable fiscal consolidation is projected over the next two years. In particular, in countries where interest rates have turned out to be higher than assumed in earlier budget plans (*e.g.* Italy, Canada, Sweden and Turkey), additional measures have already been taken to keep consolidation on track. In a number of countries where strong cyclical improvements are accompanied by relatively large reductions in structural deficits (the United Kingdom, Canada, Australia, Denmark, Greece, Sweden), large cumulative falls in the actual deficit from 1994 to 1996 are projected, ranging from 2 to 4 per cent of GDP,[2] and Norway should move into substantial surplus. Nevertheless, deficits will remain large in many countries (especially in Italy, Greece, Portugal, Spain and Sweden) and, among the 15 EU countries, by 1996, only six are expected to have deficits below the Maastricht limit of 3 per cent of GDP and only four to have debt-to-GDP ratios below 60 per cent (Table 8).

Most governments have announced medium-term fiscal consolidation targets beyond 1996. These are embodied in the OECD Secretariat's Medium-Term Reference Scenario, in which announced fiscal and monetary policy objectives are generally assumed to be achieved in the context of a favourable macroeconomic environment in which output gaps are steadily closed over the period to the year 2000.[3] (See Table 9 for a summary of its main macroeconomic features.) While reductions in fiscal deficits on an area-wide basis in the scenario are large,[4] they are just sufficient to stabilise the ratio of debt-to-GDP for the area as a whole. While debt ratios fall in some countries, these reductions are typically small and leave uncomfortably high debt levels in many countries in the year 2000 (Table 10).

Beyond 2000, ageing populations in OECD countries will put increasing stress on general government budgets, because of increased pension payments and health-care spending. The impact on government budgets will mainly depend on the nature and the degree of demographic changes, the exposure of government budgets to the effects of ageing and the response of policies to these new challenges. But it will be large nearly everywhere.

In an attempt to estimate the effect of prospective demographic changes on overall budget positions, pro-

Table 8. **Progress towards Maastricht fiscal targets**

General government financial balances and general government gross debt (Maastricht basis)[a]

As a percentage of nominal GDP

	Financial balances				Gross debt[a]			
	1993	1994	1995	1996	1993	1994	1995	1996
Austria	−4.1	−4.0	−4.5	−3.9	62.8	64.5	65.9	66.9
Belgium[b]	−6.6	−5.3	−4.3	−4.0	137.2	136.2	134.5	132.6
Denmark	−4.5	−3.9	−2.1	−1.6	80.3	75.6	75.8	75.4
Finland	−7.9	−5.5	−5.0	−3.3	57.1	60.1	66.5	70.8
France	−6.1	−6.0	−5.0	−4.1	45.8	48.5	51.2	52.6
Germany	−3.3	−2.5	−2.3	−2.2	48.2	50.1	58.0	58.1
Greece	−13.2	−12.5	−11.4	−10.0	115.1	113.6	114.0	114.0
Ireland	−2.3	−2.2	−2.5	−2.4	96.9	90.9	86.3	82.1
Italy	−9.6	−9.0	−7.8	−6.9	119.4	125.4	124.9	123.3
Luxembourg[c]	1.1	1.2	..	..	6.8	7.0	..	..
Netherlands	−3.2	−3.0	−3.3	−2.7	81.4	78.3	78.6	78.7
Portugal	−7.1	−5.7	−5.4	−5.0	66.5	69.5	69.9	69.9
Spain	−7.5	−6.6	−6.2	−5.5	59.9	62.2	65.3	67.4
Sweden	−13.4	−10.4	−9.2	−6.4	74.7	79.1	84.2	86.0
United Kingdom	−7.9	−6.5	−4.2	−2.6	48.3	52.5[d]	54.3	53.7

a) Data for general government gross debt on a Maastricht definition are provided by the Commission of the European Communities for 1993 and 1994. Estimates for 1995 and 1996 are derived by projecting forward in line with the OECD Secretariat's projections for GDP and general government financial balances while taking account, to the extent possible, of governments' policies for acquisitions of financial assets.

b) Financial balances includes proceeds of privatisations and sales of other assets (BF 32.2 billion in 1993 and BF 12.7 billion in 1994).

c) Projections not available. Both the debt and the financial balance figures were provided by the Commission of the European Communities.

d) OECD Secretariat estimates.

Figure 3. **Long-term prospects for general government primary balances**[1]

Surplus (+) or deficit (–) as a percentage of GDP

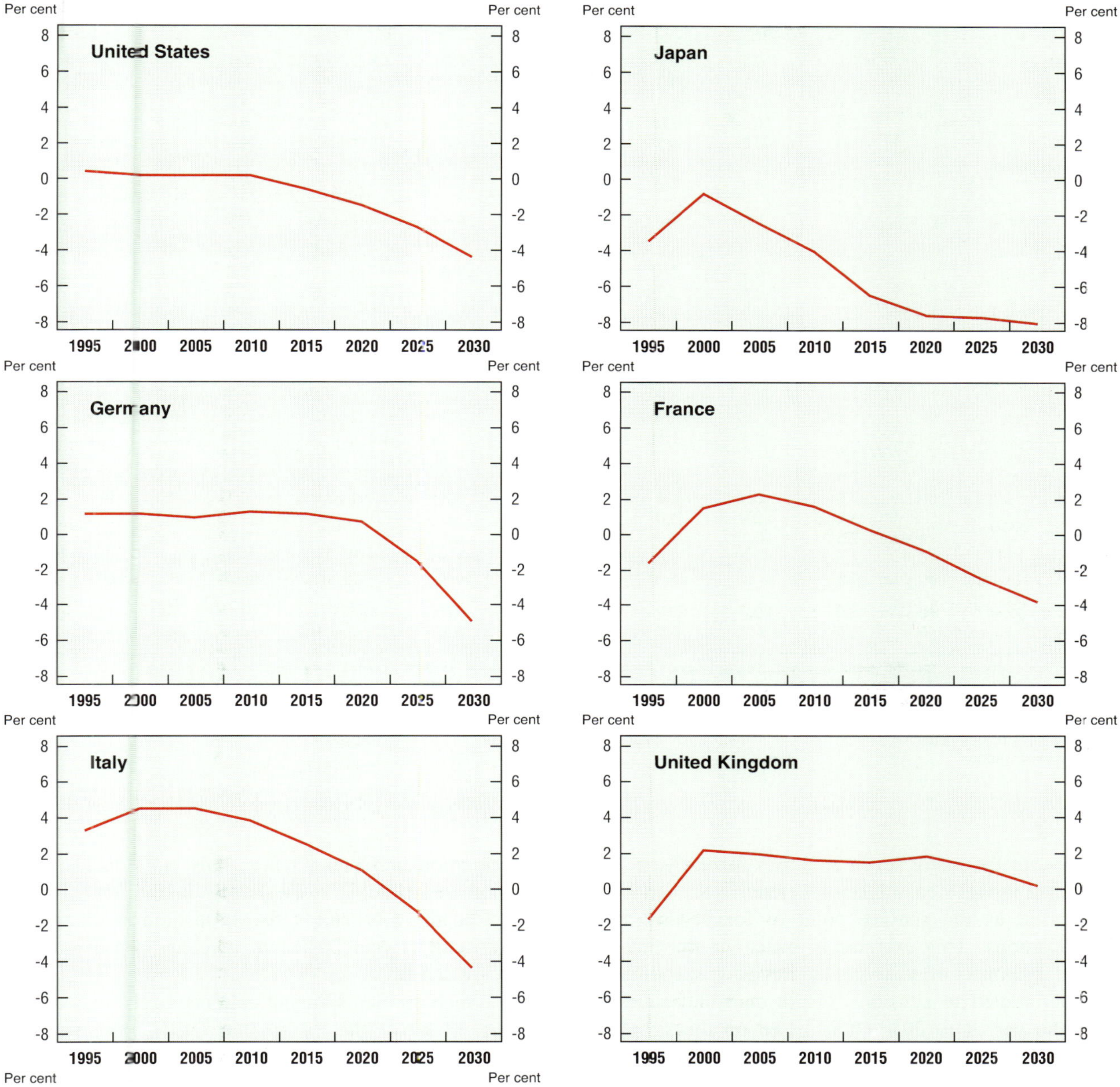

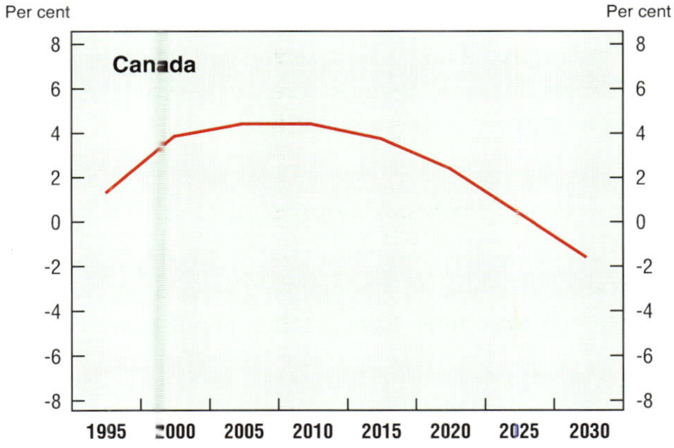

1. Primary balances in 2000 are taken from the OECD Secretariat's Medium-Term Reference Scenario (MTRS). Beyond 2000 the simulation captures demographic effects on public expenditures on pensions, health care and education, as well as the development in pension contributions and benefits to the extent they have been legislated. All other components of the primary balances are held constant as a percentage of GDP at their 2000 levels. For further details on the simulations, see the Chapter on "Effects of ageing populations on government budgets".

Table 9. **Medium-Term Reference Scenario summary**

	Real GDP growth		Inflation rate[b]		Unemployment rate[c]		Current balance[d]		Interest rates			
									Short-term		Long-term	
	Average 1997-2000	Output gap[a] by 2000	1996	2000	1996	2000	1996	2000	1996	2000	1996	2000
United States	2.3	0.1	2.7	3.0	5.7	5.8	–2.5	–2.2	6.4	5.3	6.9	7.1
Japan	3.3	–0.2	0.2	0.5	3.1	2.6	2.2	1.4	1.6	3.0	3.7	4.3
Germany	3.1	–0.1	2.3	2.4	8.7	8.0	–1.2	–1.1	5.2	5.5	7.0	6.6
France	2.9	0.1	2.0	2.2	11.5	9.3	0.8	1.4	5.4	5.5	7.3	6.6
Italy	3.0	–0.2	4.5	4.4	10.5	8.4	1.6	2.8	9.3	8.1	11.4	9.4
United Kingdom	2.8	0.1	2.7	3.0	7.6	7.0	–0.1	–0.7	7.8	7.5	8.2	7.6
Canada	3.3	0.1	2.2	2.0	9.1	8.3	–1.5	–0.3	6.6	5.3	7.5	6.7
Total of above countries	2.7	0.0	2.3	2.5	6.6	6.1	–0.3	–0.3	6.0	5.7	7.4	6.9
Australia	3.0	0.0	3.7	3.2	7.9	7.5	–5.3	–4.1	8.2	6.5	9.0	7.7
Austria	2.5	–0.1	2.7	2.9	4.2	4.0	–1.7	–1.4	5.2	5.5	7.1	6.7
Belgium	2.6	–0.1	2.2	2.4	11.8	9.7	5.8	5.9	5.6	5.5	7.7	7.0
Denmark	2.3	0.1	2.8	3.2	9.7	9.1	3.5	5.1	6.8	5.7	8.7	7.6
Finland	3.7	–0.2	2.8	3.3	14.9	12.8	1.2	1.1	6.5	6.0	8.9	7.7
Greece	2.1	0.2	7.0	4.0	9.9	7.4	–1.3	–2.1	19.0	10.5	17.0	11.0
Iceland	2.3	..	2.9	2.3	4.4	4.0	2.0	2.0	7.2	6.5	10.8	8.8
Ireland	4.6	–0.1	3.0	3.0	13.6	13.8	6.1	5.9	6.2	6.2	8.2	7.6
Mexico	5.3	..	24.0	6.9	5.2	3.4	–0.7	–2.5	35.0	12.0	35.0	14.0
Netherlands	2.6	–0.1	1.8	2.2	7.4	6.4	3.7	3.7	5.2	5.5	7.0	6.6
New Zealand	2.9	..	2.0	1.4	7.0	6.2	–1.7	–0.4	7.9	5.2	7.1	5.7
Norway	1.9	0.2	2.6	2.6	4.5	3.9	6.8	6.8	5.7	5.5	7.8	7.0
Portugal	3.0	–0.1	4.4	4.1	6.3	5.8	0.2	0.5	9.5	7.8	11.2	9.2
Spain	3.4	0.0	4.0	3.1	23.3	18.6	–1.3	–0.9	9.2	7.5	11.0	8.4
Sweden	2.5	–0.1	3.0	2.2	6.7	6.5	4.5	7.2	9.0	7.4	10.9	8.6
Switzerland	2.5	0.0	2.0	2.1	3.6	2.6	6.9	5.9	3.8	3.9	5.2	5.1
Turkey	5.5	..	45.0	15.0	12.4	10.8	1.6	–0.3	55.0	20.1	60.0	22.0
OECD Europe	3.0	0.0	2.9[e]	2.9[e]	10.6	9.0	0.8	1.0	10.1	7.2	12.0	8.5
Total OECD	2.9	0.0	3.0[e]	2.7[e]	7.6	6.8	–0.1	0.0	10.3	7.0	11.8	8.3

a) Difference between actual and potential output. No estimates of potential output are available for New Zealand. For further details, see Giorno C. *et al.*, "Potential output, output gaps and structural budget balances", *OECD Economic Studies*, No. 24, Paris, 1995.
b) Percentage changes in GDP deflator.
c) Per cent of labour force.
d) Per cent of nominal GDP.
e) Excluding Turkey.

jections for the major seven countries for the year 2000 embodied in the Medium-Term Reference Scenario have been used as the starting point of longer-term fiscal extrapolations. This exercise is meant to illustrate the budgetary impact of demographic trends on spending and receipts related to pensions, health cure and education over the period to 2030. It is based on the simplified assumption that expenditure on other items is held constant as a percentage of GDP, after adjusting for the effects of any policy changes already announced (see the chapter "Effects of Ageing Populations on Government Budgets"). In 2000, all major seven countries except Japan are projected in the Reference Scenario to have a positive primary balance (Figure 3). However, these primary balance positions are subsequently eroded, and by 2030 they range from approximate balance for the United Kingdom to deficits of around 8 per cent of GDP for Japan. Pension expenditures play a major role in this deterioration in Japan, France, Italy and Canada, while health-care spending rises sharply in the United States and Canada. Germany's fiscal position is reasonably sound until around 2020 but thereafter pension outlays increase sharply.

Such problems are not confined to the major economies. Many of the the smaller OECD countries face very similar situations regarding ageing populations, and government budgets are highly exposed to the associated cost pressures. If no early measures are taken to correct the fiscal situation, serious long-term problems could emerge in many of these countries.

Policy options for restoring fiscal sustainability

Early action to strengthen the budget positions before the pressures from ageing populations become

Table 10. **Fiscal trends in the Medium-Term Reference Scenario**

	Financial balances[a]		Gross financial liabilities[b]		Gross public debt (Maastricht criteria)[c]	
	1996	2000	1996	2000	1996	2000
United States[d]	–2.0	–2.2	63.7	64.7	–	–
Japan	–4.2	–2.0	96.2	101.6	–	–
Germany[e]	–2.2	–1.9	62.5	61.3	58.1	56.9
France	–4.1	–1.6	60.9	61.7	52.6	53.5
Italy	–6.9	–3.5	120.5	106.3	123.3	111.1
United Kingdom	–2.6	0.1	52.8	46.5	53.7	47.4
Canada	–2.4	–0.1	93.6	84.4		
Total of above countries	–3.0	–2.0	74.0	73.7	70.7	66.4
Australia	–1.0	0.5	36.5[f]	31.3[f]	–	–
Austria	–3.9	–2.2	61.4[g]	59.9[g]	66.9	65.4
Belgium	–4.0	–1.5	136.4	124.8	132.6	120.9
Denmark	–1.6	0.5	68.4[g]	62.4[g]	75.4	69.4
Finland	–3.3	–0.4	73.4[g]	88.5[g]	70.8	85.9
Greece	–10.0	–4.5	120.2[g]	115.8[g]	114.0	109.6
Ireland	–2.4	–2.1	79.1	66.1	82.1	69.1
Netherlands	–2.7	–1.2	79.5	75.7	78.7	74.9
Norway	2.7	3.7	46.5[g]	43.5[g]	–	–
Portugal	–5.0	–2.4	70.8	65.0	69.9	64.1
Spain	–5.5	–3.1	68.7[g]	71.4[g]	67.4	70.1
Sweden	–6.4	0.8	86.3	79.3	86.0	79.1
Total of above European countries	–4.0	–1.8	75.4	71.6	73.7	70.0
Total of above countries	–3.1	–1.9	74.1	73.4	–	–

a) General government fiscal surplus (+) or deficit (–), as a per cent of GDP.
b) General government gross financial liabilities according to SNA definitions, as a per cent of GDP.
c) The Maastricht definition of gross public debt is based on data provided by the Commission of the European Communities for 1993 and 1994, projected forward in line with GDP and gross financial liabilities while taking account, to the extent possible, of governments' policies for acquisitions of financial assets.
d) Excludes deposit insurance outlays.
e) Includes balances and the debt of the German Railways Fund from 1994 on, and of the Inherited Debt Fund from 1995 on.
f) Refers to fiscal year data ending 30 June. Includes indebtedness of local governments towards other levels of general government.
g) Does not exclude public-sector mutual indebtedness.

acute would be the most effective way to ensure sustainable fiscal positions over the longer term. By taking greater advantage of the opportunity for further consolidation during the growth phase of the current cycle, governments would minimise any adverse consequences on aggregate demand and leave government debt positions substantially better at the beginning of the next century than now appears likely. (The fiscal consolidation scenario reported in Figure 4, which is based on the assumption that budget deficits are on average broadly eliminated in all major regions by the year 2000, is indicative of what might be achieved.)[5] Failure to take appropriate action now will merely repeat the error made by governments in many Member countries during the latter half of the 1980s, and in the event of a cyclical downturn taking place before the end of the decade, would put public finances on an increasingly fragile footing.[6] On the other hand, greater fiscal consolidation in the immediate future would provide policies with more room for manoeuvre in the face of an eventual recession.

Fiscal consolidation efforts will require that specific measures be taken which, given an overall tax burden that is already high in many OECD countries and widespread political resistance to further increases, should give priority to expenditure reductions. On the expenditure side, a number of measures could be considered.

- In many OECD countries, there appears to be considerable scope for increasing public sector efficiency. Gains may be expected from reassessing management and financial practices, strengthening links between performance and pay, rationalising work within the public administration, eliminating overlap in the provision of public services at different government levels, charging for the provision of services, and contracting-out the provision of services to the private sector. Given the large volume of public procurement, improved methods involving, for example, greater use of competitive tendering might provide significant savings.

Figure 4. **Medium-term fiscal consolidation scenario**[1]

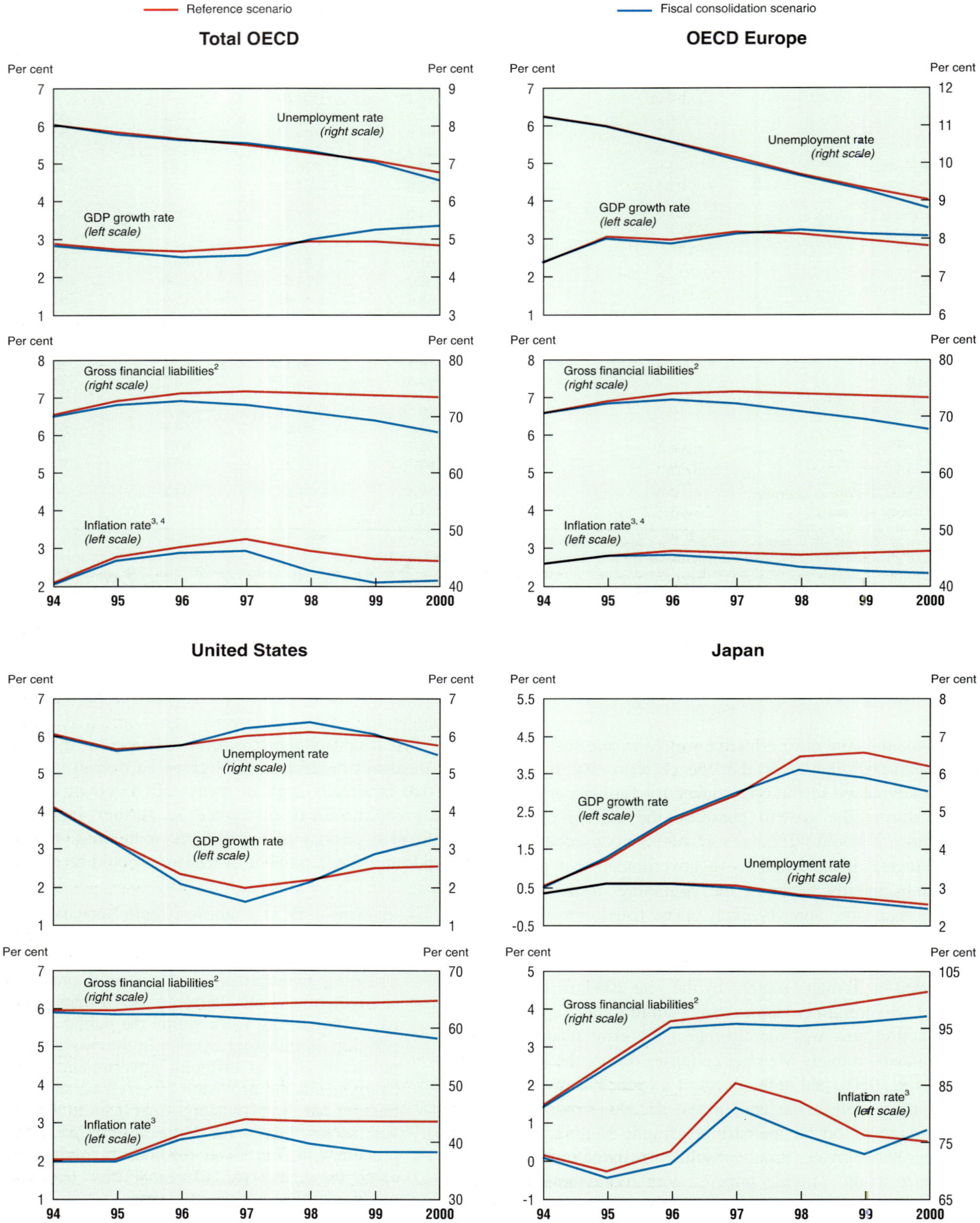

1. The medium-term fiscal consolidation scenario is based on the assumption that general government budgets are on average broadly balanced in all major regions by the year 2000.

2. As a percentage of GDP.
3. GDP deflator.
4. Excluding Turkey.

– Further cuts in industrial and agricultural subsidies may simultaneously improve overall market efficiency and lower public expenditures. Agricultural subsidies are high in nearly all OECD countries except Australia and New Zealand.
– In some countries, especially in Europe, further privatisation may yield both temporary and permanent budgetary improvements, to the extent that future subsidies to public enterprises are reduced and economic efficiency is enhanced.
– A fundamental reassessment of social transfers is required in most OECD countries. Welfare systems could be better targeted to individuals in need if eligibility requirements were tighter; work-testing of the unemployed and the disabled was more effective; means-testing was more effective; programme co-ordination was improved; and integration of benefit and tax systems was better.

Similarly, a number of options exist on the revenue side.

– Where tax rises are unavoidable, increasing indirect taxes may be preferable to increases in direct taxes, as adverse effects on growth and employment may be lower. However, care should be taken to ensure that such measures do not induce a revival of inflation pressures.
– Broadening the base of direct taxes by reducing or eliminating exemptions may be an option in many countries.
– In a number of countries, in particular in southern Europe and Mexico, the reduction of tax evasion could yield substantial revenues without altering statutory tax rates.

Policy options for reforming old-age pension systems are described in detail in the chapter ''Effects of Ageing Populations on Government Budgets'', and depending on the measures, they could improve government expenditures or revenues or both. Proposed measures include:

– increasing participation rates by avoiding policies that discourage part-time work and encourage early retirement;
– increasing working lifetimes by raising the retirement age. This would reduce pension payments and increase contributions at the same time. This measure should also be seen as a response to higher life-expectancy, to later entry of young people into the work-force and to the less physically demanding nature of many jobs due to technical change;
– reducing the generosity of pension benefits and/or increasing pension contributions or other tax rates;
– accelerating the implementation of health-care reforms with the aim of controlling costs and enhancing effectiveness.[7] This is particularly urgent in the United States and some other OECD countries (France, Canada, Finland, and Switzerland) where costs have continued to rise in recent years. These reforms involve the creation of incentives which reduce the demand for unnecessary and low-value medical services and which facilitate medical innovations which improve the health status of the population at lower overall cost.

The more radical option of moving to a fully funded pension scheme has been raised in a number of countries. This would not change the fiscal arithmetic, but building up a separate, actuarially sound, fund could help make the underlying fiscal difficulties and their inter-generational implications more transparent. It might also make it easier to persuade individuals to accept the required pension changes, since it would make pension schemes more closely resemble private saving plans where payouts are determined by what one has contributed.

Monetary policy priorities

Ensuring non-inflationary growth in the near term

Notwithstanding the elimination or the considerable narrowing of output gaps in most countries since 1993, actual inflation has generally remained subdued (see Table 5). Most countries – Italy is the only exception among the major countries – have come fairly close to reasonable price stability in recent years and, while some upward drift of inflation is likely in some, the only major increase projected over the next two years is in Mexico. Since the expansion of demand has appeared to ease towards more sustainable rates in countries where monetary policies were tightened during 1994, and exchange rate developments have weakened the outlook for Japan, and to a more limited extent, Germany and some smaller European countries with close links with Germany, the risk that the current expansion will lead to overheating appears to have ebbed. Indeed, widespread declines in long-term interest rates since late 1994, and the flattening of the yield curve in most countries where monetary conditions have tightened (Figure 5), suggest a receding of inflation fears in financial markets. Compared to Europe, declines in long-term interest rates have been more pronounced in the United States, where markets' earlier expectations of further increases in short-term rates have receded in response to weaker incoming economic data, and in Japan, where markets may even be discounting possible falls in the general price level.

Figure 5. **Yield curves**[1]

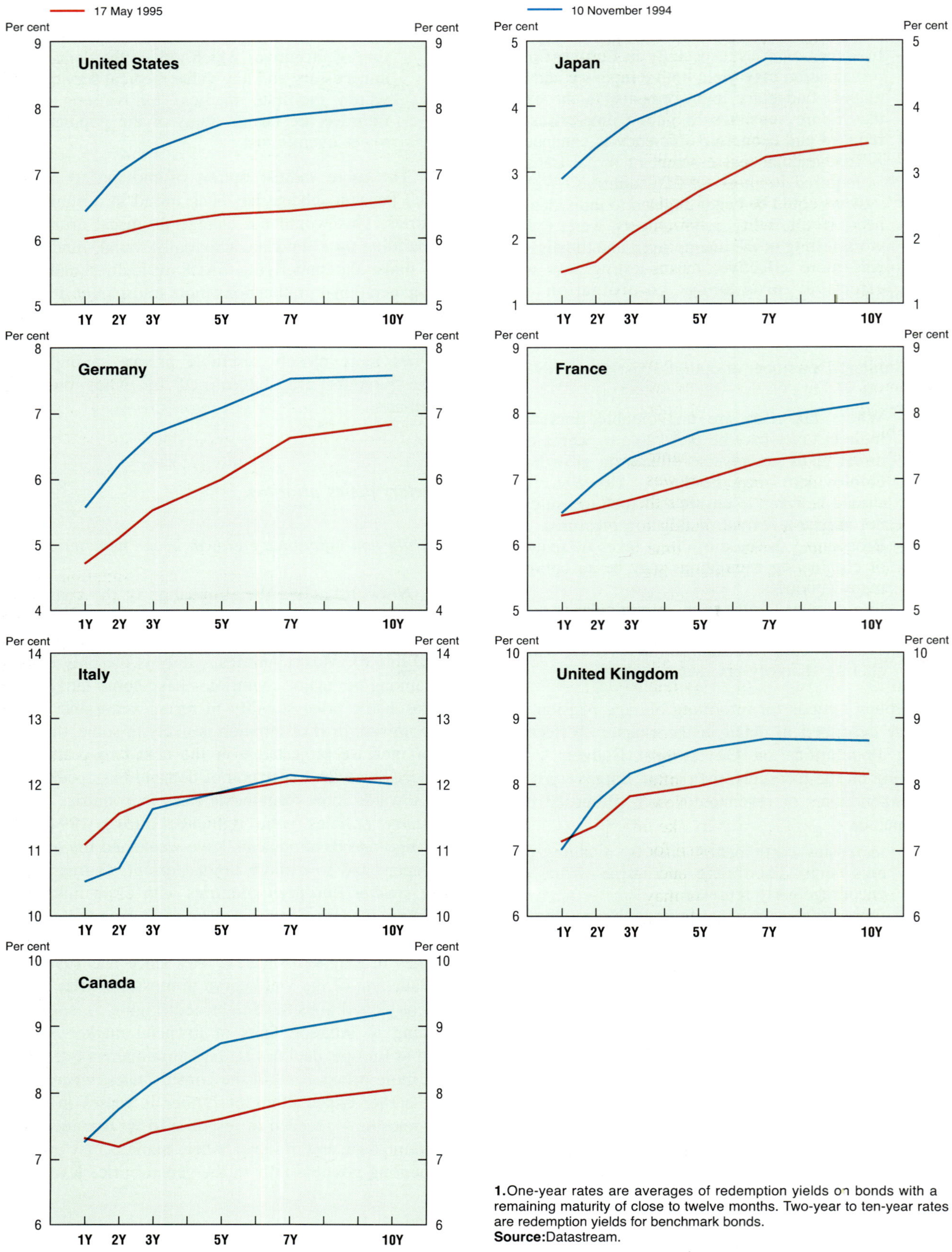

1. One-year rates are averages of redemption yields on bonds with a remaining maturity of close to twelve months. Two-year to ten-year rates are redemption yields for benchmark bonds.
Source: Datastream.

Changing perceptions about relative economic conditions in the major regions, and the likely implications for monetary policies, contributed to the recent sharp movements in exchange rates among major currencies earlier this year. The US dollar's decline, against the Deutschemark and the yen, mainly during March and April, was abrupt. However, similar episodes have occurred before and a downward trend has existed for many years, particularly *vis-à-vis* the yen (Figure 6). The decline appears to have been accentuated at least in part by an acceleration of official reserve diversification by non-OECD countries out of US dollars, which has reinforced a more general trend observed over the past years (Table 11). The less satisfactory inflation track record of the United States over the past two decades, the contrast between the persistent deterioration of its net external asset position and the strength of those of Japan and Germany (Table 12), and the long-term persistence of the US saving-investment imbalance have been the major contributors to the dollar's downward trend Given that to some degree these forces still operate, the dollar was vulnerable when market perceptions of prospects for monetary conditions in major countries began to shift. Indications that the US economy was slowing strengthened expectations that interest rates there might be at or approaching their peak, contributing to downward pressure on the dollar. At the same time, in Germany, the relatively small output gap and higher-than-expected wage settlements led to revised market expectations of higher German interest rates during the latter part of 1995, notwithstanding the weakness of M3. In Japan, while nominal interest rates were already low, markets seem to have perceived them as relatively high in real terms in a context of falling prices.

In the United States and most of the other countries where monetary policies began to tighten during 1994 to pre-empt any resurgence of inflation (the United Kingdom, Canada, Australia and New Zealand), the risks which monetary policies need to take into account appear more balanced than they have been for some time. Where activity appears to be slowing and inflation pressures remain limited, further tightening may not be necessary. However, the recent falls in long-term interest rates promise some demand stimulus in most of these countries and exchange rates are weak in some. It would therefore be premature to regard the inflation risk as having passed

In continental Europe, recent agreements in some countries may imply an acceleration of wages, albeit from low growth rates, and seem to confirm the pattern observed in previous recoveries that wage moderation ceases when unemployment stabilises. In Italy, Spain and Sweden, which have seen significant declines in the value of their currencies, a resurgence of inflation, which has already shown signs of acceleration and may worsen further next year, is clearly the major risk. At the same time, the strong Deutschemark has put pressure on Germany and other ERM countries. The Bundesbank's

Table 11. **Shares of selected currencies in international positions**

Per cent, end-year

	1977	1982	1987	1993
A. Official holdings of foreign exchange				
US dollar[a]	80.3	71.7	67.8	61.4
Deutschemark	9.3	12.9	14.3	16.1
Japanese yen	2.5	4.7	7.5	9.0
Pound sterling	1.8	2.5	2.4	3.4
French franc	1.3	1.3	0.8	2.2
Swiss franc	1.6	2.8	4.0	5.8
B. Bank's cross-border positions[b]				
US dollar	66.7	71.1	53.5	45.5
Deutschemark	16.8	11.2	12.9	15.1
Japanese yen	1.0	2.4	12.0	10.1
Pound sterling	3.0	2.9	4.2	4.6
French franc	2.0	1.6	1.9	5.3
Swiss franc	5.7	5.5	6.4	4.1

a) Includes the dollar value of holdings of ECU with the European Monetary Co-operation Fund (EMCF), which is part of the European Monetary System. Other holdings of ECU are treated as a separate reserve asset and are not shown in the table.
b) Banks reporting to the BIS only. Shares of assets and liabilities in each currency in total assets and liabilities.
Source: IMF, *Annual Report*, various issues. BIS, *International Banking and Financial Market Development*, various issues.

Table 12. **Net outstanding asset and liability positions**[a] **for selected OECD countries**

As a percentage of GDP

	1975	1985	1993
United States	4.1	1.0	–10.4
Japan	1.4	9.7	14.5
Germany	7.6	7.7	11.6
France	6.0[b]	–2.2	–3.1
Italy	–4.6	–7.6	–11.0
United Kingdom	1.9	21.9	3.8
Canada	–29.9	–35.6	–43.0
Netherlands	14.3[b]	24.0	13.0[c]
Spain	–6.4	–9.7	–16.8
Sweden	..	–20.8[d]	–46.4
Switzerland	..	111.8	102.1

a) Excluding monetary gold. Cross-country comparisons should be made with caution because of differences in the valuation of foreign direct investment positions across country.
b) 1980
c) 1992
d) 1989

Figure 6. **Bilateral movements in nominal exchange rates**
Logarithmic scale

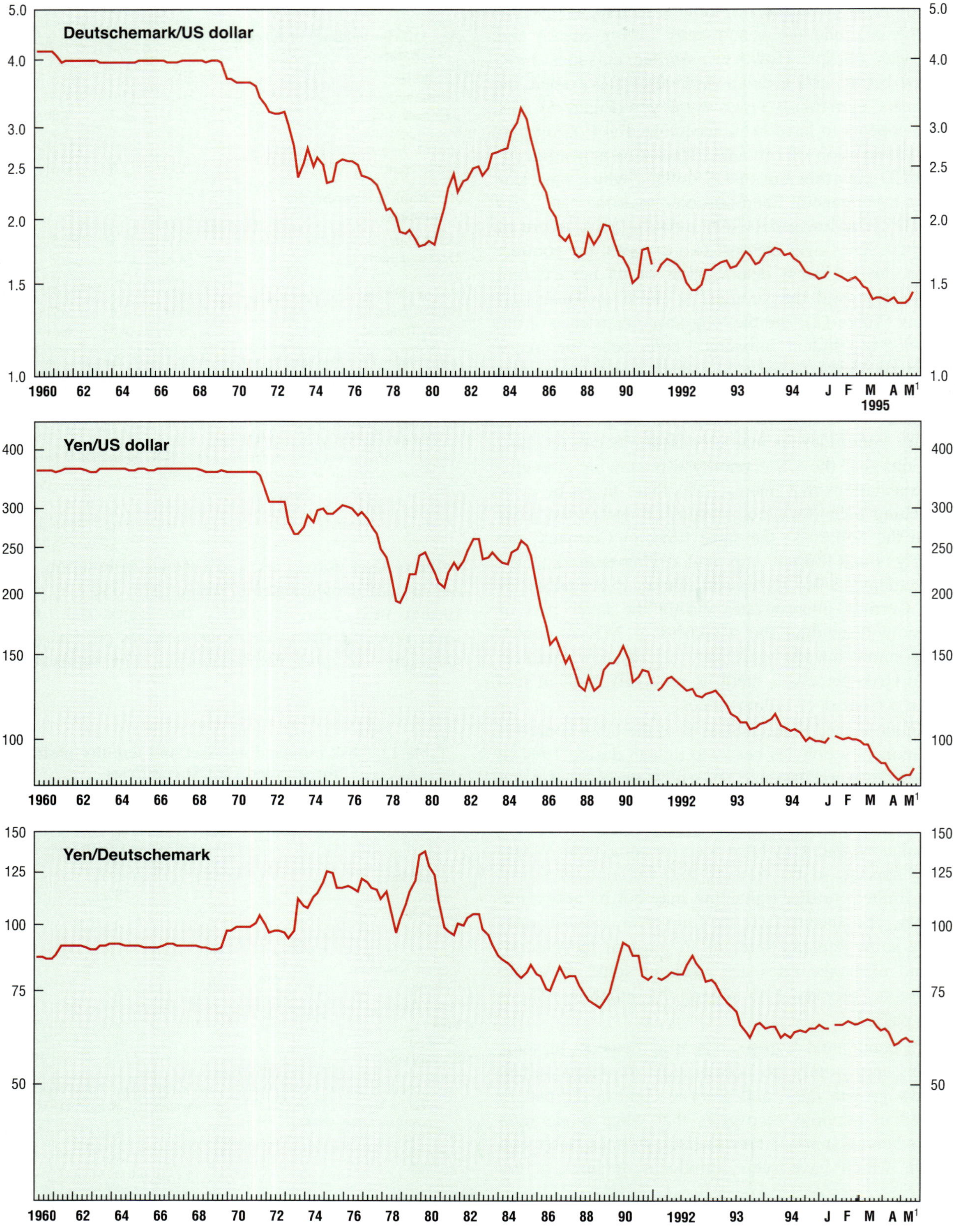

1. The last observation is the average of exchange rates from 15 to 17 May.

reduction in its discount and repurchase rates in late March has helped to ease these pressures, but the contractionary effects from Deutschemark appreciation will have to be balanced against the potential for inflation to revive as the output gap closes. Monetary policies in other ERM countries will continue to be constrained to follow policy developments in Germany. Current levels of real short-term interest rates in some of these countries remain higher than warranted on purely domestic economic grounds, and there may be scope for a narrowing of short-term interest-rate differentials *vis-à-vis* Germany. This scope will become greater if the credibility of their ERM commitment is strengthened by more ambitious fiscal consolidation efforts and structural reforms.

In Japan the recent further strengthening of the yen has come at a time when the economic recovery has already been delayed, the degree of slack is large and some banks and many non-bank financial institutions continue to behave cautiously given their weak positions. Any continued weakness of the stockmarket could aggravate this problem. The high yen has already contributed to the downward pressure on equity prices and it could exert significant deflationary pressures on the economy in the medium term. Indeed, the principal risk to price stability in Japan is that inflation could be negative, falling below the lower end of the 0 to 2 per cent range that is widely taken to characterise such stability. In this environment, both short- and long-term interest rates have declined significantly in recent months, but there may still be room, though limited, for further monetary stimulus.

Monetary management in a low inflation environment over the medium term

Monetary policy in a number of countries is increasingly focusing on maintaining the hard-won gains in lowering inflation in the early 1990s in order to realise the full benefits of an environment of low inflation/price stability. Establishing and maintaining credibility that these objectives will be met will be critical to achieving success in this regard.

Credibility of overall economic policy will be reflected, in part, in longer-term bond markets. The considerfor many years able recent falls in long-term nominal interest rates in most countries (Table 13), after the sharp rises they experienced throughout most of 1994, are encouraging in this regard. Long-term rates nonetheless remain high in many countries, relative to announced intentions of monetary policy authorities. This suggests that more is required in a number of countries before the authorities' objectives will be fully credible.

A number of factors with policy implications could be contributing to still weak credibility.

- Announced inflation objectives of central banks may not be believed (even where they are likely to succeed) because of a poor past record of keeping inflation low. If this is the case, there is a potential for severe balance-sheet problems in the future for businesses and individuals; those who have incurred current debt loads on the expectation that future inflation would be higher than currently observed would find them burdensome in the event that the authorities' low inflation objectives are met. An experience of

Table 13. **Long-term interest rates**[a]

Per cent

	1993-94 Low (1)	1994 Peak (2)	Last available (17 May 1995) (3)	Change from 1994 peak (4) = (3) – (2)
United States	5.2 (Oct. 93)	8.0 (Nov.)	6.5	–1.5
Japan	3.0 (Dec. 93)	4.8 (Oct.)	3.3	–1.5
Germany	5.6 (Dec. 93)	7.8 (Oct.)	6.8	–1.0
France	5.7 (Dec. 93)	8.3 (Nov.)	7.4	–0.9
Italy	8.4 (Feb. 94)	12.1 (Sep.)	11.7	–0.4
United Kingdom	6.1 (Dec. 93)	9.0 (Sep.)	8.1	–0.9
Canada	6.4 (Jan. 94)	9.4 (Jun.)	8.2	–1.2
Australia	6.4 (Jan. 94)	10.5 (Oct.)	8.9	–1.6
Belgium	6.5 (Jan. 94)	8.6 (Sep.)	7.6	–1.0
Denmark	7.4 (Jan. 94)	9.2 (Sep.)	8.3	–0.9
Netherlands	5.3 (Jan. 94)	7.7 (Dec.)	6.9	–0.8
Spain	8.0 (Jan. 94)	11.1 (Dec.)	11.3	0.2
Sweden	6.3 (Jan. 94)	11.2 (Sep.)	10.7	–0.5
Switzerland	4.1 (Dec. 93)	5.6 (Oct.)	4.9	–0.7

a) 10-year government bond yields. Columns (1) and (2) report weekly averages, based on daily data reported in the *Financial Times*, except for Australia, Spain and Sweden where the data are monthly and come from OECD databases. The figures in column (3) are taken from the *Financial Times* and, for Australia, Spain and Sweden, are not strictly comparable to the figures reported in columns (1) and (2). For Switzerland data for all columns are daily data from Datastream.

this nature occurred in the 1980s in several OECD countries when overly optimistic expectations of nominal income gains based on the assumption of continued high inflation failed to be realised.

- Fiscal problems in a large number of countries complicate the operation of monetary policy. If markets fear that governments will be tempted to meet debt obligations in the future through somewhat higher inflation than is now occurring, or through increases in taxes on capital income, they will exact a premium in longer-term interest rates.
- Structural rigidities in labour and product markets could also raise doubts about the ability of monetary policy to function in, and thus to sustain, a low inflation environment. Where wages and prices are relatively unresponsive to market conditions, monetary policy would have to tighten more and for longer to offset a given demand shock, with a greater loss of output. Moreover, upward pressure on prices in regulated service sectors may force monetary policies to restrain demand for manufactured goods more strongly, and to raise interest rates more sharply, to achieve overall price stability. Insofar as markets believe that this would complicate the authorities' ability to sustain their commitments to maintaining price stability, nominal interest rates would incorporate a premium above stated inflation objectives.

Policies towards financial markets

Several recent developments in financial markets have led to concerns that liberalised and globalised financial markets are increasingly prone to excessively large and abrupt swings. The crises which affected the ERM in 1992 and 1993, the Turkish crisis of 1994, the recent collapse of the Mexican peso and the pressures that some other OECD countries have experienced in bond and foreign exchange markets this year have illustrated the exposure of modern economies to shifts in sentiment in international capital markets. The collapse of Baring Brothers and large derivative losses by Metallgesellschaft, Procter and Gamble and Orange County have drawn attention to risks attached to new financial instruments, although it is not clear that all of these episodes reflect the complexities of these instruments so much as a lack of internal controls by management or a willingness to take large risks which could equally have been done with more conventional instruments. Furthermore, developments such as the unsustainable boom in real estate values during the late 1980s, which contributed to serious balance-sheet adjustment problems in a number of countries, and the large swings in real effective exchange rates of major currencies, and hence competitive positions (Figure 7), have raised questions about the strength of longer-term corrective forces operating to equilibrate asset markets.

Data on monthly changes in exchange rates, bond yields and share prices provide little support for the claim that there has been an overall increase in short-term volatility since the 1970s (Table 14). Volatility in government bond markets peaked in the early 1980s, when there were sharp movements in long-term interest rates in the United States, and, while countries such as Italy, Finland and Turkey are exceptions, volatility of effective exchange rates has also been stable or declining since then. More broadly, it has proved hard to find a firm empirical relationship between short-run volatility of exchange and bond markets on the one hand and trade flows or investment on the other.[8]

In contrast, medium-term swings and large, persistent misalignments of asset-market prices may have more significant effects on resource allocation than short-term market volatility or occasional financial stress. A persistent speculative "bubble" will often attract resources on the basis of expectations of capital gains rather than an investment's prospective usefulness or real returns. The over-investment in real estate during the 1980s in many countries stands out as a case in point. Persistent over- or under-valuation of exchange rates may also damage industries that are viable over a longer-term time frame, which in turn can increase protectionist pressures.

Concerns about short-term volatility, medium-term swings and persistent misalignments have led to proposals to reverse the process of deregulation in financial markets or to "slow" their operation in some way. Notable among these is a turnover tax designed to increase market focus on long-term values and fundamentals. The proposal appears to rest on the view that traders, fund managers and investors with a short planning horizon often drive market prices away from underlying equilibrium. Since such traders and investors make large numbers of transactions, the burden of this tax would be

Table 14. **Financial market volatility**[a]

Standard deviation of monthly percentage changes

	1970-79	1980-85	1986-89	1990-94
Effective exchange rates	1.3	1.7	1.7	1.6
Bond yields	0.3	0.5	0.4	0.3
Share prices	4.4	4.1	5.0	4.0

a) Weighted average for the major seven OECD countries

Figure 7. International competitiveness

Indices, 1991 = 100

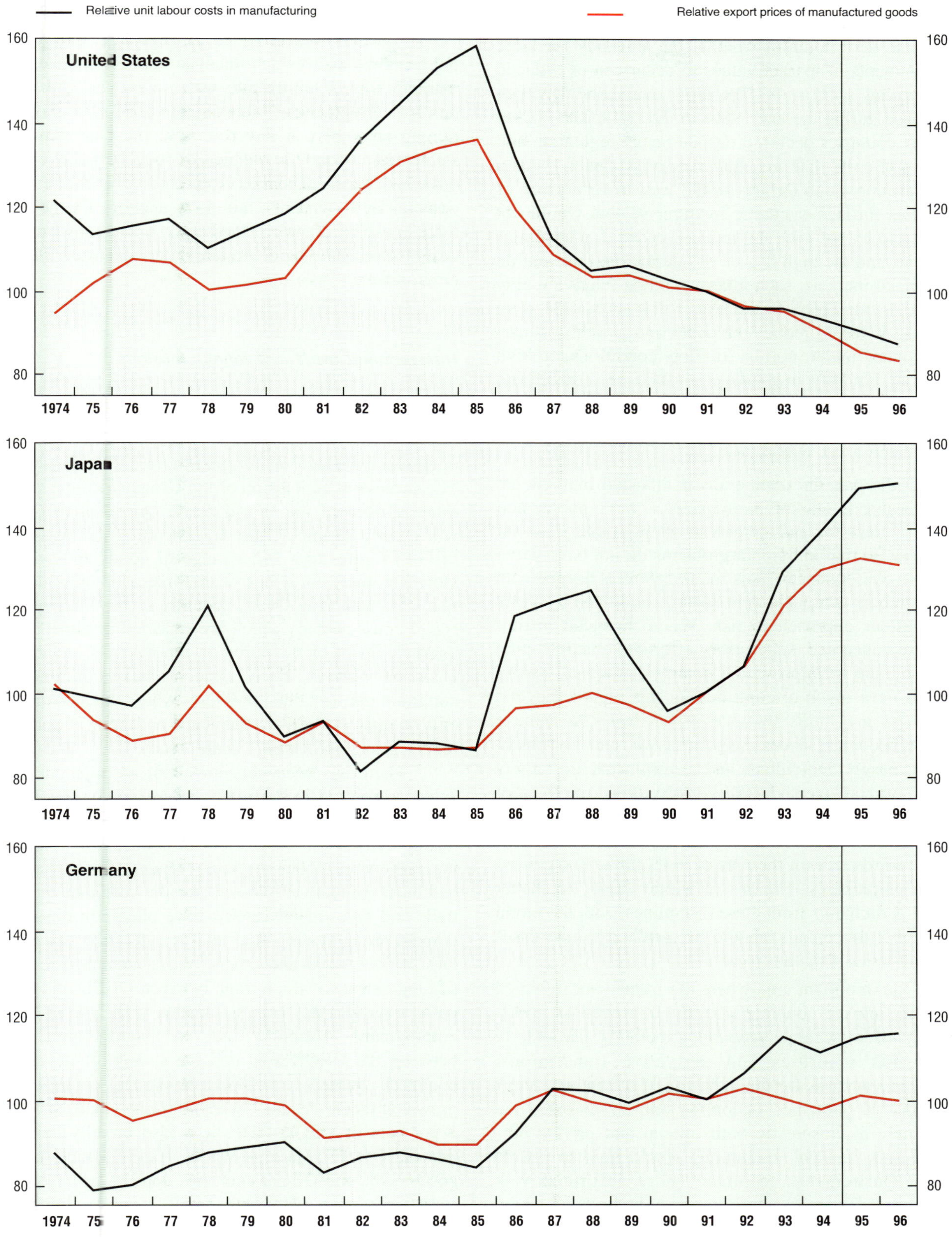

Note: A fall indicates an improvement in competitiveness.
The vertical lines indicate the end of the historical period and the beginning of the projection period.

heavy. By decreasing the return to speculation, such a tax would reduce the "noise" from short-term transactions which are not rooted in fundamentals.

There are several problems with such arguments. First, it is very doubtful whether the tendency for large misalignments of market values to occur can be reduced by imposing such a tax. The large overshooting which took place during the late 1980s in the real estate market in many countries occurred despite heavy regulation and transaction costs that are often very high. Second, given financial innovation (which would lead to replication of exposures through synthetic instruments that would not be affected by the tax), the reduced costs of telecommunications, and the high degree of international integration of financial markets, such a tax would be relatively easy to circumvent. Third, to the extent that such a tax were effective, it would reduce the depth and breadth of markets. Since, under normal trading conditions, a high degree of liquidity in markets tends to be a stabilising force, efforts to reduce this liquidity would be counter-productive. Finally, the costs of administration and collecting such a tax would be high.

If the benefits of liberalised financial markets are to be realised, market participants – both public and private – must be encouraged to adopt sound financial behaviour so that individual problems do not have wider systemic consequences. This requires both prudence with regard to borrowing and debt accumulation and a careful and cautious approach to risk. Where financial institutions are concerned, supervisory efforts to ensure capital adequacy and to improve the quality of internal control systems have much to contribute in this regard. Beyond that, there are limits to what supervisors can achieve without becoming excessively intrusive, and non-financial businesses, individuals and governments are largely free of official oversight. Ultimately, the disciplines of the market are likely to be the most powerful encouragement to sound financial management and prudent behaviour towards risk on the part of both public and private market participants. The use of public money to shelter market participants from these disciplines, with the moral hazard that this entails, should be confined to rare cases when systemic risks are clear.

One important area where the framework in which financial markets operate can be improved is transparency. More accurate accounting methods, particularly as regards securities and derivative transactions, improved standards for the inclusion of off-balance sheet positions in published accounts, and more extensive and timely disclosure by both official and private borrowers and financial institutions would help to enable market participants to make more informed risk assessments. Furthermore, to improve the basis on which regulatory and macroeconomic policy decisions are taken, better data collection at all levels – from the use of non-exchange-traded instruments to the standard macroeconomic information – would be helpful.

However well designed the regulatory and prudential frameworks in which financial markets operate, these markets will never operate well unless the wider economic environment is stable and the price system is functioning smoothly. A key role here must be played by stable macroeconomic policies, as suggested above, without which financial markets expectations of future developments will have no nominal anchor. Furthermore, these must be complemented by a broad range of well designed structural policies in order to ensure such an environment.

International trade and labour markets

An important force for strengthening competition in product markets, and hence contributing to higher rates of productivity and output growth, is international trade. The successful conclusion of the Uruguay Round and the establishment of the World Trade Organisation (WTO) will contribute importantly by extending the application of GATT rules to a wider range of goods and services. However, there are concerns that international trade, particularly with non-OECD countries, has had adverse social consequences which are reflected in either higher unemployment or pressures on wage levels, notably for unskilled workers. These concerns have contributed to continuing protectionist pressures which threaten the benefits of open trading arrangements and have in part been reflected in some "new" trade issues.

There has been concern about an apparent widespread reduction in the relative demand for low-skilled labour which in many countries has resulted in higher unemployment for such labour or contributed to increasing dispersion of income levels (Figure 8). However, it has been difficult to substantiate the role that evolving trade and investment patterns have played in this development. Several empirical analyses (carried out by the OECD Secretariat and others)[9] have attempted to quantify the extent to which trade between OECD and developing countries has been associated with falls in OECD employment. Although trade in manufactured goods between the OECD area and the sample of developing countries covered (non-OPEC developing countries) has grown in recent decades, it is still quite small, at around 2 per cent of OECD GDP. It is also broadly balanced. For the OECD area as a whole, trade in manufactured goods with non-OECD countries appears to have had a statistically significant, but small, negative impact on

Figure 8. **Changes in the dispersion of earnings**[1]

D9/D1 ratio in 1980/81 = 1.00

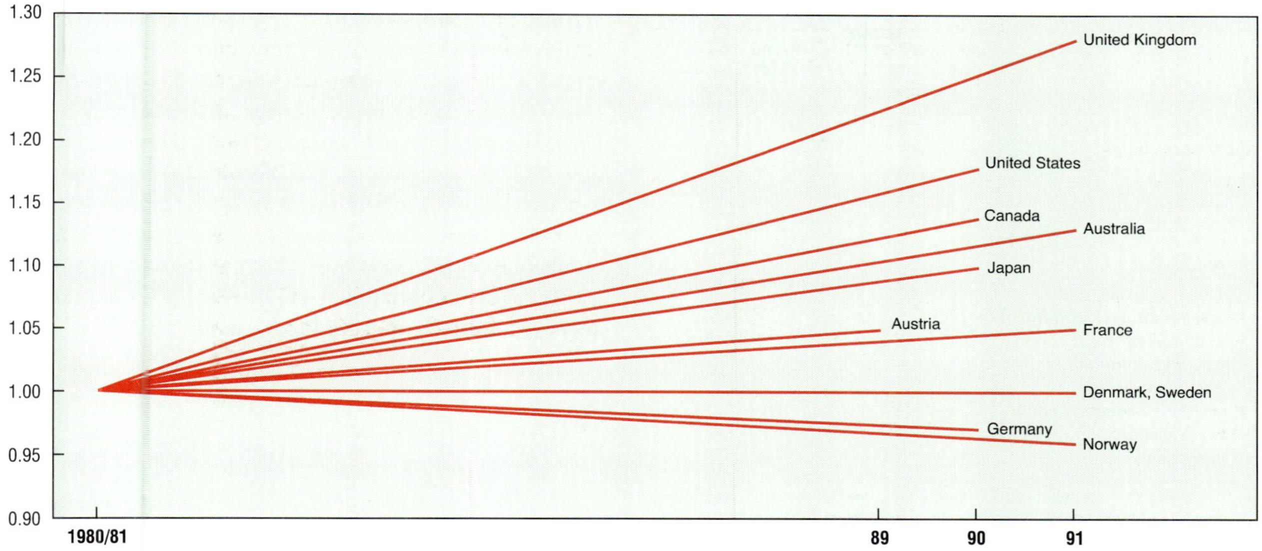

1. Change in the ratio between the earnings of someone at the bottom of the uppermost tenth of all earners, and someone at the top of the lowest tenth – these are the top and bottom "deciles" of the distribution, D9 and D1 respectively. For many countries, this ratio increased between 1981 and 1991, indicating a widening in the distribution of earnings. This may correspond to gains at the top of the distribution relative to the middle, or to losses at the bottom, or both.

Source: OECD, *Employment Outlook,* 1993, Chapter 5, table 5.2.

employment at a sectoral level (Table 15). The effects appear to be largely confined to a small number of industries, especially textiles, clothing, footwear and electronic goods. Unexpectedly, it was found that on balance, negative employment effects were most marked in industries employing (in OECD countries) a high proportion of skilled workers.

The impact of trade with non-OECD countries on the dispersion of income levels in OECD countries is difficult to assess, mainly due to data limitations. Studies focusing on total trade find no clear relationship between relative wages and trade.[10] Increased foreign competition in labour-intensive products is not found to be the major mechanism explaining widening wage distribution, although in sectors where OECD countries have typically lost or retain little market power, the impact on relative wages may be significant.[11]

Notwithstanding the relatively small impact of trade on employment and wages of low-skilled labour in OECD countries, concerns exist that some countries are obtaining comparative advantages artificially by abuse of human rights. There is also a widespread belief that irrespective of their impact on competitiveness, non-observance of certain basic standards in the workplace in any country is so reprehensible that the wider community of nations is entitled to exert pressure on the offender to change its behaviour. These considerations have led to a proposal that the WTO should have a ''social clause'' that would permit the imposition of trade sanctions on countries not observing an agreed set of labour standards.

Early fears that proponents of a social clause would press for extreme and evidently protectionist measures such as a global minimum wage and/or social security systems on a par with those in OECD countries have proved largely unfounded. The debate has centred around ''core'' standards drawn from a sub-set of conventions of the International Labour Organisation, which themselves may be too detailed for the purpose of a proposed social clause in the WTO, and may need updating. The core standards concern freedom of workers to associate and bargain collectively, prohibition of forced labour (but not all forms of prison labour), non-discrimination in employment, and elimination of child exploitation.

The proposed core labour standards are thus closely linked to human rights and only indirectly to compensation of employees. Given that most OECD countries respect these standards *de facto* (with some

Table 15. **Sensitivity of OECD manufacturing employment in various sectors to trade with non-OECD area**

	Estimated elasticities of the share in manufacturing employment with respect to[a]	
	Import penetration, from non-OECD countries[b]	Export intensity, towards non-OECD countries[b]
Industry groupings		
"High-skill"	–0.03**	–0.03**
"Medium-skill"	–0.04*	0.0
"Low-skill"	–0.01	–0.01
Selected industries[c]		
Textiles, apparel, leather	–0.16*	–
Wood products, furniture	–	–0.14*
Iron and steel	–	0.10**
Office and computing machinery	–0.19**	–0.09
Radio-TV-Communication	–0.14**	–
Other transport equipment[d]	–	–0.05**

a) The elasticities reported in this table have been estimated by regressing changes in employment in industry *i* on changes in import penetration in industry *i* and changes in export intensity of industry *i*. All variables are expressed relative to total manufacturing. The regressions pooled data for 12 OECD countries using average changes over 3 sub-periods (1973-79, 1979-85, 1985-89). ** indicates significance at the 5 per cent level, * indicates significance at the 10 per cent level. For classification of industries and further details on the methodology, see B. Larre, "The Impact of Trade on Labour Markets: an Analysis by Industry", *The OECD Jobs Study: Working Paper Series*, (forthcoming).

b) Trade *vis-à-vis* the non-OECD economies (excluding OPEC countries).

c) Only industries for which coefficients on trade variables are significantly different from zero are reported here.

d) Other than shipbuilding, motor vehicles and aircraft industries.

exceptions regarding freedom of association in some sensitive sectors), the question arises as to how the overall international competitiveness of those non-OECD countries which are not observing these core standards at present would change if they began to do so. The analysis is not straightforward. Permitting workers to bargain collectively where it was previously illegal could counter the monopsony power of employers and lead to a more socially optimal level of wages. Workers' organisations and institutions can be useful disseminators of information between employers and workers and help enhance productive efficiency. Their actions could also result in rigid wage differentials and misallocation of labour of various skill levels, as well as average wage levels too high to be compatible with full employment. The net impact on competitiveness is uncertain, and would depend on legal, institutional and customary frameworks. It is certainly not evident that forbidding workers to associate and bargain as a group confers a durable competitive advantage on a country. The impact on competitiveness of implementing the other core standards can only be modest.

This leaves open questions of whether it is appropriate to use trade sanctions, or to threaten to use them, to persuade countries to modify their behaviour. While some argue that trade sanctions will be helpful, others argue that it would be wise to explore alternatives. One argument is that even if sanctions hurt the offenders, they retard economic development there and they are also costly for the imposing countries. Since there is a correlation (admittedly not a strong one) between levels of development and observance of core standards, imposing sanctions could actually result in lower labour standards, not higher ones. These and other more practical considerations help explain the opposition to the incorporation of a "social clause" in the WTO by many OECD countries, and especially by non-Member countries.

NOTES

1. It should be noted that at shorter maturities, such as 5 years, German bond yields remain below bond yields in the United States.
2. This would also be the case in Germany if a more comprehensive definition of the public sector which includes operations of the Treuhandanstalt and other off-budget entities were considered.
3. In broad terms this scenario is very similar to the one described in "Medium-term developments in OECD countries", *OECD Economic Outlook 56,* December 1994, pp. 26-30. Principal changes, as they affect the situation in 2000, concern Mexico and Turkey, where adjustment efforts during recent financial crises have implied substantial revisions, notably to the current account in Mexico and unemployment in Turkey; Italy, where the current level of potential output in 1995 has been revised upward, leading to stronger growth over the medium term; Japan, where potential growth for the next few years has been revised downward and the fiscal starting point is substantially worse. In Norway and Sweden, the scenario reflects important changes in fiscal plans and revised assumptions about general government acquisition of financial assets, which imply substantial downward revisions in gross government debt levels. In Norway, output growth during 1997-2000 is revised downward, reflecting lower oil production plans.
4. These do not allow for any significant changes that may emerge in the United States if plans currently being discussed in Congress to balance the federal budget by 2002 are implemented.
5. The fiscal consolidation scenario assumes that Member governments make gradual improvements in the ratio of primary government balances to GDP of ¼ and ½ percentage points in 1995 and 1996 and ¾ percentage points thereafter, relative to what is assumed in the Reference Scenario. This is achieved through reductions in net transfers to households (a combination of higher social security contributions or tax rates and/or lower benefit payments).

6. The implications of slower growth and higher real interest rates for government finances were discussed in detail in *OECD Economic Outlook 55,* June 1994, pp 18-19, and *OECD Economic Outlook 56,* December 1994, pp 17-18.

7. See for instance H. Oxley and M. MacFarlan, ''Health care reform: controlling spending and increasing efficiency'', *OECD Economic Studies*, No. 24, 1995/I *(forthcoming).*

8. For a survey of work examining the impact of exchange rate volatility on trade, see International Monetary Fund, ''Exchange rate volatility and the level of international trade'', *Occasional Paper* No. 28, Washington D.C., 1984; Commission of the European Communities, ''One market, one money: an evaluation of the potential benefits and costs of forming an economic and monetary Union'', *European Economy,* No. 94, October 1990; and J. Gagnon, ''Exchange rate variability and the level of international trade'', *Journal of International Economics,* Vol. 34, May 1993. For a study examining the effect on investment, see Linda Goldberg, ''Exchange rates and investment in the United States industry'', *Review of Economics and Statistics,* November 1993.

9. See *OECD Jobs Study: Evidence and Explanations,* Part I, Chapter 3, and B. Larre *(forthcoming),* ''The impact of trade on labour markets: an analysis by industry'', *The OECD Jobs Study: Working Papers Series.* See also R.E. Baldwin, ''The effect of trade and foreign direct investment on employment and relative wages'' *OECD Economic Studies,* No. 23, Winter 1994, for a review of the literature in this area, and P. Messerlin, ''The impact of trade and capital movements on labour: evidence on the French case'', *OECD Economic Studies,* No. 24, 1995/I *(forthcoming).*

10. See R.E. Baldwin, *op. cit.* and B. Larre, *op. cit.*

11. See J. Oliveira Martins, ''Market structure, trade and industry wages'' *OECD Economic Studies,* No. 22, Spring 1994.

INVESTMENT IN THE CURRENT UPSWING IN A LONGER-TERM CONTEXT

The recent strength of business investment has given rise to inquiry about its role in this, and earlier, cycles. This chapter commences with a review of long-term trends in business investment, housing investment and purchases of consumer durables in the major countries. It then compares cyclical developments in the current recovery with those in previous recoveries. Finally, it provides a discussion of some measurement issues relevant to an assessment of the past and projected performance of investment in the major countries.

INVESTMENT TRENDS OVER THE LONGER TERM IN THE MAJOR COUNTRIES

Real business investment in the United States, Japan, the United Kingdom and Canada has displayed an upward trend as a share of real GDP over the period since 1960 (Figure 9). In the United States, this trend significantly reflects the strength of investment during the current expansion. In Japan, the longer-term trend rise has not only been stronger than that of the other major countries, but business investment has generally accounted for a much larger share of GDP than elsewhere. In the United Kingdom and Canada, real business investment accounted for a relatively low share of GDP during the 1960s and 1970s, but this share has since risen strongly. The strong increase in the UK investment share during the 1980s in part reflects the pent-up need for investment in newly privatised utilities, as well as broader structural reforms implemented during that period. In Canada, free trade agreements, first with the United States alone and then in the context of the North American Free Trade Agreement (NAFTA), appear to have provided much of the stimulus to the higher investment levels that have persisted since the mid-1980s.

Longer-term business investment trends in the major continental European countries, in contrast, have been relatively flat or falling, although an upward trend has been apparent in Germany since the mid-1970s. A force acting to dampen business investment in most of Europe after the first oil shock in 1973-74 was the sharp fall in corporate profitability, which was not reversed until the mid 1980s. In Germany, the additional stimulus provided by unification in 1990 has contributed to the stronger trend noted above.

The share of real GDP devoted to residential construction by the private sector has been consistently less than that devoted to business investment. In Japan and the major continental European countries these shares were relatively large, and in the cases of Japan and France were rising, until the early 1970s. Since then, however, there has been a decline to around 5 per cent of GDP, except in Germany, where the housing investment share has risen somewhat above that level since unification. This has brought the share of housing investment in these countries (excluding Germany) down to levels comparable to those that have consistently prevailed in the United States and Canada. The share of housing investment in GDP in the United Kingdom has been the lowest among the major countries and has displayed no trend over time, notwithstanding a history of large cycles in the housing market.

Expenditure on household durable goods as a share of real GDP has been steadily rising in most countries over the years, largely reflecting improving living standards and increasing disposable incomes. By the early 1990s, it typically accounted for between 5 and 10 per cent of GDP, with the United States at the high end of this range and Japan and France at the low end.

INVESTMENT BEHAVIOUR DURING BUSINESS CYCLES

Overview

Although divergences exist both across countries and cycles, components of total investment have tended to display some common patterns over recent business cycles. The main features are as follows:[1]

- Business investment accounts for the major part of total fixed investment in most major countries – well over 50 per cent – although this share varies widely across countries. Despite this, its contribution to GDP growth in the early phases of upswings in North America and the United Kingdom is often negative and almost always smaller than that of housing investment

Figure 9. **Trends and cycles in real spending on investment and consumer durables**

As a percentage of real GDP

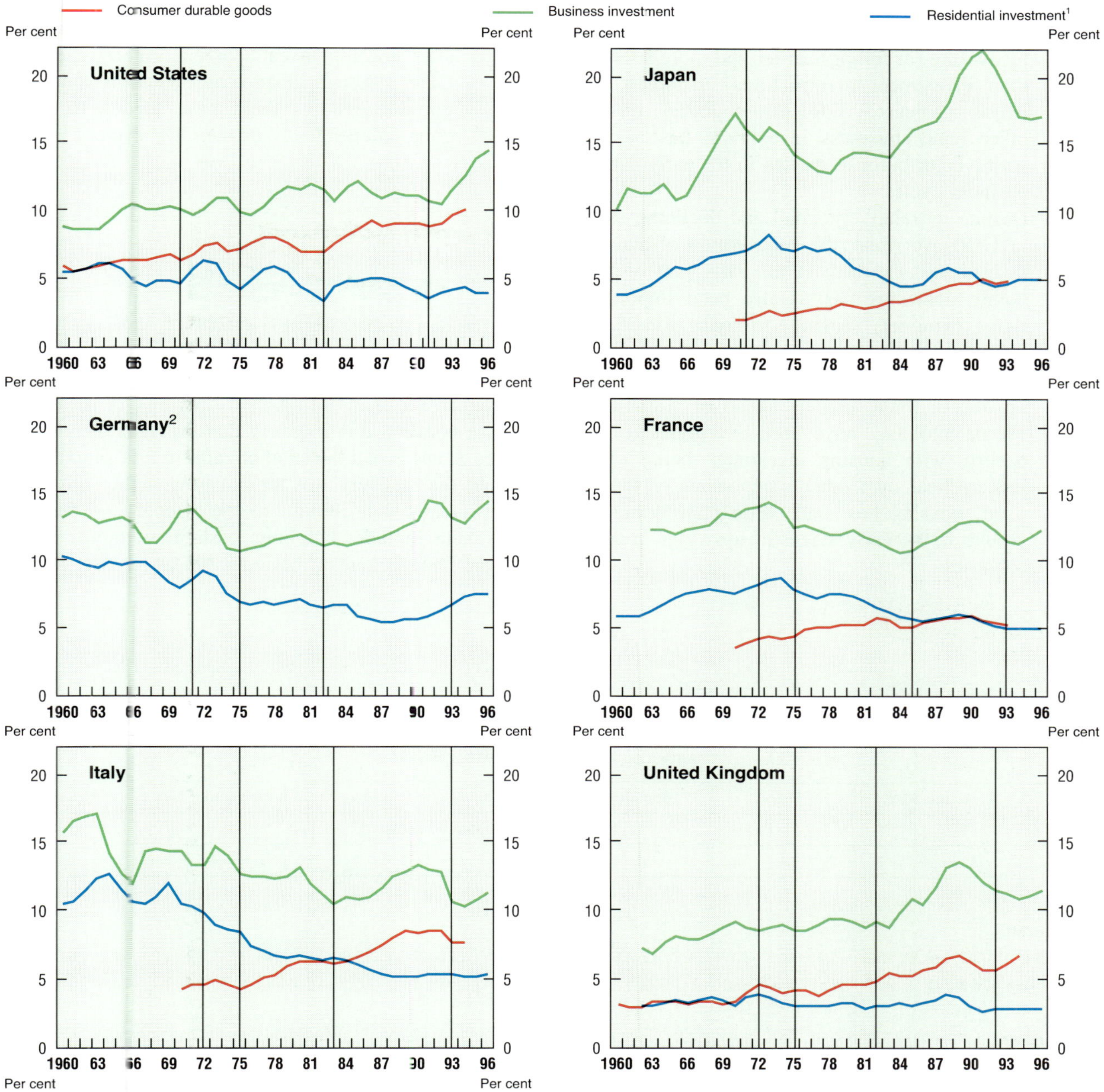

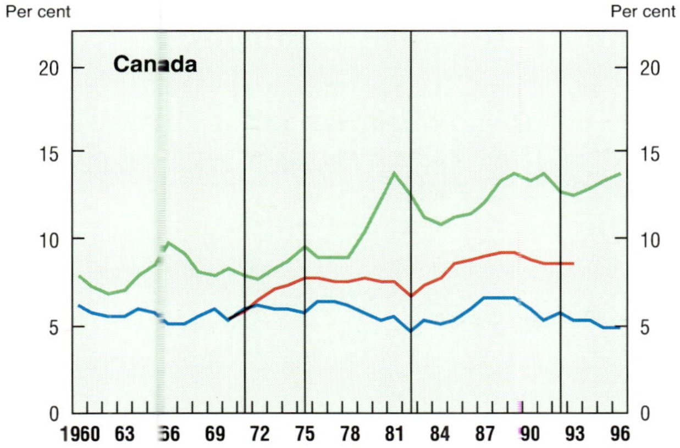

1. Residential investment by the private sector, except for Italy which includes the government sector.
2. Purchases of durables data not available for Germany.
Notes: The vertical lines show GDP troughs, based on the size of output gaps, since 1970. Information required to compute output gaps before 1970 is not available. Evidence suggests, however, that for most countries, the 1960-70 period was not characterised by significant recessions.
Base year prices: 1987 for the United States, 1985 for Japan, 1991 for Germany, 1980 for France, 1985 for Italy, 1990 for the United Kingdom and 1986 for Canada.

(Table 16). Cycles in business investment in these countries have generally lagged behind GDP cycles by two to four quarters, both in upswing and downswing episodes, with investment in machinery and equipment generally recovering (or falling) earlier and more strongly than investment in structures. In Japan and major continental European countries, on the other hand, business investment has been a strong contributor to growth in the early part of business cycles.

- Despite its relatively small and declining share of GDP over time, the contribution of housing investment to growth in the early part of economic upswings has usually been important. Being extremely sensitive to credit conditions, this component has tended to lead investment and economic recovery, in most cases picking up one to three quarters ahead of real GDP.[2] France and Italy have been exceptions to this pattern, with housing investment being much less cyclical than other components of investment; housing has made little contribution to growth in the early stages of upswings in these countries.
- Durable goods purchases have typically provided an important stimulus to growth in the early phases of upswings, often contributing as much as or more than that of housing investment. Durable goods purchases tend to pick up after housing investment but usually ahead of GDP, although Japan is an exception as durable goods purchases there have tended to move quite independently of the GDP cycle.

Is the current cycle unusual?

Business investment

Business investment – machinery and equipment in particular – has contributed more to growth in the United States and Canada in the early stages of the current expansion than during past upswings. A major difference between this recovery and previous ones in the United States is that the level of capacity utilisation at the start of the recovery was significantly higher this time. Other factors contributing to the strength of business investment include: corporate cash flow improvements (for the United States); the reduction in the user cost of

Table 16. **The contribution of various investment components to GDP growth: The current upswing compared with previous ones**[a]

Contribution to real GDP growth, per cent

	United States			Japan			Germany			France			Italy			United Kingdom			Canada		
	Number of quarters after the trough																				
	2	4	8	2	4	8	2	4	8	2	4	8	2	4	8	2	4	8	2	4	8
Business investment																					
Past cycles[b]	–3.7	6.5	15.3	15.1	18.1	21.7	14.3	12.4	9.2	31.8	22.6	15.4	21.4	25.3	16.7	–13.0	3.4	16.2	–1.2	3.6	2.7
Current cycle	26.8	18.9	35.7	n.a.[f]	n.a.[f]	n.a.[f]	6.1	22.5	29.4[c]	8.2	14.6	23.9[c]	11.2[c]	6.5[c]	18.4[c]	–12.5	30.4	7.2	14.4	30.3	21.3
Housing investment																					
Past cycles[b]	25.0	25.2	18.3	18.0	15.2	11.9	9.1	7.5	2.6	3.0	5.3	7.1	–3.4	–3.5	–2.5	15.4	0.3	1.2	21.6	15.3	10.0
Current cycle	28.5	16.8	13.9	n.a.[f]	n.a.[f]	n.a.[f]	37.9	32.0	20.9[c]	0.6	3.7	4.2[c]	0.9[c]	1.2[c]	4.3[c]	–4.0	2.1	2.8	–10.4	–8.2	–2.2
Consumer durables																					
Past cycles[b]	23.3	24.6	19.0	3.6	3.5	5.8	n.a.[d]	n.a.[d]	n.a.[d]	14.1	13.0	10.6	14.5	7.4	12.0	17.2	12.7	2.1	22.8	15.9	13.9
Current cycle	24.1	22.8	24.6	n.a.[f]	n.a.[f]	n.a.[f]	n.a.[d]	n.a.[d]	n.a.[d]	18.0	12.8	n.a.[e]	5.8	8.3	n.a.[e]	20.2	26.6	19.0	5.6	9.0	9.9

a) Business cycle troughs since 1970. Troughs are based on the size of output gaps.
b) Average contribution.
c) Projections.
d) Data on consumption of consumer durables are not available for Germany.
e) No projections are available for consumer durables.
f) For the current economic cycle, the trough is not projected to be reached before the end of the projection period.

Figure 10. **Trends in business investment**

As a percentage of GDP

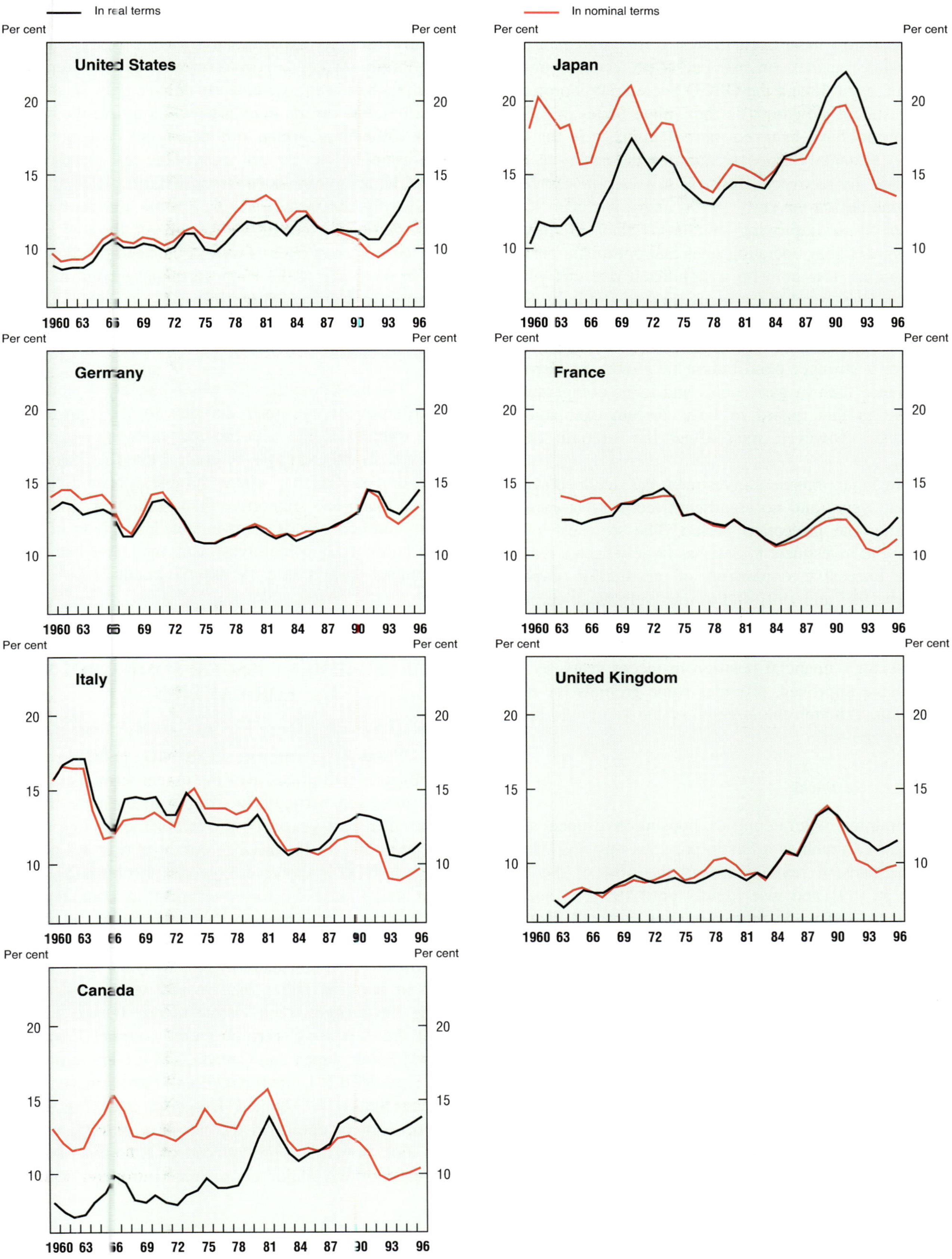

capital since the beginning of the 1990s (both the United States and Canada); tax incentives (in Canada); and the ongoing shortening of investment lives, in particular for computer equipment. For these two countries, where cyclical upswings have been maturing for around three or four years, business investment is projected to remain buoyant, even though the OECD Secretariat is projecting an investment slowdown in the United States in 1996.

Firms have behaved more cautiously in the three major continental European countries, at least in the early phases of the recovery. Business investment was generally weak during the early 1990s, and it has been slower to respond to improving conditions than in previous upswings. Higher operating rates and optimistic business expectations now point to a significant rise this year in business investment in Germany, France and Italy. Facilitated by strong profits, this is now becoming increasingly evident. Business investment is ultimately projected to make a stronger contribution to growth in Germany and France than in past cycles and to be comparable to the past in this regard in Italy. Recent exchange-rate turbulence, however, may affect the strength of the upturn.

In Japan, business investment has declined sharply in recent years and no significant recovery is expected until after the projection period. The slowness of the recovery in investment to date has largely been a reaction to the excessive expansion of production capacity between 1987 and 1991 and to relatively weak corporate profitability. Nevertheless, the growth of the capital stock has remained significant and the improvement in the business sector's financial position in recent years, as cash flows have improved, provides some grounds for future optimism, although the strength of the yen could have a negative impact.

Housing investment

In three major countries, housing investment so far has behaved much as it has in previous upswings. In the United States, it revived around the time of the GDP trough in 1991 and rose rapidly until 1994, as housing starts increased while mortgage rates declined. Housing investment flattened out in the second half of 1994, and an easing is apparent in 1995. In France and Italy housing investment has made little contribution to the recovery, consistent with the past.

In other major countries, the current cycle has been clearly atypical. In the United Kingdom and Canada, the contribution of housing investment to growth during the early phase of the upswing appears to have been small or, in the case of Canada, negative. Despite the marked improvement in housing affordability in both of these countries due to the continued weakness in house prices,[3] housing investment has been adversely affected by the lasting effects of the late 1980s debt overhang and job uncertainty. In both countries, housing investment is projected to remain sluggish in 1995 and to pick up only slightly in 1996. In Germany, on the other hand, the contribution of housing investment to growth during the upswing has been significantly higher than in the past, largely due to efforts to enlarge and improve the housing stock following German unification and to accommodate past immigration, as well as specific tax incentives. In Japan, housing rebounded strongly during 1994 after falling sharply during the early part of the decade, but it has weakened again recently. Nevertheless, the low level of long-term interest rates as well as the need for reconstruction in the wake of the Kobe earthquake point to further recovery in housing investment.

Durable goods

For most countries for which data are available, the contribution of consumer durables to GDP growth has been roughly in line with previous upswing episodes, or perhaps, slightly stronger as in the United Kingdom. The exception is Canada, where durables consumption has proved much less supportive than in the past. Job uncertainty and households' over-indebtedness, both of which have burdened housing investment, may have had a similar impact on purchases of durable goods.

MEASUREMENT ISSUES: SOME GROUNDS FOR CAUTION

Prices of investment goods have tended to rise by less than overall prices over the longer term. This difference has been particularly striking in the case of computers in recent years. To provide some background on this point, the comparative evolution of real and nominal shares in GDP is shown in Figure 10 for business investment and Figure 11 for investment in computers and office equipment. There are two main points to note.

First, recent and projected business investment behaviour looks considerably less buoyant when considered in nominal rather than in real terms. Indeed, the rising longer-term trend visible in real business investment shares is not discernible in the nominal data for the United States, Japan and Canada, and it is more muted in the case of the United Kingdom. Furthermore, in the United States, the United Kingdom and Canada, the recent cyclical upturn in the business investment share also looks much less pronounced on a nominal basis. In the case of the major continental European countries,

Figure 11. **Investment in computers and related office equipment**

As a percentage of total business investment

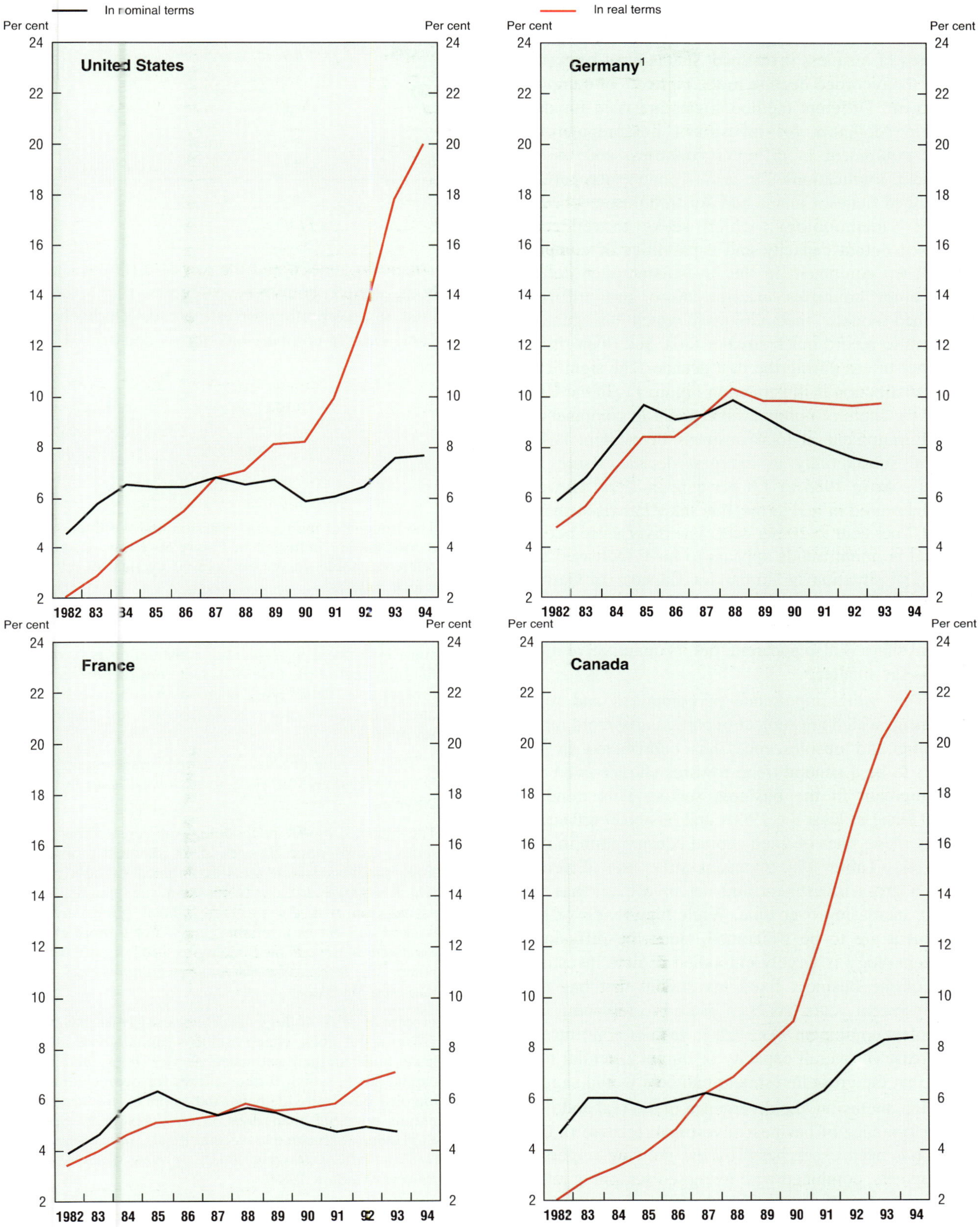

1. Includes public sector investment.

nominal shares show a slightly more muted business investment performance over the longer term, making the downward trend in France and Italy more pronounced and diminishing the rise in Germany.

Second, the divergent trends of real and nominal measures of business investment shares have been partly due to the recorded decline in the "price" of computing investment. Different methodologies are used for deriving price deflators for investment in computers and related equipment in different countries, and this has important implications for cross-country comparisons. The United States, Canada and Australia use a "hedonic pricing" methodology, which seeks to reflect the increased output capacity and capabilities of computers and related equipment in the investment price deflator. Most other countries use the more straightforward "matched-model" methodology,[4] which has generally led them to record much smaller falls, and often rises, in computer prices during the past decade. The significance of this distinction is illustrated in Figure 11. In the United States, the share of nominal investment in computers and related equipment in total business investment has not changed substantially in the past decade, rising from 6.5 per cent in 1985 to 7.8 per cent in 1994. However, when measured in real terms, this share has risen sharply, from 4.7 per cent to 20 per cent. The divergence between real and nominal trends appears to have increased since 1990. The situation is similar for Canada. In Germany and France, which use the "matched-model" methodology, the tendency for the real share to rise faster than the nominal share is also apparent, but its quantitative importance is far smaller.

The rising importance of computers and related equipment, which are subject to particularly rapid rates of scrapping and obsolescence, has contributed to what appears to be a general trend towards shorter-lived capital equipment in the business sector. This trend has existed since at least the 1960s and has been reflected in steadily rising rates of fixed capital consumption in many countries (Table 17). Consequently, the difference between gross investment and net investment has been steadily increasing over time. While high levels of gross investment are to be welcomed, since the diffusion of new technology is largely embodied in new investment, much of the business fixed investment that has taken place in recent years has been geared to replacing spent or obsolete equipment. As such it has not contributed to an increase in overall capacity or output potential to the extent that the gross investment numbers would suggest.[5]

In conclusion, the divergence in the real and nominal performance of business investment relative to GDP, which has been exacerbated by the growing importance of computers, combined with increased scrapping rates of

Table 17. **Consumption of fixed capital in the business sector**

As a percentage of real GDP

	1960-69	1970-79	1980-89	1990-94
United States	4.9	5.7	7.1	7.8
Japan	6.2	7.7	8.6	11.6
Germany	8.2	10.1	11.6	11.3
France	n.a.	6.3	7.5	8.1
Italy	n.a.	n.a.	5.0	5.7
United Kingdom	5.5	6.7	7.6	7.3
Canada	4.1	4.2	6.6	9.1

investment in general and the use of different statistical methods across countries, suggests that caution is required in interpreting investment developments over time and making comparisons across countries.

NOTES

1. The troughs of the recent recession and the three previous recessions are indicated in Figure 9. These designate the reference points in the analysis of cyclical developments which follows.
2. The early reaction of housing investment in economic upswings in part reflects national accounting procedures, since investment in residential construction is recorded as final demand at the time of actual construction, not at the time of sale. Other types of goods which have been produced but have not yet been sold are recorded as inventories.
3. In 1994 the ratio of house prices to average earnings in the United Kingdom was close to its lowest level in the past 20 years.
4. The matched-model methodology of constructing a price series records price changes of an identical product over time; products which are discontinued or new products which emerge are excluded from the sample, on the assumption that the products whose prices are being tracked will act as a reliable proxy. For a more extensive explanation of the methodologies used in pricing computers, see: *Information Technology Outlook 1994*, OECD, Paris, pp. 48-51.
5. Empirical work in the United States suggests that both the gross capital stock, which excludes capital goods after they have finished their estimated service lives, and the net capital stock, which further allows for depreciation on an ongoing basis, provide better indicators of productivity and output potential than does gross investment. See A.S. Englander, "Evaluating recent trends in capital formation", *Federal Reserve Bank of New York Quarterly Review*, Autumn 1989.

EFFECTS OF AGEING POPULATIONS ON GOVERNMENT BUDGETS

Most OECD countries will experience a rapid ageing of the population in the future, potentially putting public pension and health-care systems under increasing pressure.[1] This note examines the possible magnitude of the problem and the required policy response. Policy action to offset such pressures will have two dimensions. First, it is essential to restore sound public finances in the medium term, to create a better starting position before demographic pressures begin to be felt. Second, pension and health-care policies will have to be reviewed. For pension schemes, options include raising contributions, reducing pension payments and, perhaps most effective, increasing the age of retirement. For health, it will be necessary to explore ways of delivering care of the frail elderly in a more cost-effective manner. In both cases, policy changes should occur sooner rather than later to give people the maximum time to adjust.

Lower population growth and declining workforce

Despite considerable uncertainty about the long-term evolution of birth rates, mortality rates and immigration, the demographic patterns for the next few decades are, to a large extent, already determined, and it is generally accepted that industrial countries can expect a considerable degree of ageing during the first half of the next century[2] (Figure 12). Nevertheless, some clear differences exist among the major seven countries. In the United States and Canada – and to a lesser extent also in France and the United Kingdom – the overall population is projected to grow until around 2030 and then to stabilise; in Japan, Germany and Italy significant falls in overall population are projected. In the United States, the working-age population (adjusted for scheduled increases in retirement ages)[3] is projected to increase until 2020 and to decline slightly between 2020 and 2035 before starting to grow modestly again. Sharp falls are projected in the course of the next three decades in Japan, Germany and Italy, and moderate falls in France, the United Kingdom and Canada. In all major seven countries except the United Kingdom, elderly dependency ratios (the ratio of elderly to the ''adjusted'' working-age population) are projected almost to double by around 2030 to 2040 before stabilising or falling slightly. In Japan, Germany and France, elderly dependency ratios are projected to peak at around 0.6 and in Italy at over 0.7, while the peak for the United States, the United Kingdom and Canada is likely to be around 0.4 to 0.5.

Ageing and fiscal pressures: scenarios for the major seven countries

Ageing populations are likely to put significant pressure on public spending programmes, especially those linked to life-cycle developments, such as health care and pensions. Moreover, potential GDP growth is projected to slow down as a result of ageing, making these pressures harder to bear for the economy as a whole. Furthermore, projected high debt levels over the medium term and associated debt interest payments will exacerbate these fiscal pressures. This section builds on the medium-term scenario presented above (Tables 9 and 10)[4] to construct an illustrative long-term scenario of how the main demographically sensitive public expenditures – pensions, health and education – might evolve. Such an exercise is obviously highly speculative and relies on fairly heroic assumptions; the main point of these calculations is to provide some idea of the scale and magnitude of potential future problems.

All major seven OECD countries have multiple *public pension schemes,* either with different schemes covering different segments of the working population, or different schemes funding different components of the overall pension received (usually where benefits combine flat-rate and earnings-related components). Payroll taxes are generally levied as ''contributions'', and the pension benefit entitlements are usually based on a formula incorporating the previous earnings and the number of years of contributions made. Once a retiree's pension has been calculated, it is thereafter more or less indexed to inflation, except in Germany where it is linked to net wage growth. Countries typically also provide a flat-rate pension to those elderly who do not qualify for a pension on the basis of their earnings and contributions history, and these benefits are usually financed from general taxation receipts. Public servants often have separate pensions schemes that are funded largely from general taxation, although some contributions may be levied on employees. The age of retirement currently varies from 57 years for women in Italy, to 65 for men and women in the United States and Canada. Recognition of future pension pressures has led many countries to legislate gradual

Figure 12. **Population projections and elderly dependency ratios, 1995-2070**

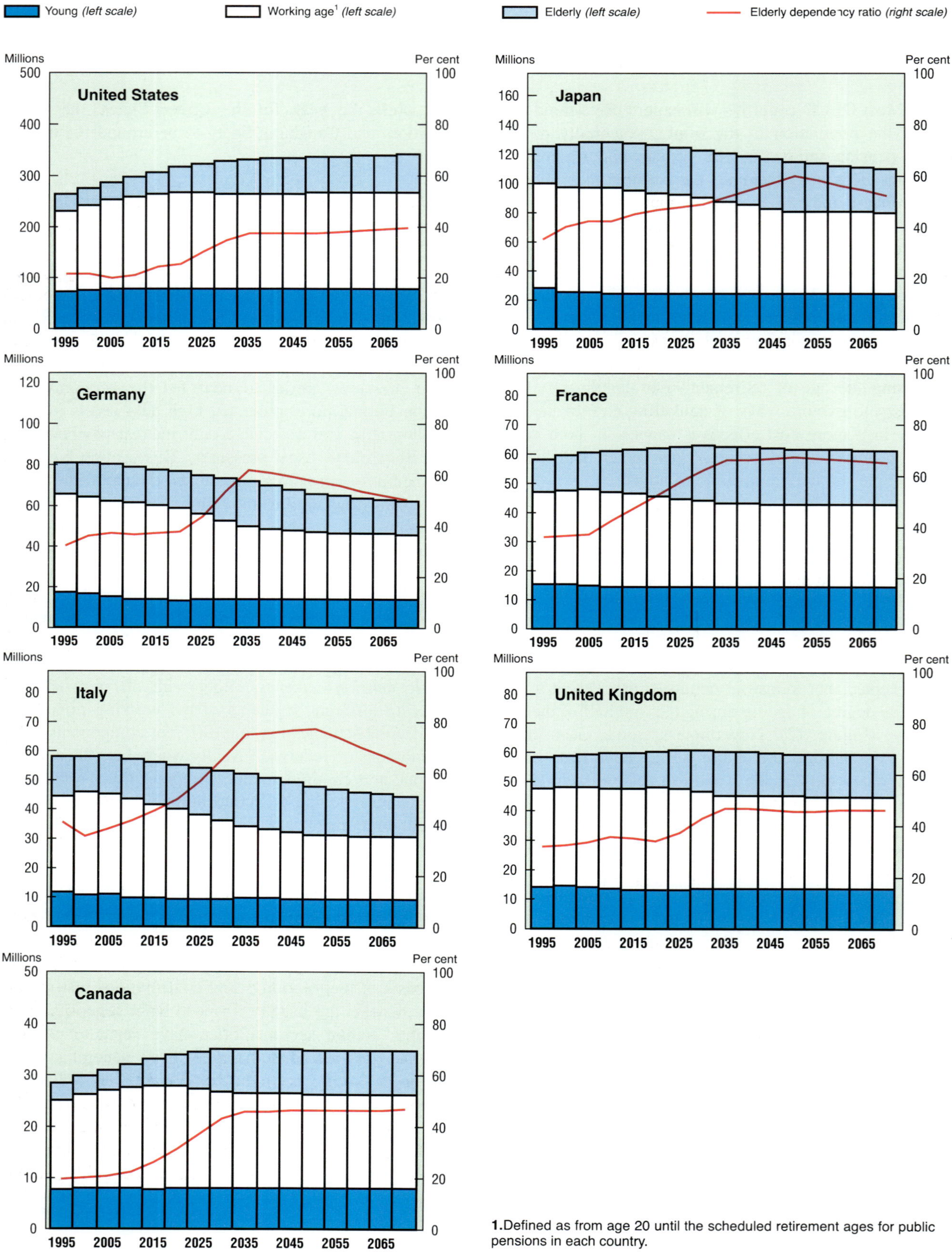

1. Defined as from age 20 until the scheduled retirement ages for public pensions in each country.

increases in retirement ages, and the retirement age will rise to 67 years in the United States and to 65 years in all other countries except France and for women in Italy, where it will be 60 years.

Scenarios illustrating the possible evolution of public pension schemes until 2070 have been constructed for the major seven countries. Despite efforts to capture as fully as possible the institutional arrangements in each country, simplifying assumptions have been necessary and the scenarios should be viewed as broadly indicative only. The scenarios for pension contributions and pension payments follow the path of the above-mentioned medium-term scenario until 2000, so that output gaps close and actual unemployment is close to structural unemployment. After 2000, the ratio of employed to the working-age population is assumed to remain constant,[5] *i.e.* percentage changes in employment are the same as those in the working-age population, and GDP growth is determined by the growth in labour productivity and changes in the working-age population.

The projected pension flows – contributions and pension payments – assuming a productivity growth rate of $1^1/_2$ per cent are shown in Figure 13. Three key features emerge. First, there is a marked difference in the magnitude of pension payments: in the United States, the United Kingdom and Canada, pension expenditure peaks at between 5 and 8 per cent of GDP, compared with pension expenditure peaks of between 15 and 20 per cent of GDP for Japan, Germany, France and Italy. This reflects both the relative generosity of pensions and the elderly dependency ratios. Second, in Japan, Germany, Italy and the United Kingdom, pension payments peak and then fall once the baby-boom generation has passed (around 2035-2050). In contrast, in the United States, France and Canada, pension expenditures reach a plateau in the second half of the period covered by the scenario. Third, despite higher contribution rates, the gap between contributions and pension payments is much larger in Japan, Germany, France and Italy than in the other three countries.

The pattern of *health-care costs* at different stages in the average life-cycle has been established in a number of studies, and it implies that as the numbers of elderly increase, total health-care costs are also likely to rise, although the effect of increased life expectancy on per capita health-care costs is more difficult to establish because it depends, in part, on the physical dimensions of the ageing process. In order to isolate and examine the effects of demographics on health-care spending,[6] per capita real public health-care spending on under 65 year-olds and on those 65 years and older is assumed to grow in line with productivity growth.[7] The per capita expenditures were then applied to the population projections for their corresponding age groups.

The scenarios of health-care costs indicate that in the United States and Canada, whose populations are growing as well as ageing, public spending on health care as a per cent of GDP would rise significantly. In the United States, the effects of ageing are exacerbated by the particularly high share of public health spending which is spent on those over 65 compared with the under 65 year-olds.

It might be expected that demographics would also affect *public spending on education,* generating some savings in those countries where school-age populations are projected to fall, notwithstanding the assumption made in the demographic projections that countries where fertility is currently below replacement rates will return to replacement rates by 2030. However, applying a similar methodology to that used for health care,[8] indicates that education spending will change very little – by, at most, around 0.3 per cent of GDP between 2000 and 2030, despite significant falls in the school-age population everywhere except in the United States and Canada.

Primary balances, debt dynamics, financial balances and net debt accumulation

The combined effects on public finances of the factors listed above are presented in Table 18. Primary balances, interest payments, financial balances and net financial liabilities are presented separately to show the evolution of debt dynamics.[9] This scenario is based on the assumption that, apart from announced policy intentions, no further measures are taken. As well, revenues and expenditures on all items in the primary balance other than pensions, health and education have been assumed to remain constant as a percentage of GDP. In this scenario outcomes over the period to 2030 differ among the major seven countries.

- In the United States, public debt levels may remain stable until around 2010 at around 40 per cent of GDP but then they would start rising to around 95 to 110 per cent of GDP by 2030 (depending on the interest-rate assumptions) despite relatively favourable demographics and a public pension scheme that is generally well financed. The increase largely reflects significant increases in public expenditures on health care.
- In Japan the primary balance, while improving over the medium term, remains in deficit and deteriorates rapidly after 2000 due to the sharp increase in pension expenditures. Adverse debt

Figure 13. **Pension payments and contributions**

As a percentage of GDP

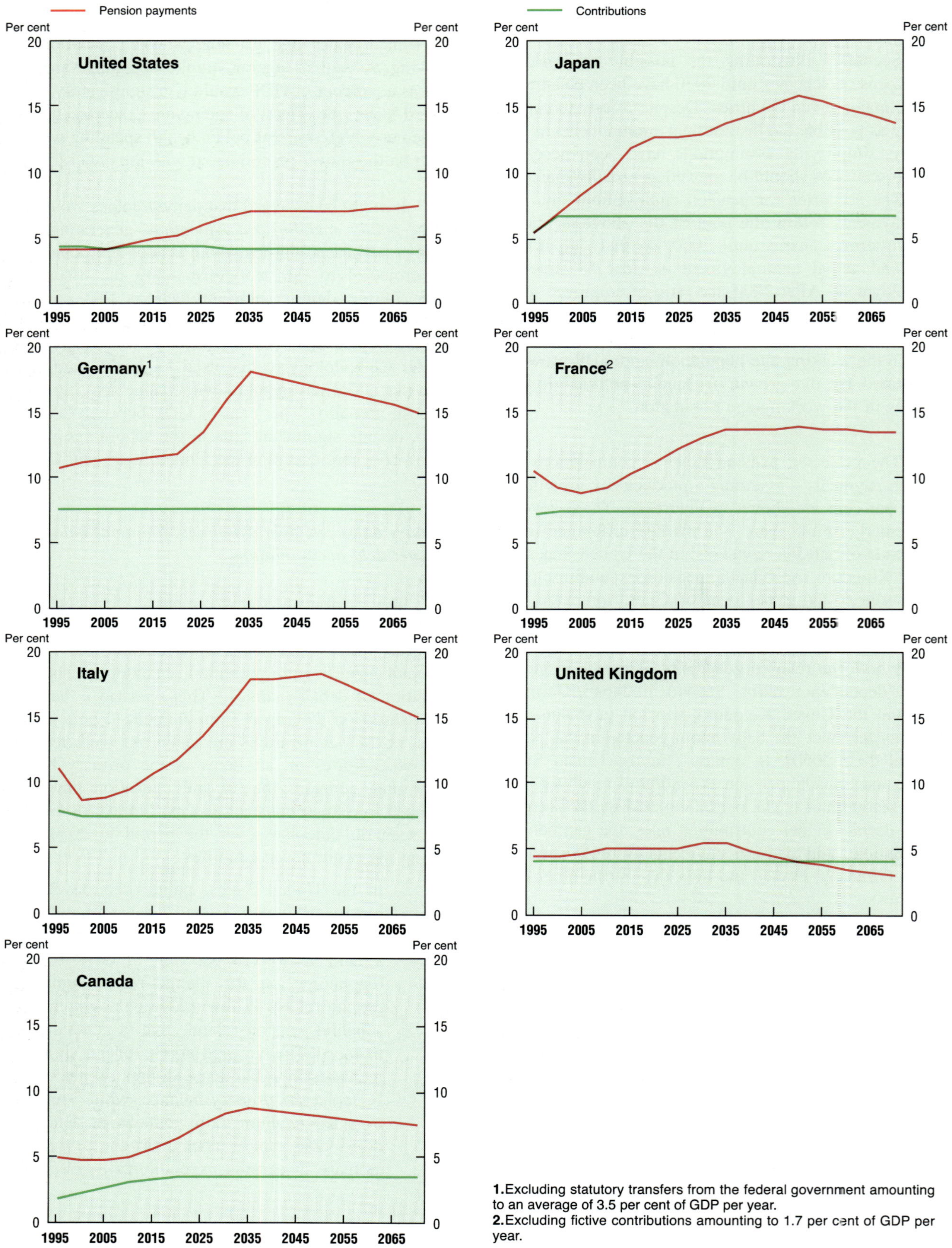

1. Excluding statutory transfers from the federal government amounting to an average of 3.5 per cent of GDP per year.

2. Excluding fictive contributions amounting to 1.7 per cent of GDP per year.

Table 18. **Fiscal indicators 1995 to 2030**[a]

Per cent of GDP

	Primary balance[b]	Interest rate/growth rate differential constant[c, d]			Interest rate constant[c]		
		Net interest payments	Financial balance[b]	Net financial liabilities	Net interest payments	Financial balance[b]	Net financial liabilities
United States							
1995	0.4	2.1	–1.8	38	2.1	–1.8	38
2000	0.1	2.4	–2.2	39	2.4	–2.2	39
2015	–0.6	2.6	–3.3	45	3.0	–3.6	47
2030	–4.3	5.0	–9.3	94	7.1	–11.4	108
Japan							
1995	–3.5	0.6	–4.1	13	0.6	–4.1	13
2000	–0.8	1.2	–2.0	24	1.2	–2.0	24
2015	–6.5	4.0	–10.5	99	4.7	–11.2	102
2030	–8.0	11.7	–19.8	289	14.7	–22.8	314
Germany							
1995	1.2	3.5	–2.3	46	3.5	–2.3	46
2000	1.2	3.1	–1.9	44	3.1	–1.9	44
2015	1.2	3.3	–2.1	49	3.4	–2.2	49
2030	–4.9	4.5	–9.4	93	6.6	–11.6	105
France							
1995	–1.6	3.3	–5.0	36	3.3	–5.0	36
2000	1.5	3.2	–1.6	41	3.2	–1.6	41
2015	0.3	2.4	–2.1	37	2.9	–2.5	40
2030	–3.8	4.8	–8.5	88	6.4	–10.2	103
Italy							
1995	3.3	11.1	–7.8	121	11.1	–7.8	121
2000	4.5	8.1	–3.5	107	8.1	–3.5	107
2015	2.5	6.0	–3.5	80	6.5	–4.0	82
2030	–4.4	8.4	–12.8	126	11.3	–15.7	146
United Kingdom							
1995	–1.7	2.6	–4.2	47	2.6	–4.2	47
2000	2.2	2.1	0.1	40	2.1	0.1	40
2015	1.6	0.7	0.9	14	0.7	0.9	14
2030	0.2	–0.8	1.0	–9	–0.8	1.1	–9
Canada							
1995	1.3	5.0	–3.7	64	5.0	–3.7	64
2000	3.8	3.9	–0.1	54	3.9	–0.1	54
2015	3.7	0.6	3.1	5	0.7	3.0	6
2030	–1.6	–0.6	–1.1	–13	–0.8	–0.8	–13

a) 2000 corresponds to the Medium-Term Reference Scenario (MTRS) (see Table 10).

b) Surplus (+) deficit (–).

c) The net interest payments from 2001 onwards have been projected in two parts. For the net interest payments on the projected stock of debt in 2000 (from the MTRS) the implicit interest rate on government debt (net interest payments as a percentage of net debt) for each country has been used. For new debt accumulated from 2001 onwards, long-term market interest rates have been applied which were derived from an average real interest rate for the major seven countries and individual inflation rates (both from the MTRS in 2000).

d) Differential derived from MTRS in 2000 and held constant thereafter. With a declining labour force, economic growth declines over the longer term and interest rates decline below the level in 2000.

dynamics result in net debt rising from about 25 per cent in 2000 to around 290 to 315 per cent of GDP by 2030.

- Germany is relatively well placed until around 2020, largely because of its comfortable primary surplus in 2000 and the relatively small deficits of the pension scheme until around 2020. While the age structure of the population deteriorates earlier, the dependency ratio does not increase significantly as the retirement age increases. But after 2020, the pension deficit deteriorates sharply and by 2030 net debt is around 95 to 105 per cent of GDP, as compared with around 45 per cent in 2000.

- France also has a reasonably good primary balance position in 2000, but the pension expenditures rise significantly, rapidly eroding the primary surplus. Adverse debt dynamics result in debt rising steeply from 40 per cent in 2000 to around 90 to 105 per cent of GDP by 2030.

- Italy is projected to generate a primary surplus sufficiently large to produce a virtuous circle of debt reduction from 120 per cent in 1995 to about 80 per cent in 2015, despite its current very high debt/GDP ratio. But the rapid increase in pension expenditures leads to a turnaround in the primary balance of around 9 per cent of GDP between 2000 and 2030. Adverse debt dynamics start to come back into play around 2015 and by 2030 net debt is 125 to 145 per cent of GDP.
- In the United Kingdom, with the advantages of a good starting position and a public pension scheme that runs only a small deficit, net debt as a per cent of GDP falls to very low levels and by 2030 even turns into a small net asset position. However, in these circumstances, the assumptions of unchanged policies for other spending and taxes may well be not realistic; policies might tend to become less restrictive with the evolution of debt thus being less favourable.
- Canada, under the assumption that announced medium-term consolidation targets are fully met, is projected to run a comfortable primary surplus by 2000. With announced pension policies including significant increases in social security contributions, the surplus will remain high until around 2020. But, thereafter, it will decline due to the continued increase in health-care and pension outlays. Nevertheless, Canada's net debt falls sharply and turns to a small net asset position by 2030. As with the United Kingdom, in these circumstances the assumptions of unchanged policies may not be realistic.

Inter-generational accounting

The interaction between population ageing and fiscal transfers can also be analysed in an inter-generational accounting framework. Essentially, the generational accounting method is aimed at assessing whether a typical member of each generation would receive back in transfers and services over their lifetime what they have paid in taxes (in net present value terms and adjusted for productivity growth), given the need eventually to satisfy an inter-temporal budget constraint that requires the present value of future tax payments (of existing and future generations) to equal the present value of all future government consumption less the initial stock of debt.[10]

The OECD Secretariat has asked experts in various countries for which generational accounting models are available (the United States, Germany, Italy, Norway and Sweden) to calculate generational accounts on a comparable basis.[11] The calculations reveal generational imbalances in favour of living generations. If policies do not change generations that are born after the base year 1993 are likely to have a significantly greater tax burden than present generations (as represented by newborn generation in the base year) in all five countries considered. But the size of the imbalance differs considerably among the countries (Table 19).[12] For example, assuming a discount rate of 5 per cent and income (or productivity) growth of 1.5 per cent, future generations in Italy have to pay net taxes more than five times as large (Case A) as the newborn generation (which clearly illustrates from a different perspective that the fiscal situation in Italy is not sustainable). In the United States and Norway, future generations have to pay 100 per cent and about 50 per cent, respectively, more net taxes than today's newborn generation. In Germany and Sweden the imbalance is smaller, although with unchanged policies, future generations will also have to bear an increase in the net tax burden of about 25 per cent and 30 per cent, respectively.

The results are sensitive to assumptions about productivity growth and the discount rate, although for most of the discount rate/productivity growth combinations assumed here, the results show a significant generational imbalance against future generations. The results are also sensitive to the assumptions about demographics as is illustrated for Italy. If the Italian fertility rate were to recover to the replacement rate over the next decade instead of by 2030 as assumed in the World Bank's projection, the generational imbalance would be considerably smaller, although still relatively large (Case B).

In most of the countries considered, future demographic changes are the major source of generational imbalances. Another source for generational imbalances is the servicing of government debt, accumulated by past and present generations. This factor is particularly important in the case of Italy. As public debt levels are already high, redressing the generational imbalances can only be achieved by changes in policies that result in a strong improvement in fiscal positions. For example, cutting pension benefits, increasing social security contributions or more general spending cuts or tax increases would help to reduce generational imbalances. Alternatively, the balance between newborns and future generations would be restored fully by immediate and permanent across-the-board public spending cuts that amounted to about 12 per cent of GDP in Italy, about 4 to 5 per cent of GDP in the

Table 19. **Generational Accounts**

Present values of life-time net tax payments per person (males)

Productivity growth (per cent)	1			1 1/2			2		
Discount rate (per cent)	3	5	7	3	5	7	3	5	7
United States									
Present generation[a] (thousands of dollars)[b]	191	105	58	217	121	66	245	139	76
Future generations (thousands of dollars)	384	226	151	422	243	157	468	262	164
Generational imbalance (in per cent)[c]	102	115	161	95	100	137	91	89	117
Germany									
Present generation (thousands of dollars)	311	168	91	362	197	107	419	231	126
Future generations (thousands of dollars)	390	211	103	446	250	126	505	293	152
Generational imbalance (in per cent)	25	26	13	23	27	18	20	27	22
Italy (Case A)[d]									
Present generation (thousands of dollars)	102	54	22	114	65	29	122	77	36
Future generations (thousands of dollars)	433	340	316	465	354	306	508	374	306
Generational imbalance (in per cent)	327	533	1336	310	446	970	315	385	741
Italy (Case B)[e]									
Present generation (thousands of dollars)	122	59	24	144	72	31	166	88	39
Future generations (thousands of dollars)	258	206	192	273	213	185	290	224	185
Generational imbalance (in per cent)	111	249	709	90	195	500	74	155	369
Norway									
Present generation (thousands of dollars)	181	97	54	207	110	61	235	126	69
Future generations (thousands of dollars)	299	130	48	376	171	72	466	216	98
Generational imbalance (in per cent)	64	34	–13	79	53	16	94	68	39
Sweden									
Present generation (thousands of dollars)	272	136	75	317	156	84	371	180	95
Future generations (thousands of dollars)	333	185	116	372	204	123	414	227	132
Generational imbalance (in per cent)	23	36	56	18	31	47	12	26	40

a) Newborns in base year.
b) In constant prices, adjusted for income growth, converted to U.S. dollars using 1993 nominal exchange rates.
c) Generational imbalance is calculated as the difference between life-time net payments for someone of the present generation and future generations (growth adjusted and in present value terms), expressed as a percentage of the net payments of the present generation. Generational imbalance in favour of the present generation is positive, generational balance corresponds to 0 and generational imbalance in favour of future generations would be negative.
d) Case A: population projection by the World Bank which assumes a return of the fertility rate to replacement rate by 2030.
e) Case B: more rapid return of fertility rate to replacement rate (by 2010) so that population falls less than in Case A.

United States, about 3 per cent in Norway, about 2 per cent in Sweden, and 1½ to 2 per cent of GDP in Germany.

Policy options

Where major fiscal pressures have been identified above, it is clear that some policy action will be needed to redress imbalances, in particular in countries where the law requires the elimination of pension deficits. Without such action government dissaving could also lead to significant reductions in national savings in some countries. Three main areas of policy action to address the threat of a burgeoning of public debt associated with the pension problem are: first, policies improving fiscal positions over the next few years (which will, of course, have an impact that will carry through into the much longer term); second, policies altering pension schemes and health-care systems; third, policies aimed at tempering the ageing effect by increasing the workforce.

Budgetary pressures can be directly addressed, either by building up a better starting position before demographic pressures mount or by raising taxes or cutting other expenditures in the longer term as the pressure develops. Achieving a lower net debt/GDP ratio and a higher primary surplus in the coming years would generate significantly more favourable debt dynamics in the longer term. For example, a permanent improvement in primary balances by 1 percentage point of GDP in 2000 would reduce net debt positions by 2030 between 40 and 55 per cent of GDP. Generating higher primary surpluses would have the particular advantage of ''buying more time'' to introduce more fundamental reforms, by delaying the time at which adverse debt dynamics emerge. If the option of offsetting the demographic pressures as they occur was chosen – *i.e.* keeping debt ratios constant at their levels in 2000 in the medium-term scenario presented in Table 10 – this would require improvements in primary balances amounting to around 5 to 9 per cent of GDP by 2030, except for the United Kingdom and Canada.

The main policy options for adjusting pension systems to future challenges include raising contribution rates, lowering pension payments (including replacement rates) and raising the retirement age.[13] The combined effects of falling working populations and rising numbers of pensioners mean that even quite major increases in contribution rates or reductions in pension payments would be insufficient to balance those schemes that face the greatest problems (Table 20). Raising contribution rates can be seen as merely a means of raising overall tax revenues and would need to be assessed against other revenue-raising options but it does focus directly on the problem. Raising retirement ages (beyond changes already scheduled) provides greater scope for rebalancing schemes, with the advantage of a two-fold impact: by increasing the working-age population and therefore both GDP itself and the contributions paid, and by decreasing the number of pensioners. Those countries with the lowest retirement ages, after current reforms are implemented, France and Italy, also face the largest pension pressures and raising retirement ages significantly would seem to offer the most scope for easing the pressure, especially as experience elsewhere indicates that raising retirement ages is a practical and feasible policy option.

In implementing any action here, early announcement of reforms would allow people the longest possible period to adjust their behaviour to pension reforms (and what these might imply for their preferred consumption and savings patterns), would minimise the adjustment cost associated with any change and spread the burden more evenly between the present workforce and the workforce in the next century. Phasing-in some reforms might also be necessary to allow people reasonable time to adjust their behaviour. The age cohort just about to retire, for example, would have little time to adjust their savings behaviour to lower public pension payments and health-care reimbursements than they would have expected.

Designing policies to contain the growth of public health expenditures as populations age is a difficult task that is likely to depend in large part on better design of health-care systems and country-specific policies to achieve greater micro-efficiency.[14] However, it would only be necessary to hold growth in per capita real public health spending to around ½ to 1 per cent lower than productivity growth in order to offset the impact of ageing on public health spending. One area where demographic pressures are likely to mount is long-term care of the frail elderly. Some of the impact may be tempered by better case management designed to ensure that the frail elderly are well cared for in the most cost-effective manner. To the extent that current policy settings work against this, either through the regulatory structure, through lack of co-ordinated structures, or through the incentives built into the structure of payments for care, there may be scope for improvement. Another issue that could be examined further is the scope for further use of income and asset[15] based means-testing for publicly

Table 20. **Pension policy options**

Net present value as a per cent of 1994 GDP[a]

	Base case	Replacement rate 10 percentage points lower[b]	Contribution rate 3 percentage points higher	Retirement age 5 years later
United States				
Contributions	136	136	164	143
Pension payments	167	141	167	135
Balance[c]	–31	–5	–4	8
Japan				
Contributions	184	184	203	198
Pension payments	294	267	294	239
Balance[d]	–110	–83	–90	–41
Germany[e]				
Contributions	212	212	235	228
Pension payments	351	294	351	294
Balance	–139	–82	–115	–66
Germany[f]				
Contributions	303	303	336	326
Pension payments	351	294	351	294
Balance	–48	9	–14	32
France[g]				
Contributions	221	221	243	238
Pension payments	319	284	319	266
Balance	–98	–63	–76	–28
France[h]				
Contributions	271	271	294	293
Pension payments	319	284	319	266
Balance	–48	–12	–25	27
Italy				
Contributions	199	199	214	214
Pension payments	312	284	312	260
Balance	–113	–85	–98	–46
United Kingdom				
Contributions	123	123	153	131
Pension payments	142	90	142	113
Balance	–19	32	12	18
Canada				
Contributions	96	96	120	103
Pension payments	195	162	195	151
Balance[i]	–99	–66	–74	–48

a) Contributions and pension payments discounted at 5 per cent. Productivity growth assumed to be 1.5 per cent.
b) For the United Kingdom, the replacement rate was lowered by 5 percentage points instead of 10 percentage points.
c) Excludes pre-existing assets of 5.8 per cent of GDP.
d) Excludes pre-existing assets of 37.1 per cent of GDP.
e) Excludes statutory transfers from the Federal Government.
f) Includes statutory transfers from the Federal Government.
g) Includes revenues from the *contribution sociale généralisée* and excludes "fictive" contributions.
h) Includes revenues from the *contribution sociale généralisée* and "fictive" contributions.
i) Excludes pre-existing assets of 5.7 per cent of GDP.

financed long-term care. It should be noted, however, that means-testing can lead to some perverse incentive structures for those around the means-test threshold. One option that has been suggested is to require current workers to make contributions to a new public "fund" from which they could draw in future years to cover their long-term care costs. Such an option might have some presentational advantages because it looks like an insurance scheme, and would provide a way of easing the burden on future taxpayers, relative to current taxpayers. However, this approach would not make any difference from a fiscal point of view, except to the extent that it implies raising additional revenue in the immediate future through taxation, which would result in a better fiscal position before demographic pressures mount.

Another policy line to deal with the pressures on government budgets that originate from ageing is to attempt to temper the ageing effect by increasing the workforce. Options that have been suggested include raising the participation rate, increasing immigration or increasing working lifetimes. Policies aimed at increasing participation rates *per se* may be difficult to design, but at least policies which discourage participation could be avoided, including those policies that discourage part-time working arrangements. The use of "early retirement" policies, currently a response to high unemployment, should also be minimised. In any case, raising the overall participation rate would not go far towards offsetting the falls in working population. Increasing immigration from countries outside the OECD area is another option, but the interaction between immigration and economic performance may be quite complex and there are likely to be practical limits on the extent to which immigration can be increased.[16]

In a number of countries, further increases in the retirement age could make a major contribution to balance pension systems. This, together with restoring sound fiscal positions in the medium term, in order to create a better starting position before demographic pressures mount, may be the most effective way of dealing with the problems ageing will pose for public finance.

NOTES

1. For a more complete description of demographic trends and of the methodology underpinning this analysis see W. Leibfritz *et al.*, "Ageing populations, pension systems and government budgets: how do they affect saving?", OECD Economics Department Working Paper (forthcoming).
2. See Bos *et al.*, *World Population Projections, 1994-95*, The International Bank for Reconstruction and Development/The World Bank (1994).
3. The working-age population is defined here as from age 20 to legislated retirement age. This differs from the standard definition of 15-64 years.
4. The medium-term scenario reported here is an updated version of the scenario described in "Medium-Term developments in OECD countries", in *OECD Economic Outlook 56*, December 1994. Revisions reflect changes in the short-term outlook and in medium-term policy objectives, but otherwise the general features of the MTRS are largely unchanged.
5. This assumption implies that the ageing of the population does not affect structural unemployment, or participation rates.
6. The results of this procedure should be regarded as indicative only – they are simply an attempt to illustrate the effects of demographics and should not be interpreted as projections of public health-care spending which would require taking other factors into account.
7. Experience during the 1980s indicates that, in fact, per capita real public expenditures on health care have risen faster than this assumption would suggest, except in Japan and Germany.
8. That is, calculating per pupil public expenditures on education for different age groups, based on data on public spending by type of education – from pre-school to post-graduate – and participation in schooling by age group for 1991. For more detail, see OECD, *Education at a Glance*, OECD Indicators (1994).
9. If real interest rates on government debt are higher than rates of economic growth, a decline of the primary surplus below a critical level would lead to a vicious spiral of higher interest payments and debt.
10. The inter-temporal budget constraint implies that over an infinite time horizon the present value of net debt must approach zero. The current value of debt may still be positive and rise, but its rate of increase must be lower than the discount rate, which implies that the primary balance must be in surplus. Generational accounts are constructed so that the present generations are not bound by the budget constraint and can continue to accumulate debt in future years. The burden of satisfying the budget constraint, thus falls entirely on the future generation (see R. Haveman, "Should Generational Accounts Replace Public Budgets and Deficits?" *Journal of Economic Perspectives*, Vol. 8, No. 1, 1994). This means that if existing generations ran primary deficits, future generations have to restore sustainability by turning primary balances into surpluses.
11. Calculations were carried out by J. Gokhale, L.J. Kotlikoff and J. Walliser (for the United States and Germany), N. Sartor (for Italy), C. John (for Sweden) and C. Gjersem (for Norway).
12. Generational accounts are shown here for men only, but have been calculated separately also for women. Differences in participation rates, life expectancies, earnings and transfers generally lead to lower life-time net tax payments of women of all generations as compared to those of men, but generational imbalances are similar for men and women.

13. The more radical option of moving to a fully funded scheme has been raised in a number of countries. However, in countries facing rapid ageing, the transition to such a scheme is particularly difficult because it involves the current working generation paying both for the currently retired and for their own retirement, *i.e.* higher taxes. Whether or not these additional taxes were paid into a separate fund would not change the overall fiscal arithmetic, but building up a separate actuarially sound fund could help to make the underlying fiscal difficulties and the intergenerational implications more transparent. In any case, such a scheme would either have to incorporate an element of intra-generational redistribution or would need to be supplemented by other provisions for those who would otherwise experience old-age poverty.

14. See M. Oxley, and M. MacFarlan, "Health care reform: controlling spending and increasing efficiency", *OECD Economics Department Working Papers,* No. 149 (1994).

15. Including housing assets which are often excluded in present means-test criteria. This may have the indirect effect of encouraging more use of home equity conversions, such as reverse mortgages and sale-leaseback, which would allow the elderly to more effectively utilise their private assets. See OECD, *Caring for Frail Elderly People* (1994).

16. Projections assume that migration rates in most countries are projected to fall quite quickly with only the United States and Canada projected to continue receiving immigrants after 2010. By 2030, migration flows are assumed everywhere to be zero. The number of working-age immigrants that would be needed in 2050 to fully offset the fall in working-age population between 2000 and 2050 (when the working population stabilises at a lower level) would be around 13 to 15 million in each case for Japan, Germany and Italy, or between 20 and 40 per cent of the working-age population.

DEVELOPMENTS IN INDIVIDUAL OECD COUNTRIES

UNITED STATES

In 1994 the United States economy turned in a strong performance, with impressive gains in real output, declining unemployment and limited inflation. But thus far this year aggregate demand has slowed to a more sustainable pace at the same time as inflation pressures may be starting to surface. The slowdown may be attributable to last year's sharp run-up in long-term interest rates, a by-product of the tightening in monetary policy. Nonetheless, the effects of this tightening may be somewhat mitigated by improved availability of credit, dollar weakness against other major currencies and the dissipation of the contractionary effects of the 1993 budget package. The outlook is for a near-term inventory correction, followed by a temporary return to above-potential rates of growth in the second half of 1995. Thereafter, despite some expansionary effects of recent declines in long-term rates, the slowdown in activity could resume, along with an edging up in unemployment, a moderate pick-up in inflation and a slight narrowing in the current account deficit, after the impact of the recent Mexican crisis wears off and the enhanced price competitiveness of US producers comes into play.

Recent developments

The economy continued to expand briskly over the second half of 1994, with real GDP growing at an annualised rate of 4¼ per cent. The strength of demand was widespread but was once again most pronounced in business fixed investment and increasingly in exports. Despite rising interest rates, firms responded to tightening operating conditions (capacity utilisation was nearing its highest level in over 15 years), and they and households took advantage of a growing availability of bank credit and improved cash flow to boost their purchases of durable goods. Businesses also continued to quicken the pace of their additions to plant capacity and to lift their stockbuilding, although the inventory-sales ratio nonetheless did no more than flatten out. Consumers also increased their spending on non-durables at a rapid rate without impinging on saving: with slowing growth in income and payroll taxes and rapid gains in personal interest income, the household saving rate actually rose to 4.7 per cent at the end of the year, the highest since early 1993. Public consumption grew at its fastest rate since 1991, as the pace of the ongoing defence drawdown

UNITED STATES
Demand and output

Percentage changes from previous period, seasonally adjusted at annual rates, volume (1987 prices)

	1991 current prices billion $	1992	1993	1994	1995	1996	1994 I	1994 II	1995 I	1995 II	1996 I	1996 II
Private consumption	3 902.5	2.8	3.3	3.5	2.7	1.9	3.6	3.1	2.6	2.3	1.7	1.9
Government consumption	1 097.4	–0.7	–0.8	–0.7	–0.3	0.3	–2.8	1.9	–1.7	0.3	0.2	0.3
Private fixed investment	746.6	5.5	11.3	12.3	10.5	4.9	13.0	9.8	12.2	8.1	4.3	3.0
Residential	189.6	16.2	8.2	8.6	–3.8	–1.2	13.4	–0.9	–4.8	–4.6	–0.7	1.3
Non-residential	557.0	2.0	12.5	13.7	15.5	6.6	12.9	13.8	18.1	12.0	5.7	3.4
Final domestic demand	5 746.5	2.5	3.7	4.1	3.5	2.2	3.9	4.0	3.5	3.0	1.9	1.8
* stockbuilding	–1.8[a]	0.1	0.3	0.6	–0.2	–0.4	1.2	0.4	–0.2	–0.7	–0.3	–0.2
Total domestic demand	5 744.7	2.5	3.9	4.7	3.3	1.8	5.1	4.4	3.2	2.3	1.6	1.6
Exports of goods and services	601.1	6.7	4.1	9.0	9.0	10.0	7.2	16.6	5.6	8.9	10.3	10.6
Imports of goods and services	621.0	8.7	10.7	13.4	8.8	5.2	13.4	15.3	7.3	6.0	4.9	5.0
* net exports	–19.9[a]	–0.3	–0.8	–0.7	–0.2	0.5	–0.9	–0.2	–0.4	0.2	0.6	0.6
GDP at market prices	5 724.8	2.3	3.1	4.1	3.2	2.3	4.3	4.3	3.0	2.6	2.3	2.2
Industrial production	–	3.3	4.1	5.3	3.7	2.0	6.4	5.4	3.9	1.8	2.0	2.1

* Contributions to changes in real GDP (as a per cent of real GDP in the previous period).
a) Actual amount.

UNITED STATES
Employment, income and inflation
Percentage changes from previous period, seasonally adjusted at annual rates

	1992	1993	1994	1995	1996	1994 I	1994 II	1995 I	1995 II	1996 I	1996 II
Employment[a,b]	0.6	1.5	3.1	1.9	1.1	4.1	2.4	2.1	1.1	1.1	1.1
Unemployment rate[b,c]	7.4	6.8	6.1	5.6	5.7	6.4	5.8	5.6	5.7	5.7	5.8
Compensation of employees	5.5	5.3	5.9	5.5	4.9	6.7	5.6	6.0	4.5	5.0	5.2
Unit labour cost	3.1	2.1	1.8	2.3	2.5	2.3	1.3	2.9	1.9	2.7	2.9
Household disposable income	6.1	5.2	5.2	6.4	5.2	5.6	7.1	6.8	4.9	5.2	5.3
GDP deflator	2.8	2.2	2.1	2.0	2.7	2.4	2.1	2.0	2.2	2.8	2.9
Private consumption deflator	3.2	2.5	2.1	2.8	3.4	2.0	2.8	2.5	3.2	3.4	3.5

a) Household basis.
b) Break in series as of January 1994.
c) As a percentage of labour force.

eased temporarily, and public construction rose at a 6 per cent annual rate. Surging export growth outpaced still robust import increases for the first time in over three years. Only the housing sector, faced with much higher interest rates on both conventional and adjustable-rate mortgages, showed any weakness, with housing starts falling off and residential investment declining for the first time since the recession.

But the momentum of demand began to wane with the coming of winter, and spending slowed substantially during the first quarter of 1995. While the growth of business investment even accelerated somewhat further to the 20 per cent range, households grew more cautious, especially with respect to interest-sensitive purchases. Despite still robust income gains, real consumer spending growth slackened to less than 1 per cent at annual rates and was actually negative for both durable and nondurable goods in the four months to March. Accordingly, the saving rate jumped to 5½ per cent in March. Similarly, new housing sales have fallen sharply, and the resultant rise of unsold homes has led to a 20 per cent fall in housing starts since December. Since last autumn, government purchases have also reverted to their medium-term weakness, with persistent declines at the federal level overwhelming moderating state and local outlays. And with the burden of the Mexican shock, exports fell for the first time in a year. Overall GDP growth was buffered by an involuntary building of inventories, especially at the wholesale level.

Until recently, the labour market continued to tighten as a result of the robust growth in output. Employment gains were averaging about 3 per cent per year, and the unemployment rate fell from 6.7 per cent in January 1994 to a trough of 5.4 per cent. For much of last year weakness in labour force participation helped push the rate down, but a rebound in labour supply growth in recent months has combined with an abrupt halt in the employment uptrend to reverse some of the fall in unemployment. Not surprisingly, the number of job losers has fallen sharply, but uncharacteristically for this point in the cycle, there has been no corresponding increase in the tendency for people to leave jobs voluntarily. This has possibly been an important factor (along with slowing benefit costs) in holding down compensation increases, which have shown virtually no signs of acceleration thus far. With business productivity up strongly in the final two quarters of 1994, unit labour costs rose only about ¾ per cent for the year – the lowest figures since 1964 – and fell by 2 per cent in manufacturing. A modest pick-up in cost inflation in the first quarter of 1995 is suggested by some indicators. Price pressures have, however, come more clearly into view. Producer prices for crude and intermediate goods began to firm in the middle of 1994, and most recently the acceleration has spread to consumer prices, especially for housing and transportation. But any broader-based move to higher rates of inflation has been mitigated by moderate increases in prices of capital goods.

On the external side the current account deficit continued to widen at a steady pace, reaching $179 billion at an annual rate (2.6 per cent of GDP) in the fourth quarter of 1994. Most of the deterioration last year came in merchandise trade, even though the downward trend was reversed late in the year as export volumes began to surge. But by then the investment income balance had shifted sharply toward deficit, led especially by earnings on foreign-owned direct investments in the United States. On the capital account, the latter part of the year was marked by accelerating direct investment inflows and higher bank borrowing from abroad, in large part to finance domestic lending, as well as renewed substantial gross capital outflows in the form of a build-up of bank

United States

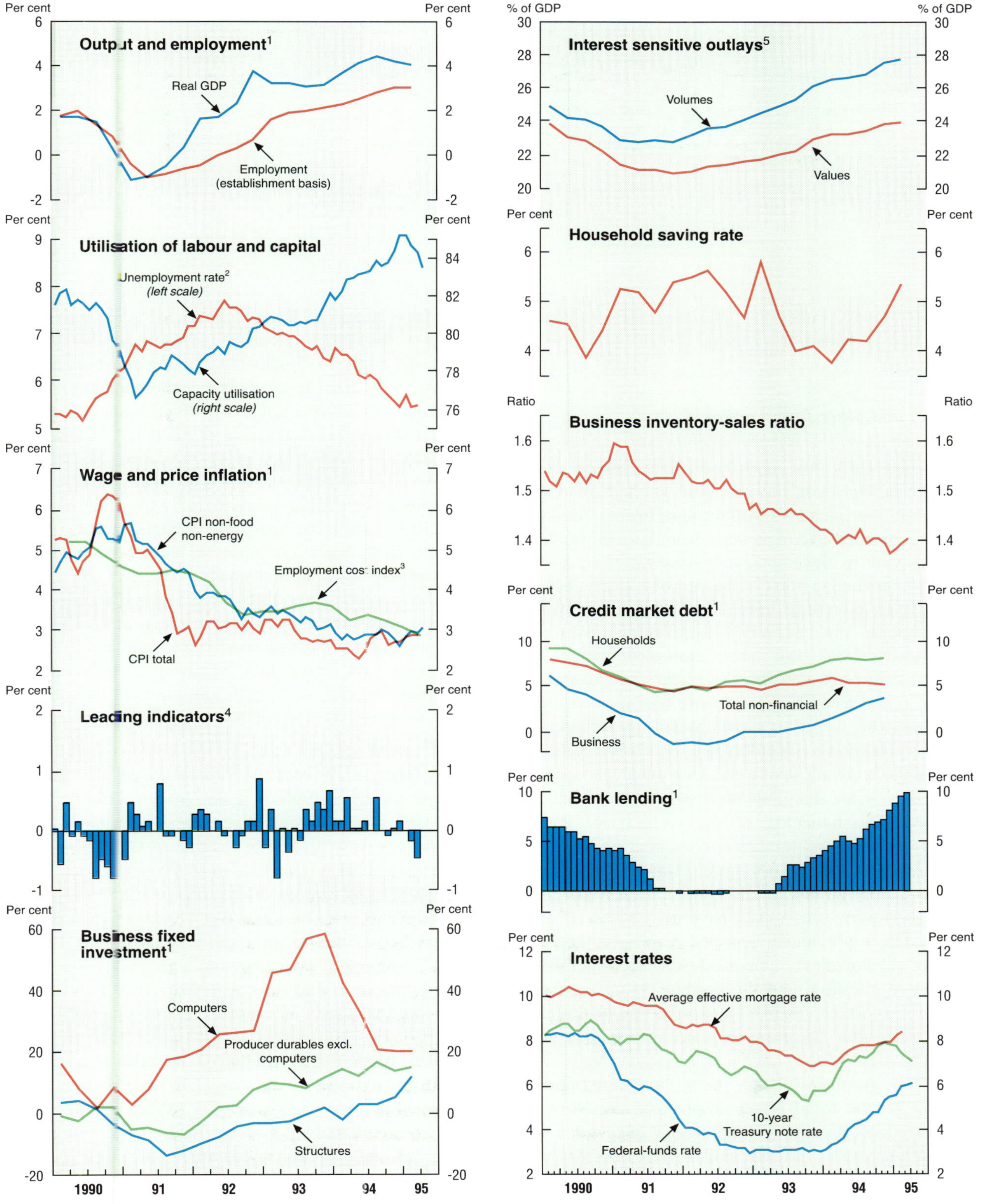

1. Year-on-year percentage change.
2. Break in series. New basis as of January 1994.
3. Total compensation of private, non-farm workers.
4. One-month percentage change.
5. Private fixed investment plus consumption of durables.

Sources: Department of Commerce; Federal Reserve Board; Congressional Budget Office; OECD, *Main Economic Indicators.*

UNITED STATES
Financial indicators

	1992	1993	1994	1995	1996	1994 I	1994 II	1995 I	1995 II	1996 I	1996 II
Household saving ratio[a]	5.2	4.6	4.2	5.0	4.8	4.0	4.4	5.2	4.8	4.9	4.8
General government financial balance[b]	–4.3	–3.4	–2.0	–1.8	–2.0	–2.0	–1.9	–1.7	–1.8	–2.0	–2.0
Current balance[b]	–1.1	–1.6	–2.3	–2.7	–2.5	–2.1	–2.5	–2.6	–2.8	–2.6	–2.5
Short-term interest rate[c]	3.4	3.0	4.3	5.9	6.4	3.6	4.9	5.7	6.2	6.4	6.4
Long-term interest rate[d]	7.0	5.9	7.1	7.1	6.9	6.6	7.6	7.2	7.0	6.9	6.8

a) As a percentage of disposable income.
b) As a percentage of GDP.
c) 3-month Treasury bills.
d) 10-year government bonds.

deposits abroad, rather than the purchase of securities which had prevailed previously.

Policies and other forces acting

Until early this year, the Federal Reserve continued to bear down on the persistent strength of demand through further increases in short-term interest rates: after policy-controlled overnight rates were boosted by ³/₄ percentage point in November, they were raised by an additional ¹/₂ percentage point at the end of January, bringing the cumulative increase in the federal funds rate to 3 percentage points since the series of tightening moves began in February 1994. But other short-term market rates reached their peak after the November change, and little further impact from the winter's rise was apparent. Long-term rates, on the other hand, peaked in November at 8 per cent and have since declined by nearly 1.5 percentage points, reaching levels not seen since the spring of 1994; thus, more than half of 1994's increase has been reversed. The flattening of the yield curve and the strength of the bond market is consistent with the view that growth is slowing to a more sustainable pace before any substantial further inflation pressures develop. In that event short-term rates would have to rise less (if at all) than had been previously expected. However, the persistence of the slowdown in demand over the winter months is open to question, and the accompanying projections allow for a further ¹/₂ percentage point rise in short rates some time after an expected late spring rebound in spending.

The groundwork has been laid for important changes on the fiscal policy front since the November 1994 elections. As expected, the federal budget deficit for fiscal 1994 (ending last September) fell to $204 billion (3.1 per cent of GDP, a full percentage point below the fiscal 1993 outcome), as the initial consolidation resulting from the 1993 Budget Act (OBRA93) was implemented. With little new fiscal action taken thus far since then, the fiscal 1995 deficit is running some 30 per cent below year-earlier levels as non-interest outlays continue to grow very modestly. On a national accounts basis the deficit shrank to 2¹/₄ per cent of GDP in calendar 1994, less than half the record 1992 imbalance. Nearly three-quarters of the improvement is estimated to have been structural, with further contributions from the automatic stabilisers and from a reduction in interest payments relative to GDP. Equal contributions have been made from expenditure restraint and greater tax effort. As a result, for the first time since 1989 the debt-to-GDP ratio for the federal government was stable last year at 51.8 per cent. Despite cyclical strength in receipts, state and local governments have made little headway in reducing their operating deficits, with the result that their overall structural surplus has dwindled to only ¹/₄ percentage point of GDP.

The Administration has released its proposed budget for fiscal 1996. It is designed to hold the deficit constant over the next five years in nominal terms, allowing a slow decline in relation to GDP. This would be achieved by further cuts in real discretionary spending, asset sales and reductions in grants to state and local governments and subsidies. Nearly half of these savings would be devoted to personal tax cuts for the "middle class" through base-narrowing changes costing some $63 billion over the next five years. But now that the Republicans are in control of Congress, it is unclear how many of the Administration's proposals will be implemented. While a balanced budget amendment to the Constitution was narrowly defeated in February, it is expected that Congress will soon finalise plans to shrink the size of the federal government by cutting both taxes and spending[1] – in part by devolving social programmes to the states – resulting in elimination of the projected deficit by 2002. Some have expressed hope that passage of the so-called "line-item veto" providing the President with the power to eliminate individual appropriation provisions may help in this regard. Other structural reforms in process include legislation to give Congress greater influence over new regulations combined with greater flexibility in their implementation, a bill to make it somewhat more difficult for the federal government to impose unfunded mandates on other levels of government, new limits on legal liabilities of doctors and various businesses and renewed attempts to decompartmentalise the telecommunications and banking sectors.

Prospects

The economy is projected to slow gradually during 1995 and 1996 as the effects of the interest rate increases work their way through: annual average real GDP growth is expected to ease from over 4 per cent in 1994 to 3¼ per cent in 1995 and 2¼ per cent in 1996. The rise in interest rates and the dissipation of stock-adjustment effects have already dampened demand for consumer durables, and this is projected to continue as the saving rate is expected to remain near recent levels. Residential investment will continue to be pulled down by the same forces; it is projected to fall somewhat further, in line with recent weakness in housing starts, before recovering late in the projection period, as lower long-term interest rates help sustain demand. Non-residential investment, however, should continue to increase for a time at its recent torrid pace, reflecting the need to relieve continuing capacity constraints, before decelerating in 1996 as slowing demand eases capacity pressures. Government consumption may have little impact on demand as further retrenchment by the federal government is offset by moderate increases at the state and local level. After its recent burst, stockbuilding could ease as firms try to return to their earlier low stock-to-sales ratios. Export growth, overall, is projected to rebound, reflecting renewed strength in market growth (with a dissipation of the Mexico shock) and increased international competitiveness resulting from recent dollar weakness. Import demand growth should moderate with the slowing economy, and the net contribution from the foreign balance should turn positive later this year as growth in the United States drops below that of its trading partners.

The unemployment rate is projected to remain near present levels before edging up in 1996. While labour market tightness can be expected to imply only modest pressure to boost real compensation rates over the projection period, productivity is likely to exhibit a cyclical slowing, and unit labour costs to pick up. Producers will probably begin to pass on these as well as higher intermediate materials costs to consumers, with the result that consumer price inflation could rise from 2 per cent in 1994 to 3½ per cent in 1996. A marked deterioration in the terms of trade as well as persistent weakness in investment goods price inflation should restrain profits growth and hold the rise in the GDP deflator to 2 per cent in 1995 and 2¾ per cent in 1996. With continuing deterioration in net investment income, the current account deficit is projected to widen to nearly $200 billion in 1995 (2.7 per cent of GDP), before edging down in 1996, as worsening terms of trade largely offset the improvement in net export volumes.

The principal risks attached to these projections concern the persistence of the slowdown in domestic demand and the degree of price pressure that may develop from projected market conditions. If the recent slowdown in final demand proves to be transitory – with renewed vigour in household spending and a reversal of the recent rise in the saving rate, for instance – then

UNITED STATES
Recent projections for the federal budget deficit
$ billion, fiscal years except as noted

	1994[a]	1995	1996	1997	1998	1999	2000
Administration[b, c]	203	193	197	213	196	197	194
Administration (calendar year)[c, d]	160	179	n.a.	n.a.	n.a.	n.a.	n.a.
Congressional Budget Office[b, c]	203	176	207	224	222	253	284
Congressional Budget Office[c, d]	174	168	201	208	207	236	261
OECD Secretariat (calendar year)[d]	159	158	176	n.a.	n.a.	n.a.	n.a.
Blue Chip Economic Indicators (calendar year)[d]	160	168	192	n.a.	n.a.	n.a.	n.a.

a) Actual estimates for 1994 as of 31 March 1995: Budget basis for fiscal 1994 – $204 billion; National accounts basis for calendar 1994 – $159 billion.
b) Budget basis.
c) Administration projections include impact of its budget proposals; Congressional Budget Office projections do not.
d) National accounts basis.

UNITED STATES
External indicators[a]

Seasonally adjusted at annual rates

	1993	1994	1995	1996	1994 I	1994 II	1995 I	1995 II	1996 I	1996 II
					$ billion					
Merchandise exports	456.9	502.7	561	636	480.7	524.7	545	576	615	657
Merchandise imports	589.4	669.1	764	834	638.3	699.9	741	786	818	850
Trade balance	–132.6	–166.4	–203	–198	–157.5	–175.2	–196	–210	–203	–194
Invisibles, net	28.7	10.7	10	10	17.4	4.0	12	7	13	7
Current balance	–103.9	–155.7	–193	–188	–140.1	–171.2	–184	–203	–190	–187
					Percentage change					
Merchandise export volumes[b]	4.6	11.0	10.2	11.5	9.6	18.0	6.6	10.2	11.9	12.0
Merchandise import volumes[b]	11.7	15.2	10.2	5.7	15.2	18.7	8.2	6.6	5.3	5.5
Export performance[c]	0.3	0.2	2.5	3.0	–1.7	4.7	0.7	4.0	2.6	2.8
Terms of trade	0.7	0.2	–2.8	–1.6	1.5	–2.7	–2.3	–4.0	–1.0	–0.6

a) For further detail, see tables in the External Trade and Payments section of the Annex.
b) Derived from values and unit values on a national accounts basis. Certain adjustments to the balance of payments basis are therefore excluded, the most important being the omission of foreign trade of the Virgin Islands.
c) Ratio between the total of export volumes and export market of total goods.

growth beyond potential rates would resume and more aggressive tightening by the Federal Reserve would be required to avoid a further pickup in inflation. This, in turn, would risk a more rapid deceleration in 1996. On the other hand, if the higher short-term interest rates (and the unusually rapid rises in bond yields in their train last year)[2] and the Mexican shock are sufficiently slowing the economy and labour and product market conditions are not as tight as thought, then no further actions by the monetary authorities might be needed and a more limited acceleration in inflation could be in train. Finally, if passed, a credible plan to reduce or even eliminate the federal budget deficit entailing a sharp cut in purchases already in fiscal 1996 would have important effects: the impact of spending cuts would no doubt be offset to some extent by the expansionary effects of lower short- and long-term interest rates but might nonetheless entail some additional near-term weakness in activity.

NOTES

1. The House of Representatives has passed a budget resolution – only the broad outlines of a seven-year budget package – which cuts spending by some $1 400 billion and taxes by $350 billion in order to eliminate the deficit by 2002. The Senate is likely to pass a different plan to reach budget balance; the two will then have to be reconciled. Substantive decisions as to how to implement the ultimate plan would then have to be included in ensuing legislation.

2. Of the six major previous episodes of tightening since 1961, only that of 1983-84 brought about such a high correlation between the size of the increases in short- and long-term rates. On average, the rise in the ten-year Treasury note rate was only about 60 per cent of that in short rates, whereas until the peak in yields in November the corresponding ratio during the 1994 episode had been 96 per cent.

JAPAN

The Japanese economy recovered extremely slowly in 1994 despite the stimulus coming from fiscal policy and continued monetary ease. One of the major factors behind the downturn – the fall in corporate investment – now appears to be ending. In addition, stable or falling prices may contribute to the growth of real earnings. These two factors together with the further easing in monetary and fiscal policy may result in stronger growth in domestic demand, though the strength of the yen will adversely affect business and consumer confidence. With imports filling much of the increased domestic demand, the current-account surplus should decline relative to GDP and there may only be a slight pick-up in output in 1995 but a better growth performance, about 2¼ per cent, in 1996 in line with the estimated growth of potential output. With considerable spare capacity, high unemployment and continued weak import prices, the price level may fall in 1995 before stabilising in 1996.

Recent developments

In the second half of 1994, output growth remained slow and, at 1 per cent, showed no acceleration from the first half of the year. Domestic demand did, however, accelerate slightly, despite a marked slowdown in private consumption reflecting a pause in salaries, as normal second-half bonus payments appear to have been paid earlier in the year. For the year as whole, the increase in consumption appears to have been helped by tax refunds and was only slightly below the growth of disposable income.

The principal element leading to the pickup in domestic demand was the marked slowdown in the decline of business investment. After falling steadily since the beginning of 1992, corporate investment grew in the last two quarters of 1994. By contrast, housing construction showed signs of weakness at the end of the year as starts in the more speculative apartment market fell. Reflecting stronger domestic demand and the high exchange rate, imports rose more rapidly than exports; as a result, the current-account surplus fell to 2.6 per cent of GDP in the second half of 1994. Weak output growth led to a fall in nearly all price indicators by the end of the year, with the GDP deflator being ¾ per cent below its level a year earlier, and to a slight rise in unemployment. However, at that time there was evidence that the labour market was stabilising, with overtime work increasing and employment rising.

JAPAN
Demand and output

Percentage changes from previous period, seasonally adjusted at annual rates, volume (1985 prices)

	1991 current prices trillion Y	1992	1993	1994	1995	1996	1994 I	1994 II	1995 I	1995 II	1996 I	1996 II
Private consumption	255.1	1.7	1.0	2.2	2.3	3.1	3.0	1.3	2.5	3.0	3.1	3.3
Government consumption	41.2	2.7	1.7	2.8	3.3	2.4	2.1	3.0	2.7	4.6	1.6	1.8
Gross fixed investment	143.4	–1.1	–1.8	–2.3	1.9	3.2	–4.6	1.2	0.8	5.0	2.5	2.7
Public[a]	30.3	15.3	16.5	5.2	4.8	4.0	5.0	2.3	2.9	11.2	1.9	1.5
Private residential	23.8	–6.7	2.5	9.6	–0.7	3.3	5.7	6.9	–6.2	3.6	3.4	3.0
Private non-residential	89.3	–4.7	–9.3	–8.8	1.2	2.7	–11.7	–1.1	1.9	2.2	2.6	3.2
Final domestic demand	439.7	0.8	0.1	0.8	2.3	3.1	0.4	1.4	2.0	3.8	2.8	3.0
* stockbuilding	3.3[b]	–0.5	–0.2	0.2	0.1	0.1	0.5	0.1	0.1	0.2	0.1	0
Total domestic demand	443.0	0.3	0	1.0	2.4	3.1	1.0	1.5	2.1	4.0	2.9	2.9
Exports of goods and services	46.8	5.2	1.3	5.0	3.5	4.9	8.8	6.8	2.0	3.3	5.5	5.4
Imports of goods and services	38.5	–0.4	2.7	8.3	10.8	9.9	9.2	10.6	10.5	11.5	9.5	9.2
* net exports	8.3[b]	0.8	–0.2	–0.4	–1.1	–0.8	0	–0.5	–1.3	–1.3	–0.7	–0.7
GDP at market prices	451.3	1.1	–0.2	0.6	1.3	2.3	1.0	1.0	0.8	2.7	2.2	2.3
Industrial production[c]	–	–6.1	–4.5	0.8	5.6	2.9	1.5	6.1	5.6	5.1	2.4	1.7

* Contributions to changes in real GDP (as a per cent of real GDP in the previous period).
a) Including public corporations.
b) Actual amount
c) Mining and manufacturing.

JAPAN
Employment, income and inflation

Percentage changes from previous period, seasonally adjusted at annual rates

	1992	1993	1994	1995	1996	1994 I	1994 II	1995 I	1995 II	1996 I	1996 II
Employment	1.1	0.2	0.1	0.1	0.3	0.2	–0.6	0.4	0.3	0.4	0.4
Unemployment rate[a]	2.2	2.5	2.9	3.1	3.1	2.9	2.9	3.1	3.1	3.1	3.1
Compensation of employees	3.7	2.3	1.8	3.0	3.2	1.8	2.7	3.0	3.4	3.1	3.2
Unit labour cost	2.5	2.5	1.3	1.7	0.9	0.8	1.7	2.2	0.7	0.9	0.9
Household disposable income	3.8	1.9	2.7	2.8	3.1	4.0	3.6	2.2	3.0	3.1	3.2
GDP deflator	1.5	0.8	0.1	–0.3	0.2	0.4	–1.6	0.3	–0.1	0.3	0.4
Private consumption deflator	2.1	1.3	0.3	–0.6	0	0.8	–1.2	–0.2	–0.7	0.2	0.3

a) As a percentage of labour force.

The slow recovery in output appears to have continued in the first quarter of 1995, with GDP expected to reverse its fourth quarter fall despite the disruption caused by the earthquake in Kobe in January. Official estimates put the damage to structures from this natural disaster at almost ¥ 10 trillion, about 0.8 per cent of the national capital stock. The Kobe area produced 5 per cent of national GDP with output being concentrated in heavy industries, such as steel and petrochemicals. Kobe was also an important port handling 30 per cent of Japan's containerised exports. In the event, the impact on production appears to have been short-lived, with spare capacity elsewhere in the country sufficient to make good losses in the Kobe area. The drop in industrial output and foreign trade was limited to January. In the first three months of the year taken together, industrial production grew at an annual rate of almost 6 per cent. However, much of this increased output was due to stock accumulation, with the growth of shipments weaker than that of production. Retail sales are still weak, suggesting that the increase in producers' stocks may have been involuntary. Moreover, consumer confidence has been reduced by the appreciation of the yen, the renewed increase in unemployment and a fall in vacancies in March. Machinery orders stopped accelerating and stabilised after two quarters of rapid growth, although remaining 4 per cent up on the same period in 1994. The rate of housing starts is now almost 3 per cent below that of a year ago following a recent drop, having weakened even in the previously buoyant area of owner-occupied houses.

Policies and other forces acting

After the significant stimulus provided in 1994 by across-the-board income tax refunds, fiscal policy has become more neutral in 1995. Tax cuts this year are based on a permanent change in the income tax schedule together with a reduced uniform percentage reduction in tax payments, a package designed with the view to benefiting middle rather than high-income groups. On the expenditure side, the 1995 Budget projects a reduction of 3 per cent in total central government expenditure compared with the initial budget for 1994. However, this fall exaggerates the tightness of policy since, excluding debt service payments and the early repayment of certain loans, the government's general spending is expected to increase by 3 per cent in FY 1995 with public works expenditure rising by 5 per cent (Table). The government introduced a supplementary budget in May 1995, increasing expenditure by ¥ 2.7 billion, mainly to start rebuilding in Kobe. As a result, overall spending of the central government is expected to rise by 7 per cent. Allowing for a likely shortfall in revenue, the budget deficit should be about the same as in 1994, at ¥ 16 trillion (3.4 per cent of GDP) and somewhat higher on a national accounts basis. As the large local government borrowing requirement will more than offset the social security surplus, the general government deficit may rise to 4¼ per cent of GDP by 1996, with the estimated structural component stable at about 2¾ per cent. Gross government debt is projected to increase to over 95 per cent of GDP in 1996, reflecting the large deficits of both central and local governments, while net debt may rise to 17 per cent of GDP.

In view of the renewed strong appreciation of the yen, and its adverse implications for economic activity, monetary policy eased further at the end of March 1995. The official discount rate was lowered by 75 basis points to 1 per cent while short-term market interest rates fell by 100 basis points to 1¼ per cent. At this level, real short-term interest rates are now as low as at the bottom of the previous interest rate cycle in 1988. Yields in the bond market also fell considerably as expectations of future growth and inflation were lowered. Reflecting these moves, banks' short-term prime rate has been reduced to 2.75 per cent; the prime rate for long-term loans fell

Japan

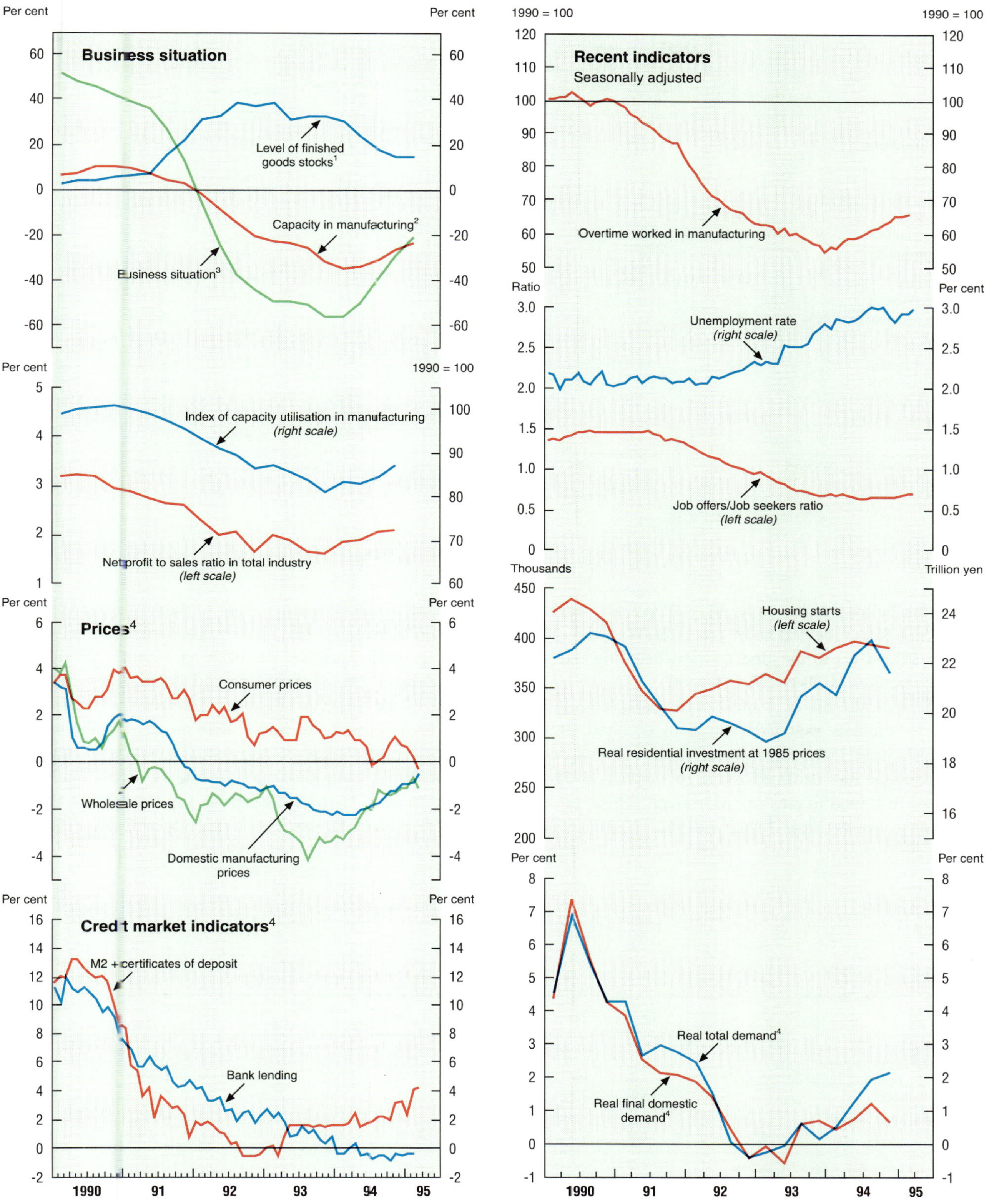

1. Per cent of replies "too high" minus per cent of replies "too low".
2. Per cent of firms with insufficient capacity minus per cent of firms with excessive capacity.
3. Per cent of replies "good" minus per cent of replies "bad".
4. Year-on-year percentage change.

Sources: Bank of Japan, *Short-Term Economic Survey of Principal Enterprises in Japan;* EPA, *Japanese Economic Indicators.*

JAPAN
The central government budget for Fiscal years 1994 and 1995
Trillion yen

	Fiscal year 1994			Fiscal year 1995			Increase FY 1994 compared with FY 1995	
	Initial Budget	Supplementary Budget	Total Budget	Initial Budget	Supplementary Budget	Total Budget	Initial Budget	Total Budget
General spending	40.9	1.0	41.9	42.1	2.7	44.8	3.1	7.1
of which:								
Public works	7.8	1.6	9.4	8.1	1.4	9.5	4.6	1.7
Local authority fundings	12.8	–0.7	12.1	13.2	–	13.2	3.6	9.6
Debt service	14.4	–	14.4	13.2	–	13.2	–7.9	–7.9
Other expenditure	5.1	–	5.1	2.4	–	2.4	–52.8	–51.0
Total expenditure	73.1	0.3	73.5	71.0	2.7	73.7	–2.9	0.4
Tax revenue	53.7	–2.8	50.8	53.7	–	53.7	0.1	5.6
Non-Tax revenue	3.3	0.3	3.6	3.4	–	3.4	1.2	–7.2
Transfers from other funds	2.4	–	2.4	1.3	–	1.3	–47.5	–47.5
Total revenue	59.4	–2.5	56.9	58.4	–	58.4	–1.8	2.5
Budgetted deficit	13.6	2.8	16.4	12.6	2.7	15.3	–7.7	–7.0
Revenue shortfall[1]	–	–	–	–	–	1.6	–	–
Projected deficit[1]	13.6	2.8	16.4	12.6	2.8	16.9	–7.7	–7.0
Construction bonds	10.5	1.8	12.3	9.7	2.3	12.0	–7.3	–2.1
Other bonds	3.1	1.0	4.1	2.9	0.6	4.9	–9.0	17.3

1. OECD Secretariat projection.
Source: Ministry of Finance.

somewhat below 3 per cent by May. The easier stance of policy was also reflected in an acceleration of the money growth (M2+CD) in the first quarter, bringing the year-on-year increase to over 3½ per cent.

Despite the fall in interest rates, bank lending continued to stagnate due to weak loan demand. Indeed, companies have markedly reduced their financial deficits as investment has declined to more normal levels and profits have started to pick up. Moreover, falling prices of investment goods have restrained the overall need to borrow, while the market share of public financial institutions is increasing. The lower money market interest rates may help to improve the banking sector's profitability and capacity to work off its bad debts. They may also improve the financial situation of borrowers thus improving the quality of the banks' loan assets. But the banking sector remains weak, as the capital position of the banks has suffered from the drop in the stock market. Although this has been partially offset by the strength of the yen which reduces the backing required for foreign currency

JAPAN
Financial indicators

	1992	1993	1994	1995	1996	1994 I	1994 II	1995 I	1995 II	1996 I	1996 II
Household saving ratio[a]	15.0	14.7	14.9	15.7	15.6	14.6	15.2	15.6	15.9	15.7	15.5
General government financial balance[b]	1.5	–1.4	–3.5	–4.1	–4.2	–3.2	–3.7	–3.9	–4.3	–4.3	–4.2
Current balance[b]	3.2	3.1	2.8	2.5	2.2	3.0	2.6	2.5	2.4	2.2	2.1
Short-term interest rate[c]	4.3	2.9	2.3	1.7	1.6	2.2	2.3	2.0	1.4	1.5	1.6
Long-term interest rate[d]	5.3	4.3	4.4	3.7	3.7	4.1	4.7	4.0	3.5	3.7	3.8

a) As a percentage of disposable income.
b) As a percentage of GDP.
c) 3-6 month CD.
d) Central government bonds.

loans, it may still take several several years for the banking sector to work off its bad debts. Overall, while the weakness of the banking sector does not appear to be a dominant factor holding back the recovery at this stage, its risk averseness is tending to weaken the response of bank credit supply to changes in monetary conditions compared with similar periods of monetary ease in the past.

The impact of one of the principal forces that have prolonged the recession – the adjustment of corporations to over-investment at the beginning of the 1990s – should wane in 1995. The volume of business investment now seems likely to stabilise, aided by the beneficial impact on profits of the growth of productivity in manufacturing. This turnaround of capital spending should generalise the increase in manufacturing output. As a result, there may be some rise in overtime work and profit-related bonuses and an end to the fall in employment. Such movements should be sufficient to sustain personal income growth, despite some slowdown in basic wage increases agreed in the spring wage round. In addition, falling prices mean that disposable income will rise faster in real than in nominal terms. However, this acceleration in domestic demand might largely be offset by the appreciation of the exchange rate which should markedly increase imports, raising foreign suppliers' penetration of the Japanese market, especially for finished consumer goods and intermediate industrial products. This process is likely to be supported by the increased Japanese direct investment in Asia, as a growing proportion of output produced by these facilities is now exported to Japan.

Prospects

On the technical assumption that the yen will stabilise at a rate of ¥ 84 to the dollar, the growth of output is projected to pick up progressively from the second half of this year, resulting in an annual growth rate of 1¼ per cent in 1995. With the momentum of the recovery increasing gradually, growth may accelerate to 2¼ per cent in 1996, so stabilising the degree of spare capacity in the economy. Potential growth has been slowing in recent years as the length of the standard working week has been shortened and will now be adversely affected by a fall in the working age population. The recovery will be led by domestic demand, which, in 1995, should benefit from the ending of the negative drag of falling investment. Although real household incomes may grow faster this year, nearly all of the increase may be saved, reflecting increased consumer uncertainty following the appreciation of the exchange rate and a growing dependence on volatile income components (such as overtime and bonus earnings). However, in 1996, as the economy adjusts to the higher exchange rate, the savings rate should stabilise, allowing an acceleration in consumption growth. Housing investment should also pick up slightly, aided by falls in interest rates. At the same time, the growth of imports should continue to be faster than that of exports. The current-account surplus is projected to decline somewhat in yen terms and in relation to GDP, falling to 2¼ per cent of GDP in 1996 but, given the improvement in the terms of trade, is unlikely to be much lower in 1996 than in 1994 in dollar terms. The impact of lower import prices, the significant degree of spare capacity in the economy and a continued high level

JAPAN
External indicators[a]
Seasonally adjusted at annual rates

	1993	1994	1995	1996	1994 I	1994 II	1995 I	1995 II	1996 I	1996 II
					$ billion					
Merchandise exports	351.3	384.0	421	447	372.5	395.5	411	430	441	453
Merchandise imports	209.8	238.2	279	314	225.2	251.2	269	289	305	322
Trade balance	141.5	145.8	142	134	147.4	144.3	142	141	136	131
Invisibles, net	–10.1	–16.5	–7	–7	–12.5	–20.5	–11	–3	–7	–7
Current balance	131.4	129.3	135	127	134.9	123.7	132	137	129	124
					Percentage change					
Merchandise export volumes[b]	–1.9	1.6	2.7	4.9	4.1	4.9	1.5	3.1	5.5	5.3
Merchandise import volumes[b]	3.3	13.7	13.2	10.3	16.8	16.0	12.3	12.2	9.8	9.6
Export performance[c]	–8.9	–10.0	–7.0	–3.1	–8.1	–8.7	–7.1	–5.1	–2.4	–2.6
Terms of trade	8.3	7.5	2.9	–0.5	8.1	–0.1	4.5	2.8	–1.7	–1.3

a) For further detail, see tables in the External Trade and Payments section of the Annex.
b) Customs basis.
c) Ratio between the total of export volumes and export market of total goods.

of unemployment should result in a fall in most price deflators in 1995, followed by a stabilisation during 1996 as import prices pick up.

The OECD Secretariat's projections are based on an effective exchange rate of the yen which is almost 16 per cent above the level of 1994. There is some risk that the scale of such an appreciation of the currency, if sustained, might force companies into a more severe adjustment of employment, stocks and output than is envisaged in the above projections. This would put more downward pressure on wages and, in turn, lessen the prospects for an acceleration of private consumption next year. As a result, the pace of the upturn would then be markedly slower. Were this appreciation to go into reverse, however, consumer confidence would increase, leading to an unwinding of the previous increase in savings. This, together with an increase in exports, would lead to an acceleration in the pace of recovery.

GERMANY

Western Germany has so far experienced a typical recovery, exports acting as the initial driving force, followed by increasing signs of a spillover into business fixed investment. Personal consumption is currently held back by the restraint on household incomes arising from fiscal consolidation, but should pick up in 1996 as the emphasis turns to tax decreases. Overall, with growth in eastern Germany continuing at a rapid pace, German growth is likely to remain buoyant, though the composition will change under the impact of exchange rate appreciation. Despite a relatively small output gap, and recent generous wage settlements, inflation pressures are likely to remain contained in the short run, due in part to the dampening effect of exchange-rate appreciation. However, meeting the medium-term goal of price stability will imply that interest rates may begin to rise later in the year. Fiscal consolidation will imply a tight rein on government spending, which should keep the general government deficit/GDP ratio at about 2¼ per cent while financing tax cuts scheduled for 1996

Recent developments

In western Germany, exports continued to be strong in the fourth quarter of 1994 and into early 1995, reflecting both export market buoyancy and competitiveness gains arising from a sharp decline in manufacturing unit labour costs during 1994. The latter reflected a surge in labour productivity in response to widespread rationalisation and restructuring in the manufacturing sector over the past two years, recouping much of the ground lost in the 1990-92 period and, up to the end of 1994, more than offsetting the adverse impact of exchange rate appreciation. Increased capacity utilisation deriving from buoyant exports has, in turn, begun to spill over into higher demand for business fixed investment, which grew strongly in the fourth quarter; order statistics suggest that this trend has continued into 1995, though export expectations weakened during the first quarter in response to the strengthening exchange rate.

Fiscal consolidation has weighed heavily on household real disposable income, with private consumption falling in the fourth quarter of 1994 and retail sales figures remaining soft in the early months of 1995.

GERMANY
Demand and output

Percentage changes from previous period, seasonally adjusted at annual rates, volume (1991 prices)

	1991 current prices billion DM	1992	1993	1994	1995	1996	1994 I	1994 II	1995 I	1995 II	1996 I	1996 II
Private consumption	1 628.4	3.0	0.5	1.3	1.0	3.0	1.9	–0.5	0.8	2.8	3.0	3.2
Government consumption	554.2	4.5	–1.2	1.2	1.8	1.3	1.8	1.6	2.2	1.2	1.2	1.4
Gross fixed investment	655.3	4.2	–4.5	4.3	5.5	5.9	5.9	5.9	7.2	5.9	5.9	5.9
Public	74.3	9.5	–2.9	0.9	1.2	2.5	3.8	–1.7	2.2	2.0	2.6	2.7
Private residential	168.1	9.6	5.6	13.0	5.3	2.5	19.8	6.3	6.0	2.8	2.6	1.9
Private non-residential	412.9	1.0	–9.2	0.6	8.4	8.5	–0.7	7.2	9.0	8.4	8.4	8.8
Final domestic demand	2 837.9	3.6	–1.0	2.0	2.4	3.4	2.8	1.3	2.5	3.2	3.3	3.5
* stockbuilding	19.4 [a]	–0.6	–0.2	0.7	0.1	0	0.5	0.6	0	0	0	0
Total domestic demand	2 857.3	3.0	–1.2	2.6	2.5	3.3	3.3	1.9	2.5	3.2	3.3	3.5
Exports of goods and services	714.2	0.2	–6.2	7.2	7.6	5.5	13.1	3.9	10.0	6.7	5.3	4.9
Imports of goods and services	717.8	3.3	–6.1	6.1	6.0	7.9	10.4	3.4	6.5	7.5	8.0	8.2
* net exports	–3.7 [a]	–0.8	0	0.2	0.4	–0.6	0.5	0.1	0.8	–0.2	–0.7	–0.9
GDP at market prices	2 853.6	2.2	–1.1	2.9	2.9	2.7	3.8	2.0	3.3	3.0	2.6	2.6
Memorandum items												
Investment in machinery and equipment	305.7	–2.4	–13.8	–1.1	6.9	7.7	0.4	4.8	7.6	7.7	7.6	7.9
Construction investment	349.6	9.9	2.8	7.9	6.3	4.8	9.4	6.5	7.0	4.8	4.8	4.7

* Contributions to changes in real GDP (as a per cent of real GDP in the previous period).
a) Actual amount.

GERMANY
Employment, income and inflation

Percentage changes from previous period, seasonally adjusted at annual rates

	1992	1993	1994	1995	1996	1994 I	1994 II	1995 I	1995 II	1996 I	1996 II
Employment	−1.8	−1.8	−0.9	0	0.5	−1.0	0	−0.2	0.5	0.5	0.5
Unemployment rate [a]	7.7	8.9	9.6	9.2	8.7	9.7	9.5	9.3	9.0	8.8	8.7
Compensation of employees	7.8	2.3	2.2	3.6	5.0	1.8	2.0	3.8	4.7	5.3	4.5
Unit labour cost	5.5	3.5	−0.7	0.6	2.2	−1.9	0	0.5	1.6	2.7	1.9
Household disposable income	8.0	3.7	2.5	3.3	5.2	2.4	1.2	3.6	4.7	5.4	5.2
GDP deflator	5.5	3.9	2.2	2.1	2.3	2.3	1.7	2.3	2.3	2.3	2.4
Private consumption deflator	4.6	3.9	2.7	2.3	2.1	2.4	2.9	2.1	1.9	2.2	2.3

a) As a percentage of labour force.

Though tourism expenditures have been quite strong, this would seem to be a reaction to the strengthening Deutschemark rather than a reflection of widespread underlying consumer optimism.

Strong growth has continued in the eastern Länder, which registered a GDP expansion of around 9 per cent in 1994. The upturn is being driven by fixed investment spending, with annual growth rates of around 16 to 17 per cent over the last 1½ years. Housing investment is the most dynamic element, though business investment has also been strong. This has pushed per capita investment spending in eastern Germany to a level which is now one-third higher than in western Germany. Over the course of 1994, exports, mainly to western Germany, accelerated sharply, growing at rates in excess of 25 per cent, albeit from a very low base. Another encouraging sign is the acceleration of manufacturing output, to a growth rate of close to 20 per cent. Nonetheless, the competitiveness of eastern production remains low on average, with overt and hidden unemployment high; moreover, private demand continues to be overwhelmingly dependent on transfers and subsidies from western Germany. Thus, growth in the new Länder cannot yet be considered to be ''self-sustaining''.

The labour market situation stabilised unusually early in the recovery. In western Germany, unemployment peaked in the second quarter of 1994, at 2.58 million persons, falling gradually thereafter as the labour force declined more than employment. In eastern Germany, employment has expanded strongly, the unemployment rate in January 1995 being 2 percentage points lower than a year earlier, leaving 1.1 million persons unemployed. At 9.2 per cent, the unemployment rate for total Germany is currently about 1 percentage point above the estimated structural rate. The recent wage agreements appear to reflect this strengthening in the labour-market situation, particularly in the case of the influential metal workers, whose annual wage increases of around 3½ per cent in both 1995 and 1996 will come on top of a shortening of working hours as of October 1995 – in total boosting hourly wage costs by 4½ per cent and 5½ per cent in 1996. Meanwhile, the 12-month rate of consumer price inflation has come down to 2¼ per cent in the first four months of 1995, compared with 2.6 per cent for the whole of 1994.

Despite the strength of exports, the current account deficit remained at 1 per cent of GDP in 1994, essentially unchanged from the previous year. A sharp improvement

GERMANY
Financial indicators

	1992	1993	1994	1995	1996	1994 I	1994 II	1995 I	1995 II	1996 I	1996 II
Household saving ratio [a]	12.9	12.3	11.0	11.0	11.0	11.2	10.7	11.0	11.0	11.0	10.9
General government financial balance [b]	−2.9	−3.3	−2.5	−2.3	−2.2	−2.2	−2.8	−2.2	−2.3	−2.2	−2.2
Current balance [b]	−1.1	−0.8	−1.1	−0.7	−1.2	−0.6	−1.7	−0.9	−0.5	−1.0	−1.4
Short-term interest rate [c]	9.5	7.3	5.4	4.8	5.2	5.6	5.2	4.9	4.7	5.0	5.4
Long-term interest rate [d]	7.9	6.5	6.9	7.1	7.0	6.5	7.4	7.2	7.0	7.0	7.0

a) As a percentage of disposable income.
b) As a percentage of GDP.
c) 3-month interbank rate.
d) Public sector bonds, 7-15 years.

Germany

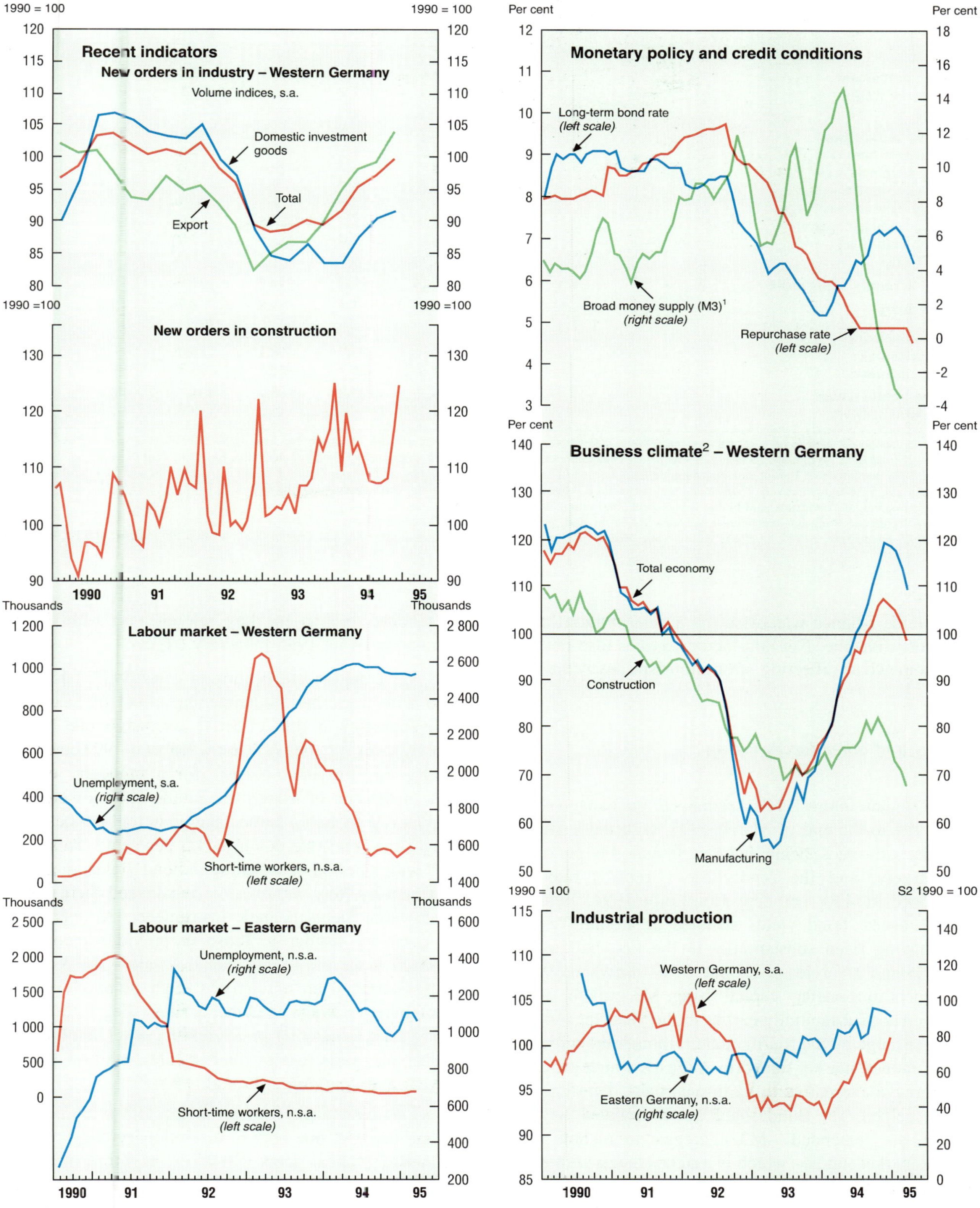

1. Change over previous six months at annual rate. Western Germany only up to December 1990. All Germany from January 1991 onwards.

2. Weighted average of present and future (six months ahead) business situation. A level of 100 corresponds to "normality".

Sources: Deutsche Bundesbank; IFO; OECD, *Main Economic Indicators.*

GERMANY
Public sector financial balances
DM billion

	1990	1991	1992	1993	1994	1995[a]	1996
General government	**–49.7**	**–93.8**	**–90.4**	**–105.1**	**–82.4**	**–80.2**	**–81.7**
Per cent of GDP	–2.1	–3.3	–2.9	–3.3	–2.5	–2.3	–2.2
of which:							
Territorial authorities	**–94.4**	**–122.7**	**–116.9**	**–137.6**	**–115.0**	**–94.8**	**–104.0**
Federal government	–48.1	–53.2	–39.3	–66.9	–50.6	–47.0	–65.0
State government west[b]	–19.4	–16.5	–16.1	–22.4	–23.0	–19.0	–22.0
Local government west	–4.2	–6.0	–10.1	–9.0	–7.5	–6.5	–5.5
State government east[b]	..	–12.4	–15.0	–19.6	–20.0	–9.5	–8.5
Local government east	..	1.9	–7.7	–4.5	–4.0	–3.5	–1.5
German unity fund	–20.0	–30.6	–22.4	–13.5	–3.0	2.0	2.5
Other funds[c]	–2.7	–5.9	–6.3	–1.7	–7.0	–11.3	–4.0
National accounts adjustments[d]	**24.3**	**5.5**	**27.9**	**22.4**	**24.0**	**13.0**	**17.0**
Social security	**20.0**	**23.4**	**–1.4**	**9.8**	**8.7**	**1.6**	**5.3**
Memorandum items							
Treuhandanstalt	–4.3	–19.9	–29.7	–38.1	–38.0	0	0
Public enterprises[e]	–9.9	–15.6	–25.7	–20.5	–11.3	0	0
Extended public sector	**–69.3**	**–128.5**	**–145.8**	**–163.7**	**–131.7**	**–80.2**	**–81.7**
As a share of GDP	–2.9	–4.5	–4.7	–5.2	–4.0	–2.3	–2.2

a) 1995 figures do not include (as a capital transfer item) the take-over by the federal government of debts of the Treuhand (DM 230 billion) and of the East German Housing fund (DM 30 billion). Inclusion of this item would imply at general government deficit in 1995 of the order of 9 to 10 per cent of GDP.
b) After 1990: west without Berlin; east including Berlin.
c) Credit fund, Economic Recovery Programme fund, financial equalisation fund, railway fund, and inherited debt fund.
d) Lending operations, dividends paid by the Bundesbank, and timing adjustments.
e) Post/Telecom and Railway Companies in the west and in the east; projections for Post/Telecom only.
Source: BMF Finanzbericht 1995; Deutsche Bundesbank, *Monthly Report*; Ministry of Finance submissions and Federal Consolidation Programme; OECD Secretariat projections.

in the trade balance was offset by a deterioration in net investment income. Net non-factor services also deteriorated somewhat, reflecting strong tourism payments.

Policies and other forces acting

Official interest rates remained unchanged from May 1994 to the end of March 1995, with the Lombard and discount rates being held at 6 and 4½ per cent, respectively, and the repurchase (''repo'') rate left unchanged at 4.85 per cent from July 1994. In these circumstances, bond yields steadied at around 7½ per cent, having risen substantially in the first half of the year, though to a lesser extent than elsewhere. With investment in monetary capital rising, M3 growth, which had overshot substantially earlier in the year, moved into its target range by the fourth quarter, though the introduction of money market funds (in August), which provided an attractive alternative to traditional bank deposits, also clearly helped. The Bundesbank has formulated the concept of an ''extended'' M3 aggregate to include such money market funds – which it watches along with other back-up indicators of inflation pressure under an overall pragmatic and flexible approach to monetary policy – but has retained M3 as the key reference variable in the formulation of its 1995 monetary targets.

M3 continued to decline in early 1995, and combined with the inflation-dampening effect of Deutschemark appreciation (the effective exchange rate having risen by over 5½ per cent between end-1994 and end-March), this provided a basis for a monetary easing. Thus, at the end of March the Bundesbank lowered the discount rate by half a percentage point to 4 per cent, and brought the repo rate down to 4.5 per cent.[1] This coincided with a period of softening in bond yields, to around 7 per cent by May, as investors rebalanced their portfolios towards Deutschemark instruments. At this level, real rates are similar to those in previous recoveries. However, since the output gap is small – the recovery having started from a relatively high output level and recent generous wage settlements suggesting little labour market slack – meeting price-stability goals may require the firming of short-term interest rates, starting later in the year and continuing through 1996.

The general government deficit fell to 2½ per cent of GDP in 1994, due both to discretionary fiscal tightening and to cyclical gains. However, government debt is still rising rapidly and this development has required a further tightening of the official stance in 1995. The increasing debt burden reflects: the take-over by the federal government of the substantial debt of the railway system in conjunction with its corporatisation in 1994 (DM 70 billion); the transfer of the debts of the Treuhandanstalt to the federal government (DM 230 billion) as of the beginning of 1995; and the transfer of a large part of the eastern German housing fund debt (DM 30 billion) in mid-year.[2] Taken together, these increases in debt entail a large increase in government interest expenditures – an estimated DM 26 billion in 1995 alone. To finance this new budgetary burden, the 7½ per cent solidarity income tax surcharge was reintroduced as of 1 January 1995 (with an expected revenue of DM 28½ billion). Although contributions to finance the new long-term care insurance (*Pflegeversicherung*) also came into effect in 1995, their effect on employers has been offset by reductions in old-age pension and health insurance contributions, and by the abolition of one public holiday.

Higher taxes, cyclical revenue gains, and underlying expenditure restraint should allow a further reduction in the government deficit to GDP ratio in 1995, to about 2¼ per cent. Thereafter, over the 1996-98 period, the intention is to reduce the government spending ratio by an amount equal to 4 per cent of GDP, in order to relieve the burden of taxation, while holding the deficit broadly stable at around 2 per cent. In 1996, the tax burden on households will fall back as income tax reductions for low-income earners (DM 15 billion), intended to ensure a "subsistence minimum" income, and termination of former indirect tax levies used for financing of coal subsidies (DM 7½ billion), are enacted – both measures resulting from recent constitutional court decisions. Moreover, there are plans for additional family support mainly via tax relief (DM 7 billion). Even though a further rise in contributions to long-term care insurance is programmed for mid-year, such tax reductions should enable a recovery of real disposable income and hence consumption in 1996. A scheduled 1996 reform of the business tax code is likely to result in only a small revenue loss (less than DM 2 billion), as it is largely self-financing, lower local business taxes being largely offset by a reduction in the investment depreciation allowance.

Prospects

Order statistics suggest exports are likely to remain strong over the near term. Thereafter, the recent strong increase in the effective exchange rate (over 9 per cent in the 12 months to May 1995), combined with rising labour costs, may start to dampen export volume growth. However, the projections for other European countries over the next two years suggest a relatively strong growth of business fixed investment, with consequent favourable product composition effects on German exports, which are heavily specialised in investment goods; this will, in turn, cushion the losses in market share likely to stem from weakened price competitiveness.

With indicators of capacity utilisation already pointing to incipient capacity strains in western Germany, and booming profitability in manufacturing, the upturn in business fixed investment is likely to continue, though weakening in reaction to the export slowdown by next year. Housing investment, by contrast, is

GERMANY
External indicators[a]
Seasonally adjusted at annual rates

	1993	1994	1995	1996	1994 I	1994 II	1995 I	1995 II	1996 I	1996 II
					$ billion					
Merchandise exports	382.6	425.3	524	564	400.4	450.1	508	541	556	573
Merchandise imports	342.9	374.5	455	507	351.6	397.4	440	470	494	521
Trade balance	39.7	50.8	70	57	48.9	52.7	68	71	62	52
Invisibles, net	–54.4	–74.5	–87	–88	–59.9	–89.0	–90	–84	–87	–89
Current balance	–14.7	–23.7	–18	–31	–11.0	–36.3	–22	–13	–25	–37
					Percentage change					
Merchandise export volumes[b]	–1.7	10.1	9.2	5.3	12.9	10.0	10.2	6.6	5.0	4.6
Merchandise import volumes[b]	–6.3	5.9	7.1	8.5	6.5	6.9	6.8	7.9	8.5	9.0
Export performance[c]	–6.2	3.8	0.2	–2.0	9.1	–1.4	1.8	–1.3	–2.1	–2.6
Terms of trade	0.5	–2.5	–0.4	–0.6	–2.4	–3.7	0.7	0.6	–1.2	–0.6

a) For further detail, see tables in the External Trade and Payments section of the Annex.
b) Customs basis.
c) Ratio between the total of export volumes and export market of total goods.

GERMANY
Projections for western and eastern Germany

Percentage change from previous year, volumes in 1991 prices

	Western Germany			Eastern Germany		
	1994	1995	1996	1994	1995	1996
Private consumption	0.8	0.6	2.8	4.5	3.6	4.4
Public consumption	1.1	1.8	1.3	1.8	1.4	1.0
Gross fixed investment	1.2	3.7	3.0	16.5	16.0	14.6
Final domestic demand	1.0	1.5	2.6	7.7	7.4	7.5
* change in stocks	0.7	0.2	0.0	0.2	–0.4	0.0
Total domestic demand	1.7	1.7	2.5	7.7	7.1	7.4
Exports of goods and services	7.7	7.9	5.0	21.4	30.3	21.9
Imports of goods and services	7.1	7.2	7.3	9.2	10.8	9.8
* change in foreign balance	0.7	0.8	–0.3	–5.0	–3.8	–4.0
GDP at market prices	2.3	2.3	2.0	9.2	9.0	9.2
Memorandum items						
GDP deflator	2.0	1.9	2.0	3.0	2.6	3.2
Private consumption deflator	2.6	2.2	2.0	3.0	2.6	2.5
Employment	–1.3	–0.4	0.3	1.1	2.0	1.6
Unemployment (per cent of labour force)	8.2	8.0	7.8	15.4	13.8	12.9

* As a percentage of GDP of the previous year.

unlikely to provide any stimulus to the expansion, being at an already high level and suffering from the phasing-out of tax incentives for owner-occupied housing at the end of 1994. Private consumption is likely to be subdued in the near term but should recover next year due to favourable wage and tax developments. Moreover, household real incomes should benefit as exchange-rate appreciation feeds into lower domestic prices.

Eastern Germany seems set to continue as the fastest-growing region in Europe. The growth of investment is likely to continue at double-digit rates, though residential investment growth may gradually slow from recent rates in excess of 30 per cent. With continued, albeit much-slowed, wage convergence, the growth of private consumption should remain robust, helped by increased confidence due to the improved labour-market situation.

While strong eastern German growth may lead to a rapid decline in unemployment there, the fall in western German unemployment may be slower. Recent adverse competitiveness shifts are likely to maintain the impetus toward rationalisation in manufacturing. Surveys indicate that the bulk of investment intentions are geared toward rationalisation rather than capacity-widening objectives in western Germany. As indicated by the wage round, disinflation may have largely run its course, although the exchange-rate appreciation may bring some further slight slowdown in the consumer price index, as may the weakening trend in raw material price increases. In eastern Germany, however, an easing of rent restrictions is likely to put upward pressure on the cost of living.

The main uncertainty attaching to the projections concerns the recent currency appreciation, which if reversed, would lead to a better than projected export performance, but could imply an upside risk to inflation. The principal deflationary risk, on the other hand, is that household savings might return to levels seen in the late 1980s and early 1990s (12 to 14 per cent), rather than remain constant at the 1994 level (11 per cent) as projected.

NOTES

1. From July 1994, the Bundesbank had been using a volume tendering system (*i.e.* meeting demands for liquidity at a pre-set interest rate) to ensure interest rate stability and avoid sending erroneous signals to the market. In reducing the repo rate at the end of March 1995, the Bundesbank also decided to switch back to variable rate repos (its preferred system of refinancing the money market). As funds will now be allocated at variable rates determined by market bidding, this change restores a certain amount of unpredictability to German short-term interest rates
2. In accounting terms, these debt take-overs should in principle be treated as "above the line" capital transfers, to reflect the fact that the debts of these formerly off-budget funds are in reality delayed expenditures of the federal government. The general government budget deficit for 1995 would then be in the order of 9-10 per cent of GDP. This would, however, misrepresent the thrust of fiscal policy in 1995, so that the OECD Secretariat's fiscal indicators do not treat the takeovers in this way.

FRANCE

With domestic demand reviving and export growth buoyant, the recovery became firmly established in the second half of 1994. Projected growth of around 3 per cent over the next two years will be driven by strong investment demand and a gradual strengthening in household consumption, based on employment gains and a fall in the saving ratio. The unemployment rate could decline by 1 percentage point by the end of 1996. Despite strong domestic demand growth, the current account will remain in sizeable surplus. With the improving labour market situation and a declining output gap, inflation is likely to settle around the current underlying rate of somewhat below 2 per cent. Projected economic growth above potential and government expenditure restraint should lead to a narrowing fiscal deficit.

Recent developments

The economic recovery strengthened significantly during 1994 – growth reaching 3.7 per cent (year-on-year) in the fourth quarter. In addition to strong external demand and a strong contribution from stockbuilding, private consumption and investment outlays also picked up. While increases in wage rates remained subdued, income growth was boosted by a brisk rise in the number of employees. On the other hand, transfer receipts slowed significantly, due to the reform of the health, pension and unemployment insurance schemes. Consumer sentiment improved gradually, reflecting better job and income prospects, and household spending was supported by a slight fall in the saving ratio. Housing investment staged a vigorous recovery in the second and third quarters of 1994. Higher mortgage interest rates since the autumn of 1994 have, however, dampened the revival of the housing market in recent months.

Business investment picked up in the second half of 1994, but was essentially flat last year on an annual average basis, reflecting another fall in industrial investment. In the manufacturing sector, greater flexibility in organising production led to a better utilisation of the existing capital stock and by early 1995 capacity utilisation was still below the long-term average. Investment in the other sectors was already more dynamic during 1994. Recent indicators point to a considerable strengthening of investment in early 1995. After severe compression in 1993, inventories remained flat during 1994, current rates

FRANCE
Demand and output

Percentage changes from previous period, seasonally adjusted at annual rates, volume (1980 prices)

	1991 current prices billion FF	1992	1993	1994	1995	1996	1994 I	1994 II	1995 I	1995 II	1996 I	1996 II
Private consumption	4 037.5	1.4	0.2	1.5	2.2	3.4	1.1	2.5	1.5	3.1	3.4	3.5
Government consumption	1 257.0	3.4	3.3	1.0	0.9	1.1	0.2	1.2	0.8	0.9	1.1	1.1
Gross fixed investment	1 436.9	–3.1	–5.8	1.1	5.8	5.8	1.3	5.5	5.7	6.4	5.7	5.5
General government	230.4	4.0	–0.3	3.3	2.0	1.9	5.0	3.7	1.5	1.5	2.0	2.0
Household	368.8	–4.2	–6.7	2.5	4.1	2.1	–0.5	8.1	3.0	2.5	2.0	1.9
Other	837.7	–4.7	–7.1	–0.2	7.9	8.7	0.8	5.0	8.4	9.8	8.5	8.2
Final domestic demand	6 731.4	0.8	–0.5	1.3	2.7	3.4	1.0	2.8	2.2	3.3	3.4	3.5
* stockbuilding	21.1[a]	–0.4	–1.8	1.5	0.5	0.2	3.9	0.6	0.5	0.5	0.2	0
Total domestic demand	6 752.5	0.4	–2.3	2.9	3.2	3.6	5.0	3.4	2.8	3.8	3.6	3.5
Exports of goods and services	1 538.1	4.9	–0.4	5.8	6.8	6.3	3.7	6.9	7.0	6.4	6.2	6.2
Imports of goods and services	1 514.5	1.1	–3.4	6.6	7.5	7.7	9.7	6.3	7.9	7.9	7.7	7.6
* net exports	23.6[a]	1.0	0.8	–0.2	–0.2	–0.5	–1.6	0.1	–0.3	–0.4	–0.5	–0.5
GDP at market prices	6 776.1	1.3	–1.5	2.7	3.0	3.2	3.3	3.6	2.5	3.4	3.1	3.1
Industrial production[b]	–	–1.0	–3.6	3.3	4.3	4.3	4.5	5.3	3.7	4.5	4.3	4.3

* Contributions to changes in real GDP (as a per cent of real GDP in the previous period).
a) Actual amount.
b) Quarterly index

FRANCE
Employment, income and inflation
Percentage changes from previous period, seasonally adjusted at annual rates

	1992	1993	1994	1995	1996	1994 I	1994 II	1995 I	1995 II	1996 I	1996 II
Employment	–0.7	–1.2	0.5	1.0	1.1	0.7	1.4	0.9	1.0	1.1	1.1
Unemployment rate [a]	10.3	11.7	12.4	12.0	11.5	12.4	12.4	12.2	11.9	11.6	11.4
Compensation of employees	3.8	1.5	2.5	4.5	4.7	2.7	3.4	4.8	4.8	4.6	4.9
Unit labour cost	2.4	3.0	–0.2	1.4	1.5	–0.7	–0.1	2.2	1.4	1.4	1.8
Household disposable income	4.4	2.6	2.9	3.9	4.6	2.6	5.0	3.3	4.1	4.6	4.9
GDP deflator	2.1	2.5	1.5	1.9	2.0	1.4	1.5	2.0	2.0	1.9	2.2
Private consumption deflator	2.4	2.2	1.8	1.6	1.7	1.9	1.5	1.7	1.6	1.7	1.9

a) As a percentage of labour force.

of inventory accumulation implying a rapidly falling stock/output ratio.

With little change in price competitiveness, manufacturing exports were primarily driven by buoyant market growth. Overall export growth was held back by the dampening effects of the European Union's agricultural reform on food exports and by losses in competitiveness against major tourism competitors. As imports recovered strongly in line with domestic demand, the foreign contribution to GDP growth turned negative in 1994. Owing to a terms of trade gain, however, the current account remained in surplus, at 3/4 per cent of GDP. Data on merchandise trade suggest a continuation of vigorous export and import growth in early 1995.

The unemployment rate peaked at 12.5 per cent in mid-1994 and fell slowly to 12.2 per cent by March 1995. The sluggishness of the decline reflects a very rapid rise in labour supply and a further fall in the number of self-employed rather than any weakness of employment. On the contrary, the number of private-sector employees has responded quickly and strongly to the economic upswing, employment growth reaching 1 1/2 per cent (year-on-year) in April 1995 overall and 3 per cent in the service sector. Many new jobs are part-time jobs, reflecting government incentives. Despite rising employment, productivity showed a strong cyclical rebound and profit margins rose further. Until April 1995, wage inflation remained moderate, and real wages continued to grow far below trend productivity. Inflation has continued its favourable development, consumer price inflation running at close to 1 3/4 per cent until April 1995: given the strength of the effective exchange rate, import price rises have remained modest, despite the sharp rise in international commodity prices, and unit labour cost increases have been minor so far. In the manufacturing sector, unit labour costs actually fell significantly over the last year.

Policies and other forces acting

After the monetary policy easing during the first half of 1994, the intervention rate and repo rate were left unchanged at 5.0 and 6.4 per cent, respectively, until early March of 1995. Despite lower short-term rates and strong domestic demand, the broad monetary aggregate rose by only 3.5 per cent in the year to February 1995, and M3 growth remains below its medium-term target rate. Also business sector credit demand was weak due to the strong profit situation. Contrary to short-term interest rate developments, long-term rates rose to 8.5 per cent in October 1994, the differential against German rates widening to close to 1 percentage point. Since then, long-term interest rates have eased back to 7 1/2 per cent and the differential has narrowed somewhat.

The weakening of the franc against the Deutschemark since autumn 1994 first led to a modest rise in short-term interest rate differentials. In March 1995, the franc fell in the wake of international and currency turbulence within the European Exchange Rate Mechanism. In order to stabilise the exchange rate, the intervention rate was raised to 8 per cent. The franc recovered and the intervention rate was cut by 1/4 percentage point in early April. Pressure on the franc renewed in the run-up to the presidential elections in early May. After the elections the franc rose against the Deutschemark, but it is currently still trading 2 per cent below its October 1994 level, and short-term interest rates declined somewhat. As other currencies depreciated against the franc the effective exchange rate remains 2 per cent above its 1994 average level. In the projections, it is assumed that currency tensions will ease now that the presidential elections are over and that short-term interest rates will fall significantly in the coming months. However, they could rise again during 1996 in line with German interest rate

France

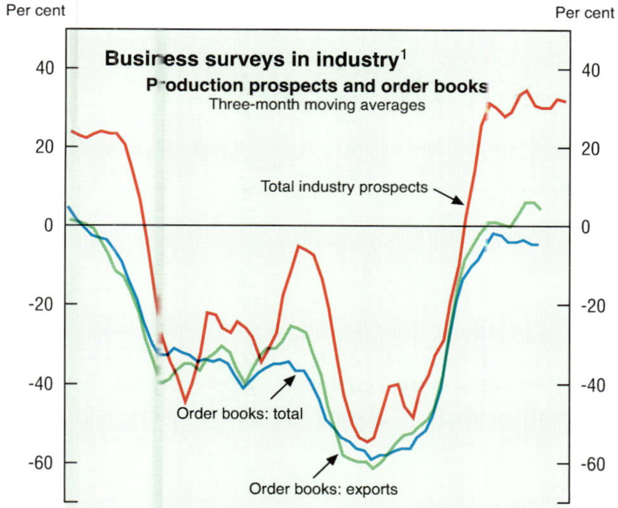

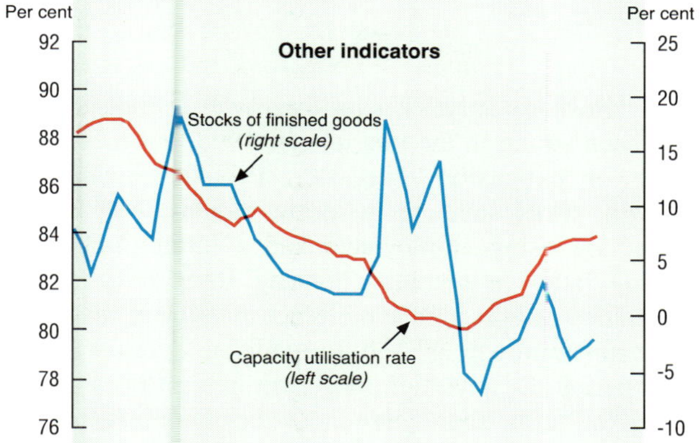

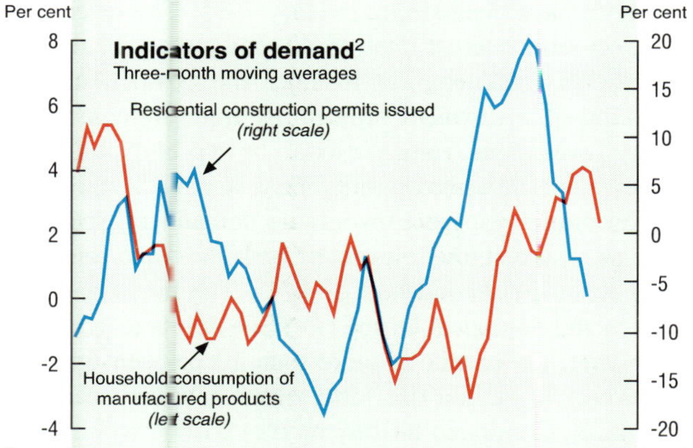

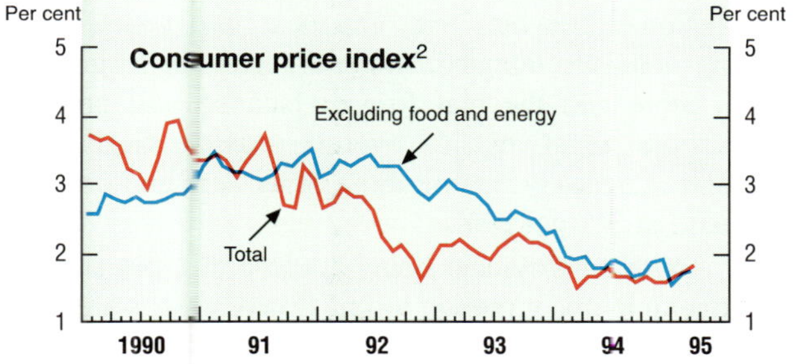

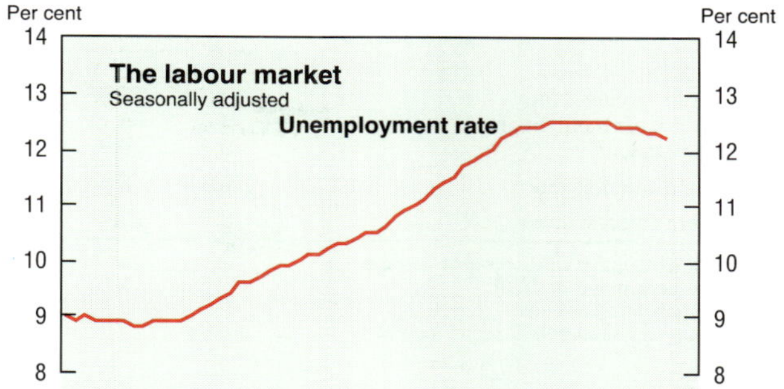

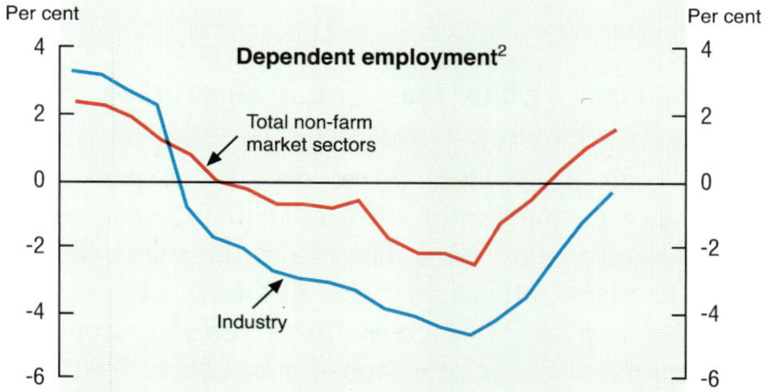

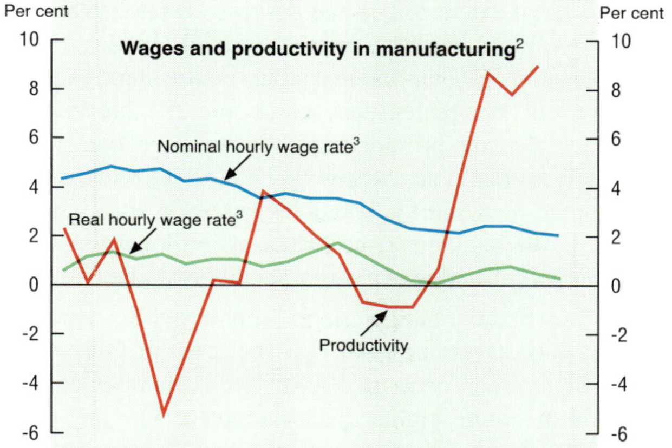

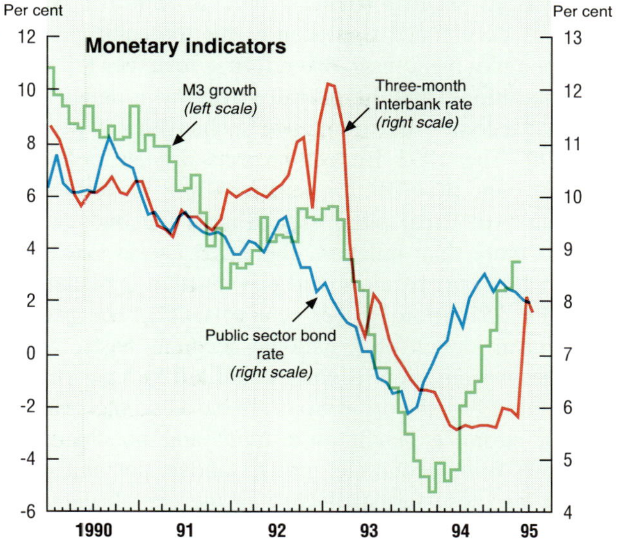

1. Balance between businessmen's optimistic (+) and pessimistic (–) answers.
2. Year-on-year percentage changes.
3. In total industry.

Sources: INSEE, *Tendances de la conjoncture;* OECD, *Financial Statistics.*

FRANCE
Financial indicators

	1992	1993	1994	1995	1996	1994 I	1994 II	1995 I	1995 II	1996 I	1996 II
Household saving ratio[a]	13.7	13.8	13.5	13.6	13.1	13.3	13.7	13.7	13.4	13.2	13.0
General government financial balance[b]	–4.0	–6.1	–6.0	–5.0	–4.1	–5.9	–6.1	–5.2	–4.7	–4.3	–3.9
Current balance[b]	0.3	0.7	0.7	0.9	0.8	0.8	0.6	0.9	0.9	0.8	0.8
Short-term interest rate[c]	10.3	8.6	5.8	6.1	5.4	6.0	5.7	6.9	5.4	5.2	5.5
Long-term interest rate[d]	9.0	7.0	7.5	7.6	7.3	6.9	8.2	7.8	7.4	7.3	7.2

a) As a percentage of disposable income.
b) As a percentage of GDP.
c) 3-month interbank rate.
d) Public and semi-public sector bonds.

developments, while long-term interest rates could decline over the projection period.

Banks have raised prime rates by 1/2 percentage point since the autumn of 1994, reflecting the earlier rise in long-term interest rates. The recent short-term interest rate hike raises refinancing costs further. It poses a new challenge to a sector which is already suffering from low profitability and large provisions for bad debts. The latter are to a large extent due to the depressed state of the real estate sector and the large number of bankruptcies during the recession. Higher interest rates could aggravate the problems of the real estate sector and the banks. The State has already provided support for five banks, the most spectacular case being the Crédit Lyonnais. The rescue plan for Crédit Lyonnais is based on state guarantees, with the bank covering losses over a long period, so that short-term budgetary costs are likely to be limited.

The State's budget deficit on a public accounts basis was on target in 1994 (at 4 per cent of GDP compared to 4 1/2 per cent in 1993), but both revenue and expenditure were higher than budgeted. On the other hand, social security finances did not improve. While spending decelerated significantly due to health, pension and unemployment insurance reforms, revenues fell short of expectations, and the overall government deficit on a national accounts basis remained unchanged at 6 per cent of GDP. The 1995 Budget projects a State deficit of 3 1/2 per cent of GDP. In line with the Government's medium-term fiscal plan, expenditures are budgeted to rise no more than inflation. Increased excise taxes will raise indirect tax receipts, and privatisation is planned to yield FF 55 billion (3/4 per cent of GDP). The general government deficit on a national accounts basis, which excludes privatisation receipts, could fall to 5 per cent of GDP. For 1996, the projections are based on the assumption of strong expenditure restraint and no change in taxation. With economic growth above potential, this should lead to a further decline in the overall deficit to close to 4 per cent in 1996. The projections are based on the 1995 budgetary statements. However, the new government is likely to amend the Budget soon.

Prospects

Business surveys point to growth in industry having been strong in the first quarter 1995, but to a slower pace of expansion thereafter. Private consumption growth, while subdued in recent months, will be bolstered by rising employment and a further fall in the saving ratio. In contrast, housing starts have already weakened due to higher mortgage rates, and residential investment growth is likely to moderate over the projection period. Despite high long-term interest rates and the sharp fall in the share price index, business investment is likely to have been strong in early 1995. The recent hike in short-term interest rates could, however, lead to some short-term weakness, for instance the postponement or shelving of investment projects by liquidity-constrained firms. Investment seems poised to be very dynamic thereafter, reflecting strong profitability, a gradual narrowing of the output gap and favourable demand prospects, as well as assumed lower levels of both short and long-term rates from the second half of 1995. The investment survey by the Statistical Office (INSEE) points to growth in industrial investment of more than 10 per cent in 1995. Stockbuilding could rise further as it is still running at a low level. Continued healthy market growth will help the expansion of exports over the next two years. Given strong domestic demand, imports are likely to grow by even more and the real foreign balance will probably contribute negatively to overall growth. GDP could expand at a steady rate of about 3 per cent and domestic demand at 3 1/2 per cent.

With employment rising at close to 1 per cent and the unemployment rate set to fall slowly, wages are likely to begin to accelerate. The acceleration should be grad-

FRANCE
External indicators[a]
Seasonally adjusted at annual rates

	1993	1994	1995	1996	1994 I	1994 II	1995 I	1995 II	1996 I	1996 II
					$ billion					
Merchandise exports	198.6	222.3	270	296	208.5	236.2	261	278	290	302
Merchandise imports	189.9	212.4	258	288	200.2	224.6	249	268	281	295
Trade balance	8.7	9.9	11	8	8.2	11.5	12	11	9	7
Invisibles, net	0.6	–0.2	3	6	2.4	–2.8	2	4	5	7
Current balance	9.2	9.7	15	13	10.6	8.7	14	15	13	14
					Percentage change					
Merchandise export volumes[b]	–1.0	6.6	8.1	6.5	4.1	9.8	7.9	6.9	6.5	6.3
Merchandise import volumes[b]	–3.8	7.0	8.6	8.4	9.6	8.4	8.7	8.6	8.4	8.2
Export performance[c]	–0.2	–2.2	–0.3	–0.9	–4.9	–0.2	–0.1	–0.8	–0.9	–1.1
Terms of trade	1.5	0.1	0.1	0.1	0.7	0.0	0.1	0.1	0.0	0.5

a) For further detail, see tables in the External Trade and Payments section of the Annex.
b) Customs basis.
c) Ratio between the total of export volumes and export market of total goods.

ual, however, given the high level of unemployment, and real wage rises should remain below trend productivity growth. The process of disinflation may be over, but inflationary pressures will probably remain low as cyclical slack is reduced only slowly and profit margins should initially absorb rises in raw materials' prices. A slight pick-up in inflation could occur towards the end of the projection period. Despite the broadly based recovery in domestic demand, the current account surplus should remain sizeable, owing to further terms-of-trade gains in 1995.

The risks attaching to the projections appear to be evenly balanced. As there has been considerable momentum behind the recovery, stockbuilding and investment could turn out to be stronger than projected. A considerably faster pace of fiscal consolidation by the new government (whose plans were not yet known at the time of writing) could influence financial market developments favourably, with positive demand effects due to lower interest rates. On the other hand, if the recent exchange market turbulence continued for a prolonged period, short-term interest rates could remain much higher than assumed, with the consequence of weaker demand growth. Finally, inflationary pressures might appear sooner than expected and improved cyclical conditions feed faster into wage and price pressures: the remaining amount of cyclical slack in goods markets, as well as the beneficial effects of labour market reforms on the level of structural unemployment within the projection period, may be overestimated.

ITALY

The recovery remained robust in the second half of 1994 and real GDP growth is projected to accelerate further in 1995 and 1996, on the basis of sustained export growth and vigorous investment. Inflation has accelerated sharply due to the effects of higher indirect taxes and additional lira depreciation. But it could resume its downward trend from the second half of 1995, against the background of an unemployment rate which is expected to remain above the estimated natural rate. Additional budgetary measures approved in March imply a significant cut in the budget deficit in 1995 and the stabilisation of the debt/ GDP ratio. Following the May pension agreement, premia on Italian interest rates have fallen. However, further structural measures will be necessary to attain the 1996 deficit target.

Recent developments

The economic upswing gained further momentum in the second half of 1994, with real GDP expanding at an annual rate of 3.7 per cent, as the export stimulus was reinforced by a strong inventory build-up. At the same time, both gross fixed investment and private consumption decelerated, mainly reflecting rising interest rates and a further drop in real wages. Judging by conjunctural indicators, particularly industrial production, output expansion may have slowed during the winter months, but from a very rapid pace.

The recovery in output has been slow to translate into an improvement in the labour market, with employment falling by 1.7 per cent in 1994 as a whole. Even though employment began to rise in the second half of 1994, the rate of unemployment continued to edge up, reaching 12.2 per cent in January 1995 from 9.6 per cent in October 1992,[1] with the increase being largest in the south. Moreover, the labour shake-out has been particularly strong in large firms (those employing 500 persons and more) in both the industrial and the service sectors, as firms responded to the recovery in production by increasing working hours and overtime, drastically reducing recourse to the Wage Supplementation Fund (CIG).[2]

Persistently high unemployment, combined with the effects of the labour agreement of July 1993, have

ITALY
Demand and output
Percentage changes from previous period, seasonally adjusted at annual rates, volume (1985 prices)

	1991 current prices trillion L	1992	1993	1994	1995	1996	1994 I	1994 II	1995 I	1995 II	1996 I	1996 II
Private consumption[a]	889.6	1.1	−2.5	1.6	1.7	2.2	2.3	1.7	1.7	1.6	2.4	2.6
Government consumption	253.2	1.0	0.7	0	0.4	0.3	−0.1	0.8	0.3	0.3	0.3	0.3
Gross fixed investment	281.9	−1.7	−13.1	−0.1	5.4	7.1	2.4	1.3	6.8	7.0	6.9	7.5
Machinery and equipment	134.0	−1.3	−19.3	5.3	9.7	7.9	10.6	7.7	10.8	9.6	7.2	7.5
Construction	147.9	−2.1	−6.3	−5.2	1.0	6.2	−5.0	−4.9	2.5	4.2	6.5	7.5
Residential	76.1	0.3	−0.8	0	3.3	6.2	0.5	1.2	3.5	5.1	6.5	6.9
Non-residential	71.8	−4.7	−12.5	−11.8	−2.3	6.1	−12.0	−13.0	1.0	2.9	6.5	8.5
Final domestic demand	1 424.7	0.5	−4.2	1.0	2.2	2.8	1.9	1.5	2.4	2.4	2.9	3.2
* stockbuilding	10.2[b]	0.3	−1.4	0.8	0.3	−0.2	0.6	3.3	−0.7	−0.7	0	0
Total domestic demand	1 434.9	0.8	−5.5	1.9	2.4	2.6	2.5	4.8	1.7	1.6	2.9	3.2
Exports of goods and services	257.0	5.0	9.4	10.9	11.0	8.2	13.1	9.9	11.7	10.8	7.7	6.7
Imports of goods and services	262.5	4.6	−7.8	9.8	9.4	7.4	12.1	14.3	8.0	7.5	7.4	7.5
* net exports	−5.5[b]	−0.1	4.6	0.3	0.5	0.3	0.3	−1.1	1.1	1.0	0.2	−0.1
GDP at market prices	1 429.5	0.7	−1.2	2.2	3.0	2.9	2.8	3.7	2.8	2.7	3.0	3.0
Industrial production	–	−0.2	−2.4	4.8	4.7	3.7	3.9	12.0	2.0	3.3	3.9	3.8

* Contributions to changes in real GDP (as a per cent of real GDP in the previous period).
a) Final consumption in the domestic market by households.
b) Actual amount.

ITALY
Employment, income and inflation
Percentage changes from previous period, seasonally adjusted at annual rates

	1992	1993	1994	1995	1996	1994 I	1994 II	1995 I	1995 II	1996 I	1996 II
Employment	–0.6	–4.2	–1.7	0.7	0.9	–3.4	0.8	0.6	0.7	1.0	1.1
Unemployment rate[a,b]	11.6	10.7	11.3	11.1	10.5	11.1	11.4	11.2	11.0	10.7	10.3
Compensation of employees	5.2	1.0	1.7	4.9	5.6	1.6	3.4	5.1	5.7	5.7	5.6
Unit labour cost	4.4	2.2	–0.4	1.8	2.6	–1.2	–0.2	2.3	2.9	2.5	2.5
Household disposable income	6.4	–0.5	5.4	5.5	6.1	8.5	5.6	5.3	5.8	6.2	6.4
GDP deflator	4.5	4.3	3.6	4.3	4.5	3.1	4.3	4.2	4.6	4.5	4.2
Private consumption deflator	5.4	4.8	4.7	5.4	4.7	4.6	4.6	6.1	4.9	4.7	4.4

a) From the fourth quarter of 1992, data are based on new definitions and therefore not comparable with earlier figures.
b) As a percentage of labour force.

kept nominal wage growth below consumer price inflation. At around 3 per cent, the growth of contractual wages in industry in 1994 again slowed relative to the previous year, although longer working hours implied an increase in the growth of average earnings in large industrial firms to 5.5 per cent. Despite a continuing decline in unit labour costs, producer price inflation has been picking up since last summer to a rate of 6.3 per cent in the twelve months to February 1995, 3.3 points above the low reached in April 1994. Consumer-price inflation stopped falling in late 1994, and picked up strongly in the first four months of 1995 so that by April, the 12-month increase in consumer prices reached 5.2 per cent, 1.6 points above the low of July 1993, largely reflecting higher indirect taxes and the effect of continued currency depreciation.

On the external side, currency depreciation and strong export market growth maintained the buoyancy of export volumes, so that – despite a rebound in import volumes and less favourable terms of trade – the trade surplus widened further in 1994. This combined with a lower deficit on invisibles to increase the current account surplus further to 1.5 per cent of GDP.

Policies and other forces acting

In response to rising inflationary pressures and exchange market turbulence, the Bank of Italy tightened monetary conditions in February 1995, raising the discount rate by ¾ point, to 8¼ per cent, and the rate on fixed term advances (Lombard rate) by 1¼ points, to 9¾ per cent. This was the second rise in policy controlled rates in a little over six months. Moreover, tight liquidity conditions in the money market consistently pushed the interbank overnight rate above the Lombard rate, which normally acts as the ceiling for interbank credit. Capital outflows prompted by political uncertainties and external developments drove the lira to new lows relative to the Deutschemark, reducing its value by 16 per cent from the year-end level by mid-March, before it regained some ground. Bond yields were also affected by the weakness of the lira, with the differential on 10-year government bonds *vis-à-vis* Germany widening to nearly 6 percentage points at the end of March, as against more than 4 percentage points at end-1994. However, the differential narrowed to under 5 percentage points in response to the agreement on pension reform of early-May.

The State budget for 1994 closed with a borrowing requirement of around L 155 trillion, equivalent to 9.5 per cent of GDP. While exceeding the original budget target by around L 12 trillion, this level was broadly in line with the revised target announced in July.[3] Faced with the prospect of a significant deficit overshoot in 1995, largely due to higher interest rates, the Dini government announced corrective budgetary measures worth L 20 trillion, or 1.1 per cent of GDP, in February 1995. The package combines tax increases worth L 15.6 trillion (L 8.7 trillion in indirect taxes, and the rest in the form of higher direct taxes and health contributions) and cuts in current non-interest spending worth L 5 trillion in 1995, with a stronger deficit reduction in 1996 and 1997, as the continuing impact of structural measures more than offsets the phasing-out of one-off measures. The government also announced an acceleration in the timetable of privatisations, envisaging the completion of privatisation of INA (insurance), IMI (banking) and ENEL (electricity) by the summer of 1995, and of STET (telecommunications) and ENI (energy) before the end of the year.

The new agreement between the government and the unions on pension reform involves a shift to a system of old-age pensions entirely financed by contributions; it also incorporates measures to impose penalties on early retirement, to harmonise treatment for all employed persons and to expand private pension funds. While the pension reform will have only a small immediate impact,

Italy

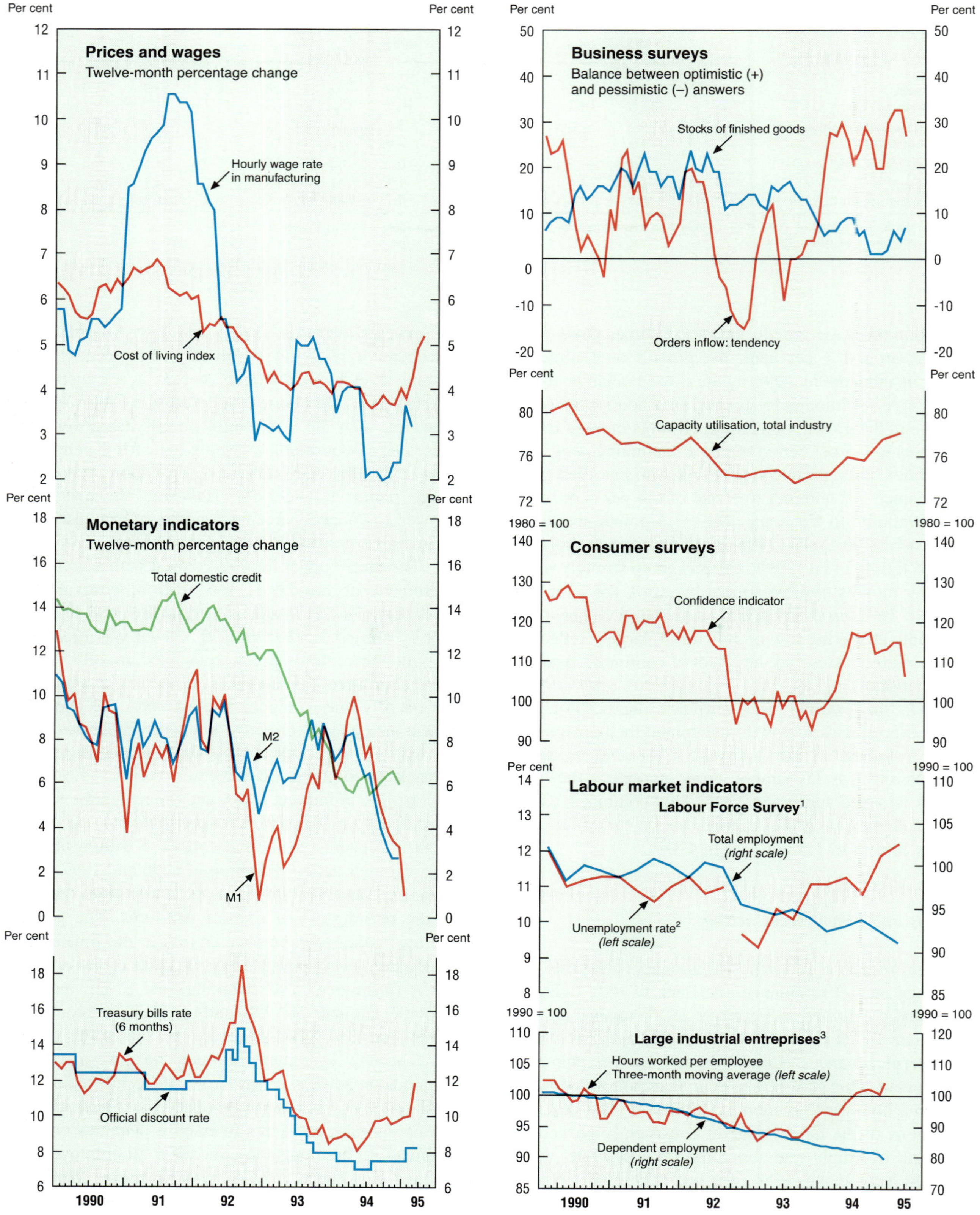

1. Not seasonally adjusted.
2. Break in series in 1991 and Q4 1992.
3. Seasonally adjusted.

Sources: Bank of Italy; OECD, *Main Economic Indicators*.

ITALY
Financial indicators

	1992	1993	1994	1995	1996	1994 I	1994 II	1995 I	1995 II	1996 I	1996 II
Household saving ratio[a]	17.7	15.7	15.0	13.8	13.6	15.4	14.6	13.9	13.6	13.6	13.7
General government financial balance[b]	–9.5	–9.6	–9.0	–7.8	–6.9	–9.1	–8.9	–8.0	–7.7	–7.1	–6.7
Current balance[b]	–2.3	1.2	1.5	1.3	1.6	1.6	1.5	1.3	1.4	1.5	1.8
Short-term interest rate[c]	14.4	10.7	8.5	9.6	9.3	8.5	8.5	9.8	9.4	9.3	9.2
Long-term interest rate[d]	13.7	11.3	10.6	12.1	11.4	9.5	11.7	12.3	11.9	11.5	11.3

a) As a percentage of disposable income.
b) As a percentage of GDP.
c) 3-month interbank rate.
d) Treasury bonds.

the savings are projected to build up over time, reaching a cumulative L 100 trillion by 2004.

Given the measures of fiscal restraint already adopted, general government net lending is expected to shrink to 7¾ per cent of GDP in 1995 and to 7 per cent in 1996, from 9 per cent in 1994. The improvement reflects both lowering of the cyclically-adjusted deficit and, to a lesser extent, the effect of the strengthening of economic recovery. These projections imply that, for 1995, the government fiscal target will be broadly met, while for 1996 they incorporate a moderate deficit overshoot given the past record of budgetary slippage. As the primary surplus climbs above 3 per cent of GDP in 1995, the public debt to GDP ratio may begin to fall. With the fiscal outlook improving and disinflation resuming, interest rates may ease from the second half of 1995; the long term differential *vis-à-vis* Germany is assumed to narrow to 4¼ percentage points by the end of 1996.

Prospects

Business surveys point to continued optimism, with firms reporting a further improvement in production prospects and orders in March. In this setting, gross fixed investment is projected to gather momentum in 1995, driven by increased profitability and higher capacity utilisation. While consumer confidence rebounded in early 1995 after weakening in the last quarter of 1994, consumer expenditure growth may not recover fully until 1996. The contribution of the net foreign balance to growth will diminish, becoming negative in the latter part of the projection period. Nevertheless, real GDP growth is projected to quicken to around 3 per cent in 1995 and 1996, from an estimated 2.2 per cent in 1994, reducing the output gap to an estimated 2 per cent in 1996.

With employment growth picking up to around 1 per cent in 1996, the unemployment rate is projected to

ITALY
External indicators[a]
Seasonally adjusted at annual rates

	1993	1994	1995	1996	1994 I	1994 II	1995 I	1995 II	1996 I	1996 II
	$ billion									
Merchandise exports	169.4	189.4	221	250	178.1	200.7	212	230	243	256
Merchandise imports	136.3	154.0	185	205	141.5	166.6	179	191	200	210
Trade balance	33.1	35.3	36	45	36.5	34.2	32	39	43	46
Invisibles, net	–21.7	–19.8	–21	–26	–21.1	–18.6	–19	–24	–27	–26
Current balance	11.3	15.5	14	19	15.4	15.6	13	15	17	20
	Percentage change									
Merchandise export volumes[b]	11.1	11.7	12.1	8.2	8.4	13.8	11.8	11.1	7.7	6.4
Merchandise import volumes[b]	–9.3	11.0	10.1	7.4	10.5	16.4	8.4	7.6	7.3	7.6
Export performance[c]	12.1	2.8	2.8	0.2	–1.4	2.6	3.1	2.6	–0.1	–1.4
Terms of trade	–1.5	–1.5	–5.0	1.5	–0.4	–6.5	–7.0	0.8	1.9	1.6

a) For further detail, see tables in the External Trade and Payments section of the Annex.
b) Customs basis.
c) Ratio between the total of export volumes and export market of total goods.

ease gradually, to 10.3 per cent by the end of 1996. The unemployment rate at which wage increases begin to accelerate being estimated at 9 per cent, labour market conditions should make for continued wage moderation. With the once-and-for-all effects of increased indirect taxes and additional currency depreciation tapering off, consumer price inflation may fall from 6 per cent in the first half of 1995 to 4½ per cent by the end of 1996, well above the official target of 2 per cent set by the government in its 3-year convergence programme of July 1994. On the external side, after a deterioration in the first half of 1995, terms of trade gains from the second half of 1995 onwards are projected to enlarge the trade surplus. The current account surplus could widen to around 1.6 per cent of GDP in 1996.

The main uncertainty attaching to the projections concerns the pace of fiscal consolidation and its impact on inflation and interest rates. On the one hand, approval by Parliament of the proposed pension reform should further strengthen market confidence, assisting the recovery of the lira and thereby alleviating inflationary pressures. With early general elections increasingly likely for the autumn, positive confidence effects could also flow from the early preparation of the 1996 budget. On the other hand, with consumer prices already accelerating in the first half of 1995, any departure from stated fiscal targets risks raising interest rates, thus hampering the convergence process.

NOTES

1. This was the first date at which newly-defined unemployment data became available. Methodological changes included an extension in the list of branches of economic activities, a more detailed questionnaire and a redefinition of "job seekers", counting as unemployed persons only those aged more than 15 who were available for work and took at least one initiative to find a job in the 30 days preceding the reference week of the quarterly labour force survey. The data from the Labour Force Survey for the period October 1992 to October 1994 have been revised in March to take into account a new population census benchmark.
2. The Wage Supplementation Fund (*Cassa Integrazione Guadagni*) pays compensation of "temporarily" laid-off workers and salaried employees in industry and many service sectors.
3. Budgetary outcomes for 1994 would have been better had it not been for unforseen expenditure and lower revenues associated with the flood which affected the northern regions in the autumn.

UNITED KINGDOM

The growth of real GDP slowed to an annual rate of around 3¼ per cent in the last quarter of 1994, following growth of over 4 per cent in the first half of the year. GDP growth in 1994 was export led; consumer spending was restrained by large tax increases and subdued consumer confidence, despite steadily falling unemployment, while private investment continued to lag the cycle. Underlying inflation fell to 2 per cent in September 1994, but rose somewhat in early 1995, while the current account moved into small surplus. GDP growth is forecast to be 3½ per cent in 1995, and 3 per cent in 1996, as the tightening of both fiscal and monetary policy takes effect. Inflation as measured by the GDP deflator is projected to rise to 2¾ per cent in 1996 and the current account to remain close to balance.

Recent developments

Real GDP increased by almost 4 per cent in 1994, compared with an estimated potential output growth of some 2½ per cent. Large tax increases considerably restricted the growth of real disposable income in 1994, despite higher employment. As in 1993, private consumption grew by around 2½ per cent, while the savings ratio fell by 1¼ points. The fall in the savings ratio appears to have been driven by the squeeze on disposable income rather than buoyant consumer confidence. Indeed, consumer confidence remained weak through 1994 and early 1995, in response to higher interest rates, a subdued housing market and limited improvements in household balance sheets. Domestic demand growth slowed in the second half of 1994, largely reflecting a fall in public investment and a smaller increase in stockbuilding. Somewhat surprisingly, consumers' expenditure slowed only marginally in the second half. New car registrations and retail sales data for early 1995 continued to point to some slowdown in private consumption. But preliminary first quarter (output-based) GDP estimates indicate that economic growth was sustained, largely reflecting a pick-up in services.

Foreign demand has been strong. Export volumes of goods and services increased by 9 per cent in 1994, reflecting strong recovery in European export markets and continuing gains in export market share. Import pen-

UNITED KINGDOM
Demand and output

Percentage changes from previous period, seasonally adjusted at annual rates, volume (1990 prices)

	1991 current prices billion £	1992	1993	1994	1995	1996	1994 I	1994 II	1995 I	1995 II	1996 I	1996 II
Private consumption	365.0	0	2.7	2.6	2.4	2.8	2.1	1.9	2.5	2.8	2.8	2.7
Government consumption	124.1	0	1.0	1.6	1.1	1.2	1.6	1.2	1.0	1.0	1.3	1.3
Gross fixed investment	97.7	–1.2	0.3	3.2	4.2	4.6	4.9	0.3	5.8	4.9	4.6	4.3
Public [a]	15.9	10.9	0.6	9.9	0.4	1.0	48.0	–13.4	8.0	1.0	1.0	1.0
Private residential	15.7	2.9	4.3	6.4	0.1	1.7	10.1	–3.1	1.0	1.5	1.7	1.8
Private non-residential	66.1	–5.1	–0.7	0.3	6.6	6.5	–6.9	6.2	6.5	7.0	6.5	6.0
Final domestic demand	586.8	–0.2	1.9	2.5	2.5	2.8	2.5	1.5	2.8	2.8	2.8	2.7
* stockbuilding	–4.9 [b]	0.5	0.3	0.5	0.3	0	0.8	0.5	0.4	0.1	0	0
Total domestic demand	581.9	0.3	2.2	3.0	2.8	2.8	3.3	2.0	3.1	2.9	2.8	2.7
Exports of goods and services	134.2	3.1	3.3	8.9	9.1	7.7	8.3	12.7	8.0	7.9	7.8	7.5
Imports of goods and services	140.8	6.2	2.8	5.9	6.6	7.0	6.4	5.3	7.0	7.2	7.0	6.8
* net exports	–6.6 [b]	–0.9	0	0.6	0.6	0.1	0.3	1.8	0.2	0.1	0.2	0.1
* compromise adjustment	0.0 [b]	0	–0.1	0.1	0	0	0.2	0	0	0	0	0
GDP at market prices [c]	575.3	–0.5	2.2	3.8	3.4	3.0	4.0	3.8	3.4	3.1	3.0	2.9
Industrial production [d]	–	–0.8	1.4	4.1	3.3	3.0	5.5	4.6	2.9	3.0	3.0	2.9

* Contributions to changes in real GDP (as a per cent of real GDP in the previous period).
a) Including nationalised industries and public corporations.
b) Actual amount.
c) Data for GDP in the past are based on a compromise estimate which is the average of the expenditure, output and income estimates of GDP. The compromise adjustment is the difference between compromise GDP and the expenditure estimate of GDP.
d) Manufacturing production.

UNITED KINGDOM
Employment, income and inflation
Percentage changes from previous period, seasonally adjusted at annual rates

	1992	1993	1994	1995	1996	1994 I	1994 II	1995 I	1995 II	1996 I	1996 II
Employment	–2.4	–0.8	0.3	1.5	1.2	–0.7	1.7	1.5	1.2	1.2	1.1
Unemployment rate [a]	9.9	10.2	9.2	8.2	7.6	9.6	8.9	8.3	8.0	7.7	7.4
Compensation of employees	3.8	3.1	3.6	4.5	5.5	4.0	3.0	4.9	5.2	5.6	5.8
Unit labour cost	4.4	0.8	–0.2	1.1	2.5	0	–0.8	1.5	2.1	2.5	2.8
Household disposable income	7.5	5.0	3.7	4.7	5.5	3.4	4.9	4.5	5.1	5.6	5.8
GDP deflator	4.3	3.4	2.0	2.3	2.7	1.8	1.8	2.4	2.6	2.7	2.9
Private consumption deflator	4.7	3.5	2.5	2.9	3.1	2.3	2.6	2.9	3.0	3.1	3.2

a) As a percentage of labour force.

etration was modest, with import growth relative to domestic demand lower than in the past. This strong visible trade performance suggests ongoing adjustments in customer-supplier relations to the lower real exchange rate prevailing since sterling left the European Exchange Rate Mechanism in September 1992. There was also a marked improvement in net investment income in 1994. Earnings related to direct investment in North America rose strongly, while earnings of overseas companies in the United Kingdom fell (reflecting losses by subsidiaries of foreign financial companies). The large UK international banking sector continued to generate strong growth in commissions and fees, boosting the services balance. The current account moved into surplus in the second half of 1994, for the first time in almost a decade.

The share of total investment in GDP in this recovery has fallen short of that of the 1981-83 recovery. Non-financial corporations have been slow to invest, with private investment up only 1.6 per cent in 1994. However, investment intentions are clearly on the rise. The financial surplus of the non-financial corporate sector was close to 2 per cent of GDP in 1994, while business surveys point to above-average capacity utilisation and high business confidence.[1]

Inflation passed its cyclical trough in late 1994. The pass through of commodity prices has been reflected in rising producer output price inflation. Retail price inflation has also picked up, though to a lesser extent. The 12-month rise in the retail price index excluding mortgage interest payments (RPIX) rose from a 27-year low of 2 per cent in September 1994 to 2.6 per cent in April 1995. Excluding in addition indirect taxes, the comparable rise was 2.1 per cent from a 1 per cent trough in October. Low underlying inflation largely reflects subdued labour cost pressures. Whole economy average earnings growth was 3½ per cent in February 1995, barely changed in over a year, and whole economy unit wage costs in the fourth quarter of 1994 were marginally down from a year earlier. Keen retail competition and a still significant output gap continue to impose discipline over business costs.

Registered unemployment has fallen steadily since December 1992, bringing registered unemployment down by over 630 000 by March 1995, and the unemployment rate to 8.4 per cent of the labour force. The growth of employment (based on the Labour Force Survey) was modest in the first two years of recovery, with job growth being predominantly part-time. But employment growth strengthened in the summer of 1994, and there was a marked shift from part-time to full-time job creation. The number of employees in September-November 1994 was 0.5 per cent up on three months earlier and 1.1 per cent over the preceding year.

Policies and other forces acting

The government's fiscal objective is to bring the public sector borrowing requirement (PSBR) back to balance over the medium term. Since 1993, there has been a substantial tightening of fiscal policy in line with this goal. The November 1994 budget announced that general government expenditure (excluding privatisation proceeds) would grow by only 0.1 per cent in real terms in FY 1995/96 (fiscal years run from April to March), with further restraint programmed until 1997/98. The tax and spending measures announced were expected to reduce public borrowing by £6.1 billion in FY 1995/96; previously announced tax changes will yield an additional £3.9 billion. The OECD Secretariat projects that the net lending of general government (excluding privatisation proceeds) will fall from 6¾ per cent of GDP in 1994 to 2½ per cent of GDP in 1996, with the structural deficit falling from 5 to 1¾ per cent. The United Kingdom is projected to satisfy the Maastricht Treaty convergence criteria for general government deficits by FY 1996/97. It

United Kingdom

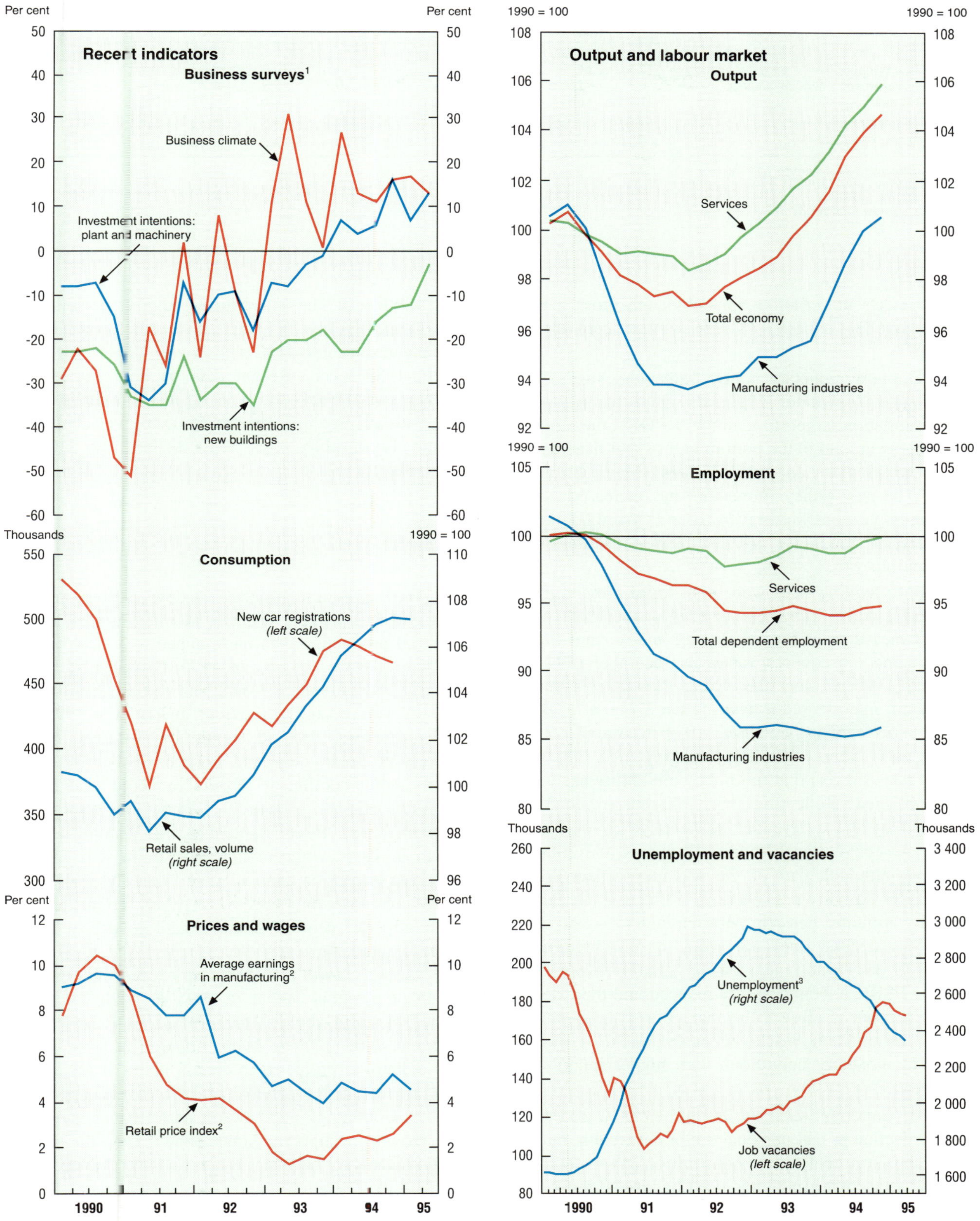

1. Balance between positive and negative answers.
2. Change over four quarters.
3. Claimants aged 18 and over.

Sources: Department of Employment, *Employment Gazette;* OECD, *Main Economic Indicators.*

UNITED KINGDOM
Financial indicators

	1992	1993	1994	1995	1996	1994 I	1994 II	1995 I	1995 II	1996 I	1996 II
Household saving ratio[a]	12.8	11.7	10.4	9.9	9.5	10.4	10.5	10.1	9.7	9.6	9.5
General government financial balance[b]	–6.1	–7.9	–6.5	–4.2	–2.6	–7.8	–5.3	–4.7	–3.8	–3.0	–2.2
Current balance[b]	–1.6	–1.9	0	–0.1	–0.1	–0.7	0.6	0	–0.3	0	–0.2
Short-term interest rate[c]	9.6	5.9	5.5	7.1	7.8	5.2	5.8	6.7	7.5	7.8	7.8
Long-term interest rate[d]	9.1	7.5	8.2	8.4	8.2	7.6	8.8	8.4	8.3	8.2	8.1

a) As a percentage of disposable income.
b) As a percentage of GDP.
c) 3-month interbank rate.
d) 10-year government bonds.

already meets the criterion for debt, with gross general government debt expected to peak at 49 per cent of GDP in 1995.

The new monetary policy framework has been in place since September 1992. Its main feature is an explicit inflation target: to maintain RPIX in the range of 1 to 4 per cent, and in the bottom half of that band by the end of the life of the current Parliament (May 1997 at the latest). The new policy framework has increased policy transparency, contributing to sound macroeconomic management conducive to sustained non-inflationary economic growth.

Base lending rates were first raised pre-emptively by 50 basis points in September 1994 – when contemporaneous measures of the retail price index were flat or falling – and subsequently raised in December 1994 and February 1995 to slow the strong growth of demand. Long-term interest rates have fallen from a peak of almost 9 per cent in September 1994 to around 8.3 per cent in early May 1995. But persisting high long-term interest rates suggest that full policy credibility has yet to be established. Reflecting this, inflation expectations measured by the differential between yields on index-linked and conventional bonds still exceed the inflation objective, although part of the gap may reflect higher volatility or liquidity risk. Sterling's effective rate depreciated by around 5 per cent between end 1994 and early May. This decline does not seem to reflect currently favourable economic fundamentals: inflation is presently low, the PSBR is being rapidly reduced and the external current account is close to balance. But if the depreciation is sustained, it would be equivalent to a modest easing in monetary conditions with higher inflationary pressure.

An important element in the 1990-92 recession was the decline in real personal sector net wealth, mainly due to the large real fall in house prices. Although real personal sector net wealth has risen by around 5 per cent since the end of 1992, it is still some 8 per cent below end-1989 levels. The real value of tangible personal sector assets (mainly housing) has remained virtually unchanged since end-1992, and is over 20 per cent below its end-1989 levels. Recent data on house prices and turnover indicate that the housing market remains sluggish, with adverse implications for consumer confidence though favourable ones with respect to inflation expectations.

Prospects

GDP growth is projected to slow to 3½ per cent in 1995, and to 3 per cent in 1996. Monthly retail sales and industrial production data had pointed to a slowdown in growth in the first quarter of 1995, but the first quarter (preliminary) estimate for GDP showed a rise of 0.8 per cent, the same as in the previous quarter. For 1995 as a whole, domestic demand should be sustained by the recovery in employment and stronger investment, while exports should continue to respond to record order books, continuing market growth in Europe and strong cost competitiveness. Fiscal tightening will restrain demand growth in 1995, while monetary restraint will have an increasing impact on demand after 1995. Even so, short-term interest rates may have to be raised further, perhaps to around 8 per cent, to slow demand growth to that of potential output beyond 1996.

Output growth is expected to exceed the estimated growth of potential output in 1995-96, with the output gap falling from about 3 per cent of GDP in 1994 to 1½ per cent of GDP by 1996. Inflation in terms of the GDP deflator is projected to remain below 3 per cent in 1995, albeit rising somewhat in 1996 as the output gap narrows. Continuing good export performance and moderate growth in import volumes should keep the current account close to balance. By end-1996, the economy could be experiencing a more sustainable rate of GDP growth, with the unemployment rate falling to around

UNITED KINGDOM
External indicators[a]
Seasonally adjusted at annual rates

	1993	1994	1995	1996	1994 I	1994 II	1995 I	1995 II	1996 I	1996 II
					$ billion					
Merchandise exports	182.1	207.0	242	268	194.1	219.8	235	249	262	275
Merchandise imports	202.2	223.1	261	289	211.3	234.9	253	269	283	296
Trade balance	–20.1	–16.1	–19	–21	–17.2	–15.0	–18	–20	–21	–22
Invisibles, net	2.4	15.9	17	20	10.6	21.2	18	17	21	19
Current balance	–17.7	–0.3	–2	–1	–6.7	6.1	0	–3	0	–3
					Percentage change					
Merchandise export volumes[b]	–0.1	11.6	8.1	7.2	16.8	10.6	7.4	7.3	7.3	7.1
Merchandise import volumes[b]	0.1	6.6	6.1	7.0	8.8	2.8	7.1	7.3	7.0	6.8
Export performance[c]	–0.3	1.8	–0.8	–0.3	5.2	–0.3	–1.1	–0.8	–0.1	–0.3
Terms of trade	1.7	–1.8	–1.6	–0.4	–3.3	–2.5	–1.4	–1.0	–0.2	–0.2

a) For further detail, see tables in the External Trade and Payments section of the Annex.
b) Customs basis.
c) Ratio between the total of export volumes and export market of total goods.

7½ per cent, close to its estimated natural rate, and the public sector borrowing requirement falling quickly to a sustainable medium-term position. Such a configuration would prepare the ground for a "soft landing" with lower inflation beyond 1996.

The risks surrounding these projections appear balanced. The main uncertainties are the timing of the projected pick-up in investment and whether inflation will remain moderate as the output gap closes. The current favourable combination of strong growth with low inflation is in part a feature of this stage of the business cycle. However, the structural reforms of the past decade have also contributed to a more flexible and less inflation-prone economy. The OECD Secretariat estimates that the natural rate of unemployment has already fallen by around 3 percentage points over the past decade to some 7 to 7½ per cent – and continuing wage moderation in the face of falling unemployment in 1994 and 1995 would be consistent with further modest declines.

NOTE

1. The Confederation of British Industry's April 1995 survey for manufacturing indicated a further rise in capacity utilisation above its long-run level and continued strength in business optimism and activity.

CANADA

Economic growth continued at a rapid pace in the second half of 1994, and the manufacturing sector has experienced a cyclical recovery of unprecedented strength over the past year. Robust activity in the United States, burgeoning global demand for industrial materials, and the highly competitive position of Canadian manufacturers boosted exports and led to a marked improvement in the external balance. At the same time, domestic demand remained relatively strong in the face of higher interest rates. However, tighter monetary conditions in recent months, along with slower growth in the United States, have started to damp economic expansion in Canada. Nonetheless, the recovery is projected to continue at a solid pace as favourable economic fundamentals – notably low inflation and declining external and budget deficits – should, over time, lead to lower interest rates, underpinning domestic demand. In addition, restored international competitiveness is likely to allow exporters to continue to gain market share in the face of projected slower market growth.

Recent developments

Real GDP expanded at an annual rate of 6 per cent in the second half of 1994, bettering the growth rate achieved in the preceding half-year. As has been the case throughout the recovery, economic growth was fuelled by exports and – to a lesser extent – by business investment. Almost half of the extraordinarily high growth in merchandise exports resulted from gains in market share in response to the sharp decline in the real exchange rate since 1991 (by more than 20 per cent in terms of relative unit labour costs). Exports of machinery and equipment and automative products, in particular, have soared since mid-1994. High capacity utilisation rates in export-oriented industries and surging profits contributed to the strength of business investment. Growth in consumer spending continued to outstrip the moderate rise in disposable income. Apart from improved consumer confidence, this appears to reflect the fact that personal net wealth has increased significantly more than incomes. Consumer demand was led by spending on durables, despite higher interest rates. However, the marked rise in mortgage rates aborted the temporary revival of residential investment that emerged in the first half of 1994. Housing starts suggest that the weakness of residential investment has continued in early 1995, and there are also signs that higher interest rates have started to damp demand for consumer durables. Although exports and manufacturing shipments have remained buoyant, labour-market statistics and other leading indicators point to a marked deceleration in overall economic expansion in the first quarter of 1995.

CANADA
Demand and output

Percentage changes from previous period, seasonally adjusted at annual rates, volume (1986 prices)

	1991 current prices billion C$	1992	1993	1994	1995	1996	1994 I	1994 II	1995 I	1995 II	1996 I	1996 II
Private consumption	412.2	1.3	1.6	3.1	2.7	3.2	3.8	2.8	2.5	3.0	3.2	3.3
Government consumption	144.4	1.2	0.5	–2.1	–1.0	–0.3	–2.4	–2.7	–0.5	–0.3	–0.5	0.1
Gross fixed investment	132.7	–2.8	–0.2	6.0	5.1	5.9	5.9	5.9	4.4	5.6	5.9	6.0
Public[a]	16.4	–0.6	4.4	4.5	9.9	5.7	1.2	9.5	10.0	10.0	5.0	3.0
Private residential	39.8	7.9	–4.4	2.9	–3.1	2.6	8.8	–4.5	–3.8	–0.2	2.8	5.0
Private non-residential	76.5	–7.5	0.7	7.7	7.4	7.1	5.8	9.8	6.5	6.8	7.3	7.1
Final domestic demand	689.4	0.4	1.0	2.7	2.5	3.1	3.0	2.4	2.3	2.9	3.1	3.3
* stockbuilding	–3.7[b]	–0.1	0.8	0.2	0.1	0	0.4	–0.3	0.4	0	0	0
Total domestic demand	685.7	0.3	1.8	2.9	2.6	3.1	3.4	2.1	2.7	2.9	3.1	3.4
Exports of goods and services	163.9	7.7	10.4	14.4	13.4	7.2	11.2	26.3	10.5	7.9	7.1	6.8
Imports of goods and services	172.5	5.9	8.8	9.6	10.2	6.7	7.6	15.3	9.5	6.8	6.7	6.6
* net exports	–8.5[b]	0.4	0.3	1.4	1.2	0.3	1.1	3.4	0.4	0.5	0.2	0.1
* error of estimate	–2.4[b]	–0.1	0	0.1	0.1	0	0.2	0.3	0	0	0	0
GDP at market prices	674.8	0.6	2.2	4.5	3.9	3.4	4.8	5.9	3.1	3.4	3.3	3.5
Industrial production	–	0.9	4.9	6.4	6.9	4.5	5.7	10.3	6.2	5.1	4.3	4.2

* Contributions to changes in real GDP (as a per cent of real GDP in the previous period).
a) Excluding nationalized industries and public corporations.
b) Actual amount.

CANADA
Employment, income and inflation

Percentage changes from previous period, seasonally adjusted at annual rates

	1992	1993	1994	1995	1996	1994 I	1994 II	1995 I	1995 II	1996 I	1996 II
Employment	–0.6	1.4	2.1	2.3	2.3	1.9	3.4	1.8	2.3	2.3	2.2
Unemployment rate[a]	11.3	11.2	10.4	9.4	9.1	10.8	9.9	9.6	9.2	9.1	9.0
Compensation of employees	2.4	2.5	3.1	4.1	4.9	3.5	3.7	4.0	4.8	4.9	5.1
Unit labour cost	1.8	0.3	–1.3	0.3	1.5	–1.2	–2.0	0.9	1.3	1.6	1.5
Household disposable income	2.8	2.8	2.1	4.3	5.2	3.4	1.2	5.4	5.1	5.2	5.3
GDP deflator	1.4	1.1	0.6	2.1	2.2	0.2	1.0	2.6	2.4	2.2	2.1
Private consumption deflator	1.3	1.7	0.7	2.0	2.0	0.1	1.0	2.4	2.2	1.9	1.9

a) As a percentage of labour force.

No further inroads into unemployment have been made in recent months as job creation slowed. This follows a fall in the unemployment rate by 1½ points to 9½ per cent during 1994, associated with employment growth of around 3 per cent. The relatively rapid decline in unemployment reflects the fact that, in contrast to previous recoveries, the pick-up in employment has not yet induced large-scale re-entry into the labour market. Nonetheless, a shift from part-time to full-time employment suggests an improvement in job opportunities and helps explain rising consumer confidence and spending. While collective wage settlements have remained subdued, the annual increase in effective earnings has edged up somewhat, although continuing to fall short of productivity growth. The resulting decline in unit labour costs, along with substantial excess capacity outside the export sector, has kept inflation low, despite upward pressure on import and producer prices stemming from currency depreciation and higher commodity prices. Although underlying inflation has picked up a little, it has only reached the middle of the official target range of 1 to 3 per cent. "Headline" inflation has moved back towards the underlying rate, as last year's cut in tobacco taxes has ceased to affect the twelve-month increase in the consumer price index. With favourable cost and price performance reinforcing the competitiveness gains stemming from a lower exchange rate, export growth has increasingly outstripped that of imports. As a result, the current-account deficit narrowed by nearly 2 percentage points during 1994 to 2¾ per cent of GDP, despite a marked rise in the investment income deficit (due to foreign-debt servicing and higher profits of foreign companies in Canada).

Policies and other forces acting

Strong economic growth has been reflected in government finances. The general government deficit dropped from a peak of 7¾ per cent in the first half of 1993 to 4½ per cent of GDP in the second half of 1994. The fiscal stance, which was broadly neutral in 1993, tightened in 1994, as evidenced by a decline in the cyclically-adjusted deficit from over 4 per cent to below 3½ per cent of GDP. This move towards restriction largely reflected discretionary spending cuts. In its February 1995 Budget, the federal government adopted drastic further expenditure restraint in order to convince financial markets that deficit reduction targets will be met in spite of higher-than-expected hikes in short-term interest rates. Measures include major cuts in government employment, transfers to provinces, and subsidies to business and agriculture. Tax increases play a minimal role in fiscal action introduced in the Budget. Assuming that in their forthcoming budgets provinces adopt similar austerity measures in response to cutbacks in transfer payments, the general government deficit could narrow to 2½ per cent of GDP by 1996. Although the fiscal tightening underlying this projection is substantial (1½ per cent of GDP over 1995-96 in terms of the cyclically-adjusted balance), this would just suffice to put the excessively high net public debt-to-GDP ratio on a downward trend from a peak of 64 per cent. Moreover, the remaining structural deficit, estimated by the OECD Secretariat to be just under 2 per cent of GDP, would still leave government finances vulnerable to any pronounced cyclical downturn.

In its monetary policy operations in the autumn of 1994, the Bank of Canada sought to hold overall monetary conditions (taking account of exchange-rate movements as well as interest rates) relatively steady. Following the rise in United States interest rates in November, the Bank increased its target range for the overnight rate only gradually, considering that the fundamentals facing the two countries were different. However, towards the end of the year, financial market concerns about Canada's fiscal and political situation reemerged against

Canada

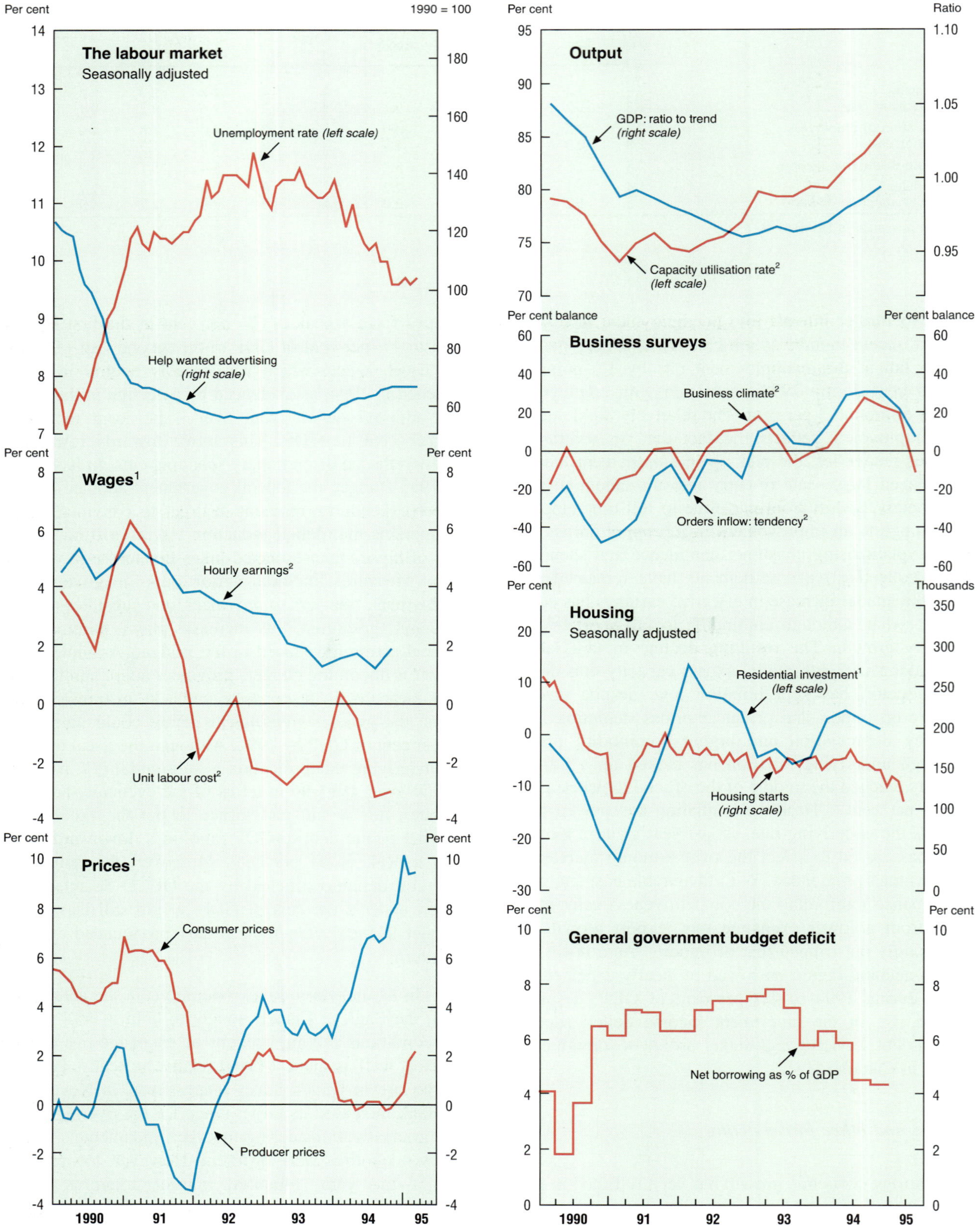

1. Year-on-year percentage change.
2. Manufacturing.

Sources: CANSIM, Statistics Canada; OECD, *Main Economic Indicators*.

CANADA
Financial indicators

	1992	1993	1994	1995	1996	1994 I	1994 II	1995 I	1995 II	1996 I	1996 II
Household saving ratio[a]	9.8	9.2	7.6	7.2	7.2	8.2	7.0	7.2	7.2	7.2	7.2
General government financial balance[b]	−7.1	−7.1	−5.3	−3.7	−2.4	−6.1	−4.5	−4.1	−3.4	−2.7	−2.1
Current balance[b]	−3.8	−4.3	−3.3	−2.2	−1.5	−3.9	−2.7	−2.4	−2.0	−1.6	−1.4
Short-term interest rate[c]	6.7	5.0	5.4	7.5	6.6	5.1	5.8	7.9	7.1	6.7	6.5
Long-term interest rate[d]	8.8	7.9	8.6	8.4	7.5	8.0	9.2	8.7	8.1	7.7	7.3

a) As a percentage of disposable income.
b) As a percentage of GDP.
c) 90-day finance company paper.
d) Long-term federal government bonds.

the background of the Mexican crisis. With the Canadian dollar coming under significant downward pressure and market interest rates rising sharply, the Bank raised the overnight rate sharply during the course of January 1995 to provide support for the currency. The February 1995 Budget had no lasting effect on financial market sentiment, in part because of the threat of sovereign credit downgrades by the major rating agencies. Short-term interest rate spreads between Canada and the United States, which had virtually disappeared in November 1994, fluctuated in the 2 per cent range from January to April 1995, implying – combined with exchange-rate movements – a significant tightening in monetary conditions. Only most recently has a stronger Canadian dollar led to a narrowing of short-term interest rate spreads. By contrast, the long-term interest-rate differential has moved in a narrow range, and bond yields have declined considerably. The projections are based on the assumption that both short-term and long-term interest rate spreads *vis-à-vis* the United States will narrow gradually as favourable economic fundamentals come into play in financial markets.

Prospects

Economic growth is projected to slow markedly during 1995 and then to stabilise at just under 3½ per cent, somewhat above the estimated rate of expansion of productive capacity. This growth profile reflects a lessening stimulus from US demand and the negative impact of past monetary tightening on economic activity; given the time lags involved, the assumed easing of interest rates in the period ahead is expected to start underpinning domestic demand only towards the end of the projection period. With buoyant corporate profits and rising capacity utilisa-

CANADA
External indicators[a]
Seasonally adjusted at annual rates

	1993	1994	1995	1996	1994 I	1994 II	1995 I	1995 II	1996 I	1996 II
					$ billion					
Merchandise exports	144.0	164.3	196	218	152.5	176.1	189	203	213	224
Merchandise imports	136.4	151.5	175	191	143.9	159.2	170	180	187	195
Trade balance	7.6	12.8	21	27	8.7	17.0	19	23	26	28
Invisibles, net	−31.4	−30.9	−34	−36	−29.9	−32.0	−32	−35	−36	−37
Current balance	−23.8	−18.1	−13	−9	−21.2	−15.0	−13	−12	−10	−8
					Percentage change					
Merchandise export volumes[b]	10.7	15.7	14.6	7.6	12.5	29.5	11.3	8.4	7.4	7.1
Merchandise import volumes[b]	11.0	12.7	11.9	6.7	10.8	18.4	11.5	6.8	6.7	6.6
Export performance[c]	0.5	1.8	4.5	1.3	−1.4	11.1	3.0	1.4	1.4	1.1
Terms of trade	1.3	0.1	1.0	1.1	−0.2	−0.1	1.3	1.4	1.1	0.7

a) For further detail, see tables in the External Trade and Payments section of the Annex.
b) Customs basis
c) Ratio between the total of export volumes and export market of total goods.

tion, business investment should remain relatively strong, although intention surveys point to some weakening in 1995. The recent rise in mortgage rates will continue to curtail housing demand in the near term, before increasing demographic requirements and improving housing affordability (due to falling interest rates) lead to some revival next year. Consumer demand will be supported by employment growth, but the fact that the household saving ratio is already at a historically low level is likely to limit the scope for a further strengthening of private consumption growth.

The strong improvement in international competitiveness – assumed in the projections to be maintained – should allow Canadian exporters to continue to gain market share, which would partly offset the adverse effect of the projected slowdown in the United States. Continued favourable export performance, together with projected more moderate import price increases, is expected to make for an ongoing decline in the current-account deficit, which may drop to 1½ per cent of GDP by 1996. Despite robust employment growth, further inroads into unemployment are projected to be limited because labour-force participation should finally recover. With continuing – though diminishing – slack in labour and product markets, inflation is expected to remain in the middle of the official target band of 1 to 3 per cent, following some pick-up in the first half of 1995.

With exports to the United States now accounting for more than 80 per cent of total merchandise exports, growth prospects in Canada are strongly influenced by the conjuncture in its major trading partner. However, with slack yet to be taken up and inflation prospects favourable, the Canadian economy is in a position to maintain stronger growth than in the United States. Whether this can be achieved will importantly depend on interest rate developments. Given the high level of Canada's public and external debt and uncertainties about the future of the federation, financial market nervousness may limit or delay the expected narrowing of interest rate differentials *vis-à-vis* the United States, despite favourable economic fundamentals.

Economic activity strengthened markedly in 1994, with growth in real GDP rising to 4.6 per cent. Concomitantly, the current-account deficit has widened substantially. So as to forestall the risks of overheating, monetary policy has been tightened and the Commonwealth Government has accelerated its deficit reduction programme. These actions should underpin a slowing of GDP growth to 3½ per cent by 1996. Underlying inflation may rise to 3¾ per cent by 1996 and the current account deficit to around 6 per cent of GDP in 1995, falling to 5½ per cent in 1996.

Recent developments. Very strong economic growth was recorded through the first three quarters of 1994, before moderating in the December quarter, when GDP(A)[1] rose by a seasonally adjusted 0.4 per cent (actual rate) bringing the rise from one year earlier to 5 per cent. Domestic demand growth, driven by private consumption and especially by investment in plant and equipment, somewhat outpaced GDP during the year, and this resulted in a widening current account deficit. Imports and retail sales data indicate that growth in domestic demand continued at a brisk pace in the first quarter of 1995. However, after an upswing spanning three years, housing investment peaked late in 1994 and leading indicators point to a slowdown in growth later in the year. Employment growth has also remained strong in recent months and is estimated to have risen by 4½ per cent (in trend terms)[2] in the year to April 1995. The seasonally adjusted unemployment rate fell to 8.3 per cent in April, well down from 10.1 per cent a year ago.

Wage inflation has quickened in recent months, with average weekly ordinary-time earnings of full-time adult employees rising by 4.4 per cent in the year to February, up from 4.1 per cent in the year to November. Nevertheless, with strong productivity growth, underlying inflation[3] has remained low, at 1.9 per cent in the year to the March quarter. Headline inflation, however, which includes mortgage and consumer debt charges, has picked up more, with the consumer price index rising by 1.7 per cent in the March quarter 1995 for an increase of 3.9 per cent from the corresponding period a year earlier.

The current-account deficit increased from 4 per cent of GDP in the first half of (calendar) 1994 to over 5 per cent in the second half. This deterioration is mainly

AUSTRALIA
Demand, output and prices[a]
Percentage changes, volume (1989/90 prices)

	1991 current prices billion A$	1992	1993	1994	1995	1996
Private consumption	235.1	3.3	2.0	4.0	3.9	3.2
Government consumption	69.6	1.4	1.3	4.6	4.5	–2.0
Gross fixed capital formation	77.7	0.5	2.5	11.1	6.0	3.7
Final domestic demand	382.5	2.4	2.0	5.6	4.5	2.4
* stockbuilding	–2.8[b]	0.5	0.6	0	0.5	0.4
Total domestic demand	379.6	3.0	2.6	5.6	5.0	2.8
Exports of goods and services	68.3	5.3	7.4	8.4	5.5	10.0
Imports of goods and services	66.0	7.6	5.2	14.7	12.0	6.8
* net exports	2.3[b]	–0.3	0.5	–1.0	–1.3	0.7
* statistical discrepancy	–1.3[b]	–0.6	0.8	0.9	0.2	0
GDP at market prices[c]	380.6	2.0	3.9	5.4	3.8	3.5
GDP implicit price deflator[c]	–	1.5	1.3	1.2	2.7	3.7
Memorandum items						
GDP average measure[d]	–	2.2	3.5	5.1	3.8	3.5
Private consumption deflator	–	1.8	2.1	1.4	2.6	3.7
Industrial production	–	0.4	6.5	9.6	7.5	6.8
Unemployment rate	–	10.7	10.9	9.7	8.7	7.9
Household saving ratio[e]	–	5.4	4.3	4.4	4.3	3.9
General government financial balance[f]	–	–4.0	–3.7	–4.6	–2.9	–1.0
Current balance[f]	–	–3.7	–3.7	–4.6	–6.0	–5.3

* Contributions to changes in real GDP (as a per cent of real GDP in the previous period).
a) Based on seasonally adjusted data for fiscal years. As a consequence of this seasonal adjustment, annual data may differ from annual unadjusted data.
b) Actual amount.
c) The income measure of GDP.
d) Average measure of the expenditure, production and income measures of GDP.
e) As a percentage of disposable income.
f) As a percentage of GDP.

attributable to a surge in import volumes, which reflects the high growth in both plant and equipment investment and private consumption.

An important factor underpinning the high growth in domestic demand during the past year has been the strength of business investment, which grew by around 17 per cent in 1994 (underpinned by a strong rise in investment in plant and equipment, which rose by around 22 per cent), and was fuelled mainly by high and rising rates of capacity utilisation and improved business balance sheet positions; survey-based measures suggest that capacity utilisation rose in 1994 to a higher rate than the average for the period since 1980. These factors are likely to continue to support the recovery in business investment, albeit at a more moderate pace following the initial correction to the low levels of investment during the early 1990s.

Policies and other forces acting. The surge in growth over the past year has brought to the fore concerns about the amount of spare capacity remaining in the economy. All estimates of the gap between actual and potential output suggest that it narrowed significantly in 1994, though there is considerable uncertainty about how much of a gap, if any, still remains. As spare capacity of both capital and labour is used up, continued growth at rates above potential, which the OECD Secretariat estimates to be a little over 3 per cent per annum, would tend to create inflationary pressures.

So as to forestall the risks of overheating, the Reserve Bank of Australia tightened monetary policy in the second half of 1994. The official cash rate was raised in three anticipatory moves by a cumulative 275 basis points between August and December 1994 to 7.5 per cent. Having fluctuated in the 10 to 10½ per cent range from November 1994 to the end of March 1995, long bond yields fell to around 9 per cent by early May. This decline was influenced by the strengthening in international bond markets as well as expectations that growth in aggregate demand may slow to more sustainable rates.

The Commonwealth Government announced in the May 1995 Budget a significant improvement in its budget balance, from an estimated deficit of A$ 12.2 billion (2.7 per cent of GDP) in FY 1994/95[4] to a surplus of A$ 0.7 billion (0.1 per cent of GDP) in FY 1995/96; excluding privatisation proceeds, a deficit of A$ 4.6 billion (0.9 per cent of GDP) is projected for FY 1995/96. Abstracting from privatisation proceeds and early debt redemptions, the discretionary tightening of fiscal policy to be effected in FY 1995/96 is estimated at around A$ 2½ billion (½ per cent of GDP). This mainly reflects tax increases. A further discretionary tightening (0.8 per cent of GDP) in fiscal policy is planned in FY 1996/97, resulting in a projected surplus (excluding privatisation proceeds) of A$ 1.3 billion (0.2 per cent of GDP).

Prospects. Output growth is projected to slow from 4½ per cent in 1994 to around 3½ per cent in 1996. This slowing reflects an easing in growth in nearly all the components of demand (including in particular government final demand and investment in dwellings and in plant and equipment). The farm sector detracted from GDP growth in the second half of 1994 owing to the drought in the eastern states, but assuming a return to normal seasonal conditions, is expected to contribute positively in 1995. Growth in total employment is projected to ease to about 2½ per cent in 1996 with the unemployment rate falling to just below 8 per cent in 1996. Tightening labour market conditions are projected to increase wage inflation and, together with a cyclical slowdown in productivity growth, to contribute to an acceleration in underlying inflation to around 3¾ per cent in 1996. The current account deficit is projected to widen to 6 per cent of GDP in 1995 but, with a return to normal seasonal conditions for the farm sector and slowing growth in imports, to fall back to 5½ per cent of GDP in 1996.

An upside risk surrounding the projections is that the tightening in monetary and fiscal policies may not be sufficient to address adequately inflationary pressures and the deterioration in the current account deficit. This risk reflects the possibility that little slack remains in the economy, as suggested by the OECD Secretariat's estimates of the output gap. A downside risk is that the large current account deficits could provoke an adverse shift in investor sentiment, which would lead to a sharper slowing in aggregate demand growth.

NOTES

1. The average of the expenditure, income and production measures of GDP.
2. All references to trend are to the smoothed series calculated by the Australian Bureau of Statistics.
3. As measured by the Treasury underlying inflation series. This excludes from the consumer price index mortgage and consumer debt charges and volatile items, including energy prices, certain fresh food groups, other goods which are subject to marked seasonal variation and an array of public sector prices or charges.
4. Fiscal years begin 1 July.

The expansion gathered speed in 1994, as exports responded to strengthening recovery in Europe and domestic demand received a boost from the 1993-94 tax reform. Recent indicators point to both ongoing export strength and a pick-up in investment activity. However, the pace of growth could gradually slacken as exchange rate appreciation limits export and investment growth and as renewed fiscal tightening, geared to achieving the Maastricht targets by 1998, squeezes household incomes and public consumption. Inflation, which slowed at the turn of the year in connection with Austria's entry into the European Union, is expected to pick up again as the output gap narrows.

Recent developments. The recovery, which began in mid-1993, continued to be buoyant throughout 1994. The 1993-94 tax cuts promoted a strong recovery of consumption growth – even though the saving rate rose by a full percentage point (to 12.7 per cent) – while investment was boosted by temporary investment tax breaks. With government consumption also growing rapidly, total domestic demand rose by 4 per cent. Exports also picked up, reflecting the strengthening upswing in western Europe and continuing demand from central and eastern Europe. The export surge has led to a revival of the manufacturing sector, first in semi-finished products and then in the investment-good producing sector. However, imports grew faster than exports, contributing to a widening of the current account deficit to 1 per cent of GDP. Weak receipts from tourism have also been a factor, with adverse relative price trends one of the chief problems afflicting this sector.

Unemployment stabilised relatively early in the recovery. Employment has been on the increase in the service and construction sectors, and it has stopped falling in manufacturing. However, a reduction in unemployment has been prevented by a steady increase in the labour force, despite restrictions on immigration, so that the unemployment rate still stood at 4.4 per cent in early 1995. Inflation, having failed to decline below 3 per cent during the recession, fell abruptly at end-year to around 2½ per cent on a 12-month basis, and the new rate was sustained in the early months of 1995. This reflected the beneficial impact of European Union (EU) membership on 1 January 1995, especially on food prices.

Policies and other forces acting. Austrian interest rates have continued to be closely bound to German rates. Thus, short-term rates were broadly unchanged between May 1994 and the end of March 1995 (with market rates rising toward end-year before falling back again in early 1995). Interest rate reductions by the Bundesbank then prompted similar cuts by the Austrian National Bank of

AUSTRIA
Demand, output and prices
Percentage changes, volume (1983 prices)

	1991 current prices billion Sch	1992	1993	1994	1995	1996
Private consumption	1 064.0	1.9	0.2	2.3	2.3	2.0
Government consumption	349.6	2.4	3.0	2.4	2.0	1.0
Gross fixed capital formation	488.4	1.3	–2.1	5.5	5.8	5.4
Final domestic demand	1 902.1	1.9	0.1	3.2	3.2	2.7
* stockbuilding	8.8[a]	–0.1	0.1	1.0	0.1	0.1
Total domestic demand	1 910.9	1.8	0.1	4.1	3.2	2.8
Exports of goods and services	770.4	2.8	–1.0	4.9	5.0	4.8
Imports of goods and services	753.0	2.6	–0.6	7.8	5.7	5.8
* net exports	17.4[a]	0.1	–0.2	–1.4	–0.5	–0.7
GDP at market prices	1 928.3	1.8	–0.1	2.7	2.8	2.3
GDP implicit price deflator	–	4.2	3.6	3.2	2.8	2.7
Memorandum items						
Private consumption deflator	–	3.9	3.5	3.3	2.3	2.5
Industrial production	–	–1.4	–1.7	3.9	4.5	5.0
Unemployment rate	–	3.6	4.2	4.4	4.3	4.2
Household saving ratio[b]	–	12.5	11.7	12.5	12.5	11.9
General government financial balance[c]	–	–2.0	–4.1	–4.0	–4.5	–3.9
Current balance[c]	–	–0.1	–0.5	–1.0	–1.4	–1.7

* Contributions to changes in real GDP (as a per cent of real GDP in the previous period).
a) Actual amount.
b) As a percentage of disposable income.
c) As a percentage of GDP.

1/2 percentage point in the discount rate, to 4 per cent, and of 1/4 percentage point each in the Lombard and GOMEX (short-term open market transactions) rates, to 5.25 and 4.45 per cent, respectively. The latter rate is now virtually equal to the German repo rate, having previously been somewhat lower, reflecting the relatively high liquidity in the Austrian banking sector last year. Austrian long-term rates (average of all maturities over one year) are around 1 1/2 percentage points above their trough in early 1994, though they continue to be at the low end of the international spectrum and the gap *vis-à-vis* the German long-term rate (7-15 year average) continues to be slightly negative. At the same time, the exchange rate has strengthened in tandem with the German mark, resulting in an appreciation of some 5 per cent in effective terms in the year to May 1995.

The 1994 general government budget deficit remained at its previous year's level of around 4 per cent of GDP. However, since economic growth turned out to be much higher than anticipated, this outcome represented a substantial increase in the cyclically-adjusted deficit. The 1995 federal budget marks a return to consolidation, forming part of a medium term programme designed to bring the general government deficit down to below 3 per cent by the end of the current legislative period in 1998. The main expenditure measures include controls on civil service expenditures, cuts in family benefits, and reductions in the availability and generosity of unemployment benefits, while the main revenue measures are increases in pension contributions, an increase in the mineral oil tax (boosting inflation in 1995 by 1/4 point), and a reduction in the business investment allowance. Such measures, together with the benefits of growth, serve to offset most of the direct budgetary cost of EU membership, which amount to some 1 1/2 per cent of GDP, limiting the increase in the 1995 general government deficit to 1/2 per cent of GDP.

Prospects. Leading indicators, especially the end-1994 jump in new orders from domestic and foreign buyers, suggest continuing strong demand growth into 1995. Moreover, recent investment surveys point to a consolidation of investment activity in the manufacturing sector. Buoyant export market growth should ensure continued investment strength throughout the projection horizon, though the recent exchange rate-related competitiveness loss will probably imply a loss of export market share in 1996. Moreover, households' real disposable income may grow by less than 2 per cent in both 1995 and 1996 due to fiscal retrenchment, which will hold down private consumption growth even though the savings rate may play its traditional cushioning role. Public consumption growth will also slow sharply. Thus, GDP growth is expected to subside from 2 3/4 per cent in 1995 to around 2 1/4 per cent in 1996. Nevertheless, the output gap will narrow relatively early due to the high starting point for GDP at the beginning of the recovery (given the shallowness of the recession). This implies that inflation could start rising again next year, the increase in consumer prices reaching perhaps 2 1/2 per cent.

A risk to the projection is that inflation could turn out to be higher than projected, due to a smaller than expected pass-through of current exchange rate appreciation into prices of imported products. If this were to be accompanied by budget slippage, the differential between Austrian and German bond yields could rise, slowing the expansion. On the other hand, a reversal of the recent exchange rate appreciation could result in a better than envisaged outcome on export and investment growth.

BELGIUM

The Belgian economy has recovered rapidly from the severe recession of 1993. Economic growth is projected to accelerate to a little over 2 1/2 per cent in 1995-96, with domestic demand progressively replacing exports as the driving force. Unemployment is expected to decline only slowly and the current-account surplus to widen further. Given the wage freeze, the amount of slack in the economy, and the recent appreciation of the Belgian franc in effective terms, serious inflation pressures seem unlikely. The general government deficit may decline significantly in 1995 but without new measures fiscal consolidation would slow in 1996.

Recent developments. The recovery from the deep recession of 1993 seems to be continuing at a sustained pace, although private consumption remains hesitant and public spending is restrained by fiscal consolidation. The upturn has been driven by a surge in exports which has buoyed most sectors of the economy. After a strong decline in 1993, business fixed investment started a major turn around in the second half of 1994, especially in manufacturing where capacity utilisation has risen rapidly and the profit situation has improved markedly. On the other hand, private consumption continues to suffer from a near-stagnation of disposable personal income in real terms and a climate of uncertainty as a result of high

BELGIUM

Demand, output and prices

Percentage changes, volume (1985 prices)

	1991 current prices billion BF	1992	1993	1994	1995	1996
Private consumption	4 243.0	2.6	−1.0	0.7	1.9	2.3
Government consumption	1 005.6	0.4	1.9	1.6	1.0	0.7
Gross fixed capital formation	1 314.5	0.1	−5.9	−0.3	6.5	4.3
Final domestic demand	6 563.1	1.8	−1.6	0.6	2.6	2.5
* stockbuilding	−8.9[a]	0.3	−0.1	0.9	0.1	0.1
Total domestic demand	6 554.2	2.1	−1.7	1.6	2.7	2.6
Exports of goods and services	4 846.5	3.9	1.6	6.3	5.6	5.4
Imports of goods and services	4 657.3	4.1	1.6	5.5	5.6	5.4
* net exports	189.2[a]	−0.3	0	0.7	0	−0.1
GDP at market prices	6 743.4	1.9	−1.7	2.3	2.7	2.6
GDP implicit price deflator	–	3.4	4.4	2.2	2.2	2.2
Memorandum items						
Private consumption deflator	–	2.1	2.6	2.4	1.9	2.0
Industrial production	–	0	−5.2	3.5	3.5	3.0
Unemployment rate	–	10.3	11.9	12.6	12.4	11.8
Household saving ratio[b]	–	21.2	22.8	22.2	22.0	21.7
General government financial balance[c]	–	−6.6	−6.6	−5.3	−4.3	−4.0
Current balance[d]	–	3.0	5.4	5.4	5.8	5.8

* Contributions to changes in real GDP (as a per cent of real GDP in the previous period).
a) Actual amount.
b) As a percentage of disposable income.
c) As a percentage of GDP. It includes the proceeds of privatisations and sales of other assets.
d) As a percentage of GDP. Balance for BLEU.

unemployment. The November 1994 survey of firms' intentions showed very strong planned increases in fixed investment in manufacturing (over 20 per cent in nominal terms), and the leading indicator of the Belgian National Bank, although a little weaker in the first quarter of 1995, points to underlying economic strength in coming months. The projected buoyancy in foreign markets should continue to support exports, but the recent appreciation of the Belgian franc in effective terms may lead to some losses in market shares. Despite the pick-up in economic activity and various measures taken by the Government to promote employment – notably in the framework of the November 1993 "global plan" – labour market conditions have improved only marginally and unemployment remains close to its peak. Consumer-price inflation has continued to decline – to 1.7 per cent (year-on-year) in April 1995.

Policies and other forces acting. Despite some turbulence in foreign exchange markets, interest differentials with Germany remained relatively stable in early 1995. But at the beginning of March, following the depreciation of the Spanish and Portuguese currencies within the European Exchange Rate Mechanism, the Belgian franc came under some pressure *vis-à-vis* the Deutschemark, prompting the Belgian National Bank to raise interest rates and tighten liquidity conditions. This response was well received by the market and pressure quickly abated. At the end of the month, with the Belgian franc back to its central rate *vis-à-vis* the Deutschemark, the Belgian National Bank was able to follow the Bundesbank and lower its rates. Official interest rates were decreased further in April and May. Interest rates are not expected to change markedly over the projection period. Short-term rates may edge up in 1996 in tandem with German rates, as the recovery matures; but long-term rates may remain around current levels, again broadly in line with German rates.

No new fiscal initiatives have been taken in the recent period, but, reflecting the impact of earlier measures (global plan) and the recovery of the economy, the general government deficit may decline significantly in 1995, to 4¼ per cent of GDP. Nonetheless, on present policies, the OECD Secretariat projects the deficit to decline only to 4 per cent in 1996, and the estimated cyclically adjusted deficit to level off at around 3 per cent. On these projections, the debt/GDP ratio declines moderately, but remains above 135 per cent in 1996.

Prospects. The outlook is for continued, robust growth, with domestic demand progressively replacing exports as the driving force. As capacity utilisation in manufacturing is already above the level of the previous cyclical peak (a little over 80 per cent) and the cash flow situation of enterprises has improved markedly, business fixed investment is likely to stage a strong recovery. This may lead to a strengthening of private consumption and a more broadly based expansion in 1996, although public consumption will continue to be restrained by fiscal consolidation. With exports losing some buoyancy, as a result of an erosion of international competitiveness, and imports picking up in line with domestic demand, the net contribution of the foreign balance to GDP growth is expected to turn slightly negative. In all, real GDP is projected to grow at a little over 2½ per cent in both 1995 and 1996, a rate somewhat above potential. Unemployment is likely to decline, but only gradually. Given the significant degree of slack in the labour market, the wage freeze in 1995-96 imposed by the global plan and the recent appreciation of the Belgian franc, serious wage-price tensions seem unlikely. Wage increases may remain below 3 per cent and consumer-price inflation may stabilise at around 2 per cent. Despite a loss of international competitiveness, the current-account surplus of the BLEU may widen – to 5¾ per cent of GDP. The main uncertainties relate to the saving ratio, which is very high and could fall more than projected, and the impact of recent exchange rate changes on exports and investment, which could be more severe than allowed for in the projections.

DENMARK

The recovery broadened in the course of 1994 to include exports and business investment, having been based principally on private consumption growth in the early stages. Against the background of an improving international outlook and historically high household and business confidence, growth rates are expected to remain above the OECD average over the projection period. With the slack in the labour market likely to be used up in 1996, inflationary pressures could emerge.

Recent developments. Following several years of depressed growth, GDP rose by 4.4 per cent in 1994, the highest growth rate for ten years. The recovery was consumption-led, fiscal reflation being accompanied by a confidence-induced increase in households' spending propensity, but was further boosted in 1994 by increasing fixed investment. Reflecting a declining export market share and strong imports, real net exports declined. The sharp rise in imports during 1994 mainly relates to the purchase of consumer durables, which comprised an unusually large number of passenger cars and other infrequent purchases of products not produced in Denmark.

Business sector employment grew by around 2 per cent in the course of 1994. Although the impact on joblessness was partly offset by a fall in public sector employment, registered unemployment fell from 12.5 per cent in mid-1994 to 10.6 per cent in February 1995, due

DENMARK
Demand, output and prices
Percentage changes, volume (1980 prices)

	1991 current prices billion DKr	1992	1993	1994	1995	1996
Private consumption	430.2	1.1	2.4	7.1	4.2	3.0
Government consumption	211.2	1.4	2.8	0.6	0.7	0.4
Gross fixed capital formation	136.7	–7.2	–2.3	3.6	6.3	5.8
Final domestic demand	778.1	–0.3	1.7	4.8	3.7	2.8
* stockbuilding	–0.7[a]	–0.2	–0.7	0.6	0.2	0.1
Total domestic demand	777.4	–0.5	1.0	5.5	3.9	2.9
Exports of goods and services	306.0	2.7	–2.0	6.9	5.6	5.3
Imports of goods and services	255.6	–0.2	–4.1	10.5	7.2	5.6
* net exports	50.4[a]	1.3	0.6	–0.6	–0.1	0.3
GDP at market prices	827.9	0.8	1.5	4.4	3.4	3.0
GDP implicit price deflator	–	2.0	1.1	1.9	2.4	2.8
Memorandum items						
Private consumption deflator	–	1.9	1.0	1.7	2.5	3.0
Industrial production	–	2.8	–2.6	10.5	5.6	4.5
Unemployment rate	–	11.2	12.2	12.1	10.6	9.7
General government financial balance[b]	–	–2.9	–4.5	–3.9	–2.1	–1.6
Current balance[b]	–	3.4	4.1	3.0	2.9	3.5

* Contributions to changes in real GDP (as a per cent of real GDP in the previous period).
a) Actual amount.
b) As a percentage of GDP.

to the effects of paid-leave schemes,[1] which reduced the labour force by an estimated 2 to 3 per cent in late 1994. Reflecting the continuing slack in the labour market, private sector wage rises remained moderate in 1994 at around 3.3 per cent. Unit labour costs declined, helping to keep headline inflation at around 2.0 per cent in 1994 – the average of the countries participating in the European Exchange Rate Mechanism (ERM).

Policies and other forces acting. The main operational target of Danish monetary policy is to maintain a stable exchange rate within the ERM. Thus, following pressure on the Danish krone at the time of the ERM-realignment in early March 1995, the official discount rate was raised by one percentage point to 6 per cent, and when German administered interest rates were lowered in late March, the Danish monetary authorities chose not to follow suit. Consequently, by early May the short-term interest rate differential *vis-à-vis* Germany stood at around 2.2 percentage points, the long-term differential being slightly lower at 1.5 percentage points. The short-term differential is expected to decline somewhat over the projection period, as turbulence in the foreign exchange markets subsides.

On the basis of announced policies, fiscal policy will be slightly restrictive in 1995 and 1996. Increased taxes and social security contributions stipulated by existing law are estimated to improve the general government budget balance by around 0.3 per cent of GDP in each year. In addition, less generous provisions for paid leave and a shift toward the take-up of active labour market measures which are less expensive to the public purse are projected to intensify the fiscal tightening. In combination with automatic budget stabilisers, this is likely to lead to an improvement in the general government budget of 2½ per cent of GDP between 1994 and 1996.

In February and March 1995 collective bargaining resulted in two-year central wage settlements covering most of the labour market. These settlements are estimated to lead to general wage increases of 3 to 3.5 per cent a year, though ensuing local bargaining rounds and wage drift are likely to add to the final outcome. In addition, employer-financed pension contributions will add around 0.5 percentage points to labour cost growth in each year.

Prospects. The recovery is likely to continue in 1995 and 1996 as private consumption is sustained by a decline in the household saving ratio toward long-term levels and export market growth remains buoyant. Early indicators for 1995 suggest that the acceleration in private investment seems to have continued, and this should gather momentum as capacity limits are approached in parts of the business sector. The resultant GDP growth rates of 3 to 3½ per cent should translate into increasing labour demand, lowering the unemployment rate to around 9½ per cent in 1996. As the slack in the labour market is gradually used up, wage increases are projected to rise, pushing consumer price inflation to 3 per cent at the end of the projection period.

The main risk to the projection relates to the labour market response during the recovery. If the slack in the labour market is smaller than assumed – or if the pick-up in labour demand is more unevenly distributed across occupations or geographic regions than expected – the increase in labour demand could translate into rising inflation earlier in the recovery. A subsidiary risk relates to interest rates and the krone which are vulnerable to financial market perceptions about inflation.

NOTE

1. These schemes, offering one year paid leave-of-absence from the labour market for employed and unemployed persons alike, were introduced with effect from January 1994.

FINLAND

Initially led by exports in the wake of the currency depreciation in the early 1990s, the economic recovery is rapidly spreading to domestic demand – although residential investment remains sluggish. Unemployment, while still very high, has been declining rapidly, giving rise to wage pressure in the exposed sectors of the economy. However, although the growth momentum is expected to continue, inflation is projected to remain subdued for some time, helped by a strengthening of the markka's exchange rate and a fall in food prices consequent on membership of the European Union.

Recent developments. After three years of sharp decline, GDP expanded by 3.9 per cent in 1994. Continuing buoyant exports – spurred by stronger activity in western Europe – remained the principal engine of recovery, but domestic demand also started to recover. At

FINLAND
Demand, output and prices
Percentage changes, volume (1990 prices)

	1991 current prices billion Mk	1992	1993	1994	1995	1996
Private consumption	274.7	–4.9	–3.9	2.0	5.1	4.8
Government consumption	118.7	–2.2	–5.3	–0.4	–1.0	–1.5
Gross fixed capital formation	110.1	–16.9	–18.6	2.8	14.7	13.9
Final domestic demand	503.5	–7.0	–7.3	1.5	5.4	5.2
* stockbuilding	–9.5 [a]	0.7	0.8	2.4	0.5	0
Total domestic demand	494.0	–6.4	–6.5	4.2	5.8	5.0
Exports of goods and services	109.3	10.0	16.7	12.5	6.9	4.0
Imports of goods and services	112.4	1.1	0.7	12.6	10.6	7.4
* net exports	–3.1 [a]	2.1	4.3	0.8	–0.5	–0.7
GDP at market prices	490.9	–3.6	–1.6	3.9	4.8	3.9
GDP implicit price deflator	–	0.7	2.4	2.5	2.5	2.8
Memorandum items						
Private consumption deflator	–	4.1	3.9	1.6	2.1	2.6
Unemployment rate	–	13.1	17.9	18.4	16.4	14.9
General government financial balance [b]	–	–5.8	–7.9	–5.5	–5.0	–3.3
Current balance [b]	–	–4.6	–1.1	1.1	1.8	1.2

* Contributions to changes in real GDP (as a per cent of real GDP in the previous period).
a) Actual amount.
b) As a percentage of GDP.

2 per cent, private consumption growth became positive for the first time since 1989, reflecting heightened confidence of households and the increasing need to replace worn-out consumer durables. Increased profitability, high levels of capacity utilisation and a favourable demand outlook boosted fixed investment in both manufacturing and commercial services. In addition, inventory formation surged as firms replenished stocks in response to accelerating output. By contrast, housing investment remained weak as the rise in long-term interest rates undermined a nascent recovery in the real estate market. Due mainly to the strengthening of domestic demand, but also reflecting advance purchases of some items in anticipation of their becoming more costly under European Union (EU) trade regulations, imports have risen at a double digit rate.

With activity gaining momentum, the unemployment rate fell from a seasonally-adjusted peak of 19.3 per cent in early 1994 to a still very high rate of 17.1 per cent last February. Under these conditions, both wage and price inflation remained low in 1994 (2 per cent and 1.1 per cent respectively) helped by a progressive strengthening of the markka's exchange rate – even though pay settlements late in the year suggest an acceleration of wage growth in tradeable sectors. With the terms of trade improving, the external current account moved into surplus (1 per cent of GDP) for the first time since 1978.

Policies and other forces acting. By April 1995 the markka had appreciated by more than 13 per cent *vis-à-vis* the Deutschemark since its trough in September 1993. As a result, the three-month Helibor, which had risen by some 50 basis points at the end of 1994, has since remained in a range of 6 to 6.1 per cent, or some 100 basis points above equivalent German rates. With uncertainties related to the EU accession removed, long-term interest rates have eased from their peak of 10 per cent in August 1994 to 9 per cent on average in the first four months of 1995, reducing the yield gap against German rates from almost 3 percentage points to around 2 percentage points. Both short and long-term differentials are assumed to remain stable over the projection period, implying some monetary tightening in line with German developments.

Despite an expected further acceleration in economic activity, the general government deficit is projected to fall only marginally in 1995 from its 1994 level of 5½ per cent of GDP. This projection is, however, distorted by a shifting of tax refunds from late 1994 to early 1995, suggesting less fiscal restraint in 1995 than actually occurs (and correspondingly overestimating the fiscal tightening in 1994). Moreover, additional expenditure in 1995 related to the EU accession – in particular to support farmers against the reduction in agricultural prices – should be temporary. Indeed, fiscal policy continues to be driven by government commitments to cut real spending (excluding EU effects) to its 1991 level by 1995 and to break the debt spiral before the end of the present decade. Assuming a normal timing of tax refunds, the general government budget balance should thus improve substantially in 1996; most recent official projections suggest that the latter may turn into a surplus of $\frac{1}{2}$ per cent of GDP, reflecting additional expenditure savings announced by the new government that took office in April 1995.

Prospects. Economic expansion is expected to become more balanced across sectors as the recovery matures, with household spending and business investment taking over from net exports as the main contributors to growth. GDP is projected to increase by $4\frac{1}{2}$ to 5 per cent in 1995 and by almost 4 per cent next year. Manufacturing industries, now starting to recruit on a large scale, should help attain overall rates of employment growth of the order of 2 to 3 per cent per annum, and the unemployment rate could fall to 14 per cent by the end of 1996. Bottlenecks in the labour market may emerge, triggering some wage pressures next year. While export growth should taper off, due mainly to capacity constraints, imports may be boosted by the pickup of private demand. As a result, projected further increases in the current account surplus will be driven mainly by terms-of-trade improvements and reduced foreign debt service. Helped by the appreciation of the markka and a fall in food prices consequent on EU membership, price inflation may remain subdued in 1995, while increasing next year.

A major uncertainty to these projections concerns the development of wages, which may prove stronger than expected if pressures building up in tradeable sectors where employment conditions are tight spill over into wages in the rest of the economy. Such an outcome could provoke an overheating in the course of 1996 – with the current account shifting back into deficit, and inflation rising.

GREECE

The economy has recovered steadily since late 1993, but at rates well below those of previous recoveries, reflecting structural distortions and macroeconomic imbalances. More stringent fiscal and monetary policies have boosted confidence and output growth is projected to accelerate as the recovery becomes more broadly based. Further progress should occur with respect to both disinflation and fiscal consolidation, but consumer price increases could still be of the order of 7 per cent in 1996 and the budget deficit close to 10 per cent of GDP.

Recent developments. GDP growth picked up to 1.5 per cent in 1994, supported primarily by exports and public investment, the latter partly financed by the European Community. The growth in equipment expenditure was brisk but it was broadly offset by a fall in housing investment. Consumer price inflation, after a marked fall to 11 per cent in early 1994, remained in the region of 10 to $10\frac{1}{2}$ per cent until early 1995. The current balance of payments deficit fell to less than $\frac{1}{2}$ per cent of GDP in 1994, due to an increase in service receipts, mainly from tourism. Moreover, sizeable capital inflows in the second half of 1994 and early 1995 made for a steep rise in official foreign exchange reserves, to the record level of $16.5 billion in March 1995.

Policies and other forces acting. Monetary settings were tightened in May 1994 following the speculative attack against the drachma, and interest rates returned to their pre-crisis levels only in November. Rates were further lowered in late 1994 and early 1995, with the 12-month Treasury bill rate falling to 16.5 per cent in May. The large interest rate differential with foreign markets resulted in corporations relying increasingly on foreign borrowing, while the rate of domestic credit expansion to the private sector decelerated to around $11\frac{1}{2}$ per cent in 1994, slightly below that of nominal GDP. The rate of growth of the broad money supply (M3) decelerated sharply to 8.1 per cent, almost at the lower limit of the target range, but this is in part attributable to large-scale portfolio adjustments. The target set for 1995 – M3 growth of 7 to 9 per cent – and the authorities' declared intention to bring the annual pace of depreciation of the drachma down to 3 per cent vis-à-vis the ECU imply restrictive monetary conditions over the projection period.

The Convergence Programme 1994-99 aims at broadly eliminating the budget deficit by the end of the period and bringing inflation down to European levels. Underpinning this Programme is a set of tax measures introduced in the first half of 1994 that are expected to broaden the tax base by curbing tax evasion. While the complete impact of these measures should be felt only as of 1995, the increase in tax receipts accelerated markedly in the second half of 1994, and the budget deficit target for the year was met, making for a general government deficit around 12.5 per cent of GDP. The 1995 Budget is based on a sharp increase in tax receipts. On the expenditure side, the authorities have announced relatively strict norms with respect to public sector wage increases – 3 per cent in January and July – as well as a stabilisation of staffing levels; but because of a carry-over from

GREECE
Demand, output and prices

Percentage changes, volume (1988 prices)

	1991 current prices billion Dr	1992	1993	1994	1995	1996
Private consumption	11 583.0	1.8	0.2	1.5	1.5	1.9
Government consumption	2 248.1	–3.0	0.3	0.2	0	0.6
Gross fixed capital formation[a]	3 359.3	–1.1	–2.5	0.7	6.4	7.2
Final domestic demand	17 190.4	0.6	–0.3	1.2	2.3	2.9
* stockbuilding	492.8[b]	–0.8	0.8	–0.1	0	0
Total domestic demand	17 683.2	–0.2	0.4	1.0	2.2	2.8
Exports of goods and services	2 726.0	8.5	–1.0	7.3	6.4	6.6
Imports of goods and services	4 561.0	2.3	2.3	3.8	5.9	6.5
* net exports	–1 835.0[b]	1.0	–1.0	0.3	–0.6	–0.8
GDP at market prices	15 848.2	0.8	–0.5	1.5	1.9	2.3
GDP implicit price deflator	–	14.1	13.5	10.9	9.5	7.0
Memorandum items						
Private consumption deflator	–	15.0	13.6	10.8	9.2	7.0
Industrial production	–	–1.5	–1.9	0.6	1.7	2.8
Unemployment rate	–	8.7	9.7	9.6	9.9	9.9
General government financial balance[c]	–	–12.3	–13.2	–12.5	–11.4	–10.0
Current balance[c]	–	–2.2	–0.8	–0.1	–1.0	–1.3

* Contributions to changes in real GDP (as a per cent of real GDP in the previous period).
a) Excluding ships operating overseas.
b) Actual amount.
c) As a percentage of GDP.

last year and seniority effects the government wage bill is nevertheless set to increase by 10 per cent. The primary surplus is expected to rise to 3 per cent of GDP in 1995. Despite a slightly rising public debt, interest payments as a percentage of GDP are projected to be broadly stabilised, reflecting a fall in interest rates. In total, the general government deficit should fall to less than 11½ per cent of GDP in 1995, and to 10 per cent of GDP in 1996, with the structural deficit estimated to fall by some 2 per cent of GDP over the two-year period. The official estimates are for a smaller deficit than projected by the OECD Secretariat, in line with lower interest rates over the period.

Prospects. Stabilisation policies should limit household disposable income and as a result private consumption is expected to remain flat in real terms in 1995, gathering speed only in 1996. Nevertheless, economic recovery may gather momentum already in the course of 1995 because of a forecast acceleration in public investment growth this year and next. Output growth could rise to around 2.3 per cent in 1996. Reflecting a more active incomes policy and moderating import prices consumer price inflation is forecast to decelerate to around 9¼ per cent in 1995 and to 7 per cent in 1996. Despite the cyclical upswing, the unemployment rate is likely to rise further, reaching 10 per cent in 1995 mainly due to the restructuring of ailing firms, but also reflecting the freeze on public sector employment – and stabilise at this level in 1996. Growing domestic demand should make for an increase in the current deficit, but it is likely to continue to be more than covered by long-term capital inflows, mainly from Greeks living abroad. The major downside risk to the projections relates to fiscal policy. Any significant slippage, on either tax receipts or expenditures, could destabilise market sentiment and thereby have a strong negative impact on growth.

Strong export growth fuelled a 3 per cent rise in real GDP in 1994. The strengthening of the economy brought about a stabilisation of the unemployment rate at around 4¾ per cent. With economic slack and a stable exchange rate, consumer prices rose only 1½ per cent in 1994, but the recent wage agreement may push that up to around 2¼ per cent this year and 2¾ per cent in 1996. Export growth is expected to moderate in 1995 owing to tightening restrictions on cod fishing, but rising domestic demand should replace the impetus provided by the export sector last year.

Recent developments. The economic recovery firmed in 1994, led by improvements in external trade. Export volumes of goods and services rose 10 per cent with gains in nearly all sectors (especially manufacturing), propelled by increased sales of marine products, rising world demand and an improvement in Iceland's competitive position. The improving economic climate was increasingly reflected in final domestic demand, which registered a 1 per cent gain following two years of sharp declines. While imports also picked up, the trade account posted a surplus of 4¾ per cent of GDP, its largest in modern history, and the current account registered its first significant surplus since 1986. The pick-up in activity was sufficient to stem the deterioration of the labour market. The unemployment rate appears to have peaked during 1994, and thus far in 1995 it has been near 1994 average levels. Nominal wages inched up by a mere 1 per cent while the consumer price index rose 1½ per cent, but in February 1995 a major accord was struck with the unions representing most of the private non-banking sector, calling for a 7 per cent average increase in base wages over two years.

Policies and other forces acting. The fishing sector continues to be constrained by falling cod quotas, reflecting shrinking fishable stocks. In recent years, this has been largely offset by shifting efforts to other species and to international waters, but this may become increasingly difficult. Fiscal policy was about neutral in 1994, and the deficit declined with the recovery. The 1995 budget, as passed in December, called for only limited further progress on deficit reduction. Although deficit-increasing measures were taken as part of the wage accords, the former government stated its intent to make future adjustments to offset the budgetary impact. Short-term interest rates drifted up slowly through most of the second half of 1994 and have risen sharply since the turn of the year. The authorities were successful at holding rates down at the long end of the maturity spectrum, although at a cost. Given the Treasury's 5 per cent interest rate ceiling for indexed bonds introduced in autumn 1993, bids were rejected for new issues as of the autumn of 1994, and the Treasury switched to ECU-linked bonds and increased borrowing abroad over this period. The new government, formed in April, moved quickly to remove the aforementioned interest rate ceiling, and rates rose to some 5¾ per

ICELAND
Demand, output and prices
Percentage changes, volume (1990 prices)

	1991 current prices billion IKr	1992	1993	1994	1995	1996
Private consumption	236.3	–4.4	–4.5	1.7	3.8	3.0
Government consumption	76.9	–0.8	2.2	1.4	2.0	2.0
Gross fixed capital formation	72.7	–11.1	–11.4	–1.1	5.3	5.8
Final domestic demand	385.9	–5.0	–4.4	1.2	3.6	3.2
* stockbuilding	1.2 [a]	–0.3	0.2	–0.3	0.1	0
Total domestic demand	387.1	–5.3	–4.2	0.9	3.8	3.2
Exports of goods and services	127.2	–1.6	6.4	10.2	2.4	2.7
Imports of goods and services	130.3	–7.8	–9.6	4.7	6.5	5.5
* net exports	–3.1 [a]	2.2	5.4	2.2	–1.0	–0.7
GDP at market prices	384.1	–3.2	1.2	3.0	2.5	2.4
GDP implicit price deflator	–	3.2	2.2	2.3	3.5	2.9
Memorandum items						
Private consumption deflator	–	4.9	4.9	1.7	2.3	2.7
Unemployment rate	–	3.0	4.3	4.7	4.5	4.4
Current balance [b]	–	–3.1	0	2.2	2.4	2.0

* Contributions to changes in real GDP (as a per cent of real GDP in the previous period).
a) Actual amount.
b) As a percentage of GDP.

cent, but it has thus far not announced any major changes in budgetary policy for this year.

Prospects. The economy is projected to expand at a moderate pace, with increases in real GDP averaging 2½ per cent over the next two years. The surge in exports may ease owing to meagre near-term prospects in the fishing sector, but domestic demand expected to take the lead, and, as a result, the contribution from the foreign balance should turn negative. However, the current account is projected to remain in surplus. The pick-up in activity may be rapid enough to lead to a small reduction in the unemployment rate. Rising wage costs, resulting from the recent wage agreements, may lead to an acceleration of consumer price inflation to 2¾ per cent in 1996. If any of the major investment projects that have been proposed go forward, then investment, imports and real GDP would probably be stronger than projected; this would lower the current-account surplus and unemployment, and would put further upward pressure on the inflation rate.

IRELAND

Ireland was the fastest-growing economy in the OECD area in 1994. The broadly-based expansion resulted in significant job gains and a decline in the unemployment rate. With a central pay agreement limiting wage increases, inflation remained subdued in 1994. GDP growth is likely to stay near 6 per cent in 1995, slowing to 5 per cent in 1996. This should lead to further progress in reducing the public debt ratio. The continuing decline in the number of jobless might, however, result in some upward pressure on wage rates and domestic prices.

Recent trends. The economic expansion, which was led by exports from the modern sector in 1993, accelerated in 1994 as the recovery in domestic demand gained momentum during the year: GDP growth reached 6 per cent, though GNP growth was ½ of a percentage point lower due to factor income outflows. As a result, employment growth picked up sharply, reducing the unemployment rate to 14½ per cent in early 1995. Buoyant domestic demand was led by increased housing investment and consumer expenditure, resulting in an unwinding of the rise in the saving rate which had

IRELAND
Demand, output and prices
Percentage changes, volume (1985 prices)

	1991 current prices million Ir£	1992	1993	1994	1995	1996
Private consumption	16 607	2.9	1.2	5.0	5.7	4.8
Government consumption	4 480	2.4	1.1	2.5	3.0	3.0
Gross fixed capital formation	4 642	–1.9	–0.4	7.2	8.5	7.0
Final domestic demand	25 730	2.0	0.9	4.9	5.8	4.9
* stockbuilding	639[a]	–2.8	–0.5	–1.2	–0.2	0.1
Total domestic demand	26 369	–1.2	0.3	3.5	5.7	5.1
Exports of goods and services	16 893	13.2	9.6	10.5	8.6	6.8
Imports of goods and services	15 072	5.4	5.9	8.5	9.3	7.5
* net exports	1 821[a]	6.1	3.8	3.1	1.3	0.9
GDP at market prices	28 189	5.0	4.1	6.0	5.8	5.0
GDP implicit price deflator	–	1.3	3.6	1.7	2.5	3.0
Memorandum items						
Private consumption deflator	–	2.8	1.6	2.4	2.6	3.0
Industrial production	–	9.2	5.6	11.9	12.8	10.0
Unemployment rate	–	15.5	15.8	14.8	13.9	13.6
Household saving ratio[b]	–	11.8	14.2	13.0	12.1	11.2
General government financial balance[c]	–	–2.2	–2.3	–2.2	–2.5	–2.4
Current balance[c]	–	4.8	7.7	6.9	6.6	6.1

* Contributions to changes in real GDP (as a per cent of real GDP in the previous period).
a) Actual amount.
b) As a percentage of disposable income.
c) As a percentage of GDP.

occurred in 1993. As the expansion became more established and broad-based, business investment increased for the first time since 1990. Inflation remained stable at 2½ per cent at the beginning of 1995, aided by the new central wage agreement which took effect at the beginning of the year as well as a gradual appreciation of the Irish pound in effective terms. Although strong domestic demand resulted in a surge of imports, the current-account surplus remained large at about 7 per cent of GDP, as export growth accelerated further in 1994.

Policies and other forces acting. Following the decline in short-term interest rates in 1994, monetary conditions were tightened at the beginning of 1995. The central bank raised its lending rate by 1 percentage point in March in response to the generalised weakness of European currencies against the Deutschemark and the potential inflationary pressures reflected in the acceleration of bank credit growth to 11 per cent at the end of 1994. Long-term rates also increased early in 1995, reflecting concerns over the exchange rate and the pickup in activity and credit demand, boosting the differential with German bond yields to more than 1½ percentage points.

Despite the buoyant state of the economy, the 1995 Budget envisages some increase in the general government deficit as income taxes on low-paid workers and their employers' payroll contributions were reduced. Such measures were aimed at improving incentives to work but, together with increases in spending, they mean that nearly all of the cyclical gain in tax revenues will be spent on permanent programme changes. Public expenditures were further increased by an amount equivalent to about ½ a per cent of GDP in response to a court ruling requiring compensation for past unequal treatment of women under the pension system. As a result, the structural budget deficit is expected to widen this year, but the government decision to limit the growth of nominal expenditure to 2 per cent above inflation in 1996 should help stabilise it subsequently. The actual deficit is projected to remain well below 3 per cent of GDP, allowing a further decline in the government debt ratio to about 80 per cent of GDP by the end of 1996 from 90 per cent at the end of 1994.

Prospects. The growth of GDP is projected to continue to be strong: 5¾ per cent in 1995 and 5 per cent in 1996. Personal consumption is likely to be sustained by tax reductions that boost real disposable income and continued employment growth, which should improve consumer sentiment and further reduce the saving ratio. The compensation payments required by the court ruling, which will continue during 1996, will also support personal consumption. Although higher interest rates may slow housing construction, business investment in structures and buildings should increase. Rapid import growth may reduce the current-account surplus to about 6 per cent of GDP in 1996. Continued employment gains, combined with a further improvement in the UK labour market that may encourage the emigration of Irish workers, could lower the unemployment rate to below 14 per cent.

The major risk to this favourable outlook is a rise in inflationary pressure. Although inflation is currently under control, the continuing decline in the number of jobless might put upward pressure on wage rates, and consequently on domestic prices. While such pressure could be alleviated by Irish workers returning from elsewhere in Europe, the pro-cyclical stance of fiscal policy will add further to strains on resources.

LUXEMBOURG

The economy is expanding at a rapid pace, with domestic demand progressively replacing exports as the driving force. Real GDP is projected to grow at around 3 per cent in 1995-96. Despite a strong increase in employment, the unemployment rate – which is very low by international standards – may decline only slowly, as most new jobs are likely to be filled by cross-border workers. Consumer-price inflation may remain subdued. The general government budget, which in 1994 was in surplus of around 2 per cent of GDP, should not change substantially.

Recent developments. The economy has recovered rapidly from the shallow downturn of 1992-93, in line with developments in surrounding countries. The upturn has been driven by a surge in exports which has boosted most sectors of the economy. Specific areas of strength have included banking and telecommunications. However, as the recovery in Europe has been strongly led by inventory accumulation and exports, it has generated little demand for the heavy steel products used almost solely for construction which are Luxembourg's area of specialisation. Hence, the steel sector is barely emerging from its severe recession. Despite the good growth performance and sustained job creation, the unemployment rate, while remaining very low by international standards, rose further in 1994 – to 2¾ per cent – as the inflow of cross-border workers continued to increase rapidly. Unit

LUXEMBOURG
Demand, output and prices
Percentage changes, volume (1990 prices)

	1991 current prices billion LF	1992	1993	1994	1995	1996
Private consumption	182.6	1.7	–0.9	2.1	3.0	3.1
Government consumption	54.4	3.5	1.8	1.2	2.0	1.9
Gross fixed capital formation	92.4	–2.1	9.9	1.7	2.5	4.2
Final domestic demand	329.4	0.9	2.5	1.8	2.7	3.2
* stockbuilding	7.7[a]	–0.2	–1.0	0.2	0	0
Total domestic demand	337.1	0.7	1.4	2.0	2.7	3.1
Exports of goods and services	300.6	1.3	–2.4	4.6	4.4	3.9
Imports of goods and services	318.9	0.2	–2.5	3.8	4.0	4.1
* net exports	–18.3[a]	1.1	0.2	0.6	0.3	–0.2
GDP at market prices	318.8	1.9	1.7	2.7	3.1	2.9
GDP implicit price deflator	–	4.5	4.7	4.0	3.0	2.7
Memorandum items						
Private consumption deflator	–	2.8	3.7	2.4	1.9	2.0
Industrial production	–	–0.9	–3.2	6.4	5.6	3.9
Unemployment rate	–	1.6	2.1	2.7	2.5	2.3

* Contributions to changes in real GDP (as a per cent of real GDP in the previous period).
a) Actual amount.

labour costs, which had increased markedly in the early 1990s and threatened the international competitive position of firms, seem to have declined in 1994 as a result of wage moderation, strong productivity gains, and cuts in employers' social security contributions. Consumer-price inflation has progressively abated, to 2.2 per cent over the 12 months to April.

Policies and other forces acting. Given the decline in unit labour costs in 1994, the recent appreciation of the Luxembourg franc in effective terms should not significantly affect the international competitiveness of the economy and its export performance. The overall position of public finance has remained quite favourable over the past few years, and compares extremely well with that of other European countries. Owing to strong tax receipts from the financial sector, the central government surplus widened to around ½ per cent of GDP in 1994, despite an important public investment programme in infrastructure and high current expenditure growth. Combined with a larger surplus of the social security system, it resulted in an overall general government surplus of nearly 2 per cent of GDP. The public debt represents less than 6 per cent of GDP and on a net basis it may be much smaller or negative. On the basis of the 1995 Budget presented in the summer of 1994, the OECD Secretariat does not expect major changes in Luxembourg's fiscal position in 1995 and 1996.

Prospects. Real GDP growth is projected to accelerate to around 3 per cent in 1995-96. Reflecting developments in neighbouring countries, exports are expected to remain buoyant, but domestic demand should progressively take the lead, and the contribution of the foreign balance to growth is projected to turn slightly negative in 1996. Investment is likely to pick up owing to high rates of capacity utilisation, a better economic climate, and persistent shortages in the housing market. Public investment is expected to rebound strongly, reflecting the start of important new projects in the rail sector. The growth of private consumption may pick up in line with personal income. The steel sector should continue to recover but the banking sector may enter a period of consolidation. The growth of employment is projected to continue at a rapid pace, but the unemployment rate is expected to decline only slowly – to 2¼ per cent in 1996 – as most new jobs may again be filled by cross-border workers. Consumer-price inflation may average around 2 per cent. These projections are highly dependent on the economic situation in neighbouring countries and the growth in export markets.

December 1994 saw a run on the Mexican peso, reflecting investors' worries about the rising current account deficit and political instability. A tightening of policies was announced in January 1995, and was reinforced in March. Recession is likely this year, as a steep decline in domestic demand more than offsets a sharp increase in net exports. The stabilisation programme, a package of international financial support and the new administration's renewed commitment to market opening are set to reassure foreign exchange and financial markets. Some stability seems to have been restored in the markets since late March. Provided that interest rates ease further over the coming months, activity should rebound in 1996, led by exports and private investment. Inflation, which has surged at the start of 1995 under the immediate impact of the depreciation, is expected to decline subsequently. The current account is likely to swing from a substantial deficit last year to near balance.

Recent developments. Economic activity recovered in 1994, with a strong contribution from all components of domestic demand, both public and private, and steadily-rising exports. Due to the appreciation in real terms of the peso and lower tariffs after the entry into force of the North American Free Trade Agreement (NAFTA), import growth was buoyant. While industrial production rose at a sustained pace, productivity enhancement resulted in labour shedding, and the open unemployment rate remained above the level prevailing in the early-1990s. Inflation stayed on a down-trend throughout the year, reaching 7 per cent for the 12 months to December 1994, a 20-year low. But the current-account deficit widened to almost 8 per cent of GDP, while the size of portfolio investment inflows created a situation of vulnerability to changes in financial market perceptions.

Investors' worries about political stability in Mexico intensified in December with the worsening of the situation in Chiapas, triggering a new wave of capital outflows. On 20 December, the new government enlarged the fluctuation band of the peso, allowing a 15 per cent devaluation; and two days later, under intensified pressure against the currency, the peso was floated. The announcement of a stabilisation package at the start of January did not suffice to restore confidence. By March the peso had fallen by 50 per cent against the dollar relative to its pre-crisis level, while nominal interest rates hovered around 80 per cent, and the stabilisation plan was reinforced. Recent indicators suggest that the stabilisation measures and the depreciation are producing their expected effects. Consumer price inflation has risen sharply, with the 12-month rise reaching 29 per cent in April,[1] and a downturn in activity seems to be in train as witnessed by a rise in open unemployment and falling imports. Exports have grown rapidly, and in the first

MEXICO
Demand, output and prices
Percentage changes, volume (1980 prices)

	1991 current prices billion NP	1992	1993	1994	1995	1996
Private consumption	621.2	3.9	0.2	3.7	–7.5	1.0
Government consumption	78.0	2.3	2.0	2.5	–9.5	–1.0
Gross fixed capital formation	168.5	7.0	–0.1	8.1	–20.8	5.1
Final domestic demand	867.7	4.4	0.3	4.5	–10.6	1.6
* stockbuilding	25.3[a]	0.7	–0.4	0	–0.8	0.3
Total domestic demand	893.0	5.1	–0.1	4.5	–11.3	1.9
Exports of goods and services	119.5	1.7	3.7	7.3	18.0	11.0
Imports of goods and services	147.4	20.9	–1.3	12.9	–25.0	9.0
* net exports	–27.8[a]	–2.8	0.9	–0.9	8.3	1.3
GDP at market prices	865.2	2.1	0.8	3.5	–2.9	3.0
GDP implicit price deflator	–	14.6	10.0	7.5	28.0	24.0
Memorandum items						
Private consumption deflator	–	14.0	9.3	6.6	35.0	27.0
Unemployment rate[b]	–	2.9	3.5	3.7	5.2	5.2
Current balance[c]	–	–7.6	–6.5	–7.8	–1.5	–0.7

* Contributions to changes in real GDP (as a per cent of real GDP in the previous period).
a) Actual amount.
b) Based on the National Survey of Urban Employment.
c) As a percentage of GDP.

quarter the trade account was slightly positive, compared with a US$4.3 billion deficit during the same period a year earlier (including net exports of in-bond industries). By mid-May, the peso had recovered by 20 per cent from its trough, and short-term interest rates were down to 55 per cent.

Policies and other forces acting. The financial balance of the public sector went from a surplus in 1993 to a small deficit in 1994, an election year, while public development banks markedly increased their loan portfolio. Against the background of rising interest rates in the United States and of repeated attacks on the peso during the year (in particular following the assassination in March of the leading candidate to the elections), the Mexican authorities pursued three lines of action: interest rates rose rapidly with the 3-month Treasury bill or Cetes rate in real terms climbing from a historical low of 2 per cent at end-February 1994 to 10 per cent in April 1994; the peso was allowed to fall to its lower limit within its band; and dollar-indexed government securities (Tesobonos) were issued to replace Cetes. But these measures turned out to be insufficient to defend the exchange rate.

The Economic Emergency Programme announced in January 1995, following the collapse of confidence in the peso, provided for a cut in public expenditure equivalent to 1.3 per cent of GDP and a tightening of monetary policy. To support macroeconomic stabilisation while preserving public expenditure for social and regional development to the maximum extent possible, a further wave of state retrenchment from economic activity, including the privatisation of ports and railways and the partial opening up of the electricity sector, was also announced. Rising concerns – not only about Mexico, but also that the Mexican crisis could trigger a run on other emerging markets – prompted the international financial community to arrange a rescue package in January.

In early March, the January stabilisation package was further strengthened in response to continuing volatility in both foreign exchange and domestic financial markets. The basic value-added tax (VAT) rate was increased from 10 to 15 per cent, gasoline and electricity prices were raised and further cuts in government spending were announced. Various measures have nonetheless been taken to cushion the impact of the adjustment for the poorer segments of the population. Taken together, these fiscal measures are estimated to yield a primary surplus of 4.4 per cent of GDP, up from 2.6 per cent in 1994. On the monetary side, the tight limit on the growth of central bank net domestic credit, adopted in January, was reaffirmed. The floating exchange rate regime was maintained. Development banks' lending to the private sector will be limited. The minimum wage was increased by 10 per cent on 1 April (in addition to the 7 per cent rise in January), while economy-wide wages will be freely negotiated between employers and employees.

Prospects. GDP may fall by about 3 per cent in 1995, as all components of domestic demand drop. The decline in output will be reflected in deteriorating labour market conditions, with employment in the formal sector of the economy as well as real wages falling significantly. As informal activities expand, however, resilience of non-wage incomes will cushion the impact on private consumption. Private investment by Mexican firms may drop sharply in 1995 as a result of high interest rates and the uncertain business climate; but continued export growth is likely to induce a recovery in investment, to the extent that foreign direct investment flows back in large amounts to take advantage of lower prices and costs.[2] The rise in Mexican external competitiveness after the peso depreciation and the sharp reduction in domestic absorption should help the current account to reach near-balance in 1995.

This outlook crucially hinges on two conditions: first that investors' confidence strengthens so that stability in financial and foreign exchange markets allows interest rates to come down further over the coming months; second that the slack in the economy continues to restrain wage adjustments, as seems to have been the case in the first months of the year, so that real depreciation is preserved. Under these conditions, the current crisis (with the adjustment to policies it has entailed, both on the macroeconomic and structural front) may be followed by a more sustainable development path.

NOTES

1. This partly reflects the value-added tax rate increase (from 10 to 15 per cent) and rises in public energy prices (petrol by 35 per cent, electricity by 20 per cent).
2. Foreign direct investment amounted to close to $8 billion in 1994, compared to $4.9 billion for 1993 (and $4.4 billion in 1992).

The economic recovery was initially export-led but investment is now taking the lead and consumption is expected to follow. After accelerating to a little over 3 per cent in 1995, real GDP growth is projected to slow to 2¾ per cent in 1996. Unemployment may decline only slowly, in part because of a fast growing labour force. Inflation is likely to remain subdued owing to wage moderation, the strength of the guilder and tax relief for business, which will reduce labour costs. The budget deficit is projected to fall below 3 per cent of GDP in 1996.

Recent developments. After a shallow downturn in 1993, economic activity rebounded strongly in 1994 and the upturn seems to be continuing at a rapid pace in 1995. The recovery was initially export-led, but more recently investment has strengthened, reflecting rising capacity utilisation and better profitability. The improvement in the business confidence index and surveys showing a planned increase in investment in manufacturing of 20 per cent in 1995 point to continued strength in this area. Private consumption has also picked up, as improved consumer confidence and a better economic outlook have progressively outweighed the dampening effects of wage moderation. The saving ratio has fallen to an exceptionally low level. Employment has responded slowly to the economic recovery, especially in the manufacturing sector where labour productivity increased by more than 7 per cent in 1994. In February 1995, the unemployment rate, at 7.4 per cent, was still close to its peak of early 1994. Producer prices have increased substantially, as prices for raw materials have risen and strong export demand has enabled exporters to widen their margins. Nonetheless, partly as a result of moderate import prices and the dampening effect of still hesitant retail sales, consumer-price inflation has edged down, to 2.3 per cent over the 12 months to April.

Policies and other forces acting. The recent appreciation of the guilder in effective terms may weigh on the export competitiveness of Dutch firms, but past experience has shown that this impact is likely to be mitigated by wage moderation, tax reductions and a good profit situation allowing export prices to fall. Moreover, thanks to the credibility of the hard currency policy, Dutch interest rates remained very close to German rates during the period of renewed tensions in the European Exchange Rate Mechanism in early 1995, and are among the lowest in Europe. Money market rates are projected to edge up in tandem with German rates as the economic recovery matures, but long term interest rates are not expected to change markedly from current levels.

NETHERLANDS
Demand, output and prices
Percentage changes, volume (1990 prices)

	1991 current prices billion Gld	1992	1993	1994	1995	1996
Private consumption	322.5	2.5	0.7	1.7	1.9	2.3
Government consumption	78.2	1.3	0.1	1.0	1.7	0.7
Gross fixed capital formation	110.5	1.1	−2.2	2.7	6.9	3.8
Final domestic demand	511.2	2.0	0	1.8	2.9	2.4
* stockbuilding	5.4[a]	−0.8	−0.5	0.7	0.3	0.3
Total domestic demand	516.5	1.2	−0.5	2.5	3.2	2.7
Exports of goods and services	293.1	2.8	1.7	5.1	5.3	4.7
Imports of goods and services	267.4	2.7	0.2	5.3	5.6	4.9
* net exports	25.7[a]	0.1	0.9	0.2	0.2	0.1
GDP at market prices	542.2	1.3	0.4	2.5	3.1	2.7
GDP implicit price deflator	–	2.6	1.6	1.9	1.8	1.8
Memorandum items						
Private consumption deflator	–	3.0	2.1	2.2	1.7	1.8
Industrial production	–	−0.7	−2.5	3.9	3.5	3.0
Unemployment rate	–	5.4	6.5	7.5	7.5	7.4
Household saving ratio[b]	–	1.9	0.7	0.4	1.2	0.8
General government financial balance[c]	–	−3.8	−3.2	−3.0	−3.3	−2.7
Current balance	–	2.1	3.1	3.9	3.8	3.7

* Contributions to changes in real GDP (as a per cent of real GDP in the previous period).
a) Actual amount.
b) As a percentage of disposable income, excluding mandatory saving through occupational pension schemes.
c) As a percentage of GDP.

In the fiscal area, the Government's medium term strategy aims to reduce the government deficit below 3 per cent of GDP in 1996, to meet the Maastricht criteria. This goal was almost achieved in 1994, and the policy focus is now shifting towards a reduction in the burden of taxes and social security contributions. This shift is partly inspired by the high level of unemployment and the belief that reducing taxes, notably the wedge between net salaries and wage costs, might be the most efficient way to improve labour market conditions. Accordingly, the Government is restraining public expenditure growth to create room for both tax cuts and reductions of the budget deficit. Taxes are to be cut by 1.5 per cent of GDP over the years 1995-98, of which ¾ per cent in 1995. Social benefits are frozen in 1995 but will be fully linked to wage developments in 1996. On this basis, and owing to the strength of the economy, the OECD Secretariat projects the general government deficit to decline to 2¾ per cent of GDP in 1996. The structural deficit may edge down to an estimated 1¾ per cent, from a little over 2 per cent this year.

Prospects. GDP growth is projected to accelerate to a little over 3 per cent in 1995, and then to slow to around 2¾ per cent in 1996, reflecting a less vigorous domestic demand and less buoyant exports. Business investment is expected to decelerate in 1996 after the sharp rebound in 1995, mainly due to lower investment in the energy sector. Fiscal consolidation will constrain government consumption and investment while the abolition of housing subsidies will have a negative impact on investment in dwellings. On the other hand, private consumption may strengthen in 1996, as the restraining effects of wage moderation will be progressively outweighed by tax cuts and growing employment. For the reasons noted above, the effects of the appreciation of the guilder on exports are likely to be limited, and as imports will be restrained by the deceleration in the growth of domestic demand, the net contribution to growth of the external balance may remain slightly positive. Despite strong job creation, unemployment may decline only slowly, as the labour force is projected to continue to grow at a rapid pace and the re-examination of persons in the disability scheme is likely to result in a shift of beneficiaries from this scheme to the unemployment scheme. Inflation pressures may remain subdued owing to wage moderation, the strength of the guilder and tax relief for enterprises which will limit labour costs. The major risk to the projections is that, with real GDP approaching potential, wage moderation might give way to a period of catching up.

NEW ZEALAND

The coming year will provide a stern test of the monetary policy framework put in place by the Reserve Bank Act and enshrined in inflation targets. Investment-led GDP growth of over 6 per cent throughout much of 1994 has been accompanied by a rise in "headline" inflation which reached 4 per cent in the first quarter of 1995. With short-term interest rates already high, the key question is whether "underlying" inflation (which excludes *inter alia* direct interest-rate effects) can be kept to the 0 to 2 target range without risking a "hard-landing" in 1996. The OECD Secretariat projections imply that a continuation of tight monetary conditions throughout 1995 will slow the economy to a more sustainable rate of growth of 3 per cent by 1996 and that, while some temporary breach is possible, underlying inflation should return to the target range by 1996.

Recent trends. The growth of real GDP in 1994 was over 6 per cent according to the preferred output measure,[1] following a 5 per cent increase in 1993. The largest contribution continues to come from fixed investment, as it has since the start of the upturn in 1991, with business investment growing by one quarter for the second year in a row. Increased private consumption, associated with rising employment, and stronger exports, based on a recovery in New Zealand's main trading partners, also made important contributions to growth in 1994. However, leading indicators point to a slowdown in activity more recently, led by weakening housing investment.

Strong output growth has been reflected in the labour market, with employment up nearly 5 per cent in the first quarter of 1995 compared with a year earlier. A recovery in labour-force participation and continued expansion in the working-age population has limited the impact of job creation on the unemployment rate, which has nevertheless fallen to 6.6 per cent from 9.1 per cent a year earlier. While a tighter labour market has led to some pick-up in nominal wages, the increase in private sector labour costs was only slightly positive in real terms in the course of 1994.

Although structural reforms have enhanced the economy's growth potential, there are signs of increased pressure on productive capacity. Despite the high levels of investment, measures of capacity utilisation based on

NEW ZEALAND
Demand, output and prices
Percentage changes, volume (1982/83 prices)

	1991 current prices million NZ$	1992	1993	1994	1995	1996
Private consumption	45 626	0.2	2.2	5.4	3.9	2.6
Government consumption	12 524	1.3	–2.6	–1.0	1.0	0.5
Gross fixed capital formation	11 820	4.1	16.5	21.0	11.7	6.5
Final domestic demand	69 970	1.2	4.7	8.5	5.8	3.5
* stockbuilding[a]	–26[b]	2.3	1.8	–0.4	0.3	–0.2
Total domestic demand	69 944	3.5	6.4	7.9	5.9	3.2
Exports of goods and services	21 194	2.1	6.1	8.7	7.1	6.9
Imports of goods and services	18 824	8.8	9.0	17.6	11.0	6.2
* net exports	2 370[b]	–2.8	–1.5	–4.5	–2.7	–0.4
GDP (expenditure) at market prices	72 314	0.8	5.1	3.8	3.8	3.1
GDP implicit price deflator	–	2.0	1.6	2.0	3.3	2.0
Memorandum items						
GDP (production)[c]	–	2.4	4.9	6.3	3.8	3.1
Private consumption deflator	–	1.7	1.0	0.5	2.9	2.0
Unemployment rate	–	10.3	9.5	8.1	7.2	7.0
Current balance[d]	–	–1.7	–2.1	–2.1	–2.1	–1.7

* Contributions to changes in real GDP (as a per cent of real GDP in the previous period).
a) Including statistical discrepancy.
b) Actual amount.
c) Considered as a more reliable indicator of total economic activity by the New Zealand Department of Statistics.
d) As a percentage of GDP.

survey evidence reached a twenty-year high in late 1994 before moderating slightly in the first quarter of 1995. This has been reflected in an excess of import over export volume growth. Nonetheless, the current-account deficit has widened little, the deterioration in the real foreign balance being largely offset by gains in the terms of trade. ''Headline'' inflation, according to the consumer price index, rose to 4 per cent in the first quarter of 1995 and the Reserve Bank's operational measure of ''underlying'' inflation (which amongst other effects excludes direct interest rate effects and government charges) moved close to the upper limit of the 0 to 2 target range.

Policies and other forces acting. In response to these developments, as well as international trends, monetary conditions have progressively tightened over the course of the past year, with short-term interest rates exceeding 9 per cent, up from a low of 4½ per cent in early 1994. Over the same period long-term rates rose much less and have eased significantly in recent months, producing a negatively sloped yield curve. Increases in interest rates and in the external value of the New Zealand dollar over the past year will tend to dampen inflation. However, although the authorities do not expect the rate of underlying inflation to overshoot the target range, they recognise that the risks are on the upside and have emphasised that there is no scope for an easing of monetary conditions in the near term.

Reflecting the strong growth and continued government spending restraint, the budget has moved into substantial surplus. On current government projections an ''operating surplus'' equivalent to 1½ per cent of GDP is projected for FY 1994/95 (ending in June), rising to 3¾ per cent in 1995/96 and 5¼ per cent in 1996/97.[2] This would enable the public-debt-to GDP ratio to be brought down below a 30 per cent target threshold in 1996/97, with the emphasis on reducing net foreign currency debt, which could be entirely eliminated by mid-1997. Providing the debt target is realised on a sustainable basis, and subject to the inflation and the current-account positions not being unfavourable, the government has announced its intention to cut taxes.

Prospects. Monetary conditions are assumed to remain tight during the remainder of 1995 and this should slow economic expansion to about 3 per cent by 1996, more in line with potential growth. Business confidence, in the past a leading indicator of cyclical turning points, has already weakened sharply for two successive quarters. The high rates of growth in investment have been partly cyclical and are unlikely to be sustained, with the downturn, particularly in residential investment, being hastened by high interest rates. Although it seems quite possible that the Reserve Bank's inflation target will be breached at some point during 1995, the projected slowing of the economy should see underlying inflation return to the target range by the beginning of 1996. It should also be consistent with a slight improvement of the current-account deficit (as a percentage of GDP) and a flattening of the yield curve as monetary conditions ease in 1996.

The major risks and uncertainties of this projection concern the difficulty of assessing the extent of inflationary pressures. As the difference between underlying and headline inflation is likely to widen during 1995, a crucial factor will be the inflation rate to which wages react.[3] There is also some concern that the disinflationary effect of the stronger New Zealand dollar is being partly offset by higher profit margins on imports. If, as a consequence, higher short-term interest rates were required to keep inflation within the target band, the possibility of a "hard landing" of the economy would increase.

NOTES

1. There is currently a major discrepancy between the two measures of GDP, with the expenditure measure showing growth of under 4 per cent in 1994. Statistics New Zealand, as well as most observers, consider that the output measure is more reliable, suggesting that the expenditure measure will subsequently be revised upwards.
2. The Fiscal Responsibility Act 1994 requires the Budget to conform with accounting standards used in financial reports of private sector companies. The "operating surplus" takes account of debt servicing costs.
3. The Reserve Bank's projections, published in March, predict that underlying inflation will peak at the upper limit of the 0 to 2 target range in the second quarter of 1995 and that headline inflation will peak at 4½ per cent.

NORWAY

The recovery of the mainland economy gathered momentum in 1994, reflecting continued buoyancy in household spending and a pick-up in international demand for traditional exports. In the course of the year the recovery also spread to mainland capital formation. While growth is projected to slow, unemployment should remain on a downward trend, and inflation might accelerate somewhat. However, if domestic demand growth does not subside as projected, there is a risk of economic overheating, with stronger pressure on wages and prices.

Recent developments. Growth of the mainland economy posted a twenty-year record of nearly 4 per cent last year, raising private sector employment for the first time since 1987. As a result, unemployment fell to a seasonally adjusted 5¼ per cent by early 1995 from its mid-1993 peak of 6¼ per cent, despite some cyclical rebound of labour force participation. Since mid-1993, the recovery has been driven by increased household demand for durables and dwellings, following a steep fall in interest rates, and by more buoyant manufacturing export markets. By contrast, mainland business investment revived only in the second half of 1994, boosted by increased levels of capacity utilisation and improved international commodity prices.

Despite increased capacity utilisation, wage inflation has so far remained within the 2½ to 3 per cent range observed since 1992. Consumer price inflation has gradually fallen from 2¼ per cent on average in 1992 to 1½ per cent in 1994 before climbing to around 2¾ per cent in early 1995 (on a twelve-month basis) subsequent to a value-added tax (VAT) increase. Resilience of domestic demand has led to a surge in merchandise imports in 1994, leaving the traditional trade balance (excluding shipping, platforms and energy) unchanged despite the pick-up in manufacturing exports. However, as energy exports soared in 1994 – lifting total (mainland and offshore) GDP growth to 5.1 per cent – and as net investment income increased in line with growing net foreign assets, the current account surplus rose from 2.1 per cent of mainland GDP in 1993 to 3.3 per cent in 1994.

Policies and other forces acting. Official projections foreshadow a reduction in the non-oil deficit of the central government from a record high of 12 per cent of mainland GDP in 1993 to 6½ per cent in 1995. While this reflected in part the business cycle, tax increases (VAT) and restraint in public consumption and income transfers also contributed. With oil revenues moving up, the general government balance is officially expected to turn from a deficit in 1993 and 1994 (of 2¾ and ¼ per cent of GDP respectively), to a surplus of 1½ per cent in 1995. In line with announced policies, some further fiscal tightening is assumed for 1996.

Since the floating of the Norwegian krone in December 1992, the exchange rate has been remarkably stable, in line with the official commitment of the monetary authorities in this regard. Apart from some turmoil in Norwegian money markets in the run-up to the referendum on accession to the European Union last November, short-term interest rates have mostly remained in a range of 5 to 5½ per cent since early 1994, with the differential against German rates at 90 basis points in early May. Moreover, long-term rates have risen by less than in other

NORWAY

Demand, output and prices

Percentage changes, volume (based on previous year prices)

	1991 current prices billion NKr	1992	1993	1994	1995	1996
Private consumption	349.7	1.8	2.3	4.4	2.9	2.5
Government consumption	147.5	4.4	1.8	2.7	1.2	1.0
Gross fixed capital formation	127.1	4.5	13.9	4.8[a]	10.1[a]	–3.1[a]
Final domestic demand	624.2	3.0	4.6	4.1	4.2	0.8
* stockbuilding	2.0[b]	–1.1	–1.4	0.5	0[a]	0[a]
Total domestic demand	626.3	1.7	3.0	4.8	4.2	0.8
Exports of goods and services	307.5	6.2	1.6	7.6	8.2	6.1
Imports of goods and services	247.1	2.8	3.2	7.2	7.3	0
* net exports	60.4[b]	1.9	–0.4	0.9	1.2	3.0
GDP at market prices	686.7	3.4	2.3	5.1	4.8	3.5
GDP implicit price deflator	–	–1.0	2.0	0.3	2.5	2.6
Memorandum items						
Mainland GDP at market prices[c]	–	2.1	2.0	3.9	2.9	2.5
Mainland GDP deflator[c]	–	1.6	1.7	2.1	2.7	2.4
Exports of energy	–	12.6	5.2	12.2	14.7	8.9
Private consumption deflator	–	2.6	1.9	1.4	2.8	2.6
Unemployment rate	–	5.9	6.0	5.5	4.9	4.5
Household saving ratio[d]	–	5.2	4.5	4.4	4.3	4.5
General government financial balance[e]	–	–2.3	–2.1	–0.2	1.4	2.7
Current balance[e]	–	2.5	2.1	3.3	4.1	6.8

* Contributions to changes in real GDP (as a per cent of real GDP in the previous period).
a) For the period 1994-96, gross fixed capital formation includes platforms under construction, while the figures on stockbuilding exclude platforms in progress.
b) Actual amount
c) GDP excluding oil and shipping.
d) As a percentage of disposable income.
e) As a percentage of GDP.

Nordic countries, with the yield on six to ten-year bonds at roughly 7¾ per cent in April 1995. Some tightening of monetary policy is expected in view of emerging inflationary pressures.

Prospects. While slowing, the recovery is projected to continue, with mainland GDP growing by nearly 3 per cent this year and 2½ per cent next. Household spending, in particular, may be less buoyant than last year, as most pent-up demand, accumulated while balance sheets were being restored, has now been satisfied. As well, capital formation on the Norwegian Continental Shelf is likely to fall, partly offset by continuing buoyant mainland business investment. While employment growth will be strong, the reduction in unemployment may be tempered by a further rebound of labour force participation. Wage growth, nonetheless, could accelerate towards the end of the projection period in response to improved profitability. Overall GDP growth will be pushed up by rapidly expanding oil and gas production, which, in conjunction with an improved investment-income balance, should also lead to further rises in the already substantial current account surplus.

The acceleration in wage growth may be stronger than expected, given the improved labour market conditions and corporate profitability. This might provoke stronger inflation pressure than predicted – the more so if domestic demand growth does not subside as projected. The risk of the economy overheating could thus prompt a tightening of monetary and fiscal policy beyond that assumed in these projections.

A mild export-led recovery took hold in 1994, supported by strengthening gross fixed investment. Private consumption may gain strength this year, stimulated by brighter employment prospects and rising incomes from self-employment. The combination of continuing export growth and reviving domestic demand is expected to raise real GDP growth to around 3 per cent in 1995. With underlying inflation falling and fiscal outcomes recently turning out better than planned, progress continues to be made towards medium-term convergence goals. However, the 1995 budget projects no further deficit reduction and risk premia on Portuguese interest rates have risen further following the escudo devaluation in March.

Recent developments. Real GDP grew by an estimated 1.2 per cent in 1994, following a decline of equal magnitude in 1993. The main stimulus to growth came from exports of goods and services, driven by strong market growth. Gross fixed investment, responding to prospects of rising output and increased profitability, staged a modest recovery, thereby reversing the fall in final domestic demand. Rising cement sales point to a recovery of construction investment, which accounts for about one half of total gross investment. Restrained by continued job insecurity and falling real wages, consumer demand was more hesitant in supporting the economic expansion. Car sales plunged in the second half of 1994. On the external side, a sharp decline in transfer receipts shifted the current account into deficit in 1994 to the extent of 1.3 per cent of GDP.

While employment picked up in the second half of 1994, job gains were too small to stop the rate of unemployment climbing to 7.1 per cent in the fourth quarter of 1994, almost 1 percentage point higher than a year earlier and 3 points above the previous unemployment low in the second quarter of 1992. The speed and size of this rise in joblessness have no precedent since the first oil price shock in the mid-1970s, although the flexibility of the Portuguese labour market has ensured that the unemployment level remains low by international standards. Increased labour market slack has had a strong disinflationary effect on nominal wage growth, which halved from 14 per cent in 1992 to 7 per cent in 1993 and eased further to around 5 per cent in 1994. Coupled with procyclical gains in productivity, nominal wage moderation enabled consumer price inflation (excluding rents) to fall to 5.2 per cent in 1994, within the official target range of 4 to 5.5 per cent. At 4 per cent, the rate recorded over the 12 months to December 1994 was the lowest in 25 years. However, the increase in the standard value-added tax

PORTUGAL

Demand, output and prices

Percentage changes, volume (1985 prices)

	1991 current prices billion Esc	1992	1993	1994	1995	1996
Private consumption	7 243.0	3.7	0.4	0.2	1.3	2.1
Government consumption	1 841.7	1.4	0	1.4	1.1	1.5
Gross fixed capital formation	3 066.5	5.4	–4.8	3.5	7.5	7.8
Final domestic demand	12 151.2	3.8	–1.0	1.2	2.9	3.6
* stockbuilding	121.6[a]	0.6	0.2	0	0.4	0
Total domestic demand	12 272.8	4.3	–0.9	1.2	3.2	3.5
Exports of goods and services	3 218.8	6.1	–5.1	6.7	10.5	7.3
Imports of goods and services	4 177.7	11.1	–3.2	4.6	8.4	6.5
* net exports	–958.9[a]	–4.0	–0.1	–0.2	–1.0	–1.1
GDP at market prices	11 313.9	1.1	–1.2	1.2	2.9	3.2
GDP implicit price deflator	–	13.5	7.4	5.0	4.5	4.4
Memorandum items						
Private consumption deflator	–	10.0	7.9	5.2	4.5	4.2
Industrial production[b]	–	–2.6	–2.4	0.2	3.0	3.5
Unemployment rate	–	4.2	5.5	6.8	6.7	6.3
Household saving ratio[c]	–	14.1	13.0	12.0	11.8	11.5
Current balance[d]	–	–0.2	0.8	–1.3	0.1	0.2

* Contributions to changes in real GDP (as a per cent of real GDP in the previous period).
a) Actual amount.
b) Industrial production index.
c) As a percentage of disposable income.
d) As a percentage of GDP.

(VAT) rate in January 1995 pushed up 12-month consumer price inflation to 4.5 per cent in March.

Policies and other forces acting. Following a substantial deficit overrun in 1993, the 1994 fiscal outcome was significantly better than expected, the general borrowing requirement subsiding to an estimated 5.7 per cent of GDP from 7.1 per cent in 1993. Stronger tax revenues more than offset the effect from higher-than-expected interest rates and lower net transfer receipts from the European Community. In 1995, the official projection points only to a stabilisation of the general government borrowing requirement, at 5.8 per cent of GDP, despite continued spending restraint, cyclical revenue gains and higher yields from VAT. This target, however, is likely to be undershot. Indeed, the OECD Secretariat projects a gradual decline of the deficit from 5.4 per cent in 1995 to 5 per cent of GDP in 1996, as output growth gathers further speed.

Monetary policy continues to be geared towards achieving inflation convergence with the best performing countries in the European Union, the stability of the nominal exchange rate being the intermediate target. In March, speculative attacks on the Spanish peseta in the context of more generalised exchange market turbulence led to a realignment of central rates in the European Exchange Rate Mechanism (ERM), including a reduction in the central value of the escudo by 3.5 per cent. This was the escudo's third devaluation since it joined the ERM in April 1992, linked, in each case, to peseta realignments. While the nominal effective exchange rate appreciated somewhat in the wake of the latest devaluation, yields on 10-year government bonds exceeded the German equivalent by around 5 percentage points in early May. With underlying inflation easing and the budgetary position improving further, risk premia should narrow, but the process could be slow if the scheduled pace of budget consolidation is not increased.

Prospects. A continued strong expansion of export markets, along with the coming-on-stream of new export capacity may lift export growth in 1995 into double figures. Together with a related acceleration in gross fixed investment, export buoyancy is projected to push real GDP growth to around 3 per cent in 1995, rising to $3^1/_4$ per cent in 1996. Stronger fixed investment will reflect both improved profitability and projects financed by the European Community. Consumer demand may firm with the brightening of employment prospects, reinforcing the domestic stimulus to economic growth. The rate of unemployment is projected to fall to 6.3 per cent in 1996, which would still exceed the estimated natural rate of unemployment (NAIRU), albeit by a small margin. The consequent deceleration of nominal wages should allow consumer-price inflation to ease in 1995 to the upper half of the 1995 official target range of 3.5 to 4.5 per cent . On the external side, rising transfer payments may shift the current account back into surplus in 1995-96, outweighing a cyclically-induced deterioration of the trade account.

The main risks attached to the projections concern interest rates, the exchange rate and fiscal consolidation. The escudo like other currencies remains vulnerable to renewed international exchange market turmoil. Investors' attitudes have remained cautious following the latest escudo devaluation, but would probably be reassured by indications that any unexpected revenue buoyancy was being used to reduce the budget deficit.

SPAIN

Recovery is underway, driven by strong export growth and, more recently, by investment. Output growth is likely to be above its potential rate in 1995-96. Economic expansion and the effects of the 1994 labour market reform should boost employment over the projection period and gradually lower the unemployment rate. Progress in disinflation and fiscal consolidation risks being slowed by pressures on the peseta in early 1995. Rising market interest rates are boosting debt-servicing costs, limiting the expected decline in the general government deficit despite public spending cuts at the beginning of 1995. Wage growth should remain moderate but increasing import prices may keep consumer price inflation above 4 per cent.

Recent developments. Growth accelerated in the fourth quarter of 1994, reaching 2 per cent for the year as a whole. Strong export volumes, the main force behind growth, contributed to a sharp improvement in business expectations, boosting private investment in the second half of the year. This and a pickup in private consumption largely offset a fall in the volume of public expenditure. Employment recovered, led by a rise in private dependent employment (around 2 per cent on a year on year basis in the first quarter of 1995), while public employment decreased by 3 per cent. Despite rapid growth of the labour force, the unemployment rate fell to $23^1/_2$ per cent, one percentage point below the level a year earlier. Underpinned by buoyant foreign demand, industrial production was up by $6^1/_2$ per cent on a 12-month

SPAIN
Demand, output and prices
Percentage changes, volume (1986 prices)

	1991 current prices billion Ptas	1992	1993	1994	1995	1996
Private consumption	34 244.4	2.1	–2.0	0.9	1.9	2.9
Government consumption	8 881.9	3.6	2.3	0.2	0.1	1.1
Gross fixed capital formation	13 041.3	–4.1	–10.5	1.1	4.5	5.9
Final domestic demand	56 167.6	0.9	–3.3	0.8	2.1	3.2
* stockbuilding	461.1 [a]	0.1	–1.0	0	0.6	0.3
Total domestic demand	56 628.7	1.0	–4.1	0.8	2.7	3.5
Exports of goods and services	9 409.4	7.3	8.3	17.7	13.2	10.7
Imports of goods and services	11 137.3	6.9	–5.1	11.0	11.3	11.0
* net exports	–1 727.9 [a]	–0.4	3.3	1.2	0.3	–0.3
GDP at market prices	54 900.8	0.7	–1.1	2.0	3.0	3.2
GDP implicit price deflator	–	6.7	4.4	4.1	4.0	3.9
Memorandum items						
Private consumption deflator	–	6.4	5.6	5.1	4.6	4.1
Industrial production	–	–2.9	–4.6	7.2	4.5	3.9
Unemployment rate	–	18.4	22.7	24.1	24.1	23.3
Household saving ratio [b]	–	10.1	12.6	12.2	12.2	11.7
General government financial balance [c]	–	–4.2	–7.5	–6.6	–6.2	–5.5
Current balance [c]	–	–3.2	–0.8	–1.1	–1.0	–1.3

* Contributions to changes in real GDP (as a per cent of real GDP in the previous period).
a) Actual amount.
b) As a percentage of disposable income.
c) As a percentage of GDP.

basis in February 1995 and, according to business climate indicators, a sharp rise is expected in production levels over the coming months. On the other hand, consumer confidence, although less negative than in 1993, remains weak, largely due to high unemployment levels.

Labour market slack and the 1994 labour market reforms have contributed to decelerating wage claims, with settlements up to March 1995 averaging 3.5 per cent in branch agreements and 2.6 per cent in agreements at the firm level. Weakness of the peseta and sharp food price rises compounded increases in value-added tax (VAT) rates and excise taxes to drive up inflation, so that in April 1995 12-month consumer price inflation stood at 5.2 per cent, slightly higher than a year earlier. Underlying inflation has been around 4$^1/_2$ per cent since mid-1994, but sharply rising producer prices point to a build-up of inflationary pressures. Underpinned by large competitiveness gains from exchange rate depreciation, Spanish export market shares expanded sharply in 1994, but a surge in imports and a deterioration in the terms of trade widened the trade deficit. However, the large surplus on the tourism account practically offset the trade deficit and the rise in net income payments, so that the current account deficit increased only slightly, to 1 per cent of GDP.

Policies and other forces acting. Since the September 1992 devaluation, the peseta has been one of the weakest currencies in the European Exchange Rate Mechanism (ERM). Reflecting market uncertainty about the evolution of the fiscal deficit and inflation, it came under heavy attack during the speculative wave sparked by the strengthening of the Deutschemark against the dollar at the beginning of 1995. This forced a 7 per cent devaluation within the ERM on 6 March. Since mid-1992, the peseta has depreciated by about 40 per cent against the Deutschemark and around 20 per cent in effective terms. Monetary policy is essentially geared towards inflation control, and interest rates were not intensively used to support the peseta during the exchange market turmoil. The intervention interest rate was raised twice, by $^3/_4$ per cent to 8 per cent in January 1995, to check inflation pressures created by rises in indirect taxes, and by $^1/_2$ per cent shortly after the devaluation. Market interest rates have increased much faster than official interest rates. Since mid-1994 short-term rates have risen by more than 1$^3/_4$ percentage points, to 9$^1/_4$ per cent in May 1995 and long-term rates have soared, from less than 8 per cent at the beginning of 1994 to 11$^1/_4$ per cent. The yield differential with the 10-year German government bond widened to over 4 percentage points from 3 percentage points in 1994. Monetary policy is now set in terms of a medium term inflation target of 3 per cent by the end of 1997. Monetary conditions might have to be tightened somewhat over the projection period due to latent inflationary pressures; fast growth of ALP (the wide liquidity measure) in the first months of 1995 would also suggest such a course. The projections assume that the long-term interest rate differential with Germany will remain larger than 4 percentage points over the projection period.

Public finances remain a central policy concern and fiscal retrenchment is the highest priority of government. The 1994 general government deficit was brought down to 6.6 per cent of GDP through significant real cuts in public investment and consumption. Public sector employment fell for the second consecutive year. The 1995 Budget aimed at lowering the general government deficit to 5.9 per cent of GDP through further adjustments in public spending. However, it was clear at the beginning of 1995 that it would be difficult to attain that target and it was decided to cut expenditure by an additional Ptas 150 billion (about 1/4 per cent of GDP); in addition, Ptas 400 billion of budgeted expenditure was frozen to cover possible fiscal slippages. Nevertheless, rising debt financing costs and the difficulty of enforcing fiscal restraint by local administrations in an election year might require further measures in order to achieve government targets. On present policy the general government deficit might still be of the order of 5½ per cent of GDP in 1996.

Prospects. Increasing capacity utilisation rates will boost private investment this year and next despite high real interest rates. With moderate wage growth and high unemployment levels, private consumption growth will accelerate only gradually. A small but positive contribution to output growth is expected from the foreign balance in 1995, as export volumes continue to be underpinned by strong export market growth and competitiveness gains from the exchange-rate depreciation. Employment should pick up significantly over the projection period but progress in reducing unemployment will be limited by the rapid labour force growth in 1995. No inflation pressures are expected from wage developments in 1995, but the weakness of the peseta and drought-induced rises in food prices may keep inflation running at around 4½ per cent in 1995, and only a small deceleration to around 4 per cent is foreseen for 1996. An increasing surplus on the tourism account is likely to broadly offset a widening of the trade deficit due to the pick-up in imports, so that the current account deficit is expected to stabilise around 1 per cent of GDP during the projection period.

These forecasts might underestimate the strength of the recovery in investment after a cumulative fall of more than 15 per cent in 1992-94. However, there is also a risk that high capital financing costs for business will prompt compensating labour adjustments. In this case, lower employment, real consumption growth and output growth could ensue. Moreover, the projections are based on a significant improvement in the general government primary balance and a gradual reduction in the deficit. If these fail to materialise, interest rates would continue to rise, reflecting losses in market confidence, with a consequent brake on output growth.

SWEDEN

Buoyant exports have continued to lead a moderate recovery, while final domestic demand remains depressed. The unemployment rate has edged down, but wage inflation is still low and the underlying rate of price increases muted. A tight fiscal stance will keep domestic demand growth modest over the projection period, and continued slack in the labour market should keep inflation in check. Nevertheless, interest rates may remain high, complicating the budget consolidation process.

Recent developments. The recovery has continued to be driven by buoyant foreign demand, with industrial production up by more than 12 per cent in February compared with a year earlier. Although industrial capacity has been boosted by surging investment, capacity utilisation continued to climb throughout 1994 to very high rates. The buoyancy of the export-oriented sectors has so far failed to give a boost to final domestic demand. A rise in the household saving ratio, related to flagging confidence, kept a lid on the growth in private consumption in 1994, and the collapse of residential construction showed no signs of abating. Although inventory accumulation gave an extraordinary boost to total domestic demand in 1994, the growth contribution may have been small as a large part of the addition to stocks appears to have been supplied from abroad.

Employment gains in the course of 1994 reduced the unemployment rate somewhat, but in the first quarter of 1995 more than 13 per cent of the labour force was still either unemployed or engaged in government labour market schemes. Although wage inflation has been drifting up in industry for several quarters, wage growth is still moderate in the economy at large. Higher world market prices and the weakness of the krona left producer prices 9.3 per cent higher in March than a year earlier. However, this has so far not been reflected in consumer prices, the consumer price index increasing by

SWEDEN
Demand, output and prices
Percentage changes, volume (1991 prices)

	1991 current prices billion SKr	1992	1993	1994	1995	1996
Private consumption	771.3	–1.4	–3.7	0.5	–0.8	0.7
Government consumption	394.4	0	–0.6	–1.0	–0.2	–0.7
Gross fixed capital formation	280.4	–10.8	–17.6	–0.4	9.8	9.3
Final domestic demand	1 446.1	–2.9	–5.3	–0.1	1.0	1.7
* stockbuilding	–21.2[a]	1.1	–0.3	1.4	–0.3	–0.2
Total domestic demand	1 424.9	–1.8	–5.6	1.4	0.7	1.5
Exports of goods and services	404.2	2.3	7.6	13.8	11.2	7.8
Imports of goods and services	381.8	1.1	–2.8	13.2	7.3	6.4
* net exports	22.4[a]	0.4	2.9	0.9	1.8	1.0
GDP at market prices	1 447.3	–1.4	–2.6	2.2	2.5	2.4
GDP implicit price deflator	–	1.1	2.6	2.9	4.0	3.0
Memorandum items						
Private consumption deflator	–	2.2	5.8	3.0	3.3	2.8
Industrial production	–	–3.5	2.6	11.8	7.5	7.0
Unemployment rate[b]	–	5.3	8.2	8.0	7.5	6.7
Household saving ratio[c]	–	7.7	7.9	8.3	7.5	7.0
General government financial balance[d]	–	–7.5	–13.4	–10.4	–9.2	–6.4
Current balance[d]	–	–3.5	–2.1	0.4	2.9	4.5

* Contributions to changes in real GDP (as a per cent of real GDP in the previous period).
a) Actual amount.
b) Based on monthly Labour Force Surveys.
c) As a percentage of disposable income.
d) As a percentage of GDP.

only 3.3 per cent in the 12 months to April; excluding the effect of hikes in net indirect taxes in January, consumer prices were up by 2.2 per cent.

Policies and other forces acting. Fiscal consolidation measures announced by the government since taking office in October aim at stabilising and subsequently reducing the state debt-to-GDP ratio from 1997 onwards, and call for a reduction in the primary structural deficit of SKr 81 billion (5¼ per cent of GDP) over the 1995-98 period. This comes on top of SKr 18 billion decided under the previous government. According to official estimates, around two-thirds of this programme should be implemented by 1996. Weak development of important tax bases will, however, imply sluggish revenue growth in 1995. All in all the tightening of the general government non-cyclical primary budget balance could amount to a cumulative 4 percentage points of GDP in 1995 and 1996.

With the aim of keeping growth of the consumer price index below 3 per cent, the maximum deviation tolerated from the target of 2 per cent, the central bank has increased its repurchasing rate in several steps from 7.4 per cent in early December to 8.4 per cent in mid-May. Further increases are expected to be required for this purpose over the projection period, and the 3-month rate could increase to 9 per cent in 1996 as European interest rates firm more generally.

Nevertheless, despite fiscal and monetary tightening, the turmoil in the international financial markets in March of this year demonstrated the vulnerability of Swedish interest rates and the exchange rate to adverse sentiment. Although the increase in the bond yield and the fall in the krona were subsequently reversed, the long-term interest rate is still high (10.6 per cent in mid-May) relative to the inflation rate and the krona is 5 per cent lower *vis-à-vis* the Deutschemark than at the beginning of the year. The high interest rate and weak currency appear to derive from a belief that the fiscal consolidation programme depends on optimistic assumptions and that further measures are required to bring down the budget deficit to a level consistent with sound public finances. Hence, the long-term interest rate differential *vis-à-vis* Germany is assumed to remain at around its current level over the short-term projection period.

Prospects. Aggregate output growth is likely to remain moderate in both 1995 and 1996, the continued buoyancy of the open sector barely taking the level of GDP to just above its pre-recession peak. Despite a projected reduction of the household saving ratio, private consumption could decline in 1995 due to a tax-induced reduction of household real disposable income. The collapse of residential construction may come to a halt in 1996, but high interest rates will keep investment growth muted in domestically-oriented sectors. However, capacity-widening capital spending is likely to be very strong in the export-oriented sectors, and export growth should remain strong, though declining with weaker market growth. As a result, the current account should register a sizeable surplus in both 1995 and 1996.

The pick-up in economic activity should be accompanied by some employment gains, but around 12 per cent of the workforce could still be either unemployed or in active programmes in 1996. The slack in the labour market should ensure that wage inflation remains low over the projection period, but high profits could translate into high wage increases in industry, with possible subsequent spillover effects into the economy at large. The evolution of consumer prices will be strongly influenced over the projection period by increases in net indirect taxes, which in 1995 will add 1 percentage point.

The principal risk to the projections concerns the course of interest rates and the exchange rate, which could either exacerbate the budget consolidation process or ease it, depending on swings in international investor confidence. There is also a risk that high projected wage settlements in industry could unduly influence wage agreements in other sectors, giving a boost to inflation.

SWITZERLAND

A turnaround of fixed investment, strong inventory accumulation and accelerating exports brought about real GDP growth of 2.1 per cent in 1994, the first year of recovery from the three-year old recession. However, with abundant room for productivity improvements, employment continued to shrink, permitting only a small decline in registered unemployment. The still substantial output gap, combined with an appreciating Swiss franc, resulted in stable consumer prices. Before gathering more strength in 1996, growth may slow somewhat in 1995, due to the effect of the Swiss franc appreciation on trade flows and the erosion of real household incomes by higher social security charges and the newly introduced value-added tax.

Recent developments. After three years of decline, fixed investment rebounded strongly in 1994, reflecting the underlying need to modernise the business capital stock as well as falling prices of imported investment goods. Construction activity was supported primarily by housing demand, with business construction still suffering from excess capacity built up in the pre-1990 boom. Strongly improving business confidence, reduced financing costs and falling import prices stimulated inventory build-up. Even government consumption provided more support to activity than expected earlier, despite announcements of government spending restraint. Recovering domestic demand induced a surge of imports and thereby a marked negative swing in the contribution of the real foreign balance to GDP growth. But with a substantial terms-of-trade gain, the current external surplus in 1994 declined by only about 1 per cent of GDP, to 7 per cent.

Total employment continued to fall in the first two quarters of 1994, but picked up in the second half-year. Notwithstanding the marked loss of jobs, measured unemployment declined gradually from a peak of 5 per cent (s.a.) at the beginning of 1994 to 4¼ per cent in the spring of 1995, owing to a shrinking labour force. The decrease in employment implied a further substantial gain in productivity and falling unit labour costs, which helped to keep average consumer price inflation at under 1 per cent in 1994.

Policies and other forces acting. Short-term interest rates remained broadly unchanged during 1994, with the three-month Euro-Swiss franc rate hovering around 4 per cent. In late 1994, the Swiss National Bank announced a new monetary target of a 1 per cent annual increase in the monetary base over the ensuing five years. Given the undershooting of the previous target throughout the preceding five-year period, the National Bank made a downward adjustment to the new target's starting point. It expects some increase in money supply growth in 1995 but even so base money will probably stay distinctly below the envisaged trajectory. The cut in the discount rate by ½ percentage point to 3 per cent in late March and the decrease in the three-month Euro-Swiss franc interest rate by about ¾ percentage point to around 3¼ per cent in April 1995 are consistent with encouraging more rapid money growth; however, judging by a host of indicators, monetary easing has been cautious, in part because the National Bank aims to avoid a price-wage spiral stemming from the introduction of a value-added tax (VAT) at the beginning of 1995. A gradual tightening may be expected for 1996, when economic growth is projected to accelerate and headline inflation to stay above the National Bank's 1 per cent objective. This would also induce some upward drift in long-term interest rates.

The financial deficit of the Confederation turned out to be nearly SF 2 billion lower than projected in 1994

SWITZERLAND
Demand, output and prices
Percentage changes, volume (1980 prices)

	1991 current prices billion SF	1992	1993	1994	1995	1996
Private consumption	190.5	–0.2	–0.8	1.3	0.7	1.5
Government consumption	46.6	–0.1	–1.7	1.4	–0.5	–0.4
Gross fixed capital formation	84.8	–5.0	–3.1	6.5	4.2	3.9
Final domestic demand	321.9	–1.5	–1.5	2.7	1.5	1.9
* stockbuilding	4.5[a]	–1.9	–0.3	1.7	0.8	0.5
Total domestic demand	326.5	–3.3	–1.8	4.4	2.3	2.4
Exports of goods and services	116.7	3.4	1.3	3.9	4.4	5.0
Imports of goods and services	112.1	–3.8	–1.0	8.8	5.5	5.0
* net exports	4.6[a]	3.1	1.0	–2.3	–0.7	–0.2
GDP at market prices	331.1	–0.3	–0.9	2.1	1.7	2.3
GDP implicit price deflator	–	2.6	2.1	1.7	1.6	2.0
Memorandum items						
Private consumption deflator	–	4.2	3.0	0.7	1.7	1.9
Industrial production	–	–0.7	–0.5	7.9	4.5	5.0
Unemployment rate	–	2.5	4.5	4.7	4.1	3.6
Current balance[b]	–	6.2	7.9	6.9	6.8	6.9

* Contributions to changes in real GDP (as a per cent of real GDP in the previous period).
a) Actual amount.
b) As a percentage of GDP.

– 1.4 instead of 2 per cent of GDP – due to stronger output growth and lower unemployment than expected but also to special factors such as postponed expenditures for infrastructure projects. A somewhat better outcome is also estimated for the cantons, while communes may broadly have met their deficit targets. This implies a fall of the general government deficit from 4¼ per cent of GDP in 1993 to 3¾ per cent in 1994. Partly as a consequence of expenditure deferment from 1994 to 1995, further improvement in the general government deficit-to-GDP ratio is unlikely before 1996.

Prospects. Economic growth is projected to slow down this year and then to accelerate somewhat. Exports are likely to remain a mainstay of activity, benefiting from vigorous export market growth, although market share losses are probable because of the recent substantial strengthening of the Swiss franc. Besides, exports seem to embody an increasing share of imported inputs from Swiss companies producing abroad (outsourcing) which gives a boost to imports. Machinery and equipment investment should continue to expand briskly because the back-log of demand has not yet been entirely eliminated, and because the abolition of the hidden tax (''taxe occulte'') on investment has increased the profitability of investment. However, leading indicators suggest a weakening of construction investment this year, partly due to the phasing out of the federal investment bonus programme. Some strengthening in building activity should be possible in 1996, when household incomes improve and business capacity utilisation increases. Little support to demand can be expected from household consumption before 1996 as real private disposable incomes are likely to remain weak in 1995 as a result of wage moderation, increased social security contributions and the introduction of a value-added tax. Government spending is set to remain constrained by ongoing efforts to reduce budget deficits. With projected terms of trade broadly unchanged, and the deteriorating real foreign balance largely offset by further strong improvements in net investment income, the current external surplus should remain at around 7 per cent of GDP in both 1995 and 1996.

The projected increase in inflation in 1995 is mainly an effect of the replacement of the turnover tax on goods by a general VAT. Owing to the appreciating exchange rate, an unchanged output gap and subdued wage growth, it is likely that the actual effect of VAT on the price level will remain below its ''mechanical'' impact. Although VAT-adjusted inflation may pick up when the effect of the Swiss franc appreciation peters out and the output gap narrows a little, measured inflation could remain roughly unchanged in 1996.

There appear to be two downside risks: first, the continuing fall in the saving ratio implicit in the projected modest growth in private consumption in 1995 may not materialise if the recent deterioration in consumer confidence were to continue; and second, the appreciating Swiss franc could entail weaker export and stronger import volumes.

The Turkish economy experienced severe stagflation in 1994. Real GDP fell by around 5½ per cent, although the recession may have hit bottom in early 1995. Inflation over the six months to April 1995 was at an annual rate of over 100 per cent. The April 1994 stabilisation programme succeeded in cutting the public sector borrowing requirement by some 4 to 5 per cent of GDP and swinging the current account into surplus. External obligations were fully met and foreign reserves rebuilt. But the public sector borrowing requirement is still some 8 per cent of GDP, and progress in structural reforms needed to support medium-term fiscal consolidation has been slow, although revised privatisation legislation could speed future progress. Turkey is scheduled to enter into a customs union with the European Union by end-1995.

Recent developments. Following the drop in output by over 11 per cent year-on-year in the second quarter of 1994, the decline moderated through the rest of the year. Nonetheless, GDP may have declined by almost 5½ per cent for the year, with severe consequences for labour markets. The resurgence of inflation since autumn 1994 is a major concern. Wholesale price inflation in the six months to April 1995 was at an annual rate of 117 per cent, albeit abating. The current account swung into surplus in the second quarter and recorded a surplus of some US$2.6 billion for 1994 as a whole, reflecting a surge in exports, a steep drop in imports and a recovery in invisibles earnings. Financial market confidence improved in early 1995, with renewed sales of 1-year government debt, falling interest rates, a marked recovery in share prices and renewed access to international capital markets.

Policies and other forces acting. The target to cut the public sector borrowing requirement (PSBR) from 12 to 6.2 per cent of GDP in 1994 was not fully met on account of higher interest rates and delays in privatisation. A substantial degree of fiscal consolidation was nonetheless achieved, with around two-thirds of the adjustment coming from expenditure cuts. Based on an inflation rate of some 22 per cent between December 1994 and December 1995, the 1995 budget targeted a PSBR for 1995 of some 5 per cent of GDP. But, with underlying inflation proving stronger, the end-year 1995 inflation target has been subsequently raised to some 40 per cent (implying an annual average of 70 per cent). Higher taxes and public-sector prices were announced to compensate for the effects of higher interest rates on the PSBR.

The Treasury successfully auctioned 9-month and 1-year government debt in the first quarter of 1995, allowing a modest lengthening of the extremely short

TURKEY
Demand, output and prices
Percentage changes, volume (1987 prices)

	1991 current prices billion TL	1992	1993	1994	1995	1996
Private consumption	434 366	3.3	7.1	–5.4	2.0	4.3
Government consumption	78 256	3.8	4.8	–3.5	–1.0	1.5
Gross fixed capital formation	149 272	4.3	21.7	–15.9	–1.8	5.3
Final domestic demand	661 894	3.6	10.6	–8.2	0.8	4.4
* stockbuilding	–6 160[a]	1.6	1.2	–4.6	1.3	0.9
Total domestic demand	655 734	5.2	11.7	–12.4	2.2	5.3
Exports of goods and services	87 215	11.0	7.7	15.2	15.0	12.0
Imports of goods and services	104 819	10.9	35.8	–21.9	12.0	14.0
* net exports	–17 604[a]	–0.3	–6.2	8.6	0.7	–0.4
* statistical discrepancy	–8 013[a]	1.0	1.7	–0.9	0	0
GDP at market prices	630 117	6.0	7.5	–5.4	2.8	4.8
GDP implicit price deflator	–	63.9	62.8	107.0	80.0	45.0
Memorandum items						
Private consumption deflator	–	63.8	63.9	106.0	80.0	45.0
Manufacturing production	–	4.2	9.2	–4.8	3.8	5.0
Unemployment rate	–	7.9	8.7	10.9	12.0	12.4
Current balance[b]	–	–0.6	–3.7	2.1	2.1	1.6

* Contributions to changes in real GDP (as a per cent of real GDP in the previous period).
a) Actual amount.
b) As a percentage of GDP.

(4-months) average maturity of domestic debt. Since February 1995, the depreciation of the Turkish lira has slowed to around 3 per cent a month. In inflation-adjusted terms, the lira in mid-March was down 25 to 30 per cent from its end-1993 level, appreciating modestly in real terms since the beginning of 1995.

Nominal interest rates on 6 month treasury bills of some 110 per cent are extremely high compared with the official end-year inflation target. This reflects deeply entrenched inflation expectations and large risk premia on Turkish lira denominated debt, due to past failures to deliver promised fiscal and monetary restraint. Such high rates of interest imply that further fiscal consolidation will be needed to avoid a steep rise in the debt-to-GDP ratio. Legislation has been passed to steadily reduce direct central bank financing of the PSBR: by 1998 only three per cent of incremental budget appropriations can be financed by the Central Bank. This constitutes an important building block in the implementation of a medium-term anti-inflationary monetary policy.

Prospects. GDP growth is projected to recover gradually in 1995 to some 2¾ per cent, led by strong exports and a rebound in agricultural output after the drought. The current account is projected to remain in significant surplus, albeit still insufficient to meet external repayment of debt principal without recourse to some foreign borrowing. For 1996, the recovery could become more broadly based, with private consumption and investment leading a pick-up in GDP growth to some 4¾ per cent. But, with the growth of potential output estimated at close to 5 per cent, the output gap has widened substantially in 1994-95. Inflation is projected to fall quickly in the course of 1995, from an annual average of 120 per cent in 1994 to around 80 per cent in 1995, and to less than 50 per cent in 1996. Attaining the inflation projection for 1995 will require monthly inflation rates falling to around 2 per cent a month in the second half of this year. These projections are conditional on achieving the targeted reductions in the PSBR and tight monetary policies.

The April 1994 stabilisation programme, introduced after the massive run on the Turkish lira, has succeeded in stabilising financial markets and establishing a current account surplus. But this stability is not assured. Much of the improvement in macroeconomic balances reflected a big drop in real incomes, one-off tax and spending measures, depressed domestic demand conditions and a large real depreciation. Broadly based and lasting economic expansion led by exports and investment will depend on quickening the pace of fundamental structural reform and medium-term fiscal consolidation. Lower inflation is essential to meet the enhanced competition resulting from the customs union with the European Union. Continuing delays in structural reform and fiscal consolidation risk renewed financial instability, the more so as international financial markets have become increasingly sensitive to sovereign risk related to large budget deficits, high inflation and dependency on foreign capital inflows.

DEVELOPMENTS IN SELECTED NON-OECD COUNTRIES

Economic recovery has continued in most countries of Central and Eastern Europe monitored by the OECD, while the Russian recession apparently levelled off in the first quarter of 1995. Strong export performance was the generally positive aspect of the upturn. On the negative side, both unemployment and inflation have remained at high levels throughout the region, except in the Czech Republic. Structural changes have been dominated by massive transfers of public assets to new owners, continued market reforms and slow but steady progress towards the consolidation of democratic institutions.

The Dynamic Asian Economies comprising Korea, Chinese Taipei, Hong Kong, Singapore, Thailand and Malaysia (DAEs) are currently being influenced by several factors. The first relates to the uncertainties with regard to the course of the reform process in China, and is of greater concern for Hong Kong and Chinese Taipei. Second, the recent depreciation of the their currencies *vis-à-vis* the yen has strengthened the DAEs' international competitiveness, which will be reflected in a boost to already-buoyant exports. Third, domestic demand also continues to expand strongly. Fourth, rapid growth together with currency depreciation is generating rising inflation pressures.

In South and Central America, the Mexican crisis has affected other countries in the area, but mainly through a reduction in capital inflows and an increase in interest rates. These effects have varied considerably within the region mostly as a result of the different policies towards capital flows followed until 1995. As the region adjusts to lower levels of capital inflows, GDP growth and inflation are now expected to fall. The current account will be affected by higher debt servicing costs while the reduction in import demand growth will be reflected in larger trade surpluses only from 1996.

CENTRAL AND EASTERN EUROPEAN COUNTRIES AND THE RUSSIAN FEDERATION

Recent developments

Preliminary estimates suggest that output growth in the countries of Central and Eastern Europe (CEECs) during 1994 was stronger than had been expected by most observers. Poland and Slovakia led the way with real GDP increases close to 5 per cent. The pace of recovery was somewhat slower in the Czech Republic, Hungary and Romania. Although Bulgarian GDP probably stagnated in 1994, a number of indicators suggest that output growth may resume this year. In contrast to the aggregate output growth in the CEECs, the Russian Federation experienced a steep decline in industrial production and GDP in 1994, with signs of stabilisation emerging only in the last quarter of the year.

Excepting the Czech Republic, high (double-digit) unemployment rates have continued to characterise the economic transition taking place in Central and Eastern Europe. The available data show that there is still no clear-cut relationship between output growth and unemployment (Table 21). This puzzle reflects the uneven character of behavioural changes in recent years as well as some statistical revisions which affect the comparability of time series data. High and persistent unemployment complicates the political economy of transition: electoral outcomes have favoured parties promising both slower reforms and improved social security.

Table 21. **Registered unemployment**

Percentage of labour force, end year

	1993	1994	1995	1996
Bulgaria	16.3	12.0	12.0	12.0
Czech Republic	3.5	3.2	4.0	4.5
Hungary	12.1	10.4	12.0	11.0
Poland	15.7	16.2	15.5	15.0
Romania	10.2	10.9	12.0	12.5
Russia[a]	5.7	9.0	12.0	14.0
Slovak Republic	14.4	14.8	14.0	13.0

a) "Open unemployment" as reported by Goskomstat's annual labour force survey. Unemployment is assessed according to the ILO definition, but under conditions of extensive informal sector activity may overestimate joblessness.

Exports have grown strongly in all CEECs, making a substantial contribution to demand. Nevertheless, household consumption and investment have played a key role in a number of countries, including the Czech Republic, Hungary and Poland. Growth in investment might be regarded as a positive sign, but a definitive judgement is not yet possible: in several countries inventory accumulation appears to be an important component of aggregate investment. In others, investment growth heavily reflects infrastructure investments stemming from the public sector, broadly defined. It remains unclear whether these developments reflect normal business cycle responses or still inadequate financial discipline of governments and of state-owned enterprises and their banks.

In the case of the Russian Federation, exports to the OECD area in 1994 were about 20 per cent higher than in 1993. According to Russian sources, the export growth was particularly strong in the metallurgy and petrochemical sectors. This pattern is consistent with the industry-level statistical data which indicate that these sectors experienced relatively low rates of output decline. Russian exports to the "traditional" markets (former Soviet Union, former CMEA partners, developing countries) have continued to fall.

On the whole, the generally strong export performance of Russia and the CEECs reflects their deepening integration into the world economy in general and the OECD area in particular (Table 22). The acceleration of growth in OECD countries has translated into growing effective demand for goods and services produced by transition economies, while their demand for products produced in OECD countries has also accelerated steadily. It can be expected that these linkages will become even more pronounced as both trade barriers and mutual ignorance of available trade opportunities continue to be reduced.

Policies and other forces acting

The major policy concerns confronting the governments vary widely in the region. Using the inflation rate as a convenient ranking indicator, one can divide the economies monitored into three groups (Table 23). At one extreme are those countries where conventional stabilisation still remains the overwhelming concern (Bulgaria, Romania, Russia). Situated at the other extreme is the Czech Republic, characterised by macroeconomic stability with full employment, where the principal policy issue is posed by strong capital inflows which complicate monetary control. The countries in between have to confront difficult choices, in particular concerning social security reforms (Hungary, Poland and Slovakia).

The middle group countries have experienced the coexistence of economic growth with high unemployment and budget deficits, which presents their policy makers with a tough dilemma. On the one hand, budgetary expenditure in real terms has to be curtailed in order to reduce inflation and move closer to a sustainable fiscal position. On the other hand, high unemployment levels and the weak political support for the reform process make substantial spending cuts risky, while long-term growth concerns dictate the need for increased public spending on human capital (education, research, health care) and infrastructure. Post-communist governments have generally responded to the emergence of mass unemployment with policies favouring early retirement (although the usual retirement age was already relatively low at 60 years for men and 55 years or less for women) and the introduction of new social benefits (unemploy-

Table 22. **Trade flows**[a]

Central and Eastern Europe and the NIS[b]	1993	1994	1995	1996
CEEC 6:[c]				
Goods export volumes (% change)	0.3	13.7	10	9.7
Goods import volumes (% change)	13.1	5.6	8.3	8.2
Exports ($ billion)	43.1	50.5	57.3	64.2
Imports ($ billion)	51.9	55.7	61.9	69.0
Current balance ($ billion)	–8.5	–5.0	–3.7	–4.4
NIS:				
Goods export volumes (% change)	15.3	10.9	8.5	5.8
Goods import volumes (% change)	4.3	8.6	9.3	8.6
Exports ($ billion)	69.5	79.2	88.9	95.9
Imports ($ billion)	58.8	64.8	72.6	81.3
Current balance ($ billion)	3.6	1.7	1.7	–2.1

a) Excludes intra-NIS trade and trade between the Czech Republic and the Slovak Republic.
b) Newly Independent States: all countries previously comprising the Soviet Union but excluding the Baltic States.
c) Poland, Hungary, Czech Republic, Slovak Republic, Romania and Bulgaria.

Table 23. **Inflation**

Percentage change in average level of consumer prices over previous year

	1993	1994	1995	1996
Bulgaria[a]	64	125	60	30
Czech Republic	21	10	9	8
Hungary	22	19	27	16
Poland	35	32	23	18
Romania	295	137	45	35
Russia[a]	840	226	102	60
Slovak Republic	23	13	10	8

a) December-on-December.

Table 24. **Current balances**

$ billion

	1993	1994	1995	1996
Bulgaria	–1.4	–0.4	–0.2	0.0
Czech Republic	0.4	0.3	0.2	0.0
Hungary	–3.5	–3.9	–3.0	–3.0
Poland	–2.3	–0.9	–0.9	–1.4
Romania	–1.2	–0.2	0.3	0.2
Slovak Republic	–0.6	–0.1	0.0	0.0
NIS	3.6	1.7	1.7	–2.1
of which:				
Russia	2.6	0.5	0.6	–1.4

ment, welfare). This approach has contained social tensions but created threats to fiscal sustainability.

Hungary faces an especially difficult adjustment challenge due to the presence of unsustainable deficits both in the budget and on the current account of the balance of payments (Table 24). The authorities addressed the twin deficit problem in March 1995, proposing an aggressive stabilisation programme. The programme tackles the balance-of-payments problem by means of a 9 per cent step devaluation – to be followed by pre-announced devaluations to the end of the year, the total devaluation amounting to some 29 per cent in the course of 1995 – and an import surcharge of 8 per cent. A tough fiscal package aims at a deficit reduction amounting to over 2 per cent of GDP and includes spending cuts resulting from an overhaul of some important social security programmes and a reduction in central government employment by some 15 per cent. It remains to be seen whether the fiscal part of the programme will be approved by the parliament so that it can be implemented. The projections presented here for the period 1995-96 assume that the government's package will be approved.

Poland and Slovakia seem to be somewhat less pressed for time with respect to radical restructuring of social security in general, and the pension system in particular. Nevertheless, given high unemployment and social expenditure levels, there is a clear need in both countries for a major reform of social security if the objective of balancing the budget over the medium-term period is to be achieved. Continued output growth in the range of 4-6 per cent is likely to increase the scope of fiscal choices facing the policy makers; however, infrastructure and human capital investment in both Poland and Slovakia remain low and need to be increased; this would leave no room for growth of social security expenditure.

The Czech Republic has achieved small fiscal surpluses in recent years while keeping the nominal exchange rate of the koruna constant. The major policy concern is posed by substantial capital inflows which the authorities are concerned not to accommodate via an appreciation of the nominal exchange rate. For the past one and a half years, the inflows have largely been sterilised so as to prevent an excessive growth of domestic liquidity which would jeopardise medium-term inflation control; this approach, however, has kept the domestic financial sector under a lot of pressure. In order to meet OECD standards and to move towards OECD Membership, the Government has submitted to the parliament a new foreign exchange law which implies a rapid move in the summer of 1995 towards full convertibility on the current account and Article VIII status in the International Monetary Fund (IMF), and a relaxation of restrictions on the capital account. Such liberalisation measures may serve to ease the pressures on monetary control arising from large capital inflows.

Strong foreign exchange inflows have also materialised in the early months of 1995 in Poland and Slovakia. Policymakers in these countries are considering moves towards greater convertibility in the next year, following the lead of the Czech Republic. Hungary has also submitted a new foreign exchange law to Parliament, going in the same direction. Restrictions on outward direct investment in the Visegrad group countries (Hungary, Poland, Czech Republic, Slovak Republic) were already relaxed with respect to member states of the European Union within the framework of the Association Agreements. Poland took steps in May towards greater market determination of the exchange rate by widening the band on the inter-bank foreign exchange market, while at the same time indicating that interest rates might be lowered somewhat.

Most transition countries moved rapidly in 1990 and 1991 from essentially non-convertible currencies to full convertibility for trade transactions, recognising the vital importance of linking the relative price structure of domestic goods and services to world market norms. But they have been much more careful in allowing citizens free access to foreign currencies for non-trade transactions, for fear of capital outflows which might jeopardise exchange-rate targets if they could not be financed from foreign exchange reserves, which were initially very low throughout the region. Underpinning these concerns has been the widespread use by households throughout the region of foreign exchange accounts, an institutional arrangement which pre-dated the transition but which has exercised an important discipline on economic policy since then.

The Visegrad countries protected themselves against capital outflows both by convertibility restrictions and by initially establishing exchange rates that, by comparison with purchasing power parity, were strongly undervalued. Despite some considerable subsequent real appreciation, capital is now being attracted by the relatively low price of many assets (including labour skills), but also by the rapidly increasing confidence that the risk of serious macroeconomic disruption or government action to expropriate foreign investors is small. These factors are acting most strongly in the case of the Czech Republic where real appreciation linked to still higher inflation in the Czech Republic than the average of partner countries is being accentuated by upward pressure on the nominal exchange rate.

While the risk of capital outflow has represented a concern to the authorities in the Visegrad countries, the problems associated with capital inflows in the course of pursuing stabilisation policies under conditions of rising capital mobility are now also attracting their attention. In particular, there is a legitimate concern, under present and foreseeable industrial conditions, to avoid a significant appreciation of the exchange rate which could be occasioned by large short-term capital inflows. While monetary instruments for sterilising such flows are limited by the underdeveloped state of the capital markets and the banking system, it should nonetheless be possible to avoid much of the dilemma by careful management of monetary policy. More generally, concern with capital flows should not be viewed as an argument in favour of exchange controls *per se* rather than appropriate economic policy. Exchange controls are in any event likely to become less and less effective over time. To prepare for this, what is needed is energetic pursuit of structural reforms that improve the capacity of domestic financial systems to operate in an open environment. To enhance the credibility of this process, a clear timetable for foreign-exchange liberalisation needs to be established in the framework of a medium-term programme for structural reforms and stabilisation.

The countries in the high-inflation group (Bulgaria, Romania and Russia) have to cope with a higher degree of financial instability than those discussed above. The Russian stabilisation programme of 1994 fell apart in the second quarter, with an acceleration of money supply growth feeding through to price inflation in the second half of the year. A flood of presidential decrees favouring special interests resulted in an erosion of fiscal discipline; this process was exacerbated by the increase of military expenditure associated with the conflict in Chechnya in the last few months of the year.

The 1995 budget passed by the Russian parliament aimed for a deficit of just under 8 per cent of GDP. However, nominal expenditures and revenues were formulated in late autumn 1994 as inflation was accelerating well above the assumed level so that nominal GDP in 1995 will exceed the projected level by more than 30 per cent, reducing the deficit, if maintained in nominal terms, to about 5½ per cent of GDP. This would represent an enormous fiscal adjustment after the estimated 1994 outturn of 11 per cent. Furthermore, the revised central bank law has imposed limits on direct financing of the deficit. Provided these limits are adhered to (without evasion through purchases of government debt on the secondary market), and the IMF standby loan (the equivalent of almost 3 per cent of GDP) and net sales of government debt to the private sector cover the deficit, the target of reducing inflation to 1-2 per cent per month by the last quarter of the year, though ambitious, is feasible. By April 1995 the monthly rate of inflation was still running at 8 per cent.

The range of variation in microeconomic reforms is perhaps just as wide as that in progress towards macroeconomic stabilisation. Second to price liberalisation, privatisation has been the key component of all reform programmes, and most countries can claim dramatic results measured by the share of the private sector in GDP by the end of 1994: some 80 per cent in the Czech Republic, more than half in Russia. It is tempting to conclude that the recoveries in GDP are a measure of the success of the privatisation programmes. Such a conclusion would be premature, not because of contrary evidence but unfortunately because direct evidence is hard to come by, and also because the nature of privatisation has varied widely.

To start with, the most dynamic sector of most transition economies has been the growth of the services sector; this sector has the major concentration of growth in new companies, as well as those privatised in small-privatisation programmes (where enterprises were usually sold to individuals). There seems little doubt that new private companies have shown more dynamic growth than either state-owned or privatised companies, though it may be difficult to be sure even of this because of high failure rates and the difficulties official statistics have in tracking the performance of small new enterprises. In Poland, where the GDP upturn appeared first, the most successful firms have come from those that were already private companies in the small private sector that existed under communism and had begun to expand in the 1980s.

In addition, where companies have been privatised to combinations of managers, workers and diverse outside investors, changes in behaviour appear only slowly. When foreign investors have brought management expertise and new markets, as well as some new investment, change is more rapid. Policymakers in almost all countries that have relied heavily on mass-privatisation or on rapid privatisation to insiders are recognising that both concentrated ownership and new investment are very important. Privatisation policy is being re-thought so as to place more emphasis on these aspects rather than on merely changing ownership. The resulting tendency in Russia to create groupings of banks and already privatised enterprises may well concentrate ownership and financial resources, and in the Russian context risks resulting in control by closed rent-seeking groups rather than the installation of outward-looking, efficiency-seeking management – it may also undermine the independent development of the financial sector. Furthermore, in countries such as Bulgaria, Romania and many members of the Commonwealth of Independent States (CIS), where very little privatisation has yet occurred, the inherently slower and more complex process of privatising only to ''real'' owners will prevent the private sector reaching a ''critical mass'' for some time, further delaying a full transition to a market-based economy.

It is true that rapid privatisation must be recognised as having severe drawbacks from the point of view of corporate governance, particularly when insider groups of managers and workers have effective control. But its role in anchoring the whole market-reform process has been important. In considering where to focus attention next, promoting effective competition for, and a market in, management – to which end the developments of secondary markets in privatisation shares is important – should be more productive than moves back towards forms of state control which could indefinitely and dangerously postpone further necessary steps in transformation.

Prospects

Russian GDP may well stabilise during 1995, even though the ambitious fiscal programme is bound to reduce domestic demand and output to some extent. Providing that financial discipline can be maintained, aggregate output growth driven by strong exports is likely to materialise in 1996. A series of microeconomic reforms taking place in Russia and the CEECs in recent years should make the positive turnaround feasible across the entire region (Tables 25 and 26).

Table 25. **Output**

Percentage change over previous year

	1993	1994	1995	1996
Bulgaria	–4.2	0.0	2.0	2.0
Czech Republic	–0.9	2.6	4.0	5.0
Hungary	–0.8	2.5	1.0	3.0
Poland	3.8	5.0	5.5	5.0
Romania	1.3	3.4	3.0	4.5
Russia	–12.0	–15.0	–5.0	2.5
Slovak Republic	–4.1	4.8	5.0	5.0

Table 26. **General government budget balances**

Percentage of GDP

	1993	1994	1995	1996
Bulgaria	–11.4 [a]	–6.8 [a]	–5.0	–5.0
Czech Republic	0.7	0.6	0.0	0.0
Hungary [c]	–6.0	–8.0	–6.0	–4.0
Poland [a, b]	–2.9	–2.7	–3.3	–2.5
Romania	–0.7	–4.0	–2.5	–2.5
Russia	–9.5	–11.0	–8.0	–6.0
Slovak Republic	–7.5	–4.0	–3.0	–2.0

a) Cash basis; excludes accrued interest on foreign debt.
b) State budget excluding local authorities but including extra-budgetary funds.
c) Excluding privatisation.

CHINA AND THE DYNAMIC ASIAN ECONOMIES

Recent trends and outlook for the Chinese economy

Since the beginning of 1995, China has embarked on its third attempt at macroeconomic stabilisation in less than two years, the previous attempts having failed to achieve a ''soft landing'', which in the case of China means bringing real GNP growth and inflation down to single-digit rates. As in the past, current macroeconomic tightening relies on selective credit rationing, mainly to contain private investment growth, and administrative measures to control food prices. In addition, financial reforms to improve the independence of the central bank and the efficiency of the commercial banks were announced in the first half of the year; these should help monetary management.

Preliminary figures suggest that economic activity has started to slow with the rate of industrial output growth in the first half of 1995 apparently decelerating to less than 20 per cent, against almost 25 per cent in the second half of 1994, and the growth of retail sales in nominal terms edging down from a rate of more than 35 per cent to about 30 per cent. However, exports have continued to grow very rapidly. Inflation remains high, with retail prices still apparently running close to 20 per cent in the first half of 1995. Soft budget constraints on loss-making state enterprises remain a major structural cause of inflation, as they result in a continued rapid expansion of the money supply, which is currently growing well beyond target range. Accommodating the losses of these enterprises has also resulted in a deterioration of the budget deficit. The calculated consolidated budget of the central government and local administrations is about 2.5 per cent of GNP (IMF definition).[1] However, a more comprehensive measure defined to include the central bank financing of the deficit of the state enterprises ("hidden deficit") suggests that the actual deficit could be much higher.[2] With a large proportion of China's external debt held in the form of public or publicly guaranteed debt, the external balance constitutes an additional possible source of strain for the overall government debt. China's foreign debt grew from around $84 billion in 1993 to around $100 billion last year.

Curbing inflation represents a top priority target for the rest of 1995. The March National People's Congress approved a new bank law strengthening the central bank's role in the fight against inflation. It also urged the implementation of a more stringent fiscal policy; and indeed the projected budget deficit for 1995 implies a decline in real terms from 1994. Even though these new measures should help, the prospects for the Chinese economy over the medium term will remain uncertain, since monetary tightening and administrative measures alone are insufficient to achieve macroeconomic stabilisation as long as a root-and-branch reform of the public sector continues to be delayed. Like the other two recent attempts to curb inflation, the current plan is in conflict with the interests of the state-owned enterprises, which are likely to exert pressures on the government to relax the credit restraints.

Economic and political uncertainties appear to have caused announced foreign direct investment (FDI) inflows to fall back. However, actual net inflows in 1995 may remain above the average since 1992 – around $24 billion – even if somewhat below the level in 1994. Over the next few years, the authorities' intention to contain foreign debt would be easier to implement if China were to attract strong FDI inflows. This is more likely if a more transparent legal framework and measures to ensure the enforcement of the rules were implemented. OECD Secretariat projections for China (Table 27) are based on the continuation of tight policies. On this basis, real GNP growth in 1995 could slow to about 10 per cent. Retail-price increases, though falling substantially, are likely to remain above 15 per cent; this is the authorities' target. The current account should remain broadly in balance.

Table 27. **China and the Dynamic Asian Economies: key economic indicators**[a]

	1993	1994	1995	1996
China				
GNP	13.0	11.8	10.0	9.0
Retail prices	13.0	21.8	17.0	13.5
Current account balance	–11.6	–0.5	0.0	–1.0
DAEs Total				
GDP/GNP	6.5	7.6	7.6	6.9
Consumer prices	4.3	5.4	5.5	5.7
Trade balance	0.8	–5.9	–8.7	–7.0
Current account balance	8.0	–1.2	–5.6	–5.0
Korea				
GDP	5.8	8.4	8.5	7.0
Consumer prices	4.8	6.2	6.0	7.0
Trade balance	1.8	–3.1	–6.0	–5.0
Current account balance	0.4	–4.8	–8.0	–7.5
Chinese Taipei				
GNP	6.0	6.1	6.3	6.4
Consumer prices	2.9	4.1	4.5	4.2
Trade balance	11.6	11.9	11.7	11.4
Current account balance	6.7	6.0	5.5	5.0
Hong Kong				
GDP	5.8	5.5	5.5	5.0
Consumer prices	8.5	8.1	9.0	8.5
Trade balance	–3.8	–10.9	–11.0	–10.4
Current account balance	7.9	2.4	2.3	3.0
Singapore				
GDP	9.9	10.1	8.5	7.5
Consumer prices	2.4	3.6	3.0	2.8
Trade balance	–8.1	–1.9	–2.0	–2.0
Current account balance	2.0	7.7	7.4	7.0
Thailand				
GDP	7.8	8.5	8.8	8.5
Consumer prices	3.5	5.1	5.0	4.5
Trade balance	–4.1	–4.6	–4.8	–4.6
Current account balance	–6.9	–8.0	–8.5	–8.5
Malaysia				
GDP	8.5	8.7	8.5	8.2
Consumer prices	3.6	3.7	4.2	4.4
Trade balance	3.4	2.7	3.4	3.6
Current account balance	–2.1	–4.5	–4.3	–4.0

a) The figures given for GDP/GNP and consumer prices are percentage changes from previous period. Trade and current account balances are in $ billion. Current account estimates for Hong Kong correspond to net exports of goods and services on a national account basis and therefore exclude investment income and transfers. The trade balance corresponds to net exports of goods on a national account basis.

Source: IMF, *International Financial Statistics*; Chinese Taipei sources; Hong Kong Census and Statistics Department, *Monthly Digest of Statistics*; OECD estimates and projections.

Recent developments and forces shaping economic activity in the Dynamic Asian Economies

Even before the financial crisis in Mexico, some Asian markets had lost buoyancy, faced with political uncertainty in China. In the days following the devaluation of the Mexican peso there were capital outflows from the DAEs and a marked drop in stock prices, ranging between 6 per cent in Singapore and 15 per cent in Korea. Nevertheless, the Asian markets seem to have weathered the crisis better than those in Latin America (see below). Stock market losses have since been completely offset in Hong Kong but markets remain volatile in other countries in the region. High levels of domestic savings and foreign reserves were two important alleviating factors, especially at the beginning of the crisis, when the acceleration of capital outflows exerted strong pressures on exchange rates. In addition, the DAEs' foreign capital inflows are mostly FDI, even though portfolio investment has grown at a faster pace during the past few years. In any case they are still able to raise money on the international credit market, even though the appreciation of the yen may entail very prudent debt management policies in some economies. In Thailand and Malaysia, more than 35 per cent of the external debt is denominated in yen, and the yen's appreciation aggravates debt servicing problems.

From early 1993 until the end of 1994, the DAEs' nominal exchange rates *vis-à-vis* the US dollar have remained relatively stable and consequently they have depreciated substantially *vis-à-vis* the yen.[3] Thanks to the improvement in relative competitiveness against Japan, which has been more marked in the case of Korea and Chinese Taipei (Figure 14, Panels A and B), the cross effects of the yen-dollar rate have been an important factor in explaining these countries' exports. New strong gains in competitiveness against Japan have occurred since the beginning of 1995, even thought the nominal exchange rate against the dollar appreciated somewhat. As a result, market share gains have been mostly concentrated in Asia and the proportion of intra-regional trade in total trade is increasing further.

Rising export revenues and capital inflows are boosting investment, and the appreciation of the yen together with capital market liberalisation are likely to make the DAEs an increasingly attractive zone for FDI flows from Japan. There seems to be evidence of this already – during the fiscal year ending in March 1995, Japanese FDI in Asia increased to $9.7 billion from $6.6 billion in the previous fiscal year. With a rising demand for skilled workers outpacing supply, surging economic activity in the DAEs is reflected in a tighter labour market, especially in Malaysia and Thailand. The associated strong rises in real incomes are spurring households' consumption. Strong domestic demand pressures are also boosting imports, especially of capital goods from Japan, which supplies 20 to 30 per cent of the region's imports.

The effects of the yen's appreciation on import prices and FDI have exacerbated inflation pressures, which were already high because of the strength of domestic demand and special factors, for example, the high level of liquidity in the money market (Hong Kong and Malaysia), and the growth of public infrastructure investment (Thailand). In Korea, inflation expectations have remained strong, given the decline in unemployment and the acceleration of wages. The DAEs' monthly rate of inflation is currently accelerating in Korea, Hong Kong, Chinese Taipei and Thailand.

Outlook and policy choices for the Dynamic Asian Economies

All in all, the DAEs' economic activity should remain robust in 1995, with prospects favourable for both exports and domestic demand. Real GDP growth is likely to remain above $7\frac{1}{2}$ per cent in 1995 before decelerating to about 7 per cent in 1996. Buoyant investment demand will be sustained by high domestic saving rates and FDI inflows, but will also be met by higher imports of capital goods. Hence, despite the favourable effects of the yen's appreciation on exports, trade and current-account balances are likely to deteriorate further. Strong activity and higher import prices due to the yen's appreciation imply that the inflation rate may increase somewhat in 1995.

Even though food prices show signs of a deceleration in East Asia, with these prices an important source of inflationary pressures in 1994, rising inflation is the most important factor conditioning short-term policy priorities. To control inflation pressures, the DAEs' authorities are likely to maintain the cautious macroeconomic policy stance that was implemented in 1994. The appreciation of the yen might be an additional factor justifying the continuation of these policies in those economies holding greater amounts of yen-denominated debt. Fiscal policies will remain conservative or neutral in most countries, except Thailand – where the budget surplus is falling relative to GDP, even though it is likely to remain roughly in balance this year – and Chinese Taipei, the only DAE to have experienced a rapid deterioration of the deficit over the past few years. With buoyant growth increasing revenues, Korea should move close to balance in 1995 after a small deficit in 1994. As Asian countries tend to encourage private investment capital for the building of infrastructure, a growing demand now evident for such investment is unlikely to cause excessive pressures on public expenditures.

Since the beginning of the year, short-term interest rates have been raised in most countries, also in reaction to pressures on exchange rates. However, monetary policy differs widely across the DAEs. In Korea and Thailand, real short-term interest rates have reached

Figure 14. **Real exchange rates for selected Asian and Latin American countries**[1]

January 1990 = 100

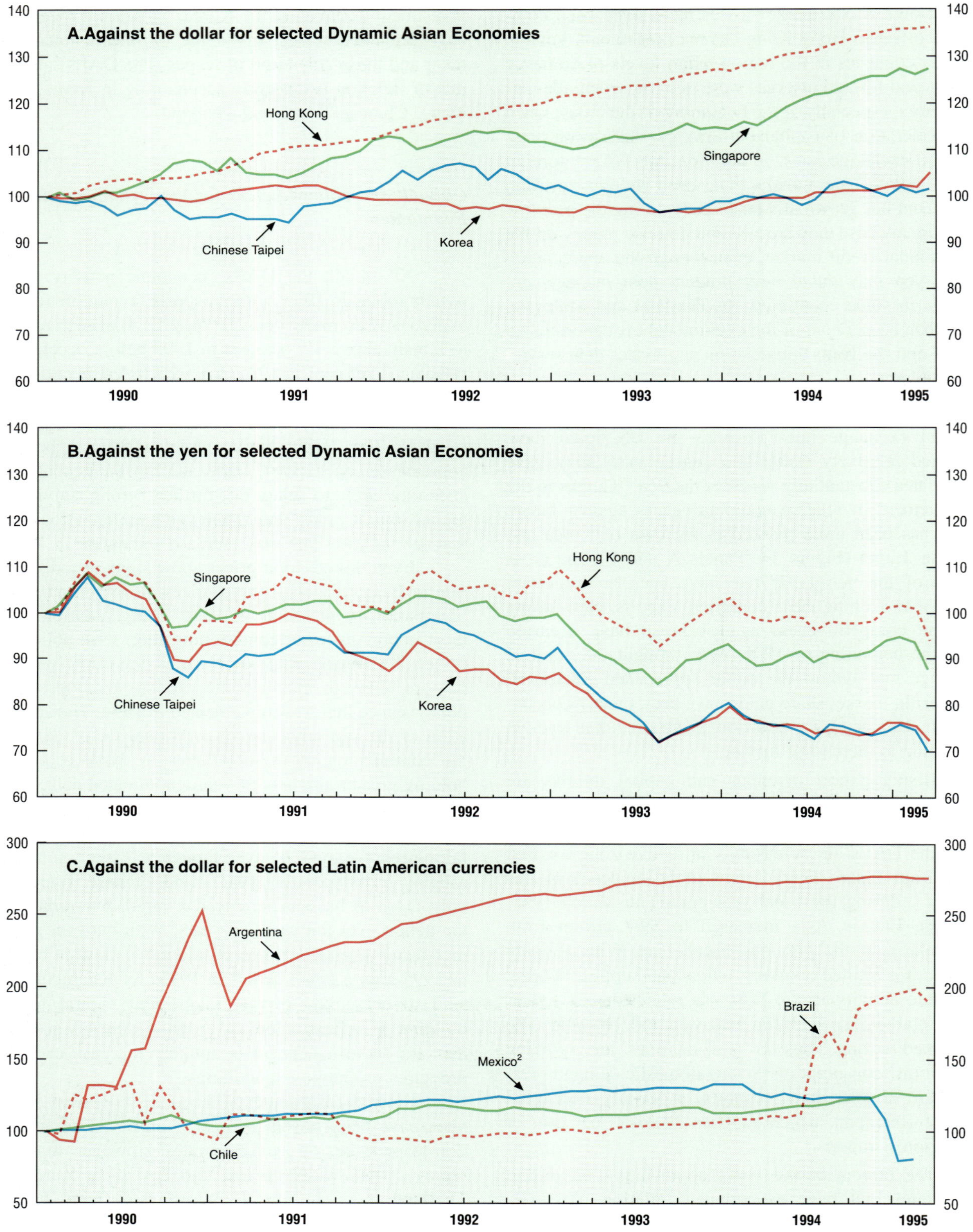

1. CPI based.
2. Mexico became an OECD country in 1994.

levels of about 10 and 8 per cent, respectively. At the other extreme, in Hong Kong, with the exchange rate pegged to the dollar and interest rates moving in tandem with rates in the United States, real interest rates are negative and money markets are excessively liquid. Similarly, short-term real interest rates are negative in Malaysia and are close to zero in Singapore. In Korea, slowing the economy to the projected rate of 7 per cent in 1996 may require that the yields on three-year corporate bonds, which were near to 15 per cent in April, rise as high as 18 per cent.

A major uncertainty for the DAEs, and especially for Hong Kong and Chinese Taipei, is the possible effects on financial markets of political instability in China, which could reduce the likelihood of a "soft landing" in that country. On the other hand, growth and export prospects in these economies should not be greatly affected by possible continued macroeconomic tightening in China as prospects for exports to OECD countries and the Asia Pacific region remain good.

SOUTH AND CENTRAL AMERICA

Macroeconomic policies in recent years

Private capital inflows into South and Central America had been substantial in the years preceding the Mexican crisis. These inflows had boosted domestic demand, caused a real appreciation of many currencies (Figure 14, Panel C) and led to current-account deficits in most of the region. To control inflationary pressures, most countries (with the main exception of Venezuela) adopted restrictive macroeconomic policies, generally entailing balanced budgets and tight monetary policy. Policy responses to capital inflows and the level of domestic savings varied considerably within the region, however. This explains, for the most part, the different degrees of vulnerability to the reduction or reversal of capital flows which occurred after December 1994.

Since 1991, Argentina has pegged its currency to the dollar through a currency board system, which legally ensured that the monetary base was fully backed by foreign currency reserves. It also allowed an almost unimpeded inflow of capital, in the hope that inflation and interest rates would converge rapidly to international levels. These rates did not fall as rapidly as expected, however, mostly as a result of a large increase in domestic demand and a fall in household savings, as stabilisation was followed by a credit boom. As the currency appreciated in real terms, the current account moved increasingly into deficit, reaching 4 per cent of GDP in 1994. In the meantime, persistently high differentials between domestic and international interest rates attracted large flows of short-term portfolio investment.

Brazil's stabilisation programme started to be implemented only in July 1994. Until then, capital inflows had been used to accumulate foreign exchange reserves, keeping the real exchange rate relatively stable. As the reserve accumulation was largely unsterilised, domestic liquidity and inflation increased rapidly. The policy response to capital inflows changed considerably with the beginning of the stabilisation programme. A new currency, introduced in July 1994, was allowed to appreciate sharply – almost 40 per cent in real terms in the second half of 1994 – leading to monthly trade deficits from November 1994. Minor restrictions on short-term capital inflows were also maintained.

In Chile, the current account deficit fell to 1½ per cent of GDP in 1994, after peaking at 5 per cent in 1993. The success in reducing external imbalances was achieved by restrictive macroeconomic policies combined with the floating of the currency within bands, intervention in the foreign exchange market and sterilisation of the monetary effects of reserve accumulation. Chile also imposed non-interest bearing reserve requirements on short-term foreign credits and on foreign currency deposits in commercial banks. This introduced distortions, but in the context of a generally liberal investment regime, helped orient capital inflows towards long-term foreign direct investment. At the same time, reforms which considerably liberalised the social security and pension systems were increasingly reflected in higher domestic saving rates – 25 per cent of GDP – decreasing the dependency on foreign capital for domestic investment and growth.

Colombia and Peru have maintained floating exchange rates in the past few years, but intervened to moderate exchange-rate appreciation, accumulating a large amount of reserves, most of it in 1994. Capital inflows helped fuel domestic demand and led to large current account deficits. The majority of these inflows took the form of long-term foreign direct investment, in large part due to important privatisation programmes, especially in Peru. In Venezuela, price and exchange controls and a banking crisis helped to undermine confidence. Coupled with one of the least liberalised regimes for foreign investment in the region, this meant that there was little capital inflow.

Policy responses to the reversal of capital flows

In early 1995, following the Mexican peso crisis, a large amount of capital flowed out of the region. Most affected was Argentina, where the currency board system implied that the resulting drop in official reserves was automatically reflected in the monetary base, leading to a liquidity squeeze. Interest rates rose sharply, causing some firms to default and some banks to fail. This created a crisis of confidence in the banking sector – withdrawals amounted to about 15 per cent of total deposits. In March 1995, a large financial support package was announced, including $4.7 billion in credits from the International Monetary Fund, the World Bank, and the Inter-American Development Bank. Part of this package was earmarked to support the banking system. The government also announced deep cuts in spending, tax increases, an acceleration of its privatisation programme, and an increase in certain import tariffs. This restored confidence and interest rates fell sharply – by mid-April overnight interest rates in the interbank market were back in the single digits, after reaching more than 70 per cent at the height of the crisis.

Capital outflows from Brazil were also significant. Initially, the government intervened to defend the currency and insulate domestic financial markets, resulting in a large drop in reserves. In March 1995, however, the government allowed the currency to depreciate – by about 5 per cent initially – and adopted an adjustable floating band, modeled on the Chilean experience. This was followed by the lifting of some restrictions on capital inflows and by a large increase in domestic interest rates. Import tariffs were also raised on a range of consumer durable goods, including automobiles After a large burst of capital outflows immediately following the devaluation, the situation appears to have stabilised – by mid-May, the currency was trading in the upper part of its band.

Chile, Colombia and Peru have been relatively little affected by capital outflows, as most of the inflows in the past few years had been in the form of foreign direct investment. Net capital inflows were much lower in the first quarter of 1995 (compared to 1994 levels), but appear to have picked up considerably after mid-April. Macroeconomic policy has not changed significantly, and most of the adjustment to lower levels of capital inflows was made through minor changes in the exchange rate and/or in domestic interest rates. Low levels of capital inflows into Venezuela in the past few years meant that the country was also little affected by the events in Mexico.

Outlook and policy choices

Macroeconomic performance in the region over the next few years will depend in part on the level at which capital flows stabilise. It is likely that inflows will be lower than in the past few years and that interest rates will remain higher than in 1994. The ensuing reduction in domestic demand growth will result in lower inflation and GDP growth rates. In the first half of 1995, trade figures for the region as a whole were strongly affected by the deficit in the Brazilian trade balance.[4] From the second half of 1995, the region's trade balance should visibly improve, as import demand growth falls and the Brazilian trade balance moves back into surplus. Current accounts will continue to be affected by increasing foreign debt servicing costs.

One of the main challenges facing the region in the next few years is to increase domestic savings in order to diminish dependency on foreign capital inflows. Steps in some countries to reform the pension and social security systems and further liberalise the financial sector should help in the medium to long term. As in many OECD countries, more assiduous fiscal consolidation would not only contribute to improve national savings, it would also reduce pressure on monetary policy, and thus allow for a reduction in real interest rates.

The outlook for Argentina improved significantly with the fiscal package announced in March 1995, which should prevent a large budget deficit in 1995. Even though growth will likely be much lower than in previous years, inflation will probably fall further towards international levels (Table 28). The trend towards a reduction in the trade and current account deficits – already visible in late 1994, mostly as a result of the trade-weighted depreciation of the peso associated with the appreciation of the Brazilian real – is projected to accelerate, as the growth of domestic demand slows down. Finally, recent steps regarding the deregulation and privatisation of pension funds are also expected to increase domestic savings in the medium term.

The adoption by Brazil of a more flexible exchange rate system should help reverse the sharp deterioration of external balances which started in late 1994.[5] This will probably entail a rise in inflation, which was already expected to move up, as domestic demand continues to grow strongly – the minimum wage was raised by more than 40 per cent in May. In the meantime, progress has been slow on the constitutional reforms which are needed to balance the budget in the medium-term and accelerate the privatisation programme. With little fiscal policy flexibility in the short-term, the government is expected to keep monetary policy extremely tight in order to prevent inflation from accelerating further. This is likely to reduce GDP growth slightly in 1995 and 1996. It is also expected that the recent increase in import tariffs will be reversed during 1996.

Table 28. **South and Central America: key economic indicators**[a]

	1993	1994	1995	1996
South and Central America[b]				
GDP	4.7	5.1	3.5	3.7
Trade balance	–1.2	3.2	2.5	4.6
Current account balance	–22.2	–21.3	–32.0	–30.0
Argentina				
GDP	6.1	6.5	1.0	2.5
Consumer prices	10.6	5.2	4.0	3.5
Trade balance	–3.7	–5.5	–1.5	0.0
Current account balance	–7.5	–11.0	–7.5	–6.0
Brazil				
GNP	5.3	5.7	4.5	4.0
Consumer prices	2490.0	940.0	35.0	35.0
Trade balance	13.1	10.4	2.5	4.0
Current account balance	–0.6	–3.5	–13.0	–12.0
Chile				
GNP	6.3	4.4	4.8	5.0
Consumer prices	12.5	10.6	8.5	8.0
Trade balance	–1.0	0.7	1.0	1.5
Current account balance	–2.4	–0.4	–0.5	0.0
Colombia				
GDP	4.6	5.3	5.5	5.5
Consumer prices	22.6	22.6	21.0	20.0
Trade balance	–1.7	–2.4	–2.5	–2.5
Current account balance	–2.2	–3.4	–4.0	–4.0
Peru				
GDP	7.0	12.5	8.0	6.0
Consumer prices	47.4	22.0	14.0	10.0
Trade balance	–0.6	–1.1	–1.8	–2.2
Current account balance	–2.2	–2.5	–3.5	–4.0
Venezuela				
GDP	–1.1	–3.3	–1.0	1.0
Consumer prices	37.5	58.0	80.0	80.0
Trade balance	3.2	8.0	8.5	8.5
Current account balance	–1.8	4.1	4.0	4.0

a) The figures given for GDP and consumer prices are percentage changes from previous period, with the exception of consumer prices in Brazil, which are expressed as changes from December to December. Trade and current account balances are in billions of dollars.

b) The figures for the South and Central America region include Venezuela. In other tables of the *Economic Outlook*, Venezuela is included in the OPEC aggregate.

GDP growth in Chile and Colombia is likely to stay at 1994 rates or even to accelerate slightly in 1995 and 1996. In Chile, strong export volume growth and high commodity prices – mainly copper – are expected to foster GDP growth and increase trade surpluses, leading to the elimination of the current-account deficit by 1996. In Colombia, GDP growth will be positively affected by increasing oil production, which should also help to close external imbalances after 1997. In Peru, growth is expected to decelerate from 1994 levels – from 12.5 to 8 per cent – as capacity utilisation reaches its limits and restrictive policies start to bear fruit. External imbalances are expected to increase as import demand for capital goods continues to grow strongly. In Venezuela, GDP is expected to fall for the third consecutive year before recovering in 1996. Inflation is expected to remain high because of large budget deficits and an increase in the money supply associated with the banking crisis which started in 1994 and which has involved the nationalisation of many banks. Imports are expected to recover in 1995 and 1996, as import and exchange controls are gradually phased out and domestic demand stops falling.

NOTES

1. See Tseng W. *et al.*, "Economic reform in China, a new phase", IMF *Occasional Paper 114*, Washington 1994.
2. For a discussion of this problem, see R.I. McKinnon, "Gradual versus rapid liberalization in Socialist economies", *Institute for Contemporary Studies*, San Francisco, 1994, and C. Wong, C. Heady and W.T. Woo, "Economic reform and fiscal management in Asia", *Asian Development Bank*, February 1993.
3. Singapore was an exception as the authorities allowed a strong appreciation of the local currency against the dollar with the result that the cross exchange rate against the yen did not depreciate.
4. Brazil accounts for about half of the region's GDP and more than a third of South and Central America's extra-regional trade.
5. Brazil's trade balance is expected to show a surplus in the second half of 1995, more than compensating for a first half deficit which may approach 1 per cent of GDP.

ANNEX

This Annex contains data on some main economic series which are intended to provide a background to the recent economic developments in the OECD area described in the main body of this report. (A complete list of Annex tables and figures is given beginning on page vii.) It also contains a section describing the OECD Secretariat's projection methods and underlying statistical concepts and sources. Data for 1995-96 are OECD Secretariat projections. The data in some of the tables have been adjusted to internationally agreed concepts and definitions in order to make them more comparable as between countries, as well as consistent with historical data shown in other OECD publications. Regional totals and sub-totals in each table are based on those countries in the table for which data are available. Aggregate measures contained in the Annex are computed on the basis of 1991 GDP weights expressed in 1991 purchasing power parities (see following page for weights). Aggregate measures for trade and payments statistics on the other hand, are based on current year exchange rates for values and base-year exchange rates for volumes.

NOTE ON STATISTICAL TREATMENT OF GERMANY

In this publication, data up to end-1990 are for western Germany only; unless otherwise indicated, they are for the whole of Germany from 1991 onwards. In tables showing percentage changes from the previous year, data refer to the whole of Germany from 1992 onwards.

COUNTRY CLASSIFICATION

	OECD
Seven major OECD countries	The United States, Japan, Germany, France, Italy, the United Kingdom and Canada
Smaller OECD countries	Australia, Austria, Belgium, Denmark, Finland, Greece, Iceland, Ireland, Luxembourg, Mexico, Netherlands, New Zealand, Norway, Portugal, Spain, Sweden, Switzerland, Turkey
OECD North America	United States, Canada, Mexico
European Union	Germany, France, Italy, United Kingdom, Austria, Belgium, Denmark, Finland, Greece, Ireland, Luxembourg, Netherlands, Portugal, Spain, Sweden
OECD Europe	European Union member countries, Iceland, Norway, Switzerland, Turkey
	Non-OECD
OPEC[a]	Algeria, Bahrain, Gabon, Indonesia, Iran, Iraq, Kuwait, the Libyan Arab Jamahiriya, Nigeria, Oman, Qatar, Saudi Arabia, the United Arab Emirates and Venezuela
Asian newly industrialising economies (ANIEs)	Chinese Taipei, Hong Kong, Korea and Singapore
Non-OPEC developing countries	
Other Asia	Non-OECD Asia and the Middle East, excluding OPEC countries and the ANIEs
Other Africa	Africa, excluding OPEC countries
Other Latin America	South and Central America, excluding OPEC countries
Central and Eastern European countries	Albania, Bulgaria, the Czech Republic, Hungary, Poland, Romania, the Slovak Republic, the Newly Independent States of the former Soviet Union, and the Baltic States

a) Historical statistics for OPEC include Ecuador up to and including 1992. Ecuador is included in Other Latin America beginning in 1993.

WEIGHTING SCHEME FOR AGGREGATE MEASURES

GDP weights used in calculating aggregate measures

Per cent

United States	36.35	Australia	1.77
Japan	14.91	Austria	0.86
Germany	8.63	Belgium	1.09
France	6.59	Denmark	0.57
Italy	6.19	Finland	0.49
United Kingdom	5.74	Greece	0.62
Canada	3.32	Iceland	0.03
		Ireland	0.27
Total of above countries	81.73	Luxembourg	0.05
		Mexico	2.79
Total of smaller countries	18.27	Netherlands	1.57
		New Zealand	0.29
OECD North America	42.46	Norway	0.45
OECD Europe	40.57	Portugal	0.65
European Union	37.40	Spain	3.15
		Sweden	0.92
Total OECD	100.00	Switzerland	0.94
		Turkey	1.75

Note: Based on 1991 purchasing power parities (PPPs). The benchmark year for the PPPs is 1990.

REFERENCE STATISTICS AND ANNUAL PROJECTIONS

Annex Table 1. **Real GDP**

Percentage changes from previous period

	Average 1970-77	1978	1979	1980	1981	1982	1983	1984	1985	1986	1987	1988	1989	1990	1991	1992	1993	1994	Projections 1995	1996
United States	3.0	4.8	2.5	–0.5	1.8	–2.2	3.9	6.2	3.2	2.9	3.1	3.9	2.5	1.2	–0.6	2.3	3.1	4.1	3.2	2.3
Japan	4.4	4.9	5.5	3.6	3.6	3.2	2.7	4.3	5.0	2.6	4.1	6.2	4.7	4.8	4.3	1.1	–0.2	0.6	1.3	2.3
Germany	2.7	3.0	4.2	1.0	0.1	–0.9	1.8	2.8	2.0	2.3	1.5	3.7	3.6	5.7	5.0	2.2	–1.1	2.9	2.9	2.7
France	3.5	3.3	3.2	1.6	1.2	2.5	0.7	1.3	1.9	2.5	2.3	4.5	4.3	2.5	0.8	1.3	–1.5	2.7	3.0	3.2
Italy	3.4	3.6	5.8	4.1	0.6	0.2	1.0	2.7	2.6	2.9	3.1	4.1	2.9	2.1	1.2	0.7	–1.2	2.2	3.0	2.9
United Kingdom	2.2	3.5	2.8	–2.2	–1.3	1.7	3.7	2.3	3.7	4.4	4.8	5.0	2.2	0.4	–2.0	–0.5	2.2	3.8	3.4	3.0
Canada	5.1	4.6	3.9	1.5	3.7	–3.2	3.2	6.3	4.8	3.3	4.2	5.0	2.4	–0.2	–1.8	0.6	2.2	4.5	3.9	3.4
Total of above countries	3.3	4.3	3.6	0.9	1.7	–0.3	2.9	4.6	3.3	2.9	3.2	4.5	3.2	2.4	1.0	1.6	1.3	3.0	2.8	2.6
Australia	3.3	4.0	4.0	2.5	3.4	–0.1	0.7	7.5	4.8	2.1	4.6	4.1	4.4	1.4	–1.5	2.0	3.9	5.4	3.8	3.5
Austria	4.1	0.1	4.7	2.9	–0.3	1.1	2.0	1.4	2.5	1.2	1.7	4.1	3.8	4.2	2.9	1.8	–0.1	2.7	2.8	2.3
Belgium	3.3	2.7	2.1	4.3	–1.0	1.5	0.5	2.2	0.8	1.4	2.0	4.9	3.5	3.2	2.3	1.9	–1.7	2.3	2.7	2.6
Denmark	2.5	1.5	3.5	–0.4	–0.9	3.0	2.5	4.4	4.3	3.6	0.3	1.2	0.6	1.4	1.3	0.8	1.5	4.4	3.4	3.0
Finland	2.9	2.2	7.3	5.3	1.6	3.6	3.0	3.1	3.3	2.4	4.1	4.9	5.7	0	–7.1	–3.6	–1.6	3.9	4.8	3.9
Greece	5.0	6.7	3.7	1.8	0.1	0.4	0.4	2.8	3.1	1.6	–0.5	4.5	4.0	–1.0	3.2	0.8	–0.5	1.5	1.9	2.3
Iceland	6.6	7.0	5.5	7.0	4.3	2.0	–2.0	4.1	3.6	6.5	8.8	–0.3	0.2	0.5	1.0	–3.2	1.2	3.0	2.5	2.4
Ireland	4.9	7.2	3.1	3.1	3.3	2.3	–0.2	4.4	3.1	–1.4	5.7	4.3	7.4	8.6	2.9	5.0	4.1	6.0	5.8	5.0
Luxembourg	2.7	4.1	2.3	0.8	–0.6	1.1	3.0	6.2	2.9	4.8	2.9	5.7	6.7	3.2	3.1	1.9	1.7	2.7	3.1	2.9
Mexico	5.8	8.2	9.2	8.3	8.8	–0.7	–4.3	3.6	2.8	–3.8	1.9	1.2	3.3	4.4	3.6	2.1	0.8	3.5	–2.9	3.0
Netherlands	3.3	2.5	2.4	0.9	–0.7	–1.4	1.4	3.1	2.6	2.7	1.2	2.6	4.7	4.1	2.3	1.3	0.4	2.5	3.1	2.7
New Zealand	2.9	–6.4	1.5	0.4	4.7	3.4	2.4	8.7	1.6	1.3	–1.1	4.2	–1.5	0.1	–3.6	0.8	5.1	3.8	3.8	3.1
Norway	4.8	4.7	5.1	4.2	0.9	0.3	4.6	5.7	5.3	4.2	2.0	–0.5	0.6	1.7	1.6	3.4	2.3	5.1	4.8	3.5
Portugal	4.9	2.8	5.6	4.6	1.6	2.1	–0.2	–1.9	2.8	5.0	5.5	5.8	5.7	4.3	2.1	1.1	–1.2	1.2	2.9	3.2
Spain	4.7	1.5	0	1.3	–0.2	1.6	2.2	1.5	2.6	3.2	5.6	5.2	4.7	3.7	2.2	0.7	–1.1	2.0	3.0	3.2
Sweden	1.8	1.8	3.8	1.7	0	1.0	1.8	4.0	1.9	2.3	3.1	2.3	2.4	1.4	–1.1	–1.4	–2.6	2.2	2.5	2.4
Switzerland	0.9	0.6	2.4	4.4	1.4	–0.9	1.0	1.8	3.7	2.9	2.0	2.9	3.9	2.3	0	–0.3	–0.9	2.1	1.7	2.3
Turkey	6.1	1.5	–0.6	–2.4	4.9	3.6	5.0	6.7	4.2	7.0	9.5	2.1	0.3	9.3	0.9	6.0	7.5	–5.4	2.8	4.8
Total of smaller countries	4.2	3.1	3.4	2.8	2.3	0.9	1.0	3.5	3.1	2.0	3.6	3.3	3.5	3.6	1.4	1.6	0.9	2.2	2.2	3.1
Total OECD	3.5	4.1	3.6	1.2	1.8	–0.1	2.6	4.4	3.3	2.7	3.3	4.3	3.2	2.6	1.0	1.6	1.2	2.9	2.7	2.7
OECD North America	3.3	5.0	3.1	0.2	2.4	–2.1	3.3	6.0	3.3	2.5	3.1	3.8	2.6	1.3	–0.4	2.1	2.9	4.1	2.8	2.5
OECD Europe	3.3	2.9	3.4	1.4	0.4	1.0	1.8	2.5	2.6	3.1	3.2	4.1	3.4	3.2	1.5	1.2	–0.2	2.4	3.0	3.0
EU	3.2	3.0	3.6	1.4	0.1	0.9	1.7	2.3	2.5	2.9	2.9	4.2	3.6	3.0	1.6	1.0	–0.6	2.7	3.0	2.9
Total OECD *less* the United States	3.8	3.7	4.2	2.3	1.8	1.2	1.8	3.3	3.4	2.6	3.4	4.5	3.7	3.4	2.0	1.2	0.1	2.2	2.4	2.9

Annex Table 2. **Nominal GDP**

Percentage changes from previous period

	Average 1970-77	1978	1979	1980	1981	1982	1983	1984	1985	1986	1987	1988	1989	1990	1991	1992	1993	1994	Projections 1995	1996
United States	10.0	13.1	11.5	8.8	11.9	3.9	8.1	10.9	6.9	5.7	6.4	7.9	7.1	5.6	3.2	5.2	5.4	6.2	5.3	5.1
Japan	14.2	10.1	8.4	8.4	7.4	4.9	4.1	6.7	6.6	4.4	4.1	6.6	6.7	7.2	6.3	2.6	0.6	0.7	1.0	2.6
Germany	8.5	7.4	8.2	6.0	4.3	3.5	5.1	4.9	4.1	5.6	3.4	5.3	6.1	9.1	9.1	7.8	2.7	5.1	5.1	5.1
France	13.4	13.8	13.7	13.2	12.7	14.6	10.5	8.9	7.7	7.9	5.3	7.5	7.4	5.7	4.1	3.5	1.0	4.2	5.0	5.2
Italy	18.1	18.3	22.2	25.1	19.7	17.5	16.2	14.6	11.7	11.0	9.3	11.0	9.3	9.9	8.9	5.2	3.1	5.9	7.4	7.5
United Kingdom	16.0	15.4	17.6	16.9	10.0	9.5	9.1	7.0	9.6	7.8	10.0	11.3	9.4	6.8	4.4	3.8	5.6	5.9	5.8	5.8
Canada	13.6	10.9	14.3	12.2	14.9	5.2	8.4	9.6	7.5	5.8	9.1	9.8	7.4	2.9	0.8	2.0	3.4	5.2	6.1	5.7
Total of above countries	12.1	12.5	12.1	10.8	11.0	6.4	8.0	9.3	7.2	6.2	6.2	8.0	7.3	6.6	4.9	4.6	3.6	4.8	4.7	4.9
Australia	15.5	11.3	13.8	14.0	13.7	11.0	8.9	14.4	11.1	9.3	12.2	12.8	12.2	6.1	0.4	3.6	5.3	6.7	6.6	7.3
Austria	11.3	5.8	9.0	8.3	6.2	7.3	6.0	6.3	5.6	5.5	4.1	5.7	6.8	7.7	7.1	6.1	3.5	6.0	5.6	5.0
Belgium	12.0	7.3	6.7	8.2	3.7	8.7	6.1	7.5	7.0	5.2	4.4	6.7	8.4	6.5	5.0	5.3	2.6	4.5	5.0	4.9
Denmark	13.0	11.5	11.4	7.8	9.1	13.9	10.4	10.3	8.8	8.4	5.0	4.6	4.8	4.1	3.6	2.8	2.6	6.4	5.9	5.8
Finland	15.9	10.7	16.3	15.6	13.2	12.4	11.5	12.1	8.9	7.0	9.0	12.3	12.1	5.8	-4.8	-2.9	0.8	6.5	7.5	6.8
Greece	18.2	20.5	23.0	19.7	19.8	25.6	19.6	23.6	21.3	19.5	13.7	20.7	19.1	19.8	22.6	15.0	12.9	12.5	11.6	9.5
Iceland	37.8	56.3	48.5	63.1	56.3	56.5	72.7	32.9	36.2	32.5	30.9	23.0	20.6	14.9	8.4	-0.1	3.4	5.4	6.1	5.3
Ireland	19.7	18.5	17.2	18.2	21.3	17.8	10.4	11.0	8.5	4.3	8.0	7.5	12.1	6.7	4.0	6.4	7.8	7.8	8.5	8.2
Luxembourg	9.3	9.4	8.8	8.8	6.6	12.1	10.0	10.9	6.0	8.8	1.9	9.9	13.1	6.2	6.1	6.5	6.4	6.8	6.2	5.7
Mexico	22.6	26.4	31.2	39.4	37.1	60.1	82.2	64.7	60.8	67.6	142.9	102.4	30.0	35.1	26.1	16.9	10.9	11.3	24.3	27.7
Netherlands	12.4	8.0	6.4	6.6	4.8	4.5	3.3	5.1	4.5	2.9	0.7	3.8	6.0	6.5	5.0	3.9	2.0	4.5	5.0	4.5
New Zealand	15.1	7.9	17.5	16.2	22.1	15.4	7.3	15.6	17.3	15.8	14.3	11.1	6.4	3.4	-1.4	2.8	6.8	5.9	7.2	5.2
Norway	13.3	11.2	12.0	19.4	15.0	10.5	11.0	12.5	10.6	2.7	9.3	3.9	6.5	6.3	4.0	2.4	4.4	5.4	7.4	6.2
Portugal	19.7	25.8	26.2	26.5	19.5	23.3	24.4	22.3	25.2	25.4	17.2	17.3	17.8	17.8	18.0	14.7	6.1	6.3	7.5	7.7
Spain	19.6	22.4	17.0	14.9	12.4	15.7	14.2	13.3	10.5	14.6	11.8	11.1	12.2	11.3	9.5	7.5	3.2	6.2	7.2	7.3
Sweden	11.5	11.5	12.1	14.9	9.5	9.3	12.0	12.0	8.7	9.3	8.0	8.9	10.6	10.3	6.4	-0.4	0	5.1	6.6	5.5
Switzerland	7.0	4.0	4.5	7.4	8.5	6.1	4.0	4.6	6.9	6.8	4.7	5.4	8.2	8.1	5.4	2.3	1.3	3.8	3.3	4.3
Turkey	27.0	48.9	74.7	83.5	51.0	32.7	32.4	58.2	59.6	45.5	46.0	73.7	75.3	73.3	60.0	73.7	75.0	95.8	85.0	52.0
Total of smaller countries	17.3	18.9	22.0	24.2	18.7	21.5	24.2	24.1	22.6	22.6	32.9	30.1	19.8	18.8	14.6	13.3	11.2	16.2	16.9	13.9
Total OECD	13.1	13.7	14.0	13.2	12.4	9.2	11.0	12.1	10.1	9.2	11.1	12.1	9.6	8.8	6.7	6.2	5.0	6.9	6.9	6.5
Total OECD *less* Turkey	12.8	13.1	12.8	11.9	11.7	8.8	10.6	11.3	9.2	8.6	10.5	10.9	8.4	7.7	5.7	5.1	3.9	5.2	5.5	5.7
OECD North America	11.1	13.8	12.9	11.0	13.7	7.7	13.4	14.4	10.5	10.1	15.6	14.5	8.7	7.3	4.5	5.7	5.6	6.5	6.7	6.6
OECD Europe	14.6	15.1	17.1	17.3	12.7	12.1	11.1	11.5	10.7	10.1	8.7	11.5	11.6	11.2	9.4	8.2	6.0	9.7	9.4	7.9
OECD Europe *less* Turkey	14.0	13.5	14.3	14.1	11.0	11.2	10.2	9.4	8.5	8.5	7.0	8.6	8.6	8.5	7.1	5.4	3.1	5.4	6.0	5.9
EU	14.2	13.7	14.6	14.2	11.0	11.3	10.3	9.5	8.5	8.6	7.1	8.7	8.7	8.5	7.2	5.5	3.1	5.5	6.0	6.0
Total OECD *less* the United States	14.9	14.1	15.4	15.8	12.7	12.3	12.6	12.7	11.9	11.3	13.8	14.5	11.1	10.7	8.7	6.8	4.8	7.3	7.8	7.3

Annex Table 3. **Real private consumption expenditure**

Percentage changes from previous period

	Average 1970-77	1978	1979	1980	1981	1982	1983	1984	1985	1986	1987	1988	1989	1990	1991	1992	1993	1994	Projections 1995	1996
United States	3.4	4.1	2.4	–0.1	1.2	1.1	4.6	4.8	4.4	3.6	2.8	3.6	1.9	1.5	–0.4	2.8	3.3	3.5	2.7	1.9
Japan	5.0	5.4	6.5	1.1	1.6	4.4	3.4	2.7	3.4	3.4	4.2	5.2	4.3	3.9	2.2	1.7	1.0	2.2	2.3	3.1
Germany	3.6	3.7	3.3	1.2	–0.6	–1.3	1.5	1.8	1.7	3.5	3.4	2.7	2.8	5.4	5.7	3.0	0.5	1.3	1.0	3.0
France	3.8	3.7	3.0	1.2	2.1	3.5	0.9	1.1	2.4	3.9	2.9	3.3	3.1	2.7	1.4	1.4	0.2	1.5	2.2	3.4
Italy	3.9	3.2	7.1	5.7	1.5	1.2	0.7	2.0	3.0	3.7	4.2	4.2	3.5	2.5	2.7	1.1	–2.5	1.6	1.7	2.2
United Kingdom	1.8	5.3	4.3	0	0.1	1.0	4.5	2.0	3.8	6.8	5.3	7.5	3.2	0.6	–2.2	0	2.7	2.6	2.4	2.8
Canada	5.9	3.4	2.9	2.2	2.3	–2.6	3.4	4.6	5.2	4.4	4.4	4.5	3.4	1.0	–1.5	1.3	1.6	3.1	2.7	3.2
Total of above countries	3.8	4.3	3.8	0.9	1.2	1.5	3.4	3.4	3.7	3.8	3.5	4.1	2.8	2.4	0.9	2.1	1.8	2.6	2.3	2.5
Australia	3.8	3.4	2.9	3.4	4.3	2.7	1.4	2.9	5.3	1.1	2.5	3.9	5.6	2.5	0.6	3.3	2.0	4.0	3.9	3.2
Austria	4.9	–1.5	4.4	1.5	0.3	1.2	5.0	–0.1	2.4	1.8	3.1	3.6	3.5	3.6	2.9	1.9	0.2	2.3	2.3	2.0
Belgium	4.1	2.3	4.8	2.0	–1.1	1.3	–1.6	1.2	1.9	2.3	3.0	2.8	3.8	2.7	3.2	2.6	–1.0	0.7	1.9	2.3
Denmark	2.2	0.7	1.4	–3.7	–2.3	1.4	2.6	3.4	5.0	5.7	–1.5	–1.0	–0.4	0	1.2	1.1	2.4	7.1	4.2	3.0
Finland	2.9	2.5	5.5	2.0	1.2	4.7	2.6	2.7	3.2	4.0	5.2	5.1	4.3	0	–3.6	–4.9	–3.9	2.0	5.1	4.8
Greece	5.1	5.7	2.6	0.2	2.0	3.9	0.3	1.7	3.9	0.7	1.2	3.6	5.6	2.1	2.3	1.8	0.2	1.5	1.5	1.9
Iceland	6.7	9.0	2.8	4.4	6.4	5.1	–5.8	3.8	4.4	7.2	16.6	–4.3	–4.2	–0.4	5.1	–4.4	–4.5	1.7	3.8	3.0
Ireland	3.9	9.1	4.4	0.4	1.7	–7.1	0.9	2.0	4.6	0.3	5.0	4.4	7.9	1.3	2.6	2.9	1.2	5.0	5.7	4.8
Luxembourg	4.5	2.9	3.5	2.8	1.7	0.4	0.5	1.4	2.7	3.4	5.0	3.9	3.9	4.0	6.5	1.7	–0.9	2.1	3.0	3.1
Mexico	5.1	8.1	8.8	7.5	7.4	–2.5	–5.4	3.3	3.6	–2.8	–0.1	1.8	6.8	6.1	4.9	3.9	0.2	3.7	–7.5	1.0
Netherlands	4.0	4.3	3.0	0	–2.5	–1.2	0.8	0.9	2.4	2.6	2.7	0.8	3.5	4.2	3.1	2.5	0.7	1.7	1.9	2.3
New Zealand	2.0	–0.7	1.8	0.3	2.3	0.6	1.3	5.6	0.7	4.7	1.3	2.2	0.9	–0.2	–1.5	0.2	2.2	5.4	3.9	2.6
Norway	4.6	–1.2	3.2	2.3	1.1	1.8	1.5	2.7	9.9	5.6	–1.0	–2.8	–2.8	2.8	0	1.8	2.3	4.4	2.9	2.5
Portugal	5.8	–2.0	0	3.7	2.9	2.4	–1.4	–2.9	0.7	6.3	6.0	5.7	3.6	6.9	4.8	3.7	0.4	0.2	1.3	2.1
Spain	5.0	0.9	1.3	0.6	–1.3	–0.1	0.3	–0.2	3.5	3.3	5.8	4.9	5.7	3.6	2.8	2.1	–2.0	0.9	1.9	2.9
Sweden	2.1	–0.7	2.4	–0.9	–0.3	0.7	–2.0	1.5	2.7	4.4	4.6	2.4	1.2	–0.4	0.9	–1.4	–3.7	0.5	–0.8	0.7
Switzerland	2.0	2.1	1.1	2.6	0.5	0	1.7	1.6	1.4	2.8	2.1	2.1	2.2	1.5	1.5	–0.2	–0.8	1.3	0.7	1.5
Turkey	6.4	2.0	–1.2	5.9	–7.6	6.9	6.7	8.1	–0.6	5.8	–0.3	1.2	–1.0	13.1	1.9	3.3	7.1	–5.4	2.0	4.3
Total of smaller countries	4.5	2.8	3.1	2.6	0.6	0.9	0.4	2.1	3.0	2.4	2.6	2.7	3.8	4.2	2.4	2.2	0.4	1.6	0.7	2.5
Total OECD	3.9	4.0	3.7	1.2	1.1	1.4	2.9	3.2	3.5	3.6	3.3	3.9	3.0	2.8	1.2	2.1	1.5	2.4	2.0	2.5
OECD North America	3.7	4.4	2.8	0.6	1.7	0.6	3.9	4.7	4.4	3.2	2.7	3.6	2.4	1.8	–0.1	2.7	2.9	3.5	2.0	1.9
OECD Europe	3.7	3.2	3.6	1.8	0	1.1	1.7	1.7	2.6	4.1	3.6	3.7	3.1	3.4	2.2	1.6	0.2	1.4	1.8	2.8
EU	3.6	3.3	3.9	1.6	0.3	0.9	1.4	1.4	2.7	4.0	3.9	4.0	3.4	3.0	2.3	1.6	–0.1	1.7	1.8	2.8
Total OECD *less* the United States	4.2	3.9	4.4	2.0	1.0	1.6	1.9	2.2	3.1	3.6	3.6	4.0	3.6	3.5	2.1	1.7	0.5	1.8	1.6	2.8

Annex Table 4. **Real public consumption expenditure**

Percentage changes from previous period

	Average 1970-77	1978	1979	1980	1981	1982	1983	1984	1985	1986	1987	1988	1989	1990	1991	1992	1993	1994	Projections 1995	Projections 1996
United States	0	1.9	1.8	2.2	1.3	1.5	2.8	3.1	6.1	5.2	3.0	0.6	2.0	3.1	1.2	–0.7	–0.8	–0.7	–0.3	0.3
Japan	5.1	5.1	4.3	3.3	4.8	2.0	3.0	2.7	1.7	4.5	0.4	2.2	2.0	1.9	1.6	2.7	1.7	2.8	3.3	2.4
Germany	3.6	3.9	3.4	2.6	1.8	–0.9	0.2	2.5	2.1	2.5	1.5	2.1	–1.6	2.2	0.3	4.5	–1.2	1.2	1.8	1.3
France	3.3	5.1	3.0	2.5	3.1	3.7	2.1	1.1	2.3	1.7	2.8	3.4	0.5	2.1	2.8	3.4	3.3	1.0	0.9	1.1
Italy	3.3	3.5	3.0	2.1	2.3	2.6	3.4	2.3	3.4	2.6	3.4	2.8	0.8	1.2	1.6	1.0	0.7	0	0.4	0.3
United Kingdom	2.7	2.2	1.9	1.7	0.3	0.9	2.1	0.8	–0.1	1.6	1.0	0.7	1.4	2.5	2.6	0	1.0	1.6	1.1	1.2
Canada	4.5	1.7	0.6	2.8	2.5	2.4	1.4	1.2	3.2	1.6	1.7	4.1	4.0	3.2	2.8	1.2	0.5	–2.1	–1.0	–0.3
Total of above countries	2.2	3.1	2.6	2.4	2.2	1.6	2.5	2.5	3.8	3.9	2.2	1.6	1.5	2.5	1.5	1.0	0.3	0.4	0.8	0.9
Australia	5.1	5.1	1.0	4.1	3.5	–0.4	5.3	4.5	5.5	4.6	2.0	3.3	2.2	4.9	2.7	1.4	1.3	4.6	4.5	–2.0
Austria	3.9	3.3	3.0	2.7	2.2	2.3	2.2	0.2	1.9	1.7	0.4	0.3	0.8	1.2	3.1	2.4	3.0	2.4	2.0	1.0
Belgium	4.4	6.0	2.5	1.5	0.6	–1.3	0.2	0.3	2.5	1.8	0.3	–0.9	0.3	0.3	2.4	0.4	1.9	1.6	1.0	0.7
Denmark	3.9	6.2	5.9	4.3	2.6	3.1	0	–0.4	2.5	0.5	2.5	0.9	–0.6	–0.4	–0.1	1.4	2.8	0.6	0.7	0.4
Finland	5.8	4.1	3.8	4.2	4.3	3.5	3.7	2.8	5.2	3.1	4.3	2.3	2.3	3.8	2.5	–2.2	–5.3	–0.4	–1.0	–1.5
Greece	7.5	3.5	5.8	0.2	6.8	2.3	2.7	3.0	3.2	–0.8	0.9	5.7	5.7	–3.3	0.3	–3.0	0.3	0.2	0	0.6
Iceland	7.9	7.1	5.5	6.1	7.3	6.0	4.9	0.5	6.4	6.8	6.5	4.6	2.9	4.2	3.2	–0.8	2.2	1.4	2.0	2.0
Ireland	6.2	7.9	4.6	7.1	0.3	3.2	–0.4	–0.7	1.8	2.6	–4.8	–5.0	–0.9	5.8	2.7	2.4	1.1	2.5	3.0	3.0
Luxembourg	3.3	1.8	2.2	3.1	1.4	1.5	1.9	2.2	2.0	3.1	2.7	3.8	1.9	3.2	3.8	3.5	1.8	1.2	2.0	1.9
Mexico	8.4	9.9	9.6	9.5	10.3	2.0	2.7	6.6	0.9	1.5	–1.2	–0.5	–0.1	2.3	3.9	2.3	2.0	2.5	–9.5	–1.0
Netherlands	2.8	3.9	2.8	0.6	2.0	0.6	1.2	–0.7	1.2	3.6	2.6	1.4	1.5	1.6	1.5	1.3	0.1	1.0	1.7	0.7
New Zealand	4.2	4.0	0.8	–0.3	2.0	0.4	2.7	2.1	1.5	2.0	–0.7	2.7	–1.1	2.7	–0.9	1.3	–2.6	–1.0	1.0	0.5
Norway	5.5	5.4	3.6	5.4	6.1	3.9	4.6	2.4	3.3	2.2	4.0	0.5	2.6	2.1	2.6	4.4	1.8	2.7	1.2	1.0
Portugal	8.1	4.4	6.4	8.0	5.5	3.7	3.8	0.2	6.4	18.6	3.8	8.0	4.4	5.7	3.0	1.4	0	1.4	1.1	1.5
Spain	5.9	5.4	4.2	4.2	3.5	5.3	3.9	2.4	5.5	5.4	8.9	4.0	8.3	6.6	5.6	3.6	2.3	0.2	0.1	1.1
Sweden	3.1	3.2	4.8	2.3	2.3	1.0	0.8	2.2	2.2	1.3	1.0	0.6	2.1	2.6	2.8	0	–0.6	–1.0	–0.2	–0.7
Switzerland	2.6	2.0	1.6	0.9	2.5	1.1	3.9	1.2	3.3	3.7	1.8	4.3	4.1	4.7	1.5	–0.1	–1.7	1.4	–0.5	–0.4
Turkey	10.2	–2.9	–2.4	–18.5	48.8	–10.6	16.6	1.9	14.1	9.2	9.4	–1.1	0.8	8.0	4.5	3.8	4.8	–3.5	–1.0	1.5
Total of smaller countries	5.9	4.7	3.8	2.0	8.6	0.9	4.1	2.4	4.3	4.1	3.2	1.7	2.6	3.7	3.2	1.8	1.4	1.0	–0.7	0.2
Total OECD	2.9	3.4	2.8	2.4	3.4	1.5	2.8	2.5	3.9	3.9	2.4	1.6	1.7	2.8	1.8	1.2	0.5	0.5	0.5	0.7
OECD North America	0.9	2.4	2.2	2.7	2.0	1.6	2.7	3.2	5.5	4.7	2.7	0.8	2.0	3.1	1.5	–0.4	–0.5	–0.6	–1.0	0.1
OECD Europe	4.0	3.7	2.9	1.6	4.3	1.3	2.7	1.6	3.0	3.0	2.9	2.2	1.2	2.6	2.2	2.2	1.0	0.7	0.9	0.9
EU	3.7	4.0	3.2	2.5	2.2	1.8	1.9	1.6	2.4	2.7	2.6	2.3	1.1	2.3	2.1	2.2	0.9	0.9	1.0	0.9
Total OECD *less* the United States	4.5	4.2	3.4	2.5	4.6	1.5	2.8	2.1	2.6	3.2	2.0	2.2	1.5	2.5	2.2	2.3	1.2	1.3	1.0	1.0

Annex Table 5. **Real total gross fixed capital formation**

Percentage changes from previous period

	Average 1970-77	1978	1979	1980	1981	1982	1983	1984	1985	1986	1987	1988	1989	1990	1991	1992	1993	1994	Projections 1995	1996
United States	4.2	10.8	4.6	–8.1	0.6	–8.0	6.6	15.9	5.0	0.4	–0.5	4.2	0.1	–1.8	–7.6	5.5	11.3	12.3	10.5	4.9
Japan	2.9	7.8	6.2	0	2.4	–0.1	–1.0	4.7	5.3	4.8	9.6	11.9	9.3	8.8	3.7	–1.1	–1.8	–2.3	1.9	3.2
Germany	–0.1	4.1	6.7	2.2	–5.0	–5.4	3.1	0.1	–0.5	3.3	1.8	4.4	6.3	8.5	5.8	4.2	–4.5	4.3	6.5	5.9
France	2.5	2.1	3.1	2.6	–1.9	–1.4	–3.6	–2.6	3.2	4.5	4.8	9.6	7.9	2.8	0	–3.1	–5.8	1.1	5.8	5.8
Italy	0.3	0.6	5.4	8.5	–3.1	–4.7	–0.6	3.6	0.6	2.2	5.0	6.9	4.3	3.8	0.6	–1.7	–13.1	–0.1	5.4	7.1
United Kingdom	0.5	3.0	2.8	–5.4	–9.6	5.4	5.0	8.9	4.2	2.6	10.3	13.9	6.0	–3.5	–9.5	–1.2	0.3	3.2	4.2	4.6
Canada	5.9	3.1	8.5	10.1	11.8	–11.0	–0.7	2.1	9.5	6.2	10.8	10.3	6.1	–3.5	–2.2	–2.8	–0.2	6.0	5.1	5.9
Total of above countries	3.0	7.2	5.1	–2.5	–0.4	–4.7	3.1	8.8	4.2	2.3	3.7	7.2	4.0	1.8	–2.8	2.1	2.8	6.1	7.1	4.9
Australia	1.6	2.9	4.0	5.4	9.1	–3.2	–8.5	10.1	9.4	–2.2	3.5	7.8	9.3	–8.2	–9.8	0.5	2.5	11.1	6.0	3.7
Austria	4.7	–4.1	3.5	3.0	–1.4	–8.2	–0.6	2.1	5.0	3.7	3.1	6.0	6.2	5.7	6.3	1.3	–2.1	5.5	5.8	5.4
Belgium	2.5	2.8	–2.7	4.6	–16.1	–1.7	–4.4	1.7	0.7	4.4	5.6	15.4	12.3	10.2	–1.4	0.1	–5.9	–0.3	6.5	4.3
Denmark	0.7	1.1	–0.4	–12.6	–19.2	7.1	1.9	12.9	12.6	17.1	–3.8	–6.6	1.0	–1.7	–5.7	–7.2	–2.3	3.6	6.3	5.8
Finland	2.1	–6.9	3.0	10.4	2.2	4.4	4.1	–2.1	2.9	–0.4	4.9	9.8	14.8	–4.1	–20.3	–16.9	–18.6	2.8	14.7	13.9
Greece	2.8	6.0	8.8	–6.5	–7.5	–1.9	–1.3	–5.7	5.2	–6.2	–5.1	8.9	8.8	10.0	–6.7	–1.1	–2.5	0.7	6.4	7.2
Iceland	9.5	–3.2	0.2	14.2	1.0	–0.5	–12.3	9.2	2.0	–1.2	19.0	–0.6	–8.3	2.8	2.1	–11.1	–11.4	–1.1	5.3	5.8
Ireland	4.6	18.9	13.6	–4.7	9.5	–3.4	–9.3	–2.5	–7.7	–2.1	–2.3	–1.6	13.5	12.8	–8.2	–1.9	–0.4	7.2	8.5	7.0
Luxembourg	1.3	1.1	3.8	12.7	–7.4	–0.5	–11.8	0.1	–9.5	31.2	14.7	14.1	8.9	2.5	9.8	–2.1	9.9	1.7	2.5	4.2
Mexico	4.9	15.2	20.2	14.9	16.2	–16.8	–28.3	6.4	7.9	–11.8	–0.1	5.8	6.4	13.1	8.3	7.0	–0.1	8.1	–20.8	5.1
Netherlands	0.3	2.5	–1.7	–0.9	–10.4	–4.1	2.0	5.3	6.7	6.9	0.9	4.5	4.9	1.6	0.2	1.1	–2.2	2.7	6.9	3.8
New Zealand	3.1	–7.7	–7.7	1.1	11.4	12.2	0.2	11.7	3.8	–1.5	1.5	0.4	6.3	–0.3	–15.2	4.1	16.5	21.0	11.7	6.5
Norway	8.2	–18.5	–5.0	–1.5	17.9	–11.0	5.8	10.9	–13.9	23.9	–2.1	1.6	–3.9	–26.8	1.7	4.5	13.9	4.8	10.1	–3.2
Portugal	3.5	6.2	–1.3	8.5	5.5	2.3	–7.1	–17.4	–3.5	11.4	16.8	11.2	4.3	6.8	2.4	5.4	–4.8	3.5	7.5	7.8
Spain	3.2	–2.7	–4.4	0.7	–2.5	2.1	–2.4	–6.9	6.1	9.9	14.0	13.9	13.6	6.6	1.3	–4.1	–10.5	1.1	4.5	5.9
Sweden	0.7	–6.8	4.5	3.5	–6.0	–0.9	1.1	7.1	5.2	0.3	8.2	6.6	11.3	1.3	–8.9	–10.8	–17.6	–0.4	9.8	9.3
Switzerland	–1.5	5.6	5.1	9.8	2.7	–2.6	4.1	4.1	5.3	7.9	7.4	6.9	5.8	2.6	–2.5	–5.0	–3.1	6.5	4.2	3.9
Turkey	8.3	–17.1	2.8	–16.7	31.6	–5.7	2.6	0.9	11.5	8.4	45.1	–1.0	2.2	15.9	1.2	4.3	21.7	–15.9	–1.8	5.3
Total of smaller countries	3.6	0.6	3.6	2.3	4.0	–3.8	–5.3	2.0	5.7	3.3	8.9	7.0	7.8	5.0	–0.8	–0.2	–1.4	2.7	1.6	5.4
Total OECD	3.1	6.0	4.8	–1.7	0.4	–4.5	1.6	7.5	4.4	2.5	4.6	7.2	4.7	2.4	–2.5	1.7	2.0	5.4	6.1	5.0
OECD North America	4.5	10.5	5.9	–5.2	2.5	–8.8	3.8	14.2	5.5	0	0.4	4.8	1.0	–0.9	–6.1	5.0	9.7	11.5	8.0	5.0
OECD Europe	1.7	0.8	3.2	1.2	–3.0	–1.8	0.6	1.4	2.8	4.6	7.3	8.0	6.8	4.0	–0.5	–0.7	–4.7	1.5	5.6	5.8
EU	1.3	1.8	3.3	1.8	–5.0	–1.5	0.3	1.2	2.5	4.1	5.6	8.5	7.2	3.9	–0.6	–0.9	–6.2	2.2	5.9	6.0
Total OECD *less* the United States	2.4	3.3	4.9	2.1	0.3	–2.5	–1.4	2.7	4.1	3.8	7.6	8.9	7.4	4.8	0.5	–0.5	–3.3	1.5	3.6	5.1

Annex Table 6. **Real gross private non-residential fixed capital formation**

Percentage changes from previous period

	Average 1970-77	1978	1979	1980	1981	1982	1983	1984	1985	1986	1987	1988	1989	1990	1991	1992	1993	1994	Projections 1995	Projections 1996
United States	3.2	13.3	8.7	–2.4	3.9	–4.6	–3.0	16.5	6.4	–4.1	–0.5	6.6	1.7	1.2	–5.7	2.0	12.5	13.7	15.5	6.6
Japan	0.3	4.5	12.9	7.9	3.8	1.3	1.7	11.7	12.1	4.4	6.7	14.8	16.6	11.4	6.6	–4.7	–9.3	–8.8	1.2	2.7
Germany	–0.1	5.5	7.5	2.8	–3.9	–4.7	4.5	–0.4	5.0	4.3	3.8	5.6	7.4	10.1	7.2	1.0	–9.2	0.6	8.4	8.5
France	2.3	1.0	2.6	4.2	–2.5	0	–4.1	–2.1	4.4	6.6	6.0	9.6	8.6	4.7	0.4	–4.7	–7.1	–0.2	7.9	8.7
Italy	1.3	2.4	7.2	9.3	–8.1	–7.2	–4.4	6.7	0.8	5.0	9.2	12.0	5.6	5.4	–0.3	–1.0	–18.6	–0.1	7.2	8.6
United Kingdom	1.8	7.9	2.8	–4.3	–5.8	7.7	–0.6	14.3	13.2	0.5	17.3	17.8	6.2	–3.1	–9.5	–5.1	–0.7	0.3	6.6	6.5
Canada	6.1	6.1	18.7	20.5	15.5	–11.4	–7.0	2.0	8.9	4.5	9.7	15.8	6.2	–2.4	1.1	–7.5	0.7	7.7	7.4	7.1
Total of above countries	2.2	8.4	8.7	2.2	1.5	–2.8	–1.6	10.9	7.3	0.5	4.2	9.8	6.4	4.1	–1.3	–1.0	0.9	4.8	9.9	6.4
Australia	0.7	9.5	3.6	5.1	16.5	2.1	–9.8	5.3	13.1	–1.3	5.9	5.4	12.7	–7.7	–14.1	–2.5	–1.0	13.7	14.0	8.9
Austria	5.7	–4.6	4.7	4.6	–2.7	–10.2	–0.9	4.1	8.6	3.7	5.8	7.3	8.8	8.3	5.1	–2.6	–6.5	6.9	7.1	6.4
Belgium	2.0	3.5	1.9	1.0	–5.5	2.2	–3.9	6.0	2.6	5.8	7.1	15.1	13.7	11.8	–2.6	–4.6	–8.4	–2.0	9.5	5.5
Denmark	3.0	1.3	–2.0	–9.6	–16.5	19.9	2.7	12.1	18.9	18.8	–5.4	–7.3	5.8	2.6	–4.5	–11.4	–2.9	2.7	9.0	7.5
Finland	1.5	–13.9	6.6	15.5	5.0	2.5	6.8	–1.7	6.3	3.6	5.2	8.5	19.1	–6.4	–24.2	–21.3	–21.3	10.6	25.7	19.7
Greece	2.3	1.3	18.3	7.2	3.0	1.7	–11.0	–1.8	9.1	–17.3	–7.0	13.3	12.7	11.3	–6.8	3.2	0.4	5.0	6.5	7.0
Iceland	..	–1.2	–3.9	12.4	3.4	0.9	–11.1	15.2	20.6	7.4	20.8	–8.5	–21.3	8.1	0.2	–14.2	–29.3	1.2	8.0	10.0
Ireland	4.0	20.9	13.5	–4.6	15.7	–3.6	–11.0	–3.0	–13.2	–2.2	2.9	7.3	14.7	14.9	–12.3	–5.9	–3.9	9.3	10.9	8.2
Luxembourg	..	..	..	..	..	..	..	..	..	..	..	..	..	..	..	..	..	..	..	..
Mexico	..	..	..	..	13.2	–22.4	–31.5	10.2	15.3	–16.6	8.1	19.4	6.9	21.1	17.9	14.8	–0.4	7.9	–22.0	6.5
Netherlands	0.8	5.0	1.1	–4.4	–12.6	–2.4	5.4	5.1	13.2	11.6	0.2	1.6	7.8	2.4	2.0	–0.7	–2.8	0.7	7.9	4.8
New Zealand	0.8	–6.8	0.3	11.6	12.8	8.8	–6.9	28.7	1.9	–4.9	12.8	1.4	11.4	–6.2	–15.1	11.2	23.8	25.4	14.3	8.1
Norway	9.1	–26.4	–6.2	–1.9	26.9	–15.2	7.2	15.2	–19.1	29.2	–5.3	1.9	–1.8	–32.4	5.3	7.0	23.1	3.7	11.3	–5.7
Portugal	..	..	..	..	..	..	..	..	..	..	..	..	..	..	..	..	..	..	..	..
Spain	3.8	1.3	–1.2	1.4	–5.5	–2.1	–0.3	–10.6	0.1	14.0	21.1	13.9	13.5	3.9	2.0	–1.4	–15.2	3.6	6.4	7.9
Sweden	4.9	–20.9	8.1	11.2	–7.1	1.3	2.7	7.2	12.7	2.3	9.3	5.8	15.0	–1.1	–15.2	–15.5	–14.3	17.5	20.0	11.0
Switzerland	–0.4	10.0	5.1	10.8	2.4	–3.6	3.4	4.1	10.6	13.3	10.8	8.9	5.2	3.3	–3.6	–8.5	–6.4	9.7	6.4	4.7
Turkey	..	..	..	..	..	..	..	..	..	..	..	..	..	..	..	..	..	..	..	..
Total of smaller countries	2.5	0.3	2.3	2.6	2.0	–4.4	–6.4	3.3	8.1	3.2	8.1	10.1	10.4	4.8	–0.4	–0.5	–5.4	6.9	4.5	7.1
Total OECD	2.3	7.1	7.7	2.3	1.6	–3.0	–2.4	9.7	7.4	1.0	4.8	9.9	7.0	4.2	–1.1	–0.9	–0.1	5.2	9.1	6.5
OECD North America	3.3	11.9	8.9	–0.5	5.4	–6.3	–5.2	14.9	7.2	–4.3	0.9	8.2	2.4	2.2	–3.6	2.1	10.7	12.8	12.4	6.7
OECD Europe	2.0	2.7	4.5	3.0	–4.5	–1.4	–0.4	3.0	5.6	5.7	8.5	10.1	8.1	4.3	–0.6	–2.8	–8.8	1.6	8.2	7.8
EU	1.9	2.9	4.6	2.8	–5.1	–1.1	–0.6	2.8	5.8	5.2	8.6	10.3	8.4	4.8	–0.6	–2.8	–9.2	1.3	8.2	8.1
Total OECD *less* the United States	1.7	3.3	7.1	5.1	0.1	–2.1	–2.0	5.6	8.0	4.0	8.0	11.8	10.2	6.0	1.6	–2.6	–7.6	0.1	5.2	6.5

Annex Table 7. **Real gross private residential fixed capital formation**

Percentage changes from previous period

	Average 1970-77	1978	1979	1980	1981	1982	1983	1984	1985	1986	1987	1988	1989	1990	1991	1992	1993	1994	Projections 1995	Projections 1996
United States	6.3	6.3	–3.3	–20.5	–8.1	–18.1	40.4	14.4	1.3	12.0	–0.4	–1.1	–3.8	–9.2	–12.9	16.2	8.2	8.6	–3.8	–1.2
Japan	4.7	5.6	–0.9	–9.2	–2.3	–0.7	–5.9	–2.1	2.6	7.8	22.6	11.9	0.5	4.7	–8.2	–6.7	2.5	9.6	–0.7	3.3
Germany	0.5	2.7	6.9	2.3	–5.0	–4.9	5.7	2.0	–9.9	–0.6	–1.2	3.7	4.9	8.5	4.3	9.6	5.6	13.0	5.3	2.5
France	3.0	6.2	4.0	–0.3	–3.1	–6.3	–2.6	–4.4	–2.1	1.3	3.3	7.1	7.1	0.3	–4.1	–4.2	–6.7	2.5	4.1	2.1
Italy	–2.2	–0.3	2.9	4.7	–0.1	–4.4	4.4	–0.5	–2.8	–2.1	–2.4	1.3	2.4	2.8	3.1	0.3	–0.8	0	3.3	6.2
United Kingdom	1.6	6.7	9.0	–5.5	–10.8	6.5	7.4	6.7	–2.7	12.0	8.1	20.5	–5.0	–16.7	–12.4	2.9	4.3	6.4	0.1	1.7
Canada	7.6	1.1	–1.0	–5.4	6.6	–16.3	17.0	0.5	9.8	13.3	16.4	2.8	4.8	–9.7	–12.5	7.9	–4.4	2.9	–3.1	2.6
Total of above countries	4.5	5.1	0.2	–10.9	–5.3	–9.8	18.9	6.4	–0.1	8.1	5.2	4.3	–0.5	–3.8	–8.3	7.2	4.2	7.7	–0.8	1.2
Australia	2.9	–3.9	9.2	11.8	2.4	–13.3	–9.8	21.4	1.9	–8.1	1.0	21.9	2.7	–12.3	–4.9	8.7	9.9	9.4	–7.0	–7.0
Austria	3.9	–4.9	3.7	4.8	2.0	–1.8	–1.7	–1.0	–1.5	2.4	1.8	8.4	–0.6	1.4	11.5	12.2	11.5	4.3	4.6	5.0
Belgium	4.2	6.2	–14.4	13.0	–41.6	–5.8	–1.6	–0.3	4.6	4.7	7.7	22.3	19.0	8.5	–0.8	12.5	–2.0	1.3	1.0	1.9
Denmark	–1.0	0.9	–0.8	–16.8	–25.7	–8.5	11.5	20.3	–2.1	21.3	–3.2	–9.4	–8.9	–13.7	–11.7	–5.0	–3.0	8.9	6.0	5.0
Finland	3.3	1.3	–1.5	4.7	–2.5	5.9	–0.3	–2.7	–3.0	–8.0	1.1	15.4	18.9	–5.7	–20.7	–16.1	–14.2	–4.0	5.1	7.0
Greece	4.3	14.0	4.7	–13.8	–22.7	–5.8	4.6	–19.7	–0.5	14.6	3.4	2.9	5.5	13.6	–15.4	–12.0	–3.5	–8.0	1.0	3.3
Iceland	8.8	9.4	6.6	5.4	–9.8	9.4	–9.1	10.4	–13.6	–13.8	14.2	14.8	2.8	–0.6	–4.9	–4.9	–7.0	2.3	6.0	6.0
Ireland	9.3	21.7	17.2	–16.8	0.2	–5.3	–4.7	6.6	–1.8	3.5	2.2	–7.2	13.3	4.9	–2.1	10.3	3.5	2.6	3.7	4.2
Luxembourg	..	..	..	..	..	..	..	..	..	..	..	..	..	..	..	..	..	..	..	..
Mexico	7.1	–6.9	9.3	4.5	7.9	1.5	–5.9	5.0	8.1	–1.6	4.4	–1.2	8.3	1.7	4.5	3.5	4.8	7.9	–22.0	6.5
Netherlands	1.3	1.5	–5.0	4.7	–9.6	–5.6	–0.4	4.5	–0.4	3.7	1.9	11.3	0.7	–2.5	–5.4	3.9	–0.5	7.5	5.2	2.8
New Zealand	1.9	–20.1	–3.5	–1.9	6.3	7.9	–1.6	18.7	–0.8	–2.7	–4.3	4.8	14.8	2.3	–15.8	5.7	16.8	11.6	4.5	3.6
Norway	5.1	9.1	2.4	–2.3	1.1	8.0	0.8	–1.4	4.1	9.6	4.0	–3.8	–17.0	–17.1	–27.3	–12.6	–5.2	33.7	20.0	10.0
Portugal	..	..	..	..	..	..	..	..	..	..	..	..	..	..	..	..	..	..	..	..
Spain	1.5	–6.0	–7.6	–2.0	–0.8	–2.0	–5.5	–5.4	6.5	2.1	6.3	11.4	3.3	6.4	–3.3	–5.2	–4.9	3.1	5.2	4.1
Sweden	–3.3	14.1	1.8	–6.0	–5.1	–2.3	–0.5	11.2	–2.5	–2.2	8.8	8.4	4.8	7.2	–2.4	–7.3	–31.0	–37.5	–22.0	8.5
Switzerland	–4.8	12.8	12.1	17.4	2.5	–6.1	6.2	7.2	3.3	1.5	4.4	3.6	5.7	–1.0	–7.0	–3.6	5.4	5.0	3.0	4.0
Turkey	..	..	..	..	..	..	..	..	..	..	..	..	..	..	..	..	..	..	..	..
Total of smaller countries	3.2	–0.1	1.1	2.6	–4.1	–3.2	–2.6	3.9	3.0	1.4	3.9	8.5	4.9	0.5	–3.7	0.6	–0.6	3.4	–2.8	3.6
Total OECD	4.4	4.3	0.3	–8.7	–5.1	–8.7	15.4	6.0	0.4	7.0	5.0	5.0	0.3	–3.1	–7.6	6.1	3.4	7.0	–1.1	1.6
OECD North America	6.6	5.0	–2.3	–17.7	–5.9	–16.7	35.5	12.7	2.4	11.2	1.2	–0.8	–2.4	–8.5	–11.7	14.7	7.0	8.1	–4.9	–0.4
OECD Europe	1.2	3.5	3.4	0.6	–5.8	–2.8	2.4	0.7	–2.8	2.7	2.5	8.0	3.1	0.4	–2.7	1.5	–0.6	4.7	3.2	3.5
EU	1.3	3.2	3.2	0.2	–6.1	–2.8	2.3	0.6	–3.0	2.6	2.4	8.2	3.3	0.7	–2.3	1.8	–0.6	4.3	3.0	3.4
Total OECD *less* the United States	2.8	3.1	2.5	–1.6	–3.3	–3.1	0.4	0.9	–0.1	4.0	8.2	8.6	2.8	0.6	–4.4	0.2	0.6	6.1	0.5	3.2

Annex Table 8. **Real total domestic demand**

Percentage changes from previous period

	Average 1970-77	1978	1979	1980	1981	1982	1983	1984	1985	1986	1987	1988	1989	1990	1991	1992	1993	1994	Projections 1995	Projections 1996
United States	2.9	4.8	2.0	–1.6	2.0	–1.4	5.2	7.8	3.6	3.0	2.7	3.0	1.8	0.8	–1.3	2.5	3.9	4.7	3.3	1.8
Japan	4.1	5.7	6.6	0.7	2.1	2.7	1.8	3.6	4.1	3.7	5.1	7.6	5.8	5.0	2.9	0.3	0	1.0	2.4	3.1
Germany	2.5	3.6	5.3	0.6	–2.3	–2.2	2.4	1.9	1.0	3.3	2.4	3.6	2.9	5.2	4.9	3.0	–1.2	2.6	2.5	3.3
France	3.3	2.8	3.8	1.6	–0.1	3.5	–0.7	0.4	2.5	4.5	3.3	4.7	3.9	2.8	0.6	0.4	–2.3	2.9	3.2	3.6
Italy	2.8	2.9	6.5	6.5	–1.1	0.6	0.2	3.5	2.8	3.0	4.2	4.4	2.8	2.5	1.9	0.8	–5.5	1.9	2.4	2.6
United Kingdom	1.8	3.9	3.6	–2.5	–1.5	2.2	4.8	2.8	2.9	4.9	5.3	7.9	2.9	–0.6	–3.1	0.3	2.2	3.0	2.8	2.8
Canada	5.6	2.6	4.5	2.4	4.4	–5.4	3.6	4.7	5.3	4.2	5.3	5.5	4.3	–0.5	–1.0	0.3	1.8	2.9	2.6	3.1
Total of above countries	3.2	4.4	3.9	0	1.0	–0.1	3.3	5.0	3.3	3.5	3.6	4.6	3.1	2.2	0.4	1.6	1.2	3.3	2.9	2.5
Australia	3.3	3.6	3.6	3.3	5.6	–0.1	–1.1	6.7	5.4	0.3	2.9	5.6	6.5	–0.7	–2.6	3.0	2.6	5.6	5.0	2.8
Austria	4.5	–2.0	4.9	3.3	–2.2	–1.1	2.8	2.7	2.2	1.8	2.6	4.3	3.2	4.2	3.1	1.8	0.1	4.1	3.2	2.8
Belgium	3.7	3.0	3.7	2.1	–4.7	0.7	–2.4	2.3	0.5	2.8	3.8	4.4	4.8	3.3	2.1	2.1	–1.7	1.6	2.7	2.6
Denmark	2.2	1.1	2.7	–4.3	–4.1	3.5	1.4	5.1	5.4	6.1	–2.2	–1.2	0.5	–1.0	–0.4	–0.5	1.0	5.5	3.9	2.9
Finland	2.4	–0.4	9.2	5.6	–0.4	4.3	2.3	2.0	2.9	2.2	5.2	6.6	7.6	–1.3	–9.2	–6.4	–6.5	4.2	5.8	5.0
Greece	4.9	5.8	4.0	–0.6	1.4	2.4	0.7	0.7	5.2	0.5	0.8	4.6	5.2	1.7	3.2	–0.2	0.4	1.0	2.2	2.8
Iceland	7.8	3.0	4.0	7.1	5.7	5.0	–8.5	6.4	3.0	4.7	15.9	–0.9	–4.5	0.9	5.0	–5.3	–4.2	0.9	3.8	3.2
Ireland	4.6	9.2	7.1	–2.3	3.0	–2.6	–2.1	1.2	1.3	0.1	1.2	1.6	8.8	6.3	0.1	–1.2	0.3	3.5	5.7	5.1
Luxembourg	2.4	7.5	–0.2	5.4	1.0	1.1	–0.1	2.9	0.5	7.6	4.0	6.7	5.9	4.8	7.4	0.7	1.4	2.0	2.7	3.1
Mexico	5.5	9.0	10.7	11.1	9.6	–8.2	–9.5	4.2	4.7	–5.6	0.7	3.3	5.5	6.5	5.3	5.1	–0.1	4.5	–11.3	1.9
Netherlands	2.8	4.0	1.6	–0.1	–4.7	–1.0	1.5	1.8	3.4	3.8	1.4	1.8	4.6	3.4	1.8	1.2	–0.5	2.5	3.2	2.7
New Zealand	3.0	–8.2	4.7	–1.2	4.4	5.0	–2.3	11.2	–0.5	2.0	0.7	1.7	4.4	–0.9	–7.3	3.5	6.4	7.9	5.9	3.2
Norway	5.2	–9.2	2.6	10.5	2.3	–0.4	–0.4	10.4	3.2	7.9	–1.3	–3.0	–2.9	–0.9	–0.5	1.7	3.0	4.8	4.2	0.8
Portugal	5.5	0.9	2.9	5.9	3.2	2.2	–5.2	–6.2	1.2	8.8	9.5	9.6	4.4	6.5	4.3	4.3	–0.9	1.2	3.2	3.5
Spain	4.7	–0.1	0.9	1.5	–2.1	1.5	0.5	–1.0	3.4	5.4	8.1	7.0	7.8	4.8	2.8	1.0	–4.1	0.8	2.7	3.5
Sweden	1.6	–1.2	5.0	1.9	–1.7	0.3	–0.5	3.6	3.3	2.4	4.0	3.0	3.5	1.1	–1.8	–1.8	–5.6	1.4	0.7	1.5
Switzerland	0.6	3.1	4.1	5.2	–0.8	–0.9	2.3	2.2	2.5	5.6	3.6	2.8	4.1	2.3	–0.5	–3.3	–1.8	4.4	2.3	2.4
Turkey	6.7	–3.5	–0.8	3.4	2.4	1.4	5.8	6.4	3.2	7.0	8.9	–1.3	1.5	14.6	–0.9	5.2	11.7	–12.4	2.2	5.3
Total of smaller countries	4.2	2.0	3.9	3.7	1.2	–0.6	–0.9	2.9	3.4	2.6	4.0	3.7	4.9	4.3	1.2	1.8	0.2	1.6	0.9	3.0
Total OECD	3.4	4.0	3.9	0.7	1.1	–0.2	2.6	4.6	3.3	3.3	3.6	4.4	3.4	2.6	0.5	1.7	1.0	3.0	2.5	2.6
OECD North America	3.3	4.9	2.7	–0.5	2.7	–2.2	4.1	7.3	3.8	2.6	2.8	3.2	2.3	1.1	–0.9	2.5	3.5	4.6	2.3	1.9
OECD Europe	3.1	2.3	4.1	1.8	–1.3	0.8	1.4	2.1	2.5	4.1	4.1	4.5	3.6	3.4	1.3	1.2	–1.2	1.9	2.8	3.2
EU	3.0	2.7	4.3	1.5	–1.5	0.9	1.2	1.7	2.4	3.9	3.9	4.9	3.8	2.9	1.4	1.1	–1.9	2.4	2.8	3.1
Total OECD *less* the United States	3.6	3.4	5.0	2.0	0.5	0.5	1.0	2.8	3.2	3.5	4.2	5.2	4.3	3.6	1.6	1.2	–0.6	2.0	2.1	3.1

Annex Table 9. **Real exports of goods and services**

Percentage changes from previous period

	Average 1970-77	1978	1979	1980	1981	1982	1983	1984	1985	1986	1987	1988	1989	1990	1991	1992	1993	1994	Projections 1995	1996
United States	6.3	9.5	8.6	9.2	1.7	–9.0	–3.6	6.9	1.2	6.6	10.5	15.8	11.9	8.2	6.3	6.7	4.1	9.0	9.0	10.0
Japan	10.6	–0.3	4.3	17.0	12.5	0.9	4.8	14.8	5.4	–4.9	0.1	7.0	9.0	7.3	5.2	5.2	1.3	5.0	3.5	4.9
Germany	5.7	2.9	4.3	5.2	7.2	3.9	–0.8	8.2	7.6	–0.6	0.4	5.5	10.2	11.0	10.9	0.2	–6.2	7.2	7.6	5.5
France	7.7	5.9	7.5	2.7	3.7	–1.7	3.7	7.0	1.9	–1.4	3.1	8.1	10.2	5.4	4.1	4.9	–0.4	5.8	6.8	6.3
Italy	7.0	8.7	8.3	–8.8	7.9	–2.4	2.3	8.5	3.2	2.5	4.7	5.4	8.8	7.0	0.5	5.0	9.4	10.9	11.0	8.2
United Kingdom	5.7	1.9	3.8	–0.2	–0.7	0.8	1.8	6.5	6.0	4.5	5.8	0.5	4.7	5.0	–0.7	3.1	3.3	8.9	9.1	7.7
Canada	4.7	13.6	5.0	2.7	4.4	–2.2	6.4	17.7	6.0	4.5	3.5	9.5	0.8	4.1	1.0	7.7	10.4	14.4	13.4	7.2
Total of above countries	7.2	6.3	6.8	7.4	4.8	–3.8	0	9.0	3.3	2.6	5.9	10.4	9.9	7.6	5.2	5.2	2.7	8.2	8.0	7.9
Australia	4.0	3.3	11.8	–1.6	–4.2	9.6	–4.5	16.5	10.7	4.7	11.8	3.3	3.3	8.1	12.7	5.3	7.4	8.4	5.5	10.0
Austria	6.4	7.3	11.7	5.2	4.9	2.7	3.2	6.1	6.9	–2.7	2.4	9.0	10.3	8.1	5.9	2.8	–1.0	4.9	5.0	4.8
Belgium	5.8	3.3	7.5	2.9	2.5	1.3	2.8	5.5	1.1	5.5	6.5	8.5	7.3	4.1	2.6	3.9	1.6	6.3	5.6	5.4
Denmark	4.1	1.2	8.4	5.2	8.2	2.5	4.9	3.5	5.0	0	5.1	7.8	4.2	6.9	7.7	2.7	–2.0	6.9	5.6	5.3
Finland	4.4	8.9	8.8	8.4	4.9	–1.1	2.5	5.4	1.2	1.2	2.7	3.7	1.3	1.4	–6.6	10.0	16.7	12.5	6.9	4.0
Greece	12.1	16.4	6.7	6.9	–5.9	–7.2	8.0	16.9	1.3	14.0	16.0	9.0	4.5	1.5	15.6	8.5	–1.0	7.3	6.4	6.6
Iceland	5.0	15.2	6.3	2.7	3.3	–8.9	10.5	2.5	11.0	5.9	3.8	–3.4	2.6	–0.1	–5.8	–1.6	6.4	10.2	2.4	2.7
Ireland	6.9	12.3	6.5	6.4	2.0	5.5	10.5	16.6	6.6	2.9	13.7	8.9	10.3	8.9	5.2	13.2	9.6	10.5	8.6	6.8
Luxembourg	2.9	2.7	9.7	–1.4	–4.8	–0.3	5.3	18.0	9.5	3.2	6.5	7.5	6.9	2.6	3.6	1.3	–2.4	4.6	4.4	3.9
Mexico	7.7	11.6	12.1	6.1	11.6	21.8	13.6	5.7	–4.5	5.6	9.5	5.8	2.3	3.6	4.6	1.7	3.7	7.3	18.0	11.0
Netherlands	5.6	3.3	7.4	1.5	1.5	–0.1	3.5	7.3	5.3	1.8	3.6	9.0	6.6	5.3	4.7	2.8	1.7	5.1	5.3	4.7
New Zealand	3.7	1.5	6.5	3.8	3.7	1.6	7.8	8.0	7.5	0.4	4.5	5.4	–3.1	7.1	7.1	2.1	6.1	8.7	7.1	6.9
Norway	5.9	12.2	2.6	2.1	1.4	–0.1	7.6	8.2	6.9	1.6	1.2	5.5	10.7	8.1	6.1	6.2	1.6	7.6	8.2	6.1
Portugal	0.3	9.1	33.0	2.2	–4.4	4.7	13.6	11.6	6.7	6.3	10.6	7.9	13.3	10.5	0.5	6.1	–5.1	6.7	10.5	7.3
Spain	7.4	10.7	5.6	2.3	8.2	5.0	10.0	11.7	2.7	1.9	6.3	5.1	3.0	3.2	7.9	7.3	8.3	17.7	13.2	10.7
Sweden	3.5	7.8	6.1	–0.5	2.1	5.8	9.8	6.8	1.4	3.7	4.3	2.5	3.1	1.6	–2.3	2.3	7.6	13.8	11.2	7.8
Switzerland	4.3	3.6	2.4	5.1	4.8	–2.9	1.1	6.3	8.3	0.4	1.7	5.8	5.0	3.0	–0.7	3.4	1.3	3.9	4.4	5.0
Turkey	3.4	27.3	–6.8	–4.5	63.5	34.0	13.1	25.4	–1.9	–5.1	26.4	18.4	–0.3	2.6	3.7	11.0	7.7	15.2	15.0	12.0
Total of smaller countries	5.9	9.6	7.6	2.4	9.9	8.8	7.2	10.7	2.9	2.5	8.8	7.3	4.2	4.6	5.3	5.2	4.6	9.9	10.2	8.4
Total OECD	7.0	6.9	6.9	6.5	5.8	–1.5	1.4	9.3	3.2	2.6	6.4	9.8	8.8	7.0	5.2	5.2	3.1	8.5	8.4	8.0
OECD North America	6.3	9.9	8.6	8.5	2.6	–6.5	–1.7	7.7	1.2	6.3	9.9	14.7	10.4	7.6	5.8	6.4	4.6	9.4	10.0	9.9
OECD Europe	6.3	6.6	6.0	0.8	7.0	2.3	3.6	8.8	4.3	1.2	4.9	6.1	7.4	6.3	4.3	4.0	2.0	8.9	8.8	7.1
EU	6.4	5.6	6.7	1.0	4.5	1.0	3.1	8.0	4.4	1.5	4.1	5.5	7.8	6.6	4.5	3.7	1.7	8.8	8.6	6.9
Total OECD *less* the United States	7.3	5.5	6.0	4.9	8.1	2.8	4.2	10.7	4.5	0.2	4.1	6.4	7.1	6.4	4.6	4.4	2.5	8.2	8.1	6.8

Annex Table 10. **Real imports of goods and services**

Percentage changes from previous period

	Average 1970-77	1978	1979	1980	1981	1982	1983	1984	1985	1986	1987	1988	1989	1990	1991	1992	1993	1994	Projections 1995	Projections 1996
United States	4.9	9.2	1.3	–4.7	4.9	0	12.5	25.0	6.3	6.6	4.6	3.7	3.8	3.6	–0.5	8.7	10.7	13.4	8.8	5.2
Japan	6.2	6.9	12.9	–7.8	0.4	–2.5	–3.0	10.4	–1.4	2.4	7.8	18.7	17.6	8.6	–4.1	–0.4	2.7	8.3	10.8	9.9
Germany	5.0	5.5	9.2	3.6	–3.1	–1.1	1.4	5.2	4.5	2.7	4.2	5.1	8.3	10.3	11.6	3.3	–6.1	6.1	6.0	7.9
France	5.8	3.0	10.1	2.5	–2.1	2.6	–2.7	2.7	4.5	7.1	7.7	8.6	8.1	6.1	3.0	1.1	–3.4	6.6	7.5	7.7
Italy	3.5	4.8	11.7	2.9	–1.2	–0.3	–1.4	12.3	3.9	2.9	9.1	6.8	7.6	8.0	3.4	4.6	–7.8	9.8	9.4	7.4
United Kingdom	3.8	4.2	9.6	–3.6	–2.8	4.9	6.6	9.9	2.6	6.9	7.8	12.6	7.4	0.5	–5.3	6.2	2.8	5.9	6.6	7.0
Canada	7.5	7.4	11.4	4.9	8.5	–15.2	9.0	17.1	8.7	7.6	7.0	13.8	6.3	2.0	3.1	5.9	8.8	9.6	10.2	6.7
Total of above countries	5.2	7.2	6.7	–2.8	1.9	–0.7	5.7	16.2	4.2	5.3	6.1	8.3	7.8	5.4	0.4	5.3	4.3	10.2	8.7	6.9
Australia	4.0	3.5	2.1	5.1	9.7	5.6	–10.4	21.3	4.5	–4.7	1.7	16.6	20.2	–3.8	–2.5	7.6	5.2	14.7	12.0	6.8
Austria	7.5	0.1	11.7	6.2	–0.8	–3.3	5.5	9.9	6.2	–1.2	4.7	9.4	8.5	7.8	6.3	2.6	–0.6	7.8	5.7	5.8
Belgium	6.3	3.6	9.3	0	–3.0	0.1	–1.3	5.8	0.7	7.6	8.8	8.0	8.8	4.2	2.4	4.1	1.6	5.5	5.6	5.4
Denmark	2.7	0.1	5.0	–6.8	–1.7	3.8	1.8	5.5	8.1	6.8	–2.0	1.5	4.5	1.2	4.1	–0.2	–4.1	10.5	7.2	5.6
Finland	2.8	–3.7	18.4	8.3	–4.7	2.5	3.0	1.0	6.8	2.6	9.2	11.1	8.9	–0.6	–11.7	1.1	0.7	12.6	10.6	7.4
Greece	7.7	7.2	7.2	–8.0	3.6	7.0	6.6	0.2	12.8	3.8	16.6	8.0	9.2	11.3	10.6	2.3	2.3	3.8	5.9	6.5
Iceland	8.0	3.6	2.5	3.0	7.1	–0.6	–9.7	9.1	9.4	1.0	23.3	–4.6	–10.3	1.0	5.4	–7.8	–9.6	4.7	6.5	5.5
Ireland	5.9	15.7	13.9	–4.5	1.7	–3.1	4.7	9.9	3.2	5.6	6.2	4.9	12.7	5.5	1.3	5.4	5.9	8.5	9.3	7.5
Luxembourg	2.6	7.0	6.4	3.9	–2.9	–0.3	1.2	13.9	7.0	6.1	7.8	8.5	6.1	4.3	8.1	0.2	–2.5	3.8	4.0	4.1
Mexico	4.3	21.9	29.9	31.9	17.7	–37.9	–33.8	17.8	11.0	–7.6	5.1	36.7	21.3	19.7	16.8	20.9	–1.3	12.9	–25.0	9.0
Netherlands	4.2	6.3	6.0	–0.4	–5.9	1.0	3.9	5.0	6.5	3.5	4.2	7.6	6.7	4.2	4.1	2.7	0.2	5.3	5.5	4.9
New Zealand	3.8	–6.1	17.4	–1.6	3.1	7.0	–7.8	16.4	0.6	2.5	10.0	–1.8	14.4	3.3	–3.7	8.8	9.0	17.6	11.0	6.2
Norway	6.6	–13.1	–0.7	3.3	1.5	3.7	0	9.5	5.9	9.9	–7.3	–1.7	0.9	2.2	1.7	2.8	3.2	7.2	7.3	0
Portugal	3.9	0.2	12.6	6.9	2.3	3.9	–6.1	–4.4	1.4	17.3	20.2	16.5	7.9	13.7	5.4	11.1	–3.2	4.6	8.4	6.5
Spain	7.2	–1.0	11.4	3.3	–4.2	4.8	–0.3	–1.8	7.9	14.4	20.1	14.4	17.3	7.8	9.0	6.9	–5.1	11.0	11.2	11.0
Sweden	2.6	–5.5	11.6	0.4	–5.4	3.0	0.8	5.3	6.9	4.5	7.7	5.3	7.4	0.7	–4.9	1.1	–2.8	13.2	7.3	6.4
Switzerland	3.3	10.9	6.8	7.2	–1.3	–2.6	4.4	7.1	5.1	7.1	5.5	5.3	5.4	2.9	–1.7	–3.8	–1.0	8.8	5.5	5.0
Turkey	10.6	–29.9	–7.3	69.3	12.5	8.3	16.9	19.7	–6.6	–3.5	23.0	–4.5	6.9	33.0	–5.2	10.9	35.8	–21.9	12.0	14.0
Total of smaller countries	5.8	1.7	10.4	13.2	3.2	–3.0	–3.7	9.0	5.5	3.2	10.0	12.6	12.4	9.4	4.2	7.4	2.9	7.0	3.7	7.9
Total OECD	5.4	6.2	7.4	0.1	2.1	–1.1	4.0	14.9	4.5	4.9	6.8	9.1	8.6	6.2	1.1	5.7	4.0	9.6	7.8	7.1
OECD North America	5.2	9.9	4.0	–1.5	6.0	–3.7	9.2	23.9	6.8	5.8	4.8	6.6	5.1	4.5	0.9	9.3	9.7	13.1	6.7	5.6
OECD Europe	5.2	2.1	9.2	4.7	–1.8	1.9	1.7	6.6	4.2	5.4	8.7	7.8	8.4	7.5	3.5	4.0	–1.5	6.2	7.6	7.7
EU	4.9	3.6	10.1	1.5	–2.5	1.7	1.0	5.9	4.6	5.7	8.3	8.6	8.7	6.4	4.1	3.9	–3.4	7.4	7.5	7.5
Total OECD *less* the United States	5.5	4.4	10.9	2.9	0.5	–1.7	–1.0	9.0	3.4	3.9	8.1	12.2	11.4	7.6	2.1	3.9	0.2	7.5	7.2	8.2

Annex Table 11. **Output gaps**[a]

Deviations of actual GDP from potential GDP as a percentage of potential GDP

	1980	1981	1982	1983	1984	1985	1986	1987	1988	1989	1990	1991	1992	1993	1994	Projections 1995	Projections 1996
United States	–0.9	–1.5	–5.8	–4.1	–0.9	–0.6	–0.5	0.1	1.6	2.1	1.3	–1.1	–1.0	–0.5	1.2	1.8	1.4
Japan	0.7	0.3	–0.3	–1.6	–1.6	–0.9	–2.6	–2.8	–0.2	1.1	2.7	4.1	2.8	0.5	–1.4	–2.9	–3.1
Germany	1.8	–0.4	–3.3	–3.4	–2.3	–1.9	–1.4	–1.8	–0.6	0.2	2.3	3.8	2.5	–1.2	–1.1	–0.9	–1.0
France	0.8	–0.8	0.8	–0.7	–1.7	–2.1	–2.0	–2.1	–0.3	1.3	1.3	–0.2	–1.0	–4.4	–3.6	–2.8	–1.9
Italy	3.9	1.9	–0.8	–2.5	–2.7	–2.4	–1.8	–0.7	0.6	1.8	1.7	0.8	–0.8	–4.1	–4.0	–3.0	–2.1
United Kingdom	–0.8	–3.8	–3.8	–2.1	–2.0	–0.7	1.3	3.7	6.0	5.6	3.3	–1.3	–3.9	–4.4	–3.1	–2.1	–1.6
Canada	0.5	0.5	–5.9	–5.6	–2.2	–0.2	0.2	1.6	3.7	3.5	0.8	–3.4	–5.0	–5.1	–3.2	–1.9	–1.1
Total of above countries	0.3	–0.8	–3.5	–3.1	–1.5	–1.0	–1.0	–0.6	1.2	1.9	1.8	0.5	–0.3	–1.4	–0.8	–0.5	–0.5
Australia	0.7	0.7	–2.8	–5.0	–0.8	0.6	–0.7	0.4	1.0	1.8	0.1	–3.9	–4.4	–2.9	–0.4	0.4	0.7
Austria	2.4	–0.6	–1.8	–1.8	–2.5	–1.9	–2.3	–2.4	–0.1	1.8	2.2	1.5	0.3	–1.8	–1.2	–0.6	–0.6
Belgium	3.5	1.2	0.6	–0.9	–0.8	–1.8	–2.5	–2.8	–0.6	0.4	1.3	1.3	1.0	–2.6	–2.5	–1.9	–1.7
Denmark	0.0	–2.8	–1.9	–1.3	0.7	2.3	3.2	1.0	–0.2	–1.2	–1.8	–2.4	–3.7	–3.9	–1.8	–0.5	0.0
Finland	1.9	–0.2	–0.2	–0.9	–1.3	–0.6	–0.6	0.9	3.3	6.4	5.6	–2.4	–5.8	–7.3	–5.7	–3.7	–2.5
Greece	5.0	1.5	–2.3	–4.5	–3.4	–2.3	–2.0	–3.3	–0.4	1.6	–1.2	0.0	–0.9	–2.8	–2.8	–2.4	–1.7
Ireland	–0.4	0.0	–1.3	–3.6	–2.1	–1.7	–5.7	–3.5	–3.4	–0.7	2.6	0.6	0.5	–0.3	0.1	0.3	0.3
Netherlands	1.2	–0.7	–2.8	–2.3	–0.6	0.4	0.6	–0.7	–1.0	0.8	2.0	1.5	0.2	–1.8	–1.5	–0.9	–0.9
Norway[b]	1.4	0.7	–0.6	–0.1	1.3	5.1	6.0	4.6	0.8	–2.7	–2.5	–4.3	–3.8	–3.3	–1.5	–0.9	–0.7
Portugal	3.5	2.5	2.1	–0.6	–5.0	–5.1	–3.6	–1.6	0.6	2.9	4.0	3.3	1.7	–1.9	–3.1	–2.7	–2.1
Spain	–3.7	–5.4	–5.5	–5.2	–5.2	–4.5	–3.5	–0.7	1.3	2.8	3.4	2.8	0.7	–2.5	–3.0	–2.6	–2.3
Sweden	0.8	–0.7	–1.2	–1.0	1.5	1.8	2.4	3.6	4.1	4.4	3.7	1.3	–1.2	–4.6	–3.5	–2.7	–2.3
Switzerland	0.0	–0.7	–3.2	–3.6	–3.5	–1.6	–0.5	–0.4	0.3	3.4	3.7	1.5	–0.3	–2.6	–2.0	–2.1	–1.7
Total of above European countries	1.1	–0.9	–2.0	–2.4	–2.2	–1.7	–1.1	–0.5	1.0	2.0	2.2	1.1	–0.4	–3.2	–2.7	–2.0	–1.6
Total of above OECD countries	0.3	–0.9	–3.3	–3.1	–1.6	–1.1	–1.0	–0.5	1.1	1.9	1.9	0.5	–0.4	–1.6	–1.0	–0.7	–0.6

a) For further details, see Giorno *et al.*, ''Potential output, output gaps and structural budget balances'', *OECD Economic Studies,* No. 24, 1995/I (forthcoming).
b) Mainland Norway.

Annex Table 12. **Compensation per employee in the business sector**

Percentage changes from previous period

	Average 1970-77	1978	1979	1980	1981	1982	1983	1984	1985	1986	1987	1988	1989	1990	1991	1992	1993	1994	Projections 1995	1996
United States	7.5	8.2	8.7	9.3	9.1	6.8	4.9	4.7	3.5	3.8	4.1	5.1	3.2	4.8	4.0	5.5	3.7	3.4	2.9	3.7
Japan	15.8	7.5	6.0	5.8	6.8	4.2	2.4	4.2	3.4	2.8	2.9	3.2	4.0	5.3	4.3	1.1	0.7	1.2	2.5	2.5
Germany[a]	9.4	5.7	6.1	6.9	4.8	4.8	3.8	3.8	3.1	3.7	3.3	3.2	3.0	4.2	4.8	10.3	4.3	3.7	3.9	4.7
France	13.5	12.0	12.7	15.0	14.2	13.4	10.1	8.1	6.8	4.1	4.0	4.3	4.2	5.1	4.4	3.8	2.1	1.2	2.6	3.3
Italy	18.9	15.6	19.5	20.2	20.5	16.6	15.9	11.9	10.4	7.0	7.7	7.8	9.3	8.5	8.6	6.2	3.6	4.4	4.8	5.1
United Kingdom	16.0	13.7	16.6	19.1	13.2	9.0	7.9	6.1	8.6	8.4	6.3	8.1	8.6	10.0	8.1	4.9	2.3	2.6	3.6	4.4
Canada	10.9	4.9	6.9	9.5	12.2	10.2	4.7	5.1	5.4	3.0	6.7	6.6	5.2	4.2	4.6	3.2	2.0	2.0	2.5	3.0
Total of above countries	11.3	9.0	9.6	10.4	10.0	7.7	5.8	5.5	4.7	4.2	4.3	5.0	4.3	5.5	4.8	5.0	2.9	2.8	3.1	3.7
Australia	15.0	8.0	7.9	10.7	12.4	18.1	5.4	8.9	5.7	7.5	6.6	6.8	6.1	6.5	3.2	4.1	3.3	2.0	3.8	4.5
Austria	12.0	8.2	6.7	7.9	7.8	5.6	5.7	5.4	5.3	7.5	4.3	3.2	4.9	3.8	6.3	5.3	3.5	3.5	5.1	4.9
Belgium	14.5	7.0	7.8	8.7	7.8	7.4	5.7	8.6	5.2	4.6	3.3	2.1	4.3	6.2	7.5	6.0	4.1	2.5	2.7	2.8
Denmark	13.2	9.7	10.5	11.1	8.7	11.2	9.0	6.0	4.8	5.1	7.2	3.5	4.5	5.4	4.3	3.8	2.9	3.8	4.0	4.2
Finland	18.9	6.5	11.9	14.0	14.2	9.0	9.3	10.1	10.4	7.6	8.0	9.8	10.5	9.4	3.8	4.8	3.6	2.6	5.2	5.5
Greece	17.2	22.4	21.6	14.6	20.4	26.4	21.4	18.1	22.5	12.2	10.0	16.7	22.1	14.5	13.7	10.5	7.9	12.5	10.0	7.8
Ireland	18.9	16.1	18.7	20.0	17.4	14.0	13.9	11.6	9.8	5.1	6.2	7.5	6.3	4.2	3.5	6.2	6.1	4.9	4.8	5.0
Mexico	..	..	..	..	25.3	45.1	60.5	50.1	45.2	65.6	115.0	84.7	16.9	22.0	19.9	23.9	11.0	9.3	25.0	24.0
Netherlands	12.9	7.2	6.1	6.0	4.1	6.5	3.9	0.3	1.7	2.6	1.4	1.1	0.7	3.1	4.5	4.7	3.2	1.7	2.0	2.0
New Zealand	14.2	12.5	15.1	17.9	21.4	10.0	3.2	4.1	12.4	18.5	13.0	11.1	5.9	0.1	1.2	3.0	1.0	1.7	3.5	3.1
Norway	12.7	7.5	4.4	12.7	9.4	11.4	7.6	7.4	7.0	10.3	9.5	7.3	4.6	5.3	4.8	3.4	1.0	3.1	3.3	3.8
Portugal	24.8	18.9	20.9	20.1	20.6	19.3	20.8	21.2	19.5	19.0	14.1	9.6	13.1	14.3	11.2	18.4	7.8	5.6	4.8	4.6
Spain	20.4	24.9	18.1	15.8	16.3	15.5	15.5	9.7	8.0	9.4	6.7	6.2	5.4	8.7	8.7	9.8	7.3	3.5	3.9	4.5
Sweden	12.4	11.4	8.3	14.7	10.5	5.5	8.0	9.8	8.4	8.3	7.4	8.1	12.2	9.8	6.3	3.7	5.1	5.4	5.3	3.9
Switzerland	9.3	5.0	4.8	5.8	5.6	6.1	3.4	2.8	3.5	4.8	5.1	4.9	5.5	6.2	7.6	5.5	3.1	2.6	2.1	2.7
Total of above smaller countries[b]	15.8	13.2	11.5	12.1	14.2	17.8	18.2	15.4	14.0	17.7	24.8	19.4	8.3	9.7	8.9	9.7	5.8	4.5	7.5	7.5
Total of above North American countries[b]	7.8	7.9	8.6	9.3	10.4	9.6	8.5	7.8	6.4	7.8	11.6	10.4	4.2	5.9	5.1	6.5	4.0	3.6	4.4	5.0
Total of above European countries	14.6	12.1	12.8	13.9	12.3	10.8	9.5	7.6	7.2	6.2	5.5	5.7	6.2	6.9	6.6	6.8	3.7	3.3	3.8	4.3
Total of above OECD countries[b]	12.0	9.6	9.9	10.7	10.7	9.4	7.9	7.2	6.3	6.4	7.8	7.4	5.0	6.2	5.5	5.8	3.4	3.1	3.9	4.3

a) Up to and including 1991, data concern western Germany; subsequent data concern total Germany.
b) Total excludes Mexico prior to 1981.

Annex Table 13. **Unit labour costs in the business sector**

Percentage changes from previous period

	Average 1970-77	1978	1979	1980	1981	1982	1983	1984	1985	1986	1987	1988	1989	1990	1991	1992	1993	1994	Projections 1995	Projections 1996
United States	6.4	8.5	10.1	10.9	8.1	7.8	1.4	2.8	3.0	2.5	3.7	4.2	3.1	4.9	3.6	2.8	2.3	1.8	2.1	2.4
Japan	11.5	3.5	1.5	3.1	4.1	2.0	1.4	0.3	–1.0	0.9	–0.4	–1.4	1.2	2.2	1.6	1.1	1.0	0.6	1.2	0.3
Germany[a]	5.6	3.1	3.1	7.6	4.6	4.5	0.1	0.8	1.6	2.6	2.4	–0.1	0.7	1.3	2.2	5.9	3.8	–0.5	0.7	2.2
France	9.7	8.2	8.8	13.0	11.8	10.4	8.7	5.0	4.0	1.5	1.9	0.4	1.1	3.5	3.3	1.2	1.8	–1.5	0.4	1.1
Italy	15.6	11.6	14.0	17.4	19.7	17.0	15.5	9.0	8.3	4.5	4.5	4.1	6.0	7.1	8.2	4.1	1.8	0.1	1.7	2.9
United Kingdom	12.9	10.8	14.7	20.8	10.0	4.3	2.7	5.7	5.4	3.2	3.3	6.4	9.6	10.2	6.9	3.0	0.4	–0.1	1.7	2.6
Canada	7.9	3.7	7.8	11.5	11.2	9.9	1.4	1.2	3.3	2.8	5.0	4.7	4.8	5.1	4.2	1.6	1.2	–0.6	1.0	2.0
Total of above countries	8.7	7.3	8.2	10.5	8.4	7.1	3.0	3.0	2.8	2.4	2.7	2.6	3.1	4.5	3.7	2.7	1.9	0.7	1.5	1.9
Australia	12.6	3.4	5.0	11.1	10.6	18.0	2.1	3.4	4.3	9.3	3.7	6.5	6.8	6.7	2.4	1.1	–0.8	–0.3	2.9	3.6
Austria	7.0	9.2	2.3	5.2	8.8	5.7	1.9	3.7	2.2	7.2	2.9	–1.2	1.5	1.9	4.7	5.5	4.4	1.0	2.5	2.9
Belgium	10.3	3.6	6.0	3.2	6.4	3.7	3.9	5.5	4.8	3.6	1.8	–1.6	2.3	4.2	5.2	3.3	4.5	–0.3	0.3	1.0
Denmark	9.7	8.7	6.9	10.4	7.4	7.3	5.8	3.3	3.3	4.3	8.0	1.4	2.1	2.1	0.5	2.6	–0.7	–1.5	2.2	2.4
Finland	14.8	2.6	5.5	10.9	13.7	5.9	5.9	6.7	6.2	3.9	3.4	4.4	4.3	8.7	5.8	0	–2.4	–2.0	3.6	3.8
Greece	11.8	14.4	18.2	14.1	27.3	24.8	22.4	15.1	19.8	10.7	10.5	13.2	17.4	17.6	7.0	11.3	9.7	12.2	8.5	6.2
Ireland	13.1	10.1	18.3	17.9	11.5	12.9	10.9	4.1	2.7	7.3	0.4	3.2	–1.6	–1.0	0	2.0	1.9	1.4	1.3	1.8
Mexico	..	..	..	..	21.9	45.3	63.4	47.7	44.3	69.5	112.8	84.2	14.3	17.5	18.5	23.7	11.0	6.9	26.4	22.3
Netherlands	8.6	5.1	4.7	5.8	3.0	5.0	–0.1	–3.1	0.6	1.9	2.2	0.1	–2.2	1.3	3.6	4.3	2.7	–1.3	–0.2	0.2
New Zealand	13.1	20.0	15.0	17.3	16.3	7.2	–0.7	–2.0	15.0	16.1	15.7	2.3	4.5	1.0	3.7	2.9	–2.2	2.5	3.1	1.9
Norway	9.2	6.0	–0.3	9.8	9.2	10.6	4.3	4.5	2.6	11.3	11.0	8.8	2.9	1.9	4.0	0.3	–1.7	0.6	2.1	2.7
Portugal	21.0	14.9	15.3	17.1	19.1	16.5	25.7	23.5	15.2	12.6	10.7	5.8	8.7	11.9	12.1	7.0	6.8	3.9	2.5	2.3
Spain	15.1	20.7	15.9	10.4	12.7	11.9	11.3	5.8	3.9	8.0	3.9	3.6	4.5	7.3	6.3	6.5	3.4	0.3	1.9	3.0
Sweden	10.6	8.8	4.7	14.2	10.4	3.7	5.8	5.0	7.2	6.3	4.9	7.0	11.1	9.3	5.7	–0.4	0.4	1.8	5.0	3.1
Switzerland	7.6	5.4	3.3	3.5	6.6	7.8	2.2	1.9	1.6	3.1	4.1	2.9	2.4	5.0	7.5	3.2	1.1	–1.3	1.0	1.5
Total of above smaller countries[b]	11.9	10.3	8.7	9.6	12.6	16.2	16.5	12.2	11.7	17.5	23.0	17.3	6.1	7.9	7.4	7.3	3.8	1.7	6.4	5.9
Total of above North American countries[b]	6.5	8.1	9.9	10.9	9.2	10.4	5.5	5.7	5.7	6.9	11.0	9.5	3.9	5.8	4.7	4.1	2.7	1.9	3.6	3.7
Total of above European countries	10.9	9.0	9.4	12.6	10.9	8.9	6.8	5.0	4.7	3.9	3.4	2.7	4.0	5.4	5.1	4.0	2.4	–0.1	1.4	2.2
Total of above OECD countries[b]	9.2	7.7	8.3	10.4	9.1	8.7	5.3	4.5	4.3	4.9	6.2	5.1	3.6	5.1	4.3	3.5	2.2	0.9	2.4	2.6

a) Up to and including 1991, data concern western Germany; subsequent data concern total Germany and total economy.
b) Total excludes Mexico prior to 1981.

Annex Table 14. **GDP deflators**

Percentage changes from previous period

	Average 1970-77	1978	1979	1980	1981	1982	1983	1984	1985	1986	1987	1988	1989	1990	1991	1992	1993	1994	Projections 1995	Projections 1996
United States	6.8	7.9	8.7	9.4	10.0	6.2	4.1	4.5	3.6	2.7	3.2	3.9	4.5	4.3	3.8	2.8	2.2	2.1	2.0	2.7
Japan	9.3	5.0	2.7	4.6	3.7	1.7	1.4	2.3	1.6	1.8	0	0.4	1.9	2.2	2.0	1.5	0.8	0.1	–0.3	0.2
Germany	5.6	4.3	3.8	5.0	4.2	4.4	3.2	2.1	2.1	3.2	1.9	1.5	2.4	3.2	3.9	5.5	3.9	2.2	2.1	2.3
France	9.5	10.1	10.1	11.4	11.4	11.7	9.7	7.5	5.7	5.2	3.0	2.8	3.0	3.1	3.3	2.1	2.5	1.5	1.9	2.0
Italy	14.2	14.1	15.5	20.2	19.0	17.3	15.0	11.6	8.8	7.9	6.0	6.6	6.2	7.6	7.7	4.5	4.3	3.6	4.3	4.5
United Kingdom	13.5	11.6	14.4	19.5	11.4	7.6	5.2	4.6	5.7	3.3	5.0	6.0	7.1	6.4	6.5	4.3	3.4	2.0	2.3	2.7
Canada	8.1	6.0	10.0	10.6	10.8	8.7	5.0	3.1	2.6	2.4	4.7	4.6	4.8	3.1	2.7	1.4	1.1	0.6	2.1	2.2
Total of above countries	8.5	7.8	8.2	9.8	9.2	6.7	4.9	4.6	3.8	3.2	2.9	3.3	4.0	4.1	3.9	3.0	2.3	1.7	1.8	2.3
Australia	11.8	7.1	9.5	11.2	10.0	11.1	8.2	6.5	6.0	7.1	7.3	8.3	7.4	4.6	2.0	1.5	1.3	1.2	2.7	3.7
Austria	6.9	5.7	4.1	5.2	6.5	6.2	3.9	4.9	3.1	4.3	2.4	1.6	2.9	3.3	4.0	4.2	3.6	3.2	2.8	2.7
Belgium	8.4	4.4	4.5	3.8	4.7	7.1	5.6	5.2	6.1	3.8	2.3	1.8	4.8	3.1	2.7	3.4	4.4	2.2	2.2	2.2
Denmark	10.2	9.9	7.6	8.2	10.1	10.5	7.7	5.6	4.3	4.6	4.7	3.4	4.2	2.7	2.2	2.0	1.1	1.9	2.4	2.8
Finland	12.6	8.3	8.5	9.8	11.5	8.5	8.3	8.8	5.4	4.6	4.7	7.0	6.1	5.8	2.5	0.7	2.4	2.5	2.5	2.8
Greece	12.6	12.9	18.6	17.7	19.8	25.1	19.1	20.3	17.6	17.6	14.2	15.6	14.5	21.0	18.8	14.1	13.5	10.9	9.5	7.0
Iceland	29.2	46.1	40.8	52.4	49.8	53.4	76.2	27.6	31.4	24.4	20.3	23.4	20.4	14.3	7.3	3.2	2.2	2.3	3.5	2.9
Ireland	14.1	10.5	13.7	14.7	17.4	15.2	10.7	6.4	5.2	5.8	2.1	3.1	4.4	–1.7	1.1	1.3	3.6	1.7	2.5	3.0
Luxembourg	6.5	5.1	6.4	7.9	7.2	10.8	6.8	4.4	3.0	3.8	–1.0	4.0	6.0	3.0	3.0	4.5	4.7	4.0	3.0	2.7
Mexico	15.9	16.8	20.2	28.7	26.0	61.3	90.4	59.0	56.5	74.1	138.5	99.9	25.8	29.4	21.7	14.6	10.0	7.5	28.0	24.0
Netherlands	8.8	5.4	3.9	5.6	5.5	6.1	1.9	1.8	1.8	0.2	–0.5	1.2	1.2	2.3	2.7	2.6	1.6	1.9	1.8	1.8
New Zealand	11.8	15.3	15.7	15.8	16.6	11.7	4.8	6.4	15.5	14.3	15.6	6.6	8.1	3.3	2.3	2.0	1.6	2.0	3.3	2.0
Norway	8.1	6.3	6.6	14.6	14.0	10.2	6.1	6.4	5.0	–1.4	7.2	4.4	5.9	4.5	2.4	–1.0	2.0	0.3	2.5	2.6
Portugal	14.1	22.3	19.4	20.9	17.6	20.7	24.6	24.7	21.7	19.5	11.1	10.9	11.4	13.0	15.5	13.5	7.4	5.0	4.5	4.4
Spain	14.3	20.6	16.9	13.4	12.6	13.9	11.8	11.6	7.7	11.1	5.9	5.6	7.1	7.3	7.1	6.7	4.4	4.1	4.0	4.0
Sweden	9.6	9.5	7.9	13.0	9.5	8.2	10.0	7.6	6.6	6.9	4.8	6.5	8.0	8.9	7.6	1.1	2.6	2.9	4.0	3.0
Switzerland	6.0	3.4	2.0	2.9	6.9	7.1	3.0	2.8	3.1	3.8	2.6	2.4	4.2	5.7	5.5	2.6	2.1	1.7	1.6	2.0
Turkey	19.7	46.7	75.8	88.1	44.0	28.2	26.2	48.2	53.1	36.0	33.3	70.1	74.9	58.7	58.5	63.9	62.8	107.0	80.0	45.0
Total of smaller countries	12.6	15.3	18.0	20.8	16.1	20.5	23.0	19.9	18.9	20.2	28.2	26.0	15.8	14.7	13.0	11.5	10.2	13.6	14.4	10.4
Total OECD	9.3	9.2	10.0	11.8	10.5	9.2	8.2	7.4	6.6	6.3	7.5	7.5	6.2	6.0	5.6	4.5	3.8	3.9	4.1	3.7
Total OECD *less* Turkey	9.1	8.6	8.8	10.5	9.9	8.9	7.9	6.6	5.7	5.8	7.1	6.3	4.9	5.1	4.6	3.5	2.7	2.1	2.8	3.0
OECD North America	7.5	8.3	9.6	10.8	11.1	10.0	9.8	7.9	7.0	7.4	12.2	10.2	5.9	5.9	4.9	3.5	2.6	2.3	3.8	4.0
OECD Europe	10.9	11.8	13.2	15.7	12.3	11.1	9.1	8.7	7.9	6.8	5.3	7.2	8.0	7.7	7.8	6.9	6.2	7.1	6.2	4.7
OECD Europe *less* Turkey	10.5	10.2	10.3	12.4	10.8	10.3	8.4	6.9	5.8	5.5	4.0	4.3	4.9	5.3	5.5	4.3	3.7	2.6	2.8	2.9
EU	10.6	10.4	10.5	12.6	10.9	10.4	8.5	7.0	5.9	5.6	4.0	4.3	4.9	5.3	5.5	4.5	3.7	2.7	2.9	2.9
Total OECD *less* the United States	10.7	10.0	10.7	13.2	10.7	11.0	10.6	9.1	8.2	8.4	10.0	9.6	7.1	7.0	6.6	5.5	4.7	5.0	5.3	4.3

Annex Table 15. **Private consumption deflators**

Percentage changes from previous period

	Average 1970-77	1978	1979	1980	1981	1982	1983	1984	1985	1986	1987	1988	1989	1990	1991	1992	1993	1994	Projections 1995	Projections 1996
United States	6.5	7.3	8.9	10.4	8.9	5.8	4.8	4.0	3.9	3.1	4.2	4.2	4.9	5.1	4.2	3.2	2.5	2.1	2.8	3.4
Japan	10.3	4.5	3.6	7.5	4.5	2.7	2.0	2.5	2.2	0.4	0.2	–0.1	1.8	2.6	2.5	2.1	1.3	0.3	–0.6	0
Germany	5.4	2.6	4.2	5.8	6.2	5.1	3.2	2.5	1.8	–0.6	0.5	1.3	2.9	2.6	3.7	4.6	3.9	2.7	2.3	2.1
France	9.3	9.1	10.8	13.3	13.0	11.5	9.7	7.7	5.7	2.7	3.2	2.6	3.4	2.9	3.2	2.4	2.2	1.8	1.6	1.7
Italy	13.9	13.3	14.7	20.4	18.0	17.1	14.8	12.0	9.0	6.3	5.3	5.7	6.4	6.2	6.8	5.4	4.8	4.7	5.4	4.7
United Kingdom	13.3	9.5	13.6	16.2	11.2	8.7	4.8	5.0	5.3	4.0	4.3	5.0	5.9	5.5	7.4	4.7	3.5	2.5	2.9	3.1
Canada	6.9	7.6	8.5	10.0	11.2	10.2	6.3	3.9	3.7	3.8	4.0	3.8	4.7	4.3	4.8	1.3	1.7	0.7	2.0	2.0
Total of above countries	8.4	7.1	8.3	10.8	9.1	6.8	5.3	4.5	4.0	2.6	3.1	3.2	4.2	4.3	4.2	3.3	2.6	2.0	2.2	2.5
Australia	11.2	8.5	9.4	10.4	9.2	10.4	9.3	6.4	6.7	8.5	7.8	6.9	6.6	6.0	3.7	1.8	2.1	1.4	2.6	3.7
Austria	6.9	4.2	4.5	6.4	7.6	6.0	3.4	5.6	3.3	1.9	1.0	1.4	2.7	3.1	3.4	3.9	3.5	3.3	2.3	2.5
Belgium	8.1	4.2	3.9	6.4	8.7	7.8	7.1	5.7	5.9	0.7	1.9	1.6	3.6	3.7	2.5	2.1	2.6	2.4	1.9	2.0
Denmark	10.5	9.2	10.4	10.7	12.0	10.2	6.7	6.4	4.3	2.9	4.6	4.0	4.3	2.7	2.4	1.9	1.0	1.7	2.5	3.0
Finland	12.6	8.0	7.7	11.2	11.9	9.4	8.7	7.4	6.1	3.1	3.6	4.6	5.0	6.0	5.6	4.1	3.9	1.6	2.1	2.6
Greece	11.6	12.8	16.5	21.9	22.7	20.6	18.1	17.9	18.2	22.3	15.7	14.2	14.3	19.4	18.8	15.0	13.6	10.8	9.2	7.0
Iceland	27.7	43.3	46.3	55.6	51.0	51.9	82.6	31.6	32.6	19.8	15.9	25.9	23.2	16.2	5.3	4.9	4.9	1.7	2.3	2.8
Ireland	14.0	7.9	14.9	18.6	19.6	15.0	9.2	7.4	5.0	3.8	2.3	2.9	3.2	1.5	2.5	2.8	1.6	2.4	2.6	3.0
Luxembourg	7.1	3.4	4.9	7.5	8.6	10.6	8.3	6.5	4.3	1.3	1.7	2.7	3.6	3.6	2.9	2.8	3.7	2.4	1.9	2.0
Mexico	15.3	16.4	17.6	24.8	26.3	57.7	89.5	65.3	59.0	83.1	133.5	109.6	23.4	28.3	21.8	14.0	9.3	6.6	35.0	27.0
Netherlands	8.5	4.5	4.3	6.9	6.3	5.3	2.8	2.1	2.2	0.3	0.2	0.5	1.2	2.2	3.2	3.0	2.1	2.2	1.7	1.8
New Zealand	11.4	12.2	14.0	17.9	14.7	15.5	7.2	7.3	17.2	12.3	14.0	6.9	6.4	6.0	2.3	1.7	1.0	0.5	2.9	2.0
Norway	8.4	7.8	5.1	10.0	13.5	11.0	8.4	6.4	5.9	7.7	7.9	6.2	4.3	4.8	4.1	2.6	1.9	1.4	2.8	2.6
Portugal	14.5	21.3	25.2	21.6	20.2	20.3	25.8	28.5	19.4	13.0	9.6	11.4	11.8	11.7	12.5	10.0	7.9	5.2	4.5	4.2
Spain	14.2	19.1	16.5	15.7	14.6	14.6	12.6	11.9	7.1	9.4	5.7	5.0	6.6	6.5	6.4	6.4	5.6	5.1	4.6	4.1
Sweden	9.2	11.6	7.9	13.8	12.1	10.5	10.8	7.7	7.0	5.2	5.6	6.1	7.0	9.9	10.3	2.2	5.8	3.0	3.3	2.8
Switzerland	6.1	0.7	4.5	4.5	6.6	5.5	2.6	3.3	3.7	0.3	1.5	2.3	3.5	5.3	5.7	4.2	3.0	0.7	1.7	1.9
Turkey	18.9	52.3	78.6	87.9	44.4	27.4	25.7	49.1	50.9	30.3	48.6	59.5	82.8	60.1	57.9	63.8	63.9	106.0	80.0	45.0
Total of smaller countries	12.3	15.4	18.1	21.2	17.2	19.8	23.3	21.1	19.2	20.3	28.9	26.1	15.7	14.7	13.2	11.6	10.6	13.6	15.4	10.8
Total OECD	9.1	8.6	10.1	12.7	10.6	9.2	8.6	7.6	6.8	5.8	7.8	7.4	6.3	6.2	5.9	4.8	4.1	4.1	4.6	4.0
Total OECD *less* Turkey	8.9	7.8	8.9	11.4	10.0	8.9	8.3	6.8	6.0	5.4	7.1	6.4	4.9	5.3	4.9	3.7	3.0	2.3	3.3	3.3
OECD North America	7.1	7.9	9.4	11.3	10.2	9.5	10.5	8.0	7.5	8.4	12.6	11.1	6.1	6.6	5.4	3.7	2.9	2.3	4.8	4.8
OECD Europe	10.7	10.9	13.4	16.2	13.3	11.3	9.2	9.1	7.7	4.9	5.5	6.2	8.2	7.2	7.7	7.0	6.5	7.5	6.4	4.7
OECD Europe *less* Turkey	10.3	9.0	10.4	12.9	11.9	10.5	8.4	7.3	5.7	3.7	3.5	3.8	4.8	4.8	5.4	4.5	3.9	3.1	3.1	2.9
EU	10.4	9.2	10.6	13.2	12.0	10.6	8.5	7.4	5.7	3.8	3.5	3.8	4.8	4.7	5.5	4.5	3.9	3.2	3.1	2.9
Total OECD *less* the United States	10.6	9.4	10.9	14.1	11.6	11.2	10.9	9.7	8.5	7.4	9.9	9.2	7.1	6.9	6.8	5.7	5.0	5.2	5.7	4.4

Annex Table 16. **Consumer prices**[a]

Percentage changes from previous period

	Average 1970-75	1976	1977	1978	1979	1980	1981	1982	1983	1984	1985	1986	1987	1988	1989	1990	1991	1992	1993	1994
United States	6.7	5.7	6.5	7.6	11.3	13.5	10.3	6.1	3.2	4.3	3.5	1.9	3.7	4.1	4.8	5.4	4.2	3.0	3.0	2.6
Japan	11.4	9.4	8.2	4.2	3.7	7.8	4.9	2.7	1.9	2.2	2.0	0.6	0.1	0.7	2.3	3.1	3.3	1.7	1.3	0.7
Germany[b]	6.1	4.6	3.7	2.7	4.1	5.5	6.3	5.3	3.3	2.4	2.2	–0.1	0.2	1.3	2.8	2.7	3.5	4.0	4.1	3.0
France	8.8	9.6	9.4	9.1	10.8	13.6	13.4	11.8	9.6	7.4	5.8	2.7	3.1	2.7	3.6	3.4	3.2	2.4	2.1	1.7
Italy[c]	10.6	16.7	19.3	12.4	15.7	21.2	19.3	16.4	14.9	10.6	8.6	6.1	4.6	5.0	6.6	6.1	6.5	5.3	4.2	3.9
United Kingdom	13.0	16.5	15.8	8.3	13.4	18.0	11.9	8.6	4.6	5.0	6.1	3.4	4.1	4.9	7.8	9.5	5.9	3.7	1.6	2.5
Canada	7.3	7.5	8.0	8.9	9.1	10.2	12.4	10.8	5.8	4.3	4.0	4.2	4.4	4.0	5.0	4.8	5.6	1.5	1.8	0.2
Total of above countries	8.3	8.2	8.5	7.3	9.9	12.7	10.3	7.2	4.7	4.7	4.0	2.1	2.9	3.4	4.5	5.0	4.3	3.0	2.7	2.3
Australia	10.2	13.5	12.3	7.9	9.1	10.2	9.6	11.2	10.1	3.9	6.7	9.1	8.5	7.3	7.5	7.3	3.2	1.0	1.8	1.9
Austria	7.3	7.3	5.5	3.6	3.7	6.3	6.8	5.4	3.3	5.7	3.2	1.7	1.4	1.9	2.6	3.3	3.3	4.0	3.6	3.0
Belgium	8.4	9.2	7.1	4.5	4.5	6.7	7.1	8.7	7.7	6.3	4.9	1.3	1.6	1.2	3.1	3.4	3.2	2.4	2.8	2.4
Denmark	9.3	9.0	11.1	10.0	9.6	12.3	11.7	10.1	6.9	6.3	4.7	3.7	4.0	4.5	4.8	2.6	2.4	2.1	1.3	2.0
Finland	11.7	14.4	12.6	7.8	7.5	11.6	12.0	9.6	8.3	7.1	5.9	2.9	4.1	5.1	6.6	6.1	4.3	2.9	2.2	1.1
Greece	12.3	13.0	12.4	12.6	19.1	24.7	24.5	21.0	20.2	18.5	19.3	23.0	16.4	13.5	13.7	20.4	19.5	15.9	14.4	10.9
Iceland[d]	24.7	28.9	30.3	43.8	44.4	58.5	51.8	50.2	84.0	30.9	32.0	22.1	18.3	25.7	20.8	15.5	6.8	4.0	4.0	1.6
Ireland	13.3	18.0	13.6	7.7	13.2	18.3	20.4	17.1	10.5	8.6	5.5	3.8	3.1	2.1	4.1	3.3	3.2	3.1	1.4	2.3
Luxembourg	7.2	9.8	6.7	3.1	4.5	6.3	8.1	9.4	8.7	5.6	4.1	0.3	–0.1	1.4	3.4	3.7	3.1	3.2	3.6	2.2
Mexico	11.8	14.6	28.8	17.6	18.4	25.8	28.2	58.7	102.3	65.3	57.8	86.2	131.8	114.2	20.0	26.7	22.7	15.5	9.8	7.0
Netherlands	8.6	8.8	6.4	4.1	4.2	6.5	6.7	5.9	2.7	3.3	2.3	0.1	–0.7	0.7	1.1	2.5	3.2	3.2	2.6	2.8
New Zealand	10.2	16.8	14.4	11.9	13.8	17.1	15.4	16.1	7.4	6.1	15.4	13.2	15.7	6.4	5.7	6.1	2.6	1.0	1.3	1.8
Norway	8.4	9.1	9.1	8.1	4.8	10.9	13.7	11.3	8.4	6.3	5.7	7.2	8.7	6.7	4.6	4.1	3.4	2.3	2.3	1.4
Portugal	15.4	19.3	27.2	22.5	23.9	16.6	20.0	22.4	25.5	28.8	19.6	11.8	9.4	9.7	12.6	13.4	11.4	8.9	6.5	5.2
Spain	12.1	17.6	24.5	19.8	15.7	15.6	14.5	14.4	12.2	11.3	8.8	8.8	5.2	4.8	6.8	6.7	5.9	5.9	4.6	4.7
Sweden	8.0	10.2	11.4	10.0	7.2	13.7	12.1	8.6	8.9	8.0	7.4	4.2	4.2	5.8	6.4	10.5	9.3	2.3	4.6	2.2
Switzerland	7.7	1.7	1.3	1.1	3.6	4.0	6.5	5.6	3.0	2.9	3.4	0.8	1.4	1.9	3.2	5.4	5.8	4.0	3.3	0.8
Turkey[e]	15.6	17.1	27.1	45.3	58.7	110.2	36.6	32.1	31.4	48.4	45.0	34.6	38.9	73.7	63.3	60.3	66.0	70.1	66.1	106.3
Total of smaller countries	9.1	10.0	10.1	7.9	8.0	10.3	10.5	10.4	8.8	8.4	8.0	8.1	11.0	16.7	10.8	14.0	15.2	16.5	18.7	35.4
Total OECD	8.8	9.2	10.1	8.7	11.0	14.7	11.6	10.0	9.3	8.1	7.0	5.9	7.8	8.6	6.3	6.8	6.1	4.8	4.2	4.3
Total OECD *less* Turkey	8.7	9.1	9.8	8.1	10.1	13.0	11.1	9.6	8.9	7.4	6.2	5.3	7.2	7.5	5.2	5.9	5.1	3.6	3.1	2.6
OECD North America	6.8	5.9	6.6	7.7	11.1	13.3	10.5	6.5	3.5	4.5	3.8	2.7	5.4	7.2	5.7	6.7	5.7	4.0	3.6	2.9
OECD Europe	9.9	11.8	12.8	10.3	12.5	17.4	13.5	11.5	9.4	9.0	7.9	5.2	5.0	6.8	7.9	8.2	7.9	7.3	6.3	7.7
OECD Europe *less* Turkey	9.7	11.6	12.2	8.8	10.4	13.3	12.3	10.6	8.4	7.2	6.1	3.7	3.3	3.7	5.2	5.7	5.1	4.2	3.4	3.0
European Union	9.8	11.9	12.5	9.0	10.6	13.5	12.4	10.7	8.5	7.3	6.1	3.7	3.3	3.7	5.3	5.7	5.1	4.2	3.4	3.1
Total OECD *less* the United States	12.7	14.7	15.4	10.2	10.7	16.1	13.4	15.0	16.5	12.1	10.3	9.5	11.3	12.2	7.3	7.8	7.4	6.1	5.1	5.5

a) Aggregates were computed using the previous year's consumer expenditure expressed in private consumption purchasing power parities.
b) Western Germany.
c) Index for households of wage and salary earners.
d) Excluding rent.
e) Until 1981: Istanbul index (154 items); from 1982, Turkish index.

Annex Table 17. **Oil and other primary commodity markets**

	1979	1980	1981	1982	1983	1984	1985	1986	1987	1988	1989	1990	1991	1992	1993	1994	Projections 1995	1996
Oil market conditions[a] (in million barrels per day)																		
Demand																		
OECD[b]	42.0	38.8	36.6	34.9	34.3	35.0	34.6	35.7	36.4	37.5	37.9	38.0	38.2	38.8	39.1	40.0	40.5	. .
of which: North America[b]	20.9	19.4	18.5	17.6	17.2	17.7	17.6	18.1	18.6	19.2	19.3	18.9	18.6	18.9	19.2	19.7	19.9	. .
Europe	14.8	13.7	12.7	12.2	12.0	12.0	11.9	12.4	12.5	12.7	12.8	13.0	13.4	13.6	13.6	13.7	13.9	. .
Pacific	6.3	5.7	5.4	5.1	5.1	5.3	5.1	5.2	5.3	5.6	5.8	6.1	6.2	6.3	6.3	6.6	6.6	. .
Non-OECD[c]	23.4	23.8	24.2	24.4	24.7	25.0	25.5	26.1	26.9	27.6	28.2	28.5	28.7	28.4	28.1	28.2	28.8	. .
Total	65.4	62.6	60.8	59.3	59.0	60.0	60.1	61.8	63.3	65.1	66.1	66.5	66.8	67.2	67.2	68.2	69.2	. .
Supply																		
OECD[b]	14.9	15.0	15.1	15.4	16.0	16.8	17.1	16.9	16.9	16.7	16.0	15.9	16.4	16.6	16.8	17.6	17.8	. .
Total OPEC	31.5	27.6	23.6	19.9	18.6	18.8	17.6	19.9	19.7	21.8	23.8	25.1	25.4	26.5	27.0	27.3	. .	. .
Former USSR	11.7	12.1	12.3	12.3	12.4	12.3	12.0	12.3	12.6	12.5	12.2	11.5	10.4	9.0	7.9	7.2	6.9	. .
Other non-OECD[c]	8.7	9.4	9.6	10.6	11.1	11.9	12.6	12.9	13.3	13.8	14.1	14.6	14.8	15.2	15.9	16.3	. .	. .
Total	66.8	64.1	60.6	58.2	58.1	59.8	59.2	62.0	62.4	64.8	66.1	67.0	66.9	67.2	67.5	68.5	. .	. .
Trade																		
OECD net imports[b]	27.8	24.3	21.4	19.0	18.0	18.5	17.3	19.1	19.8	20.7	22.0	22.3	21.8	22.2	22.5	22.5	. .	. .
Former USSR net exports	3.0	3.2	3.2	3.2	3.2	3.2	2.9	3.4	3.6	3.6	3.4	3.0	2.1	2.1	2.2	2.4	2.4	. .
Other non-OECD net exports[c]	25.5	22.1	18.1	15.2	14.2	14.9	13.8	15.7	15.1	16.9	18.5	19.7	19.7	20.2	20.4	20.2	. .	. .
Price																		
OECD crude oil import price (cif, $ per bl)[d]	19.3	32.9	36.3	33.9	30.0	29.0	27.5	15.0	17.9	14.8	17.5	22.3	19.3	18.5	16.4	15.6	17.7	18.0
Prices of other primary commodities[e] (indices of dollar prices, 1991 = 100)																		
Food and tropical beverages	126	173	141	104	111	107	91	98	92	114	115	106	100	97	98	118	123	123
of which: Food	110	168	136	95	101	92	76	78	84	109	113	105	100	99	99	111	114	114
Tropical beverages	221	207	170	161	169	193	176	218	142	143	124	108	100	85	92	161	178	181
Agricultural raw materials	96	106	92	80	85	85	79	79	92	101	100	106	100	97	95	107	123	122
Minerals, ores and metals	97	107	90	78	84	78	75	71	84	123	123	111	100	96	82	93	111	112
Total	113	145	119	93	100	96	85	88	90	114	114	107	100	97	94	110	120	120
Memorandum item																		
Export prices of OECD manufactures (dollar index)	68	75	71	69	67	65	65	77	87	93	92	100	100	103	97	99	108	111

a) Based on data published in IEA, Oil Market Report, May 1995; Annual Statistical Supplement, September 1993.
b) Not including Mexico.
c) Including Mexico.
d) By technical assumption, oil price is set to rise at the same rate as OECD manufactured export prices as of 1995 I.
e) Indices through 1994 I are based on data compiled by UNCTAD; OECD Secretariat estimates and projections from 1995 to 1996.

Annex Table 18. **Labour force**[a]

Percentage changes from previous period

	1991 Labour force (thousands)	1978	1979	1980	1981	1982	1983	1984	1985	1986	1987	1988	1989	1990	1991	1992	1993	1994	Projections 1995	Projections 1996
United States[b]	125 312	3.3	2.7	1.9	1.6	1.4	1.2	1.8	1.7	2.1	1.7	1.5	1.8	0.8	0.4	1.3	0.8	2.3	1.5	1.2
Japan	65 062	1.5	1.2	1.0	1.0	1.2	2.0	0.7	0.6	1.0	1.0	1.4	1.7	1.8	1.9	1.1	0.6	0.4	0.4	0.4
Germany	39 113	0.6	1.2	1.5	1.3	0.9	0.2	0.2	0.8	1.0	0.7	0.8	0.7	2.2	1.7	–0.8	–0.5	–0.1	–0.3	0.2
France	25 032	0.7	0.9	0.6	0.8	1.1	0	0.6	0.5	0.6	0.5	0.5	0.7	0.5	0.6	0.4	0.3	1.3	0.6	0.5
Italy	24 060	0.4	1.5	1.2	1.2	0.4	1.2	0.5	0.5	1.7	0.8	1.1	0.1	1.1	0.4	0	–5.3	–1.0	0.5	0.2
United Kingdom	28 564	0.5	0.9	0.4	–0.3	–0.4	0.7	2.5	1.4	0.3	1.0	1.2	0.9	0.1	–0.6	–0.6	–0.5	–0.8	0.3	0.5
Canada	14 408	3.7	3.2	3.0	2.9	0.6	1.6	1.9	2.1	1.9	1.9	2.0	1.8	1.3	0.6	0.5	1.3	1.1	1.2	1.9
Total of above countries	321 552	1.9	1.8	1.4	1.2	1.0	1.1	1.3	1.2	1.4	1.2	1.3	1.4	1.1	0.8	0.6	0	1.0	0.8	0.8
Australia	8 542	1.1	1.1	2.8	1.7	1.5	1.3	1.8	2.7	3.4	2.2	2.7	3.6	2.4	0.6	0.7	0.6	1.7	1.7	1.7
Austria	3 596	1.3	1.2	0.4	1.2	2.1	–0.4	0.2	–0.2	0.9	1.3	0.1	0.5	2.2	2.0	2.2	1.3	0.7	0.5	0.4
Belgium	4 210	0.7	1.2	0.3	0.6	0.6	0.4	–0.1	–0.5	–0.1	0.1	0.3	0.4	0.8	0.7	0.6	0.6	0.3	0.3	0.2
Denmark	2 822	2.0	0	0.4	1.0	1.2	1.0	1.3	1.4	1.3	0.8	0.2	0.2	–0.7	–0.5	0.4	0.5	–0.3	0.2	0.2
Finland	2 533	0	1.1	1.8	1.3	1.5	0.6	0.7	0.8	0.1	–0.6	–0.3	0.5	–0.1	–0.9	–1.2	–0.7	–0.2	0.5	0.4
Greece	3 933	0.6	1.1	2.3	6.6	1.0	3.4	0.7	0.6	–0.1	–0.1	2.0	0.2	0.8	–1.7	2.6	2.1	1.2	1.0	1.0
Iceland	136	3.0	1.0	3.2	4.9	3.0	1.2	1.7	3.2	2.8	5.6	–2.6	–0.6	0	6.1	–5.1	0.2	1.5	1.0	1.0
Ireland	1 320	1.8	2.0	1.1	2.0	1.9	0.8	0	–0.4	0.5	0.8	–1.4	–1.7	1.7	1.6	2.2	0.9	1.5	1.2	1.6
Luxembourg	167	–0.1	0.7	0.5	0.7	0	–0.1	0.6	0.6	1.0	1.5	1.1	0.6	1.3	1.5	0.4	0.2	1.5	0.2	0.5
Mexico[c]	11 403	..	..	..	..	..	..	..	..	..	..	4.3	2.9	2.1	5.0	4.3	3.6	2.9	2.6	3.0
Netherlands	6 125	0.8	1.3	1.6	0.8	0.8	1.4	0.1	–0.2	1.6	1.2	2.1	0.9	2.0	2.0	1.6	1.9	1.7	1.4	1.5
New Zealand	1 629	0.5	1.6	0.7	1.5	1.1	0.7	1.9	2.5	0.1	0.9	–1.6	–1.0	1.6	1.4	0.4	1.1	2.7	2.2	1.6
Norway	2 126	1.9	1.2	0.2	1.8	1.1	0.9	1.0	1.7	2.9	2.0	0.6	–1.3	–0.6	–0.7	0.2	0	1.0	0.8	0.7
Portugal[d]	4 803	0.6	1.5	2.0	0.1	–0.2	4.3	0.7	–0.3	0.1	1.0	1.1	1.5	1.8	2.4	–6.4	–0.6	1.2	0.7	0.6
Spain	15 073	0.2	0.1	0	0.2	1.2	1.1	0.6	0.8	1.7	2.4	1.6	1.3	1.4	0.4	0.5	1.1	0.9	1.0	0.8
Sweden	4 552	0.8	1.4	1.3	0.2	0.5	0.4	0.4	0.8	–0.8	1.2	1.1	1.3	1.1	–0.5	–1.9	–3.3	–1.2	1.2	0.5
Switzerland	3 599	0.9	1.1	2.2	2.3	0.7	0.5	1.2	1.8	1.2	1.1	1.1	1.0	1.3	0.5	–0.8	–0.6	–1.2	0.1	0.6
Turkey[e]	19 967	1.4	0.2	0.6	–0.2	0.9	1.8	1.4	1.2	2.7	2.8	1.6	2.0	1.4	0.1	1.1	1.8	–1.8	1.8	1.8
Total of smaller countries[f]	96 535	0.9	0.8	1.0	0.9	1.0	1.4	0.9	0.9	1.5	1.7	1.6	1.5	1.4	1.0	0.8	1.1	0.5	1.4	1.3
Total OECD[f]	418 087	1.7	1.6	1.3	1.2	1.0	1.2	1.2	1.1	1.4	1.3	1.4	1.4	1.2	0.8	0.7	0.3	0.9	0.9	0.9
OECD North America[f]	151 123	3.3	2.7	2.0	1.7	1.4	1.2	1.8	1.7	2.0	1.7	1.8	1.9	0.9	0.8	1.5	1.1	2.3	1.5	1.4
OECD Europe	191 731	0.7	1.0	0.9	0.8	0.7	0.9	0.9	0.8	1.1	1.1	1.0	0.8	1.1	0.5	–0.1	–0.5	–0.1	0.6	0.6
EU	165 904	0.6	1.0	0.9	0.8	0.6	0.8	0.8	0.7	0.9	0.9	1.0	0.7	1.1	0.6	–0.2	–0.8	0.1	0.4	0.4
Total OECD *less* the United States[f]	292 775	1.0	1.1	1.1	1.0	0.8	1.2	0.9	0.9	1.2	1.2	1.3	1.2	1.4	1.0	0.4	0.1	0.3	0.7	0.8

a) For sources and definitions, see "Sources and Methods".
b) Break in series as of January 1994.
c) Data based on the National Survey of Urban Employment which in 1992 covered 32 urban areas and about 12 million persons.
d) Break in series in 1992.
e) The figures incorporate important revisions to Turkish data; see "Sources and Methods".
f) Totals exclude Mexico prior to 1988.

Annex Table 19. **Labour force participation rates**[a]

	Average 1970-77	1978	1979	1980	1981	1982	1983	1984	1985	1986	1987	1988	1989	1990	1991	1992	1993
United States	66.8	70.0	70.7	71.0	71.2	71.5	71.6	72.2	72.7	73.5	74.1	74.7	75.6	75.8	75.8	76.1	76.0
Japan	71.2	71.5	71.8	71.8	72.1	72.3	73.0	72.7	72.5	72.4	72.5	72.8	73.3	74.1	75.2	75.9	76.1
Germany	68.7	67.9	68.1	68.3	68.1	67.8	67.3	67.0	67.4	68.0	68.4	68.7	68.6	69.1	70.9	69.9	69.7
France	67.8	68.6	68.7	68.4	68.0	67.8	66.9	66.6	66.4	66.5	66.5	66.4	66.5	66.6	66.7	66.8	66.7
Italy	58.6	59.3	59.7	60.3	60.6	60.0	59.9	59.3	59.1	59.9	60.4	60.5	60.8	61.3	61.5	61.4	58.2
United Kingdom	73.1	73.9	74.1	74.0	73.4	72.7	72.7	73.8	74.7	74.7	75.3	76.1	76.7	76.7	75.9	75.4	75.0
Canada	67.6	71.1	72.1	73.0	73.9	73.3	73.6	74.2	75.1	75.8	76.5	77.3	77.8	77.9	77.3	76.5	76.3
Total of above countries	67.9	69.3	69.8	70.0	70.1	70.1	70.1	70.3	70.6	71.0	71.5	71.9	72.5	72.8	73.1	73.1	72.8
Australia	69.9	70.0	69.7	70.5	70.4	70.1	69.8	69.9	70.6	71.7	71.9	72.4	73.6	74.2	74.0	73.7	73.5
Austria	67.4	67.2	67.6	67.3	67.1	67.7	66.8	66.3	65.8	66.2	66.9	66.8	67.0	67.7	68.2	69.3	69.8
Belgium	62.4	62.4	62.8	63.0	63.3	63.0	62.8	62.3	62.0	61.8	61.8	61.8	62.1	62.6	63.1	63.4	63.7
Denmark	76.1	79.8	79.3	79.2	79.4	79.9	80.3	81.1	81.9	82.6	82.9	82.8	82.8	81.9	81.2	81.2	81.3
Finland	71.8	74.0	74.5	75.5	76.0	76.5	76.5	76.5	76.9	76.8	76.3	76.1	76.5	76.1	75.0	73.9	73.2
Greece	56.9	55.5	55.4	55.9	58.7	58.7	59.9	59.8	59.6	59.1	58.7	59.5	59.2	59.2	57.3	57.8	58.6
Iceland	71.5	73.6	73.1	74.3	76.7	77.6	77.3	77.6	79.3	80.8	84.0	80.1	78.6	78.0	81.6	77.2	77.0
Ireland	63.5	62.3	62.4	62.3	62.6	63.0	62.7	62.0	61.3	61.4	61.6	60.5	59.7	60.5	60.6	61.4	61.5
Luxembourg	..	61.2	61.7	61.5	61.4	61.2	60.6	60.7	60.7	60.8	61.5	61.7	61.8	62.1	62.1	..	..
Mexico	..	..	..	..	..	..	..	..	..	..	..	..	..	..	..	..	..
Netherlands	60.3	57.7	57.6	57.7	57.4	57.3	57.4	56.8	56.0	56.4	56.5	57.2	57.4	58.2	59.1	59.6	60.4
New Zealand	65.1	65.6	66.4	66.0	66.5	66.2	65.3	65.4	66.4	66.2	66.1	64.6	63.5	63.8	63.8	63.3	63.3
Norway	70.2	75.1	75.6	75.3	76.1	76.4	76.5	76.7	77.5	79.2	80.3	80.1	78.7	78.0	77.1	76.9	76.6
Portugal	65.6	68.6	68.8	68.6	68.1	67.5	69.9	69.9	69.4	69.2	69.5	70.0	71.7	72.2	73.4	68.5	67.8
Spain	59.8	57.6	57.0	56.3	56.0	56.0	55.8	55.5	55.4	55.8	56.6	57.0	57.3	57.6	57.6	57.5	57.7
Sweden	76.4	79.3	80.1	80.8	80.6	80.7	80.9	81.0	81.6	80.9	81.7	82.3	82.9	83.0	82.2	80.5	77.5
Switzerland	75.8	73.6	73.7	74.4	75.1	74.7	74.4	74.7	75.5	75.8	76.0	76.2	77.6	78.0	77.4	76.1	75.2
Turkey[b]	71.6	71.3	69.2	68.2	65.8	64.1	62.9	61.6	60.2	60.9	60.9	60.1	59.6	58.9	57.5	56.6	56.9
Total of smaller countries	66.5	66.2	65.7	65.5	65.0	64.6	64.4	64.0	63.6	64.0	64.2	64.2	64.4	64.4	63.9	63.5	63.5
Total OECD	67.5	68.6	68.9	69.0	69.0	68.8	68.8	68.8	69.0	69.4	69.8	70.1	70.6	70.8	71.0	70.9	70.7
OECD North America	66.9	70.1	70.8	71.2	71.5	71.7	71.8	72.4	72.9	73.7	74.4	75.0	75.8	76.0	76.0	76.2	76.1
OECD Europe	66.7	66.7	66.7	66.6	66.3	65.8	65.5	65.3	65.2	65.5	65.9	66.0	66.1	66.3	66.5	66.0	65.5
EU	66.0	66.0	66.1	66.2	66.0	65.7	65.5	65.4	65.5	65.8	66.2	66.4	66.7	67.0	67.4	67.0	66.4
Total OECD *less* the United States	67.8	68.1	68.1	68.1	68.0	67.7	67.6	67.4	67.4	67.7	68.0	68.2	68.5	68.7	69.0	68.8	68.4

a) For sources and definitions, see ''Sources and Methods''.
b) The figures incorporate important revisions to Turkish data; see ''Sources and Methods''.

Annex Table 20. **Employment**[a]

Percentage changes from previous period

	1991 Employment (thousands)	1978	1979	1980	1981	1982	1983	1984	1985	1986	1987	1988	1989	1990	1991	1992	1993	1994	Projections 1995	Projections 1996
United States[b]	116 869	4.4	2.9	0.5	1.1	–0.9	1.3	4.1	2.0	2.3	2.6	2.3	2.0	0.5	–0.9	0.6	1.5	3.1	1.9	1.1
Japan	63 680	1.3	1.3	1.0	0.8	1.0	1.7	0.6	0.7	0.8	1.0	1.7	2.0	2.0	1.9	1.1	0.2	0.1	0.1	0.3
Germany	36 511	0.8	1.7	1.6	–0.1	–1.2	–1.4	0.2	0.7	1.4	0.7	0.8	1.5	3.0	2.5	–1.8	–1.8	–0.9	0	0.5
France	22 671	0.5	0.2	0.1	–0.5	0.4	–0.2	–0.9	–0.1	0.5	0.4	1.0	1.4	1.0	0	–0.7	–1.2	0.5	1.0	1.1
Italy	21 410	0.3	1.0	1.3	0.2	–0.3	0.2	0.4	0.4	0.5	–0.2	1.1	0.1	1.8	0.9	–0.6	–4.2	–1.7	0.7	0.9
United Kingdom	26 216	1.2	1.4	–0.9	–3.4	–1.9	–0.2	2.3	1.0	0.3	2.4	3.4	2.7	0.4	–3.1	–2.4	–0.8	0.3	1.5	1.2
Canada	12 916	3.4	4.2	3.0	2.9	–3.2	0.6	2.7	3.0	3.0	2.7	3.2	2.1	0.6	–1.9	–0.6	1.4	2.1	2.3	2.3
Total of above countries	300 273	2.3	2.0	0.7	0.4	–0.5	0.7	2.0	1.3	1.4	1.7	2.0	1.8	1.2	0	–0.1	0	1.2	1.2	0.9
Australia	7 734	0.3	1.4	2.9	2.0	0	–1.8	2.9	3.6	3.5	2.2	3.8	4.7	1.5	–2.1	–0.7	0.3	3.1	2.8	2.6
Austria	3 471	0.9	1.2	0.7	0.6	1.2	–1.0	0.1	0	1.4	0.6	0.3	1.0	2.1	1.7	2.1	0.6	0.5	0.6	0.5
Belgium	3 819	0.1	0.9	–0.1	–1.9	–1.3	–1.0	–0.2	0.6	0.7	0.5	1.5	1.6	1.4	0.1	–0.4	–1.3	–0.4	0.5	0.9
Denmark	2 526	1.0	1.2	–0.5	–1.3	0.4	0.3	1.7	2.5	2.6	0.9	–0.6	–0.6	–1.0	–1.5	–0.4	–0.7	–0.1	1.9	1.2
Finland	2 340	–1.4	2.5	3.2	1.1	1.0	0.6	1.0	1.0	–0.3	–0.3	0.3	1.6	–0.1	–5.2	–7.1	6.1	0.8	2.9	2.2
Greece	3 632	0.4	1.1	1.4	5.2	–0.8	1.1	0.4	1.0	0.4	–0.1	1.7	0.4	1.3	–2.3	1.4	1.0	1.2	0.7	1.0
Iceland	134	2.9	1.0	3.3	4.8	2.6	0.9	1.5	3.6	3.1	5.8	–2.8	–1.6	–0.1	6.5	–6.7	–1.1	1.1	1.2	1.1
Ireland	1 125	2.5	3.2	1.0	–0.9	0.2	–2.1	–1.8	–2.5	0.5	0.6	0.3	–0.1	3.3	–0.1	1.2	0.6	2.6	2.4	1.9
Luxembourg	195	–0.6	0.5	0.7	0.3	–0.3	–0.3	0.5	1.3	2.5	2.7	3.4	2.7	4.1	4.1	2.5	1.8	2.7	2.8	2.7
Mexico[c]	11 080	..	..	..	..	..	..	..	..	..	..	4.7	3.5	2.3	4.9	4.2	2.9	2.7	1.0	3.0
Netherlands	5 790	0.9	1.4	1.2	–1.1	–2.1	–1.3	0.5	1.3	2.5	1.6	2.3	1.8	3.0	2.6	1.6	0.7	0.6	1.5	1.6
New Zealand	1 461	–0.6	1.4	–0.1	0.7	0.9	–1.0	2.7	3.5	–0.4	0.8	–3.2	–2.6	0.9	–1.4	0.4	2.0	4.2	3.2	1.9
Norway	2 009	1.6	1.1	0.5	1.5	0.4	0.1	1.3	2.3	3.5	1.9	–0.6	–3.0	–1.0	–1.0	–0.3	0	1.5	1.4	1.2
Portugal[d]	4 604	–0.2	1.2	2.2	0.5	–0.1	4.0	–0.1	–0.5	0.1	2.6	2.6	2.2	2.2	2.9	–6.4	–2.0	–0.1	0.8	1.0
Spain	12 609	–1.7	–1.7	–3.0	–3.0	–1.3	–1.1	–1.8	–0.9	2.2	3.1	2.9	4.1	2.6	0.2	–1.9	–4.3	–0.9	1.1	1.7
Sweden	4 430	0.4	1.5	1.3	–0.2	–0.1	0.1	0.7	1.0	–0.7	1.6	1.4	1.5	0.9	–1.7	–4.1	–6.8	–0.9	1.8	1.3
Switzerland	3 559	1.0	1.1	2.3	2.3	0.5	0	1.0	1.9	1.4	1.2	1.2	1.1	1.3	–0.1	–2.2	–2.6	–1.4	0.7	1.2
Turkey[e]	18 420	1.4	1.5	1.3	0.9	1.1	1.0	1.5	1.7	1.9	2.3	1.5	1.9	2.0	0.3	1.0	0.9	–4.1	0.5	1.3
Total of smaller countries[f]	88 909	0.3	0.9	0.6	0.1	–0.1	0	0.6	1.1	1.6	1.8	2.0	2.2	1.8	0.5	–0.2	–0.6	–0.2	1.2	1.7
Total OECD[f]	389 182	1.9	1.7	0.7	0.3	–0.4	0.6	1.7	1.2	1.5	1.7	2.0	1.9	1.3	0.1	–0.1	–0.1	0.9	1.2	1.1
OECD North America[f]	140 865	4.3	3.0	0.7	1.3	–1.1	1.2	4.0	2.1	2.4	2.6	2.5	2.2	0.6	–0.5	0.8	1.6	3.0	1.9	1.4
OECD Europe	175 442	0.5	1.0	0.5	–0.6	–0.5	–0.2	0.4	0.6	1.0	1.3	1.6	1.6	1.6	0.1	–1.2	–1.7	–0.8	0.9	1.1
EU	151 320	0.4	0.9	0.3	–0.9	–0.8	–0.4	0.3	0.5	0.9	1.1	1.7	1.7	1.6	0.1	–1.5	–2.0	–0.4	0.9	1.0
Total OECD *less* the United States[f]	272 313	0.8	1.2	0.8	0	–0.3	0.2	0.7	0.9	1.1	1.3	1.8	1.9	1.7	0.5	–0.4	–0.8	–0.1	0.8	1.1

a) For sources and definitions, see "Sources and Methods".
b) Break in series as of January 1994.
c) Data based on the National Survey of Urban Employment which in 1992 covered 32 urban areas and about 12 million persons.
d) Break in series in 1992.
e) The figures incorporate important revisions to Turkish data; see "Sources and Methods".
f) Totals exclude Mexico prior to 1988.

Annex Table 21. **Unemployment rates: commonly used definitions**[a]

	1991 Unemployment (thousands)	1978	1979	1980	1981	1982	1983	1984	1985	1986	1987	1988	1989	1990	1991	1992	1993	1994	Projections 1995	1996
United States[b]	8 443	6.1	5.8	7.2	7.6	9.7	9.6	7.5	7.2	7.0	6.2	5.5	5.3	5.5	6.7	7.4	6.8	6.1	5.6	5.7
Japan	1 382	2.2	2.1	2.0	2.2	2.3	2.7	2.7	2.6	2.8	2.9	2.5	2.3	2.1	2.1	2.2	2.5	2.9	3.1	3.1
Germany	2 602	3.7	3.2	3.2	4.5	6.4	7.9	7.9	8.0	7.7	7.6	7.6	6.9	6.2	6.7	7.7	8.9	9.6	9.2	8.7
France	2 361	5.2	5.8	6.2	7.4	8.0	8.3	9.7	10.2	10.4	10.5	10.0	9.4	8.9	9.4	10.3	11.7	12.4	12.0	11.5
Italy[c]	2 650	7.3	7.8	7.7	8.5	9.2	10.0	10.1	10.2	11.2	12.1	12.1	12.1	11.5	11.0	11.6	10.7	11.3	11.1	10.5
United Kingdom	2 348	4.5	4.0	5.3	8.3	9.7	10.5	10.7	11.0	11.0	9.8	7.8	6.1	5.9	8.2	9.9	10.2	9.2	8.2	7.6
Canada	1 493	8.4	7.5	7.5	7.6	11.0	11.9	11.3	10.5	9.6	8.8	7.8	7.5	8.1	10.4	11.3	11.2	10.4	9.4	9.1
Total of above countries	21 279	5.0	4.8	5.5	6.3	7.7	8.1	7.4	7.3	7.3	6.9	6.3	5.8	5.8	6.6	7.3	7.3	7.2	6.8	6.6
Australia	809	6.4	6.1	6.0	5.7	7.1	9.9	8.9	8.1	8.0	8.0	7.1	6.1	7.0	9.5	10.7	10.9	9.7	8.7	7.9
Austria	125	1.8	1.8	1.6	2.2	3.1	3.7	3.8	3.6	3.1	3.8	3.6	3.1	3.2	3.5	3.6	4.2	4.4	4.3	4.2
Belgium	391	7.2	7.5	7.9	10.2	11.9	13.2	13.2	12.3	11.6	11.3	10.3	9.3	8.7	9.3	10.3	11.9	12.6	12.4	11.8
Denmark	296	7.3	6.2	7.0	9.2	9.8	10.4	10.1	9.0	7.8	7.8	8.6	9.3	9.6	10.5	11.2	12.2	12.1	10.6	9.7
Finland	193	7.3	6.0	4.7	4.9	5.4	5.4	5.2	5.0	5.4	5.1	4.5	3.5	3.5	7.6	13.1	17.9	18.4	16.4	14.9
Greece	301	1.8	1.9	2.8	4.0	5.8	7.9	8.1	7.8	7.4	7.4	7.7	7.5	7.0	7.7	8.7	9.7	9.6	9.9	9.9
Iceland	2	0.4	0.4	0.3	0.4	0.7	1.0	1.3	0.9	0.6	0.5	0.6	1.6	1.8	1.4	3.0	4.3	4.7	4.5	4.4
Ireland	195	8.2	7.1	7.3	9.9	11.4	14.0	15.5	17.4	17.4	17.5	16.1	14.7	13.3	14.7	15.5	15.8	14.8	13.9	13.6
Luxembourg	2	0.8	0.7	0.7	1.0	1.3	1.6	1.7	1.7	1.5	1.7	1.6	1.4	1.3	1.4	1.6	2.1	2.7	2.5	2.3
Mexico[d]	322	..	..	4.7	4.2	4.8	4.6	4.4	4.2	3.9	3.8	3.5	2.9	2.7	2.8	2.9	3.5	3.7	5.2	5.2
Netherlands	335	3.8	3.6	4.0	5.8	8.5	11.0	10.6	9.2	8.4	8.0	7.8	6.9	6.0	5.5	5.4	6.5	7.5	7.5	7.4
New Zealand	168	1.7	1.8	2.5	3.3	3.6	5.3	4.5	3.5	4.0	4.1	5.6	7.1	7.8	10.3	10.3	9.5	8.1	7.2	7.0
Norway	116	1.8	1.9	1.7	2.0	2.7	3.4	3.2	2.6	2.0	2.1	3.2	4.9	5.2	5.5	5.9	6.0	5.5	4.9	4.5
Portugal	199	7.9	8.2	8.0	7.7	7.5	7.8	8.5	8.7	8.6	7.1	5.8	5.1	4.7	4.1	4.2	5.5	6.8	6.7	6.3
Spain	2 464	7.0	8.6	11.5	14.3	16.4	18.2	20.1	21.5	21.0	20.5	19.5	17.3	16.3	16.3	18.4	22.7	24.1	24.1	23.3
Sweden	122	2.2	2.1	2.0	2.5	3.2	3.5	3.1	2.9	2.7	2.1	1.8	1.5	1.7	2.9	5.3	8.2	8.0	7.5	6.7
Switzerland	39	0.3	0.3	0.2	0.2	0.4	0.9	1.1	0.9	0.8	0.7	0.6	0.5	0.5	1.1	2.5	4.5	4.7	4.1	3.6
Turkey[e]	1 547	9.8	8.6	8.1	7.1	7.0	7.7	7.6	7.1	7.9	8.3	8.4	8.5	8.0	7.7	7.9	8.7	10.9	12.0	12.4
Total of smaller countries[f]	7 626	6.2	6.1	6.5	7.2	8.2	9.5	9.7	9.5	9.4	9.3	8.4	7.8	7.4	7.9	8.8	10.4	11.0	11.2	10.9
Total OECD[f]	28 904	5.2	5.1	5.7	6.5	7.8	8.4	7.9	7.8	7.8	7.4	6.8	6.3	6.2	6.9	7.6	8.0	8.1	7.8	7.6
OECD North America[f]	10 258	6.3	6.0	7.2	7.6	9.8	9.8	7.9	7.5	7.3	6.5	5.6	5.3	5.6	6.8	7.4	7.0	6.3	6.0	6.0
OECD Europe	16 288	5.5	5.5	5.9	7.2	8.3	9.3	9.7	9.8	9.9	9.8	9.2	8.5	8.0	8.5	9.5	10.7	11.3	11.0	10.6
EU	14 584	5.2	5.3	5.9	7.5	8.8	9.8	10.3	10.4	10.4	10.3	9.6	8.7	8.2	8.8	10.0	11.1	11.5	11.1	10.6
Total OECD *less* the United States[f]	20 462	4.9	4.8	5.1	6.0	7.0	7.9	8.1	8.1	8.1	8.0	7.4	6.8	6.4	7.0	7.7	8.6	8.9	8.8	8.5

a) For sources and definitions, see "Sources and Methods".
b) Break in series as of January 1994.
c) Break in series in 1991 and 1992.
d) Data based on the National Survey of Urban Employment which in 1992 covered 32 urban areas and about 12 million persons.
e) The figures incorporate important revisions to Turkish data; see "Sources and Methods".
f) Totals exclude Mexico prior to 1988.

Annex Table 22. **Standardised unemployment rates**

Per cent of total labour force

	1975	1976	1977	1978	1979	1980	1981	1982	1983	1984	1985	1986	1987	1988	1989	1990	1991	1992	1993	1994
United States	8.3	7.6	6.9	6.0	5.8	7.0	7.5	9.5	9.5	7.4	7.1	6.9	6.1	5.4	5.2	5.4	6.6	7.3	6.7 |	6.0
Japan	1.9	2.0	2.0	2.2	2.1	2.0	2.2	2.4	2.6	2.7	2.6	2.8	2.8	2.5	2.3	2.1	2.1	2.2	2.5	2.9
Germany[a]	3.6	3.7	3.6	3.5	3.2	2.9	4.2	5.9	7.7 |	7.1	7.1	6.4	6.2	6.2	5.6	4.8	4.2[b]	4.6[b]	6.1[b]	6.9[b]
France[a]	4.0	4.4	4.9	5.2	5.8	6.2	7.4	8.1	8.3	9.7	10.2	10.4	10.5	10.0	9.4	8.9	9.4	10.4	11.6	12.5
Italy	5.8	6.6	7.0	7.1	7.6	7.5	7.8	8.4 |	8.8	9.4	9.6	10.5	10.9	11.0	10.9	10.3	9.9	10.5 |	10.2 |	..
United Kingdom[a]	4.3	5.6	6.0	5.9	5.0	6.4	9.8	11.3	12.4 |	11.7	11.2	11.2	10.3	8.6	7.2	6.9	8.8	10.1	10.5	9.6
Canada	6.9	7.1	8.1	8.3	7.4	7.5	7.5	10.9	11.9	11.2	10.5	9.5	8.8	7.7	7.5	8.1	10.3	11.3	11.2	10.3
Major seven countries	5.4	5.4	5.4	5.1	4.9	5.5	6.3	7.7	8.1 |	7.3	7.2	7.1	6.7	6.1	5.7	5.6	6.3	6.9	7.0 |	6.9
Australia	4.8	4.7	5.6	6.2	6.2	6.0	5.7	7.1	9.9	8.9	8.2	8.0	8.0	7.2	6.1	6.9	9.5	10.7	10.8	9.7
Belgium[a]	5.0	6.4	7.4	7.9	8.2	8.8	10.8	12.6 |	12.1	12.1	11.3	11.2	11.0	9.7	8.0	7.2	7.2	7.7	8.6	9.7
Finland	2.2	3.8	5.8	7.2	5.9	4.6	4.8 |	5.3	5.4	5.2	5.0	5.3	5.0	4.5	3.4	3.4	7.5	13.0	17.7	18.2
Ireland	..	..	..	..	..	..	..	..	14.0	15.5	17.0	17.0	16.7 |	16.2	14.7	13.3	14.7	15.5	15.6	14.7
Netherlands[a]	5.2	5.5	5.3	5.3	5.4	6.0	8.5	11.4 |	12.0	11.8	10.6	9.9	9.6 |	9.1	8.3	7.5	7.0	5.6	6.2	7.2
New Zealand	..	..	..	..	..	..	..		..	..	..	4.0	4.1	5.6	7.1	7.7	10.2	10.4	9.6	8.1
Norway	2.3	1.7	1.4	1.8	2.0 |	1.6	2.0	2.6	3.4	3.1	2.6	2.0	2.1	3.2	4.9	5.2	5.5	5.9	6.0	5.4
Portugal	..	..	..	..	..	..	..	..	7.8	8.4	8.5	8.4	7.0	5.7	5.0	4.6	4.1 |	4.1	5.5	6.8
Spain	3.6	4.5	5.1	6.8	8.4	11.1	13.8	15.6	17.0	19.7	21.1	20.8	20.1	19.1	16.9	15.9	16.0	18.1	22.4	23.8
Sweden	1.6	1.6	1.8	2.2	2.1	2.0	2.5	3.2	3.5	3.1	2.8	2.7 |	1.9	1.6	1.4	1.5	2.7	4.8 |	8.2	8.0
Total OECD	5.3	5.4	5.4	5.2	5.1	5.8	6.7	8.2	8.6 |	8.0	7.8	7.7	7.3	6.7	6.2	6.1	6.7	7.4 |	7.8 |	7.8
Memorandum item																				
EU[c]	4.3	5.0	5.4	5.6	5.7	6.4	8.1	9.4	10.0 |	10.4	10.5	10.5	10.2	9.6	8.7	8.1	8.5	9.4 |	10.7 |	11.4

a) Series based on EC Labour Force Surveys: see corresponding notes in *Quarterly Labour Force Statistics.*
b) Western Germany.
c) EU: only countries shown – Germany, France, Italy, United Kingdom, Belgium, Ireland, Netherlands, Portugal, Spain and Sweden – are included in the area total.
Note: These unemployment rates are based on the ILO/OECD Guidelines. The unemployed are defined as persons of working age who are without work, available for work and actively seeking employment; unemployment is expressed as a percentage of total labour force including all members of the armed forces. Break is marked by (|). The data above are averages of quarterly or monthly figures. For a detailed description of the sources and methods used, see *Standardized Unemployment Rates, Sources and Methods* (OECD, 1985).

Annex Table 23. **Labour force, employment and unemployment**

Millions

	1978	1979	1980	1981	1982	1983	1984	1985	1986	1987	1988	1989	1990	1991	1992	1993	1994	Projections 1995	Projections 1996
Labour force																			
Major seven countries	266.8	271.7	275.5	278.9	281.6	284.8	288.4	291.8	295.9	299.6	303.5	307.6	310.9	321.6	323.6	323.7	327.1	329.6	332.1
Total of smaller countries[a]	73.7	74.3	75.1	75.7	76.5	77.6	78.2	78.9	80.1	81.5	82.5	83.6	84.8	85.1	85.4	86.1	86.2	87.2	88.2
Total OECD[a]	340.6	346.0	350.6	354.6	358.1	362.3	366.6	370.7	376.1	381.1	386.0	391.2	395.7	406.7	409.0	409.8	413.3	416.9	420.3
OECD North America[a]	113.5	116.6	119.0	121.0	122.6	124.1	126.4	128.6	131.2	133.5	135.6	138.0	139.1	139.7	141.5	142.7	145.9	148.0	149.8
OECD Europe	163.8	165.4	166.9	168.1	169.3	170.7	172.2	173.5	175.4	177.4	179.2	180.6	182.6	191.7	191.6	190.7	190.5	191.5	192.7
EU	141.8	143.2	144.6	145.8	146.7	147.8	149.0	150.0	151.3	152.6	154.1	155.1	156.8	165.9	165.5	164.3	164.5	165.2	165.9
Total OECD *less* the United States[a]	238.3	241.0	243.6	245.9	247.9	250.8	253.1	255.3	258.2	261.3	264.4	267.3	270.9	281.4	282.0	281.8	282.3	283.9	285.8
Employment																			
Major seven countries	253.5	258.5	260.3	261.2	259.8	261.7	267.0	270.4	274.3	278.9	284.3	289.6	293.0	300.3	300.0	300.0	303.6	307.2	310.1
Total of smaller countries[a]	69.2	69.8	70.2	70.3	70.2	70.2	70.6	71.4	72.6	73.9	75.1	76.6	77.9	77.8	77.2	76.3	75.8	76.7	77.8
Total OECD[a]	322.7	328.3	330.5	331.5	330.0	331.9	337.6	341.8	346.9	352.8	359.5	366.2	370.9	378.1	377.2	376.4	379.4	383.9	387.9
OECD North America[a]	106.4	109.6	110.4	111.8	110.6	111.9	116.4	118.9	121.7	124.9	127.8	130.4	131.1	129.8	130.4	132.3	136.4	139.1	140.7
OECD Europe	154.7	156.3	157.0	156.0	155.1	154.8	155.5	156.5	158.1	160.1	162.6	165.3	168.0	175.4	173.3	170.3	169.0	170.5	172.3
EU	134.4	135.7	136.1	134.8	133.8	133.3	133.7	134.3	135.5	137.0	139.2	141.6	143.9	151.3	149.1	146.0	145.5	146.8	148.4
Total OECD *less* the United States[a]	226.7	229.4	231.2	231.1	230.5	231.1	232.6	234.6	237.3	240.3	244.5	248.9	253.0	261.2	259.6	257.0	256.4	258.5	261.1
Unemployment																			
Major seven countries	13.3	13.2	15.2	17.6	21.8	23.1	21.4	21.4	21.6	20.7	19.1	18.0	17.9	21.3	23.6	23.7	23.4	22.4	22.1
Total of smaller countries[a]	4.5	4.5	4.9	5.5	6.3	7.4	7.6	7.5	7.6	7.6	7.4	7.0	6.8	7.3	8.2	9.8	10.4	10.5	10.4
Total OECD[a]	17.9	17.7	20.1	23.1	28.1	30.4	29.0	28.9	29.2	28.4	26.6	25.0	24.7	28.6	31.8	33.5	33.9	33.0	32.4
OECD North America[a]	7.1	7.0	8.6	9.2	12.1	12.2	10.0	9.7	9.5	8.6	7.8	7.6	8.1	9.9	11.0	10.4	9.5	8.9	9.1
OECD Europe	9.0	9.1	9.9	12.2	14.1	15.9	16.7	17.0	17.3	17.3	16.6	15.4	14.6	16.3	18.3	20.3	21.4	21.1	20.4
EU	7.3	7.6	8.5	10.9	12.9	14.4	15.3	15.7	15.8	15.7	14.9	13.6	12.9	14.6	16.5	18.3	19.0	18.3	17.5
Total OECD *less* the United States[a]	11.7	11.6	12.4	14.8	17.4	19.7	20.5	20.6	21.0	20.9	19.9	18.5	17.8	20.1	22.4	24.7	25.9	25.5	24.7

a) The aggregate measures do not include Mexico because of a potential bias present in Mexican unemployment, employment and labour force statistics created by the limited coverage of the National Survey of Urban Employment.

Annex Table 24. **Capital income shares in the business sector**[a]

	Average 1970-77	1978	1979	1980	1981	1982	1983	1984	1985	1986	1987	1988	1989	1990	1991	1992	1993	1994	Projections 1995	Projections 1996
United States	31.9	33.2	32.8	31.7	32.4	31.2	32.8	33.6	33.8	33.9	33.5	33.3	34.1	33.5	33.1	33.1	33.1	33.3	33.2	33.4
Japan	34.6	30.3	30.4	30.9	30.3	29.8	29.6	30.3	31.7	32.0	31.6	32.3	32.3	32.0	31.8	31.2	30.6	30.2	28.9	28.7
Germany[b]	34.0	33.7	33.5	31.3	30.9	31.2	33.2	34.0	34.5	35.1	34.6	35.6	36.3	37.1	37.7	37.5	37.5	39.2	40.0	40.1
France[c]	31.2	29.9	30.0	28.3	28.2	28.5	29.2	30.7	31.9	34.9	35.5	36.9	38.1	37.6	37.9	38.3	38.3	39.8	40.5	41.0
Italy[d]	31.0	34.9	35.5	36.0	35.3	35.4	34.5	36.4	36.6	38.6	38.4	38.8	38.3	37.3	36.6	36.7	37.0	39.7	41.0	41.7
United Kingdom[c]	29.7	32.5	31.3	29.2	28.9	30.7	32.3	31.9	32.1	31.0	31.6	31.2	29.9	28.4	27.1	27.7	29.8	30.9	31.3	31.2
Canada[d]	34.5	36.0	37.7	38.0	36.6	35.3	38.1	39.3	38.6	37.7	37.5	37.1	36.6	35.1	33.5	32.7	32.7	33.8	34.9	35.1
Total of above countries	32.4	32.7	32.5	31.7	31.7	31.2	32.3	33.1	33.6	34.0	33.8	34.1	34.4	33.9	33.5	33.5	33.6	34.2	34.3	34.4
Australia	32.4	32.1	34.5	33.9	33.4	28.8	32.7	34.6	35.2	35.0	36.9	38.3	38.6	37.2	36.7	37.0	38.1	38.3	37.5	37.5
Austria[d]	32.7	30.2	31.3	31.4	29.5	30.0	31.2	31.5	35.8	35.0	34.6	36.4	36.7	37.2	36.9	35.6	34.6	35.7	36.1	36.1
Belgium	33.6	29.4	28.7	28.4	26.8	29.2	30.9	31.1	32.1	32.7	32.6	35.0	35.9	35.2	33.2	32.7	32.2	32.8	33.9	34.6
Denmark	31.5	30.1	29.8	28.5	30.2	33.0	34.3	35.6	35.8	34.9	32.5	33.7	35.5	36.7	37.3	37.5	38.1	39.9	40.1	40.3
Finland[d]	26.7	29.5	31.3	30.4	28.7	30.1	29.7	30.0	28.4	28.2	28.4	29.1	30.0	27.7	24.6	25.1	29.3	32.5	32.7	32.0
Greece	50.3	45.2	43.9	45.7	42.1	39.2	38.8	41.1	40.3	44.0	44.5	45.0	43.5	42.2	46.8	48.0	49.5	48.6	48.8	48.9
Ireland	22.6	26.3	23.4	19.6	22.8	24.1	23.9	24.7	26.6	24.2	27.0	26.9	28.7	28.5	28.5	27.7	29.5	29.5	30.7	32.0
Mexico	..	..	..	25.4	20.7	24.7	36.2	37.1	38.2	39.3	42.3	45.2	47.8	50.6	56.2	52.8	53.2	53.3	54.7	55.9
Netherlands[d]	30.0	29.9	29.7	29.7	32.0	33.5	35.0	38.4	39.2	37.9	38.0	38.5	40.6	40.9	40.1	38.5	37.4	38.9	39.5	40.1
New Zealand[d]	36.7	33.4	33.5	31.0	31.3	34.4	37.0	41.7	42.3	41.4	37.0	40.0	41.6	42.9	42.6	42.4	45.3	45.0	45.1	45.3
Norway[e]	20.9	20.7	23.8	23.3	23.5	22.7	23.2	23.7	23.6	23.5	22.8	23.4	24.9	25.7	25.6	26.1	28.9	29.3	28.4	27.6
Portugal[d]	27.0	28.0	31.1	30.4	28.3	28.1	26.9	27.3	29.5	30.8	29.1	30.0	30.8	29.7	32.3	35.1	35.4	35.7	36.8	38.2
Spain	31.7	30.6	30.7	32.3	31.5	33.0	32.5	36.0	37.6	38.2	38.9	40.0	40.9	40.6	40.6	40.1	41.0	42.9	43.7	44.1
Sweden	28.8	24.7	27.4	26.4	25.9	29.6	31.8	33.1	32.3	31.8	31.2	31.5	29.6	27.4	28.7	31.0	33.7	34.6	34.7	33.3
Switzerland[c]	26.8	21.6	20.7	20.1	20.2	19.8	20.1	20.7	21.8	22.1	21.2	20.7	22.2	22.6	21.4	20.6	21.1	23.3	24.0	24.7
Total of above smaller countries[f]	31.3	29.7	30.3	29.5	28.3	29.4	32.1	33.9	34.9	35.1	35.7	37.0	38.1	38.2	39.1	38.4	39.2	40.1	40.7	41.1
Total of above North American countries[f]	32.1	33.5	33.2	31.8	32.0	31.1	33.4	34.3	34.5	34.5	34.4	34.4	35.2	34.8	34.7	34.4	34.4	34.6	34.8	35.0
Total of above European countries	31.5	31.7	31.7	30.8	30.4	31.1	31.9	33.2	33.8	34.7	34.7	35.4	35.7	35.4	35.3	35.3	35.9	37.5	38.3	38.6
Total of above OECD countries[f]	32.2	32.2	32.2	31.3	31.1	30.9	32.2	33.3	33.8	34.2	34.2	34.6	35.0	34.6	34.5	34.3	34.5	35.2	35.3	35.5

a) Difficulties in making an appropriate imputation for the labour income of the self-employed mean that great care is needed in interpreting cross-country differences in the level of capital income shares. For details, see "Sources and Methods".
b) Up to and including 1990, data concern western Germany; data from 1991 concern the whole of Germany and the whole economy and exclude the employment adjustment for unpaid family workers for which data are not available.
c) Excluding the employment adjustment for unpaid family workers for which data are not available.
d) Excluding the employment adjustment for unpaid family workers prior to 1974 for Portugal, 1975 for Canada, 1977 for Italy and Finland, 1985 for Austria, 1986 for New Zealand and 1987 for the Netherlands.
e) Mainland business sector (*i.e.* excluding shipping as well as crude petroleum and gas extraction).
f) Total excludes Mexico prior to 1980.

Annex Table 25. **Rates of return on capital in the business sector**[a]

	Average 1970-77	1978	1979	1980	1981	1982	1983	1984	1985	1986	1987	1988	1989	1990	1991	1992	1993	1994	Projections 1995	1996
United States	15.8	15.8	15.3	13.9	13.6	12.5	13.8	15.2	15.6	15.7	15.9	16.2	16.8	16.6	16.3	17.1	18.1	18.9	19.1	19.3
Japan	18.7	14.9	14.5	14.3	13.8	13.4	13.3	13.8	14.5	14.7	14.5	15.0	15.2	14.9	14.8	14.1	13.6	13.4	12.8	12.9
Germany[b]	13.6	13.0	12.9	11.6	11.0	10.8	11.5	11.9	12.0	12.5	12.3	12.8	13.1	13.7	13.9	13.7	13.2	14.1	14.6	14.4
France[c]	12.8	11.5	11.5	10.5	10.3	10.2	10.4	10.9	11.4	12.8	13.1	13.9	14.7	14.5	14.4	14.6	14.1	14.7	15.2	15.6
Italy[d]	11.5	12.4	13.0	13.0	12.1	12.2	12.2	13.2	13.3	14.7	14.8	15.2	15.0	14.7	14.6	14.5	13.9	14.9	15.3	15.9
United Kingdom[c]	10.2	10.1	9.5	8.4	8.1	9.0	9.9	9.9	10.2	9.7	10.2	10.3	9.8	9.4	9.1	9.9	11.1	11.9	12.4	12.6
Canada[d]	14.9	16.0	17.6	18.9	18.2	16.0	18.0	19.5	19.5	19.2	19.8	20.1	19.5	18.0	17.3	17.1	17.4	18.4	19.4	19.7
Total of above countries	15.1	14.3	14.1	13.2	12.8	12.2	13.0	13.9	14.3	14.6	14.7	15.1	15.5	15.2	15.0	15.3	15.6	16.2	16.4	16.6
Australia	12.2	10.7	11.6	11.1	11.0	8.9	9.8	11.3	11.2	10.6	11.4	12.4	13.2	12.5	11.8	12.0	12.4	13.0	12.6	12.8
Austria[d]	13.1	10.8	11.2	10.9	9.8	9.6	10.0	10.0	11.3	11.1	10.8	11.4	11.5	11.7	11.6	11.1	10.6	11.1	11.4	11.4
Belgium	13.0	11.3	10.9	10.8	9.7	10.4	10.9	11.1	11.6	12.1	12.2	13.4	13.7	13.5	12.5	12.3	11.8	12.0	12.4	12.7
Denmark	10.7	9.2	9.0	8.1	8.1	9.1	9.5	10.2	10.3	10.1	9.2	9.6	10.0	10.3	10.1	10.1	9.9	10.8	11.1	11.3
Finland[d]	8.1	7.9	8.9	8.7	8.2	8.6	8.6	8.8	8.4	8.3	8.3	8.7	9.1	8.0	6.4	6.3	7.3	8.5	9.2	9.4
Greece	41.3	30.6	29.8	29.3	24.4	22.5	19.6	19.9	19.1	19.7	19.6	20.5	19.0	18.5	20.3	20.5	21.3	21.2	21.4	21.5
Ireland	8.4	9.0	8.0	6.3	7.4	7.8	7.8	8.1	8.8	8.0	9.5	9.4	10.1	10.6	10.4	10.5	11.7	12.1	13.2	14.2
Netherlands[d]	13.7	13.9	13.5	13.3	14.0	14.7	15.4	17.3	17.9	17.4	16.8	17.1	18.4	18.8	18.5	17.5	16.7	17.5	17.7	18.0
New Zealand[d]	15.1	10.8	11.4	10.1	10.4	11.3	12.0	14.1	14.3	14.4	13.1	16.1	17.4	17.6	16.9	16.9	18.8	20.4	21.2	20.9
Norway[e]	8.2	6.5	7.6	7.3	7.1	6.5	6.6	7.0	6.7	6.9	6.5	6.4	6.4	6.7	6.6	6.6	7.2	7.4	7.2	6.9
Spain	18.8	16.3	15.9	15.4	14.1	14.8	13.9	15.5	15.7	17.0	18.0	18.9	19.5	19.4	19.2	18.6	18.4	18.9	19.1	19.3
Sweden	11.4	8.1	9.3	9.1	8.7	9.7	10.2	11.0	10.7	10.7	10.6	10.9	10.3	9.5	10.1	11.1	11.6	12.3	12.9	12.2
Switzerland[c]	11.6	9.0	9.0	8.6	8.6	8.3	8.4	8.8	9.2	9.7	9.3	8.9	9.3	9.7	9.0	8.5	8.7	9.5	9.8	10.1
Total of above smaller countries	15.0	12.8	12.9	12.4	11.8	11.8	11.8	12.8	13.1	13.3	13.5	14.1	14.6	14.4	14.2	13.9	14.0	14.5	14.8	14.9
Total of above North American countries	15.7	15.8	15.5	14.3	14.0	12.8	14.2	15.6	15.9	16.0	16.2	16.5	17.0	16.7	16.4	17.1	18.1	18.8	19.2	19.3
Total of above European countries	13.2	12.3	12.2	11.5	10.9	11.1	11.3	12.0	12.2	12.8	13.0	13.5	13.7	13.6	13.5	13.5	13.4	14.2	14.6	14.8
Total of above OECD countries	15.1	14.1	13.9	13.1	12.7	12.1	12.8	13.8	14.1	14.4	14.6	15.0	15.3	15.1	14.9	15.1	15.4	16.0	16.2	16.4

a) Difficulties in making an appropriate imputation for the labour income of the self-employed and in deriving a consistent measure of the capital stock across countries mean that great care is needed in interpreting cross-country differences in the levels of rates of return. For details, see "Sources and Methods".
b) Western Germany.
c) Excluding the adjustment to employment for unpaid family workers for which data are not available.
d) Excluding the adjustment to employment for unpaid family workers prior to 1975 for Canada, 1977 for Italy and Finland, 1985 for Austria, 1986 for New Zealand and 1987 for the Netherlands.
e) Mainland business sector (*i.e.* excluding shipping as well as crude petroleum and gas extraction).

Annex Table 26. **Household saving rates**[a]

Percentage of disposable household income

	1977	1978	1979	1980	1981	1982	1983	1984	1985	1986	1987	1988	1989	1990	1991	1992	1993	1994	Projections 1995	Projections 1996
United States	6.5	7.1	7.2	8.1	9.1	8.9	6.9	8.3	6.6	6.2	4.5	4.5	4.1	4.3	5.1	5.2	4.6	4.2	5.0	4.8
Japan	21.8	20.8	18.2	17.9	18.4	16.7	16.1	15.8	15.6	16.1	14.7	14.3	14.6	14.1	15.1	15.0	14.7	14.9	15.7	15.6
Germany	12.2	12.1	12.7	12.8	13.6	12.7	10.9	11.4	11.4	12.3	12.6	12.8	12.4	13.8	12.7	12.9	12.3	11.0	11.0	11.0
France[b]	18.7	20.4	18.8	17.6	18.0	17.3	15.9	14.5	14.0	12.9	10.8	11.0	11.7	12.5	13.2	13.7	13.8	13.5	13.6	13.1
Italy[b]	26.5	26.9	26.1	23.0	21.8	20.4	22.3	20.6	18.9	18.2	17.8	16.9	16.7	18.2	18.2	17.7	15.7	15.0	13.8	13.6
United Kingdom[b]	9.2	10.9	12.1	13.4	12.6	11.3	9.7	11.1	10.7	8.7	7.1	5.7	7.2	8.4	10.5	12.8	11.7	10.4	9.9	9.5
Canada	11.4	12.6	13.2	13.6	15.4	18.2	14.8	15.0	13.3	10.7	9.2	9.7	10.4	9.7	9.6	9.8	9.2	7.6	7.2	7.2
Australia	11.6	11.7	11.0	10.4	9.3	8.3	8.4	9.3	7.5	7.3	5.6	6.2	6.5	7.5	5.8	5.4	4.3	4.4	4.3	3.9
Austria	8.0	11.3	11.2	10.5	8.1	10.3	8.3	8.2	8.3	10.9	12.4	11.6	12.8	13.8	13.9	12.5	11.7	12.5	12.5	11.9
Belgium	18.8	19.1	18.1	19.6	19.2	16.5	16.7	15.8	13.9	15.2	14.3	15.0	18.1	18.0	20.7	21.2	22.8	22.2	22.0	21.7
Denmark	6.1	6.8	7.2	8.0	12.3	18.7	17.2	16.7	12.4	4.8	3.2	8.0	12.3	15.7	15.8	15.4	18.1	17.8	16.2	14.7
Finland	2.4	3.7	3.9	5.4	4.5	5.2	5.8	4.5	3.8	2.5	2.9	–1.2	–0.6	0.4	5.1	7.1	6.6	3.7	5.6	4.6
Greece	..			..	..	..	..	..	..	..	..	..	..	..	..	..	..	..	..	..
Iceland	..	..	..	..	..	..	..	..	..	..	..	..	..	..	..	..	..	..	..	..
Ireland	15.0	15.2	13.1	10.9	12.1	15.2	13.6	13.3	10.9	11.4	11.1	9.6	7.4	10.0	10.7	11.8	14.2	13.0	12.1	11.2
Luxembourg	..	..	..	..	..	..	..	..	..	..	..	..	..	..	..	..	..	..	..	..
Mexico	..	..	..	..	..	..	..	..	..	..	..	..	..	..	..	..	..	..	..	..
Netherlands[c]	3.8	3.1	2.7	1.8	2.8	4.8	1.8	0.5	–0.2	1.4	1.4	1.8	4.0	5.9	1.1	1.9	0.7	0.4	1.2	0.8
New Zealand	..	..	..	..	..	..	..	..	..	..	..	..	..	..	..	..	..	..	..	..
Norway	4.7	8.4	4.6	3.4	4.5	3.8	4.3	5.2	–2.7	–6.1	–6.2	–2.4	0.9	0.9	2.6	5.2	4.5	4.4	4.3	4.5
Portugal	17.7	22.2	25.0	25.5	25.2	25.0	23.2	23.6	24.6	22.3	21.8	17.6	16.3	17.5	16.3	14.1	13.0	12.0	11.8	11.5
Spain[b]	12.8	13.9	12.5	10.8	11.8	12.8	12.3	11.4	11.2	11.5	8.8	10.1	8.4	10.5	11.6	10.1	12.6	12.2	12.2	11.7
Sweden	4.1	4.5	2.9	6.7	5.1	1.7	2.4	2.1	2.3	1.3	–2.8	–4.8	–4.9	–0.6	3.1	7.7	7.9	8.3	7.5	7.0
Switzerland	3.9	4.6	3.7	3.3	4.6	6.2	5.8	5.8	5.7	7.0	8.4	9.9	11.0	12.2	13.0	12.7	12.0	11.1	10.8	11.0
Turkey	..	..	..	..	..	..	..	..	..	..	..	..	..	..	..	..	..	..	..	..

a) National definition except the United States.
b) Gross saving.
c) Excluding mandatory saving through occupational pension schemes.

Annex Table 27. **Gross national saving as a percentage of GDP**

	1977	1978	1979	1980	1981	1982	1983	1984	1985	1986	1987	1988	1989	1990	1991	1992	1993
United States	19.6	21.2	21.3	19.8	20.8	18.5	17.1	19.0	17.6	16.1	16.1	16.6	16.6	15.6	15.7	14.6	14.9
Japan	32.0	32.3	31.5	31.1	31.5	30.6	29.8	30.8	31.7	32.0	32.6	33.9	34.3	34.6	35.1	34.0	32.5
Germany	21.7	22.6	22.8	21.7	20.3	20.2	21.2	21.7	22.0	23.8	23.5	24.3	25.7	24.9	22.2	21.6	19.9
France	24.4	24.6	24.6	23.6	21.1	19.7	19.1	19.0	18.9	20.1	20.0	21.1	21.8	21.5	20.9	19.8	18.7
Italy	26.0	26.3	26.3	24.7	22.5	22.0	22.2	22.3	21.6	21.4	20.8	20.8	20.0	19.6	18.6	17.2	18.0
United Kingdom	18.5	18.4	19.0	17.7	16.7	16.7	17.1	16.8	17.6	16.0	15.9	15.4	15.4	14.4	13.5	12.8	12.7
Canada	20.9	21.1	23.1	22.9	22.6	19.5	18.8	20.2	19.6	18.1	19.0	20.6	19.4	16.4	13.9	12.8	13.3
Australia	20.7	21.5	21.9	21.4	20.3	17.2	19.4	19.2	18.6	19.2	21.0	22.4	20.4	17.5	15.5	15.6	16.5
Austria	24.3	25.3	25.7	25.8	24.3	24.0	22.6	23.5	23.2	23.8	23.8	24.6	25.2	26.3	25.8	25.1	24.1
Belgium	20.8	20.6	18.6	17.5	14.1	13.7	14.7	15.8	15.2	17.1	17.5	19.8	21.3	21.2	21.2	21.3	22.3
Denmark	18.9	18.8	16.6	14.9	12.4	12.1	13.4	15.1	14.9	16.1	16.1	16.6	16.9	17.8	17.5	17.8	17.2
Finland	22.9	23.2	25.2	26.0	24.9	23.3	22.8	23.8	22.8	22.2	22.1	24.0	24.8	23.0	15.1	12.1	13.6
Greece	24.5	26.3	28.3	29.1	24.6	16.7	16.8	15.4	13.1	14.5	14.5	17.3	15.9	13.8	15.2	15.3	15.5
Iceland	26.5	24.9	23.3	24.0	21.5	19.0	18.3	16.3	14.6	17.2	15.1	15.0	15.0	15.8	14.2	14.3	15.9
Ireland	20.3	20.2	18.0	15.1	12.9	16.0	15.8	15.7	14.9	14.9	16.3	15.9	16.3	20.0	20.7	18.5	20.8
Luxembourg	42.1	44.6	43.8	44.2	45.8	59.3	63.8	63.8	64.1	62.2	55.1	57.8	61.6	62.5	59.4	60.2	..
Mexico	19.7	19.8	20.8	22.2	21.4	22.4	24.7	22.5	22.5	18.2	22.0	19.3	18.8	19.2	17.8	16.1	15.8
Netherlands	22.8	21.4	20.7	20.5	21.0	21.6	22.0	23.7	24.3	24.4	22.6	24.2	26.1	26.0	24.8	23.5	23.2
New Zealand	20.9	19.5	20.1	18.6	20.7	19.7	20.9	20.2	18.1	19.3	19.2	18.9	16.6	15.1	14.5	18.6	21.0
Norway	22.3	23.4	25.3	29.6	29.4	27.7	28.3	31.0	29.6	23.0	23.4	22.7	24.6	24.1	23.6	21.0	21.9
Portugal	19.7	24.8	27.8	26.9	22.4	20.6	20.0	18.8	21.0	24.7	27.1	25.3	26.8	26.6	25.4	25.3	..
Spain	23.2	23.9	22.8	20.8	19.2	19.6	19.7	20.9	20.6	21.6	21.6	22.6	21.9	21.7	21.0	19.1	18.7
Sweden	17.8	17.6	17.8	17.8	15.6	14.2	16.1	17.9	17.5	18.1	18.2	18.8	19.2	17.7	15.8	13.4	12.3
Switzerland	26.5	27.0	26.6	26.7	28.4	28.1	27.9	28.9	29.8	31.1	31.7	32.8	33.7	33.1	31.6	29.7	29.4
Turkey	16.6	15.0	15.0	12.1	19.2	18.4	15.5	16.3	20.7	23.9	24.3	28.9	26.4	21.5	19.3	20.9	20.1
Total OECD	22.6	23.4	23.5	22.4	22.3	21.0	20.5	21.4	21.1	20.7	20.9	21.6	21.7	20.9	20.4	19.3	..
OECD North America	19.7	21.1	21.4	20.2	21.0	18.9	17.8	19.3	18.1	16.4	16.7	17.1	17.0	15.9	15.7	14.5	14.9
OECD Europe	22.3	22.7	22.7	21.6	20.3	19.8	19.9	20.3	20.5	21.1	20.9	21.7	22.0	21.3	20.1	19.1	..
EU	22.5	22.9	23.0	21.8	20.0	19.5	19.8	20.1	20.1	20.7	20.5	21.1	21.5	21.0	19.8	18.7	..

Annex Table 28. **General government total outlays**[a]

As a percentage of nominal GDP

	1978	1979	1980	1981	1982	1983	1984	1985	1986	1987	1988	1989	1990	1991	1992	1993	1994	Projections 1995	Projections 1996
United States[b]	30.0	29.9	31.8	32.1	33.9	33.9	32.6	33.2	33.7	33.4	32.5	32.4	33.3	34.0	35.0	34.5	33.5	33.4	33.6
Japan	30.0	31.1	32.0	32.8	33.0	33.3	32.3	31.6	32.0	32.2	31.6	30.9	31.7	31.4	32.3	34.3	35.8	37.4	38.4
Germany[c]	47.3	47.2	47.9	48.7	49.0	47.8	47.4	47.0	46.4	46.7	46.3	44.8	45.1	47.9	48.6	49.4	49.0	49.1	48.6
France	44.6	45.0	46.1	48.6	50.3	51.4	51.9	52.2	51.3	50.9	50.0	49.1	49.8	50.5	52.2	55.0	54.9	53.9	53.0
Italy	42.4	41.6	41.9	45.9	47.6	48.7	49.3	50.9	50.7	50.2	50.3	51.3	53.2	53.5	53.6	56.6	53.9	52.7	51.2
United Kingdom	41.4	40.9	43.0	44.2	44.5	44.7	45.1	44.0	42.4	40.7	37.9	37.5	39.9	40.7	43.1	43.7	42.9	41.6	40.5
Canada	38.7	37.3	38.8	39.8	44.8	45.3	45.0	45.3	44.6	43.5	42.5	43.1	46.0	49.3	50.1	49.7	47.4	46.1	45.1
Total of above countries	35.0	35.0	36.4	37.4	38.8	39.0	38.3	38.4	38.4	38.1	37.2	36.9	38.0	38.9	39.9	40.6	40.0	40.0	39.9
Australia	32.7	31.6	31.5	31.5	32.9	35.2	35.5	36.4	37.2	35.3	33.7	33.0	34.7	37.1	37.7	37.3	37.5	36.9	35.6
Austria	49.0	48.2	48.1	49.5	50.1	50.4	50.0	50.9	51.6	51.9	50.2	49.0	48.6	49.6	50.5	52.7	51.5	52.2	51.6
Belgium[d]	55.9	57.7	58.6	63.7	63.8	63.8	62.5	62.2	61.5	59.8	57.3	55.0	54.8	56.3	56.2	56.7	56.4	55.5	54.9
Denmark	50.7	53.2	56.2	59.8	61.2	61.6	60.4	59.3	55.7	57.3	59.4	59.6	58.6	59.2	61.3	63.8	63.9	61.9	61.2
Finland	39.9	38.4	38.1	39.0	40.8	42.4	42.0	43.8	44.7	45.0	44.0	42.0	45.4	53.9	59.1	60.6	58.7	56.6	54.6
Greece	28.3	29.4	29.7	34.5	35.8	37.7	40.0	43.3	42.4	42.3	42.5	43.8	46.1	43.4	44.8	47.3	47.9	47.6	46.6
Ireland	42.9	45.1	48.9	50.2	53.0	53.0	51.3	52.4	53.2	50.6	47.4	40.6	41.2	42.1	42.6	43.0	43.8	42.4	40.8
Netherlands	51.6	53.3	55.2	57.1	59.1	59.7	58.1	56.5	56.1	57.7	56.3	53.8	54.0	54.6	55.3	55.7	54.4	52.2	50.7
Norway	50.9	49.5	47.5	47.1	47.5	47.6	45.5	44.8	48.9	50.5	52.5	53.5	53.8	55.5	57.4	57.0	55.6	52.5	51.1
Portugal	36.2	36.0	25.5	43.7	42.8	47.7	44.1	43.1	43.7	42.4	42.0	40.6	43.1	47.9	49.9	51.8	51.5	51.7	51.2
Spain	29.0	30.1	32.2	34.9	36.6	37.7	38.1	41.1	40.7	39.6	39.5	40.9	42.0	43.5	44.4	47.6	45.6	44.7	44.0
Sweden	58.6	60.0	60.1	62.6	64.8	64.5	62.0	63.3	61.6	57.8	58.1	58.3	59.1	61.3	67.3	72.6	68.8	68.2	65.7
Total of above smaller countries	41.2	41.9	42.3	45.3	46.7	47.8	47.2	48.1	48.0	47.2	46.5	46.0	46.9	48.6	50.1	51.9	50.8	49.8	48.7
Total of above European countries	43.7	43.9	44.7	47.2	48.3	48.7	48.7	49.0	48.3	47.8	47.0	46.5	47.6	48.9	50.2	52.1	51.0	50.2	49.2
Total of above OECD countries	35.8	35.9	37.2	38.5	39.9	40.1	39.4	39.7	39.7	39.3	38.5	38.1	39.2	40.2	41.3	42.1	41.5	41.3	41.0

a) Current outlays plus net capital outlays.
b) Excludes deposit insurance outlays.
c) Includes outlays of the German Railways Fund from 1994 on and of the Inherited Debt Fund from 1995 on.
d) Includes proceeds of privatisations and sales of other assets (BF 32.2 billion in 1993 and BF 12.7 billion in 1994).

Annex Table 29. **General government current receipts**[a]

As a percentage of nominal GDP

	1978	1979	1980	1981	1982	1983	1984	1985	1986	1987	1988	1989	1990	1991	1992	1993	1994	Projections 1995	Projections 1996
United States	30.2	30.3	30.5	31.1	30.5	29.9	29.7	30.1	30.2	31.0	30.5	30.9	30.8	30.7	30.7	31.1	31.5	31.6	31.6
Japan	24.5	26.3	27.6	29.0	29.4	29.6	30.2	30.8	31.0	32.6	33.1	33.4	34.6	34.4	33.8	32.9	32.3	33.3	34.1
Germany	44.8	44.6	45.0	45.0	45.7	45.3	45.5	45.8	45.0	44.8	44.1	44.9	43.0	44.6	45.7	46.0	46.5	46.8	46.3
France	42.5	44.1	46.1	46.7	47.6	48.2	49.2	49.3	48.6	49.0	48.3	47.9	48.3	48.3	48.2	48.8	48.9	48.9	48.9
Italy	31.9	31.5	33.3	34.4	36.2	38.0	37.8	38.3	39.1	39.3	39.6	41.4	42.3	43.3	44.0	47.0	44.9	44.9	44.3
United Kingdom	37.0	37.7	39.6	41.6	42.1	41.4	41.3	41.2	40.0	39.3	38.9	38.5	38.7	38.1	37.0	35.8	36.4	37.4	37.9
Canada	35.5	35.3	36.1	38.3	38.8	38.4	38.5	38.5	39.2	39.7	40.0	40.3	41.9	42.7	43.1	42.6	42.2	42.4	42.7
Total of above countries	32.4	32.9	33.7	34.6	34.8	34.6	34.7	35.1	35.1	35.7	35.4	35.8	36.0	36.2	36.2	36.4	36.4	36.8	36.9
Australia	30.0	29.4	30.0	31.0	32.4	31.3	32.5	33.6	34.5	35.2	34.9	34.2	35.2	34.2	33.7	33.6	32.9	34.1	34.6
Austria	46.2	45.8	46.4	47.8	46.7	46.4	47.5	48.5	48.0	47.6	47.1	46.2	46.5	47.1	48.4	48.6	47.5	47.6	47.8
Belgium	49.2	50.2	49.3	50.8	52.8	52.3	53.3	53.5	52.3	52.4	50.6	48.8	49.4	49.8	49.5	50.1	51.1	51.2	50.9
Denmark	50.4	51.5	52.9	52.9	52.0	54.4	56.3	57.3	59.1	59.7	60.0	59.1	57.1	57.1	58.5	59.3	60.0	59.7	59.6
Finland	43.9	41.4	41.0	42.6	42.8	43.0	45.0	46.8	48.1	46.1	48.1	48.3	50.8	52.5	53.2	52.7	53.1	51.6	51.3
Greece	26.5	27.0	27.1	25.9	29.2	30.3	31.4	31.4	31.9	32.6	30.6	29.0	32.0	31.9	32.5	34.1	35.4	36.1	36.6
Ireland	33.7	34.3	36.9	37.5	39.9	41.8	42.0	41.6	42.3	42.1	42.9	38.9	39.0	40.0	40.4	40.6	41.6	39.9	38.4
Netherlands	49.1	49.7	51.3	52.0	52.5	53.8	52.3	52.6	52.6	52.6	52.1	49.1	49.0	51.8	51.5	52.6	51.4	49.0	48.0
Norway	50.8	50.8	53.2	51.8	51.9	51.8	53.0	55.1	54.7	55.2	55.1	55.0	56.3	55.2	55.1	54.9	55.3	53.9	53.8
Portugal	29.2	29.7	31.1	33.0	35.1	37.4	37.0	35.6	37.2	36.8	38.4	38.3	37.6	41.4	46.6	44.7	45.7	46.3	46.1
Spain	27.0	28.3	29.9	31.2	31.2	33.1	32.8	34.2	34.7	36.4	36.3	38.1	37.9	38.6	40.2	40.1	39.0	38.6	38.5
Sweden	58.2	57.1	56.1	57.4	57.8	59.5	59.0	59.5	60.4	62.1	61.6	63.7	63.3	60.2	59.8	59.2	58.4	59.0	59.2
Total of above smaller countries	38.7	39.0	39.8	40.8	41.5	42.4	42.6	43.4	43.9	44.5	44.2	43.9	44.2	44.7	45.4	45.5	45.1	44.9	44.8
Total of above European countries	39.7	40.1	41.4	42.3	43.1	43.7	43.9	44.3	44.0	44.1	43.8	44.0	43.9	44.6	45.0	45.5	45.3	45.4	45.2
Total of above OECD countries	33.2	33.7	34.5	35.5	35.7	35.6	35.8	36.2	36.2	36.8	36.6	36.9	37.1	37.3	37.4	37.6	37.6	37.9	37.9

a) Current receipts exclude capital receipts.

Annex Table 30. **General government financial balances**

Surplus (+) or deficit (–) as a percentage of nominal GDP

	1978	1979	1980	1981	1982	1983	1984	1985	1986	1987	1988	1989	1990	1991	1992	1993	1994	Projections 1995	Projections 1996
United States[a]	0.1	0.4	-1.3	-1.0	-3.4	-4.1	-2.9	-3.1	-3.4	-2.5	-2.0	-1.5	-2.5	-3.2	-4.3	-3.4	-2.0	-1.8	-2.0
Japan	-5.5	-4.7	-4.4	-3.8	-3.6	-3.6	-2.1	-0.8	-0.9	0.5	1.5	2.5	2.9	3.0	1.5	-1.4	-3.5	-4.1	-4.2
Germany[b]	-2.4	-2.6	-2.9	-3.7	-3.3	-2.6	-1.9	-1.2	-1.3	-1.9	-2.2	0.1	-2.1	-3.3	-2.9	-3.3	-2.5	-2.3	-2.2
France	-2.1	-0.8	0.0	-1.9	-2.8	-3.2	-2.8	-2.9	-2.7	-1.9	-1.7	-1.2	-1.6	-2.2	-4.0	-6.1	-6.0	-5.0	-4.1
Italy	-10.4	-10.2	-8.6	-11.6	-11.3	-10.7	-11.6	-12.6	-11.6	-11.0	-10.7	-9.9	-10.9	-10.2	-9.5	-9.6	-9.0	-7.8	-6.9
United Kingdom	-4.4	-3.3	-3.4	-2.6	-2.5	-3.3	-3.9	-2.8	-2.4	-1.4	1.0	0.9	-1.2	-2.6	-6.1	-7.9	-6.5	-4.2	-2.6
Canada	-3.2	-2.0	-2.8	-1.5	-5.9	-6.9	-6.5	-6.8	-5.4	-3.8	-2.5	-2.9	-4.1	-6.6	-7.1	-7.1	-5.3	-3.7	-2.4
Total of above countries	-2.6	-2.1	-2.7	-2.8	-4.0	-4.3	-3.5	-3.3	-3.3	-2.4	-1.8	-1.1	-2.0	-2.7	-3.7	-4.2	-3.6	-3.2	-3.0
Australia	-2.7	-2.2	-1.5	-0.6	-0.4	-4.0	-3.0	-2.7	-2.8	-0.1	1.2	1.1	0.5	-2.9	-4.0	-3.7	-4.6	-2.9	-1.0
Austria	-2.8	-2.4	-1.7	-1.8	-3.4	-4.0	-2.6	-2.5	-3.7	-4.3	-3.0	-2.8	-2.2	-2.4	-2.0	-4.1	-4.0	-4.5	-3.9
Belgium[c]	-6.8	-7.5	-9.3	-13.0	-11.0	-11.5	-9.2	-8.7	-9.2	-7.4	-6.6	-6.3	-5.4	-6.5	-6.6	-6.6	-5.3	-4.3	-4.0
Denmark	-0.4	-1.7	-3.3	-6.9	-9.1	-7.2	-4.1	-2.0	3.4	2.4	0.6	-0.5	-1.5	-2.1	-2.9	-4.5	-3.9	-2.1	-1.6
Finland	4.0	3.0	2.9	3.6	2.0	0.6	3.0	3.0	3.5	1.1	4.1	6.3	5.4	-1.5	-5.8	-7.9	-5.5	-5.0	-3.3
Greece	-1.8	-2.4	-2.6	-8.6	-6.5	-7.3	-8.7	-11.8	-10.5	-9.8	-11.9	-14.8	-14.0	-11.5	-12.3	-13.2	-12.5	-11.4	-10.0
Ireland	-9.2	-10.9	-12.1	-12.7	-13.1	-11.2	-9.4	-10.8	-10.9	-8.5	-4.5	-1.7	-2.2	-2.1	-2.2	-2.3	-2.2	-2.5	-2.4
Netherlands	-2.5	-3.6	-3.9	-5.1	-6.6	-5.9	-5.9	-3.9	-3.5	-5.1	-4.2	-4.7	-5.0	-2.8	-3.8	-3.2	-3.0	-3.3	-2.7
Norway	-0.1	1.3	5.7	4.7	4.4	4.2	7.5	10.2	5.8	4.7	2.6	1.4	2.5	-0.2	-2.3	-2.1	-0.2	1.4	2.7
Portugal	-7.0	-6.3	5.6	-10.8	-7.7	-10.3	-7.1	-7.5	-6.5	-5.6	-3.6	-2.3	-5.5	-6.5	-3.3	-7.1	-5.7	-5.4	-5.0
Spain	-2.0	-1.8	-2.2	-3.7	-5.4	-4.6	-5.2	-6.9	-6.0	-3.1	-3.3	-2.8	-4.1	-4.9	-4.2	-7.5	-6.6	-6.2	-5.5
Sweden	-0.5	-2.9	-4.0	-5.3	-7.0	-5.0	-2.9	-3.8	-1.2	4.2	3.5	5.4	4.2	-1.1	-7.5	-13.4	-10.4	-9.2	-6.4
Total of above smaller countries	-2.6	-2.9	-2.4	-4.6	-5.2	-5.4	-4.5	-4.7	-4.1	-2.7	-2.3	-2.1	-2.7	-4.0	-4.7	-6.4	-5.6	-4.9	-3.9
Total of above European countries	-4.0	-3.7	-3.3	-5.0	-5.2	-5.0	-4.8	-4.7	-4.3	-3.7	-3.2	-2.5	-3.6	-4.4	-5.2	-6.5	-5.7	-4.8	-4.0
Total of above OECD countries	-2.6	-2.2	-2.7	-3.0	-4.2	-4.5	-3.6	-3.5	-3.4	-2.5	-1.9	-1.2	-2.1	-2.8	-3.8	-4.5	-3.9	-3.4	-3.1
General government financial balances excluding social security																			
United States[a,d,e]	0.3	0.5	-1.2	-0.8	-3.3	-4.1	-3.0	-3.4	-3.8	-3.0	-2.9	-2.5	-3.5	-4.2	-5.1	-4.2	-2.9	-2.8	-3.0
Japan[d]	-7.9	-7.3	-7.0	-6.6	-6.3	-6.3	-4.8	-3.9	-3.9	-2.3	-1.6	-0.8	-0.6	-0.8	-2.0	-4.9	-7.0	-7.6	-7.7

a) Excludes deposit insurance outlays.
b) Includes balances of the German Railways Fund from 1994 on and of the Inherited Debt Fund from 1995 on.
c) Includes proceeds of privatisations and sales of other assets (BF 32.2 billion in 1993 and BF 12.7 billion in 1994).
d) OECD Secretariat estimates, derived from fiscal year data converted to a calendar year basis. The coverage of the social security systems is not the same in the United States and Japan.
e) Includes the surplus of state and local government pension schemes.

Annex Table 31. **General government structural balances**[a]

Surplus (+) or deficit (–) as a percentage of potential GDP

	1978	1979	1980	1981	1982	1983	1984	1985	1986	1987	1988	1989	1990	1991	1992	1993	1994	Projections 1995	Projections 1996
United States[b]	–0.8	–0.5	–1.1	–0.4	–1.3	–2.4	–2.4	–2.9	–3.2	–2.5	–2.6	–2.3	–3.1	–3.5	–3.9	–3.2	–2.4	–2.5	–2.6
Japan[c]	–5.4	–5.2	–4.7	–4.0	–3.5	–2.9	–1.4	–0.4	0.2	1.7	1.6	2.0	1.7	1.5	0.3	–1.6	–2.9	–2.8	–2.8
Germany[c,d]	–3.2	–4.4	–3.9	–3.5	–1.5	–0.7	–0.7	–0.2	–0.6	–0.9	–1.9	0.0	–3.2	–4.9	–4.3	–2.7	–1.9	–1.8	–1.7
France	–2.7	–1.8	–0.4	–1.5	–3.2	–2.8	–1.9	–1.7	–1.7	–0.7	–1.4	–1.9	–2.2	–2.1	–3.5	–3.8	–3.9	–3.4	–3.0
Italy	–10.3	–10.8	–9.7	–12.2	–11.1	–9.9	–10.6	–11.7	–11.0	–10.7	–10.9	–10.6	–11.6	–10.5	–9.2	–7.9	–7.4	–6.7	–6.1
United Kingdom	–5.4	–4.8	–3.2	–0.7	–0.2	–1.8	–2.6	–2.2	–2.9	–3.2	–1.9	–2.0	–3.1	–2.2	–4.2	–5.6	–4.8	–3.0	–1.7
Canada	–4.3	–3.3	–3.1	–1.7	–2.9	–3.9	–5.2	–6.7	–5.5	–4.6	–4.4	–4.7	–4.5	–4.7	–4.1	–4.1	–3.4	–2.7	–1.7
Total of above countries	–3.2	–3.1	–2.9	–2.4	–2.6	–2.9	–2.8	–2.8	–2.9	–2.2	–2.3	–1.9	–2.9	–3.1	–3.6	–3.4	–3.1	–2.9	–2.7
Australia	–2.7	–2.6	–1.8	–0.8	0.4	–2.1	–2.4	–2.9	–2.6	–0.2	0.9	0.5	0.3	–1.5	–2.1	–2.3	–4.2	–3.0	–1.3
Austria	–2.6	–3.4	–2.8	–1.5	–2.5	–3.1	–1.3	–1.5	–2.5	–3.0	–3.0	–3.7	–3.2	–3.2	–2.2	–3.2	–3.4	–4.3	–3.5
Belgium[e]	–7.2	–8.2	–11.7	–13.9	–11.4	–10.9	–8.7	–7.6	–7.5	–5.7	–6.3	–6.5	–6.2	–7.2	–7.3	–5.0	–3.8	–3.2	–3.0
Denmark	–0.9	–2.9	–3.4	–5.4	–8.0	–6.4	–4.4	–3.3	1.7	1.8	0.6	0.1	–0.5	–0.8	–0.8	–2.1	–2.7	–1.8	–1.6
Finland	5.5	3.0	2.1	3.7	2.1	1.0	3.6	3.2	3.8	0.7	2.6	3.6	2.8	–0.2	–2.4	–3.6	–2.2	–2.9	–1.9
Greece	–4.2	–4.7	–4.2	–9.2	–5.7	–5.6	–7.2	–10.8	–9.6	–8.3	–11.7	–15.5	–13.5	–11.5	–11.9	–11.9	–11.1	–10.2	–9.2
Ireland	–10.7	–11.7	–11.9	–12.8	–12.3	–9.1	–8.2	–9.8	–7.5	–6.5	–2.6	–1.3	–3.4	–2.4	–2.5	–2.2	–2.2	–2.7	–2.5
Netherlands	–3.4	–4.8	–4.7	–4.7	–4.7	–4.2	–5.4	–4.1	–4.0	–4.7	–3.5	–5.1	–6.3	–3.8	–4.0	–1.9	–1.9	–2.7	–2.1
Norway[f]	–2.8	–4.2	–4.1	–4.4	–4.4	–5.9	–3.7	–2.7	–0.8	–0.7	0.3	–1.4	–2.8	–4.8	–6.8	–7.5	–6.3	–5.0	–4.6
Portugal	–6.8	–6.9	4.7	–11.9	–8.6	–10.1	–5.1	–5.3	–4.9	–4.9	–3.8	–3.4	–7.2	–8.1	–4.2	–6.4	–4.3	–4.0	–4.0
Spain	–1.8	–0.6	–0.5	–1.0	–2.6	–1.8	–2.4	–4.3	–3.9	–2.7	–4.0	–4.5	–6.2	–6.7	–4.7	–5.8	–4.6	–4.4	–4.0
Sweden	0.1	–3.9	–4.6	–4.7	–6.0	–4.2	–4.0	–5.2	–3.0	1.7	0.5	2.2	1.5	–2.1	–6.5	–9.5	–7.5	–7.0	–4.6
Total of above smaller countries	–2.8	–3.4	–3.0	–4.3	–4.3	–4.3	–3.8	–4.3	–3.6	–2.6	–2.8	–3.3	–4.1	–4.7	–4.5	–4.9	–4.4	–4.1	–3.4
Total of above European countries	–4.5	–4.8	–3.9	–4.5	–4.2	–3.9	–3.8	–3.9	–3.8	–3.5	–3.7	–3.5	–4.9	–5.0	–5.1	–4.9	–4.3	–3.8	–3.2
Total of above OECD countries	–3.2	–3.1	–2.9	–2.7	–2.8	–3.1	–2.9	–3.0	–3.0	–2.2	–2.4	–2.1	–3.0	–3.3	–3.7	–3.6	–3.3	–3.1	–2.8

a) OECD Secretariat estimates of the structural component of general government financial balances. The estimates are surrounded by large margins of error, reflecting uncertainty as to the present size and future growth of potential output, and the degree to which elimination of the output gap would translate into enhanced tax revenues and reduced expenditure. For a discussion of the methodology, see the section on fiscal policy in "Sources and Methods".

b) Excludes deposit insurance outlays. Receipts relating to Operation Desert Storm, amounting to 0.6 per cent of GDP in 1991, are excluded.

c) Excludes expenditure related to Operation Desert Storm in 1991 amounting to 0.2 per cent of GDP for Japan and 0.4 per cent of GDP for Germany.

d) Includes balances of the German Railways Fund from 1994 on and of the Inherited Debt Fund from 1995 on.

e) Includes proceeds of privatisations and sales of other assets (BF 32.2 billion in 1993 and BF 12.7 billion in 1994).

f) As a percentage of mainland potential GDP. The financial balances shown exclude revenues from oil production.

Annex Table 32. **General government primary balances**

Surplus (+) or deficit (–) as a percentage of nominal GDP

	1978	1979	1980	1981	1982	1983	1984	1985	1986
United States [a]	1.2	1.5	–0.1	0.5	–1.8	–2.4	–0.9	–1.0	–1.4
Japan [b,c]	–4.9	–3.9	–3.4	–2.5	–2.2	–2.0	–0.3	0.9	0.7
Germany [b]	–1.5	–1.4	–1.6	–2.1	–1.3	–0.3	0.4	1.1	1.0
France	–1.5	0.0	0.8	–0.7	–1.6	–1.4	–0.9	–0.8	–0.6
Italy	–6.0	–5.8	–3.9	–6.1	–4.8	–3.7	–4.1	–5.2	–3.8
United Kingdom	–1.8	–0.5	–0.3	0.7	0.7	–0.2	–0.5	0.5	0.7
Canada	–1.5	–0.3	–0.9	0.9	–3.0	–4.0	–2.9	–2.8	–1.2
Total of above countries	–1.3	–0.7	–1.1	–0.9	–1.9	–2.0	–1.0	–0.7	–0.8
Australia [b]	–2.1	–1.5	–0.6	0.4	0.5	–2.8	–1.4	–0.8	–0.6
Austria	–1.1	–0.6	0.0	0.2	–1.1	–1.7	0.2	0.4	–0.8
Belgium [b,c,d]	–2.9	–3.1	–4.0	–5.9	–2.7	–3.0	–0.2	0.9	1.1
Denmark [e]	–0.8	–1.2	–2.8	–5.1	–6.5	–2.9	1.7	4.1	8.5
Finland	2.9	2.0	1.9	2.5	0.9	–0.3	2.1	2.1	2.4
Greece [b,c]	–0.2	–0.3	–0.3	–5.6	–4.0	–3.8	–4.3	–6.7	–5.0
Ireland [c]	–6.5	–7.6	–8.5	–8.3	–7.6	–5.7	–3.5	–4.3	–4.2
Netherlands	–0.5	–1.6	–1.5	–2.1	–2.8	–1.7	–1.4	0.8	1.2
Norway	–0.3	1.3	5.9	4.6	4.0	3.9	6.4	8.7	3.8
Portugal	–4.6	–3.8	8.4	–6.0	–3.0	–4.7	0.2	0.9	2.3
Spain [b]	–1.9	–1.6	–1.9	–3.3	–5.0	–3.8	–3.8	–4.2	–2.7
Sweden	–1.7	–4.1	–4.4	–4.9	–5.4	–3.1	–0.5	–0.8	1.0
Total of above smaller countries	–1.6	–1.7	–1.0	–2.7	–2.9	–2.8	–1.3	–0.8	–0.1
Total of above European countries	–2.3	–1.9	–1.2	–2.4	–2.2	–1.8	–1.2	–0.9	–0.4
Total of above OECD countries	–1.3	–0.8	–1.1	–1.1	–2.0	–2.1	–1.0	–0.7	–0.7

	1987	1988	1989	1990	1991	1992	1993	1994	Projections 1995	Projections 1996
United States [a]	–0.5	–0.1	0.5	–0.4	–1.0	–2.2	–1.5	–0.1	0.4	0.3
Japan [b,c]	1.8	2.6	3.4	3.5	3.3	1.7	–1.1	–3.1	–3.5	–3.5
Germany [b]	0.5	0.2	2.3	–0.1	–1.3	–0.4	–0.7	0.3	1.2	1.3
France	0.3	0.5	1.0	0.8	0.4	–1.2	–3.0	–2.7	–1.6	–0.8
Italy	–3.6	–3.1	–1.5	–1.8	–0.5	1.4	2.0	1.2	3.3	3.9
United Kingdom	1.7	3.6	3.3	1.2	–0.5	–4.1	–5.7	–3.9	–1.7	–0.1
Canada	0.4	1.8	1.9	1.3	–1.4	–2.3	–2.4	–0.5	1.3	2.6
Total of above countries	0.0	0.6	1.4	0.5	–0.1	–1.1	–1.5	–1.0	–0.3	0.0
Australia [b]	2.0	3.0	3.0	2.3	–1.2	–2.6	–2.6	–2.7	–0.9	1.1
Austria	–1.2	0.2	0.3	1.0	0.9	1.4	–0.5	–0.6	–1.0	–0.2
Belgium [b,c,d]	2.3	2.6	3.3	4.3	2.9	3.1	2.9	4.1	4.3	4.5
Denmark [e]	6.9	4.8	3.3	1.8	1.4	0.0	–0.9	–0.7	1.3	1.8
Finland	0.2	3.2	5.1	3.6	–3.4	–7.8	–8.4	–4.8	–3.9	–1.2
Greece [b,c]	–2.9	–4.4	–7.2	–3.8	–1.8	–0.2	–0.2	2.2	2.9	3.4
Ireland [c]	–1.8	1.9	4.4	4.0	3.6	2.9	2.5	1.7	1.4	1.2
Netherlands	–0.2	0.7	–0.3	–0.6	1.8	0.7	1.6	1.5	1.3	1.9
Norway	2.1	–1.0	–1.0	0.9	–1.8	–3.7	–3.0	–0.4	1.3	2.9
Portugal	2.2	3.5	4.1	1.9	1.0	4.5	–0.3	–0.2	0.0	0.0
Spain [b]	–0.3	–0.3	0.3	–0.8	–1.3	–0.3	–2.6	–1.7	–1.1	–0.2
Sweden	6.0	4.5	5.9	4.3	–1.0	–7.4	–11.9	–7.6	–5.6	–2.2
Total of above smaller countries	1.1	1.3	1.5	1.1	–0.1	–0.7	–1.9	–1.0	–0.2	0.9
Total of above European countries	0.1	0.5	1.3	0.3	–0.4	–0.8	–1.7	–1.0	0.2	1.0
Total of above OECD countries	0.2	0.7	1.4	0.6	–0.1	–1.0	–1.6	–1.0	–0.3	0.1

a) Excludes deposit insurance outlays.
b) OECD Secretariat estimates.
c) Where net interest payments are not available net property income paid is used instead.
d) Includes proceeds of privatisations and sales of other assets (BF 32.2 billion in 1993 and BF 12.7 billion in 1994).
e) The primary balance excludes not only net interest payments, but also dividends received.

Annex Table 33. **General government net debt interest payments**

As a percentage of nominal GDP

	1978	1979	1980	1981	1982	1983	1984	1985	1986	1987	1988	1989	1990	1991	1992	1993	1994	Projections 1995	Projections 1996
United States	1.1	1.1	1.2	1.5	1.7	1.7	2.0	2.1	2.0	2.0	1.9	2.0	2.1	2.2	2.1	1.9	1.9	2.1	2.3
Japan [a,b]	0.6	0.8	1.0	1.3	1.4	1.6	1.8	1.7	1.6	1.3	1.1	0.9	0.6	0.4	0.3	0.3	0.4	0.6	0.8
Germany [a,c]	0.9	1.1	1.3	1.6	2.0	2.3	2.3	2.3	2.3	2.4	2.3	2.2	2.0	2.0	2.5	2.6	2.8	3.5	3.5
France	0.6	0.8	0.8	1.2	1.2	1.7	1.9	2.1	2.1	2.2	2.1	2.2	2.4	2.5	2.9	3.2	3.3	3.3	3.3
Italy	4.4	4.4	4.7	5.5	6.6	7.0	7.5	7.4	7.8	7.4	7.6	8.4	9.1	9.7	10.9	11.6	10.2	11.1	10.8
United Kingdom	2.6	2.8	3.1	3.3	3.2	3.1	3.3	3.4	3.1	3.0	2.7	2.4	2.3	2.1	2.1	2.2	2.6	2.6	2.5
Canada	1.6	1.7	1.9	2.3	2.9	2.9	3.5	4.0	4.2	4.2	4.3	4.8	5.3	5.2	4.8	4.7	4.8	5.0	5.0
Total of above countries	1.3	1.4	1.6	1.9	2.2	2.3	2.5	2.6	2.6	2.5	2.4	2.5	2.5	2.6	2.6	2.6	2.6	2.9	3.0
Australia [a]	0.6	0.8	0.9	0.9	0.9	1.2	1.6	1.9	2.2	2.1	1.8	1.9	1.8	1.6	1.3	1.1	1.9	2.0	2.2
Austria	1.6	1.8	1.7	1.9	2.3	2.3	2.7	2.9	2.9	3.1	3.2	3.1	3.2	3.3	3.4	3.6	3.4	3.5	3.7
Belgium [a,b]	3.8	4.4	5.4	7.0	8.3	8.6	9.0	9.7	10.2	9.7	9.3	9.5	9.7	9.3	9.7	9.5	9.4	8.6	8.5
Denmark [d]	–0.5	0.5	0.5	1.8	2.6	4.3	5.8	6.1	5.1	4.5	4.2	3.8	3.4	3.5	2.9	3.6	3.2	3.4	3.4
Finland	–1.1	–1.0	–1.0	–1.1	–1.0	–1.0	–0.9	–0.9	–1.0	–0.9	–0.9	–1.2	–1.8	–2.0	–2.0	–0.5	0.8	1.1	2.1
Greece [a,b]	1.6	2.1	2.3	3.1	2.5	3.5	4.4	5.2	5.5	6.9	7.5	7.6	10.3	9.7	12.1	13.0	14.7	14.3	13.5
Ireland [b]	2.7	3.3	3.5	4.5	5.5	5.5	5.9	6.5	6.7	6.7	6.3	6.1	6.1	5.7	5.1	4.8	3.8	3.9	3.6
Netherlands	2.0	2.0	2.4	3.0	3.8	4.2	4.4	4.7	4.7	4.9	4.9	4.4	4.4	4.6	4.6	4.7	4.5	4.6	4.7
Norway	–0.3	0.1	0.2	–0.2	–0.4	–0.3	–1.0	–1.5	–2.0	–2.6	–3.6	–2.5	–1.6	–1.6	–1.4	–0.9	–0.2	–0.1	0.1
Portugal	2.4	2.6	2.8	4.8	4.8	5.5	7.4	8.4	8.7	7.9	7.1	6.4	7.4	7.5	7.8	6.8	5.5	5.3	5.1
Spain [a]	0.2	0.2	0.3	0.3	0.4	0.7	1.5	2.7	3.3	2.9	3.0	3.1	3.3	3.6	3.9	4.9	4.9	5.1	5.3
Sweden	–1.3	–1.1	–0.4	0.3	1.6	1.9	2.4	3.0	2.2	1.7	1.0	0.5	0.1	0.1	0.1	1.5	2.8	3.7	4.2
Total of above smaller countries	0.9	1.1	1.4	1.9	2.3	2.7	3.2	3.9	4.0	3.8	3.7	3.6	3.8	3.8	4.0	4.4	4.6	4.7	4.8
Total of above European countries	1.7	1.9	2.1	2.6	2.9	3.3	3.6	3.8	3.9	3.8	3.7	3.7	3.9	4.0	4.4	4.8	4.7	5.0	5.0
Total of above OECD countries	1.3	1.4	1.5	1.9	2.2	2.4	2.6	2.8	2.8	2.7	2.6	2.6	2.7	2.7	2.8	2.9	2.9	3.2	3.2

a) OECD Secretariat estimates.
b) Net property income paid rather than net interest payments is used as the latter is not available.
c) Includes interest payments of the German Railways Fund from 1994 on and of the Inherited Debt Fund from 1995 on.
d) Net interest payments including dividends received are used.

Annex Table 34. **General government gross financial liabilities**[a]

As a percentage of nominal GDP

	1978	1979	1980	1981	1982	1983	1984	1985	1986	1987	1988	1989	1990	1991	1992	1993	1994	Projections 1995	Projections 1996
United States	39.2	37.2	37.7	37.0	41.0	43.6	44.9	48.2	51.4	52.6	53.3	53.9	55.6	59.3	62.5	64.3	63.2[b]	63.0	63.7
Japan	41.9	47.0	52.0	56.8	60.9	66.6	67.9	68.7	72.3	74.9	72.9	70.6	69.8	67.7	71.2	75.1	81.7[b]	88.9	96.2
Germany[c]	30.1	30.8	32.8	36.5	39.6	41.1	41.7	42.5	42.5	43.8	44.4	43.2	43.4	42.7	47.3	51.8	54.6[b]	62.5	62.5
France	31.0	31.4	30.9	30.1	34.1	35.3	37.1	38.6	39.3	40.7	40.6	40.6	40.1	41.1	45.6	52.9	56.8[b]	59.5	60.9
Italy	62.4	61.5	59.0	61.1	66.4	72.0	77.4	84.3	88.2	92.6	94.9	97.9	100.5	103.9	111.4	120.2	122.6[b]	122.1	120.5
United Kingdom	58.6	54.9	54.1	54.3	53.7	53.7	55.1	53.4	51.7	49.2	42.8	37.2	35.0	35.5	41.4[b]	47.4	51.6	[e] 53.4	52.8
Canada	46.4	43.7	44.3	45.0	50.1	55.5	59.2	64.7	68.5	69.2	68.9	69.9	73.1	80.6	88.2	94.0	94.6[b]	94.6	93.6
Total of above countries	41.6	41.3	42.3	43.4	47.2	50.3	52.0	54.4	56.9	58.4	58.1	57.6	58.4	60.2	64.4	68.3	70.1	72.5	74.0
Australia[d]	..	..	..	..	..	..	..	..	..	31.4	27.2	24.4	23.4	24.2	27.0	30.7	35.0[b]	36.3	36.5
Austria[e]	33.9	36.0	37.2	39.3	41.6	46.0	47.8	49.6	53.7	57.2	57.5	56.7	56.2	56.6	56.1	58.3[b]	59.0	60.4	61.4
Belgium	69.7	75.3	81.1	95.0	104.9	115.7	120.5	124.5	129.3	133.7	134.2	130.8	130.7	132.6	134.4	141.3	140.1	138.3[b]	136.4
Denmark[e]	21.9	27.0	33.5	43.6	53.0	61.6	65.9	64.1	58.3	55.9	58.0	58.5	59.7	60.9[b]	63.1	66.8	68.7	68.8	68.4
Finland[e]	11.6	11.8	11.9	12.2	14.6	16.3	16.0	16.7	17.5	18.6	17.6	15.2	14.8	23.2	42.4	56.2	62.7	69.1[b]	73.4
Greece[e]	24.5	23.0	23.1	27.3	30.0	34.4	41.2	48.3	48.8	53.8	66.4	69.7	77.7	81.7	88.6	117.1	119.8[b]	120.2	120.2
Ireland	64.6	69.8	71.3	75.9	81.6	95.4	99.6	102.7	116.3	116.3	112.3	102.1	96.0	95.3	90.7	92.7	87.9[b]	83.3	79.1
Netherlands	40.2	42.0	45.1	49.5	54.6	60.9	65.0	68.4	69.9	73.5	76.2	76.3	76.5	76.4	77.1	78.5	79.0[b]	79.4	79.5
Norway[e]	60.0	62.9	52.2	47.4	42.2	38.8	38.7	40.7	51.1	42.7	42.6	42.7	39.2	38.5	41.8	50.7[b]	47.7	48.3	46.5
Portugal	33.1	22.6	33.0	41.6	44.6	49.7	55.4	58.5	56.5	63.6	65.3	62.8	60.4	62.2	63.2	67.8[b]	70.4	70.8	70.8
Spain[e]	14.4	16.5	18.3	24.0	30.4	38.7	45.4	50.8	51.8	51.2	47.4	48.7	48.7	49.9	53.0	59.4[b]	63.5	66.5	68.7
Sweden	34.5	39.6	44.3	52.1	61.7	65.5	67.0	67.6	67.1	59.1	53.5	48.4	44.4	53.7	69.8	74.6[b]	79.4	84.5	86.3
Total of above smaller countries	32.2	33.8	35.8	40.6	45.7	51.3	55.3	58.4	59.6	60.2	59.4	58.3	57.9	59.9	63.7	69.9	72.4	73.9	74.5
Total of above European countries	40.7	40.7	41.3	44.0	47.8	51.1	53.9	56.2	57.2	58.3	57.7	56.9	56.8	57.9	62.9	69.5	72.4	75.3	75.4
Total of above OECD countries	40.3	40.3	41.5	43.0	47.0	50.4	52.4	55.0	57.3	58.6	58.2	57.7	58.3	60.2	64.3	68.5	70.4	72.7	74.1

a) This table previously appeared under the title **Gross Public Debt**. The title has been changed to more accurately reflect the nature of the data shown, which includes all financial liabilities as defined by the System of National Accounts (where data permits) and covers the general government sector, which is a consolidation of central government, state and local government and the social security sector. It should be noted that the definition of debt applied under the Maastricht Treaty differs from the System of National Accounts definition shown here. Estimates of general government gross debt according to the Maastricht definition are shown in Annex Table 61.

b) OECD Secretariat estimates starting from this year.

c) Includes the debt of the German Railways Fund from 1994 on and of the Inherited Debt Fund from 1995 on.

d) Debt data refer to fiscal years ending 30 June. Data include indebtedness of local government towards other levels of general government.

e) Does not exclude public sector mutual indebtedness.

Annex Table 35. **General government net financial liabilities**[a]

As a percentage of nominal GDP

	1978	1979	1980	1981	1982	1983	1984	1985	1986	1987	1988	1989	1990	1991	1992	1993	1994	Projections 1995	Projections 1996
United States	21.3	19.1	18.8	18.8	21.5	24.0	25.0	27.1	29.4	30.9	30.9	29.9	31.5	33.4	36.2	38.1	37.7[b]	37.6	38.2
Japan	11.3	14.9	17.3	20.6	23.1	26.0	27.0	26.5	26.2	21.3	17.7	14.8	9.5	5.3	4.4	5.8[b]	9.2	13.2	17.1
Germany[c]	9.4	11.6	11.8	15.0	17.8	19.5	20.4	20.8	21.2	22.4	23.4	22.0	22.1	22.1	27.7	35.1	37.9[b]	45.8	45.8
France	1.9	–0.2	–3.3	0.0	2.1	4.5	7.5	10.8	13.8	13.0	14.1	14.8	16.3	17.6	21.0	27.7	32.5[b]	36.0	38.3
Italy	57.4	56.0	53.9	57.2	63.7	69.2	74.9	81.9	86.0	90.5	93.0	96.1	99.0	102.6	110.0	118.6	121.0[b]	120.5	119.0
United Kingdom	52.3	47.8	47.0	46.3	46.2	46.3	47.9	46.6	45.3	42.6	36.0	30.6	28.8	30.2[b]	35.2	41.2	45.4	47.1	46.6
Canada	11.5	13.0	13.3	11.7	17.7	24.1	28.4	34.7	38.6	39.7	38.4	40.3	44.0	49.8	57.1	62.0	64.2[b]	64.2	63.1
Total of above countries	21.3	20.6	20.5	21.8	24.7	27.4	29.1	30.9	32.5	32.6	31.8	30.6	30.8	31.5	34.6	38.3	40.0	41.9	42.9
Australia[d]	..	..	..	..	..	..	..	..	..	19.4	16.5	13.4	11.6	12.3	15.3	19.6	24.0[b]	25.3	25.5
Belgium	57.2	63.1	69.6	84.3	94.2	105.2	109.6	112.5	117.4	121.5	122.0	119.1	119.0	119.9	122.0	127.9	127.8	126.0[b]	124.2
Denmark	–2.2	1.8	7.3	16.6	26.4	33.3	36.8	34.4	28.5	25.6	26.8	26.1	26.6	27.8[b]	29.9	33.7	35.5	35.7	35.3
Finland[e]	–26.6	-23.4	-23.6	-23.6	-21.6	-20.5	-20.4	-21.5	-22.6	-22.0	-24.0	-27.9	-30.7	-28.9	-20.0	-11.9	-5.7	–0.3[b]	3.0
Netherlands[e]	19.7	21.5	24.5	26.9	30.8	35.9	39.2	42.3	45.5	51.0	54.0	55.8	56.8	56.0	57.7	59.8	60.3[b]	60.7	60.8
Norway[e]	6.7	9.8	0.4	–2.2	–4.7	–8.4	–12.5	–16.0	–21.1	–21.4	–21.3	–20.6	–21.7	–21.0	–18.2	–15.3[b]	–14.3	–14.7	–16.5
Spain	3.5	5.8	6.1	9.2	13.0	18.5	22.0	27.5	30.4	30.8	31.4	30.9	31.8	33.6	36.4	42.7[b]	46.8	49.9	52.0
Sweden	–25.3	–19.8	–11.6	–3.3	6.4	12.7	15.2	15.6	14.2	7.8	1.4	–4.8	–5.0	–2.3	6.8	12.9[b]	23.4	31.5	36.3
Total of above smaller countries[f]	13.9	16.5	18.2	21.9	25.8	30.9	33.6	36.3	38.1	39.0	39.3	37.9	38.1	39.2	42.3	48.4	51.5	53.2	54.1
Total of above European countries[f]	23.9	23.9	23.5	26.5	29.9	33.2	36.0	38.4	40.1	40.9	40.9	40.1	40.8	41.8	46.6	53.6	56.9	60.0	60.4
Total of above OECD countries[f]	20.3	20.1	20.2	21.8	24.8	27.8	29.7	31.6	33.2	33.4	32.7	31.5	31.7	32.4	35.6	39.6	41.5	43.3	44.3

a) This table previously appeared under the title **Net Public Debt**. The title has been changed to more accurately reflect the nature of the data shown, which includes all financial liabilities as defined by the System of National Accounts (where data permits) and covers the general government sector, which is a consolidation of central government, state and local government and the social security sector.
b) OECD Secretariat estimates starting from this year.
c) Includes the debt of the German Railways Fund from 1994 on and of the Inherited Debt Fund from 1995 on.
d) Debt data refer to fiscal years ending 30 June.
e) Financial assets exclude shares and holdings on public corporations.
f) Including gross financial liabilities for Austria, Greece and Ireland.

Annex Table 36. **Short- and long-term interest rates**[a]

	1981	1982	1983	1984	1985	1986	1987	1988	1989	1990	1991	1992	1993	1994	Projections 1995	1996
Short-term rates																
United States	14.0	10.6	8.6	9.5	7.5	6.0	5.8	6.7	8.1	7.5	5.4	3.4	3.0	4.3	5.9	6.4
Japan	7.4	7.0	6.7	6.5	6.6	5.1	4.2	4.5	5.4	7.7	7.2	4.3	2.9	2.3	1.7	1.6
Germany	12.1	8.9	5.8	6.0	5.4	4.6	4.0	4.3	7.1	8.5	9.2	9.5	7.3	5.4	4.8	5.2
France	15.3	14.6	12.5	11.7	9.9	7.7	8.3	7.9	9.4	10.3	9.6	10.3	8.6	5.8	6.1	5.4
Italy	19.3	19.9	18.3	17.3	15.3	13.4	11.3	10.8	12.6	12.0	12.0	14.4	10.7	8.5	9.6	9.3
United Kingdom	13.9	12.3	10.1	9.9	12.2	10.9	9.7	10.3	13.9	14.8	11.5	9.6	5.9	5.5	7.1	7.8
Canada	18.3	14.4	9.5	11.2	9.6	9.2	8.4	9.6	12.2	13.0	9.0	6.7	5.0	5.4	7.5	6.6
Australia	15.1	16.6	12.2	12.2	16.2	16.4	13.5	12.9	17.7	14.4	10.1	6.5	5.1	5.7	8.2	8.2
Austria	11.4	8.8	5.4	6.5	6.2	5.3	4.3	4.6	7.5	8.5	9.1	9.3	7.2	5.0	4.8	5.2
Belgium	15.3	14.0	10.4	11.4	9.5	8.1	7.1	6.7	8.8	9.6	9.4	9.4	8.2	5.7	5.5	5.6
Denmark	15.2	16.8	12.7	11.7	10.2	9.1	10.1	8.5	9.8	10.8	9.7	11.5	10.3	6.2	6.4	6.8
Finland	11.5	11.8	14.6	16.5	13.5	12.7	10.0	10.0	12.6	14.0	13.1	13.3	7.8	5.4	6.0	6.5
Ireland	15.2	16.3	13.2	13.2	11.9	12.5	10.8	8.0	10.0	11.3	10.4	14.3	9.1	5.9	6.3	6.2
Mexico	30.8	45.7	59.5	49.7	63.7	90.5	102.8	62.1	44.8	35.0	19.8	15.9	15.5	14.7	50.0	35.0
Netherlands	11.7	8.5	5.7	6.2	6.4	5.7	5.4	4.8	7.4	8.7	9.3	9.4	6.9	5.2	4.9	5.2
New Zealand	15.3	17.0	13.1	15.0	23.3	19.1	21.1	15.4	13.5	13.9	10.0	6.7	6.3	6.7	9.2	7.9
Norway	..	15.6	12.5	12.6	12.0	15.0	14.3	13.2	11.3	11.4	10.6	14.5	7.7	5.5	5.4	5.7
Spain	16.2	16.3	20.0	14.9	12.2	11.7	15.8	11.7	15.0	15.2	13.2	13.3	11.7	8.0	9.0	9.2
Sweden	..	13.3	11.4	11.9	14.2	9.8	9.4	10.1	11.5	13.7	11.6	12.9	8.4	7.4	8.6	9.0
Switzerland	8.2	4.4	3.3	3.8	4.4	3.6	3.2	2.6	6.4	8.3	7.6	7.2	4.3	3.5	3.5	3.8
Long-term rates																
United States	13.9	13.0	11.1	12.4	10.6	7.7	8.4	8.8	8.5	8.6	7.9	7.0	5.9	7.1	7.1	6.9
Japan	8.4	8.3	7.8	7.3	6.5	5.1	5.0	4.8	5.2	7.0	6.4	5.3	4.3	4.4	3.7	3.7
Germany	10.1	8.9	8.1	8.0	7.0	6.2	6.2	6.5	7.0	8.8	8.5	7.9	6.5	6.9	7.1	7.0
France	16.3	16.0	14.4	13.4	11.9	9.1	10.2	9.2	9.2	10.4	9.5	9.0	7.0	7.5	7.6	7.3
Italy	19.4	20.2	18.3	15.6	13.7	11.5	10.6	10.9	12.8	13.5	13.1	13.7	11.3	10.6	12.1	11.4
United Kingdom	14.9	13.1	11.3	11.3	11.1	10.1	9.6	9.7	10.2	11.8	10.1	9.1	7.5	8.2	8.4	8.2
Canada	15.0	14.4	11.8	12.7	11.1	9.5	9.9	10.2	9.9	10.8	9.8	8.8	7.9	8.6	8.4	7.5
Australia	14.0	15.3	14.1	13.6	13.9	13.4	13.2	12.1	13.4	13.2	10.7	9.2	7.3	9.0	9.3	9.0
Austria	10.6	9.9	8.2	8.0	7.8	7.3	6.9	6.7	7.1	8.7	8.6	8.3	6.6	6.7	7.1	7.1
Belgium	13.4	13.4	11.9	12.2	11.0	8.6	8.2	8.0	8.6	10.1	9.3	8.7	7.2	7.7	8.0	7.6
Denmark	20.1	21.4	15.1	14.5	11.6	10.1	11.3	9.6	9.8	10.6	9.3	8.9	7.2	7.9	8.9	8.7
Finland	11.0	11.0	10.8	11.1	10.7	8.9	7.9	10.3	12.1	13.2	11.9	12.1	8.2	8.4	9.0	8.9
Ireland	17.3	17.1	13.9	14.6	12.6	11.1	11.3	9.5	8.9	10.1	9.2	9.1	7.7	8.2	8.7	8.2
Mexico	..	56.3	56.3	56.3	63.7	90.5	102.8	62.1	44.8	34.9	19.7	16.1	15.6	13.8	50.0	35.0
Netherlands	11.5	9.9	8.2	8.1	7.3	6.4	6.4	6.2	7.2	9.0	8.8	8.1	6.2	6.7	7.1	7.0
New Zealand	12.8	12.9	12.2	12.6	17.6	16.7	15.7	13.1	12.8	12.5	9.9	8.4	6.9	7.7	7.9	7.1
Norway	12.3	13.2	12.9	12.2	12.6	13.3	13.3	12.9	10.8	10.7	10.0	9.6	6.9	7.4	7.9	7.8
Spain	15.8	16.0	16.9	16.5	13.4	11.4	12.8	11.7	13.8	14.6	12.8	11.7	10.2	10.0	11.5	11.0
Sweden	13.5	13.0	12.3	12.3	13.0	10.3	11.4	11.2	11.3	13.6	10.9	10.4	8.5	9.5	10.9	10.9
Switzerland	5.6	4.8	4.4	4.5	4.7	4.2	4.0	4.0	5.2	6.4	6.2	6.4	4.6	5.0	5.0	5.2

a) For sources and definitions, see "Sources and Methods".

Annex Table 37. **Nominal exchange rates (*vis-à-vis* the US dollar)**

Average of daily rates

	Monetary unit	1982	1983	1984	1985	1986	1987	1988	1989	1990	1991	1992	1993	1994	Projections[a] 1995	Projections[a] 1996
United States	*Dollar*	1.000	1.000	1.000	1.000	1.000	1.000	1.000	1.000	1.000	1.000	1.000	1.000	1.000	1.000	1.000
Japan	*Yen*	249.1	237.5	237.6	238.6	168.5	144.6	128.2	138.0	144.8	134.5	126.7	111.2	102.2	86.9	83.7
Germany	*Deutschemark*	2.427	2.553	2.846	2.944	2.172	1.797	1.756	1.880	1.616	1.659	1.562	1.653	1.623	1.404	1.379
France	*Franc*	6.572	7.621	8.739	8.984	6.927	6.009	5.956	6.380	5.446	5.641	5.294	5.662	5.552	4.973	4.916
Italy	*Lira*	1353	1519	1757	1909	1491	1297	1302	1372	1198	1241	1232	1572	1613	1664	1667
United Kingdom	*Pound*	0.573	0.660	0.752	0.779	0.682	0.612	0.562	0.611	0.563	0.567	0.570	0.666	0.653	0.623	0.620
Canada	*Dollar*	1.233	1.232	1.295	1.366	1.389	1.326	1.231	1.184	1.167	1.146	1.209	1.290	1.366	1.372	1.358
Australia	*Dollar*	0.986	1.109	1.141	1.432	1.496	1.429	1.281	1.265	1.282	1.284	1.362	1.473	1.369	1.363	1.373
Austria	*Schilling*	17.06	17.97	20.01	20.69	15.27	12.64	12.34	13.23	11.37	11.67	10.99	11.63	11.42	9.88	9.70
Belgium-Luxembourg	*Franc*	45.70	51.13	57.76	59.43	44.69	37.34	36.77	39.40	33.42	34.16	32.15	34.56	33.46	28.93	28.40
Denmark	*Krone*	8.33	9.14	10.36	10.59	8.09	6.84	6.73	7.31	6.19	6.40	6.04	6.48	6.36	5.54	5.42
Finland	*Markka*	4.813	5.565	6.003	6.196	5.070	4.396	4.186	4.288	3.823	4.043	4.486	5.721	5.223	4.336	4.252
Greece	*Drachma*	66.7	87.9	112.7	138.1	139.5	135.2	141.6	162.1	158.2	182.1	190.5	229.1	242.2	228.4	230.5
Iceland	*Krona*	12.30	24.85	31.73	41.54	41.10	38.68	43.03	56.68	58.36	59.10	57.62	67.64	70.00	63.82	63.02
Ireland	*Pound*	0.704	0.805	0.923	0.946	0.747	0.672	0.657	0.706	0.605	0.622	0.588	0.683	0.670	0.617	0.610
Mexico[b]	*Peso*	0.052	0.155	0.192	0.327	0.639	1.418	2.281	2.495	2.841	3.022	3.095	3.115	3.389	5.930	5.870
Netherlands	*Guilder*	2.670	2.854	3.209	3.322	2.450	2.026	1.977	2.121	1.821	1.870	1.758	1.857	1.820	1.573	1.544
New Zealand	*Dollar*	1.332	1.496	1.767	2.026	1.917	1.695	1.529	1.674	1.678	1.729	1.860	1.851	1.687	1.503	1.482
Norway	*Krone*	6.451	7.296	8.160	8.594	7.392	6.737	6.517	6.903	6.258	6.482	6.214	7.092	7.057	6.286	6.209
Portugal	*Escudo*	79.4	110.8	146.4	169.9	148.2	140.8	143.9	157.1	142.3	144.4	134.8	160.7	166.0	147.9	146.1
Spain	*Peseta*	109.8	143.5	160.8	170.1	140.0	123.5	116.5	118.4	101.9	103.9	102.4	127.2	134.0	125.0	123.1
Sweden	*Krona*	6.282	7.667	8.273	8.602	7.124	6.340	6.129	6.446	5.918	6.045	5.824	7.785	7.716	7.289	7.250
Switzerland	*Franc*	2.030	2.099	2.350	2.457	1.798	1.491	1.463	1.635	1.389	1.434	1.406	1.477	1.367	1.161	1.133
Turkey	*Lira*	161	224	363	520	669	855	1419	2120	2606	4169	6861	10966	29778	44867	55174
Hong Kong	*Dollar*	6.070	7.265	7.818	7.791	7.804	7.795	7.806	7.799	7.789	7.770	7.739	7.735	7.728	7.734	7.734
Korea	*Won*	731.1	775.7	806.0	870.0	881.0	825.0	730.3	669.2	708.0	733.2	780.0	802.4	804.3	769.0	762.3
Singapore	*Dollar*	2.140	2.113	2.133	2.200	2.177	2.106	2.013	1.949	1.812	1.727	1.628	1.615	1.527	1.403	1.389
Chinese Taipei	*Dollar*	38.95	40.07	39.60	39.85	37.84	31.92	28.57	26.28	26.63	26.55	25.02	26.35	26.45	25.61	25.39
	ECU	1.024	1.125	1.272	1.322	1.019	0.867	0.846	0.908	0.788	0.809	0.773	0.854	0.843	0.755	0.745
	SDR	0.906	0.936	0.975	0.986	0.853	0.774	0.742	0.780	0.738	0.731	0.710	0.716	0.699	0.645	0.637

a) On the technical assumption that exchange rates remain at their levels of 2 May 1995, except for Greece and Turkey where exchange rates vary according to official exchange rate policy.
b) From 1982 until 1991 a dual exchange rate for the Mexican peso against the dollar was in effect: the authorities controlled rate applicable to a set of current account transactions and a free market rate. The figures in the table refer to the market rate.

Annex Table 38. **Effective exchange rates**[a]

Indices 1991 = 100, average of daily rates

	1982	1983	1984	1985	1986	1987	1988	1989	1990	1991	1992	1993	1994	Projections[b] 1995	1996
United States	93.0	101.7	107.9	113.0	99.1	89.2	89.8	97.3	98.4	100.0	101.4	107.2	106.3	103.3	101.6
Japan	58.0	64.4	67.1	69.5	90.7	96.7	106.6	102.4	95.1	100.0	105.8	125.7	135.3	153.2	157.5
Germany	75.0	79.4	79.0	80.6	89.6	93.7	94.0	92.8	99.4	100.0	104.5	108.5	110.0	117.7	118.7
France	99.4	93.2	90.9	92.7	97.0	96.4	95.8	95.4	100.4	100.0	103.2	106.5	107.8	110.5	110.4
Italy	109.0	106.1	102.0	97.2	100.1	98.9	96.6	97.4	101.0	100.0	97.3	81.8	78.7	68.8	67.7
United Kingdom	117.2	109.8	105.3	105.7	99.2	95.3	101.6	99.0	97.9	100.0	96.5	88.4	89.0	85.3	84.7
Canada	92.5	94.8	91.9	89.2	83.7	84.8	90.8	96.0	97.6	100.0	96.3	91.0	85.5	84.0	84.5
Australia	156.5	144.5	147.5	119.6	96.8	91.2	99.4	103.5	99.4	100.0	92.5	85.6	89.6	83.2	81.4
Austria	85.4	87.6	87.8	90.3	95.3	95.6	96.4	95.9	100.8	100.0	101.4	103.7	104.3	108.3	108.8
Belgium-Luxembourg	85.8	84.2	82.7	84.9	92.4	94.5	94.3	93.9	101.6	100.0	100.9	101.9	104.2	110.0	110.7
Denmark	90.2	91.0	87.8	88.1	94.2	96.5	95.9	93.7	101.0	100.0	102.9	104.6	105.0	109.8	110.6
Finland	98.5	93.5	94.7	96.1	94.4	93.9	96.0	99.6	101.8	100.0	87.2	75.2	81.4	89.4	90.0
Greece	297.8	247.3	212.7	184.4	143.6	128.1	124.9	117.1	109.8	100.0	92.0	83.0	77.8	75.8	74.3
Iceland	593.6	328.6	271.1	208.5	172.4	159.0	136.3	111.3	100.2	100.0	99.0	93.9	89.0	88.8	88.8
Ireland	101.4	97.3	91.7	91.6	97.7	95.5	94.1	93.8	100.1	100.0	102.2	95.8	96.1	97.0	97.1
Mexico[c]	6 853.3	2 154.7	1 801.7	1 111.8	526.2	229.2	130.9	122.8	106.9	100.0	96.7	97.1	89.7	49.5	49.7
Netherlands	80.3	82.5	81.2	82.6	90.8	94.1	93.9	94.2	100.7	100.0	102.2	104.9	105.8	111.7	112.5
New Zealand	139.5	132.0	115.8	106.1	96.3	100.5	108.7	105.8	101.8	100.0	92.1	96.6	102.2	108.5	109.2
Norway	112.7	112.0	111.1	109.1	103.0	96.7	99.9	101.5	102.5	100.0	99.2	98.5	97.5	99.9	100.0
Portugal	204.0	164.2	133.5	121.4	112.1	104.2	101.4	100.0	98.2	100.0	103.2	98.7	95.0	97.7	97.8
Spain	103.8	86.6	85.3	84.6	82.9	81.8	87.8	93.1	98.5	100.0	97.3	86.2	80.7	79.2	79.6
Sweden	112.1	99.4	101.3	101.5	100.7	97.8	97.8	99.2	98.8	100.0	101.1	81.3	80.5	77.0	76.4
Switzerland	86.4	91.2	90.2	91.1	96.9	99.9	98.6	93.9	101.4	100.0	97.0	99.1	106.1	114.0	115.4
Turkey	3 176.4	2 424.6	1 652.9	1 246.9	776.0	497.7	293.9	208.7	156.2	100.0	59.2	40.6	15.9	8.9	7.1
Hong Kong	147.5	129.9	124.7	128.3	112.4	103.0	99.3	103.3	99.6	100.0	99.0	104.6	103.0	96.7	95.7
Korea	118.0	115.3	115.6	109.1	94.7	92.8	100.5	111.9	102.7	100.0	92.1	90.9	89.0	86.9	86.6
Singapore	90.5	96.6	100.7	99.9	88.5	85.3	86.0	91.9	95.5	100.0	103.8	107.7	112.2	114.9	114.8
Chinese Taipei	77.0	78.0	81.4	83.0	77.3	85.9	92.6	103.9	100.4	100.0	102.8	99.5	97.2	94.3	94.0

a) For the details on the method of calculation, see the section on effective exchange rates in ''Sources and Methods''.
b) On the technical assumption that exchange rates remain at their levels of 2 May 1995, except for Greece and Turkey where exchange rates vary according to official exchange rate policy.
c) From 1982 until 1991 a dual exchange rate for the Mexican peso against the dollar was in effect: the authority-controlled rate applicable to a set of current-account transactions and a free market rate. The figures in the table refer to the market rate.

Annex Table 39. **Export volumes**

Total goods, customs basis, percentage changes from previous period

	1977	1978	1979	1980	1981	1982	1983	1984	1985	1986	1987	1988	1989	1990	1991	1992	1993	1994	Projections 1995	1996
United States[a]	0.0	10.4	11.2	10.0	–1.7	–10.7	–4.3	6.2	1.6	4.2	10.0	19.3	11.8	7.3	7.6	7.4	4.6	11.0	10.2	11.5
Japan	9.5	–1.0	–0.9	18.5	10.7	–2.3	8.4	15.4	5.0	–0.5	0.4	4.3	4.3	5.2	2.4	1.6	–1.9	1.6	2.7	4.9
Germany	4.0	3.4	5.1	1.7	6.8	3.4	0.4	8.6	5.9	1.5	2.6	6.3	7.9	1.4	–3.1	2.0	–1.7	10.1	9.2	5.3
France	6.5	4.9	8.3	3.3	3.9	–2.8	3.6	7.0	2.4	–1.1	3.7	9.0	9.1	5.3	3.9	4.7	–1.0	6.6	8.1	6.5
Italy	7.9	9.3	8.7	–3.4	4.4	0.9	4.5	5.1	6.3	1.8	3.1	8.6	5.5	2.6	0.8	3.6	11.1	11.7	12.1	8.2
United Kingdom	9.7	2.7	4.0	1.2	–1.3	3.2	1.8	8.5	5.8	4.0	5.5	2.5	5.4	6.5	0.5	2.1	–0.1	11.6	8.1	7.2
Canada	9.4	10.2	1.8	–0.3	3.4	–0.5	7.4	18.6	6.4	3.8	3.6	9.3	1.2	4.6	1.5	8.3	10.7	15.7	14.6	7.6
Total of above countries	5.7	5.1	5.8	5.4	3.9	–1.9	2.2	9.5	4.6	1.7	4.0	8.7	7.2	4.6	2.0	4.1	2.1	9.3	9.0	7.6
Australia	0.8	0.7	13.0	–0.2	–5.8	9.6	–5.9	16.4	14.0	3.9	10.4	3.1	2.0	6.2	14.6	6.3	6.1	8.0	5.9	11.0
Austria	3.6	10.0	12.4	4.7	4.9	1.7	4.3	9.4	9.6	1.1	2.1	7.6	14.4	10.2	6.5	3.8	–2.5	11.1	8.8	5.6
Belgium-Luxembourg	2.2	3.6	6.0	0.0	0.5	1.6	4.0	5.4	4.2	4.2	6.2	7.5	8.1	3.1	4.0	0.0	–3.4	6.8	6.7	5.7
Denmark	4.0	2.4	9.6	9.0	7.0	2.0	7.6	5.4	4.6	1.4	2.4	5.0	7.5	5.9	7.5	4.6	–1.3	5.6	4.6	4.8
Finland	10.3	7.0	10.1	9.7	2.5	–2.9	4.0	9.7	0.9	0.4	1.6	3.3	–0.1	2.9	–9.1	9.0	18.6	13.0	6.5	4.2
Greece	–1.1	15.8	5.9	9.8	–15.9	2.5	9.7	22.1	0.8	16.9	10.9	–32.9	39.1	–3.0	13.8	9.5	–4.2	5.7	7.0	5.9
Iceland[b]	9.5	13.8	10.2	5.2	4.1	–17.0	14.7	–1.4	13.7	16.3	15.7	–2.2	0.3	4.9	–0.9	–4.0	0.7	13.1	2.9	2.2
Ireland	18.2	11.7	8.2	7.2	1.1	5.8	12.0	17.9	5.3	2.8	18.1	8.7	9.2	7.7	6.8	11.4	10.0	9.5	8.4	6.7
Mexico	19.9	53.3	16.1	35.7	22.2	12.7	25.8	9.1	–5.8	4.0	–12.9	–10.4	2.2	1.5	3.4	–2.9	9.5	12.1	18.4	11.6
Netherlands	–1.6	2.9	10.0	1.0	0.6	–0.6	4.4	7.4	5.9	4.3	2.7	9.2	6.3	4.5	5.1	2.4	3.7	6.8	4.2	4.3
New Zealand	2.7	2.0	7.2	5.1	1.3	3.1	5.3	4.7	10.7	–1.7	2.7	4.2	–3.1	6.0	10.5	2.2	4.4	10.1	9.5	8.0
Norway	–3.9	23.7	5.5	5.4	–1.7	–0.8	12.5	9.1	–14.1	1.8	13.9	4.6	15.0	6.7	6.6	8.0	5.2	12.3	10.4	7.0
Portugal	4.1	9.9	26.3	6.9	–2.5	11.8	19.1	14.5	10.6	7.8	11.7	9.3	20.5	12.6	0.6	7.6	0.7	14.3	12.3	7.2
Spain	13.0	15.1	11.1	0.3	10.0	7.2	9.3	16.8	3.4	–3.2	8.0	6.9	4.2	12.9	11.8	5.6	9.7	23.2	13.1	10.8
Sweden	–3.1	6.6	8.9	1.3	1.1	4.0	12.0	7.8	3.2	2.8	2.6	3.3	2.5	0.1	–2.5	1.1	10.5	15.7	12.3	7.5
Switzerland	12.2	3.1	4.2	4.5	2.6	–5.0	–0.5	7.9	7.8	0.0	1.7	7.4	7.8	3.4	–2.6	3.5	1.0	3.9	5.1	4.6
Turkey[b]	–22.4	16.6	–11.3	15.0	81.5	29.3	5.2	29.5	14.7	–21.1	21.9	8.7	0.8	0.8	6.9	5.6	6.0	10.3	19.5	13.1
Total of smaller countries	3.3	7.6	8.8	4.5	3.3	2.5	7.1	9.4	3.8	2.2	3.9	4.7	6.8	4.9	4.4	3.4	3.9	10.2	8.6	7.0
Total OECD	5.0	5.8	6.6	5.2	3.7	–0.7	3.5	9.5	4.4	1.9	4.0	7.6	7.1	4.7	2.7	3.9	2.6	9.6	8.9	7.4
OECD North America	2.8	12.1	9.3	9.3	1.1	–6.6	1.5	9.4	1.8	4.1	5.5	13.7	8.4	6.2	5.9	6.9	6.2	12.2	11.8	10.6
OECD Europe	5.0	5.2	6.9	1.7	3.6	1.5	3.5	8.2	4.8	1.7	4.1	6.4	7.4	4.0	1.2	3.2	1.9	10.1	8.9	6.4
EU	5.0	4.9	7.1	1.5	3.5	1.7	3.4	8.0	5.0	1.9	3.9	6.4	7.2	4.0	1.2	3.1	1.8	10.3	8.9	6.4
Total OECD *less* the United States	5.9	5.0	5.7	4.2	4.8	1.2	4.8	10.0	4.8	1.5	3.1	5.8	6.2	4.2	1.7	3.2	2.2	9.3	8.6	6.6

a) Derived from values and unit values on a national accounts basis.
b) OECD Secretariat estimates.

Annex Table 40. **Import volumes**

Total goods, customs basis, percentage changes from previous period

	1977	1978	1979	1980	1981	1982	1983	1984	1985	1986	1987	1988	1989	1990	1991	1992	1993	1994	Projections 1995	1996
United States[a]	11.4	9.9	1.4	-5.3	4.4	-1.2	13.8	25.2	5.9	8.6	4.2	4.0	4.4	2.4	0.7	10.4	11.7	15.2	10.2	5.7
Japan	3.2	6.2	11.1	-5.9	-2.4	-0.7	1.2	10.8	0.5	9.7	9.0	16.7	7.9	5.0	3.9	-0.6	3.8	13.7	13.2	10.3
Germany	2.5	6.2	7.5	0.4	-4.6	0.4	4.0	5.4	4.4	5.2	5.1	6.3	7.0	8.8	8.2	2.3	-6.3	5.9	7.1	8.5
France	-0.6	3.7	10.6	2.4	-3.7	2.9	-2.7	2.6	4.6	7.4	7.7	9.0	8.0	5.7	2.9	0.6	-3.8	7.0	8.6	8.4
Italy	-0.8	5.1	13.7	10.2	-8.3	-0.1	1.2	7.5	8.6	2.8	10.2	3.7	9.6	4.1	2.9	3.3	-9.3	11.0	10.1	7.4
United Kingdom	-0.1	3.9	8.0	-6.0	-4.8	5.1	6.4	10.7	3.9	7.1	7.1	13.6	7.9	0.5	-5.4	6.4	0.1	6.6	6.1	7.0
Canada	0.9	3.8	9.3	-4.4	1.4	-16.4	11.0	19.7	10.4	7.6	6.3	14.2	5.4	0.4	3.0	7.3	11.0	12.7	11.9	6.7
Total of above countries	3.5	6.3	7.5	-1.7	-2.0	-0.5	5.6	12.8	5.2	7.1	6.3	8.2	6.7	4.1	2.4	4.9	2.1	10.9	9.5	7.4
Australia	1.9	4.2	3.0	7.1	10.6	4.9	-12.5	22.0	8.2	0.5	-3.4	12.7	25.6	-2.6	-3.8	7.9	7.5	17.1	12.5	6.4
Austria	9.9	-2.2	10.7	7.7	-4.0	-0.8	7.9	8.4	5.4	5.2	5.3	7.8	10.2	11.0	2.9	3.2	-1.0	12.8	6.2	5.8
Belgium-Luxembourg	4.6	2.5	6.0	2.6	-3.7	1.7	-1.4	6.1	4.4	6.9	6.9	6.2	6.8	5.2	4.1	1.0	-1.4	5.2	6.6	5.7
Denmark	-1.2	-0.3	4.9	-6.9	-2.4	2.3	3.0	3.9	8.0	6.7	-1.8	-1.8	2.4	2.9	5.2	3.7	-3.2	12.5	8.4	5.5
Finland	7.2	4.4	19.1	12.4	-6.3	1.3	3.3	-0.1	5.8	5.5	9.0	9.0	10.6	-3.9	-16.9	-2.1	-3.7	14.6	11.5	7.4
Greece	6.0	5.2	9.0	-7.6	-1.2	15.0	4.6	0.9	15.4	3.2	17.9	-23.0	33.0	13.9	11.0	6.3	14.1	3.8	5.2	6.3
Iceland[b]	19.5	-2.1	2.5	6.8	8.9	-2.5	-9.6	4.6	10.9	9.4	25.9	-5.4	-12.1	6.8	7.3	-5.0	-15.3	8.6	8.2	5.7
Ireland	11.8	13.6	13.7	-5.0	1.6	-4.4	3.5	9.2	3.4	0.6	10.3	6.5	10.9	7.1	0.7	5.1	6.5	9.1	9.8	8.1
Mexico	-15.5	27.8	33.2	39.7	27.7	-37.9	-26.5	36.8	13.8	-18.0	-22.3	40.1	14.9	21.7	31.4	22.8	0.7	11.2	-24.6	8.9
Netherlands	2.4	6.0	6.6	-1.3	-6.1	1.0	4.5	5.4	7.2	3.9	5.3	8.0	6.9	4.8	4.7	1.6	1.1	5.3	6.4	5.2
New Zealand	-3.7	-8.6	18.1	-2.3	2.9	6.3	-6.7	19.9	0.0	-1.5	10.3	-7.7	21.5	7.7	-9.4	10.5	4.1	18.5	11.4	7.0
Norway	7.6	-11.1	4.8	11.2	-3.8	3.5	-3.4	13.5	10.5	14.6	-2.2	-9.3	-5.8	10.3	2.5	3.4	0.6	16.3	5.3	-1.2
Portugal	12.8	-1.9	7.1	11.9	6.9	5.9	-10.4	-5.5	6.7	19.3	27.9	22.2	8.3	15.9	6.0	13.4	-5.8	6.7	9.5	6.8
Spain	-2.6	-3.4	15.7	4.7	-4.4	3.7	-0.8	-0.9	7.2	18.2	26.8	18.4	16.6	9.7	11.6	9.0	-7.7	17.1	11.8	10.9
Sweden	-6.5	-10.8	19.1	1.6	-5.0	4.6	2.2	3.3	9.3	3.8	6.1	4.5	6.5	0.5	-5.8	0.6	1.9	12.9	6.9	6.7
Switzerland	10.1	9.7	7.8	8.3	-4.9	2.2	5.9	8.5	3.8	8.5	6.0	4.5	7.0	1.9	-1.4	-5.1	-0.9	8.4	5.7	4.9
Turkey[b]	5.4	-30.8	-8.4	21.7	23.5	2.1	11.9	23.5	8.1	-7.2	14.8	-2.5	8.9	28.8	-3.7	7.2	40.5	-26.3	10.9	14.4
Total of smaller countries	2.2	1.5	9.6	4.7	-1.0	-1.5	-0.1	7.7	6.9	5.1	6.3	7.1	9.5	6.3	3.8	4.2	0.5	8.9	5.6	6.6
Total OECD	3.1	4.8	8.1	0.3	-1.7	-0.8	3.8	11.2	5.7	6.5	6.3	7.8	7.5	4.8	2.8	4.7	1.6	10.3	8.4	7.2
OECD North America	7.7	9.4	4.5	-2.3	5.9	-8.0	10.4	24.8	7.1	6.9	3.4	6.9	5.0	2.9	2.8	10.7	10.7	14.5	8.1	6.0
OECD Europe	1.6	3.1	9.1	1.9	-4.5	1.8	2.3	6.0	5.7	6.2	7.5	7.2	8.0	5.7	3.0	2.8	-2.8	7.6	7.7	7.3
EU	1.1	3.4	9.4	1.3	-4.7	1.9	2.2	5.5	5.7	6.0	7.7	7.8	8.4	5.6	3.3	3.1	-3.5	7.9	7.8	7.5
Total OECD *less* the United States	1.5	3.7	9.6	1.5	-2.9	-0.7	1.7	7.9	5.6	5.9	6.9	8.9	8.3	5.3	3.4	3.3	-1.0	8.9	7.8	7.6

a) Derived from values and unit values on a national accounts basis.
b) OECD Secretariat estimates.

Annex Table 41. **Export prices (average unit values)**

Total goods, percentage changes, national currency terms

	1977	1978	1979	1980	1981	1982	1983	1984	1985	1986	1987	1988	1989	1990	1991	1992	1993	1994	Projections 1995	Projections 1996
United States	5.0	6.4	13.9	11.7	7.7	0.7	0.8	2.5	–3.1	–2.4	3.5	6.0	2.0	0.0	–0.5	–2.0	–2.0	–0.4	1.2	1.7
Japan	–0.6	–4.0	9.8	10.6	2.8	5.5	–6.6	0.1	–0.6	–15.4	–6.0	–2.5	6.9	4.2	–0.3	–0.1	–4.7	–1.0	–8.9	–2.2
Germany	2.6	0.9	5.3	9.6	6.2	4.4	1.3	3.4	3.9	–3.3	–2.7	0.9	4.5	–1.1	–0.6	–0.6	–4.7	–0.9	–2.0	0.4
France	10.3	6.5	10.2	11.5	13.4	12.8	10.0	9.6	4.2	–3.5	–0.6	2.7	4.9	–1.9	–0.1	–2.3	–2.5	2.2	1.4	1.8
Italy	19.6	8.0	16.9	19.3	22.9	15.1	6.2	11.1	9.2	–4.3	0.3	2.2	9.6	2.4	2.7	0.8	8.7	2.6	6.5	4.8
United Kingdom	15.9	7.6	10.1	15.2	8.3	6.4	7.5	7.0	5.2	–10.5	3.9	0.4	8.4	3.9	0.5	1.3	9.6	0.6	2.7	2.7
Canada	6.5	8.8	20.8	17.2	6.5	0.5	–0.1	3.7	0.5	–2.7	1.3	–0.2	1.5	–1.7	–5.0	2.5	5.1	4.5	4.5	2.7
Total of above countries	6.5	3.7	11.2	12.4	8.4	5.5	1.7	4.4	1.9	–6.1	–0.4	1.6	5.0	0.7	–0.4	–0.5	–0.6	0.4	–0.4	1.2
Australia	11.2	2.3	19.8	13.8	3.6	3.7	9.4	3.7	17.7	2.3	3.0	10.8	5.2	1.8	–5.0	–1.5	3.3	–5.8	5.9	5.6
Austria	2.5	–0.7	4.0	5.0	6.1	4.2	–0.4	3.7	2.7	–4.2	–2.1	4.0	–1.6	–1.4	–3.6	–1.8	–1.8	–1.4	1.8	2.7
Belgium-Luxembourg	2.8	1.3	11.1	10.8	8.7	13.7	7.2	7.0	1.5	–6.9	–4.7	2.7	7.9	–3.1	–1.9	–1.4	–1.5	–0.1	–1.2	1.3
Denmark	5.7	5.6	7.8	13.8	11.9	11.1	4.9	6.1	3.4	–4.3	–0.9	0.2	5.7	–1.5	–0.4	–1.8	–0.2	0.7	0.4	2.4
Finland	14.8	6.4	12.4	10.8	11.1	7.3	6.4	6.3	2.6	–2.2	2.1	4.9	7.7	–1.2	0.8	6.1	5.4	1.0	1.8	2.1
Greece	10.4	4.6	7.8	43.3	22.8	21.1	20.0	14.8	14.9	8.4	5.4	22.2	15.1	8.3	9.4	6.7	8.0	7.7	7.9	5.1
Iceland[a]	26.5	49.6	46.6	52.0	38.1	57.2	92.3	25.3	29.8	14.5	1.6	19.1	28.2	11.4	1.0	–1.2	3.1	5.8	5.5	3.3
Ireland	15.2	5.6	9.0	10.6	14.5	12.4	8.5	9.0	4.1	–6.1	–3.4	5.5	8.8	–8.7	–2.0	–0.5	7.2	1.8	2.2	2.7
Mexico	50.8	–3.3	20.9	29.8	13.5	116.2	96.8	37.9	49.1	79.0	178.1	83.4	19.3	28.7	6.5	6.4	3.3	9.0	51.7	8.2
Netherlands	3.0	–1.9	8.7	13.3	15.6	4.1	–0.3	5.9	1.3	–16.9	–6.1	0.4	5.1	–0.9	–0.8	–3.4	–2.5	0.5	–1.2	0.8
New Zealand	14.7	6.3	21.3	15.4	13.1	10.4	5.6	13.5	8.8	–2.3	5.9	6.3	13.1	–1.4	–4.2	8.2	2.5	–3.1	3.0	2.1
Norway	6.7	5.8	16.8	30.6	15.4	7.3	3.7	9.4	43.9	–25.0	–3.5	0.0	12.4	3.7	–3.4	–8.5	0.8	–3.1	2.6	1.7
Portugal	35.4	24.3	31.2	23.4	13.6	15.3	29.0	30.7	15.7	3.3	8.4	10.4	5.8	2.9	0.2	–2.2	2.2	4.6	2.4	2.4
Spain	17.6	12.3	9.6	19.1	16.4	10.1	15.9	13.1	6.1	–4.3	2.4	4.6	4.8	–2.6	–1.4	0.5	4.6	5.2	4.7	4.0
Sweden	8.2	7.8	10.3	9.8	10.2	10.0	13.5	7.0	4.1	–1.0	3.3	5.1	6.6	2.1	0.4	–3.0	7.9	4.5	8.7	4.2
Switzerland	1.6	–3.9	1.0	5.7	6.0	4.9	2.5	4.7	2.0	0.5	–1.0	2.2	5.6	1.3	2.3	1.0	0.1	–0.7	–1.5	1.9
Turkey[a]	30.0	50.6	76.4	123.4	28.9	37.8	31.8	55.5	39.9	52.6	43.1	74.6	47.9	36.1	56.2	69.2	59.4	173.1	76.5	44.5
Total of smaller countries	9.8	3.4	11.6	15.5	11.6	13.4	11.1	9.8	8.7	–2.7	5.5	8.2	7.6	1.3	0.1	–0.1	2.0	2.7	5.0	3.3
Total OECD	7.4	3.6	11.3	13.3	9.3	7.7	4.2	5.9	3.7	–5.2	1.2	3.4	5.7	0.9	–0.2	–0.4	0.1	1.0	1.0	1.8
OECD North America	8.1	6.2	15.9	14.1	7.8	6.1	5.6	4.9	0.7	1.6	10.6	8.9	3.1	1.4	–1.0	–0.5	–0.1	1.3	4.8	2.4
OECD Europe	8.7	4.3	9.6	13.5	11.4	8.8	5.9	7.5	5.4	–5.6	–0.8	2.4	6.5	0.0	0.2	–0.5	1.1	1.6	1.6	2.3
EU	8.9	4.3	9.5	12.8	11.4	8.7	5.8	7.2	4.5	–5.8	–1.0	2.1	6.1	–0.4	–0.2	–0.7	0.8	1.0	1.2	2.0
Total OECD *less* the United States	7.9	3.1	10.8	13.6	9.6	9.1	4.9	6.6	5.1	–5.7	0.7	2.9	6.5	1.1	–0.2	–0.1	0.5	1.3	1.0	1.8

a) OECD Secretariat estimates.

Annex Table 42. **Import prices (average unit values)**

Total goods, percentage changes, national currency terms

	1977	1978	1979	1980	1981	1982	1983	1984	1985	1986	1987	1988	1989	1990	1991	1992	1993	1994	Projections 1995	1996
United States	10.1	5.8	18.3	23.4	3.1	–5.3	–4.4	–1.4	–3.7	–0.7	7.5	4.9	2.8	2.4	–2.1	–1.7	–2.6	–0.6	4.1	3.4
Japan	–4.1	–17.6	30.0	40.4	0.7	4.6	–9.3	–2.8	–4.3	–36.6	–7.9	–5.4	11.8	11.4	–9.1	–6.9	–12.4	–7.9	–11.4	–1.8
Germany	3.6	–2.9	11.3	17.0	13.8	0.6	–0.4	5.9	2.6	–16.0	–6.1	0.9	7.4	–2.6	2.1	–3.3	–5.2	1.6	–1.5	1.0
France	13.4	2.7	11.9	22.7	19.5	12.6	8.2	10.1	1.5	–14.3	–1.1	2.5	7.1	–2.0	–0.6	–3.2	–3.9	2.1	1.4	1.6
Italy	16.9	6.6	18.9	26.0	32.1	12.5	3.5	12.9	7.4	–15.9	–1.6	7.5	6.4	–0.5	0.9	–0.7	10.4	4.1	12.1	3.3
United Kingdom	16.6	4.3	9.2	11.2	7.9	7.2	7.9	8.4	3.8	–5.8	2.5	–0.3	5.9	3.0	–0.4	–0.5	7.7	2.4	4.4	3.1
Canada	12.4	13.6	14.2	16.3	12.0	3.5	–1.3	4.6	1.7	0.0	–1.9	–1.9	–0.3	0.7	–3.1	1.7	3.8	4.4	3.5	1.6
Total of above countries	8.8	0.9	16.1	22.3	10.5	2.8	–0.4	4.0	0.3	–12.6	–0.3	1.7	5.8	1.5	–1.6	–2.4	–1.9	0.4	1.3	1.9
Australia	20.7	6.7	14.2	14.8	4.7	7.3	6.9	2.2	23.5	16.4	7.4	–0.9	–4.6	2.6	2.4	0.4	7.0	–6.3	3.6	3.3
Austria	3.7	0.7	5.3	8.9	10.2	0.2	–2.8	3.9	4.2	–10.0	–4.2	1.8	3.6	–2.7	3.5	–2.7	–4.0	–1.3	0.3	2.3
Belgium-Luxembourg	1.9	1.8	10.3	13.8	13.8	13.3	7.4	7.7	–0.2	–13.2	–5.4	3.1	7.1	–1.8	–1.3	–3.2	–4.4	0.9	–1.1	1.0
Denmark	7.6	2.6	13.4	21.4	16.7	9.5	3.2	8.1	2.5	–9.8	–4.2	2.5	7.1	–3.0	0.0	–3.0	–1.4	2.3	0.9	2.5
Finland	16.6	10.7	13.9	18.0	12.3	4.3	7.1	4.4	3.6	–9.7	–2.4	1.8	3.6	1.8	2.5	10.3	12.9	–0.1	1.1	2.0
Greece	5.9	7.2	22.6	34.5	16.8	24.0	17.0	21.1	18.4	14.5	–2.7	21.1	12.1	9.4	9.7	7.0	7.2	7.8	7.2	5.5
Iceland[a]	18.3	55.2	55.1	54.6	40.6	60.0	94.7	22.6	30.7	11.4	5.9	18.3	31.9	14.0	–0.7	–0.9	10.2	5.7	1.7	2.0
Ireland	18.4	5.7	14.2	18.4	19.4	8.1	4.4	10.7	2.5	–9.0	–3.7	4.6	8.6	–5.2	2.3	–2.3	5.9	4.8	1.2	1.6
Mexico	60.7	13.8	17.6	12.0	5.9	120.9	111.6	36.8	50.0	164.2	152.7	80.4	9.6	21.8	5.2	5.0	0.0	8.0	61.9	6.5
Netherlands	3.0	–2.3	11.6	14.9	14.9	1.0	0.1	5.8	0.9	–17.7	–5.0	–0.6	5.2	–2.0	–0.6	–2.5	–3.2	0.8	–1.3	1.0
New Zealand	10.2	3.6	12.9	29.2	14.1	11.5	8.4	13.6	10.8	–2.4	–4.4	–0.9	7.8	0.8	1.1	6.6	–0.3	–8.0	0.3	2.0
Norway	7.9	4.9	10.1	12.9	6.7	4.4	3.8	3.0	0.1	0.1	2.8	2.9	6.1	1.0	–1.6	–2.1	1.0	0.5	4.0	2.5
Portugal	29.4	23.1	34.4	28.0	19.8	17.0	34.3	35.4	7.1	–8.7	6.3	7.0	7.8	3.2	0.2	–5.1	3.3	3.0	2.7	2.5
Spain	18.8	9.5	2.6	36.4	29.0	12.7	21.3	11.9	2.1	–17.9	–3.2	–1.5	2.3	–3.4	–2.8	–3.1	5.8	6.6	5.1	3.8
Sweden	14.3	14.8	10.7	14.2	9.5	11.6	15.2	5.8	2.6	–8.6	4.2	4.3	5.9	1.9	–1.1	–4.2	12.4	4.1	6.0	3.9
Switzerland	6.1	–10.5	6.7	11.9	7.2	–1.2	–0.7	4.2	4.3	–9.3	–3.6	4.9	8.1	–0.4	0.1	2.0	–1.9	–4.8	–1.5	2.1
Turkey[a]	22.2	54.8	90.3	150.0	37.0	42.1	29.5	53.5	39.8	35.6	43.2	71.8	51.6	34.8	56.0	67.7	47.9	177.7	75.0	45.3
Total of smaller countries	11.6	4.5	12.2	19.6	14.3	12.6	12.1	10.3	6.4	–4.0	4.0	7.1	6.4	0.9	1.2	–0.1	1.4	3.5	5.3	3.2
Total OECD	9.6	2.0	14.9	21.5	11.7	5.7	3.2	5.9	2.1	–10.1	1.0	3.3	6.0	1.3	–0.7	–1.7	–0.9	1.3	2.5	2.3
OECD North America	13.5	7.7	17.5	21.2	4.8	2.0	1.8	2.0	0.2	6.3	12.3	7.7	2.7	3.4	–1.8	–0.6	–1.3	0.9	7.2	3.3
OECD Europe	9.8	2.4	12.1	19.3	16.3	7.3	5.5	8.8	3.3	–12.6	–2.3	2.8	6.8	–0.7	0.8	–1.6	0.7	3.0	2.5	2.4
EU	9.8	2.6	11.7	18.8	16.7	7.4	5.5	8.7	3.0	–13.4	–2.8	2.2	6.4	–1.1	0.4	–2.3	0.4	2.3	2.1	2.0
Total OECD *less* the United States	9.5	1.1	14.1	21.0	13.9	8.5	5.2	7.8	3.6	–12.2	–0.5	2.9	6.8	1.1	–0.4	–1.7	–0.5	1.8	2.1	2.0

a) OECD Secretariat estimates.

Annex Table 43. **Competitive positions: relative unit labour costs**[a]

Indices, 1991 = 100

	1977	1978	1979	1980	1981	1982	1983	1984	1985	1986	1987	1988	1989	1990	1991	1992	1993	1994	Projections 1995	Projections 1996
United States	117	110	114	118	125	136	145	153	158	132	113	105	106	103	100	96	96	94	91	88
Japan	105	121	102	90	93	81	88	88	86	119	122	125	109	96	100	106	129	139	149	151
Germany	84	88	89	90	83	86	88	86	84	92	103	102	99	103	100	106	115	111	115	116
France	102	103	105	110	108	104	104	105	107	109	109	103	99	102	100	100	102	100	102	101
Italy	95	90	91	88	88	89	94	92	90	91	91	90	94	99	100	95	78	75	66	65
United Kingdom	72	79	94	115	119	112	102	98	100	94	95	101	101	97	100	98	89	92	88	87
Canada	94	84	81	82	85	94	94	86	82	79	85	92	96	97	100	92	84	79	76	76
Australia	113	103	97	98	110	118	112	119	99	83	82	92	101	102	100	90	80	81	76	76
Austria	122	120	115	112	112	112	111	108	107	112	112	106	102	102	100	100	100	102	106	104
Belgium-Luxembourg	152	150	147	137	123	102	92	91	92	97	99	96	93	101	100	100	99	102	108	108
Denmark	98	100	99	86	81	79	80	80	82	91	101	98	94	103	100	100	98	99	105	106
Finland	107	90	90	90	94	97	95	98	97	94	92	94	99	104	100	77	62	67	76	77
Mexico	138	136	142	151	180	139	70	84	77	62	63	78	85	89	100	112	121	121	82	96
Netherlands	134	132	129	121	109	112	111	100	97	105	111	107	100	101	100	104	106	103	109	108
New Zealand	112	117	117	114	116	114	111	96	92	92	104	114	104	101	100	88	91	98	105	104
Norway	109	104	97	99	103	106	106	104	103	104	105	110	106	103	100	99	96	96	99	99
Portugal	92	78	71	75	82	81	76	72	74	76	75	78	82	89	100	109	108	110	117	118
Spain	82	84	101	95	92	90	78	80	79	79	80	85	92	100	100	102	90	86	86	88
Sweden	119	110	103	102	103	90	81	83	86	86	86	90	94	97	100	98	72	73	73	73
Switzerland	70	84	80	70	70	77	86	84	83	89	94	96	91	98	100	97	99	108	117	119
Korea	73	74	81	71	64	70	71	67	68	57	61	74	101	100	100	94	93	94	96	101
Chinese Taipei	69	59	66	72	78	80	74	87	82	74	83	94	107	103	100	107	104	104	101	103
Hong Kong	86	87	81	81	111	111	95	93	106	83	75	77	87	93	100	101	115	122	123	128
Singapore	79	77	77	76	82	98	108	114	119	87	80	81	89	93	100	107	106	115	121	125

a) In manufacturing, expressed in a common currency.

Annex Table 44. **Competitive positions: relative export prices**[a]

Indices, 1991 = 100

	1977	1978	1979	1980	1981	1982	1983	1984	1985	1986	1987	1988	1989	1990	1991	1992	1993	1994	Projections 1995	1996
United States	107	100	101	103	115	124	131	134	136	120	109	103	104	101	100	97	95	91	86	84
Japan	90	101	92	88	93	87	87	86	87	96	97	100	97	93	100	106	121	129	133	131
Germany	97	100	100	99	91	92	92	89	89	98	102	100	98	102	100	103	100	98	101	100
France	101	103	104	104	100	97	96	97	99	103	104	103	100	103	100	101	101	104	106	106
Italy	87	85	86	89	92	91	90	90	90	92	92	89	95	99	100	99	90	88	82	83
United Kingdom	84	90	97	107	107	101	98	95	97	93	94	99	97	99	100	98	100	102	99	100
Canada	115	108	106	106	106	103	105	103	100	96	99	103	105	102	100	96	97	97	99	100
Australia	140	125	124	121	117	109	112	116	102	94	101	114	113	106	100	89	88	88	86	87
Austria	118	115	113	110	107	108	106	104	103	107	109	112	103	105	100	100	103	100	107	109
Belgium-Luxembourg	106	107	110	108	101	96	97	96	94	98	99	98	100	103	100	102	100	102	106	107
Denmark	105	106	102	94	90	89	92	89	90	98	101	99	96	102	100	102	105	106	111	113
Finland	91	83	83	85	90	92	89	90	91	91	93	97	102	101	100	92	83	90	100	100
Mexico	94	97	101	100	96	101	70	76	66	84	92	98	97	102	100	103	112	113	101	110
Netherlands	118	114	114	112	108	109	107	102	97	97	104	104	100	102	100	100	99	100	103	103
New Zealand	100	97	101	100	103	103	104	104	100	94	100	115	113	109	100	97	101	105	118	120
Norway	108	103	101	106	106	102	100	105	100	95	96	112	116	105	100	95	91	91	95	94
Portugal	114	107	108	111	113	108	105	104	106	105	103	103	98	99	100	102	96	95	99	99
Spain	84	80	85	84	77	78	74	76	79	86	88	91	91	96	100	103	97	92	94	96
Sweden	105	99	100	101	101	93	90	91	92	94	95	97	98	99	100	100	88	89	92	93
Switzerland	77	88	83	77	78	82	86	84	82	92	97	96	91	98	100	100	103	110	116	118
Korea	100	98	105	98	102	100	98	100	96	92	94	101	111	101	100	96	97	98	95	97
Chinese Taipei	91	88	93	94	96	93	89	93	89	84	92	99	105	100	100	100	100	101	98	100
Hong Kong	143	131	127	126	125	122	112	120	119	108	105	100	102	99	100	100	103	103	100	101
Singapore	132	132	128	125	136	137	139	135	128	100	99	96	97	101	100	98	99	100	97	99

a) For manufactured goods, expressed in a common currency.

Annex Table 45. **Export performance for total goods**[a]

Percentage changes from previous period

	1977	1978	1979	1980	1981	1982	1983	1984	1985	1986	1987	1988	1989	1990	1991	1992	1993	1994	Projections 1995	1996
United States	-3.7	4.2	2.6	4.4	-7.4	-6.0	-3.3	-3.7	-2.3	0.6	5.5	6.4	2.4	1.9	0.1	0.4	0.3	0.2	2.5	3.0
Japan	0.0	-10.6	-4.3	13.9	4.1	-3.5	2.9	1.6	0.1	-6.6	-5.3	-5.3	-3.7	0.1	-5.2	-7.9	-8.9	-10.0	-7.0	-3.1
Germany	-1.1	-4.3	-1.8	-3.6	5.7	1.5	-1.6	1.1	1.4	-2.6	-3.4	-2.0	-0.8	-4.1	-5.1	-0.8	-6.2	3.8	0.2	-2.0
France	1.8	-0.8	2.3	-2.1	2.5	-3.4	2.3	0.4	-0.5	-6.2	-3.2	0.2	0.9	-0.3	-0.5	-0.2	-0.2	-2.2	-0.3	-0.9
Italy	1.9	1.8	4.0	-6.7	1.7	-1.2	3.7	-0.6	2.8	-4.0	-2.7	-0.3	-3.0	-4.1	-2.9	-0.4	12.1	2.8	2.8	0.2
United Kingdom	2.3	-2.9	-4.2	-2.8	-4.4	1.3	-0.4	1.6	2.3	-1.5	0.5	-3.3	-2.6	1.3	-3.3	-2.5	-0.3	1.8	-0.8	-0.3
Canada	-0.9	-1.4	2.1	2.9	-0.3	0.2	-2.4	-0.9	1.1	-1.5	1.3	3.3	-4.5	0.7	-0.4	-1.4	0.5	1.8	4.5	1.3
Total of above countries	-0.4	-2.3	-0.2	1.1	0.3	-1.7	0.0	0.0	0.6	-3.1	-1.3	-0.4	-1.1	-0.8	-2.8	-1.9	-1.8	-0.5	0.1	-0.1
Australia	-4.5	-2.6	4.4	-1.7	-8.1	9.2	-3.9	5.7	13.1	3.6	5.5	-3.2	-6.0	4.1	10.2	1.4	0.8	-2.3	-4.1	1.8
Austria	-1.2	-1.5	5.1	0.6	4.4	0.1	0.9	2.8	4.9	-1.1	-3.2	-0.8	4.9	2.4	4.1	3.5	1.3	1.6	0.0	-2.4
Belgium-Luxembourg	-1.7	-2.2	-1.5	-4.0	0.9	-0.3	1.4	-1.1	-0.8	-1.4	-0.5	-1.8	-0.4	-3.1	-0.5	-3.3	-1.2	-1.8	-1.8	-1.9
Denmark	2.6	-0.6	1.5	6.9	7.4	-0.5	4.6	-0.5	-0.9	-2.8	-3.1	-0.7	0.2	0.9	4.8	1.3	-0.2	-3.5	-3.0	-1.9
Finland	6.4	6.4	-2.2	8.3	0.6	-2.9	1.6	0.2	-3.3	-4.3	-3.6	-2.5	-7.5	-1.0	-10.3	6.1	22.0	4.3	-2.0	-2.9
Greece	-5.1	8.6	-4.9	8.2	-16.1	-0.7	13.6	12.6	-3.5	16.5	5.7	-36.7	28.1	-10.6	9.6	10.4	0.3	-3.4	-1.1	-1.5
Iceland	8.0	8.9	4.6	8.1	1.5	-19.9	12.2	-6.4	9.4	10.4	9.8	-6.7	-4.0	-0.4	-3.9	-8.0	1.6	4.6	-2.7	-3.7
Ireland	13.2	6.3	-1.3	6.7	-0.6	4.2	7.1	8.9	2.3	-1.7	8.7	-4.0	3.7	4.7	3.9	6.9	10.1	0.1	0.4	-0.4
Mexico	6.3	35.8	6.5	36.9	20.6	12.9	29.2	-6.8	-8.6	-1.0	-17.9	-10.2	-0.9	-0.9	7.0	-9.7	-0.2	-1.1	7.8	5.4
Netherlands	-4.4	-2.0	2.5	-1.4	3.0	-1.4	2.7	2.3	2.2	0.3	-2.7	2.3	-0.8	-1.1	1.4	-0.9	6.2	-1.1	-3.3	-2.7
New Zealand	-1.1	-3.6	0.4	0.7	-4.6	2.9	6.3	-3.6	9.1	0.0	-0.7	-3.5	-13.0	3.6	7.6	-3.0	-0.5	-0.4	0.2	0.1
Norway	1.7	24.9	0.3	12.2	7.3	2.8	12.9	-0.1	-13.2	-5.4	8.7	-0.2	8.5	2.6	4.5	5.4	4.0	8.5	4.5	0.5
Portugal	3.4	7.0	17.3	1.9	-2.3	11.1	15.1	7.6	5.9	0.3	3.3	-0.5	11.5	7.6	-2.1	3.9	4.8	2.7	3.1	-0.5
Spain	7.2	10.8	5.1	-5.6	9.5	0.7	4.8	12.9	-2.7	-13.9	-0.3	-0.4	-1.1	2.4	1.9	-1.6	9.7	14.5	4.5	3.1
Sweden	-0.4	2.9	1.5	-2.9	2.0	2.0	8.8	0.0	-1.9	-2.9	-2.3	-2.7	-4.5	-4.2	-4.4	-3.2	10.6	5.3	3.5	0.6
Switzerland	4.8	2.6	-6.8	0.9	1.0	-5.6	-5.9	-3.8	5.2	-4.1	-4.8	-1.3	-0.8	-1.5	-7.7	0.4	1.5	-6.5	-3.6	-3.3
Turkey	-26.0	7.5	-17.6	11.7	82.8	28.9	2.3	22.3	11.4	-24.8	14.6	2.0	-7.0	-5.2	1.4	2.4	8.9	1.0	10.1	4.9
Total of smaller countries	0.3	3.1	0.7	1.7	3.6	1.0	4.8	1.6	0.1	-2.7	-1.9	-2.1	-0.5	-0.4	0.8	-0.4	4.3	0.9	0.1	-0.4
Total OECD	-0.1	-0.9	0.0	1.3	1.2	-1.0	1.3	0.4	0.4	-3.0	-1.5	-0.9	-0.9	-0.7	-1.8	-1.5	-0.2	-0.1	0.1	-0.2
OPEC	9.5	-4.8	-2.5	-15.4	-12.6	-5.3	-9.2	-6.4	0.0	12.7	-3.0	6.0	-3.5	1.5	6.6	1.4	-2.0	-1.5	-1.7	-1.4
ANIEs[b]	6.2	6.4	-0.1	6.9	2.7	3.8	7.4	4.1	-4.1	9.3	12.8	1.1	-5.8	0.1	2.1	-2.8	2.0	-1.3	0.1	1.2
Other Asia[c]	-2.1	0.0	4.2	2.2	1.5	7.8	0.8	-0.7	3.1	5.2	2.3	-1.0	4.8	1.6	6.4	5.1	4.8	0.2	-0.4	0.4
Latin America[c]	1.4	5.4	2.2	2.2	1.9	-0.3	3.4	4.5	-1.2	-14.0	7.2	8.1	0.8	-4.6	-0.7	-1.5	2.2	-1.7	-0.9	1.1
Africa[c]	7.1	2.6	-0.1	30.3	-7.5	0.6	6.7	-3.2	-2.4	2.5	1.5	-4.3	-2.4	0.0	1.5	-0.2	1.0	-0.9	-1.9	-1.3
Central and Eastern Europe	6.3	43.1	-3.4	-4.7	2.1	7.6	5.0	-0.4	-6.3	13.4	-0.9	2.3	-5.1	-5.6	-10.3	-17.7	5.5	1.2	0.6	-0.2
Total of non-OECD countries	6.0	2.3	-0.7	-3.3	-4.1	1.3	1.1	-0.4	-1.9	6.5	4.3	2.0	-2.6	-0.5	2.0	-1.5	2.2	-0.8	-0.5	0.3
World	1.4	0.0	-0.2	0.2	-0.1	-0.4	1.3	0.3	-0.1	-0.8	0.0	-0.1	-1.4	-0.7	-0.8	-1.5	0.4	-0.3	-0.1	-0.1
OECD North America	-2.8	4.0	2.8	5.8	-4.3	-3.2	0.1	-3.0	-2.1	0.1	1.8	3.9	0.5	1.4	0.4	-0.7	0.3	0.5	3.3	2.8
OECD Europe	0.7	-0.5	-0.2	-2.2	2.9	-0.2	1.4	1.3	0.9	-3.4	-1.9	-1.4	-0.7	-1.8	-2.3	-0.5	1.6	1.7	0.2	-1.0
EU	0.4	-1.2	0.1	-2.8	2.5	-0.2	1.5	1.4	1.0	-3.2	-2.1	-1.5	-0.8	-1.8	-2.2	-0.7	1.4	1.9	0.2	-1.0
Total OECD *less* the United States	0.5	-1.7	-0.5	0.7	3.0	-0.3	2.0	1.1	0.8	-3.6	-2.5	-1.9	-1.5	-1.2	-2.2	-1.9	-0.3	-0.2	-0.4	-0.9

a) Export performance is the ratio between export volumes and export markets for total goods. The export volume concept employed is the sum of the exports of food, raw materials, energy and manufactures. The calculation of export markets is based on a weighted average of import volumes in each exporting country's markets, with weights based on trade flows in 1991. The export market for total goods facing each country is calculated as the weighted sum of the individual export markets for food, raw materials, energy and manufactures, where the weights correspond to the commodity export structure of the exporting country in the previous year.
b) ANIEs include Chinese Taipei, Hong Kong, Korea and Singapore.
c) Not including OPEC countries.

Annex Table 46. **Shares in world exports and imports**

Percentage, values for total goods

	1977	1978	1979	1980	1981	1982	1983	1984	1985	1986	1987	1988	1989	1990	1991	1992	1993	1994	Projections 1995	1996
A. Exports																				
United States	11.6	11.6	11.5	11.6	12.5	12.1	11.9	12.2	11.9	11.0	10.6	11.7	12.4	11.7	12.3	12.2	12.7	12.5	11.9	12.2
Japan	7.7	7.9	6.5	6.8	8.0	7.8	8.5	9.3	9.6	10.3	9.6	9.6	9.2	8.5	9.2	9.3	10.1	9.8	9.3	8.9
Germany	12.0	12.4	11.8	10.8	10.1	10.8	10.7	10.2	10.8	12.9	13.2	12.7	12.4	12.7	11.7	11.9	10.7	10.6	11.2	10.9
France	6.1	6.3	6.2	5.9	5.5	5.4	5.4	5.2	5.4	6.0	6.1	6.0	5.9	6.3	6.2	6.4	5.8	5.8	6.1	6.0
Italy	4.1	4.3	4.4	4.0	4.0	4.2	4.2	4.0	4.2	4.8	4.8	4.7	4.7	5.0	4.9	4.9	4.7	4.6	4.6	4.7
United Kingdom	5.2	5.4	5.4	5.7	5.3	5.4	5.3	5.1	5.4	5.2	5.4	5.3	5.1	5.4	5.4	5.2	4.9	5.0	5.0	5.0
Canada	4.1	3.9	3.7	3.5	3.9	4.0	4.4	4.9	4.9	4.4	4.1	4.2	4.2	3.8	3.7	3.7	4.1	4.1	4.2	4.2
Other OECD countries	18.1	18.6	18.5	18.0	17.5	18.5	18.4	18.5	18.9	20.0	20.3	20.0	19.8	20.7	20.4	20.4	19.5	19.7	20.5	20.6
Non OECD Asia	7.6	8.0	8.1	8.3	9.2	9.8	10.7	11.5	11.3	11.5	12.7	13.4	13.6	13.1	14.3	14.8	16.5	17.1	16.9	17.4
Latin America	3.9	3.5	3.5	3.5	3.5	3.3	3.5	3.5	3.2	2.7	2.5	2.7	2.7	2.5	2.4	2.4	2.5	2.5	2.4	2.4
OPEC	14.7	12.1	14.4	15.2	14.1	12.1	10.1	9.0	8.3	5.4	5.1	4.4	4.8	5.5	5.0	5.0	4.7	4.4	4.2	4.1
Other non OECD countries	5.0	6.0	6.0	6.7	6.3	6.6	6.8	6.5	6.0	5.9	5.6	5.2	5.1	4.9	4.4	3.8	3.9	3.9	3.7	3.7
B. Imports																				
United States	14.5	14.3	13.6	12.9	14.0	14.0	15.7	18.3	18.5	18.2	17.4	16.6	16.4	15.0	14.5	14.8	16.4	16.7	16.4	16.1
Japan	6.2	5.9	6.4	6.7	6.8	6.7	6.6	6.7	6.4	5.7	5.8	6.2	6.4	6.3	6.2	5.7	6.1	6.2	6.2	6.3
Germany	10.0	10.1	10.5	10.1	8.9	8.9	9.0	8.6	8.8	9.6	9.8	9.4	9.2	10.0	10.5	10.4	8.9	8.7	9.0	9.1
France	6.7	6.6	6.9	7.1	6.4	6.5	6.1	5.7	5.8	6.3	6.7	6.5	6.5	6.9	6.7	6.5	5.7	5.7	6.0	6.0
Italy	4.0	4.0	4.4	4.8	4.4	4.4	4.2	4.2	4.5	4.5	4.8	4.7	4.7	4.9	4.8	4.7	3.8	3.8	3.8	3.8
United Kingdom	5.7	5.7	5.9	5.5	4.9	5.1	5.3	5.3	5.4	5.7	6.0	6.4	6.2	6.1	5.6	5.5	5.2	5.1	5.1	5.1
Canada	3.8	3.5	3.4	3.1	3.4	3.1	3.5	3.9	4.1	4.0	3.7	3.9	3.9	3.5	3.5	3.4	3.8	3.7	3.7	3.6
Other OECD countries	22.8	22.0	22.5	22.1	20.6	20.5	19.7	19.2	19.9	21.6	22.3	22.0	21.9	23.0	22.7	22.6	21.1	20.9	21.2	21.2
Non OECD Asia	8.0	8.6	8.9	9.3	10.2	10.4	11.3	11.4	11.9	11.1	11.6	12.9	13.5	13.2	14.7	15.7	17.8	18.4	18.1	18.5
Latin America	4.9	4.6	4.7	5.0	5.2	4.6	4.0	3.5	3.0	2.9	2.8	2.5	2.5	2.5	2.6	2.8	3.0	3.1	3.0	2.9
OPEC	7.0	6.7	5.5	6.0	7.2	7.9	7.0	5.9	4.9	4.0	3.4	3.4	3.2	3.1	3.4	3.6	3.6	3.5	3.4	3.4
Other non OECD countries	6.4	7.9	7.3	7.5	8.0	7.8	7.5	7.2	6.7	6.4	5.7	5.6	5.5	5.6	4.7	4.3	4.5	4.3	4.1	4.0

Annex Table 47. **Trade balances**

$ billion

	1977	1978	1979	1980	1981	1982	1983	1984	1985	1986	1987	1988	1989	1990	1991	1992	1993	1994	Projections 1995	1996
United States	-31.1	-33.9	-27.6	-25.5	-28.0	-38.5	-67.1	-112.5	-122.2	-145.1	-159.6	-127.0	-115.2	-109.0	-74.1	-96.1	-132.6	-166.4	-203.1	-198.4
Japan	17.3	24.6	1.8	2.1	20.0	18.1	31.5	44.3	56.0	92.8	96.4	95.0	76.9	63.5	103.0	132.3	141.5	145.8	141.6	133.5
Germany	18.4	23.0	15.2	8.0	15.5	24.2	19.4	21.7	27.9	54.1	67.7	76.4	75.1	69.4	18.0	26.5	39.7	50.8	69.6	57.0
France	-2.8	0.7	-2.1	-13.0	-10.1	-15.5	-8.2	-4.1	-5.4	-2.8	-9.2	-8.5	-10.1	-12.9	-8.8	2.9	8.7	9.9	11.4	8.0
Italy	0.4	3.4	-0.1	-15.9	-10.8	-7.9	-1.7	-5.2	-5.5	4.7	0.2	-0.7	-1.7	1.2	-0.2	3.1	33.1	35.3	35.6	44.8
United Kingdom	-4.1	-3.1	-7.1	3.2	6.5	3.3	-2.3	-7.1	-4.3	-14.0	-18.9	-38.2	-40.4	-33.4	-18.1	-23.0	-20.1	-16.1	-18.7	-21.2
Canada	3.2	4.2	4.2	8.0	6.4	14.8	14.8	16.0	12.6	7.7	9.0	8.1	6.0	8.3	3.7	6.1	7.6	12.8	21.1	27.1
Total of above countries	1.3	19.0	-15.7	-33.1	-0.5	-1.4	-13.7	-46.9	-40.9	-2.5	-14.5	5.1	-9.4	-13.0	23.5	51.8	77.9	72.2	57.4	50.8
Australia	1.0	0.1	2.5	1.4	-2.2	-2.1	0.0	-0.8	-1.0	-1.8	0.3	-0.6	-3.4	0.4	3.5	1.5	-0.1	-3.3	-6.0	-2.7
Austria	-3.8	-3.3	-4.3	-6.3	-4.5	-3.1	-3.4	-3.3	-2.6	-3.5	-4.2	-4.6	-5.0	-5.9	-7.6	-7.7	-6.7	-8.0	-6.3	-6.8
Belgium-Luxembourg	-2.4	-2.5	-4.1	-5.0	-4.1	-2.9	-1.2	-0.8	-0.2	1.1	0.8	1.9	1.2	0.8	0.5	2.7	5.3	3.1	3.9	4.8
Denmark	-2.7	-2.4	-3.4	-2.0	-0.9	-0.8	0.2	-0.2	-0.7	-1.1	0.8	1.9	2.4	4.9	4.7	7.2	8.0	7.2	8.1	8.5
Finland	0.4	1.1	0.4	-0.6	0.3	0.2	0.2	1.5	0.9	1.6	1.4	1.1	-0.2	0.7	2.4	3.9	6.4	7.7	8.9	8.7
Greece	-3.2	-3.5	-5.0	-5.6	-5.4	-4.8	-4.3	-4.2	-5.1	-4.4	-5.5	-6.1	-7.4	-10.2	-10.1	-11.6	-12.6	-13.1	-15.5	-17.3
Iceland	-0.1	0.0	0.0	0.0	0.0	-0.2	0.0	0.0	0.0	0.1	-0.1	0.0	0.1	0.1	0.0	0.0	0.2	0.3	0.3	0.3
Ireland	-0.8	-1.1	-2.3	-2.2	-2.2	-1.1	-0.2	0.3	0.6	1.1	2.6	3.8	4.0	4.0	4.2	6.8	8.1	8.8	10.5	11.5
Mexico	-1.0	-1.7	-2.8	-3.8	-4.9	6.2	13.3	12.0	7.1	3.7	7.2	0.3	-2.6	-4.4	-11.3	-20.7	-18.9	-23.2	-4.1	-3.4
Netherlands	-0.2	-1.5	-1.4	-1.4	3.8	4.8	4.3	5.5	5.4	7.2	5.1	8.5	8.1	10.2	10.7	11.4	12.9	15.7	18.0	17.9
New Zealand	0.0	0.5	0.4	0.3	0.2	-0.3	0.3	-0.5	0.0	0.1	0.6	2.1	1.0	0.9	2.1	1.7	1.7	1.4	1.8	2.2
Norway	-4.1	-0.5	0.1	1.9	3.0	2.4	4.4	5.2	4.7	-2.1	-0.7	-0.2	3.8	7.6	8.7	9.3	7.2	7.4	9.5	13.2
Portugal	-2.0	-2.1	-2.6	-4.0	-7.0	-4.8	-3.0	-2.1	-1.5	-1.7	-3.6	-5.5	-4.9	-6.8	-7.9	-9.5	-6.9	-6.2	-7.3	-8.0
Spain	-6.1	-4.1	-5.7	-11.7	-10.0	-9.3	-7.6	-4.3	-4.2	-6.4	-12.8	-18.0	-24.6	-29.5	-30.8	-30.8	-15.7	-15.2	-17.0	-19.9
Sweden	0.3	2.6	-0.7	-2.2	0.1	-0.4	1.9	3.4	2.3	5.1	4.5	4.8	4.0	3.4	6.3	6.7	7.7	9.6	15.8	18.5
Switzerland	0.2	0.6	-1.7	-5.0	-2.5	-1.3	-2.3	-2.3	-2.0	-2.0	-3.1	-3.2	-4.1	-3.2	-2.1	2.7	5.1	5.5	6.1	6.3
Turkey	-3.8	-2.1	-2.6	-4.6	-3.9	-2.7	-3.0	-2.9	-3.0	-3.1	-3.2	-1.8	-4.2	-9.6	-7.3	-8.2	-14.2	-4.1	-3.9	-5.8
Total of smaller countries	-28.2	-19.7	-33.0	-50.8	-40.1	-20.0	-0.3	6.4	0.8	-6.0	-10.0	-15.6	-31.8	-36.6	-34.3	-34.6	-12.4	-6.5	22.9	27.9
Total OECD	-26.9	-0.6	-48.7	-83.9	-40.6	-21.5	-14.0	-40.5	-40.1	-8.5	-24.5	-10.4	-41.3	-49.6	-10.7	17.2	65.5	65.7	80.3	78.8
OECD North America	-28.9	-31.5	-26.2	-21.3	-26.5	-17.4	-39.0	-84.4	-102.5	-133.7	-143.4	-118.6	-111.9	-105.2	-81.7	-110.7	-143.9	-176.7	-186.0	-174.7
OECD Europe	-16.3	5.7	-27.3	-66.4	-32.1	-19.7	-6.8	1.0	7.4	34.1	21.6	11.6	-3.8	-9.3	-37.7	-7.6	66.3	98.5	128.9	120.5
EU	-8.6	7.6	-23.2	-58.8	-28.7	-18.0	-5.9	1.1	7.6	41.1	28.7	16.8	0.6	-4.2	-36.8	-11.5	67.9	89.4	116.8	106.5
Total OECD *less* the United States	4.2	33.3	-21.1	-58.4	-12.5	17.0	53.2	72.0	82.1	136.6	135.0	116.5	74.0	59.4	63.3	113.3	198.1	232.1	283.4	277.1

Annex Table 48. **Non-factor services, net**

$ billion

	1977	1978	1979	1980	1981	1982	1983	1984	1985	1986	1987	1988	1989	1990	1991	1992	1993	1994	Projections 1995	1996
United States	3.9	4.2	3.0	6.1	11.9	12.3	9.3	3.3	0.1	6.3	7.6	12.1	24.9	30.2	45.6	55.7	56.8	60.0	65.6	72.0
Japan	–6.1	–8.3	–11.5	–12.2	–12.8	–11.6	–12.2	–12.0	–12.0	–14.4	–22.4	–32.3	–39.0	–45.5	–44.4	–46.3	–45.4	–49.9	–52.4	–58.5
Germany	–5.3	–5.8	–9.4	–9.3	–7.0	–6.0	–5.5	–3.7	–3.0	–4.3	–8.0	–11.0	–9.4	–13.2	–17.4	–27.3	–31.6	–38.6	–44.6	–45.8
France	4.6	8.1	8.9	9.3	7.0	6.8	7.8	7.1	8.9	9.7	10.0	10.3	12.5	14.2	15.1	17.6	14.7	17.6	22.0	24.1
Italy	2.8	4.1	5.7	4.7	3.6	3.8	5.0	4.6	4.5	5.3	5.1	2.9	0.8	–1.2	–0.1	–4.6	–0.1	1.2	1.4	2.7
United Kingdom	5.3	7.1	8.3	8.5	7.6	5.3	5.8	5.6	8.2	9.1	10.2	7.0	5.5	6.6	6.5	7.2	7.8	7.3	10.2	13.6
Canada	–3.3	–3.2	–2.6	–3.2	–3.2	–3.5	–3.8	–4.1	–4.1	–4.3	–5.3	–5.7	–7.8	–10.3	–11.1	–11.3	–10.9	–8.4	–6.6	–7.5
Total of above countries	1.9	6.2	2.3	4.0	7.1	7.2	6.5	0.8	2.6	7.3	–2.7	–16.5	–12.5	–19.2	–5.7	–9.0	–8.6	–10.8	–4.4	0.6
Australia	–2.1	–2.2	–2.3	–2.6	–3.0	–3.1	–2.6	–3.5	–3.4	–2.9	–2.7	–2.5	–4.5	–3.7	–2.8	–2.8	–1.7	–2.3	–3.2	–3.2
Austria	2.1	3.1	3.6	5.2	3.7	4.3	4.1	3.5	2.9	4.4	5.0	5.3	6.3	8.1	9.3	9.8	7.9	7.7	6.4	6.0
Belgium-Luxembourg	2.0	1.8	1.7	1.5	1.3	1.9	2.1	1.7	1.7	2.8	3.1	3.1	3.1	4.2	4.8	5.7	5.8	9.0	12.0	12.8
Denmark	1.2	1.3	1.4	1.3	1.2	0.9	0.8	0.7	0.7	0.3	0.5	1.2	0.9	2.6	3.9	4.1	2.8	2.4	2.7	3.1
Finland	0.1	0.3	0.3	0.3	0.4	0.3	0.1	–0.2	–0.4	–0.6	–1.0	–1.5	–2.1	–3.0	–3.4	–2.7	–1.8	–1.9	–2.3	–2.9
Greece	1.3	1.7	2.1	2.5	2.3	1.9	1.4	1.4	1.2	1.7	2.7	2.9	2.4	3.6	4.1	5.0	6.6	7.2	8.7	9.9
Iceland	0.1	0.1	0.0	0.0	0.0	0.0	0.1	0.0	0.0	0.1	0.0	0.0	0.0	0.0	0.0	0.0	0.0	0.1	0.1	0.1
Ireland	0.0	–0.1	–0.2	–0.4	–0.2	–0.2	–0.2	–0.2	–0.2	–0.5	–0.8	–1.1	–1.4	–1.2	–1.2	–1.6	–1.6	–1.5	–1.6	–1.6
Mexico	1.2	1.2	1.1	–0.8	–2.2	–0.7	0.8	1.2	1.0	1.2	2.2	2.7	2.9	1.9	2.6	2.7	4.0	3.8	9.3	11.2
Netherlands	1.4	1.2	0.3	0.2	1.0	1.1	0.6	0.6	0.2	–0.9	–0.2	–0.7	0.8	2.2	0.4	0.3	1.0	1.3	3.0	4.1
New Zealand	–0.4	–0.5	–0.6	–0.8	–0.8	–0.8	–0.5	–0.4	–0.3	–0.5	–0.5	–0.6	–0.8	–0.8	–0.9	–1.0	–0.7	–0.4	–0.6	–0.7
Norway	0.2	0.1	1.1	1.6	1.4	0.7	–0.1	–0.2	0.0	–0.5	–1.1	–0.6	0.1	0.4	0.5	–1.2	–0.2	–0.5	–0.8	–0.8
Portugal	0.1	0.3	0.5	0.6	0.5	0.2	0.4	0.5	0.8	0.9	1.2	1.0	1.2	1.4	1.1	0.9	0.9	0.4	0.5	0.8
Spain	3.5	5.1	6.1	6.0	5.9	5.8	6.3	7.6	7.6	11.2	12.9	13.3	12.0	12.2	12.9	13.2	11.8	14.7	17.6	19.3
Sweden	–1.1	–0.9	0.2	0.5	0.2	–0.4	0.0	–0.1	–0.6	–1.9	–1.8	–2.4	–3.2	–3.5	–2.8	–3.0	–0.9	–1.0	–0.5	0.0
Switzerland	0.9	0.6	0.2	0.2	0.3	0.4	0.9	0.8	1.1	1.4	1.7	0.6	0.1	–0.5	0.0	0.4	1.6	1.7	1.9	2.7
Turkey	–0.2	0.2	0.3	0.1	0.8	0.9	0.8	0.9	1.3	1.3	1.8	3.3	3.4	4.2	4.4	4.8	5.6	5.2	6.2	8.1
Total of smaller countries	10.3	13.3	15.9	15.5	12.7	13.3	15.0	14.5	13.5	17.6	23.1	24.1	21.3	27.9	33.1	34.7	41.1	46.0	59.3	69.0
Total OECD	12.1	19.5	18.2	19.5	19.8	20.5	21.4	15.3	16.1	25.0	20.3	7.6	8.8	8.7	27.3	25.8	32.5	35.2	54.9	69.6
OECD North America	1.8	2.2	1.5	2.1	6.5	8.2	6.4	0.4	–3.0	3.2	4.6	9.1	20.0	21.9	37.1	47.1	49.9	55.4	68.3	75.7
OECD Europe	18.9	28.2	31.1	33.0	29.9	27.8	30.4	30.7	34.9	39.5	41.3	33.9	33.0	36.9	38.3	28.9	30.4	32.4	42.9	56.3
EU	17.9	27.3	29.5	31.0	27.3	25.7	28.7	29.2	32.5	37.3	38.9	30.6	29.4	32.8	33.3	24.8	23.5	25.8	35.5	46.2
Total OECD *less* the United States	8.3	15.3	15.2	13.4	7.9	8.2	12.1	12.0	16.0	18.7	12.8	–4.5	–16.1	–21.5	–18.3	–29.9	–24.3	–24.8	–10.7	–2.5

Annex Table 49. **Investment income, net**

$ billion

	1977	1978	1979	1980	1981	1982	1983	1984	1985	1986	1987	1988	1989	1990	1991	1992	1993	1994	Projections 1995	1996
United States	18.0	20.4	30.9	30.1	32.9	29.8	31.1	30.0	19.7	11.8	7.9	11.6	13.7	20.7	14.8	4.5	3.9	-15.2	-20.6	-25.1
Japan	0.1	0.9	2.0	0.9	-0.8	1.7	3.1	4.2	6.8	9.5	16.7	21.0	23.4	23.2	26.7	36.2	41.4	40.9	52.1	59.1
Germany	-1.1	1.4	0.4	1.0	-0.4	-2.0	1.1	3.1	2.7	4.0	3.3	3.7	11.1	16.8	17.9	14.4	11.9	1.9	1.5	1.8
France	0.7	1.4	2.4	3.7	2.6	1.1	-0.5	-1.3	-1.2	-0.5	-0.4	0.1	0.5	-3.0	-5.1	-7.7	-8.1	-9.6	-9.0	-7.7
Italy	-1.1	-1.1	-0.5	-0.6	-3.2	-3.9	-3.9	-3.9	-4.0	-6.2	-6.6	-7.1	-8.3	-14.7	-17.5	-20.8	-16.2	-15.3	-16.4	-21.4
United Kingdom	0.5	1.5	2.6	-0.4	2.5	2.5	4.3	5.8	2.9	6.8	6.1	7.9	5.5	1.7	-0.4	7.5	2.4	17.2	16.2	16.1
Canada	-4.3	-5.2	-6.1	-6.7	-9.5	-10.3	-12.6	-12.3	-12.8	-13.7	-15.4	-19.8	-21.2	-19.6	-16.6	-16.8	-20.7	-23.4	-27.9	-29.8
Total of above countries	12.7	19.4	31.7	27.8	24.2	19.0	22.6	25.6	14.2	11.6	11.7	17.5	24.8	25.3	19.9	17.5	14.7	-3.5	-4.1	-6.9
Australia	-1.7	-2.0	-2.5	-2.7	-2.9	-2.6	-3.3	-4.3	-4.7	-5.0	-6.0	-8.4	-11.4	-13.3	-12.4	-10.4	-8.8	-9.5	-11.6	-13.8
Austria	-0.3	-0.5	-0.5	-0.5	-0.5	-0.4	-0.4	-0.4	-0.3	-0.7	-0.9	-0.9	-0.9	-1.0	-1.5	-1.2	-1.0	-0.9	-1.2	-1.1
Belgium-Luxembourg	0.5	0.6	0.4	-0.1	-0.1	-0.2	-0.2	-0.1	-0.1	0.1	0.4	0.4	1.3	0.8	1.5	0.9	3.0	3.5	3.6	3.1
Denmark	-0.5	-0.9	-1.3	-1.8	-2.0	-2.2	-2.0	-2.2	-2.6	-3.5	-4.1	-4.2	-4.3	-5.7	-5.6	-5.6	-4.7	-4.3	-4.4	-3.7
Finland	-0.6	-0.7	-0.7	-0.9	-1.1	-1.3	-1.2	-1.1	-1.1	-1.4	-1.6	-1.8	-2.7	-3.7	-4.6	-5.4	-5.0	-4.3	-4.0	-3.9
Greece	-0.1	-0.1	-0.2	-0.3	-0.6	-0.7	-0.8	-0.9	-1.1	-1.3	-1.4	-1.5	-1.5	-1.6	-1.7	-2.0	-1.2	-1.6	-1.9	-1.8
Iceland	-0.1	-0.1	-0.1	-0.1	-0.1	-0.1	-0.1	-0.2	-0.1	-0.2	-0.2	-0.2	-0.2	-0.3	-0.3	-0.2	-0.2	-0.2	-0.2	-0.2
Ireland	-0.3	-0.5	-0.7	-0.8	-1.0	-1.5	-1.6	-1.9	-2.2	-2.8	-3.2	-4.2	-4.7	-5.3	-4.7	-5.7	-5.6	-6.2	-7.7	-8.8
Mexico	-2.2	-2.8	-4.0	-6.6	-10.2	-12.4	-9.4	-10.4	-9.3	-7.8	-7.1	-7.6	-8.7	-8.9	-8.9	-9.8	-11.2	-12.3	-12.3	-12.9
Netherlands	0.3	-0.2	-0.2	-0.3	-0.4	-0.1	0.2	-0.1	0.6	0.4	0.2	-0.7	1.3	0.8	1.0	0.1	0.7	2.0	1.3	1.7
New Zealand	-0.4	-0.6	-0.5	-0.5	-0.6	-0.7	-0.9	-1.1	-1.3	-1.5	-2.0	-2.1	-1.9	-1.6	-2.5	-2.0	-2.4	-2.9	-3.5	-3.6
Norway	-0.9	-1.4	-1.8	-1.9	-1.8	-1.9	-1.7	-1.5	-1.0	-1.1	-1.2	-2.0	-2.5	-2.7	-2.6	-3.4	-3.4	-1.7	-1.4	-0.8
Portugal	-0.2	-0.3	-0.4	-0.6	-1.0	-1.3	-1.1	-1.2	-1.2	-1.0	-0.9	-0.9	-0.7	-0.2	0.1	0.6	0.0	-0.1	-0.3	-0.1
Spain	-0.7	-1.0	-1.1	-1.5	-2.3	-2.3	-2.5	-2.4	-1.8	-2.0	-2.8	-3.5	-3.0	-3.8	-4.8	-6.6	-5.1	-9.0	-10.5	-12.1
Sweden	-0.5	-0.7	-0.8	-1.4	-2.2	-1.7	-1.8	-1.9	-2.0	-1.9	-1.4	-1.6	-2.2	-4.3	-6.2	-9.8	-9.0	-6.0	-6.4	-5.7
Switzerland	3.1	4.1	5.0	5.3	6.0	6.0	6.2	6.7	6.8	8.5	10.5	13.3	12.7	14.8	15.3	14.9	14.4	14.2	17.4	18.8
Turkey	-0.3	-0.4	-1.0	-1.1	-1.4	-1.5	-1.4	-1.4	-1.3	-1.6	-1.8	-2.0	-1.7	-1.8	-1.9	-1.6	-1.5	-1.8	-2.3	-2.4
Total of smaller countries	-5.0	-7.5	-10.5	-15.9	-22.3	-24.9	-22.0	-24.4	-22.7	-22.7	-23.6	-27.9	-31.4	-37.7	-39.8	-47.4	-41.2	-41.1	-45.4	-47.4
Total OECD	7.7	11.8	21.2	12.0	1.9	-5.9	0.6	1.1	-8.5	-11.2	-12.0	-10.4	-6.6	-12.5	-19.9	-29.9	-26.5	-44.6	-49.4	-54.3
OECD North America	11.5	12.3	20.8	16.8	13.2	7.1	9.1	7.3	-2.4	-9.8	-14.6	-15.7	-16.2	-7.8	-10.7	-22.1	-27.9	-50.9	-60.8	-67.9
OECD Europe	-1.8	1.1	1.4	-2.3	-6.9	-11.3	-7.4	-5.0	-6.9	-4.3	-6.0	-5.2	-0.5	-13.0	-21.1	-31.7	-28.7	-22.2	-25.7	-28.2
EU	-3.5	-1.1	-0.7	-4.5	-9.6	-13.8	-10.3	-8.5	-11.2	-10.0	-13.3	-14.3	-8.7	-23.0	-31.6	-41.2	-38.0	-32.7	-39.1	-43.6
Total OECD *less* the United States	-10.3	-8.6	-9.7	-18.1	-31.0	-35.7	-30.5	-28.9	-28.1	-22.9	-19.9	-22.0	-20.2	-33.2	-34.7	-34.4	-30.4	-29.4	-28.8	-29.2

Annex Table 50. **Current balances**

$ billion

	1977	1978	1979	1980	1981	1982	1983	1984	1985	1986	1987	1988	1989	1990	1991	1992	1993	1994	Projections 1995	1996
United States	–14.5	–15.1	–0.3	2.3	5.0	–13.4	–44.5	–99.8	–126.4	–151.2	–167.1	–128.2	–102.8	–91.7	–6.9	–68.4	–103.9	–155.7	–193.4	–188.2
Japan	10.9	16.5	–8.8	–10.8	4.8	6.8	20.8	35.0	49.2	85.8	87.0	79.6	57.2	35.8	72.9	117.6	131.4	129.3	134.6	126.6
Germany	3.9	9.1	–5.3	–13.2	–3.6	5.0	4.5	9.8	17.0	40.5	46.1	49.5	57.2	48.9	–19.2	–21.6	–14.7	–23.7	–17.5	–31.2
France	–0.4	7.0	5.2	–4.2	–4.7	–12.2	–4.8	–1.2	–0.3	1.8	–5.0	–4.8	–4.7	–9.8	–6.1	3.9	9.2	9.7	14.5	13.5
Italy	2.3	6.0	5.8	–10.4	–9.6	–7.0	1.0	–2.9	–4.0	2.0	–2.2	–6.3	–11.8	–17.0	–23.6	–27.8	11.3	15.5	14.1	18.6
United Kingdom	–0.3	2.2	–1.0	6.6	13.6	8.1	5.3	2.0	2.9	–1.3	–8.1	–29.6	–36.8	–33.8	–14.4	–17.3	–17.7	–0.3	–1.5	–1.3
Canada	–4.1	–4.3	–4.1	–1.0	–5.1	2.3	–1.4	–0.6	–4.5	–10.1	–11.8	–17.1	–22.8	–21.6	–24.1	–21.9	–23.8	–18.1	–12.5	–9.1
Total of above countries	–2.1	21.4	–8.4	–30.5	0.4	–10.4	–19.1	–57.7	–66.1	–32.4	–61.2	–56.9	–64.6	–89.4	–21.5	–35.5	–8.1	–43.2	–61.7	–71.1
Australia	–3.1	–4.4	–2.6	–4.1	–8.3	–7.9	–5.9	–8.6	–8.7	–9.2	–7.4	–10.0	–17.4	–14.8	–9.8	–10.6	–10.4	–14.9	–20.7	–19.5
Austria	–2.2	–0.7	–1.1	–1.7	–1.3	0.7	0.2	–0.2	–0.1	0.2	–0.2	–0.2	0.2	1.2	0.1	–0.1	–0.9	–2.0	–3.5	–4.3
Belgium-Luxembourg	–0.6	–0.8	–3.1	–4.9	–4.2	–2.4	–0.4	0.0	0.7	3.1	2.8	3.5	3.6	3.7	4.8	6.6	11.3	12.2	16.2	17.2
Denmark	–1.7	–1.4	–3.0	–2.5	–1.9	–2.2	–1.2	–1.6	–2.7	–4.5	–3.0	–1.3	–1.1	1.3	2.2	4.8	5.5	4.4	5.2	6.7
Finland	–0.1	0.7	–0.2	–1.4	–0.5	–1.0	–1.1	0.0	–0.8	–0.7	–1.7	–2.7	–5.8	–6.9	–6.7	–4.9	–1.0	1.1	2.3	1.6
Greece	1.1	–1.0	–1.9	–2.2	–2.4	–1.9	–1.9	–2.1	–3.3	–1.7	–1.2	–1.0	–2.6	–3.5	–1.6	–2.1	–0.7	–0.1	–1.1	–1.6
Iceland	–0.1	0.0	0.0	–0.1	–0.2	–0.3	–0.1	–0.1	–0.1	0.0	–0.2	–0.2	–0.1	–0.1	–0.3	–0.2	0.0	0.1	0.2	0.2
Ireland	–0.5	–0.8	–2.1	–2.1	–2.6	–1.9	–1.2	–1.0	–0.7	–0.8	–0.1	0.1	–0.5	0.1	1.5	2.4	3.7	3.6	4.0	4.1
Mexico	–1.9	–3.2	–5.5	–10.4	–16.2	–5.9	5.9	4.2	0.8	–1.4	4.2	–2.4	–5.8	–7.4	–14.9	–24.8	–23.4	–28.8	–3.9	–2.4
Netherlands	0.6	–1.6	–2.3	–2.9	2.7	4.2	3.9	4.9	5.1	4.9	2.9	5.0	8.0	10.1	7.6	6.8	9.4	12.9	15.0	15.6
New Zealand	–0.8	–0.5	–0.7	–0.9	–1.2	–1.7	–1.0	–1.9	–1.6	–1.7	–1.7	–0.3	–1.3	–1.0	–0.6	–0.7	–0.9	–1.1	–1.3	–1.1
Norway	–5.0	–2.1	–1.0	1.1	2.2	0.6	2.0	2.9	3.1	–4.5	–4.1	–3.9	0.2	3.9	5.1	2.9	2.2	3.6	5.5	9.6
Portugal	–0.9	–0.4	0.0	–1.1	–4.6	–3.1	–1.5	–0.6	0.3	1.2	0.4	–1.0	0.2	–0.2	–0.7	–0.2	0.7	–1.2	0.1	0.2
Spain	–1.9	1.6	1.1	–5.1	–4.8	–4.2	–2.5	2.0	2.7	3.9	–0.1	–3.7	–10.9	–16.9	–16.7	–18.3	–4.2	–5.2	–5.5	–8.1
Sweden	–2.1	–0.2	–2.4	–4.4	–2.9	–3.5	–0.8	0.5	–1.3	–0.1	–0.2	–0.8	–3.4	–6.6	–4.8	–8.7	–4.0	0.9	6.5	10.6
Switzerland	3.5	4.4	2.4	–0.6	2.8	4.1	3.8	4.4	5.0	6.9	7.6	9.0	7.0	8.6	10.6	15.1	18.3	18.1	21.6	23.4
Turkey	–3.1	–1.3	–1.4	–3.4	–1.9	–1.0	–1.8	–1.4	–1.0	–1.5	–0.8	1.6	1.0	–2.6	0.3	–0.9	–6.4	2.6	3.3	3.1
Total of smaller countries	–21.0	–11.8	–23.6	–46.7	–45.4	–27.5	–3.5	1.3	–2.5	–6.0	–2.7	–8.3	–28.7	–31.2	–23.9	–33.0	–0.8	6.2	43.8	55.2
Total OECD	–23.2	9.6	–32.1	–77.2	–45.0	–37.8	–22.6	–56.4	–68.6	–38.4	–63.9	–65.2	–93.3	–120.6	–45.5	–68.6	–8.9	–37.0	–17.9	–15.9
OECD North America	–20.4	–22.6	–9.9	–9.1	–16.3	–17.0	–40.0	–96.2	–130.1	–162.7	–174.6	–147.7	–131.4	–120.8	–45.9	–115.1	–151.1	–202.6	–209.8	–199.7
OECD Europe	–9.8	20.6	–10.2	–52.3	–24.0	–18.0	3.5	15.3	22.6	49.4	32.9	13.2	–0.4	–19.8	–62.0	–59.8	22.0	52.2	79.3	77.8
EU	–5.0	19.5	–10.1	–49.4	–26.9	–21.5	–0.5	9.5	15.5	48.5	30.4	6.7	–8.5	–29.5	–77.7	–76.6	7.9	27.8	48.8	41.6
Total OECD *less* the United States	–8.7	24.7	–31.8	–79.5	–50.0	–24.4	21.9	43.4	57.7	112.8	103.2	63.0	9.5	–28.9	–38.5	–0.2	95.0	118.7	175.5	172.3

Note: The balance-of-payments data in this table are derived from OECD countries' submissions and publications. They are based on the concepts and definitions of the IMF *Balance of Payments Manual.*

Annex Table 51. **Current balances as a percentage of GDP**

	1977	1978	1979	1980	1981	1982	1983	1984	1985	1986	1987	1988	1989	1990	1991	1992	1993	1994	Projections 1995	Projections 1996
United States	–0.7	–0.7	0.0	0.1	0.2	–0.4	–1.3	–2.6	–3.1	–3.5	–3.7	–2.6	–2.0	–1.7	–0.1	–1.1	–1.6	–2.3	–2.7	–2.5
Japan	1.6	1.7	–0.9	–1.0	0.4	0.6	1.8	2.8	3.6	4.3	3.6	2.7	2.0	1.2	2.2	3.2	3.1	2.8	2.5	2.2
Germany	0.8	1.4	–0.7	–1.6	–0.5	0.8	0.7	1.6	2.7	4.5	4.2	4.2	4.8	3.3	–1.1	–1.1	–0.8	–1.1	–0.7	–1.2
France	–0.1	1.4	0.9	–0.6	–0.8	–2.2	–0.9	–0.2	–0.1	0.2	–0.6	–0.5	–0.5	–0.8	–0.5	0.3	0.7	0.7	0.9	0.8
Italy	1.0	2.0	1.6	–2.3	–2.3	–1.7	0.2	–0.7	–0.9	0.3	–0.3	–0.8	–1.4	–1.6	–2.1	–2.3	1.2	1.5	1.3	1.6
United Kingdom	–0.1	0.7	–0.2	1.2	2.5	1.7	1.2	0.4	0.6	–0.2	–1.2	–3.5	–4.4	–3.5	–1.4	–1.6	–1.9	0.0	–0.1	–0.1
Canada	–2.0	–2.0	–1.8	–0.4	–1.7	0.8	–0.4	–0.2	–1.3	–2.8	–2.8	–3.5	–4.1	–3.8	–4.1	–3.8	–4.3	–3.3	–2.2	–1.5
Total of above countries	–0.1	0.4	–0.1	–0.5	0.0	–0.2	–0.3	–0.8	–0.9	–0.3	–0.6	–0.5	–0.5	–0.6	–0.1	–0.2	0.0	–0.2	–0.3	–0.3
Australia	–3.0	–3.8	–2.0	–2.7	–4.8	–4.7	–3.6	–4.7	–5.4	–5.4	–3.7	–4.0	–6.2	–5.0	–3.3	–3.7	–3.7	–4.6	–6.0	–5.3
Austria	–4.5	–1.2	–1.6	–2.1	–2.0	1.1	0.3	–0.3	–0.2	0.3	–0.2	–0.2	0.2	0.7	0.1	–0.1	–0.5	–1.0	–1.4	–1.7
Belgium-Luxembourg	–0.7	–0.9	–2.8	–4.2	–4.4	–2.7	–0.5	–0.1	0.9	2.8	2.0	2.3	2.3	1.9	2.4	3.0	5.4	5.4	5.8	5.8
Denmark	–3.7	–2.5	–4.5	–3.7	–3.2	–4.0	–2.1	–3.0	–4.7	–5.5	–2.9	–1.2	–1.1	1.0	1.7	3.4	4.1	3.0	2.9	3.5
Finland	–0.3	1.9	–0.3	–2.7	–1.0	–2.0	–2.3	–0.1	–1.4	–1.0	–1.9	–2.6	–5.1	–5.1	–5.5	–4.6	–1.1	1.1	1.8	1.2
Greece	–3.4	–2.5	–4.1	–4.6	–5.4	–4.2	–4.5	–5.3	–8.2	–3.5	–2.2	–1.5	–3.9	–4.3	–1.8	–2.2	–0.8	–0.1	–1.0	–1.3
Iceland	–2.6	0.9	–0.9	–2.4	–4.4	–8.3	–2.2	–4.8	–3.9	0.5	–3.5	–3.6	–1.5	–2.2	–4.7	–3.1	0.0	2.2	2.4	2.0
Ireland	–5.0	–6.2	–12.3	–10.5	–13.4	–9.3	–5.9	–5.5	–3.4	–3.1	–0.3	0.2	–1.4	0.2	3.3	4.8	7.7	6.9	6.6	6.1
Mexico	–2.2	–2.9	–3.9	–5.4	–6.5	–2.2	5.1	2.6	0.8	–0.9	3.0	–1.4	–2.9	–3.1	–5.2	–7.6	–6.5	–7.8	–1.5	–0.7
Netherlands	0.5	–1.1	–1.4	–1.7	1.9	3.0	2.9	3.8	3.9	2.8	1.3	2.2	3.5	3.5	2.6	2.1	3.1	3.9	3.8	3.7
New Zealand	–5.6	–2.9	–3.5	–4.4	–5.0	–7.2	–4.4	–8.6	–7.1	–6.3	–4.9	–0.7	–3.1	–2.2	–1.5	–1.7	–2.1	–2.1	–2.1	–1.7
Norway	–14.0	–5.2	–2.2	1.9	3.8	1.1	3.7	5.3	5.4	–6.5	–4.8	–4.3	0.3	3.5	4.8	2.5	2.1	3.3	4.1	6.8
Portugal	–5.0	–2.1	–0.2	–3.8	–16.8	–11.7	–6.1	–2.6	1.4	3.4	1.1	–2.2	0.3	–0.3	–0.8	–0.2	0.8	–1.3	0.1	0.2
Spain	–1.4	1.0	0.6	–2.4	–2.6	–2.4	–1.6	1.3	1.6	1.7	0.0	–1.1	–2.9	–3.4	–3.2	–3.2	–0.8	–1.1	–1.0	–1.3
Sweden	–2.6	–0.3	–2.2	–3.5	–2.6	–3.6	–0.9	0.6	–1.4	–0.1	–0.1	–0.4	–1.8	–2.8	–2.0	–3.5	–2.1	0.4	2.9	4.5
Switzerland	5.7	5.1	2.6	–0.5	3.0	4.2	4.0	4.8	5.4	5.0	4.4	4.9	4.0	3.8	4.6	6.2	7.9	6.9	6.8	6.9
Turkey	–5.1	–1.8	–2.0	–5.0	–2.6	–1.4	–2.9	–2.4	–1.5	–1.9	–0.9	2.0	0.9	–1.7	0.2	–0.6	–3.7	2.1	2.1	1.6
Total of smaller countries	–2.2	–1.0	–1.8	–3.1	–3.1	–2.0	–0.3	0.1	–0.2	–0.4	–0.1	–0.4	–1.2	–1.1	–0.8	–1.0	0.0	0.2	1.2	1.4
Total OECD	–0.4	0.2	–0.4	–1.0	–0.6	–0.5	–0.3	–0.7	–0.8	–0.3	–0.5	–0.5	–0.6	–0.7	–0.3	–0.4	0.0	–0.2	–0.1	–0.1
OECD North America	–0.9	–0.9	–0.3	–0.3	–0.5	–0.5	–1.0	–2.3	–2.9	–3.4	–3.4	–2.7	–2.2	–1.9	–0.7	–1.7	–2.1	–2.6	–2.6	–2.4
OECD Europe	–0.5	0.8	–0.3	–1.4	–0.7	–0.6	0.1	0.5	0.8	1.2	0.7	0.2	0.0	–0.3	–0.8	–0.7	0.3	0.7	0.9	0.8
EU	–0.3	0.8	–0.3	–1.5	–0.9	–0.7	0.0	0.4	0.6	1.3	0.6	0.1	–0.2	–0.4	–1.1	–1.0	0.1	0.4	0.6	0.5
Total OECD *less* the United States	–0.3	0.6	–0.7	–1.5	–1.0	–0.5	0.5	0.9	1.2	1.7	1.3	0.7	0.1	–0.3	–0.3	0.0	0.7	0.9	1.1	1.0

Annex Table 52. **Structure of current account balances of major world regions**[a]

$ billion

	1977	1978	1979	1980	1981	1982	1983	1984	1985	1986	1987	1988	1989	1990	1991	1992	1993	1994	Projections 1995	1996
Trade balance																				
OECD	–27	–1	–49	–84	–41	–21	–14	–41	–40	–9	–25	–10	–41	–50	–11	17	66	66	80	79
Non-OECD *of which:*	52	24	84	122	66	24	24	52	42	13	48	32	39	41	24	6	–15	–16	–10	–11
OPEC	64	50	118	175	127	66	46	54	55	10	28	18	42	73	43	37	43	39	46	44
ANIEs[b]	–2	–4	–8	–11	–11	–8	–3	4	9	19	26	22	19	7	3	2	2	–4	–7	–6
Other Asia[c]	–8	–14	–19	–28	–31	–28	–30	–27	–38	–30	–23	–29	–29	–23	–22	–24	–41	–38	–37	–36
Latin America[c]	1	–1	–4	–9	–7	–4	6	14	15	9	7	20	19	16	10	4	–4	–5	–6	–4
Africa[c]	–2	–5	–3	–5	–15	–13	–8	–8	–4	–3	–4	–8	–10	–11	–10	–14	–14	–15	–16	–16
Central and Eastern Europe	0	–3	–1	1	3	11	13	14	6	8	14	9	–3	–20	1	1	0	6	9	7
World[d]	25	23	35	38	25	3	10	12	2	4	23	21	–2	–9	13	24	51	50	70	67
Services and private transfers, net																				
OECD	18	28	37	30	19	8	14	9	–1	4	–1	–13	–6	–15	–6	–21	–11	–30	–14	–7
Non-OECD *of which:*	–41	–48	–60	–73	–92	–92	–81	–82	–75	–60	–55	–58	–67	–72	–92	–83	–82	–92	–104	–111
OPEC	–37	–44	–51	–64	–73	–72	–62	–60	–53	–39	–40	–39	–45	–52	–70	–67	–68	–66	–66	–70
ANIEs[b]	4	4	4	3	5	7	6	4	3	6	7	8	8	10	10	13	16	15	15	14
Other Asia[c]	3	4	4	10	8	9	8	5	6	6	5	3	3	4	5	3	0	0	–2	–2
Latin America[c]	–8	–9	–12	–14	–22	–27	–25	–25	–23	–23	–21	–23	–25	–24	–21	–17	–20	–24	–33	–34
Africa[c]	–5	–4	–5	–7	–8	–8	–7	–6	–6	–9	–7	–6	–6	–7	–5	–2	–1	–2	–3	–4
Central and Eastern Europe	2	2	1	–1	–2	–2	–1	0	–1	–1	–1	–1	–1	–2	–11	–12	–9	–14	–15	–16
World[d]	–23	–20	–23	–43	–73	–84	–67	–73	–75	–56	–56	–71	–73	–87	–98	–105	–93	–122	–119	–118
Official transfers, net																				
OECD	–14	–18	–20	–23	–23	–25	–23	–25	–28	–34	–38	–42	–46	–56	–28	–65	–64	–73	–84	–87
Non-OECD *of which:*	4	2	5	2	5	5	6	8	12	13	15	16	17	12	–5	23	25	23	22	23
OPEC	–4	–6	–6	–9	–8	–6	–6	–5	–4	–3	–1	–1	–1	–10	–34	–2	0	–1	–1	–1
ANIEs[b]	0	0	0	0	0	0	0	0	0	0	0	0	0	0	0	0	0	0	0	0
Other Asia[c]	5	5	7	7	8	8	7	7	9	9	8	8	8	9	9	9	8	8	8	9
Latin America[c]	0	0	1	1	1	1	1	1	1	1	2	2	2	3	4	4	4	3	3	3
Africa[c]	3	3	3	4	4	3	4	4	5	6	6	7	8	10	11	9	8	8	9	10
Central and Eastern Europe	0	0	0	0	0	0	0	0	0	0	0	0	0	0	6	4	4	4	3	2
World[d]	–10	–15	–15	–21	–19	–19	–16	–17	–16	–21	–24	–26	–29	–44	–33	–41	–39	–50	–62	–65
Current balance																				
OECD	–23	10	–32	–77	–45	–38	–23	–56	–69	–38	–64	–65	–93	–121	–45	–69	–9	–37	–18	–16
Non-OECD *of which:*	15	–22	29	52	–22	–62	–50	–22	–21	–34	7	–11	–11	–19	–73	–54	–72	–85	–93	–100
OPEC	23	0	61	102	46	–11	–22	–10	–3	–33	–13	–23	–4	10	–62	–32	–25	–28	–21	–27
ANIEs[b]	2	0	–4	–8	–6	–2	3	8	12	25	33	31	27	17	13	14	17	11	7	8
Other Asia[c]	0	–6	–7	–11	–15	–11	–15	–14	–23	–15	–10	–17	–18	–10	–8	–13	–33	–30	–30	–30
Latin America[c]	–7	–10	–15	–23	–29	–30	–18	–10	–7	–13	–12	–1	–4	–6	–7	–9	–20	–25	–36	–34
Africa[c]	–4	–6	–5	–8	–19	–18	–10	–10	–5	–6	–4	–7	–9	–8	–5	–8	–7	–9	–10	–10
Central and Eastern Europe	2	–1	0	0	1	9	12	14	5	8	14	8	–4	–23	–4	–6	–5	–4	–3	–7
World[d]	–8	–13	–3	–25	–67	–100	–73	–79	–89	–72	–57	–76	–105	–140	–119	–122	–81	–122	–111	–116

a) Historical data for the OECD area are aggregates of reported balance of payments data by each individual country. Because of various statistical problems as well as a large number of non-reporters among non-OECD countries, trade and current balances estimated on the basis of these countries' own balance of payments records may differ from corresponding estimates shown in this table.
b) ANIEs include Chinese Taipei, Hong Kong, Korea and Singapore.
c) Not including OPEC countries.
d) Reflects statistical errors and asymmetries. Given the very large gross flows of world balance of payments transactions, statistical errors and asymmetries easily give rise to world totals (balances) that are significantly different from zero.

Annex Table 53. **Stocks of foreign assets and liabilities**

$ billion, end period

	1981	1982	1983	1984	1985	1986	1987	1988	1989	1990	1991	1992	1993
							Assets [a]						
Major seven countries													
United States	899	999	1 124	1 135	1 211	1 366	1 498	1 666	1 874	1 964	2 044	2 062	2 268
Japan	209	228	272	341	438	727	1 072	1 469	1 771	1 858	2 007	2 035	2 180
Germany	244	249	238	239	336	495	657	682	856	1 091	1 138	1 168	1 268
France [b]	169	180	179	182	215	255	337	339	472	707	724	802	851
Italy	96	87	95	103	119	156	195	209	269	352	398	371	416
United Kingdom	623	667	700	716	853	1 058	1 295	1 397	1 534	1 738	1 764	1 777	2 033
Canada	70	75	76	82	86	98	117	144	164	182	198	190	207
Selected other OECD countries													
Australia [c]	11	16	20	19	19	27	40	59	68	72	72	68	73
Belgium-Luxembourg	192	191	188	195	254	337	447	435	523	658	..	..	..
Denmark	15	15	17	18	30	38	53	59	68	94	107	110	120
Finland	10	11	11	14	18	21	30	32	36	47	46	42	44
Netherlands	114	136	132	131	167	214	271	275	324	391	423	431	..
Norway	17	18	17	20	28	32	41	38	41	48	47	46	..
Spain	40	33	31	39	42	52	74	82	98	130	158	163	208
Sweden [b]	22	21	24	23	28	34	48	56	101	141	151	132	136
Total of above countries	2 732	2 926	3 124	3 257	3 845	4 910	6 175	6 944	8 199	9 475	..	..	..
							Liabilities						
Major seven countries													
United States	630	740	867	991	1 171	1 434	1 648	1 918	2 230	2 318	2 487	2 658	2 926
Japan	198	203	235	267	308	547	831	1 178	1 478	1 530	1 623	1 522	1 570
Germany	221	223	210	201	289	405	496	480	594	744	819	891	1 047
France [b]	141	191	198	203	227	254	334	348	497	761	824	874	890
Italy	111	108	113	120	151	192	239	258	342	465	529	510	525
United Kingdom	568	602	625	629	753	916	1 184	1 285	1 446	1 744	1 761	1 748	1 998
Canada	185	186	192	198	210	235	273	319	357	394	430	422	444
Selected other OECD countries													
Australia [c]	52	54	64	68	76	93	130	170	189	203	217	209	225
Belgium-Luxembourg	192	194	192	198	258	340	448	431	515	646	..	..	..
Denmark	33	34	36	39	58	75	99	104	114	143	163	158	279
Finland	19	20	21	24	28	34	48	53	63	84	90	89	92
Netherlands	92	108	103	101	137	179	229	233	282	343	373	389	..
Norway	32	32	29	29	35	43	57	59	62	66	62	57	..
Spain	58	54	52	55	59	68	94	109	138	201	253	264	288
Sweden [b]	36	39	44	43	53	63	84	101	142	202	219	209	216
Total of above countries	2 569	2 788	2 980	3 165	3 812	4 877	6 194	7 045	8 448	9 844	..	..	..

a) Excluding monetary gold.
b) As from 1989 due to change in concept and definitions, the figures are not comparable with those of previous periods.
c) Fiscal year ending end-June.

Annex Table 54. **Semiannual demand and output projections**

Percentage changes from previous period, seasonally adjusted at annual rates, volume

	1994	1995	1996	1994 I	1994 II	1995 I	1995 II	1996 I	1996 II
Private consumption									
United States	3.5	2.7	1.9	3.6	3.1	2.6	2.3	1.7	1.9
Japan	2.2	2.3	3.1	3.0	1.3	2.5	3.0	3.1	3.3
Germany	1.3	1.0	3.0	1.9	–0.5	0.8	2.8	3.0	3.2
France	1.5	2.2	3.4	1.1	2.5	1.5	3.1	3.4	3.5
Italy	1.6	1.7	2.2	2.3	1.7	1.7	1.6	2.4	2.6
United Kingdom	2.6	2.4	2.8	2.1	1.9	2.5	2.8	2.8	2.7
Canada	3.1	2.7	3.2	3.8	2.8	2.5	3.0	3.2	3.3
Major seven countries	2.6	2.3	2.5	2.9	2.1	2.2	2.6	2.4	2.6
OECD North America	3.5	2.0	1.9	3.6	3.3	1.5	1.7	1.9	2.2
OECD Europe	1.4	1.8	2.8	1.4	1.2	1.7	2.5	2.9	2.9
EU	1.7	1.8	2.8	1.9	1.4	1.7	2.4	2.8	2.9
Total OECD	2.4	2.0	2.5	2.7	2.2	1.8	2.3	2.5	2.7
Public consumption									
United States	–0.7	–0.3	0.3	–2.8	1.9	–1.7	0.3	0.2	0.3
Japan	2.8	3.3	2.4	2.1	3.0	2.7	4.6	1.6	1.8
Germany	1.2	1.8	1.3	1.8	1.6	2.2	1.2	1.2	1.4
France	1.0	0.9	1.1	0.2	1.2	0.8	0.9	1.1	1.1
Italy	0	0.4	0.3	–0.1	0.8	0.3	0.3	0.3	0.3
United Kingdom	1.6	1.1	1.2	1.6	1.2	1.0	1.0	1.3	1.3
Canada	–2.1	–1.0	–0.3	–2.4	–2.7	–0.5	–0.3	–0.5	0.1
Major seven countries	0.4	0.8	0.9	–0.6	1.7	0.1	1.2	0.7	0.8
OECD North America	–0.6	–1.0	0.1	–2.3	1.2	–2.4	–0.3	0.2	0.5
OECD Europe	0.7	0.9	0.9	0.6	0.9	0.9	0.8	0.9	1.0
EU	0.9	1.0	0.9	0.8	1.1	1.0	0.8	0.9	0.9
Total OECD	0.5	0.5	0.7	–0.2	1.2	0	0.9	0.6	0.8
Investment									
United States	12.3	10.5	4.9	13.0	9.8	12.2	8.1	4.3	3.0
Japan	–2.3	1.9	3.2	–4.6	1.2	0.8	5.0	2.5	2.7
Germany	4.3	6.5	5.9	5.9	5.9	7.2	5.9	5.9	5.9
France	1.1	5.8	5.8	1.3	5.5	5.7	6.4	5.7	5.5
Italy	–0.1	5.4	7.1	2.4	1.3	6.8	7.0	6.9	7.5
United Kingdom	3.2	4.2	4.6	4.9	0.3	5.8	4.9	4.6	4.3
Canada	6.0	5.1	5.9	5.9	5.9	4.4	5.6	5.9	6.0
Major seven countries	6.1	7.1	4.9	6.4	6.0	7.9	6.7	4.5	4.0
OECD North America	11.5	8.0	5.0	12.7	8.3	8.9	6.2	4.9	4.4
OECD Europe	1.5	5.6	5.8	2.4	3.0	6.7	6.1	5.7	5.6
EU	2.2	5.9	6.0	3.6	4.1	6.7	6.2	5.9	5.9
Total OECD	5.4	6.1	5.0	6.0	5.3	6.7	6.0	4.9	4.6
Total domestic demand									
United States	4.7	3.3	1.8	5.1	4.4	3.2	2.3	1.6	1.6
Japan	1.0	2.4	3.1	1.0	1.5	2.1	4.0	2.9	2.9
Germany	2.6	2.5	3.3	3.3	1.9	2.5	3.2	3.3	3.5
France	2.9	3.2	3.6	5.0	3.4	2.8	3.8	3.6	3.5
Italy	1.9	2.4	2.6	2.5	4.8	1.7	1.6	2.9	3.2
United Kingdom	3.0	2.8	2.8	3.3	2.0	3.1	2.9	2.8	2.7
Canada	2.9	2.6	3.1	3.4	2.1	2.7	2.9	3.1	3.4
Major seven countries	3.3	2.9	2.5	3.8	3.3	2.8	2.8	2.4	2.4
OECD North America	4.6	2.3	1.9	5.1	4.0	1.8	1.5	2.0	2.2
OECD Europe	1.9	2.8	3.2	2.4	2.3	2.9	3.1	3.2	3.2
EU	2.4	2.8	3.1	3.4	3.0	2.6	2.9	3.2	3.2
Total OECD	3.0	2.5	2.6	3.5	3.0	2.3	2.6	2.6	2.7

Annex Table 54. *(cont'd)* **Semiannual demand and output projections**

Percentage changes from previous period, seasonally adjusted at annual rates, volume

	1994	1995	1996	1994 I	1994 II	1995 I	1995 II	1996 I	1996 II
Exports of goods and services									
United States	9.0	9.0	10.0	7.2	16.6	5.6	8.9	10.3	10.6
Japan	5.0	3.5	4.9	8.8	6.8	2.0	3.3	5.5	5.4
Germany	7.2	7.6	5.5	13.1	3.9	10.0	6.7	5.3	4.9
France	5.8	6.8	6.3	3.7	6.9	7.0	6.4	6.2	6.2
Italy	10.9	11.0	8.2	13.1	9.9	11.7	10.8	7.7	6.7
United Kingdom	8.9	9.1	7.7	8.3	12.7	8.0	7.9	7.8	7.5
Canada	14.4	13.4	7.2	11.2	26.3	10.5	7.9	7.1	6.8
Major seven countries	8.2	8.0	7.9	8.5	12.3	6.3	7.5	8.1	8.0
OECD North America	9.4	10.0	9.9	7.4	16.7	7.3	9.3	10.0	10.1
OECD Europe	8.9	8.8	7.1	10.1	9.0	9.2	7.9	6.9	6.6
EU	8.8	8.6	6.9	9.9	8.7	9.1	7.7	6.8	6.4
Total OECD	8.5	8.4	8.0	8.8	11.8	7.2	7.8	8.1	8.0
Imports of goods and services									
United States	13.4	8.8	5.2	13.4	15.3	7.3	6.0	4.9	5.0
Japan	8.3	10.8	9.9	9.2	10.6	10.5	11.5	9.5	9.2
Germany	6.1	6.0	7.9	10.4	3.4	6.5	7.5	8.0	8.2
France	6.6	7.5	7.7	9.7	6.3	7.9	7.9	7.7	7.6
Italy	9.8	9.4	7.4	12.1	14.3	8.0	7.5	7.4	7.5
United Kingdom	5.9	6.6	7.0	6.4	5.3	7.0	7.2	7.0	6.8
Canada	9.6	10.2	6.7	7.6	15.3	9.5	6.8	6.7	6.6
Major seven countries	10.2	8.7	6.9	11.2	11.7	7.9	7.5	6.7	6.7
OECD North America	13.1	6.7	5.6	14.2	13.8	4.7	4.2	5.9	6.9
OECD Europe	6.2	7.6	7.7	7.5	7.0	8.0	8.1	7.6	7.4
EU	7.4	7.5	7.5	9.5	8.2	7.2	7.4	7.6	7.6
Total OECD	9.6	7.8	7.1	10.7	10.8	7.0	7.0	7.1	7.4
GDP									
United States	4.1	3.2	2.3	4.3	4.3	3.0	2.6	2.3	2.2
Japan	0.6	1.3	2.3	1.0	1.0	0.8	2.7	2.2	2.3
Germany	2.9	2.9	2.7	3.8	2.0	3.3	3.0	2.6	2.6
France	2.7	3.0	3.2	3.3	3.6	2.5	3.4	3.1	3.1
Italy	2.2	3.0	2.9	2.8	3.7	2.8	2.7	3.0	3.0
United Kingdom	3.8	3.4	3.0	4.0	3.8	3.4	3.1	3.0	2.9
Canada	4.5	3.9	3.4	4.8	5.9	3.1	3.4	3.3	3.5
Major seven countries	3.0	2.8	2.6	3.4	3.4	2.6	2.8	2.5	2.5
OECD North America	4.1	2.8	2.5	4.2	4.5	2.3	2.3	2.5	2.6
OECD Europe	2.4	3.0	3.0	2.9	2.7	3.2	3.1	3.0	2.9
EU	2.7	3.0	2.9	3.5	3.1	3.1	3.0	2.9	2.9
Total OECD	2.9	2.7	2.7	3.2	3.2	2.5	2.7	2.7	2.7
Nominal GDP									
United States	6.2	5.3	5.1	6.8	6.5	5.0	4.8	5.1	5.2
Japan	0.7	1.0	2.6	1.4	-0.6	1.0	2.6	2.5	2.7
Germany	5.1	5.1	5.1	6.2	3.7	5.7	5.4	4.9	5.1
France	4.2	5.0	5.2	4.8	5.1	4.6	5.4	5.1	5.3
Italy	5.9	7.4	7.5	6.0	8.2	7.1	7.4	7.7	7.3
United Kingdom	5.9	5.8	5.8	5.9	5.7	5.8	5.7	5.7	5.8
Canada	5.2	6.1	5.7	5.0	6.9	5.8	5.9	5.6	5.7
Major seven countries	4.8	4.7	4.9	5.4	4.9	4.5	4.8	4.9	5.0
OECD North America	6.5	6.7	6.6	6.5	7.7	6.4	6.4	6.7	6.7
OECD Europe	9.7	9.4	7.9	11.1	9.8	9.7	8.6	7.8	7.4
OECD Europe *less* Turkey	5.4	6.0	5.9	6.1	5.7	6.1	6.0	5.9	5.9
EU	5.5	6.0	6.0	6.1	5.7	6.1	6.0	5.9	5.9
Total OECD	6.9	6.9	6.5	7.6	7.3	6.9	6.8	6.5	6.4
Total OECD *less* Turkey	5.2	5.5	5.7	5.6	5.6	5.5	5.7	5.7	5.8

Annex Figure 1. Recent consumer-price developments[1]

OECD area[2]

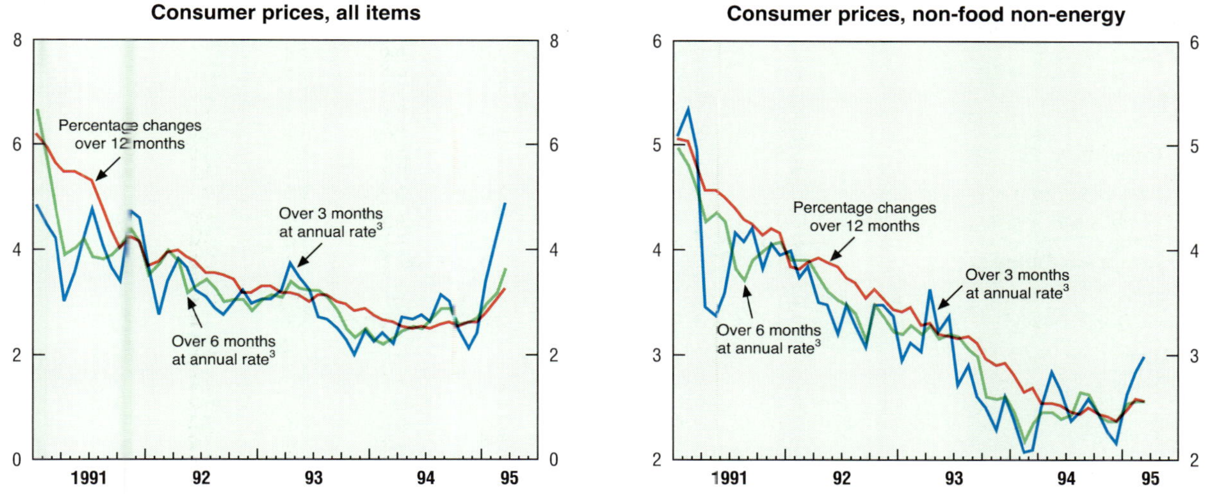

Individual countries

Non-food non-energy prices

Percentage changes from corresponding month of previous year

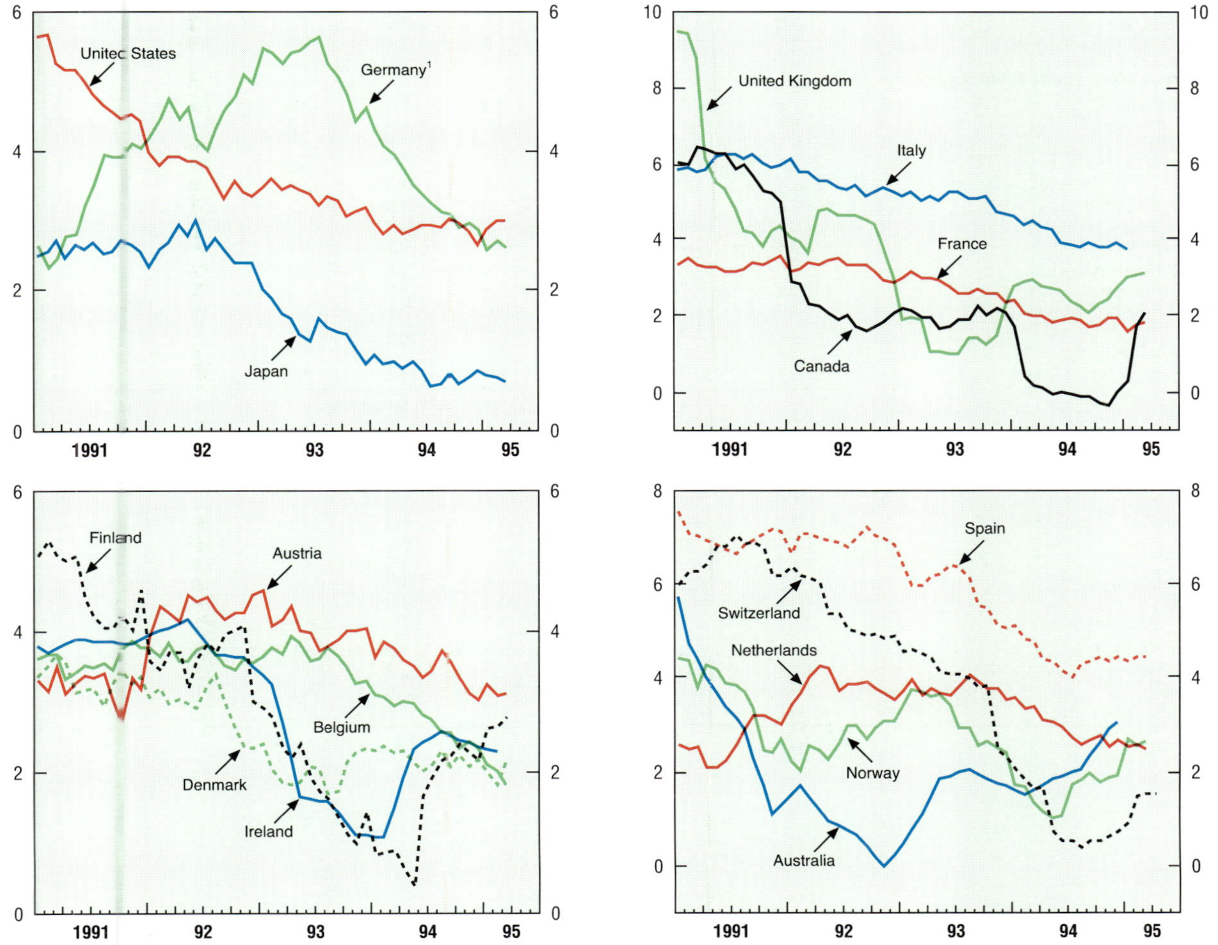

1. Data used for Germany concern western Germany.
2. Excluding Turkey.
3. Seasonally adjusted.

Annex Table 55. **Semiannual price, cost and unemployment projections**

Percentage changes from previous period, seasonally adjusted at annual rates

	1994	1995	1996	1994 I	1994 II	1995 I	1995 II	1996 I	1996 II
Private consumption deflator									
United States	2.1	2.8	3.4	2.0	2.8	2.5	3.2	3.4	3.5
Japan	0.3	–0.6	0	0.8	–1.2	–0.2	–0.7	0.2	0.3
Germany	2.7	2.3	2.1	2.4	2.9	2.1	1.9	2.2	2.3
France	1.8	1.6	1.7	1.9	1.5	1.7	1.6	1.7	1.9
Italy	4.7	5.4	4.7	4.6	4.6	6.1	4.9	4.7	4.4
United Kingdom	2.5	2.9	3.1	2.3	2.6	2.9	3.0	3.1	3.2
Canada	0.7	2.0	2.0	0.1	1.0	2.4	2.2	1.9	1.9
Major seven countries	2.0	2.2	2.5	2.0	2.0	2.2	2.3	2.6	2.7
OECD North America	2.3	4.8	4.8	2.1	3.0	5.6	5.3	4.7	4.6
OECD Europe	7.5	6.4	4.7	8.3	7.4	6.6	5.4	4.7	4.3
OECD Europe *less* Turkey	3.1	3.1	2.9	3.0	3.1	3.2	2.9	2.9	2.9
EU	3.2	3.1	2.9	3.1	3.1	3.2	2.9	2.9	3.0
Total OECD	4.1	4.6	4.0	4.4	4.1	5.1	4.4	4.0	3.8
Total OECD *less* Turkey	2.3	3.3	3.3	2.2	2.4	3.7	3.4	3.3	3.3
GDP deflator									
United States	2.1	2.0	2.7	2.4	2.1	2.0	2.2	2.8	2.9
Japan	0.1	–0.3	0.2	0.4	–1.6	0.3	–0.1	0.3	0.4
Germany	2.2	2.1	2.3	2.3	1.7	2.3	2.3	2.3	2.4
France	1.5	1.9	2.0	1.4	1.5	2.0	2.0	1.9	2.2
Italy	3.6	4.3	4.5	3.1	4.3	4.2	4.6	4.5	4.2
United Kingdom	2.0	2.3	2.7	1.8	1.8	2.4	2.6	2.7	2.9
Canada	0.6	2.1	2.2	0.2	1.0	2.6	2.4	2.2	2.1
Major seven countries	1.7	1.8	2.3	1.9	1.4	1.9	2.0	2.3	2.4
OECD North America	2.3	3.8	4.0	2.2	3.1	4.0	4.0	4.1	4.0
OECD Europe	7.1	6.2	4.7	8.0	6.9	6.4	5.4	4.7	4.3
OECD Europe *less* Turkey	2.6	2.8	2.9	2.5	2.5	2.9	3.0	2.9	2.9
EU	2.7	2.9	2.9	2.5	2.6	3.0	3.0	2.9	3.0
Total OECD	3.9	4.1	3.7	4.3	3.9	4.4	3.9	3.8	3.6
Total OECD *less* Turkey	2.1	2.8	3.0	2.0	2.1	3.0	3.0	3.0	3.0
Unit labour costs (total economy)									
United States	1.8	2.3	2.5	2.3	1.3	2.9	1.9	2.7	2.9
Japan	1.3	1.7	0.9	0.8	1.7	2.2	0.7	0.9	0.9
Germany	–0.7	0.6	2.2	–1.9	0	0.5	1.6	2.7	1.9
France	–0.2	1.4	1.5	–0.7	–0.1	2.2	1.4	1.4	1.8
Italy	–0.4	1.8	2.6	–1.2	–0.2	2.3	2.9	2.5	2.5
United Kingdom	–0.2	1.1	2.5	0	–0.8	1.5	2.1	2.5	2.8
Canada	–1.3	0.3	1.5	–1.2	–2.0	0.9	1.3	1.6	1.5
Major seven countries	0.8	1.7	2.1	0.8	0.7	2.2	1.7	2.2	2.3
OECD North America	1.9	3.4	3.6	2.4	1.6	4.4	3.3	3.6	3.7
OECD Europe	3.8	4.7	4.0	3.8	3.5	5.4	4.5	4.1	3.6
OECD Europe *less* Turkey	0	1.5	2.3	–0.6	0.4	1.7	2.2	2.3	2.2
EU	0	1.5	2.3	–0.6	0.4	1.7	2.3	2.4	2.3
Total OECD	2.6	3.7	3.3	2.7	2.3	4.5	3.4	3.4	3.2
Total OECD *less* Turkey	1.0	2.4	2.6	1.0	1.1	3.0	2.5	2.7	2.7
	Per cent of labour force								
Unemployment									
United States	6.1	5.6	5.7	6.4	5.8	5.6	5.7	5.7	5.8
Japan	2.9	3.1	3.1	2.9	2.9	3.1	3.1	3.1	3.1
Germany	9.6	9.2	8.7	9.7	9.5	9.3	9.0	8.8	8.7
France	12.4	12.0	11.5	12.4	12.4	12.2	11.9	11.6	11.4
Italy	11.3	11.1	10.5	11.1	11.4	11.2	11.0	10.7	10.3
United Kingdom	9.2	8.2	7.6	9.6	8.9	8.3	8.0	7.7	7.4
Canada	10.4	9.4	9.1	10.8	9.9	9.6	9.2	9.1	9.0
Major seven countries	7.2	6.8	6.6	7.3	7.0	6.9	6.8	6.7	6.6
OECD North America	6.3	6.0	6.0	6.6	6.0	5.9	6.0	6.0	6.0
OECD Europe	11.3	11.0	10.6	11.3	11.2	11.1	10.9	10.7	10.5
EU	11.5	11.1	10.6	11.6	11.4	11.2	11.0	10.7	10.4
Total OECD	8.1	7.8	7.6	8.2	7.9	7.9	7.8	7.7	7.6

Annex Figure 2. **Capacity utilisation in manufacturing**

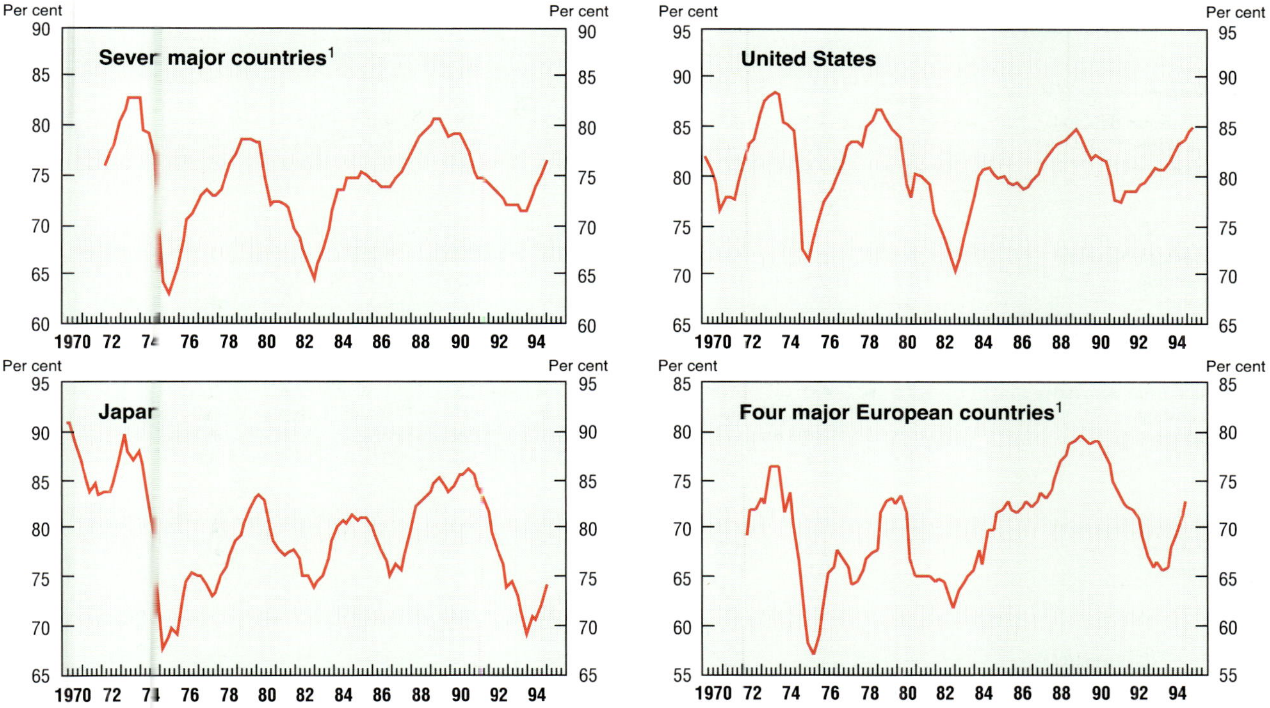

1. Data for Germany concern western Germany.

Note: Cross-country comparisons of capacity utilisation levels may be misleading owing to conceptual and methodological differences in the construction of the indices. For further details, see Methodological notes of *Main Economic Indicators* and *Sources and Methods,* No. 37 (Business Surveys), April 1983.

Annex Figure 3. **Real commodity prices**[1]

Index 1960 = 100

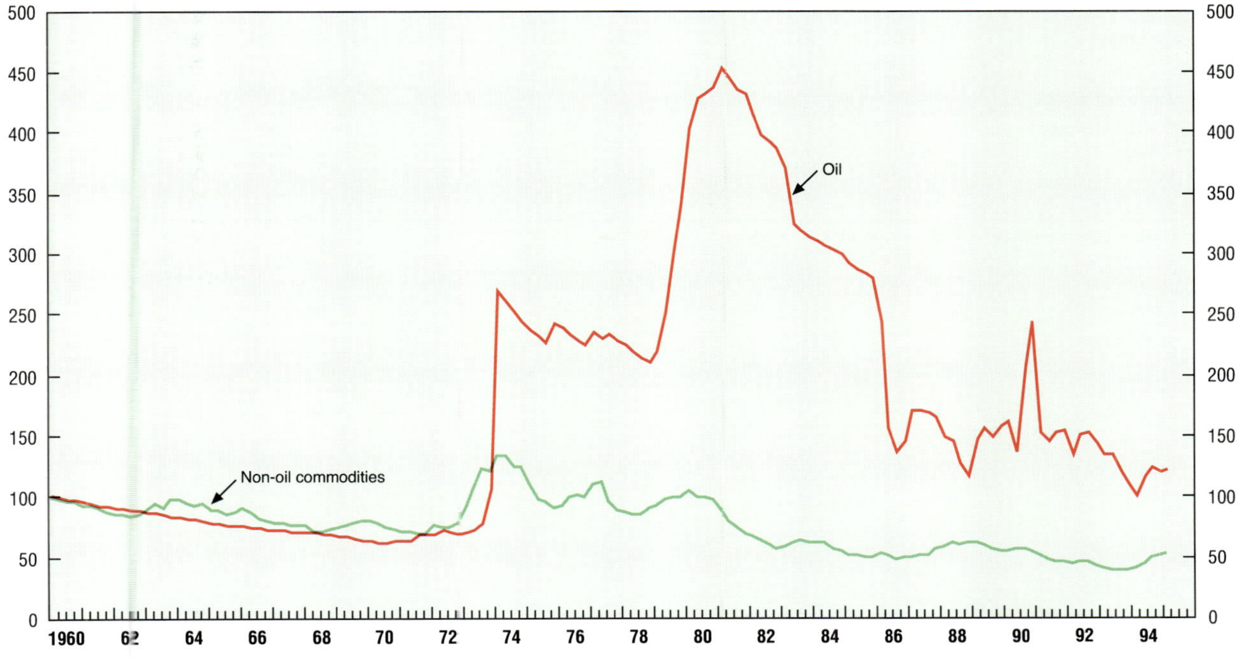

1. Deflated by the GDP deflator for the seven major countries (German data concern western Germany).

Annex Table 56. **Contributions to changes in real GDP in major OECD countries**

As a per cent of real GDP in the previous period, seasonnally adjusted at annual rates

	1992	1993	1994	1995	1996	1994 I	1994 II	1995 I	1995 II	1996 I	1996 II
United States											
Final domestic demand	2.5	3.7	4.2	3.5	2.2	3.9	4.0	3.5	3.0	2.0	1.8
Stockbuilding	0.1	0.3	0.6	–0.2	–0.4	1.2	0.4	–0.2	–0.7	–0.3	–0.2
Net exports	–0.3	–0.8	–0.7	–0.2	0.5	–0.9	–0.2	–0.4	0.2	0.6	0.6
GDP	2.3	3.1	4.1	3.2	2.3	4.3	4.3	3.0	2.6	2.3	2.2
Japan											
Final domestic demand	0.8	0.1	0.7	2.3	3.1	0.4	1.4	2.0	3.7	2.8	3.0
Stockbuilding	–0.5	–0.2	0.2	0.1	0.1	0.5	0.1	0.1	0.2	0.1	0.0
Net exports	0.8	–0.2	–0.4	–1.1	–0.8	0.0	–0.5	–1.3	–1.3	–0.7	–0.7
GDP	1.1	–0.2	0.6	1.3	2.3	1.0	1.0	0.8	2.7	2.2	2.3
Germany											
Final domestic demand	3.5	–1.0	2.0	2.4	3.3	2.8	1.3	2.5	3.2	3.3	3.5
Stockbuilding	–0.6	–0.2	0.7	0.1	0.0	0.5	0.6	0.0	0.0	0.0	0.0
Net exports	–0.8	0.0	0.2	0.4	–0.6	0.5	0.1	0.8	–0.2	–0.7	–0.9
GDP	2.2	–1.1	2.9	2.9	2.7	3.8	2.0	3.3	3.0	2.6	2.6
France											
Final domestic demand	0.8	–0.5	1.3	2.7	3.4	1.0	2.8	2.2	3.3	3.4	3.5
Stockbuilding	–0.4	–1.8	1.5	0.5	0.2	3.9	0.6	0.5	0.5	0.2	0.0
Net exports	1.0	0.8	–0.2	–0.2	–0.5	–1.6	0.1	–0.3	–0.4	–0.5	–0.5
GDP	1.3	–1.5	2.7	3.0	3.2	3.3	3.6	2.5	3.4	3.1	3.1
Italy											
Final domestic demand	0.5	–4.4	1.0	2.1	2.8	1.9	1.4	2.3	2.4	2.8	3.1
Stockbuilding	0.3	–1.4	0.8	0.3	–0.2	0.6	3.3	–0.7	–0.7	0.0	0.0
Net exports	–0.1	4.6	0.3	0.5	0.3	0.3	–1.1	1.1	1.0	0.2	–0.1
GDP	0.7	–1.2	2.2	3.0	2.9	2.8	3.7	2.8	2.7	3.0	3.0
United Kingdom											
Final domestic demand	–0.2	2.0	2.6	2.5	2.8	2.5	1.5	2.8	2.8	2.8	2.7
Stockbuilding	0.5	0.3	0.5	0.3	0.0	0.8	0.5	0.4	0.1	0.0	0.0
Net exports	–0.9	0.0	0.6	0.6	0.1	0.3	1.8	0.2	0.1	0.2	0.1
Compromise adjustment	0.0	–0.1	0.1	0.0	0.0	0.2	0.0	0.0	0.0	0.0	0.0
GDP	–0.5	2.2	3.8	3.4	3.0	4.0	3.8	3.4	3.1	3.0	2.9
Canada											
Final domestic demand	0.4	1.1	2.7	2.5	3.1	3.0	2.4	2.3	2.9	3.1	3.3
Stockbuilding	–0.1	0.8	0.2	0.1	0.0	0.4	–0.3	0.4	0.0	0.0	0.0
Net exports	0.4	0.3	1.4	1.2	0.3	1.1	3.4	0.4	0.5	0.2	0.1
Error of estimate	–0.1	0.0	0.1	0.1	0.0	0.2	0.3	0.0	0.0	0.0	0.0
GDP	0.6	2.2	4.5	3.9	3.4	4.8	5.9	3.1	3.4	3.3	3.5
Total of above countries											
Final domestic demand	1.7	1.4	2.6	2.9	2.7	2.6	2.7	2.8	3.1	2.5	2.5
Stockbuilding	–0.1	0.1	0.7	0.1	–0.2	1.2	0.6	0.1	–0.3	–0.2	–0.3
Net exports	0.0	–0.2	–0.3	–0.2	0.1	–0.4	0.0	–0.3	–0.1	0.2	0.2
GDP	1.6	1.3	3.0	2.8	2.6	3.4	3.4	2.6	2.8	2.5	2.5

Note: Components may not add to GDP due to rounding.

Annex Table 57. **Contributions to changes in real GDP in other OECD countries**

As a per cent of real GDP in the previous period

	1993	1994	1995	1996
Australia				
Final domestic demand	1.9	5.5	4.4	2.4
Stockbuilding	0.6	0.0	0.5	0.4
Net exports	0.5	–1.0	–1.3	0.7
GDP	3.9	5.4	3.8	3.5
Austria				
Final domestic demand	0.1	3.2	3.2	2.8
Stockbuilding	0.1	1.0	0.1	0.1
Net exports	–0.2	–1.4	–0.5	–0.7
GDP	–0.1	2.7	2.8	2.3
Belgium				
Final domestic demand	–1.6	0.7	2.6	2.5
Stockbuilding	–0.1	0.9	0.1	0.1
Net exports	0.0	0.7	0.0	–0.1
GDP	–1.7	2.3	2.7	2.6
Denmark				
Final domestic demand	1.5	4.4	3.4	2.6
Stockbuilding	–0.7	0.6	0.2	0.1
Net exports	0.6	–0.6	–0.1	0.3
GDP	1.5	4.4	3.4	3.0
Finland				
Final domestic demand	–7.0	1.4	4.8	4.7
Stockbuilding	0.8	2.4	0.5	0.0
Net exports	4.3	0.8	–0.5	–0.7
GDP	–1.6	3.9	4.8	3.9
Greece				
Final domestic demand	–0.4	1.3	2.5	3.2
Stockbuilding	0.8	–0.1	0.0	0.0
Net exports	–1.0	0.3	–0.6	–0.8
GDP	–0.5	1.5	1.9	2.3
Iceland				
Final domestic demand	–4.3	1.1	3.4	3.0
Stockbuilding	0.2	–0.3	0.1	0.0
Net exports	5.4	2.2	–1.0	–0.7
GDP	1.2	3.0	2.5	2.4
Ireland				
Final domestic demand	0.8	4.1	4.7	4.0
Stockbuilding	–0.5	–1.2	–0.2	0.1
Net exports	3.8	3.1	1.3	0.9
GDP	4.1	6.0	5.8	5.0
Luxembourg				
Final domestic demand	2.5	1.8	2.8	3.2
Stockbuilding	–1.0	0.2	0.0	0.0
Net exports	0.2	0.6	0.3	–0.2
GDP	1.7	2.7	3.1	2.9
Mexico				
Final domestic demand	0.3	4.4	–10.5	1.4
Stockbuilding	–0.4	0.0	–0.8	0.3
Net exports	0.9	–0.9	8.3	1.3
GDP	0.8	3.5	–2.9	3.0

	1993	1994	1995	1996
Netherlands				
Final domestic demand	0.0	1.7	2.7	2.2
Stockbuilding	–0.5	0.7	0.3	0.3
Net exports	0.9	0.2	0.2	0.1
GDP	0.4	2.5	3.1	2.7
New Zealand				
Final domestic demand	4.9	8.7	6.2	3.8
Stockbuilding	1.8	–0.4	0.3	–0.2
Net exports	–1.5	–4.5	–2.7	–0.4
GDP	5.1	3.8	3.8	3.1
Norway				
Final domestic demand	4.3	3.9	4.0	0.8
Stockbuilding	–1.6	0.6	0.0	0.0
Net exports	–0.5	0.6	–0.9	2.7
GDP	2.3	5.1	4.8	3.5
Portugal				
Final domestic demand	–1.2	1.4	3.5	4.3
Stockbuilding	0.2	0.0	0.4	0.0
Net exports	–0.1	–0.2	–1.0	–1.1
GDP	–1.2	1.2	2.9	3.2
Spain				
Final domestic demand	–3.5	0.8	2.2	3.3
Stockbuilding	–1.0	0.0	0.6	0.3
Net exports	3.3	1.2	0.3	–0.3
GDP	–1.1	2.0	3.0	3.2
Sweden				
Final domestic demand	–5.2	–0.1	0.9	1.6
Stockbuilding	–0.3	1.4	–0.3	–0.2
Net exports	2.9	0.9	1.8	1.0
GDP	–2.6	2.2	2.5	2.4
Switzerland				
Final domestic demand	–1.6	2.8	1.5	2.0
Stockbuilding	–0.3	1.7	0.8	0.5
Net exports	1.0	–2.3	–0.7	–0.2
GDP	–0.9	2.1	1.7	2.3
Turkey				
Final domestic demand	10.7	–8.5	0.8	4.3
Stockbuilding	1.2	–4.6	1.3	0.9
Net exports	–6.2	8.6	0.7	–0.4
GDP	7.5	–5.4	2.8	4.8
OECD Europe				
Final domestic demand	–0.7	1.3	2.4	3.0
Stockbuilding	–0.4	0.4	0.2	0.0
Net exports	0.9	0.8	0.4	0.0
GDP	–0.2	2.4	3.0	3.0
Total OECD				
Final domestic demand	1.2	2.5	2.5	2.7
Stockbuilding	0.2	0.7	0.2	–0.2
Net exports	–0.2	–0.2	0.1	0.2
GDP	1.2	2.9	2.7	2.7

Note: Totals may not add-up due to statistical discrepancy.

Annex Figure 4. **Measures of relative competitive position**

Indices in US$ terms; 1991 = 100

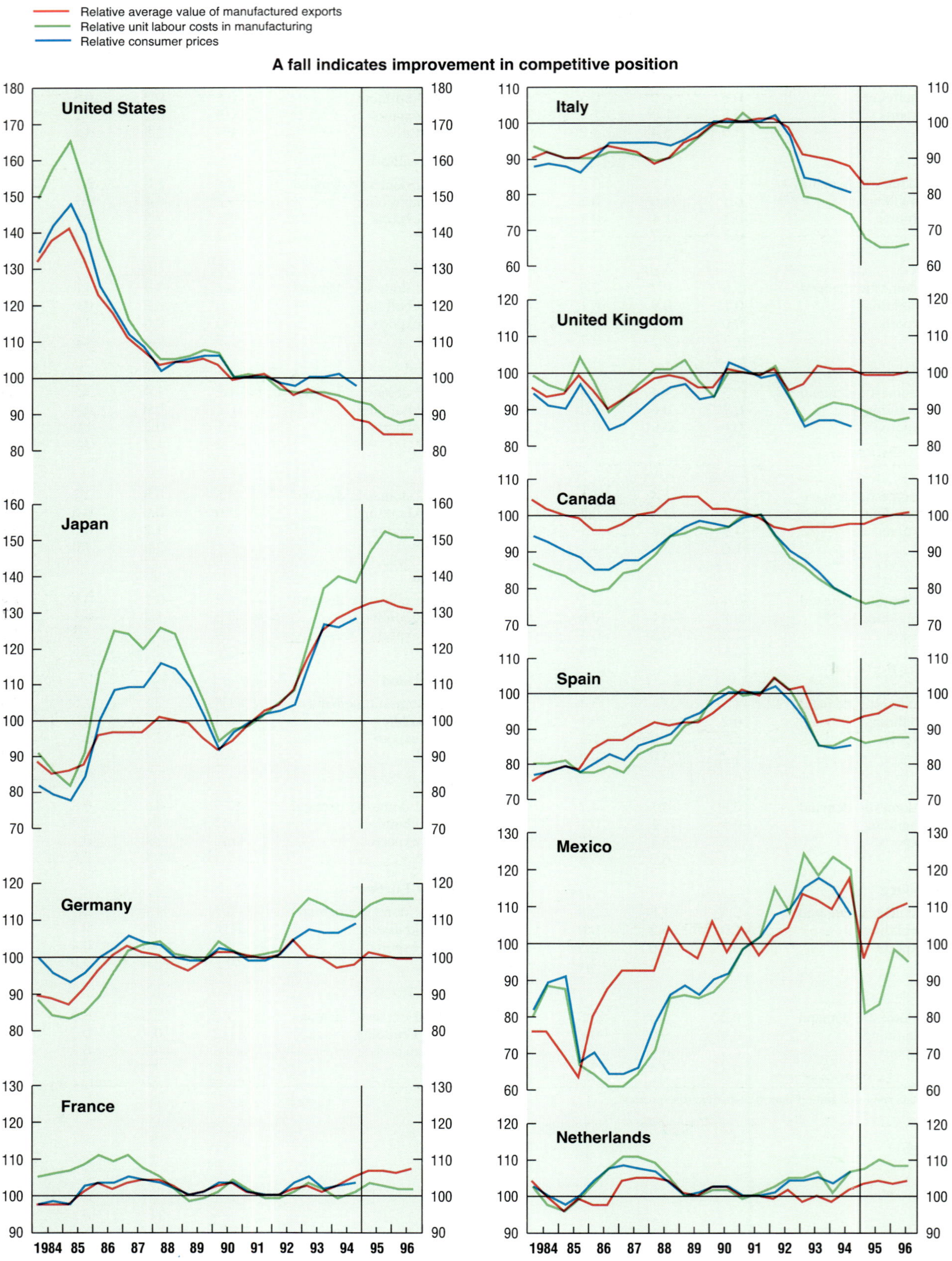

Note: The vertical line indicates the end of the historical period and the beginning of the projection period.

Annex Figure 4 *(cont'd)*. **Measures of relative competitive position**

Indices in US$ terms; 1991 = 100

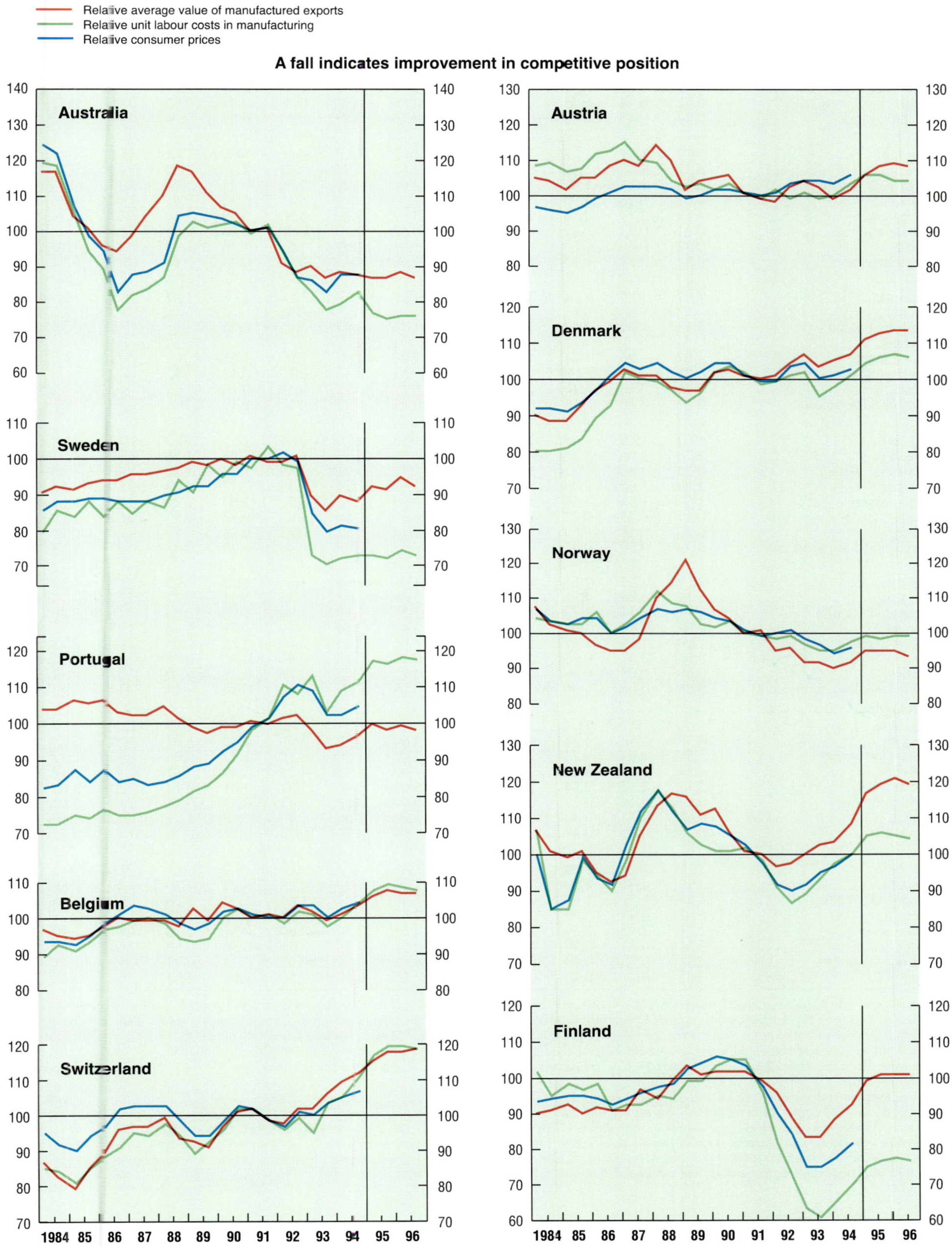

Note: The vertical line indicates the end of the historical period and the beginning of the projection period.

Annex Table 58. **Household saving, net wealth and indebtedness**[a]

	1982	1983	1984	1985	1986	1987	1988	1989	1990	1991	1992	1993	1994
United States													
Saving ratio	8.9	6.9	8.3	6.6	6.2	4.5	4.5	4.1	4.3	5.1	5.2	4.6	4.2
Net wealth	4.89	4.93	4.73	4.88	5.00	5.06	5.00	5.17	4.85	5.08	5.01	5.02	..
Net financial wealth	2.52	2.59	2.43	2.57	2.66	2.67	2.66	2.80	2.62	2.82	2.82	2.84	..
Real assets	2.37	2.34	2.30	2.31	2.34	2.40	2.35	2.37	2.23	2.26	2.19	2.17	..
Financial assets	3.24	3.33	3.18	3.38	3.52	3.56	3.58	3.76	3.57	3.78	3.77	3.82	..
Corporate equities	0.43	0.46	0.39	0.49	0.57	0.54	0.55	0.62	0.55	0.74	0.81	0.88	..
Liabilities	0.72	0.74	0.75	0.82	0.86	0.89	0.92	0.95	0.95	0.95	0.95	0.97	..
Home mortgages	0.44	0.45	0.45	0.48	0.52	0.56	0.59	0.61	0.62	0.64	0.64	0.65	..
Japan													
Saving ratio	16.7	16.1	15.8	15.6	16.1	14.7	14.3	14.6	14.1	15.1	15.0	14.7	14.9
Net wealth	5.38	5.43	5.50	5.61	6.34	7.54	7.95	8.71	8.55	7.85	7.06	6.83	..
Net financial wealth	1.36	1.47	1.57	1.65	1.83	2.01	2.22	2.52	2.23	2.24	2.12	2.17	..
Real assets	4.02	3.96	3.93	3.96	4.51	5.53	5.73	6.19	6.32	5.61	4.94	4.66	..
Financial assets	2.18	2.31	2.44	2.53	2.75	3.02	3.30	3.63	3.39	3.39	3.23	3.30	..
Corporate equities	0.21	0.24	0.27	0.30	0.42	0.52	0.70	0.90	0.58	0.55	0.35	0.33	..
Liabilities	0.82	0.85	0.88	0.89	0.92	1.01	1.07	1.11	1.16	1.15	1.11	1.12	..
Home mortgages	0.34	0.35	0.35	0.36	0.37	0.40	0.43	0.46	0.48	0.48	0.49	0.51	..
Germany													
Saving ratio	12.7	10.9	11.4	11.4	12.3	12.6	12.8	12.4	13.8	12.7	12.9	12.3	11.0
Net wealth	..	..	..	..	..	..	..	..	..	..	..	..	..
Net financial wealth	1.52	1.60	1.65	1.73	1.78	1.76	1.82	1.85	1.78	..	..	..	..
Real assets	..	..	..	..	..	..	..	..	..	..	..	..	..
Financial assets	1.67	1.76	1.81	1.89	1.94	1.93	1.99	2.03	1.96	..	..	..	..
Equities	0.07	0.09	0.09	0.13	0.15	0.11	0.13	0.15	0.12	..	..	..	..
Liabilities	0.15	0.16	0.16	0.16	0.17	0.17	0.17	0.18	0.18	..	..	..	..
Long-term bank credit	0.10	0.10	0.10	0.10	0.11	0.11	0.12	0.12	0.12	..	..	..	..
France													
Saving ratio	17.3	15.9	14.5	14.0	12.9	10.8	11.0	11.7	12.5	13.2	13.7	13.8	13.5
Net wealth	3.76	3.86	3.84	3.88	4.14	4.01	4.16	4.24	3.96	4.16	4.16	4.51	..
Net financial wealth	0.77	0.86	0.87	0.98	1.24	1.12	1.31	1.47	1.24	1.42	1.47	1.85	1.68
Real assets	2.99	3.00	2.98	2.90	2.89	2.89	2.85	2.77	2.72	2.73	2.69	2.66	..
Financial assets	1.35	1.44	1.50	1.62	1.88	1.85	2.12	2.31	2.07	2.22	2.26	2.64	2.47
Equities	0.17	0.25	0.32	0.43	0.66	0.60	0.85	1.03	0.83	0.97	0.98	1.29	1.07
Liabilities	0.58	0.58	0.63	0.63	0.64	0.73	0.81	0.83	0.84	0.79	0.79	0.79	0.79
Medium- and long-term credit	0.39	0.39	0.41	0.43	0.43	0.47	0.49	0.49	0.49	0.48	0.47	0.48	0.47
Italy[b]													
Saving ratio	20.4	22.3	20.6	18.9	18.2	17.8	16.9	16.7	18.2	18.2	17.7	15.7	15.0
Net wealth[c]	5.19	4.88	4.88	5.04	4.90	5.04	5.11	5.35	5.31	5.47	5.85	..	..
Net financial wealth	1.11	1.14	1.22	1.39	1.56	1.55	1.65	1.96	1.96	2.03	2.10	2.40	..
Real assets[c]	4.08	3.74	3.65	3.65	3.34	3.49	3.46	3.39	3.35	3.44	3.75	..	..
Financial assets	1.19	1.22	1.31	1.48	1.66	1.66	1.77	2.24	2.25	2.33	2.41	2.73	..
Equities	0.06	0.07	0.08	0.15	0.23	0.16	0.17	0.49	0.46	0.48	0.50	0.61	..
Liabilities	0.08	0.08	0.09	0.09	0.10	0.11	0.12	0.28	0.29	0.30	0.31	0.32	..
Medium- and long-term credit	0.05	0.05	0.06	0.06	0.07	0.08	0.09	0.13	0.14	0.14	0.14	0.15	..
United Kingdom													
Saving ratio	11.3	9.7	11.1	10.7	8.7	7.1	5.7	7.2	8.4	10.5	12.8	11.7	10.4
Net wealth	4.34	4.66	4.78	4.91	5.29	5.67	6.32	6.40	5.72	5.57	5.29	5.65	..
Net financial wealth	1.50	1.63	1.74	1.79	2.01	2.01	1.98	2.18	1.83	1.96	2.12	2.52	..
Real assets	2.84	3.03	3.04	3.12	3.28	3.66	4.34	4.22	3.89	3.61	3.17	3.14	..
Financial assets	2.17	2.37	2.54	2.65	2.93	3.01	3.06	3.31	3.01	3.14	3.24	3.62	..
Domestic equities	0.23	0.26	0.27	0.27	0.35	0.40	0.37	0.41	0.33	0.34	0.35	0.43	..
Liabilities	0.68	0.74	0.80	0.86	0.92	1.00	1.08	1.13	1.18	1.17	1.12	1.10	..
Mortgages	0.40	0.47	0.48	0.52	0.58	0.64	0.70	0.73	0.77	0.78	0.77	0.77	..
Canada													
Saving ratio	18.2	14.8	15.0	13.3	10.7	9.2	9.7	10.4	9.7	9.6	9.8	9.2	7.6
Net wealth	3.99	4.04	4.00	3.98	4.16	4.25	4.26	4.28	4.28	4.38	4.49	4.60	4.72
Net financial wealth	1.47	1.57	1.61	1.64	1.70	1.70	1.67	1.67	1.70	1.76	1.83	1.89	1.94
Real assets	2.52	2.47	2.39	2.34	2.46	2.55	2.59	2.61	2.59	2.62	2.66	2.71	2.78
Financial assets	2.21	2.32	2.34	2.39	2.51	2.58	2.58	2.60	2.65	2.73	2.83	2.90	2.98
Equities	0.51	0.53	0.53	0.55	0.59	0.61	0.59	0.56	0.56	0.59	0.62	0.69	0.74
Liabilities	0.74	0.75	0.73	0.75	0.81	0.88	0.91	0.93	0.95	0.97	0.99	1.01	1.04
Mortgages	0.45	0.47	0.45	0.46	0.50	0.55	0.57	0.59	0.61	0.64	0.67	0.68	0.71

a) Households and private unincorporated enterprises. The saving ratio is expressed as a percentage of household nominal disposable income, whereas the remaining variables are expressed as a simple ratio to household nominal disposable income. Assets and liabilities refer to year-end nominal values. Real assets and net wealth include durable goods for the United States, Italy, the United Kingdom, and Canada. Data for Germany exclude acquisition of real assets and associated liabilities; it is estimated that inclusion of household mortgages would increase the ratio of total liabilities to income to about 0.70 per cent in 1985.

b) Beginning in 1989, the financial accounts statistics for Italy are constructed with new sources and with a new methodology. They are, therefore, not comparable with the historical series.

c) Do not include the real assets of private unincorporated enterprises.

Sources: United States, Federal Reserve, *Balance Sheets for the U.S. Economy;* Japan, Economic Planning Agency, *Annual Report on National Accounts;* Germany, Deutsche Bundesbank, *Ergebnisse der gesamtwirtschaftlichen Finanzierungsrechnung der Deutschen Bundesbank;* France, INSEE, *25 ans de Comptes de Patrimoine (1969-1993)* and *Rapport sur les Comptes de la Nation;* Italy, Banca d'Italia, *Supplementi al Bolletino Statistico;* Cambridge University Press, *Saving and the Accumulation of Wealth;* OECD, *Financial Accounts of OECD countries;* United Kingdom, Central Statistical Office, *United Kingdom National Accounts, Financial Statistics;* Canada, Statistics Canada, *National Balance Sheet Accounts.*

Annex Figure 5. **Stock prices and long-term interest rates**

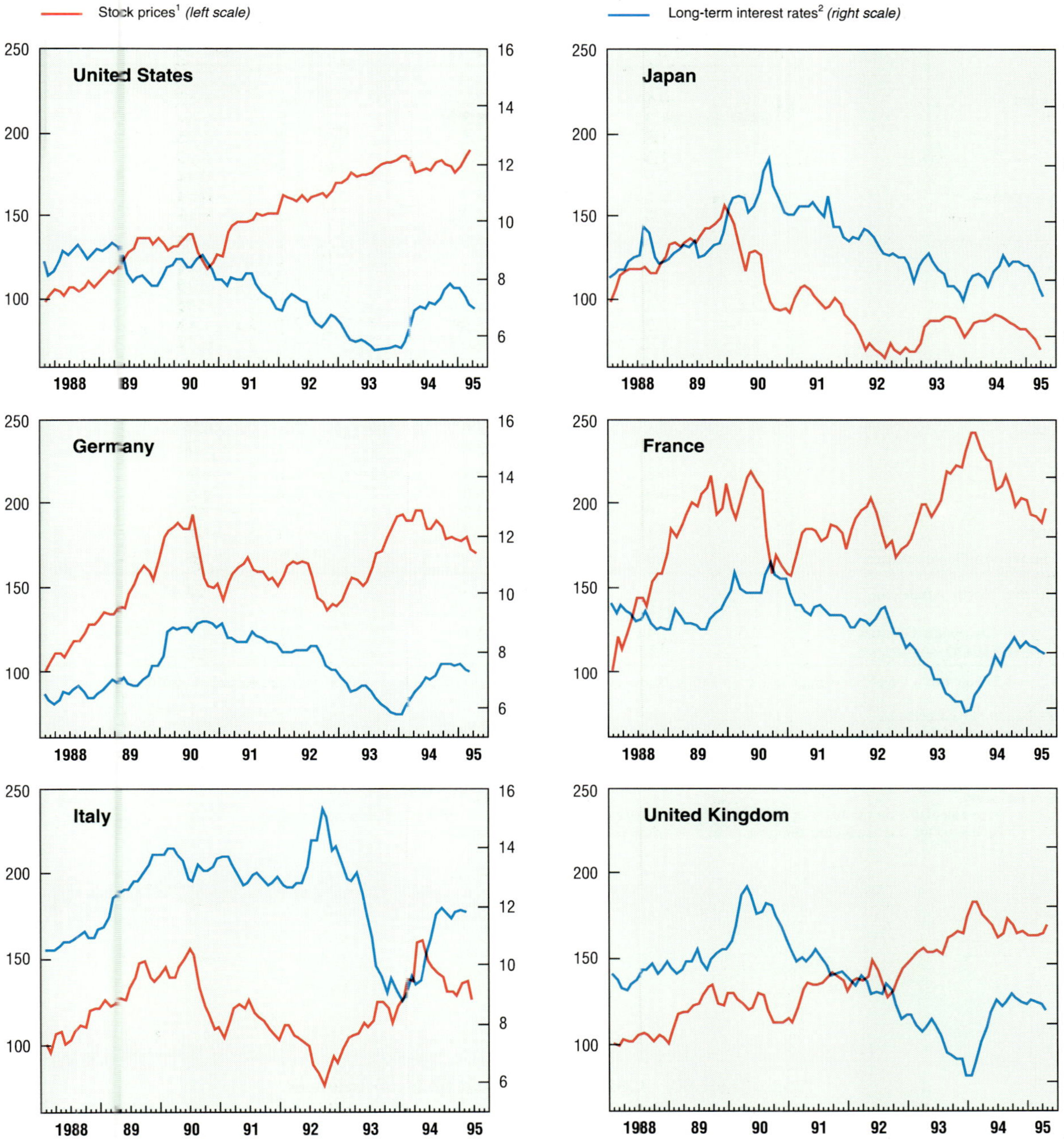

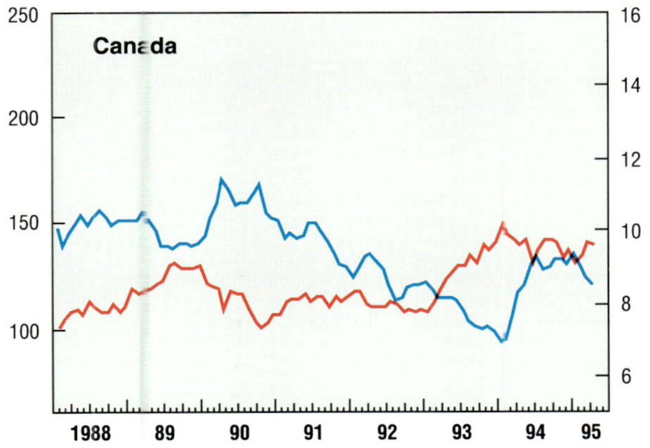

1. January 1988 = 100.
NYSE for the United States, Tokyo stock exchange for Japan, all shares for Germany, INSEE for France, Milan stock exchange for Italy, Financial Times 500 for United Kingdom, Toronto stock exchange for Canada.
2. 10-year government bond yield for the United States, Japan, Italy and United Kingdom, 8-15 year public sector bonds for Germany, public and semi-public sector bonds for France, over 10-year government bonds for Canada.

Annex Table 59. **Productivity in the business sector**

Percentage changes at annual rates

	Total factor productivity[a]			Labour productivity[b]			Capital productivity		
	1960[c]-73	1973-79	1979-93[d]	1960[c]-73	1973-79	1979-93[d]	1960[c]-73	1973-79	1979-93[d]
United States	1.6	–0.4	0.4	2.2	0	0.8	0.2	–1.3	–0.5
Japan	5.6	1.3	1.4	8.3	2.9	2.5	–2.6	–3.4	–1.9
Germany[e]	2.6	1.8	1.0	4.5	3.1	1.7	–1.4	–1.0	–0.6
France	3.7	1.6	1.2	5.3	2.9	2.2	0.6	–1.0	–0.7
Italy	4.4	2.0	1.0	6.3	2.9	1.8	0.4	0.3	–0.7
United Kingdom	2.6	0.6	1.4	3.9	1.5	2.0	–0.3	–1.5	0.2
Canada	1.9	0.6	–0.3	2.9	1.5	1.0	0.1	–1.1	–2.8
Total of above countries[f]	2.9	0.6	0.8	4.3	1.4	1.5	–0.5	–1.5	–0.8
Australia	2.3	1.0	0.5	3.4	2.3	1.2	0.2	–1.5	–0.7
Austria	3.3	1.2	0.7	5.8	3.2	1.7	–2.0	–3.1	–1.5
Belgium	3.8	1.4	1.4	5.2	2.7	2.3	0.6	–1.9	–0.7
Denmark	2.3	0.9	1.3	3.9	2.4	2.3	–1.4	–2.6	–0.8
Finland	4.0	1.9	2.1	5.0	3.2	3.2	1.4	–1.6	–0.8
Greece	3.1	0.9	–0.2	9.1	3.4	0.7	–8.8	–4.2	–2.1
Ireland	3.6	3.0	3.3	4.8	4.1	4.1	–0.9	–1.2	0.2
Netherlands	3.5	1.8	0.8	4.8	2.8	1.3	0.8	0	–0.2
New Zealand	0.7	–2.1	0.4	1.6	–1.4	1.6	–0.7	–3.2	–1.4
Norway[g]	2.3	1.4	0	3.8	2.5	1.3	0	–0.3	–1.9
Portugal	5.4	–0.2	1.6	7.4	0.5	2.4	–0.7	–2.5	–0.8
Spain	3.2	0.9	1.6	6.0	3.2	2.9	–3.6	–5.0	–1.5
Sweden	2.0	0	0.8	3.7	1.4	1.7	–2.2	–3.2	–1.4
Switzerland	2.0	–0.4	0.4	3.2	0.8	1.0	–1.4	–3.5	–1.3
Total of above smaller countries[f]	3.0	0.9	1.1	5.0	2.5	2.0	–1.5	–2.8	–1.1
Total of above North American countries[f]	1.6	–0.4	0.4	2.3	0.1	0.9	0.2	–1.3	–0.7
Total of above European countries[f]	3.3	1.4	1.2	5.1	2.6	2.0	–0.7	–1.4	–0.7
Total of above OECD countries[f]	2.9	0.6	0.9	4.4	1.6	1.6	–0.7	–1.7	–0.9

a) TFP growth is equal to a weighted average of the growth in labour and capital productivity. The sample-period averages for capital and labour shares are used as weights.
b) Output per employed person.
c) Or earliest year available, *i.e.* 1961 for Australia, Greece and Ireland; 1962 for Japan, the United Kingdom and New Zealand; 1964 for Spain; 1965 for France and Sweden; 1966 for Canada and Norway and 1970 for Belgium and the Netherlands.
d) Or latest available year, *i.e.* 1991 for Norway and Switzerland; 1992 for Italy, Australia, Austria, Belgium, Ireland, New Zealand, Portugal and Sweden and 1994 for the United States, western Germany and Denmark.
e) Western Germany.
f) Aggregates were calculated on the basis of 1992 GDP for the business sector expressed in 1992 purchasing power parities.
g) Mainland business sector (*i.e.* excluding shipping as well as crude petroleum and gas extraction).

Annex Table 60. **Central government financial balances**

Surplus (+) or deficit (–) as a percentage of nominal GDP

	1989	1990	1991	1992	1993	1994	1995	1996
United States[a]	–2.3	–3.0	–3.5	–4.7	–3.8	–2.4	–2.2	–2.4
excluding social security[a,b]	–3.4	–4.0	–4.5	–5.5	–4.6	–3.2	–3.2	–3.4
Japan[c]	–1.2	–0.3	–0.2	–2.2	–2.9	–3.7	–4.0	–4.0
Germany	–0.9	–2.0	–1.9	–1.3	–2.1	–1.5	–1.3	–1.8
France	–1.5	–1.5	–1.7	–3.0	–4.5	–4.8	–4.0	–3.5
Italy	–10.7	–10.1	–10.3	–10.4	–9.9	–9.5	–7.8	–6.9
United Kingdom	+1.2	–1.1	–2.3	–6.9	–7.9	–6.7	–4.4	–2.8
Canada	–3.2	–3.9	–4.6	–4.2	–4.6	–3.4	–2.4	–1.7
Total of above countries	–2.3	–2.7	–3.1	–4.3	–4.3	–3.6	–3.2	–3.0

a) Excludes deposit insurance outlays.
b) OECD Secretariat estimates, derived from fiscal year data converted to a calendar year basis.
c) For the fiscal years beginning 1 April of the year shown.

Annex Table 61. **Maastricht definition general government gross public debt**[a]

As a percentage of nominal GDP

	1990	1991	1992	1993	1994	Projections 1995	Projections 1996
Austria	58.4	58.7	58.4	62.8	64.5	65.9	66.9
Belgium	130.8	130.1	131.1	137.2	136.2	134.5	132.6
Denmark[b]	59.6	64.6	69.0	80.3	75.6	75.8	75.4
Finland	14.5	23.0	41.5	57.1	60.1	66.5	70.8
France	35.4	35.7	39.6	45.8	48.5	51.2	52.6
Germany	43.8	41.5	44.1	48.2	50.1	58.0	58.1
Greece	82.6	85.8	92.1	115.1	113.6	114.0	114.0
Ireland	96.8	96.9	94.2	96.9	90.9	86.3	82.1
Italy	97.9	101.3	108.4	119.4	125.4	124.9	123.3
Luxembourg	5.4	4.9	5.8	6.8	7.0	. .	. .
Netherlands	78.8	78.9	79.9	81.4	78.3	78.6	78.7
Portugal	68.6	69.3	61.7	66.5	69.5	69.9	69.9
Spain	45.1	45.8	48.3	59.9	62.2	65.3	67.4
Sweden	44.9	46.9	59.4	74.7	79.1	84.2	86.0
United Kingdom[c]	. .	35.6	41.8	48.3	52.5	54.3	53.7

a) General government gross debt according to the definition applied under the Maastricht Treaty is based on estimates in national currencies provided by the Commission of the European Communities for 1990 to 1994 and projected forward in line with the the OECD Secretariat's projections for GDP, general government financial balances and governments' policies for acquisitions of financial assets. These data may differ from the gross financial liabilities figures shown in Annex Table 34. For further details, see *OECD Economic Outlook* No. 55, page 17.

b) In accordance with the Maastricht definition, government held deposits at the central bank, securities (other than government securities) held by the Social Pension Fund and public debt on behalf of public enterprises are included.

c) OECD Secretariat estimates starting in 1994.

Annex Table 62. **Monetary and credit aggregates**[a]**: recent trends and targets**

Percentage changes, seasonally adjusted at annual rates

		Annual change (to 4th quarter)				Latest twelve months		From target base period	Current target or projection
		1991	1992	1993	1994				
United States	M2	2.9	2.0	1.7	1.0	1.	(Mar. 1995)	1.7	1-5
	M3	1.2	0.5	1.0	1.4	2.4	(Mar. 1995)	4.6	0-4
	BC	–0.1	0.0	3.5	7.6	10.0	(Mar. 1995)		
Japan	M2 + CD	2.2	–0.5	1.6	2.7	3.5	(Mar. 1995)	3.7	3-4
	BC	4.5	2.2	0.6	–0.5	–0.3	(Feb. 1995)		
Germany	M3	5.2	9.5	7.5	5.7	0.3	(Mar. 1995)	–2.7	4-6
	BC	10.7	8.1	7.9	5.5	4.2	(Mar. 1995)		
France	M3	3.9	5.3	–2.2	1.2	3.2	(Mar. 1995)	2.2	around 5
	BC	7.5	3.0	–3.3	–1.8	–2.0	(Feb. 1995)		
Italy	M2	8.7	6.1	8.2	2.4	6.3	(Mar. 1995)		
	BC	13.8	4.7	6.2	4.6	4.6	(Dec. 1994)		
United Kingdom	M0	2.8	2.8	5.5	7.0	6.6	(Mar. 1995)	6.9	0-4
	M4	5.7	3.8	4.2	4.4	4.5	(Mar. 1995)	5.2	3-9
	BC	6.0	–2.5	2.9	2.4	2.4	(Dec. 1994)		
Canada	M2	5.0	3.7	3.5	2.8	3.7	(Mar. 1995)		
	BC	3.9	0.9	3.5	7.8	7.4	(Mar. 1995)		

a) BC = commercial banks credit to economy. For more details see "Sources and Methods".

Annex Table 63. **Export market growth and performance in manufactured goods**

Percentage changes from previous year

	(1) Import volume				(2) Export market growth[a]				(3) Export volume				(4) Export performance[b]			
	1993	1994	1995	1996	1993	1994	1995	1996	1993	1994	1995	1996	1993	1994	1995	1996
United States	13.1	17.7	11.4	6.0	5.0	11.8	8.1	8.4	6.5	13.2	10.7	12.7	1.4	1.3	2.5	3.9
Japan	6.8	19.8	18.0	11.6	7.6	12.8	10.4	8.2	–2.1	1.4	2.9	4.9	–9.0	–10.1	–6.9	–3.0
Germany	–11.7	8.9	8.6	8.9	0.7	10.0	9.1	7.6	–6.0	14.3	9.6	5.4	–6.6	3.9	0.4	–2.1
France	–5.0	8.2	10.1	9.0	–1.3	10.0	9.2	7.8	–3.1	9.4	9.3	6.8	–1.9	–0.6	0.1	–0.9
Italy	–12.4	14.4	10.6	7.9	–0.6	9.4	9.3	8.2	12.3	13.2	12.5	8.3	12.9	3.5	2.8	0.2
United Kingdom	2.0	8.6	6.8	7.4	0.5	10.5	9.9	7.8	–0.5	10.8	8.5	7.4	–1.0	0.2	–1.2	–0.4
Canada	11.3	14.8	12.8	6.8	11.5	16.6	11.1	6.4	13.8	17.4	15.9	7.7	2.2	0.6	4.4	1.2
Total of the above countries	1.7	13.6	10.9	7.7	3.3	11.4	9.4	7.9	1.3	10.9	9.3	7.9	–2.0	–0.4	0.0	0.0
Australia	6.6	17.1	12.5	6.3	7.6	14.0	12.2	9.4	7.7	9.6	5.9	11.5	0.1	–3.9	–5.7	1.9
Austria	–1.1	14.0	6.4	5.7	–4.1	9.5	9.1	8.3	–4.2	11.7	9.3	5.6	–0.1	1.9	0.2	–2.5
Belgium-Luxembourg	–1.3	5.2	7.3	6.1	–2.6	9.5	9.2	8.1	–3.7	7.2	7.1	5.8	–1.1	–2.1	–1.9	–2.1
Denmark	–3.1	12.6	8.9	5.6	–1.1	11.1	8.9	7.1	–0.8	5.6	3.8	4.3	0.2	–4.9	–4.7	–2.6
Finland	–2.9	12.3	12.7	7.5	0.4	11.2	9.1	7.4	18.9	12.0	6.2	3.9	18.5	0.7	–2.7	–3.2
Greece	12.3	4.1	5.5	7.1	–3.3	9.5	9.3	8.2	–5.1	2.1	8.5	6.6	–1.7	–6.8	–0.8	–1.5
Iceland	–18.6	11.0	9.9	6.9	–1.8	10.6	8.6	7.0	–1.4	14.4	4.4	3.5	0.3	3.5	–3.8	–3.3
Ireland	7.4	9.6	10.8	8.8	0.0	10.6	9.0	7.5	9.4	10.4	9.8	8.1	9.4	–0.2	0.8	0.6
Mexico	0.2	12.1	–25.6	8.9	11.6	16.7	11.4	6.2	11.1	13.4	19.3	11.6	–0.6	–2.7	6.9	5.1
Netherlands	0.7	6.0	7.3	5.1	–2.9	9.5	8.9	7.7	4.1	8.6	4.2	4.2	7.1	–0.8	–4.3	–3.3
New Zealand	2.3	20.1	13.2	8.0	7.5	15.4	12.4	8.3	7.0	13.1	12.1	8.2	–0.5	–1.8	–0.4	–0.1
Norway	–1.0	17.9	5.8	–2.1	0.9	10.9	9.3	7.4	3.6	12.1	6.1	5.0	2.6	1.1	–2.8	–2.3
Portugal	–8.4	5.4	10.6	7.7	–4.4	10.9	9.4	8.1	1.3	11.2	13.7	7.5	5.9	0.3	3.8	–0.5
Spain	–14.0	19.3	13.9	11.8	–2.7	9.1	8.9	7.9	6.5	26.6	14.2	11.3	9.4	16.0	4.9	3.1
Sweden	2.7	15.7	8.5	6.9	–0.2	11.3	9.2	6.9	9.8	18.6	13.2	7.6	9.9	6.6	3.7	0.7
Switzerland	–0.8	8.4	5.7	4.8	–0.9	10.7	9.7	8.3	0.6	3.3	5.7	4.7	1.4	–6.7	–3.7	–3.3
Turkey	33.8	–29.0	12.1	15.5	–3.6	10.5	9.5	8.3	6.9	10.9	20.6	13.7	10.9	0.4	10.0	5.0
Total of smaller countries	–0.5	9.5	6.0	6.8	–0.7	10.8	9.5	7.8	3.4	11.2	9.1	7.0	4.1	0.4	–0.4	–0.7
Total OECD	1.1	12.4	9.4	7.4	2.3	11.2	9.4	7.9	1.8	11.0	9.3	7.7	–0.5	–0.2	–0.1	–0.2
OPEC	2.5	4.6	9.3	9.0	5.5	12.2	11.0	8.9	6.2	6.2	4.4	4.9	0.7	–5.3	–6.0	–3.7
ANIEs[c]	11.2	12.8	11.9	11.4	7.7	13.3	11.2	8.5	10.1	11.6	11.2	9.9	2.2	–1.5	0.0	1.3
Other Asia	11.0	10.7	11.0	10.6	7.8	13.3	11.5	9.3	12.2	12.4	10.3	9.5	4.1	–0.7	–1.1	0.1
Latin America	8.1	9.5	9.5	5.1	6.2	12.3	9.8	7.2	6.8	7.1	7.1	8.2	0.5	–4.5	–2.5	1.0
Africa	5.0	2.6	6.5	4.9	–0.1	10.5	9.9	7.9	0.7	5.1	4.4	5.5	0.9	–4.9	–5.1	–2.2
Central and Eastern Europe	6.8	7.1	9.2	9.2	–1.9	10.2	9.7	8.4	4.8	10.8	9.2	7.9	6.8	0.5	–0.4	–0.4
Total of non-OECD countries	8.8	9.6	10.5	9.6	6.3	12.8	11.0	8.6	9.4	10.9	10.0	9.2	2.9	–1.7	–0.9	0.5
World	3.2	11.6	9.7	8.0	3.2	11.6	9.7	8.0	3.4	11.0	9.4	8.0	0.2	–0.5	–0.3	0.0
OECD North America	11.7	16.7	9.0	6.3	6.7	13.1	8.9	7.8	8.2	14.1	12.3	11.5	1.4	0.9	3.1	3.4
OECD Europe	–4.6	9.1	8.7	7.6	–0.7	10.0	9.3	7.8	0.2	11.9	9.4	6.6	0.9	1.7	0.1	–1.1
EU	–5.3	9.6	8.8	7.9	–0.7	10.0	9.2	7.8	0.1	12.4	9.5	6.6	0.8	2.2	0.3	–1.1
Total OECD *less* the United States	–2.3	10.7	8.8	7.9	1.8	11.1	9.7	7.8	0.8	10.5	9.0	6.6	–1.0	–0.6	–0.7	–1.1

a) The calculation of export markets is based on a weighted average of import volumes [panel (1) above] in each exporting country's markets, with weights based on manufacturing trade flows in 1991.

b) Export performance [panel (4) above] is derived for each country as the ratio of export volumes [panel (3) above] to export markets [panel (2) above].

c) ANIEs include Chinese Taipei, Hong Kong, Korea and Singapore.

Annex Table 64. **Geographical structure of OECD trade**

Percentage of nominal GDP

Area or country	Source/destination		Source of imports 1962	1972	1982	1992	1993	Destination of exports 1962	1972	1982	1992	1993
OECD	**OECD**		**6.09**	**8.02**	**10.37**	**11.16**	**10.10**	**5.81**	**7.87**	**10.02**	**10.99**	**10.24**
	of which:	Europe	3.85	5.23	6.65	7.40	6.28	3.99	5.30	6.90	7.55	6.62
		North America[a]	1.81	2.03	2.66	2.53	2.60	1.40	2.06	2.40	2.73	2.91
		Other	0.43	0.76	1.07	1.22	1.22	0.42	0.51	0.72	0.71	0.71
	Non-OECD		**2.40**	**2.47**	**4.79**	**3.45**	**3.52**	**2.40**	**2.37**	**4.35**	**3.34**	**3.57**
	of which:	DAEs[b] + China	0.19	0.35	0.86	1.40	1.49	0.25	0.41	0.84	1.32	1.50
		OPEC	0.66	0.81	2.15	0.72	0.67	0.33	0.41	1.42	0.56	0.50
USA	**OECD**		**1.84**	**3.47**	**4.91**	**5.81**	**6.03**	**2.22**	**2.94**	**4.18**	**5.14**	**4.99**
	of which:	Europe	0.78	1.27	1.65	1.86	1.84	1.09	1.25	1.89	1.96	1.81
		North America[a]	0.74	1.37	1.97	2.25	2.41	0.81	1.19	1.44	2.20	2.27
		Other	0.31	0.84	1.29	1.71	1.79	0.33	0.49	0.84	0.98	0.92
	Non-OECD		**1.02**	**1.12**	**2.83**	**3.13**	**3.24**	**1.55**	**1.18**	**2.56**	**2.40**	**2.44**
	of which:	DAEs[b] + China	0.08	0.33	0.87	1.75	1.84	0.11	0.22	0.67	1.08	1.14
		OPEC	0.26	0.22	0.99	0.56	0.53	0.18	0.23	0.73	0.37	0.33
Japan	**OECD**		**5.37**	**3.99**	**4.41**	**3.10**	**2.75**	**3.94**	**5.23**	**6.22**	**5.13**	**4.52**
	of which:	Europe	1.00	0.82	0.93	1.04	0.88	1.11	1.57	2.01	1.97	1.54
		North America[a]	3.60	2.37	2.77	1.68	1.54	2.56	3.36	3.71	2.93	2.77
		Other	0.77	0.80	0.72	0.39	0.33	0.27	0.29	0.50	0.22	0.21
	Non-OECD		**3.88**	**3.72**	**7.67**	**3.26**	**2.96**	**4.13**	**4.17**	**6.49**	**4.15**	**4.04**
	of which:	DAEs[b] + China	0.84	0.73	1.61	1.52	1.46	1.29	1.67	2.39	2.81	2.84
		OPEC	1.12	1.50	4.45	1.06	0.89	0.52	0.61	2.00	0.52	0.41
Europe	**OECD**		**11.52**	**13.75**	**18.04**	**17.89**	**16.55**	**10.42**	**13.43**	**17.07**	**17.19**	**16.81**
	of which:	Europe	8.72	11.38	14.69	15.00	13.69	8.59	11.37	14.78	15.02	14.41
		North America[a]	2.25	1.76	2.44	1.78	1.80	1.38	1.68	1.83	1.63	1.82
		Other	0.55	0.62	0.91	1.10	1.07	0.45	0.38	0.46	0.54	0.59
	Non-OECD		**4.25**	**3.84**	**6.38**	**3.86**	**4.13**	**3.48**	**3.29**	**5.73**	**3.71**	**4.35**
	of which:	DAEs[b] + China	0.24	0.27	0.62	1.06	1.19	0.25	0.26	0.47	0.78	1.03
		OPEC	1.17	1.35	2.81	0.74	0.71	0.54	0.59	2.10	0.74	0.72

a) North America now includes Mexico.
b) DAEs are the Dynamic Asian Economies (Chinese Taipei, Hong Kong, Korea, Malaysia, Singapore, Thailand).

SOURCES AND METHODS

The analysis in the *Economic Outlook* and the projections on which it is based are the work of the OECD Economics Department. The following notes describe various technical aspects of the projection methods used, and underlying statistical concepts, sources and methods.

PROJECTION METHODS

While taking into account official and unofficial national projections for Member countries, the OECD *Economic Outlook* projections are based on the OECD Secretariat's independent assessment of the world economy. This draws on individual country, general economic and area analyses. Emphasis is placed on the role of international trade and financial linkages, to ensure that projections for each country are consistent with global developments.

The *Economic Outlook* projections are specifically conditional on technical assumptions about exchange rates, energy prices, and the choice of economic policies – fiscal, monetary and structural:

- Exchange rates against the US dollar are generally assumed to remain constant over the projection period, at the level prevailing on a prespecified cut-off date, chosen in the course of the exercise, except for those countries with stated or *de facto* policies.
- The price of crude oil is set on the basis of a technical assumption described in the text.
- Fiscal and monetary policy assumptions for individual countries are generally based upon stated official policies, with public sector expenditure and revenue projections being based upon the most recent budgetary statements.

The OECD Secretariat's world macroeconomic model, INTERLINK[1], is used to help to ensure national and international consistency, though a considerable amount of country-specific expertise and judgement is brought to bear in the construction of the underlying individual country assessments.

A preliminary version of the *Economic Outlook* projections is presented to and discussed by the OECD Working Group on Short-Term Economic Prospects, where Member country delegates provide their analyses and detailed comments, drawing on national authority evidence and projections.

In presenting half-yearly demand, output and price projections, all estimates reported in the *Economic Outlook* are seasonally adjusted and shown in terms of percentage changes at annual rates. Further definitional notes relating to reporting conventions, in particular the measurement of semiannual rates of growth, are given below.

The domestic economy

Macroeconomic developments reflect the interaction of many economic variables and relationships. The following paragraphs describe those which are particularly important to OECD Secretariat projections.

Domestic expenditure

Two broad categories of domestic expenditure are distinguished, consumption and investment, subdivided into various private and public sector components. The projections of private consumption typically depend on real personal disposable income, changes in the rate of inflation, monetary and financial conditions, and also leading indicators of consumer confidence and retail sales. Particular attention is given to current trends in personal and business sector savings rates and asset holdings. Private investment is, for most countries, subdivided into business fixed investment, residential construction and stockbuilding. Business fixed investment is typically assessed in relation to non-financial variables (sales, output and capacity utilisation) and financial variables (cash flow and interest rates) but also gives weight to business survey information. Projections for residential construction take account of demographic trends, housing stocks, real income and financial conditions, and also draw on cyclical indicators for the construction sector. Projections of stockbuilding are usually made with reference to relevant stock-output and stock-sales ratios, taking account of recent trends, financial factors and specific supply-side influences.

Government non-wage expenditures, divided into non-wage consumption and investment, are treated as being exogenous policy assumptions, specified in either nominal or real terms. In a number of cases, an independent assessment is made of expected out-turns versus stated policy goals. Government wage expenditures may be set either in terms of nominal targets for the total wage bill or as the product of government employment and associated wage projections.

Methods involved in the analysis of external influences on output and real GDP, *i.e.* those coming from goods and services trade, are described below in the section concerning foreign trade.

Employment, wages and prices

Employment and other labour market trends are commonly assessed in relation to changes in the levels of actual and expected output. Important additional elements relate to labour and factor productivity trends, capacity constraints and real factor costs. Unemployment rate projections are given by the combination of employment and labour supply projections, with the latter assessed judgmentally on the basis of demographic trends and participation rate assumptions.

Wage and earnings assessments take into account a number of key factors. Extensive use is made of the pattern of current wage settlement as a leading indicator, with pressure of demand in the labour market, productivity rates and the terms of trade also influencing the overall projection of real wages and compensation per employee. The projections of unit labour costs used in the assessment of prices and inflation take account of those for employment, productivity growth, wage rates and social contributions. Public sector wage projections are generally based on announced policies but may also be assumed to adjust in line with private sector wages.

The assessment of domestic prices and inflation trends depends crucially on unit costs, the levels of demand and supply potential (see below) and foreign prices. In making individual price projections, allowance is also made for a number of special factors affecting prices in individual countries – harvest yields, changes in taxes and subsidies and administered price regimes. The overall set of domestic expenditure deflators in conjunction with goods and services trade prices and corresponding real expenditure components are then combined to give projections of total domestic demand and output deflators. The specific treatment of trade prices is discussed in more detail in the section concerning foreign trade.

Supply potential and output gaps (Annex Table 11)

As outlined in the relevant chapter of *Economic Outlook* 56, the OECD Secretariat has recently carried out a major reassessment of its methods for measuring potential output and output gaps for use in its analyses of inflation pressure and structural budget balances. The revised output gap measures, reported now in Annex Table 11 are based on the methodology set out in "Potential Output, Output Gaps and Structural Budget Balances", by Claude Giorno, Pete Richardson, Deborah Roseveare and Paul van den Noord, OECD *Economic Studies*, No. 24, 1995/1.

The output gap is measured as the percentage difference between actual GDP in constant prices, and estimated potential GDP. The latter is based on a production function approach, taking into account the capital stock, changes in labour supply, factor productivities and underlying non-accelerating wage rates of unemployment or the NAWRU for each Member country. It should be stressed that the estimated levels of potential are subject to significant margins of error.

Sectoral accounts

Appropriation accounts for the household and government sectors are projected for the seven major OECD economies and some smaller countries. Both accounts are constructed by identifying the different sources of income and expenditures, savings and net lending.

Household income consists primarily of the wage compensation of employees, self-employment income, and transfers. Property and other income – essentially dividends and interest – are evaluated in the light of business income and debt interest flows. The sum of these elements is adjusted for direct taxes and transfers paid to give household disposable income. The latter is then split between household consumption and savings. Household taxes and transfers are typically projected on the basis of movements in the appropriate nominal bases and corresponding marginal tax and transfer rates. There is some variation in the detail of the treatment of transfers as between the larger and smaller economies. Social security receipts are projected on the basis of the unemployment rate, prices and wage compensation levels. Household net lending is obtained by subtracting housing investment from household savings.

For the United States a full disaggregation of revenues and expenditures is made as between State and Local and Federal accounts, with wage and non-wage expenditures also split between defence and non-defence spending. For the other major economies a relatively standardised total general government approach (described below) is adopted, while for some smaller economies there is a less detailed treatment of transfers, subsidies and property income. For a number of countries, specific allowance is also given to revenues and tax receipts from sectors of specific importance, for example, oil and gas.

The current receipts of the government sector are in general defined as the sum of direct taxes on household and business sectors, indirect taxes, social security, and other transfer receipts and interest-related property income. Indirect taxes are projected on the basis of weighted expenditures, combined with corresponding marginal tax elasticities. Business sector taxes are assessed on the basis of projected business income, making some allowance for the lags between accruals and payments. Social security and other transfer receipts are linked directly to the corresponding household sector payments, while property income is in general assumed to grow broadly in line with nominal GDP.

Current disbursements are made up of current consumption, transfer payments, subsidies and interest payments. For the major economies, interest payments are assessed on the basis of the stocks of outstanding debt, the rate of roll-over in the stock and the relevant interest rates. Government net lending is then derived as current savings, less nominal investment, capital consumption and other miscellaneous capital transactions. The stock of government net financial liabilities is finally obtained as the cumulation of net lending, subject to statistical discrepancies.

Domestic monetary policies

For the major economies, prevailing monetary policies are examined against a range of monetary indicators. Typically, assumptions are made about the choice and stance of policy, taking into account recent policy announcements with respect to the choice of monetary targets, associated target ranges and instruments, by national authorities. Increasingly, this involves a strong interdependent element, given for example the importance of interest rates, exchange rates, output and prices to international transmission mechanisms. Effectively this means that international financial linkages are increasingly important in the overall global assessment, and hence the assumptions for short- and long-term interest rates and/or monetary aggregates for virtually all OECD countries may hinge critically on the assessment of monetary policy in the three largest ones.

Further details of a wider range of statistical and methodological issues are described below in the Monetary Aggregates and Interest Rates section.

Foreign trade

Particular attention is given in the forecasting exercise to ensuring the consistency of international trade volume and price projections, trade representing a principal channel through which developments in one country affect other economies. Six categories of international trade are customarily distinguished: manufactures; energy; food; raw materials; non-factor services; and other services. Various adjustment and reconciliation procedures are involved in linking customs-basis foreign trade projections to the national-accounts basis projections for individual countries.

The projections for total goods trade are based on a split into the following specific SITC categories:

- food: 0 + 1
- raw materials: 2 + 4
- energy: 3
- manufactures: 5 + 6 + 7 + 8 + 9

Projections for these components are weighted together using moving weights based on 1991 trade flows. These are approximately comparable to figures published in the OECD's *Monthly Statistics of Foreign Trade* (Series "A"). The paragraphs below summarise how projections for these components are prepared. The structural specifications of equations used in the foreign trade projections are set out, for each country, in the OECD Secretariat's INTERLINK Reference Manual.

a) *Goods: volumes*

i) *Manufactures*

The initial projections of import volume growth for manufactured goods are derived from equations (in logarithm level form) in which the main explanatory variables are activity (demand) and lagged competitive position. The activity variable in the import equations is specified so that a distinction is made for most countries between the short-and long-term response of imports to a change in demand (*i.e.* demand is split into two components: a moving average, and the ratio of actual demand to this moving average). In addition, for some countries a lagged dependent variable is included in the specification. Export volume projections are based on developments in export markets and competitive positions. For each exporting country, export market growth is defined as a weighted average of real import growth in other countries, while competitiveness effects are proxied by changes in relative prices. These are measured by the ratio of each country's export prices to a weighted average of its competitors' export prices. The weights are derived through a double weighting procedure described in the section of effective exchange rates below.

Expenditure elasticities for imports are, in general, estimated in the range of 1.5 to 2.5, while most of the price elasticities (import prices relative to domestic prices) range from –0.4 to –0.9, the response being lagged over two to three years. For export volumes, price elasticities (export prices relative to competitors' prices) are typically taken to be in the range of –1.0 to –2.0, lagged over three years, while market growth elasticities for most countries are close to unity.

ii) *Energy*

International trade in energy is concentrated in oil, and the forecasting effort is focused accordingly. It is assumed that OPEC is the marginal supplier, with other producers setting prices relative to those of OPEC such that they are always able to sell their full capacity output.

The demand for oil is projected, in collaboration with the International Energy Agency, from relationships which link oil consumption to the real cost of imported oil. Judgmental adjustment is then made to reflect any unusual weather conditions and new developments in energy substitution.

With oil demand determined, net oil imports are obtained by subtracting expected domestic production and adjusting for any expected change in stocks. The movement in oil imports is then added to the projected movements of imports of other forms of energy.

iii) *Food and raw materials*

Import volumes of food are assumed to follow projected movements in real private consumption; import volumes of raw materials are assumed to follow movements in industrial production. While some allowance is made for the effects of large changes in competitiveness, trade volumes of food and raw materials are generally assumed to be relatively insensitive to changes in competitiveness over the projection period. Food and raw material exports are based on, *inter alia,* export market growth for these commodities, with an allowance for factors affecting supply.

b) *Goods: unit values*

i) *Manufactures*

Projections for unit values of exports of manufactured goods are based initially on movements in unit labour costs, import prices, and competitors' export prices – the first two being subject to lags of up to one year. Some allowance is made for exceptionally high or low rates of capacity utilisation.

Import unit values are derived as weighted averages of foreign costs and domestic prices. The resulting import price projections are then modified to reflect time lags in the translation of exchange rate changes into import prices. In those countries where competitiveness has changed sharply, an allowance is made for price discrimination by foreign suppliers in the first half-year, partly reversed over the next two half-years. The export and import price equations have been estimated to ensure consistency at the world level. (For more details, see "Import and export price equations of manufactures", *OECD Economics and Statistics Department Working Papers,* No. 43, Richard Herd.)

ii) *Energy*

The customary technical assumption is that, in the near term, oil prices are determined by market conditions, including announced OPEC decisions, and thereafter follow prices of OECD exports of manufactured goods. Adjustments are made to reflect natural gas and coal contracts and thereby allow for the lag between the movements of other fossil fuels and oil prices.

iii) *Food and raw materials*

In general, food and raw material unit values (in dollars) are derived from projected movements of spot commodity prices. Current OECD Secretariat estimates suggest that about three-quarters of the change in spot industrial materials prices is passed through into OECD import unit values of raw materials within about six months.

Equations for OECD export unit values for food and raw materials utilise domestic cost pressure variables as well as world spot commodity prices as explanatory variables. In addition, food export unit value equations for EU countries are adjusted for the effects of the Common Agricultural Policy. Import unit values for food and raw materials are trade-weighted averages of partner-country export unit values.

c) *Services*

Projections of non-factor services are based on equations of broadly similar specification to those used for manufactures trade. Volumes of non-factor service debits depend both on projected movements of import-content-weighted real expenditure, and the price of import of services relative to domestic prices. Non-factor service credits depend on market growth for services and each country's export prices of services relative to those of its competitors. A service trade share matrix based on 1989 flows is used to calculate market growth and competitors' prices. Export prices of services for each country are assumed to move in line with its total expenditure price deflator. Service export prices for non-OECD zones are assumed to move with the average for the OECD area. Import prices are then calculated from export prices using the service trade share matrix. Import elasticities of non-factor services with respect to import-content-weighted expenditure components are around 1.2, with price elasticities of –0.7 to –0.8 lagged over 1 ½ years. Non-factor service export projections are based on market growth in partner countries, with market growth elasticities around unity and price elasticities of –0.4 to –0.5 lagged over 1 ½ years. Projections for investment income are based on equations that take account of external assets and liabilities and rates of return. Movements in external assets and liabilities are linked to capital outflows and current-account balances.

d) *Non-OECD*

Trade volumes and prices of the non-OECD area are projected on the basis of six country groupings (see Country Classification for details). Individual projections are made for some important non-OECD countries. Import and export prices for each group reflect world prices weighted according to the commodity structure of trade. Export volumes for each group are projected on the basis of the growth of their markets, with account taken, in some cases, of changes in competitiveness. For groups with large external assets, import volumes are in line with assessment of development plans. For other groups, import volumes are projected taking account of export revenues, the level of external financing and import prices.

EFFECTIVE EXCHANGE RATES

The calculation of effective exchange rates uses a system of weights based on a double-weighting principle, which is also used to calculate price and cost competitiveness indicators. The effective exchange rates take account of both export and import competitiveness.

Twenty-four OECD Member countries (Belgium-Luxembourg is treated as one country) and four of the dynamic Asian economies (Hong Kong, Korea, Singapore and Chinese Taipei) are included in the calculation of effective exchange rates. Thirty markets are considered: the 24 OECD countries and the six non-OECD zones.

For each year, starting in 1970, a 28 × 30 (country × market) matrix has been constructed, based on ISIC data. Each diagonal element represents the production of manufactured goods (net of exports) of individual countries and each off-diagonal element represents the exports of manufactured goods from one country (row) to any other OECD country or non-OECD zones (column). This basic matrix is then used to compute a new intermediate matrix for each country which gives a measure of the relative importance of the other 27 competitors in the 30 markets. The obtained intermediate matrix is then weighted by the relative share of the 30 markets for the country involved. This gives a global weighting system for each year since 1970.

Geometric indices of effective exchange rates are then computed: indices of nominal exchange rates are weighted each year with the weighting matrix of the previous year. For 1970, the indices are weighted with the 1970 weighting matrix. This gives a set of effective exchange rates based on moving weights.

A fuller description of this methodology is given in "OECD's indicators of international trade and competitiveness", *OECD Economics Department Working Papers*, No. 120, Martine Durand, Jacques Simon and Colin Webb.

FISCAL POLICY

Government financial liabilities

The figures for gross financial liabilities (Annex Table 34) refer to the debt and other liabilities (short-and long-term) of all of the institutions contained in the general government sector of the national accounts. This sector is the aggregate of the central and local government sectors and the social security sector. The gross data for the individual government sectors is consolidated where national sources permit such a consolidation. The figures for net financial liabilities (Annex Table 35) measure the gross financial liabilities of the general government sector less the financial assets held by the general government sector. Such assets may be cash, bank deposits, loans to the private sector, participations in private sector companies, holdings in public corporations or foreign exchange reserves (depending on the institutional structure of the country concerned, see footnotes to Annex Table 35). If it has not been possible to consolidate the gross financial liabilities data, assets may include debt issued by one institution in the general government sector but held by another institution in the general government sector (see footnotes to Annex Table 34 for the non-consolidated countries).

Gross debt according to the convergence criteria set out in the Maastricht Treaty (Annex Table 61) comprises currency and deposits, bills and short-term bonds, other short-term loans and other medium- and long-term loans, defined according to the European System of Integrated Economic Accounts (ESA). Financial liabilities such as trade credits extended to the government are not included.

Cyclical and non-cyclical components of general government financial balances (Annex Table 31)

The budget balance can be decomposed into a cyclical and a non-cyclical, or structural, component. The decomposition is aimed at separating cyclical influences on the budget balances resulting from the divergence between actual and potential output (the output gap), from those which are non-cyclical. Changes in the latter can be seen as a cause rather than an effect of output fluctuations and may be interpreted as indicative of discretionary policy adjustments. It should be noted, however, that changes in resource revenues – as a result of oil price changes, for example – and in interest payments – as a result of past debt accumulation or changes in interest rates – are neither cyclical nor purely discretionary. Yet these changes are reflected in the evolution of the structural component of the budget balance.

The structural budget balance is derived by (re-)calculating the items on the government appropriation account which would be obtained if output (GDP) were at its potential level. Denoting a cyclically-adjusted variable by an asterisk, revenues (T) and expenditures (G) are recalculated as follows:

$$T_t^* = T_t\,(GDP_t^*/GDP_t)^{\alpha} \qquad \alpha > 0$$
$$G_t^* = G_t\,(GDP_t^*/GDP_t)^{\beta} \qquad \beta < 0$$

where α and β are respectively the elasticity of current receipts and expenditure with respect to nominal output growth. The cyclical adjustment is carried out for the main revenue items separately (*i.e.* corporate taxes, personal income taxes, indirect taxes and social security contributions), and for the unemployment-related expenditure.

The structural budget balances are reported as a percentage of potential output as described earlier. It should be stressed that the estimated structural budget balances are surrounded by large margins of uncertainty. This is due not only to the usual risks to the projection of actual output, but also reflects uncertainty as to the present size and future growth of potential output, and the degree to which elimination of the output gap would translate into enhanced tax revenues and reduced expenditures. For a further discussion of these issues, see "Potential Output, Output Gaps and Structural Budget Balances", *op. cit.*

The primary balance (Annex Table 32) is obtained by netting net interest payments from the overall balance.

MONETARY AGGREGATES AND INTEREST RATES

Monetary and credit aggregates (Annex Table 62)

M1 is the narrowly defined money supply, *i.e.* currency plus domestic demand deposits. M2, M2 + CD, M3 and M4 are broadly-defined money stocks, which add to M1 domestic savings deposits and other managed liabilities of banks and other financial institutions, and certificates of deposit (CD) in Japan, France and the United Kingdom. In the United Kingdom, M0 is currency in circulation with the public plus bankers' operational balances with the central bank. Monetary aggregates are obtained from national data sources.

Bank credit: United States: commercial banks loans; Japan: commercial banks loans and discount; Germany: bank credit to economy, excluding Central Bank, short-, medium- and long-term; France: bank credit to economy, total; Italy: commercial and saving banks, credit to private sector; United Kingdom: bank credit to industry and other sectors; Canada: chartered banks, credit to economy. Bank credit information is obtained from OECD, *Main Economic Indicators* and Banque de France.

Latest twelve-month changes are calculated from the most recent 3-month average relative to the corresponding 3-month average a year earlier. Changes from target base period are calculated as the latest monthly figure relative to the fourth quarter of the previous year, except for the United Kingdom and Japan which are changes over the previous twelve months. For the United States and Germany, targets are for Q4 to Q4 annual growth rates; for Japan, the figure is not a target but a projection for growth from Q2 to Q2; for France, the figure is a medium-term objective; for the United Kingdom, the current target or monitoring range is expressed in terms of changes over the previous 12 months.

Interest rates

The following interest rates are reported in Annex Table 36.

Short-term rates: United States: 3-month Treasury bills; Japan: 3-6 month CD; Germany, France, United Kingdom: 3-month interbank rates; Italy: interbank deposits; Canada: 90-day finance company paper; Austria: day-to-day money; Belgium: 3-month Treasury certificates; Denmark: 3-month interbank rate; Finland: 3-month Helibor; Ireland: 91-day Exchequer bills up to 1983, 3-month interbank rate from 1984; Mexico: 3-month Treasury certificates; Netherlands: 3-month Aibor; Norway: call money rate; Spain: 3-month interbank loans; Sweden: 3-month Treasury discount notes; Switzerland: 3-month deposits; Australia: 90-day bank-accepted bills; New Zealand: 90-day bank bills.

Long-term rates: United States, Japan and United Kingdom: 10-year government bonds; Germany: 8-15 year public sector bonds; France: public and semi-public sector bonds; Italy: Treasury bonds; Canada: over 10-year long-term federal government bonds; Austria: public sector bonds; Belgium: central government bonds (more than 5 years); Denmark: central government bonds (10 years); Finland: non-central government taxable public bonds (as from 1994, taxable 5-year central government bonds); Ireland: 15-year government bonds; Mexico: 1-year Treasury certificates; Netherlands: 5-8 year central government bonds; Norway: 6-10 year central government bonds; Spain: government bonds (more than 2 years); Sweden: 5-year yield of long-term government bonds; Switzerland: private sector bonds; Australia: 10-year bonds; New Zealand: 10-year government bonds.

Sources: OECD, *Main Economic Indicators* and *Financial Statistics*. Some series are not strictly comparable over time due to changes in definitions or in institutional arrangements. For further details, see OECD *Financial Statistics, Methodological Supplement,* 1991-92.

LABOUR FORCE DATA

This section outlines the sources and definitions of the data concerning labour markets. Where different series are available, those chosen are the ones which the OECD Economics Department finds most useful for policy analysis and forecasting, usually because they are the most commonly cited, and are frequently published. The data are not always consistent with the national authorities' definitions and those published in the OECD's quarterly and annual publication *Labour Force Statistics* (LFS). Exceptions are noted below.

For most countries the source of these data is a labour force survey of a sample of households in which both components of the unemployment rate (UNR), unemployment levels (UN) and labour force (LF), are measured simultaneously. For the remaining countries, one of the components of the identity LF = UN + ET (employment) is derived from the other two, which are generally estimated from different sources. The term "total" is used with reference to labour force and employment to indicate that all armed forces (conscripts as well as professional military) are included. In some countries (indicated below), employment and labour force include professional military, but exclude conscripts. "Civilian" labour force and employment data exclude all military personnel. Participation rates are calculated as the labour force divided by the total working-age population; where the count of the working-age population, the labour force, the employed and the unemployed is normally restricted to individuals 16 through 64 years of age. Unless otherwise specified, annual data refer to the average of either monthly or quarterly data; semiannual data shown for the seven largest countries are averages of monthly or quarterly seasonally-adjusted figures.

United States

Unemployment, civilian employment and civilian labour force are from the monthly *Current Population Survey* of persons aged 16 and over. The data are seasonally-adjusted by the Bureau of Labor Statistics. All layoffs are included in unemployment. Since January 1994, the data have been based on a new survey methodology, and are not directly comparable with data for previous years. For a full discussion of the implications of the change see box 1 in the OECD *Economic Survey of the United States* (November 1994).

Japan

Unemployment, employment and labour force (including national "self-defence" forces) are from the monthly Labour Force Survey of persons aged 15 and over. The data are seasonally-adjusted by the OECD Secretariat.

Germany

Data on employment (GDP basis) and unemployment are based on national accounts statistics. The labour force (LF) is derived as the sum of total employment (dependent and self-employed) and unemployment. Seasonal adjustment is done by the OECD Secretariat. Up to 1991, data on employment and unemployment refer to western Germany only.

France

INSEE provides OECD with quarterly series on civilian employment. They are seasonally adjusted by the OECD and an interpolated annual series of the armed forces is added in order to arrive at total employment. Monthly seasonally adjusted data corresponding to ILO guidelines are also sent by INSEE. The labour force is the sum of total employment and unemployment.

Italy

Employment, unemployment and labour force are from the quarterly Labour Force Survey of persons aged 14 and over. The definition of unemployment was revised in 1986 and in 1992 to be more in line with ILO and Eurostat guidelines. The employment figures from the quarterly Labour Force Survey differ from those in the national accounts source, *Conti Economici Trimestrali,* ISTAT. The latter are used for derived variables such as labour productivity and labour costs. A standard labour unit has been defined which measures the average volume of work carried out by a full-time worker.

United Kingdom

Seasonally-adjusted unemployment, total employment and total labour force (working population) are from the Department of Employment publication, *Employment Gazette.* The unemployment figures refer to claimants at Unemployment Benefit Offices. They exclude students seeking vacation work and those persons temporarily stopped from work. Employment data are based on quarterly surveys of employers and households. Self-employment is derived from the 1981 Census of Population and the Labour Force Surveys; it excludes unpaid family workers. Total employment equals the sum of employees, participants in work-related government training programmes, self-employment and the armed forces. The national unemployment rate refers to unemployed claimants aged 18 and over as a percentage of the total labour force.

Canada

Unemployment, civilian employment and civilian labour force are from the monthly Labour Force Survey of persons aged 15 and over. Unemployment also includes persons who, while not actively looking for work in the preceding four weeks, were available for work, but were on temporary layoff or had a new job to start in four weeks or less. The data are seasonally-adjusted by the national authorities.

Australia

Unemployment, total employment and the total labour force are from the monthly household Labour Force Survey of persons aged 15 and over. Only persons laid-off for less than four weeks (because of bad weather or plant breakdown) are included among the employed; all other layoffs are considered as unemployed or out of the labour force. The national unemployment rate is calculated with reference to the civilian labour force.

Austria

Unemployment, total employment and total labour force are from the quarterly Labour Force Survey (microcensus) of persons aged 15 and over. The figures have been adjusted by the OECD Secretariat for breaks in the employment series at 1969/70, 1981/82 and 1983/84.

Belgium

Data on unemployment are based on administrative sources, complemented by surveys. They refer to end-of-June, and comprise fully unemployed persons entitled to benefits, other unemployed obliged to register and voluntarily registered persons. The mid-year estimate of the total labour force comprises domestic employment (including all armed forces), plus Belgian border workers working abroad, less foreign border workers working in Belgium, plus unemployment.

Denmark

Unemployment refers to the registered unemployed aged 16 to 66 years and includes the partially unemployed converted to full-time equivalents. Unemployment and total employment figures, corresponding to national accounts concepts, are compiled from the Danish Central Register of Labour Market Statistics (CRAM). Total labour force is then derived from the identity LF = ET + UN. The national rate refers to all registered unemployed expressed as a percentage of the CRAM estimate of total labour force. The *Economic Outlook* statistics differ from those published in LFS, which are based on the spring Labour Force Survey.

Finland

Unemployment, civilian employment and civilian labour force are from the monthly Labour Force Survey of persons aged 15 to 74. The labour force concept underlying the national unemployment rate includes the professional military but excludes conscripts. Unemployment figures exclude persons over the age of 56 receiving a preretirement unemployment pension and not actively seeking work.

Greece

Unemployment, total employment and total labour force are compiled from the annual Labour Force Survey. The figures are completed or revised in line with the latest census results. All data refer to the second quarter of each year.

Iceland

The unemployed are registrations. Civilian employment, expressed in person-years (that is, full-time equivalents), is compiled from accident insurance statistics. The labour force is derived from the identity LF = ET + UN.

Ireland

Unemployment, total employment and total labour force figures are derived from the annual Labour Force Survey and relate to mid-April of each year. The national unemployment rate is calculated by the Irish Statistical Agency in line with ILO and Eurostat guidelines.

Luxembourg

National employment excludes non-resident persons working in Luxembourg and includes nationals working over the border and international civil servants. Data are those provided by the Administration de l'emploi and the national statistical agency (STATEC). Unemployment refers to those registered at the employment agencies and resident in Luxembourg. The labour force is derived from the identity LF = ET + UN.

Mexico

Unemployment, employment, and labour force are from the National Survey of Urban Employment covering in 1992 32 urban areas, *i.e.* some 12 million persons, compared to 23-30 million according to Census data: 23 million in the 1990 Census, 30 million in the National Employment Survey of 1991 (that records more of the self-employed, part-time workers in the informal economy). In 1994, the coverage was extended to 39 urban areas. The employment figures from the Urban Employment Survey also differ from those in the national accounts. The latter, which put total employment around 25 million, are used for derived variables such as labour productivity and labour costs. General government employees are from the national accounts; self-employment is the difference between total employment in the national accounts and the number of employees in social insurance statistics.

Netherlands

Unemployment refers to the standardised unemployed, excluding part-time unemployed (defined as persons seeking work for less than 20 hours per week), and the unemployed temporarily engaged in state-run unemployment relief programmes. There are breaks in the series at 1983, 1984 and 1989. Since the beginning of 1989 the official series is based on the monthly survey undertaken by the Central Bureau of Statistics. Estimates for 1987 and 1988, in line with the new measurement methods, have been made by the OECD Secretariat. Total employment is taken from the Labour Force Survey. The total labour force is then derived from the identity LF = ET + UN. The employment figures from the Labour Force Survey differ from those in the national accounts source. The latter, expressed in man-years, are used for derived variables such as labour productivity and labour costs.

New Zealand

Unemployment, civilian employment and civilian labour force are from the Quarterly Survey of Households. Prior data for total employment and unemployment have been chain-linked with the new series.

Norway

Data on unemployment, employment and labour force are taken from the Quarterly Labour Force Surveys of persons aged 16 to 74. The seasonally-adjusted rate of unemployment is calculated by the OECD Secretariat on the basis of national aggregate statistics, and differs somewhat from the corresponding figure published by the Central Bureau of Statistics, Oslo, which is based on an aggregation of labour force statistics seasonally-adjusted at the regional and occupational levels.

Portugal

Unemployment, civilian employment and civilian labour force are derived from the quarterly Labour Force Survey of persons aged 15 and over. There are breaks in the series in 1973/74, 1982/83 and 1991/92. The data shown refer to continental Portugal; the professional army is included, conscripts are excluded. Figures reported in the *Economic Outlook* adopt the narrow definition of unemployment which applies a one-month reference period for job search.

Spain

Unemployment, employment and labour force are from the quarterly Labour Force Survey of persons aged 16 and over. Permanent inmates at institutions, notably religious establishments, are excluded from the survey. Temporary inmates are included in their original household (approximately 1 per cent of inmates are missed by the survey) as are professional military. Prior to 1988, data exclude the provinces of Ceuta and Melilla.

Sweden

Unemployment and employment data are from the monthly Labour Force Survey of persons aged 16 to 64. There are breaks in the series in 1986 and 1993. Data for earlier years published in the *Economic Outlook* have been revised accordingly. A further minor adjustment was made in January 1993. The labour force is derived from the identity LF = ET + UN. Both the numerator and the denominator of the national unemployment rate and the Swedish labour force data published in LFS are based on the results of the Labour Force Survey.

Switzerland

Unemployment refers to the monthly registered unemployed, including the partially unemployed. Civilian employment figures, including permanent military personnel, are established using the census of enterprises, the census of population and the quarterly employment survey of enterprises. The labour force is derived from the identity LF = ET + UN.

Turkey

In 1989, the State Planning Organisation revised the labour market statistics from 1978 onwards. The new series on civilian employment, civilian labour force and unemployment are based on the provisional results of the 1988 Household Labour Force

Survey and sectoral value-added and productivity statistics. Since 1988, labour market statistics are derived from the biannual household Labour Force Surveys. Annual figures refer to the results of the October surveys.

COST AND PRICE DATA

Average compensation (Annex Table 12)

Average compensation is calculated as wage and non-wage labour costs, as estimated in the national accounts, per employed person.

Capital income shares and rates of return on capital (Annex Tables 24 and 25)

The estimates of capital income are derived from OECD *National Accounts* statistics. They refer to income generated from production, and hence exclude inflation gains and losses accruing to enterprises from holdings of tangible and financial assets and liabilities. The difference between value-added calculated at factor cost (*i.e.* excluding net indirect taxes) and labour income – the gross operating surplus of enterprises – is taken as the measure of income from capital. A labour income component equal to average business-sector compensation has been imputed to self-employed persons after excluding from the latter unpaid family workers. For those countries where data on numbers of unpaid family workers are not available either for the whole or part of the period covered (see notes to the tables), the bias due to this inclusion is unlikely to be significant.

An adjustment to exclude the operating surplus of the housing sector has not been made owing to the paucity of data; however, estimates based on available data suggest that excluding this item might typically reduce capital income shares by around 6 percentage points, and the estimated rates of return on capital by around 3 percentage points.

The capital stock estimates which are used to compute the rates of return cover only assets included in non-residential gross fixed capital formation and hence exclude dwellings, inventories, monetary working capital, land and natural resources. The historical capital stock data are obtained from national sources whenever possible. For the projection period they have been extrapolated using the perpetual inventory method, which involves accumulating past investment and dropping out assets at the end of their service lives.

Evaluation of the capital stock is based on replacement cost. It should be noted that cross-country differences exist in respect to the assumed service lives of the different capital assets (structures and plant/equipment) and the deflation methods applied[2].

USE OF NATIONAL STATISTICS

National accounts

The figures shown in the country tables on Demand and Output follow, in general, the OECD *Standardised System*[3] definitions. One important deviation from the *Standardised System* is the line "public investment" which includes, whenever possible, fixed capital formation by both general government and government-owned and controlled enterprises. The latter's definition and coverage may vary as between countries.

a) *United States*

Official quarterly national accounts, published by the Bureau of Economic Analysis of the US Department of Commerce, are available through the first quarter of 1995. The appropriation account for households is based on OECD definitions and differs slightly from official US figures. Briefly, OECD disposable income equals US disposable income minus consumer interest payments and net foreign transfers. OECD Secretariat estimates of the savings ratio may thus differ by one- or two-tenths of a percentage point from estimates based on the official US definition. Government fixed investment expenditures (including those of government enterprises) are included in "government expenditure", and no allowance is made for depreciation of government fixed capital. The investment figures, therefore, refer to the private sector only.

b) *Japan*

Annual and quarterly national accounts are published by the Economic Planning Agency. Figures from the second quarter of 1994 to the fourth quarter of 1994 are preliminary estimates published by the Economic Planning Agency.

c) *Germany*

The historical figures for Germany are based on official data published by the Statistisches Bundesamt. Historical seasonally-adjusted quarterly components of demand and GDP for western Germany are available through the fourth quarter of 1994. National accounts data, not seasonally-adjusted, for eastern Germany are available from the second half of 1990 through the fourth quarter of 1994. Seasonal adjustment for eastern German data is done by the OECD Secretariat.

d) *France*

Quarterly accounts based on the *Enlarged System of National Accounts* (ESNA) are available through the fourth quarter of 1994. Industrial production figures refer to the official quarterly index of industrial production and not to the value added in the industrial sector.

e) *Italy*

The definitions used are those of the OECD *System of National Accounts*. Half-yearly series, in constant prices, through the second half of 1994, are based on quarterly national accounts published by the *Istituto Centrale di Statistica* (ISTAT).

f) *United Kingdom*

National accounts data through the fourth quarter of 1994 are taken from *Economic Trends*, CSO. The three official estimates of GDP, output, expenditure and income are averaged to yield a "compromise" GDP estimate.

g) *Canada*

Official quarterly national accounts through the fourth quarter of 1994 are published by Statistics Canada. Over the projection period, the residual error is assumed to remain constant from the second half of 1994.

Current statistics

Unless otherwise stated, all the national statistics quoted in the *Economic Outlook* are taken from the *Main Economic*

Indicators published monthly by the OECD Secretariat (MEI). Starting in September 1967, supplements to MEI have been published describing in detail the sources and methods of these statistics. The following notes are therefore confined to some methodological points of special importance for the understanding of the text.

Index of industrial production

The figures shown include, as far as possible, mining, manufacturing and public utilities (electricity, gas and water), but exclude construction. The exact coverage, the weighting system and the methods of calculation vary from country to country but the divergences are less important than in the case of the price and the wage indices[4]. With the exception of certain smaller countries, the indices are seasonally adjusted by national statistical offices using different methods usually derived from the US Bureau of the Census Method II.

Seasonal adjustment

Some of the series used have been seasonally adjusted, notably in the area of foreign trade but also in some cases for industrial production, unemployment and consumer prices. The method used is the X-11 variant of the US Bureau of the Census Method as programmed for computer use by the Agency. (Further details may be found in Technical Paper No. 15 of the Bureau of the Census.) Where appropriate, series are also corrected for calendar variations.

CALCULATION AND DEFINITION OF SEMIANNUAL GROWTH RATES

Although quarterly and higher frequency data are commonly shown in the *Economic Outlook* for some countries and variables, most of the data reported are either annual or semiannual and are presented in terms of percentage growth rates. The calculation and presentation of growth rate information, particularly that relating to semiannual series, is sometimes a source of confusion and the following paragraphs therefore provide specific clarification on the measurement principles involved.

Annual growth rates are commonly defined as the percentage change in a variable between two consecutive years. Similarly, semiannual growth rates can be calculated as the percentage changes between two consecutive half-years. It is often convenient, however, to convert such measures of semiannual growth into a form which is more readily comparable with annual growth figures, *i.e.* to express them at *annual rates.* Mathematically, this is done by squaring the semiannual growth factor (which is obtained by dividing the current value of a variable by its value in the preceding half year) and subtracting unity. In effect, the semiannual growth rate is *compounded* over two half-years to provide an indication of the annual rate of growth which would result from the continuation of the semiannual rate of growth over a one-year period.

In terms of simple algebra, if a variable has a value of X_t in one half-year and X_{t+1} in the next, the formula for the semiannual rate of growth for period t+1, expressed at an *annual rate,* is given by:

$$g(t+1) = [(X_{t+1}/X_t)^2 - 1.0]*100.$$

For example, recent statistics for the Industrial Production index in the United Kingdom are as follows:

	1988		1989		1990	
	I	II	I	II	I	II
Industrial production (1985 = 100 basis)	111.7	116.4	118.8	119.0	119.9	116.7

Given the above formula, the growth between the first and second halves of 1989 expressed at an *annual rate,* is computed as $[(119.0/118.8)^2 - 1.0]*100$, or 0.3 per cent. Corresponding rates of growth for each of the years and half-years in question are, on a similar basis, as follows:

	1989	1990	1988		1989		1990	
			I	II	I	II	I	II
Industrial production (growth rates)	4.3	–0.5	5.2	8.6	4.2	0.3	1.5	–5.3

Such a numerical example helps illustrate the usefulness of semiannual growth rates in highlighting movements in an economic variable during the course of a year. It also demonstrates that annual growth rates for a specific year do not usually correspond to the average of the semiannual growth rates *during* that year. In the above example, the annual rate of growth for 1989, at 4.3 per cent, is higher than the average of the two semiannual rates of growth experienced during 1989, at 2.2 per cent. This is because year-on-year rates of growth are influenced by the levels of a variable achieved in both halves of the preceding year, whereas the average of the corresponding two semiannual rates are influenced only by the level achieved in the second half of the preceding year. This feature is known as a ''carry over'' effect.

There is however a useful rule of thumb which can be used to approximately convert semiannual rates of growth to corresponding year-on-year growth rates. Known as the ''quarter-half-quarter'' rule, this approximates the year-on-year growth rate by weighting together the semiannual growth rates for the second semester of the preceding year and those of the first and second semesters of the year in question, with weights of one quarter, one half and one quarter, respectively. Applying this rule to the above example gives annual rates of growth for 1989 and 1990 of 4.3 per cent (*i.e.* 8.6/4 + 4.2/2 + 0.3/4) and –0.5 per cent (*i.e.* 0.3/4 + 1.5/2 – 5.3/4), respectively, coinciding with the actual measured rates. In using this rule, it is important to bear in mind that some degree of approximation is involved, particularly where large variations in semiannual growth rates are concerned.

Other measures of growth rates are, of course, used in commenting and presenting economic statistics. Quarter-on-quarter growth rates are often referred to, which may in turn be expressed at annual rates, by raising the quarterly growth factor to the power four, subtracting unity and multiplying by 100. Analogous measures also exist for monthly rates of growth or inflation, expressed also at annual rates. In some countries, notably the United States, public interest may also focus on growth rates between the final quarters of successive years, commonly referred to as the growth rate *in* the year in question. In others, growth rates measured in relation to the corresponding month, quarter or semester of the previous year are also commonly used.

NOTES

1. Recent descriptions of the scope, structure and properties of the OECD Secretariat's INTERLINK model and the underlying empirical studies are given by Richardson (1988), OECD (1988), and associated *Economics Department Working Papers.*
2. A full description of the sources and methods for the capital stock data is contained in Keese *et al.* (1991).
3. For detailed definitions, see United Nations, *A System of National Accounts,* New York, 1968.
4. A quarterly supplement to *Main Economic Indicators* provides an internationally comparable selection of industrial output indices for branches and a number of categories.

REFERENCES

Giorno C., P. Richardson, D. Roseveare, P. van den Noord (1995), ''Potential output, output gaps and structural budget balances'', *OECD Economic Studies,* No. 24, 1995/1.

Keese, M., G. Salou and P. Richardson (1991), ''The Measurement of Output and Factors of Production for the Business Sector in OECD Countries'', *OECD Department of Economics and Statistics Working Papers,* No. 99.

OECD (1988), ''OECD INTERLINK System, Reference Manual'' (January).

Richardson, P. (1988), ''The Structure and Simulation Properties of OECD's INTERLINK Model'', *OECD Economic Studies,* No. 10 (Spring).

EMPLOYMENT OPPORTUNITIES

Economics Department, OECD

The Economics Department of the OECD offers challenging and rewarding opportunities to economists interested in applied policy analysis in an international environment. The Department's concerns extend across the entire field of economic policy analysis, both macroeconomic and microeconomic. Its main task is to provide, for discussion by committees of senior officials from Member countries, documents and papers dealing with current policy concerns. Within this programme of work, three major responsibilities are:

- to prepare regular surveys of the economies of individual Member countries;
- to issue full twice-yearly reviews of the economic situation and prospects of the OECD countries in the context of world economic trends;
- to analyse specific policy issues in a medium-term context for the OECD as a whole, and to a lesser extent for the non-OECD countries.

The documents prepared for these purposes, together with much of the Department's other economic work, appear in published form in the *OECD Economic Outlook, OECD Economic Surveys, OECD Economic Studies* and the Department's *Working Papers* series.

The Department maintains a world econometric model, INTERLINK, which plays an important role in the preparation of the policy analyses and twice-yearly projections. The availability of extensive cross-country data bases and good computer resources facilitates comparative empirical analysis, much of which is incorporated into the model.

The Department is made up of about 80 professional economists from a variety of backgrounds and Member countries. Most projects are carried out by small teams and last from four to eighteen months. Within the Department, ideas and points of view are widely discussed; there is a lively professional interchange, and all professional staff have the opportunity to contribute actively to the programme of work.

Skills the Economics Department is looking for:

a) Solid competence in using the tools of both microeconomic and macroeconomic theory to answer policy questions. Experience indicates that this normally requires the equivalent of a PH.D. in economics or substantial relevant professional experience to compensate for a lower degree.

b) Solid knowledge of economic statistics and quantitative methods; this includes how to identify data, estimate structural relationships, apply basic techniques of time series analysis, and test hypotheses. It is essential to be able to interpret results sensibly in an economic policy context.

c) A keen interest in and extensive knowledge of policy issues, economic developments and their political/social contexts.

d) Interest and experience in analysing questions posed by policy-makers and presenting the results to them effectively and judiciously. Thus, work experience in government agencies or policy research institutions is an advantage.

e) The ability to write clearly, effectively, and to the point. The OECD is a bilingual organisation with French and English as the official languages. Candidates must have excellent knowledge of one of these languages, and some knowledge of the other. Knowledge of other languages might also be an advantage for certain posts.

f) For some posts, expertise in a particular area may be important, but a successful candidate is expected to be able to work on a broader range of topics relevant to the work of the Department. Thus, except in rare cases, the Department does not recruit narrow specialists.

g) The Department works on a tight time schedule with strict deadlines. Moreover, much of the work in the Department is carried out in small groups. Thus, the ability to work with other economists from a variety of cultural and professional backgrounds, to supervise junior staff, and to produce work on time is important.

General information

The salary for recruits depends on educational and professional background. Positions carry a basic salary from FF 305 700 or FF 377 208 for Administrators (economists) and from FF 438 348 for Principal Administrators (senior economists). This may be supplemented by expatriation and/or family allowances, depending on nationality, residence and family situation. Initial appointments are for a fixed term of two to three years.

Vacancies are open to candidates from OECD Member countries. The Organisation seeks to maintain an appropriate balance between female and male staff and among nationals from Member countries.

For further information on employment opportunities in the Economics Department, contact:

Administrative Unit
Economics Department
OECD
2, rue André-Pascal
75775 Paris Cedex 16
FRANCE

E-Mail: compte.esdadmin@oecd.org

Applications citing ''ECOU'', together with a detailed *curriculum vitæ* in English or French, should be sent to the Head of Personnel at the above address.

EMPLOYMENT OPPORTUNITIES

Vacancies occur regularly in the OECD Secretariat in the following areas:

Agricultural Economics
Balance of Payments
Computing and Communications
Development Economics
Econometrics
Education Policies
Energy Economics
Environment
Fiscal Policy
Industrial Economics
Labour Economics
Macro-economics
Monetary Economics
National Accounts
Nuclear Physics/Engineering
Public Management
Social Affairs
Statistics
Territorial Studies

Qualifications

Relevant advanced university degree; at least two years' relevant professional experience; very good knowledge of one of the official languages of the Organisation (English and French) and ability to draft well in that language; good knowledge of the other would be an advantage.

Initial appointment

Two or three years.

Basic annual salary

From FF 305 700 (Administrator) and from FF 438 348 (Principal Administrator), supplemented by allowances depending on residence and family situation.

Vacancies are open to both male and female candidates from OECD Member countries.

Applications, in English or French (specifying area of specialisation and enclosing detailed *curriculum vitæ*), should be marked "PROF" and sent to:

Human Resource Management Division
OECD
2, rue André-Pascal
75775 Paris CEDEX 16
France

OTHER ECONOMIC PERIODICALS

Economics Department, OECD

OECD ECONOMIC SURVEYS by the Economic and Development Review Committee.
Detailed surveys of trends and prospects for OECD Member countries.

Each country study (1995)	France: FF 100	Other countries: FF 130	US$24	DM 39
Subscription for 1995				
(10 00 01 1) ISSN 0376-6438	France: FF 1 200	Other countries: FF 1 300	US$240	DM 398

OECD ECONOMIC STUDIES
This half-yearly publication, produced by the Economics Department of the OECD Secretariat, contains articles featuring applied macroeconomic and statistical analysis, generally with an international or cross-country dimension. Many articles appearing in *OECD Economic Studies* are based on background papers produced for the OECD's intergovernmental committees.

Single issue 1995	France: FF 140	Other countries: FF 180	US$31	DM 53
1995 Subscription				
(13 00 00 1) ISSN 0255-0822	France: FF 250	Other countries: FF 270	US$49	DM 94

	TITLES	AUTHORS
No. 23/Winter 1994		
	The effects of trade and foreign direct investment on employment and relative wages	Robert E. Baldwin
	The EC's internal market: implementation and economic effects	Peter Hoeller and Marie-Odile Louppe
	Costs and benefits of moving from low inflation to price stability	Malcolm Edey
	Estimating pension liabilities: a metodological framework	Randall S. Jones, Robert E. King and Michael Klein
	A survey of the trade and environment nexus: global dimensions	John Beghin, David Roland-Holst and Dominique van der Mensbrugghe
(13 94 23 1) ISSN 0255-0822		
No. 22/Spring 1994		
	Active labour market policy and unemployment – a framework for the analysis of crucial design features	Lars Calmfors
	Medium-term determinants of OECD productivity	A. Steven Englander and Andrew Gurney
	OECD productivity growth: medium-term trends	A. Steven Englander and Andrew Gurney
	Market structure, trade and industry wages	Joaquim Oliveira Martins
	Monetary policy credibility and price uncertainty: the New Zealand experience of inflation targeting	Andreas M. Fischer and Adrian B. Orr
	The effects of net transfers on low incomes among non-elderly families	Michael F. Förster
(13 94 22 1) ISBN 92-64-14293-2		
No. 21/Winter 1993		
	Employment regulation and patterns of work in EC countries	David Grubb and William Wells
	Unemployment persistence	Jørgen Elmeskov and Maitland MacFarlan
	The role of real and nominal rigidities in macroeconomic adjustment: a comparative study of the G3 economies	Dave Turner, Pete Richardson and Sylvie Rauffet
	Interpreting unemployment: the role of labour-force participation	Jørgen Elmeskov and Karl Pichelmann
	Centralisation of wage bargaining and macroeconomic performance – a survey	Lars Calmfors
(13 93 21 1) ISBN 92-64-14108-1		

SELECTED PUBLICATIONS

Economics Department, OECD

GLOBAL WARMING: Economic Dimensions and Policy Responses
This report addresses the policy follow-up of the Framework Convention on Climate Change signed at Rio de Janeiro in June 1992, requiring signatories to reduce the threat of global warming by defining adequate policy actions and evaluating their economic consequences. It briefly summarises the debate, discusses current options for reducing carbon emissions, explores future responses to the threat of global warming, and examines the implications of a carbon tax for international trade and fiscal policies. Finally, it examines the scope for international co-operation and joint policy implementation of this Convention.
Annexes provide detailed background material and technical information.
January 1995, 156 pages (11 95 01 1) ISBN 92-64-14377-7 France: FF 220 Other countries: FF 285 US$53 DM 87

ASSESSING STRUCTURAL REFORM: Lessons for the Future
The OECD examines structural policies of Member countries as part of its regular surveillance of their economic policies. This report summarises the work in this area over the 1990-93 period. It includes an overview that suggests some factors that need to be kept in mind in designing structural reforms (notably the fact that delay can increase the transition costs of reforms that are in any event unavoidable) and some of the things left to do (particularly in areas such as labour markets, agriculture and the public sector). It also includes a substantial stastistical annex and a country-by-country description of measures taken during the period.
March 1994, 186 pages (11 94 01 1) ISBN 92-64-14090-5 France: FF 190 Other countries: FF 250 US$42 DM 74

PROGRESS IN STRUCTURAL REFORM. An Overview
Structural reform remains at the centre of the economic policy agenda. The progress achieved in recent years has yielded visible results in terms of improved economic performance, but much remains to be done and a new thrust of reform is needed to ensure sustained growth with high levels of employment. This report examines four priority areas for action in this respect: unemployment and the labour market; international trade; public sector reform; and policies to limit environmental damage.
October 1992, 112 pages (11 92 02 1) ISBN 92-64-13763-7 France: FF 110 Other countries: FF 140 US$28 DM 45

REFORMING THE ECONOMIES OF CENTRAL AND EASTERN EUROPE
This is a comprehensive survey of the main issues facing central and eastern European countries in their transition to market economies. It provides an appraisal of economic and social reform in the Czech and Slovak Federal Republic, Hungary, Poland, and, with less detail, in Bulgaria, Romania and the former USSR. Although these countries have started introducing reforms, progress has been slow in building the institutional framework of a market economy, in developing the necessary management skills, and in transforming attitudes of the general public. Macroeconomic stability has been difficult to achieve or to sustain. The report argues that OECD governments can best contribute to the development of these countries by ensuring greater access to OECD markets and by improving the focus and co-ordination of their assistance efforts.
January 1992, 120 pages (11 92 01 1) ISBN 92-64-13613-4 France: FF 80 Other countries: FF 100 US$21 DM 33

ECONOMIES IN TRANSITION. Structural Adjustment in OECD Countries
During the past decade, policy in most OECD countries has sought to make economies more flexible and efficient through the strengthening of market mechanisms. Structural adjustment has been regularly monitored in recent years in the annual Country Surveys prepared by the Economic and Development Review Committee of the OECD. This volume synthesises the main developments noted in these Surveys, with chapters on labour markets, financial markets, industrial adjustment and fiscal policy. It explores more broadly the potential of microeconomic policy changes for improving economic performance and represents a major contribution to the comparative analysis of structural change and adjustment.
March 1989, 216 pages (11 89 01 1) ISBN 92-64-13204-X France: FF 160 Other countries: FF 210 US$34 DM 66

THE OECD CATALOGUE OF PUBLICATIONS and supplements ''New Publications'' will be sent free of charge on request, addressed either to OECD Publications Service, 2, rue André-Pascal, 75775 Paris Cedex 16, FRANCE, or to the OECD Distributor in your country.

WORKING PAPERS

Economics Department, OECD

This series of *Working Papers* is designed to make available to a wider readership selected studies which the Department has prepared for use within OECD. Authorship is generally collective, but main individual authors are named. From *Working Paper* No. 26 onwards, papers are generally available on request in their original language, English or French, with a summary in the other. Earlier papers are available in both English and French.

Enquiries should be addressed to:

OECD
Economics Department
2, rue André-Pascal
75775 Paris Cedex 16
FRANCE

153. *Markets for tradeable CO_2 emission quotas principles and practice*
Graciela Chichilnisky and Geoffrey Heal (February 1995)

152. *Estimating potential output, output gaps and structural budget balances*
Claude Giorno, Pete Richardson, Deborah Roseveare and Paul van den Noord (January 1995)

151. *NO_x/SO_x emissions and carbon abatement*
Christophe Complainville and Joaquim Oliveira Martins (December 1994)

150. *The determinants and properties of monetary conditions: direct survey evidence from New Zealand*
Andreas Fischer and Adrian Orr (December 1994)

149. *Health care reform: controlling spending and increasing efficiency*
Howard Oxley and Maitland Macfarlan (December 1994)

148. *Macroeconomic performance and fiscal policy adjustments in the medium term: alternative medium-term scenarios*
Pete Richardson, Claude Giorno and Stephan Thurman (October 1994)

147. *The EC's internal market: implementation, economic consequences, unfinished business*
Peter Hoeller and Marie-Odile Louppe (August 1994)

146. *OECD model comparison project (II) on the costs of cutting carbon emissions.*
Comparison of model structure and policy scenarios: green and 12RT
Alan Mann and Joaquim Oliveira Martins (August 1994)

145. *An international sectoral data base for fourteen OECD countries* (second edition)
F.J.M. Meyer zu Schlochtern and J.L. Meyer zu Schlochtern (June 1994)

144. *Fiscal policy, government debt and economic performance*
Willi Leibfritz, Deborah Roseveare and Paul van den Noord (June 1994)

143. *GREEN: the reference manual*
Dominique van der Mensbrugghe (May 1994)

142. *Pension liabilities in the seven major economies*
Paul van den Noord and Richard Herd (December 1993)

141. *The distribution system in Sweden*
Sören Wibe (October 1993)

140. *The distribution sector in the United Kingdom*
John A. Dawson (October 1993)

139. *The Italian distribution system*
Luca Pellegrini and Angelo M. Cardani (October 1993)

138. *The French distribution industry and the openness of the French Economy*
Patrick Messerlin (October 1993)

137. *The German distribution system*
Josef Lachner, Uwe Chr. Täger, Günter Weitzel (October 1993)

136. *A study of the distribution system in Japan*
Masayoshi Maruyama (October 1993)

135. *An analysis of the U.S. distribution system*
Roger R. Betancourt (October 1993)

134. *Market structure, international trade and relative wages*
Joaquim Oliveira Martins (October 1993)

133. *The economic analysis of institutions and organisations – in general and with respect to country studies*
Oliver E. Williamson (September 1993)

132. *High and persistent unemployment: assessment of the problem and its causes*
Jørgen Elmeskov (September 1993)

131. *Centralization of wage bargaining and macroeconomic performance: a survey*
Lars Calmfors (September 1993)

130. *Unemployment and labour force participation – trends and cycles*
Jørgen Elmeskov and Karl Pichelmann (June 1993)

129. *Trends and cycles in labour productivity in the major OECD countries*
Giuseppe Nicoletti and Lucrezia Reichlin (June 1993)

128. *International integration of financial markets and the cost of capital*
Mitsuhiro Fukao (March 1993)

127. *The international spillovers of capital income taxation: an applied general equilibrium analysis*
François Delorme, Lawrence H. Golder and Philippe Thalmann (January 1993)

126. *The future of capital income taxation in a liberalised financial environment*
David Carey, Jean-Claude Chouraqui and Robert P. Hagemann (January 1993)

125. *Global effects of the European carbon tax*
Giuseppe Nicoletti and Joaquim Oliveira Martins (December 1992)

124. *The Chinese economic area: economic integration without a free trade agreement*
Randall Jones, Robert King and Michael Klein (July 1992)

123. *New issues, new results: the OECD's second survey of the macroeconomic costs of reducing CO_2 emissions*
Peter Hoeller, Andrew Dean and Masahiro Hayafuji (July 1992)

122. *Costs of reducing CO_2 emissions: evidence from six global models*
Andrew Dean and Peter Hoeller (July 1992)

121. *Results for the OECD comparative modelling project from the Whalley-Wigle Model*
John Whalley (University of Western Ontario) and Randall Wigle (Wilfrid Laurier University) (July 1992)

120. *OECD's indicators of international trade and competitiveness*
Martine Durand, Jacques Simon and Colin Webb (July 1992)

119. *Les indicateurs de compétitivité et de commerce internationaux de l'OCDE*
Martine Durand, Jacques Simon and Colin Webb (July 1992)

118. *The cost of reducing CO_2 emissions: a comparison of carbon tax curves with GREEN*
Joaquim Oliveira Martins, Jean-Marc Burniaux, John P. Martin and Giuseppe Nicoletti (July 1992)

117. *Adjustment under fixed exchange rates: application to the European Monetary Union*
A. Steven Englander and Thomas Egebo (July 1992)

116. *GREEN: a multi-sector, multi-region, dynamic general equilibrium model for quantifying the costs of curbing CO_2 emissions: a technical manual*
Jean-Marc Burniaux, John P. Martin, Giuseppe Nicoletti and Joaquim Oliveira Martins (May 1992)

115. *The costs of reducing CO_2 emissions: evidence from GREEN*
Jean-Marc Burniaux, John P. Martin, Giuseppe Nicoletti and Joaquim Oliveira Martins (May 1992)

114. *Carbon taxes and CO_2 emissions targets: results from the IEA Model*
E. Lakis Vouyoukas, IEA (April 1992)

113. *Use of the Edmonds-Reilly Model to model energy-related greenhouse gas emissions*
D.W. Barns, J.A. Edmonds and J.M. Reilly, Pacific Northwest Laboratory, Washington, D.C. (April 1992)

112. *The welfare effects of fossil carbon restrictions: results from a recursively dynamic trade model*
Thomas Rutherford, University of Western Ontario (April 1992)

111. *Global 2100: alternative scenarios for reducing carbon emissions*
Alan S. Manne, Stanford University (April 1992)

110. *Energy taxation and price distortions in fossil fuel markets: some implications for climate change policy*
Peter Hoeller and Jonathan Coppel (April 1992)

109. *The information content of interest rate spreads across financial systems*
Frank Browne and Warren Tease (April 1992)

108. *Is there a future for capital income taxation?*]
Jack M. Mintz (March 1992)

107. *A "credit crunch"? The recent slowdown in bank lending and its implications for monetary policy*
Paul Francis O'Brien and Frank Browne (March 1992)

106. *Energy prices, taxes and carbon dioxide emissions*
Peter Hoeller and Markku Wallin (July 1991)

105. *Savings trends and measurement issues*
Jørgen Elmeskov, Jeffrey Shafer and Warren Tease (July 1991)

104. *GREEN – a multi-region dynamic general equilibrium model for quantifying the costs of curbing CO_2 emissions: a technical manual*
Jean-Marc Burniaux, John P. Martin, G. Nicoletti and J. Oliveira Martins (June 1991)

103. *The costs of policies to reduce global emissions of CO_2: initial simulation results with GREEN*
Jean-Marc Burniaux, John P. Martin, G. Nicoletti and J. Oliveira Martins (June 1991)

102. *Patterns of recoveries for the major seven OECD countries*
Marco Mira d'Ercole (June 1991)

101. *P-Star as an indicator of inflationary pressure*
Peter Hoeller and Pierre Poret (March 1991)

100. *Old age income maintenance*
Murray Petrie and Peter Sturm (April 1991)

MAIN SALES OUTLETS OF OECD PUBLICATIONS
PRINCIPAUX POINTS DE VENTE DES PUBLICATIONS DE L'OCDE

ARGENTINA – ARGENTINE
Carlos Hirsch S.R.L.
Galería Güemes, Florida 165, 4° Piso
1333 Buenos Aires Tel. (1) 331.1787 y 331.2391
Telefax: (1) 331.1787

AUSTRALIA – AUSTRALIE
D.A. Information Services
648 Whitehorse Road, P.O.B 163
Mitcham, Victoria 3132 Tel. (03) 873.4411
Telefax: (03) 873.5679

AUSTRIA – AUTRICHE
Gerold & Co.
Graben 31
Wien I Tel. (0222) 533.50.14
Telefax: (0222) 512.47.31.29

BELGIUM – BELGIQUE
Jean De Lannoy
Avenue du Roi 202
B-1060 Bruxelles Tel. (02) 538.51.69/538.08.41
Telefax: (02) 538.08.41

CANADA
Renouf Publishing Company Ltd.
1294 Algoma Road
Ottawa, ON K1B 3W8 Tel. (613) 741.4333
Telefax: (613) 741.5439
Stores:
61 Sparks Street
Ottawa, ON K1P 5R1 Tel. (613) 238.8985
211 Yonge Street
Toronto, ON M5B 1M4 Tel. (416) 363.3171
Telefax: (416)363.59.63

Les Éditions La Liberté Inc.
3020 Chemin Sainte-Foy
Sainte-Foy, PQ G1X 3V6 Tel. (418) 658.3763
Telefax: (418) 658.3763

Federal Publications Inc.
165 University Avenue, Suite 701
Toronto, ON M5H 3B8 Tel. (416) 860.1611
Telefax: (416) 860.1608

Les Publications Fédérales
1185 Université
Montréal, QC H3B 3A7 Tel. (514) 954.1633
Telefax: (514) 954.1635

CHINA – CHINE
China National Publications Import
Export Corporation (CNPIEC)
16 Gongti E. Road, Chaoyang District
P.O. Box 88 or 50
Beijing 100704 PR Tel. (01) 506.6688
Telefax: (01) 506.3101

CHINESE TAIPEI – TAIPEI CHINOIS
Good Faith Worldwide Int'l. Co. Ltd.
9th Floor, No. 118, Sec. 2
Chung Hsiao E. Road
Taipei Tel. (02) 391.7396/391.7397
Telefax: (02) 394.9176

CZECH REPUBLIC – RÉPUBLIQUE TCHEQUE
Artia Pegas Press Ltd.
Narodni Trida 25
POB 825
111 21 Praha 1 Tel. 26.65.68
Telefax: 26.20.81

DENMARK – DANEMARK
Munksgaard Book and Subscription Service
35, Nørre Søgade, P.O. Box 2148
DK-1016 København K Tel. (33) 12.85.70
Telefax: (33) 12.93.87

EGYPT – ÉGYPTE
Middle East Observer
41 Sherif Street
Cairo Tel. 392.6919
Telefax: 360-6804

FINLAND – FINLANDE
Akateeminen Kirjakauppa
Keskuskatu 1, P.O. Box 128
00100 Helsinki
Subscription Services/Agence d'abonnements :
P.O. Box 23
00371 Helsinki Tel. (358 0) 12141
Telefax: (358 0) 121.4450

FRANCE
OECD/OCDE
Mail Orders/Commandes par correspondance:
2, rue André-Pascal
75775 Paris Cedex 16 Tel. (33-1) 45.24.82.00
Telefax: (33-1) 49.10.42.76
Telex: 640048 OCDE

Orders via Minitel, France only/
Commandes par Minitel, France exclusivement :
36 15 OCDE

OECD Bookshop/Librairie de l'OCDE :
33, rue Octave-Feuillet
75016 Paris Tel. (33-1) 45.24.81.81
(33-1) 45.24.81.67

Documentation Française
29, quai Voltaire
75007 Paris Tel. 40.15.70.00

Gibert Jeune (Droit-Économie)
6, place Saint-Michel
75006 Paris Tel. 43.25.91.19

Librairie du Commerce International
10, avenue d'Iéna
75016 Paris Tel. 40.73.34.60

Librairie Dunod
Université Paris-Dauphine
Place du Maréchal de Lattre de Tassigny
75016 Paris Tel. (1) 44.05.40.13

Librairie Lavoisier
11, rue Lavoisier
75008 Paris Tel. 42.65.39.95

Librairie L.G.D.J. - Montchrestien
20, rue Soufflot
75005 Paris Tel. 46.33.89.85

Librairie des Sciences Politiques
30, rue Saint-Guillaume
75007 Paris Tel. 45.48.36.02

P.U.F.
49, boulevard Saint-Michel
75005 Paris Tel. 43.25.83.40

Librairie de l'Université
12a, rue Nazareth
13100 Aix-en-Provence Tel. (16) 42.26.18.08

Documentation Française
165, rue Garibaldi
69003 Lyon Tel. (16) 78.63.32.23

Librairie Decitre
29, place Bellecour
69002 Lyon Tel. (16) 72.40.54.54

Librairie Sauramps
Le Triangle
34967 Montpellier Cedex 2 Tel. (16) 67.58.85.15
Tekefax: (16) 67.58.27.36

GERMANY – ALLEMAGNE
OECD Publications and Information Centre
August-Bebel-Allee 6
D-53175 Bonn Tel. (0228) 959.120
Telefax: (0228) 959.12.17

GREECE – GRÈCE
Librairie Kauffmann
Mavrokordatou 9
106 78 Athens Tel. (01) 32.55.321
Telefax: (01) 32.30.320

HONG-KONG
Swindon Book Co. Ltd.
Astoria Bldg. 3F
34 Ashley Road, Tsimshatsui
Kowloon, Hong Kong Tel. 2376.2062
Telefax: 2376.0685

HUNGARY – HONGRIE
Euro Info Service
Margitsziget, Európa Ház
1138 Budapest Tel. (1) 111.62.16
Telefax: (1) 111.60.61

ICELAND – ISLANDE
Mál Mog Menning
Laugavegi 18, Pósthólf 392
121 Reykjavik Tel. (1) 552.4240
Telefax: (1) 562.3523

INDIA – INDE
Oxford Book and Stationery Co.
Scindia House
New Delhi 110001 Tel. (11) 331.5896/5308
Telefax: (11) 332.5993
17 Park Street
Calcutta 700016 Tel. 240832

INDONESIA – INDONÉSIE
Pdii-Lipi
P.O. Box 4298
Jakarta 12042 Tel. (21) 573.34.67
Telefax: (21) 573.34.67

IRELAND – IRLANDE
Government Supplies Agency
Publications Section
4/5 Harcourt Road
Dublin 2 Tel. 661.31.11
Telefax: 475.27.60

ISRAEL
Praedicta
5 Shatner Street
P.O. Box 34030
Jerusalem 91430 Tel. (2) 52.84.90/1/2
Telefax: (2) 52.84.93

R.O.Y. International
P.O. Box 13056
Tel Aviv 61130 Tel. (3) 49.61.08
Telefax: (3) 544.60.39

Palestinian Authority/Middle East:
INDEX Information Services
P.O.B. 19502
Jerusalem Tel. (2) 27.12.19
Telefax: (2) 27.16.34

ITALY – ITALIE
Libreria Commissionaria Sansoni
Via Duca di Calabria 1/1
50125 Firenze Tel. (055) 64.54.15
Telefax: (055) 64.12.57
Via Bartolini 29
20155 Milano Tel. (02) 36.50.83

Editrice e Libreria Herder
Piazza Montecitorio 120
00186 Roma Tel. 679.46.28
Telefax: 678.47.51

Libreria Hoepli
Via Hoepli 5
20121 Milano Tel. (02) 86.54.46
Telefax: (02) 805.28.86

Libreria Scientifica
Dott. Lucio de Biasio 'Aeiou'
Via Coronelli, 6
20146 Milano Tel. (02) 48.95.45.52
Telefax: (02) 48.95.45.48

JAPAN – JAPON
OECD Publications and Information Centre
Landic Akasaka Building
2-3-4 Akasaka, Minato-ku
Tokyo 107 Tel. (81.3) 3586.2016
Telefax: (81.3) 3584.7929

KOREA – CORÉE
Kyobo Book Centre Co. Ltd.
P.O. Box 1658, Kwang Hwa Moon
Seoul Tel. 730.78.91
Telefax: 735.00.30

MALAYSIA – MALAISIE
University of Malaya Bookshop
University of Malaya
P.O. Box 1127, Jalan Pantai Baru
59700 Kuala Lumpur
Malaysia Tel. 756.5000/756.5425
Telefax: 756.3246

MEXICO – MEXIQUE
Revistas y Periodicos Internacionales S.A. de C.V.
Florencia 57 - 1004
Mexico, D.F. 06600 Tel. 207.81.00
Telefax: 208.39.79

NETHERLANDS – PAYS-BAS
SDU Uitgeverij Plantijnstraat
Externe Fondsen
Postbus 20014
2500 EA's-Gravenhage Tel. (070) 37.89.880
Voor bestellingen: Telefax: (070) 34.75.778

NEW ZEALAND
NOUVELLE-ZÉLANDE
Legislation Services
P.O. Box 12418
Thorndon, Wellington Tel. (04) 496.5652
Telefax: (04) 496.5698

NORWAY – NORVÈGE
Narvesen Info Center – NIC
Bertrand Narvesens vei 2
P.O. Box 6125 Etterstad
0602 Oslo 6 Tel. (022) 57.33.00
Telefax: (022) 68.19.01

PAKISTAN
Mirza Book Agency
65 Shahrah Quaid-E-Azam
Lahore 54000 Tel. (42) 353.601
Telefax: (42) 231.730

PHILIPPINE – PHILIPPINES
International Book Center
5th Floor, Filipinas Life Bldg.
Ayala Avenue
Metro Manila Tel. 81.96.76
Telex 23312 RHP PH

PORTUGAL
Livraria Portugal
Rua do Carmo 70-74
Apart. 2681
1200 Lisboa Tel. (01) 347.49.82/5
Telefax: (01) 347.02.64

SINGAPORE – SINGAPOUR
Gower Asia Pacific Pte Ltd.
Golden Wheel Building
41, Kallang Pudding Road, No. 04-03
Singapore 1334 Tel. 741.5166
Telefax: 742.9356

SPAIN – ESPAGNE
Mundi-Prensa Libros S.A.
Castelló 37, Apartado 1223
Madrid 28001 Tel. (91) 431.33.99
Telefax: (91) 575.39.98

Libreria Internacional AEDOS
Consejo de Ciento 391
08009 – Barcelona Tel. (93) 488.30.09
Telefax: (93) 487.76.59

Llibreria de la Generalitat
Palau Moja
Rambla dels Estudis, 118
08002 – Barcelona
(Subscripcions) Tel. (93) 318.80.12
(Publicacions) Tel. (93) 302.67.23
Telefax: (93) 412.18.54

SRI LANKA
Centre for Policy Research
c/o Colombo Agencies Ltd.
No. 300-304, Galle Road
Colombo 3 Tel. (1) 574240, 573551-2
Telefax: (1) 575394, 510711

SWEDEN – SUÈDE
Fritzes Customer Service
S–106 47 Stockholm Tel. (08) 690.90.90
Telefax: (08) 20.50.21

Subscription Agency/Agence d'abonnements :
Wennergren-Williams Info AB
P.O. Box 1305
171 25 Solna Tel. (08) 705.97.50
Telefax: (08) 27.00.71

SWITZERLAND – SUISSE
Maditec S.A. (Books and Periodicals - Livres et périodiques)
Chemin des Palettes 4
Case postale 266
1020 Renens VD 1 Tel. (021) 635.08.65
Telefax: (021) 635.07.80

Librairie Payot S.A.
4, place Pépinet
CP 3212
1002 Lausanne Tel. (021) 341.33.47
Telefax: (021) 341.33.45

Librairie Unilivres
6, rue de Candolle
1205 Genève Tel. (022) 320.26.23
Telefax: (022) 329.73.18

Subscription Agency/Agence d'abonnements :
Dynapresse Marketing S.A.
38 avenue Vibert
1227 Carouge Tel. (022) 308.07.89
Telefax: (022) 308.07.99

See also – Voir aussi :
OECD Publications and Information Centre
August-Bebel-Allee 6
D-53175 Bonn (Germany) Tel. (0228) 959.120
Telefax: (0228) 959.12.17

THAILAND – THAÏLANDE
Suksit Siam Co. Ltd.
113, 115 Fuang Nakhon Rd.
Opp. Wat Rajbopith
Bangkok 10200 Tel. (662) 225.9531/2
Telefax: (662) 222.5188

TURKEY – TURQUIE
Kültür Yayinlari Is-Türk Ltd. Sti.
Atatürk Bulvari No. 191/Kat 13
Kavaklidere/Ankara Tel. 428.11.40 Ext. 2458
Dolmabahce Cad. No. 29
Besiktas/Istanbul Tel. 260.71.88
Telex: 43482B

UNITED KINGDOM – ROYAUME-UNI
HMSO
Gen. enquiries Tel. (071) 873 0011
Postal orders only:
P.O. Box 276, London SW8 5DT
Personal Callers HMSO Bookshop
49 High Holborn, London WC1V 6HB
Telefax: (071) 873 8200
Branches at: Belfast, Birmingham, Bristol, Edinburgh, Manchester

UNITED STATES – ÉTATS-UNIS
OECD Publications and Information Center
2001 L Street N.W., Suite 650
Washington, D.C. 20036-4910 Tel. (202) 785.6323
Telefax: (202) 785.0350

VENEZUELA
Libreria del Este
Avda F. Miranda 52, Aptdo. 60337
Edificio Galipán
Caracas 106 Tel. 951.1705/951.2307/951.1297
Telegram: Libreste Caracas

Subscription to OECD periodicals may also be placed through main subscription agencies.

Les abonnements aux publications périodiques de l'OCDE peuvent être souscrits auprès des principales agences d'abonnement.

Orders and inquiries from countries where Distributors have not yet been appointed should be sent to: OECD Publications Service, 2 rue André-Pascal, 75775 Paris Cedex 16, France.

Les commandes provenant de pays où l'OCDE n'a pas encore désigné de distributeur peuvent être adressées à : OCDE, Service des Publications, 2, rue André-Pascal, 75775 Paris Cedex 16, France.

5-1995

OECD PUBLICATIONS, 2 rue André-Pascal, 75775 PARIS CEDEX 16
PRINTED IN FRANCE
(12 95 57 1) ISBN 92-64-14484-6 - No. 47923 1995
ISSN 0474-5574

OECD ECONOMIC OUTLOOK

Statistics and projections on microcomputer diskette

The full set of historical time series data and projections underlying the *Economic Outlook* is regularly available on microcomputer diskette at the same time as its publication. A basic version of the *Economic Outlook* diskette contains approximately 3 500 macroeconomic time series for OECD countries and non-OECD zones, beginning in 1980 and extending to the end of the published forecast horizon. In addition, the *Economic Outlook Reference Supplement* contains data for most OECD countries and the majority of National Accounts and other country-specific statistics, starting as early as 1960. This supplement provides data in a form which is fully compatible with other *Economic Outlook* files, permitting a wide variety of analyses and statistical applications, *e.g.* for modelling and longer-term comparative and graphical analyses.

The general subject and country coverage for both versions are as follows:

Subject coverage

- Gross national product and its components
- Government and households appropriation accounts
- Fiscal and monetary indicators
- Labour market and supply indicators
- Wages, prices and profitability
- International trade and payments

Country coverage

- 25 OECD countries
- OECD area aggregations
- Non-OECD zones

Prices and subscription information

Annual subscription, two issues per year, in June and December:

including *Reference Supplement:*	£375	US$620	FF 3 400	DM 1 030
excluding *Reference Supplement:*	£250	US$410	FF 2 250	DM 680

Subscriptions, which also include the printed version of the *Economic Outlook,* may be made at any time of the year. For special conditions (Academics, Government Agencies, and Commercial Redistribution Rights) contact OECD Publications service.

Diskette format

Data are provided on diskettes suitable for IBM PC-compatible microcomputers ($5^1/_4$ or $3^1/_2$ inches). These include a simple programme to translate these series into a variety of formats which can be read and used by most PC software packages.

Send your order to:

OECD
Publications, Electronic Editions
2, rue André-Pascal
75775 Paris Cedex 16
FRANCE

Other OECD Statistical Series on Diskette

International Trade and Competitiveness Indicators (ITCI)

The *International Trade and Competitiveness Indicators* statistical series are designed for use in a wide range of empirical analyses related to the international trade performance of OECD Member countries. The set of diskettes includes principal series for external trade classified by four broad SITC commodity groups (basic materials, food, fuels and manufactures) in nominal and constant-price value terms, along with corresponding price deflators, market shares and competitiveness indicators. These statistics are available in a consistent quarterly form for OECD countries. The length of individual series is determined by the availability of individual country source information, but in general all series are available from 1975 onwards.

The ITCI diskettes are accompanied by relevant user instructions and detailed Sources and Methods material based upon *Working Paper*, No. 120. The set of diskettes is updated to take account of new information and data revisions on a twice-yearly basis, at an annual subscription rate of £250, US$410, FF 2 250, DM 680.

Business Sector Data Base (BSDB)

The *Business Sector Data Base* contains data for 24 OECD Member countries related to business-sector value added, employment, investment, factor prices and capital stocks, from 1960 to the present day, and are stored in quarterly form. The underlying data base was developed for use in the analysis of production and supply issues in the context of the OECD's regular surveys and assessments, and related empirical studies.

The BSDB diskettes are accompanied by relevant user instructions and detailed Sources and Methods material, based upon *Working Paper*, No. 99. The BSDB is available in two issues per year, with an annual subscription of £275, US$455, FF 2 500, DM 755.